BUSINESS
DATA
COMMUNICATIONS

BUSINESS DATA COMMUNICATIONS

Fifth Edition

David A. Stamper

 **ADDISON-WESLEY**

An imprint of Addison Wesley Longman, Inc.

Reading, Massachusetts • Menlo Park, California • New York • Harlow, England
Don Mills, Ontario • Sydney • Mexico City • Madrid • Amsterdam

Executive Editor: Michael Roche
Assistant Editor: Ruth Berry
Senior Production Supervisor: Juliet Silveri
Project Coordination: Electronic Publishing Services Inc., NYC
Text Designer and Illustrations: Electronic Publishing Services Inc., NYC
Design Manager: Regina Hagen
Cover Designer: Cindy Nelson and Kevin Toler, Black & Copper
Cover Illustration: © Bill Frymire/Masterfile
Compositor: Electronic Publishing Services Inc., NYC
Senior Marketing Manager: Tom Ziolkowski
Senior Marketing Coordinator: Deanna Storey
Manufacturing Manager: Sheila Spinney

Photo credits: pp. 45, 47, 48, 74, 108, 174, 178: Dave Stamper; p. 55: Courtesy of Gabriel Electronics Inc.; p. 271: Courtesy of Wyse Technology; p. 272: Courtesy of International Business Machines Corporation. Unauthorized use not permitted. p. 290: Courtesy of Atlantic Research Corporation; p. 291: Courtesy of Electrodata, Inc.; p. 381: © Dow Jones & Company, Inc. All Rights Reserved.

Library of Congress Cataloging-in-Publication Data

Stamper, David A.
    Business data communications / David A. Stamper. — 5th ed.
        p.   cm.
    Includes index.
    ISBN 0-8053-7732-8
    1. Data transmission systems.   2. Business enterprises—Computer
  networks.   I. Title.
TK5105.S734   1999
004.6—DC21   98-7257
                                                                          CIP

Many of the designations used by manufacturers and sellers to distinguish their products are claimed as trademarks. Where those designations appear in the book and Addison Wesley Longman was aware of a trademark claim, those designations have been printed in initial caps or in all caps.

Reprinted with corrections, April 1999

ISBN 0-8053-7732-8

3456789—RNV—02010099

TO VIRGINIA

BRIEF CONTENTS

DETAILED CONTENTS

PREFACE

Business Data Communications, Fifth Edition, is designed for an introductory course in data communication, a required course in the information system curriculum. Previous editions have been used at over 200 universities, colleges, and community colleges. The text provides a balanced approach, emphasizing both the technical aspects of data communication and related managerial issues.

Data communication continues to be one of the most dynamic segments of the computer industry. One need only look at the high-flying (and sometimes crash-and-burn) technical companies on the stock exchanges to verify this. Many of these growth companies are involved in the communication segment of the market. In the 1990s the focus was on network interconnection and Internet-related services. Widespread use of the Internet by businesses and individuals has spurred communication providers to expand their offerings. The industry continues to increase the speeds of both switched and dedicated communication links. These changes are the focal point of the new material in this edition.

This edition retains the fundamental structure and organization of previous editions: The chapters are arranged to follow the seven-layer Open Systems Interconnection reference model from the bottom up. In the first editions the focus was on wide area network technologies. As local area networks expanded, so did our coverage of LANs, and in the fourth edition we recognized this by dividing the network coverage into two sections: LANs and WANs. That separation continues in this edition. The two sections mirror each other and each is developed along the layers of the OSI reference model. This edition has expanded coverage in both LAN and WAN technologies. We include some of the new LAN capabilities and have added two chapters in the WAN section dedicated to Internet usage and technologies. In addition, recognizing the changes in the computer industry since the publication of the previous edition, we have expanded and updated topics in the area of common carrier services.

NEW AND EXPANDED IN THIS EDITION

Emphasis on the Internet

In 1990 there were several hundred thousand Internet nodes and the Internet was still a vehicle for the exchange of scholarly information. Today, there are over 20 million nodes and the Internet reaches virtually every country in the world. The Internet is now a place of business, recreation, communication, and other personal and commercial pursuits. It has become such a ubiquitous part of our society that it deserves considerable attention in a data communication book. In this edition you will find two chapters devoted to the Internet: one on Internet use and commerce and one on the technologies underlying the Internet.

Emphasis on Local Area Networks

LANs continue to expand in use and technology. Since the previous edition, the speed of communication over Ethernet LANs has jumped two orders of magnitude; we have progressed from 10-Mbps through 100-Mbps to 1-Gbps speeds. Switching technology has further expanded the overall bandwidth and has provided the ability to define virtual LANs. We have added new developments to the LAN section while maintaining the coverage of basic technologies.

As the scope of data communication expands, we need to address the new technologies; meanwhile, the older technologies continue to be used and ordinarily merit attention as well. For the first-time student, these older concepts are not a part of their background and must be explained along with the newer developments. However, it is impractical to keep all of the old and augment it with the new. Therefore, readers of previous editions will notice that some coverage has been dropped. The chapter on system analysis and the product life cycle, a fixture since the first edition, has been dropped to give proper attention to newer topics. The part openers have also been cut to make way for new topics. Furthermore, slightly less coverage is given to some of the older topics.

PEDAGOGY AND LEARNING AIDS

Chapter Introductions, Summary, Review Questions, Problems and Exercises, Key Terms

Each chapter opens with an introduction and learning objectives and closes with a summary of key points and a list of Key Terms. Each chapter also contains two sets of end-of-chapter questions. Review Questions stimulate discussion and reflection on key points in the chapter. Problems and Exercises provide specific research topics or situational problem-solving to augment chapter material. Over 500 Key Terms are indicated in bold throughout each chapter and are defined in the margins for easy reference.

Case Study

This icon identifies a realistic case study based on the fictional Syncrasy Corporation, which appears in numerous chapters to illustrate data communication applications. The case study chronicles a vigorous young company as it grows and diversifies, and provides a business context for students to apply the different technologies described in the text to the changing communication needs of a realistic situation.

SUPPLEMENTS

Instructor's Guide
The accompanying Instructor's Guide contains over 150 PowerPoint slides to illustrate key figures and concepts from the text, as well as the following features:

- Over 635 multiple-choice and fill-in test questions and answers
- Objectives and Teaching Suggestions
- Answers to selected Review Questions and Exercises

For more information about the fifth edition of *Business Data Communications* and its supplements, or to request the software described above, please contact your Addison Wesley Longman Sales and Marketing Representative, or call the publisher directly.

ACKNOWLEDGMENTS

I am grateful to the numerous people who contributed to the fifth edition of this textbook. I wish to thank the reviewers of the fifth edition, who were instrumental in providing suggestions and constructive criticisms for improving the text as we built on the foundation laid by the earlier editions. These people gave willingly of their time, and the fifth edition of *Business Data Communications* is much improved as a result of their contributions:

Bodie Farah, Eastern Michigan University

Michael Jeffries, University of Tampa

Celeste Dubeck-Smith, Northern Virginia Community College

Jay Benson, Anne Arundel Community College

Hugo Moortgat, San Francisco State University

Much appreciation goes to the editorial and production departments of Addison Wesley Longman and the staff of Electronic Publishing Services. In particular, I wish to thank the following for their ideas, assistance, and support:

Rob Anglin (EPS)

Ruth Berry

Deneen Celecia

Kerry Connor

Gina Hagen

Michelle Hudson

Carol Anne Peschke (EPS)

Mike Roche

Deanna Storey

Last, but not least, I wish to thank all of you—faculty, students, and business professionals alike—who have used this book. Over time, I have received many suggestions for improvements from you, both formally and informally. Your comments are sincerely appreciated.

David A. Stamper

CHAPTER 1

Introduction to Data Communication

CHAPTER OBJECTIVES

After studying this chapter you should be able to

- Differentiate between telecommunication and data communication
- Discuss several significant data communication historical events
- Identify the essential elements of communication
- Describe different types of data communication applications
- Discuss the requirements of an online system
- List the seven layers of the OSI reference model
- Define some functions for each of the seven layers of the OSI reference model
- Describe how a message is passed from one application to another using the OSI reference model

A data processing system may be viewed as an integration of subsystems that aid in solving business or scientific problems. Common subsystems include the operating system, database management system, languages, applications, and data communication. Each subsystem is implemented as a combination of software and hardware. This text discusses one part of the data processing system, the data communication subsystem, along with its interfaces with the other subsystems. What is meant in this text by the term *data communication?* Although the terms *telecommunication* and *data communication* have become almost synonymous in some circles, they have distinct meanings. James Martin gives a broad definition of telecommunication:

> Any process that permits the passage from a sender to one or more receivers of information of any nature delivered in any easy to use form

(printed copy, fixed or moving pictures, visible or audible signals, etc.) by any electromagnetic system (electrical transmission by wire, radio, optical transmission, guided waves, etc.). Includes telegraphy, telephony, video-telephony, data transmission, etc.

data communication
The transmission of data to and from computers and components of computer systems.

This definition is too broad for the scope of this book. We define **data communication** as the subset of telecommunication involving the transmission of data to and from computers and components of computer systems. More specifically, data communication is the transmission of data through a conducted medium such as wires, coaxial cables, or fiber optic cables or by the use of radiated electromagnetic waves such as broadcast radio, infrared light, and microwaves. We discuss other facets of telecommunication such as telephone systems and broadcast radio only as they pertain to the transmission of computer data.

In reading this book, be aware that the field of data communication is so extensive that entire books are devoted to each chapter topic presented here. This text is intended to provide an overview of the entire field of data communication and to familiarize you with the terminology and capabilities of data communication systems. Your mastery of this material will enable you to participate in discussions about how to configure data communication components.

Based on the belief that a knowledge of history helps clarify the events of today, we start our discussion of data communication with a historical overview of the telecommunication industry and key data communication events.

HISTORY OF THE TELECOMMUNICATION INDUSTRY

The history of data communication differs significantly from that of other computer technologies, such as languages, hardware, database management, and applications. Data communication development is a joint venture between the communication industry and the computer industry.

The modern telecommunication industry began in 1837 with the invention of the telegraph by Samuel Morse. This invention led to building a telecommunication infrastructure of poles and wires and further development of communication hardware and protocols. The invention of the telegraph was followed by the invention of the telephone by Alexander Graham Bell in 1876, and the development of wireless communication technology by Guglielmo Marconi in the 1890s. These pioneering efforts set the stage for today's communication industry. Because telephone companies have been the primary source of long-distance communication circuits, this history begins with the state of telephone companies at the start of the computer era.

At the beginning of the computer era, the communication industry was already well established. Telephone and telegraph companies had developed a network of communication facilities throughout the industrialized world. In the United States and many other countries, telephone companies had been given exclusive rights to install lines and provide services in specific geographical areas, with government agencies exercising control over tariffs and the services provided. This situation appeared to benefit both the telephone companies and consumers. The goal of the system was to provide affordable service. However, some users paid less than the actual cost of service whereas others paid more, because of the following pricing structure.

Every person was to have access to telephone service at a reasonable cost. Service was to be provided to all geographical areas, regardless of remoteness or population density. Small remote towns were to have the same type of service as large metropolitan communities, at about the same rates. If the total cost of installing lines and switching equipment in a small town had been borne entirely by users in that town, the cost of service would have been prohibitive to most residents. Therefore, losses incurred in such a town were offset by profits from other geographical areas. The three major sources of profit in the United States were the major metropolitan areas, businesses, and long-distance service. The large metropolitan areas were profitable because of economies of scale and density of installations. Business rates were much higher than rates for individuals because the value received was ostensibly greater (because the telephone was being used to generate income) and because businesses could afford to pay more. Long-distance tariffs were set high to subsidize the portions of the system operating at a loss. Thus, the service provided was generally good and prices were reasonable for each class of user. (Note that two of these profitable segments—business and long distance—also pertain to data communication.)

In addition to having exclusive rights to transmission facilities, the telephone companies in the United States and numerous other countries had exclusive rights to attach equipment to the telephone networks. This gave them a monopoly on the equipment needed to transmit and receive data, such as modems. (A modem changes a computer signal from digital to analog format for transmission along a **medium** such as telephone lines, and another modem converts the signal back to digital format at the receiving end. Modems are discussed further in Chapter 2.) These exclusive rights allowed telephone companies to turn the sale or lease of such equipment to profit, which is what U.S. telephone companies did.

In the United States telephone companies were viewed as "natural" monopolies, meaning that it was considered wasteful to have two or more telephone companies servicing the same location. The price attached to the monopoly was that telephone companies such as American Telephone & Telegraph (AT&T) were prohibited from involvement in certain business segments, such as the computer industry. Partly because of this monopoly on equipment, as well as the special status given providers of data transmission facilities, the growth of data communication was somewhat slower than that of other computer-related technologies. The development of databases, languages, operating systems, and hardware components was strong from the 1950s through the early 1970s, but large-scale expansion of data communication systems really did not occur until the 1970s. The growth experienced then was primarily the result of three developments:

- Large-scale integration of circuits reduced the cost and size of terminals and communication equipment.

medium In data communication, the carrier of data signals. Twisted-pair wires, coaxial cables, and fiber optic cables are the most common LAN media.

- Development of software systems made the establishment of data communication networks easy.
- Competition among providers of transmission facilities reduced the cost of data circuits.

Without these developments data communication systems would not have been affordable for many computer users. Consider the transmission costs in 1968 and 1973, just before and just after competition appeared. In 1968 AT&T charged an average of $315 for 100 miles of leased telephone line. In 1973 the average cost of the same line was as low as $85. A simple teletypewriter (TTY) terminal that sold for $2595 in 1971 could be replaced in 1975 for $750, and the 1975 terminal had more features than the older model.

HISTORY OF DATA COMMUNICATION

Significant data communication events are shown on the timeline in Table 1–1. The most significant of these are discussed in this section.

The Transistor

transistor A solid-state device used to control the flow of electricity in electronic equipment.

The invention of the **transistor** by Walter H. Brattain, John Bardeen, and William Shockley at Bell Laboratories in 1947 was fundamental to the electronics we use in computers and communication equipment. The transistor replaced vacuum tubes, which were large and produced significant amounts of heat; in contrast, the transistor is small and produces little heat, characteristics that are essential to the electronic equipment that forms the basis of our computer and communication industry.

The Hush-a-Phone Case

Hush-a-Phone case A U.S. case that set a precedent regarding attaching equipment to telephone networks.

A 1948 court case not specifically related to data communication eventually had a significant impact on that industry: the **Hush-a-Phone case.** Recall that U.S. telephone companies had a legal monopoly over all equipment attached to their networks, to keep anyone from attaching devices that might interfere with or destroy signals and equipment in the network. The Hush-a-Phone Company developed and marketed a passive device (no electrical or magnetic components) that could be installed over the transmitting telephone handset to block out background noise and provide more privacy; AT&T threatened to suspend service for users and distributors of the device. Hush-a-Phone appealed to the Federal Communications Commission (FCC). After several hearings, the FCC decided in favor of AT&T. In 1956, however, an appeals court overturned the FCC ruling and decided in favor of the Hush-a-Phone Company, holding that no harm to the AT&T network would result from use of such a device. This precedent opened the door for other companies to attach equipment to the telephone networks. The telephone regulations as modified by this decision stated that the telephone company could not prohibit a customer from using a device for his or her convenience as long as the devices did not injure the telephone system, involve direct elec-

Table 1–1 History of Data Communications

1837:	Invention of the telegraph
1876:	Invention of the telephone
1890s:	Development of wireless technology
1939:	ABC computer operational
1940:	Data communication performed using COMPLEX computer
1944:	MARK I computer operational
1946:	ENIAC computer operational
1947:	Invention of the transistor
1948:	First commercial computer installed, the UNIVAC I
1953:	First private commercial computer installed, UNIVAC at General Electric Corporation
1954:	IBM introduces remote job entry (RJE)
1956:	Hush-a-Phone decision in favor of Hush-a-Phone Company
1958:	First U.S. communications satellite sent into orbit Start of SAGE radar early warning system
1959:	FCC approves private microwave communication networks
1963:	First geosynchronous orbiting satellite, SYNCOM II MCI files with FCC to provide communication services
1964:	SABRE airline reservation system completed Packet switching network concept proposed by the Rand Corporation
1966:	IBM's binary synchronous (BISYNC or BSC) protocol announced
1968:	Carterphone case concludes in favor of Carter Electronics
1969:	ARPANET, first packet switching network (later to become the Internet), begins operation
1972:	Ethernet LAN specifications formulated IBM's synchronous data link control (SDLC) protocol announced
1974:	IBM announces its systems network architecture (SNA)
1975:	General Telephone and Electronics' Telenet public packet distribution network (PDN) becomes operational Personal computers introduced, the Altaire 8800
1981:	IBM PC introduced
1982:	Microcomputer LANs appear
1984:	AT&T divestiture
1985:	Cellular radio telephones are introduced
1990:	A prototype of the Internet World Wide Web is introduced
1992:	The Internet grows to 1 million host computers
1993:	The Internet grows to 2 million host computers
1995:	The Internet grows to over 4 million host computers
1996:	The Telecommunications Reform Act of 1996 is passed

trical connection to the system, provide a recording device on the line, or connect the telephone company line with any other communication device.

Competition for Long-Distance Transmission

In 1963 Microwave Communications Incorporated (MCI) filed with the FCC to provide microwave communication services between Chicago and St. Louis, their goal being to sell data transmission circuits to private industry. AT&T objected to MCI's petition because MCI could operate at much lower overhead than AT&T; MCI, unlike AT&T, would not have to serve lower-volume markets such as rural areas in Montana, Wyoming, Idaho, Texas, and Kansas. Despite AT&T's objections, MCI received approval for the communication link in 1970. Since then, MCI has expanded into other major metropolitan areas. It added an individual telephone service (Execunet) in 1975, by which date MCI had service to 24 cities. This era of heavy competition for data transmission circuits in the United States has led to lower rates for data communication users.

The Carterphone Case

Carterphone (or Carterfone) case A U.S. case regarding attaching devices to a telephone company's network.

Another court case that helped open data communication to competition occurred in 1966: the **Carterphone case.** Carter Electronics Company had been marketing a radio telephone system that allowed communication between a moving vehicle and a base station via radio-wave transmission. Because the original Carterphone was unable to forward a mobile call to another location, the company introduced a device that could pass on the radio transmission through a telephone network. AT&T objected to attaching the Carterphone to its network on the grounds of potential harm to the network and violation of the FCC prohibition against connecting an outsider's communication device to AT&T's telephone line. The 1968 ruling was in favor of Carter Electronics. As an outgrowth of the decision, it became legal for any device to be attached to the telephone network provided the telephone companies were allowed to install a protective device between the "foreign" equipment and the network. This provision later was changed to allow connection of FCC-approved equipment without any protective devices, which made it legal to attach other manufacturers' communication equipment to the network and led to improved products at lower prices. As another side effect of the Carterphone decision, individuals were allowed to purchase and install their own telephones.

Local Area Networks

local area network (LAN) A communication network in which all components are located within several kilometers of each other, that uses high transmission speeds, generally 1 Mbps or higher.

wide area network (WAN) A network that typically covers a wide geographical area and operates at speeds lower than LAN speeds.

A **local area network (LAN),** like the example shown in Figure 1–1, is a communication network whose components are all located within several kilometers of each other. LANs differ from the oldest type of network, a **wide area network (WAN).** A WAN typically covers a wide geographical area and operates at speeds lower than those of a LAN. Major uses of LANs include exchange of data at high speed between computers within a local area, factory or production control, office automation, and financial systems.

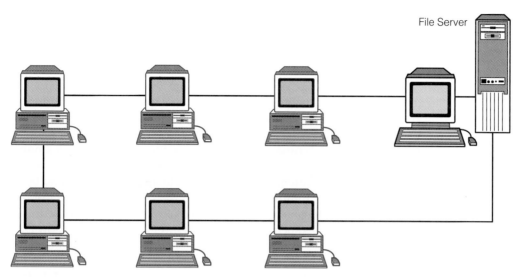

Figure 1–1
Local Area Network

The original specifications for Ethernet, one of the most publicized and implemented LANs, were published by the Xerox Corporation in 1972. Later, Digital Equipment Corporation (DEC) and Intel joined Xerox in developing Ethernet further. In the early 1980s microcomputer and LAN technologies were merged. Today microcomputer LANs form a significant portion of government, academic, and corporate computing power. LANs are discussed in greater detail in Chapters 6–9.

Data Link Protocols

A **data link protocol** governs the flow of data between sending and receiving stations. The original data communication protocols were borrowed from the telegraph and telephone industries. In 1967 IBM introduced the binary synchronous (BISYNC or BSC) protocol for use in remote job entry applications, and it was later expanded for use in other applications. In 1972 IBM introduced the synchronous data link control (SDLC) protocol, which has become the prototype for many current data link protocols. Data link protocols are discussed in more detail in Chapters 7 and 11.

data link protocol Convention that governs data flow between a sending and a receiving station.

Microcomputers

Microcomputers were introduced in 1975 with the Altaire 8800. Microcomputer technology proliferated in the 1980s and is continuing in the 1990s. A wide variety of microcomputer software and hardware, coupled with increased processing and storage capacity and low costs, have made microcomputers an important element in data communication networks. In many installations they have replaced terminals. In addition, the introduction of

LANs with microcomputers as workstations has created many changes in the ways offices process data.

The Internet

Internet A specific collection of interconnected networks spanning nearly all the countries of the world.

The **Internet** of today is vastly different from what it was originally intended to be. The Internet began in 1969 as the **Arpanet,** a network funded by the U.S. Defense Department's Advanced Research Projects Agency (ARPA). The Arpanet linked leading universities and research organizations together, and its primary use was to provide communication among scientists and researchers. By the mid-1980s there were over 500 host nodes on the Internet and additional communication tools and protocols had been developed to make communication easier. In the 1990s the character of the Internet changed extensively. Thousands of new nodes were added and more sophisticated tools such as Web browsers were developed to allow easier access to data. Most significantly, the Internet became a communication facility for businesses and individuals as well as for scientists. In the early days, using the Internet for commercial purposes was discouraged; today, the Internet's primary use is for business and personal activities. A wealth of data—good and bad, accurate and inaccurate—is easily available to anyone with a computer, modem, or similar connection device and an Internet service provider (see Chapters 13 and 14).

Arpanet A network funded by the U.S. Defense Department that linked leading universities and research organizations together.

The Telecommunications Act of 1996

Telecommunications Act of 1996 Legislation that allowed more competition among communication services, allowed local phone companies to provide long-distance service, deregulated cable television rates, and allowed some cable and telephone companies to combine.

The **Telecommunications Act of 1996** signaled a major change in the way in which telecommunication companies in the United States could operate. The major provisions allowed

- more competition among intrastate and interstate communication services
- regional Bell operating companies (RBOC) to provide long-distance services
- deregulation of cable television company rates
- cable television companies and telephone companies to combine in some areas

A consequence of this act has been the merger of telecommunication, cable television, and entertainment companies as companies in these three industries prepare to position themselves to become service providers in the next century (see Chapter 4).

ESSENTIAL FEATURES OF COMMUNICATION

Data communication has several important features. Communication of any type requires a message, a sender, a receiver, and a medium. In addition, the message should be understandable and there should be some means of error detection. Figure 1–2 illustrates the sender, receiver, medium, and message in a telephone connection.

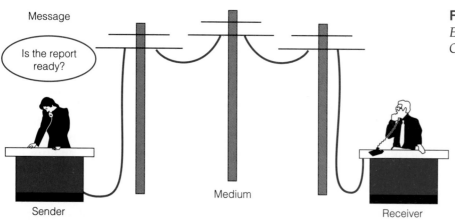

Figure 1–2
Essential Features of Communication

Message

For two entities to communicate, there must be a message, which can assume several forms and be of varying length. Types of data communication messages include a file, a request, a response, status, control, and correspondence. These are illustrated in Figure 1–3. Let us briefly look at each of them.

A File With **remote job entry (RJE),** one of the first applications of data communication, messages were transmitted from a remote location to a processor. The message was the entire card file. In computer networks, where several processors are connected, it is not unusual for complete or partial files to be transferred between processing units.

remote job entry (RJE)
An application of data communication in which batches of data are collected at a remote site and transmitted to a host for processing.

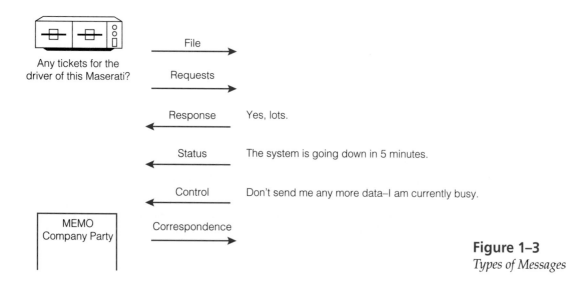

Figure 1–3
Types of Messages

A Request   In online transaction processing, a user may request that the computer processor take some type of action, such as display information, update the database, access a Web page, or logon or logoff.

A Response   A request ordinarily receives a return message or response. For an information inquiry, the response is either the information requested or an error message saying why the data was not returned (such as "security violation," "Internet site not found," "information not on file," or "hardware failure"). For a database update transaction, the response could be either an explicit message that the action was performed, an error message, or an implicit acknowledgment that the transaction has been performed successfully, such as "progressing to the next transaction."

Status   A status message, which can be sent to either all users or only selected users, reveals the functional status of the system. If a system must be halted for scheduled maintenance, a status message might be broadcast to all users, enabling them to bring their work to an orderly halt.

Control   Control messages are transmitted between system components. An automatic teller machine (ATM) might indicate to the controlling computer that it is out of cash; a printer might indicate that its buffer, or information storage area, is full and cannot receive additional data; or a network computer might notify other computers that a new computer has been added to the network and is available to accept and send messages.

Correspondence   Correspondence involves messages sent from user to user. Such messages include those sent on electronic mail (e-mail) systems, where memos and correspondence may be routed between employees of a company. Some systems transmit document images, provide bulletin board message posting, or enable telephone-like interactive communication.

Sender

The sender is the transmitter of the message, either a person or a machine. Often the sender is a computer or terminal with enough intelligence to originate a message or response without human intervention. The sender can also be a system user, sensor, badge reader, or other input device.

Receiver

Receivers include computers, terminals, remote printers, people, and devices such as drill presses, furnaces, and air conditioners. A message and a sender can exist without a receiver; however, without a receiver, no communication takes place. For example, signals have been beamed into space in an attempt to contact other intelligent life forms, but until these signals are received, no communication has occurred. In a computer system a message could be sent to all terminals saying that a new system feature is available, but if all terminals happen to be turned off at that time, no communication has occurred.

Medium

Messages are carried from sender to receiver through some medium of communication. In oral communication, sound waves are transmitted through air (the medium). Data communication uses several media to transmit data, including wires, radio waves, and light pulses. Media are discussed more thoroughly in Chapter 2.

Understandability

Even if all the components discussed here are present, if the message is not understood correctly, then accurate communication has not taken place. In human communication the most obvious obstacle is language differences, for which a translator or interpreter may be necessary. Computer systems have similar obstacles to communication. For instance, data can be represented by any of several different codes; the two most common are the American Standard Code for Information Interchange (ASCII) and the Extended Binary Coded Decimal Interchange Code (EBCDIC). Sometimes it is necessary to translate from one code to another to ensure that data is interpreted correctly. If two applications in a network are not using the same record formats for message interpretation, then the message will not be understood or will be incorrectly understood.

Error Detection

In human communication, receivers can often detect errors because humans have the ability to reason and interpret. Grammatical errors, misspellings, and even some misstatements can usually be corrected by a human receiver. (If a teacher mistakenly gives the distance between the earth and the sun as 93 million light years rather than 93 million miles, we would probably realize the error and, presumably, correct it.) But computer networks do not reason. Even when a human computer operator realizes that a received message is erroneous, that operator may be unable to correct the error. When the receiver is a piece of hardware, incapable of reasoning and unable to detect or correct errors, it becomes necessary to use special schemes for determining whether an original message has been distorted during transmission. All such schemes involve transmitting additional information along with the data, which increases the chances of detecting errors without eliminating the possibility that the received data may be erroneous. Error detection is discussed in Chapter 3.

DATA COMMUNICATION APPLICATIONS

There are several broad classes of data communication applications: batch, data entry, distributed, inquiry/response, interactive, and sensor based. Note that the classes are not mutually exclusive; some transactions may fall into more than one class.

Batch Applications

Batch applications, including RJE, are characterized by large data transfers in two directions. Information from a batch of inventory cards might be transferred from a warehouse to a remote computer center, and in return the warehouse would receive an updated inventory list. In some batch applications, large amounts of data flow in one direction only. When a sales representative records sales on a portable computer terminal but waits until the end of the workday to transmit the entire day's orders, a large amount of data flows in one direction and little or no data flows in the other direction.

Data Entry Applications

Data entry applications consist of lengthy inputs with short responses. In a credit authorization system in Australia, input for a batch of receipts consists of credit card number, merchant number, and charge amount, plus the batch total. The system then calculates its own batch total and compares it with the input total; if the figures agree, the only response is a prompt to continue entering the next batch.

Distributed Applications

Distributed applications are characterized not so much by input and output size as by whether data or processing or both are distributed among several processing units. Thus, requests as well as data flow between several system components, with possibly some parallelism in data access and processing. Order entry is an example of this type of processing. When an order for an item is entered, the system tries to determine whether the item is in stock in any of its several regionally located warehouses. Because each warehouse has a computer system and maintains its local inventory, the system inquires into these remote databases to find a location with enough stock to fill the order. The system then updates the inventory at the location(s) from which the order is to be filled, updates the invoicing and accounts receivable at the accounting location, and supplies the ordering location with a shipment date and other relevant data. Client/server computing (see Chapter 5) is one example of a distributed processing application architecture.

Office automation systems are a special case of distributed systems, with both data and processing distributed among several different components. Applications include word processing, communication between members of the corporation via e-mail, spreadsheet analysis, graphics, desktop publishing, and facsimile generation for presentations, reports, and contracts.

Inquiry/Response Applications

In **inquiry/response applications,** inputs generally have only a few characters and output responses have many. Inquiry/response applications involve requests to display information. For example, a police inquiry might consist of a driver's license number and the response could be several thousand characters of information detailing the driver's name, address, driving record, and so on. In a hospital application, a nurse might enter the nurse's station number (a few characters) and the output would probably consist of several thousand characters giving each patient's name, status, medical requirements, and so on.

Interactive Applications

An **interactive application** is characterized by short inputs and outputs. The computer system prompts the user for an input, eliciting a short response. Because the sender and receiver are essentially conversing with each other, this application is sometimes called conversational. Interactive applications are often used for online transaction processing with terminals that cannot locally store an entire screenful of information. Applications in which the user's response dictates the next prompt, such as certain computerized games, are also interactive.

interactive application An application characterized by short inputs and outputs.

Sensor-Based Applications

Sensor-based applications involve special data collection devices for such uses as controlling temperature in buildings, monitoring and maintaining patient condition in hospitals, and controlling manufacturing processes. The processor receives data from the sensors and, if necessary, takes control action.

sensor-based application An application in which the processor receives data from sensors and, if necessary, acts on that data.

Combined Applications

The typical computer in a network of large systems supports more than one type of activity. It might have a batch-processing requirement and one or more types of on-line applications. One task in designing a data communication system is to balance the workload to ensure effective and efficient use. Effective use means minimizing idle time for system components. It is not effective to have a data communication line idle for long periods and then have many users attempting to use it at once. Efficient use means using the components in an optimal manner. Efficient uses of a data communication line include compressing the data before transmitting it or eliminating sources of data errors. These goals can be reached through good design and management, and we discuss techniques for reaching these goals in Chapters 17–18.

Good management often requires that tradeoffs be made. If batch jobs must run concurrently with data communication applications, a manager may configure a computer system so batch applications do not run as efficiently as possible so that transaction-oriented applications are optimized.

REQUIREMENTS OF AN ONLINE SYSTEM

Although data communication applications are diverse, most have certain basic requirements: performance, consistency, flexibility, availability, reliability, recovery, and security.

Performance

System performance can be measured in several ways. Two very common measures are response time and transaction rate (or throughput). **Response time** is the interval between entering a message and getting the response. Some define the measurement interval as being from the end of the entry to the appearance of the first response character; others define it as the interval from the end of the entry to receipt of the final response character. The difference between the two can be significant. For example, if the speed of the communication circuit is 200 characters per second and the response consists of 1200 characters, the response time by the first definition is 6 seconds less than that by the second definition. Response time has two major components: the time required for data transmission and the time required for processing. (Each component has subcomponents.) This text deals only with data transmission time.

Response times are quoted for transactions of a given type. In a hospital application there are response times for each of the following transactions:

- patient admission
- patient discharge
- patient lookup
- room occupants

One transaction type may have different response times in different systems. This happens because of hardware differences or because the transactions are implemented in different ways. Table 1–2 illustrates the work Transaction A may do to admit a patient at one hospital and Table 1–3 shows the work a patient admission transaction, Transaction B, does at another hospital. The work accomplished by these two transactions is different; therefore, their response times differ. When comparing or evaluating transaction response times, you also need to evaluate the work done by those transactions.

Throughput, or transaction rate, is the amount of work performed by the system per unit of time. It may appear that fast response time and high throughput are equivalent. Actually, the opposite is sometimes true. For example, transactions in which customers are involved need quick response time. Optimizing the speed of such transactions might slow down other processing activity, such as batch reporting. Although response time in customer transactions might be reduced, the total amount of work accom-

response time The amount of time required to receive a reply to a request.

throughput The amount of work performed by a system per unit of time.

Table 1–2   Activities for Transaction A

Obtain vacant room list header from memory location
Read vacant room record
Read patient record
Update vacant room list header in memory from room record
Rewrite room record linked to patient record
Rewrite patient record

Table 1–3 Activities for Transaction B

Obtain vacant room header from memory
Read vacant room record
Read patient record
Update vacant room header from room record
Rewrite room record linked to patient record
Read related charge record for room
Write charge record for patient
Read standard patient issue record
Write patient charge record for issue of supplies
Rewrite patient record

plished may decline. In a truly successful system, both response time and throughput are optimal.

There are other measures of performance, such as turnaround time and instruction rate; however, these measures are not typically used to rate data communication applications.

Consistency

Consistency describes a system that works predictably both with respect to the people who use the system and with respect to response times. Inconsistent response time is extremely annoying to system users and is sometimes worse than a slow but consistent response time. Of course, complete consistency is difficult to achieve because of occasional periods of heavy processing. One common system design objective is for the response time of most transactions of a given type to be lower than a certain threshold, such as 3 s. It would be quite disconcerting if 50% of these transactions took 3 s, 20% took 10 s, 15% took 30 s, 10% took 1 min, and 5% took more than a minute. Such inconsistency not only is frustrating but also limits the effectiveness of the system.

consistency A consistent system works predictably with respect to both response times and the people who use the system.

Flexibility

One common aspect of online systems is that they change. Users might want to alter the types of transactions available, change the data format, expand an application, or add new applications. **Flexibility** means that both growth and change must be accommodated with minimal impact on existing applications and users. The ability to increase processing power, terminals, communication circuits, and database capacity is critical to the long-term success of a system, and the network implementation ought to accommodate such changes. One of the best ways to ensure this ability is to use industry-standard network architectures and protocols. This method also helps when adding or upgrading nodes and gives users a wider variety of options from which to choose.

flexibility The ability to have both growth and change with minimal impact on existing applications and users.

Availability

Availability requires that an online system be continuously available to the user community during the workday. In some cases this means 24

availability A system is available when all components a user needs to satisfy the request are usable.

hours a day, every day of the year. In certain applications, if the online system is unavailable it can result in significant financial loss to a business. For example, an airline might be unable to sell seats on a flight if the reservation system is down, or it may overbook a flight, which will cause extra work for the employees and possible penalty payments to travelers for their inconvenience.

Reliability

reliability The probability that a system will continue to function over a given time period.

Reliability, an important system attribute, is a measure of the frequency of system failure and in some ways combines consistency and availability. A system failure is any event that prohibits users from processing transactions. This includes any hardware breakdown, such as a processor failure in a system that is not fault-tolerant, as well as an application or system software failure or the failure of the medium (such as a faulty data communication line). **Mean time between failure (MTBF)** is a measure of the average time until a given component may be expected to fail, and **mean time to repair (MTTR)** is the average time required to fix a failed component. Both figures are important in determining the frequency of failure and the time required to return the system to successful operation.

mean time between failure (MTBF) The average amount of time a given component may be expected to operate before failing.

mean time to repair (MTTR) The average time required to fix a failed component.

One way to improve the reliability of data communication systems is to increase **fault tolerance,** which is the ability to continue processing despite component failure. There are levels of fault tolerance. In a fully fault-tolerant system, single points of failure do not cause system failure because every component in the system has a backup component that takes over if a failure occurs. Fault-tolerant WANs are formed by combining fault-tolerant hardware with fault-tolerant software, and fault tolerance is also available for LANs. Fault tolerance is usually confined to a LAN's file servers, which may not be fully fault tolerant. For example, fault tolerance is sometimes provided at the disk level only.

fault tolerance Combined hardware and software techniques that improve the reliability of a system.

Recovery

recovery The act of restoring a system to operational status following a failure.

Recovery addresses the fact that all systems, even those built for continuous operation, can fail. In some cases it may not be the system that fails but either the source of power or the people who operate the system. Regardless of the cause, the system must be able to recover to a consistent point at which the database has no partially updated transactions, no transactions have been processed twice, and no transactions have been lost. System users also should be advised of the state of all work they had in progress at the time of failure, to keep them from submitting a duplicate transaction or failing to reenter a transaction not received before the failure.

Security

security Security is a delaying tactic. Physical security is intended to deny access to a facility. Transmission and data security are intended to restrict access to authorized users. Typical security measures include identification and authentication (passwords), data encryption, and user profiles. Security does not prevent unauthorized access to a system, but makes it more difficult.

Security has become increasingly important as the microcomputer has made computer networks accessible to almost everyone. As more businesses use data communication, the number of accessible computer systems continues to grow, thus making a vast amount of sensitive information available, including financial data and classified military information. Unfortunately, security has not always received a high priority in system and network design, so making up for these deficiencies is necessary in the development of future systems and the enhancement of existing ones. System security is discussed in more detail in Chapter 19.

INTRODUCTION TO NETWORKS

This section discusses two definitions of computer networks and some functions common to them. The functions described are the bases for later chapters.

Computer Networks

What exactly is a computer network? First, a computer network can be defined as a single computer, called a host, together with communication circuits, communication equipment, and terminals (see Figure 1–4). A network can also be defined as two or more computers connected via a communication medium, together with associated communication links, terminals, and communication equipment (see Figures 1–5 and 1–6). In these cases the computers are called nodes. In Figures 1–4 and 1–5, the communication links are depicted by lines attached to the nodes. These are sample configurations only; actually, a wide variety of configurations is in use, and several viable

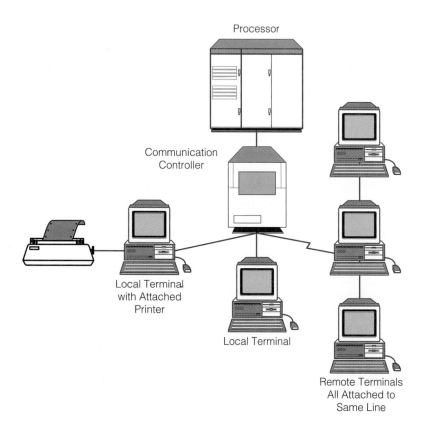

Processor

Communication
Controller

Local Terminal
with Attached
Printer

Local Terminal

Remote Terminals
All Attached to
Same Line

Figure 1–4
*Simple Data
Communication System*

Figure 1–5
Network of Computers

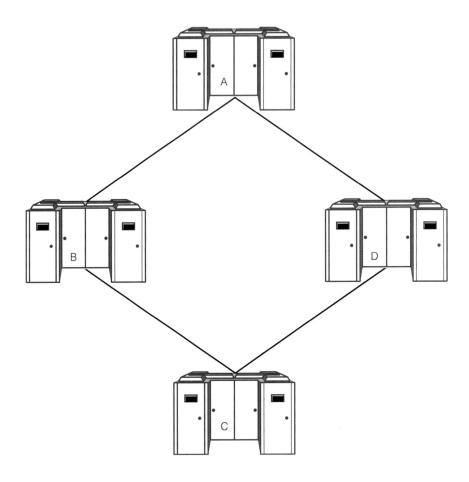

configurations may exist for one application. In addition, an entity may have several networks, such as several LANs and a WAN. It is common to interconnect networks to provide communication among all network users, such as between LAN users on one LAN and LAN users on another LAN or between a LAN user and a WAN user. Such a network of networks is illustrated in Figure 1–6 and by the Internet, which connects several regional networks into one large supernetwork. The Internet is discussed in Chapters 13 and 14.

Data Communication Applications and Configurations

The following discusses several different applications and configurations of computer equipment. The sections covering LANs and WANs provide details on network configurations and where they are used.

Company A

This company is an attorney's office with 12 partners and 22 support staff. The partnership maintains most of its documentation on a LAN. Each at-

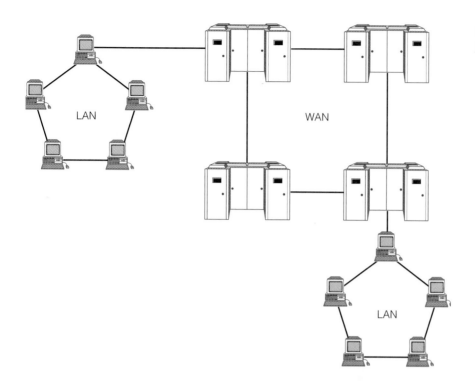

Figure 1–6
Interconnected Networks

torney and administrative support person has a microcomputer workstation that is attached to the network. Personal documents are stored on individuals' local disks, whereas documents that are subject to sharing are
stored on the network's file server. The file server is a repository for shared
files such as completed contracts and wills, templates for legal documents
and spreadsheets, and program files including word processors, spreadsheets, and desktop publishing. The file server also provides sharing of
other resources such as printers, fax machines, and modems to be shared
among the LAN users. Company A, like all the companies we are profiling,
also has a connection to the Internet. Company A's network is represented
by Figure 1–7.

Company B

This company provides a service to trucking companies that enables their
drivers to cash scrip at truck stops throughout the country. The advantages
are that drivers do not need to carry large amounts of cash for long trips,
truck-stop owners are guaranteed against losses from bad checks, and the
trucking companies need not provide significant cash advances to their
drivers. The communication network consists of approximately 50 terminals located in the same building as the host computer in Company B's office. Truck-stop employees can telephone data entry personnel on a
toll-free number to receive authorization to pay the driver (or advice to call

Figure 1–7
Company A's Network

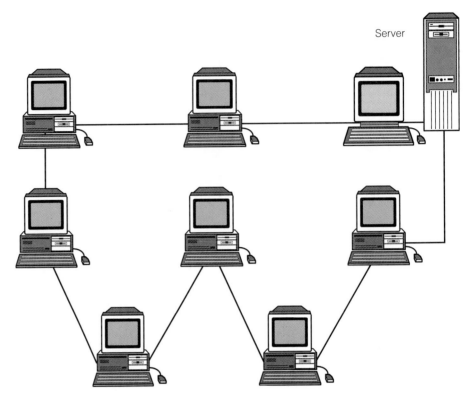
Server

common carrier A public utility that provides public transmission media, such as telephone and satellite companies.

the police). The total amount of money allocated to the driver is updated after each transaction. All links between computer and terminals are local and are controlled by Company B, rather than being leased or purchased from a **common carrier** such as a telephone company. The Company B configuration is generally represented by Figure 1–8.

Company C

This service company is involved in the automated preparation of tax returns. Its clients are accounting firms who contract to use Company C's computer facilities and software. Depending on the size of the accounting firm, clients may choose to have a private, dedicated communication link to the host computer, or they can share a communication link with other users. Clients who share a telephone link compete with each other for access to the available telephone lines. Suppose 50 lines are shared by 150 clients and each client typically uses the connection fewer than 2 hours per day. Because of time zone differences, the workday is 12 hours long and the average use of the facility is 50% (300 hours of the 600 available connection hours). Ordinarily there is not much competition for these shared lines. But just before the April 15 income tax filing deadline, clients may dramatically increase their use of the system, so availability of the communication links might

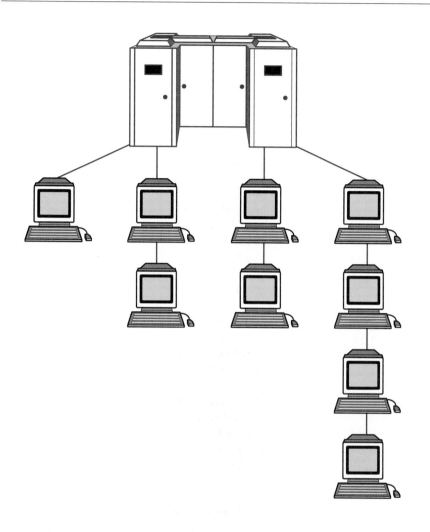

Figure 1–8
Company B's Network

twisted-pair wires One of the most common LAN media, in which pairs of wires are twisted together to minimize signal distortion from adjacent wire pairs in the sheath. The two basic types of twisted-pair wires are unshielded and shielded.

fiber optic cable A transmission medium that provides high data rates and low errors. Glass or plastic fibers are woven together to form the core of the cable. This core is surrounded by a glass or plastic layer called the cladding. The cladding is covered with plastic or other material for protection. The cable requires a light source, most commonly laser and light-emitting diodes.

become a problem. For a client who needs a line more than 2 hours per day, it is probably more economical to use a dedicated line. The Company C configuration is depicted in Figure 1–9.

Company D

This multinational company manufactures and markets large computer systems. Every large sales office has a LAN and a demonstration computer, and all of these LANs and demonstration computers as well as the computers in the software development facility, home office, and manufacturing plants are linked in one large network, consisting of more than 200 WAN nodes, 3000 LAN nodes, and 1500 terminals. In addition to long-distance telephone lines and local, private lines, Company D uses **twisted-pair wires** and **fiber optic cable** for the LAN media and satellite communication for long-distance, high-volume transmissions between manufacturing plants and divisional offices. Company D has chosen an Internet-like user

Figure 1–9
Company C's Network

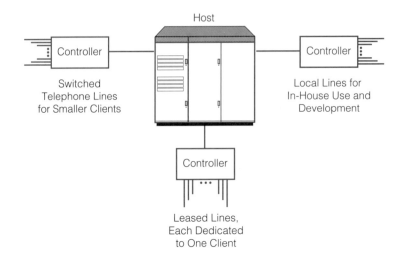

Host

Controller

Switched
Telephone Lines
for Smaller Clients

Controller

Local Lines for
In-House Use and
Development

Controller

Leased Lines,
Each Dedicated
to One Client

intranet A private network that uses Internet protocols and technology.

environment for its network. Users have Web browsers, which can efficiently locate information they are looking for. A private network that uses Internet protocols and technology is sometimes called an **intranet.** The Company D configuration is generally represented by Figure 1–10.

These four companies have very different network configurations, yet each network is efficient and cost-effective for the business that uses it. Companies A, B, and C could have installed a network similar to that of Company D, but by doing so they would have to spend considerably more for their networks and thus might lose their competitive edge.

Many alternatives are available to a network designer, and several configurations will probably solve the communication requirements. A few such alternatives might be highly cost-effective, some may be only mediocre, and a few might drive the company into bankruptcy. It is important to realize that several "right" approaches usually exist.

System Complexity

file server A computer that allows microcomputers on a network to share resources such as data, programs, and printers. The file server's software, rather than the operating system of the microcomputer, controls access to shared files.

Data communication systems may be simple or complex. A simple system might be composed of a single processor and some terminals, all located within a single building or a small local area network (LAN). Figure 1–4 illustrates the hardware components of a processor with terminals that are connected with user-provided wiring. Figure 1–11 illustrates a microcomputer LAN with a dedicated file server and six workstations. A **file server** allows the microcomputers to share resources such as data, programs, and printers. A more elaborate system might consist of several LANs, each of which is attached to a mainframe or minicomputer, which in turn is connected in a WAN. Also attached to the WAN processors are terminals that are distributed both locally and remotely. A network of this type is commonly called an **enterprise network,** which is two or more LANs connected to each other or one or more LANs connected to a WAN or to each other. Figure 1–6 depicts a system that meets this description. The computers and

enterprise network A network of two or more LANs connected to each other, or one or more LANs connected to a WAN.

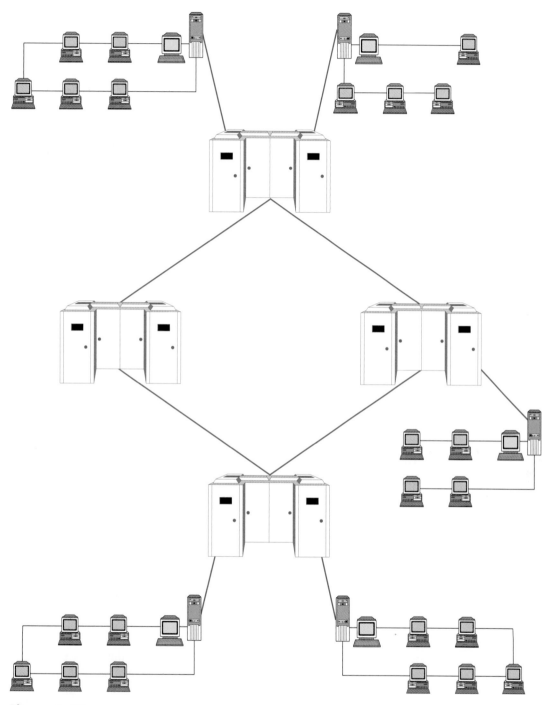

Figure 1–10
Company D's Network

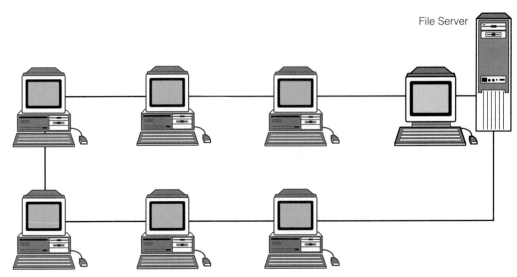

File Server

Figure 1–11
LAN with File Server and Six Workstations

terminals in this figure are connected via an assortment of private wires, communication lines leased from a common carrier (such as a telephone company), and microwave and satellite transmission. These three figures indicate the variety and complexity of communication systems. The illustrated components are discussed in detail in later chapters.

Hierarchy of Functions

Regardless of the scope of a network and the equipment and media used, all networks share common functions. To contend with the growing number of different computer networks being developed, and in the belief that these diverse systems eventually need to be connected, the **International Standards Organization (ISO)** has identified and stratified the functions that every network must fulfill. This model makes it easier to develop interfaces among these different networks.

The ISO recommendation is called the **Open Systems Interconnection (OSI) reference model,** or the OSI reference model. The reference model does more than describe network interconnections; it also defines a network architecture. Many ISO standards relating to the reference model have been established and more are being formulated. When the standards process is completed, network developers will have an alternative to proprietary corporate network architectures such as IBM's systems network architecture (SNA). Details and examples of this reference model are found in many of the following chapters. A brief description is provided here because the OSI reference model and standards arising from it are used for the development of networks. This discussion also provides an overview of communication systems.

The basic objective of a network of computers is for an application on one node to communicate with an application or device on another node. Although this may sound simple, some complexities are involved. You have just seen that

International Standards Organization (ISO) An organization that is active in setting communication standards.

Open Systems Interconnection (OSI) reference model A seven-layered set of functions for transmitting data from one user to another, specified by the ISO to facilitate interconnection of networks.

many different WAN and LAN implementations are possible, and so are many different types of interfaces. This means that you need one type of hardware and software to connect to one type of LAN and a different set of hardware and software to connect to a different type of LAN or to a particular WAN. Because of the variety of network types available and the frequent need to interconnect them, a thriving business has been created for establishing connections among networks. Building network interfaces is much simpler if the network is designed around an open architecture. An **open architecture** is one in which the network specifications are available to any company. This allows a variety of companies to design hardware and software components that can easily be integrated into new and existing networks based on the open architecture.

open architecture Architecture whose network specifications are available to any company. This allows a variety of companies to design hardware and software components that can be easily integrated into new and existing networks.

The Functions of Communication

To help motivate an understanding of the OSI reference model, consider how a worker might send a message from his or her office to a colleague in another location. This simple act can closely resemble sending a message in a network. A possible scenario for this transmission might be as follows:

1. The worker writes a message on a tablet and delivers it to her or his administrative assistant.

2. The administrative assistant makes the memo presentable by typing it, correcting grammatical mistakes, and so on. The administrative assistant places the memo in an interoffice envelope and places the envelope in the outgoing mailbox.

3. The mail room clerk picks up the mail, takes it to the mail room, sorts it, and determines a route for the message. Possible routings are internal mail, postal mail, and private express mail carriers. Because this message must go to a distant office and no priority is assigned, the clerk places the interoffice envelope in an external mailing envelope, possibly with other correspondence for that office, addresses it, and deposits the envelope in the external mailbox.

4. The mail carrier picks up the mail, including the worker's message, and takes it to the post office, where it is sorted and placed on an outgoing mail truck.

5. The post office physically delivers the mail to the mail room of the destination office. That mail room clerk opens the outer envelope and sorts its contents.

6. The mail room clerk delivers the memo in its interoffice envelope to the recipient's administrative assistant.

7. The recipient's administrative assistant takes the memo out of the envelope and prepares the memo for the recipient. The administrative assistant may time-stamp the memo, summarize it, make comments, set a priority for the recipient's reading it, and so on.

8. The recipient receives the memo, reads it, and reacts to the worker's message.

The preceding scenario describes a variety of different functions necessary to move a message from the sender's desk to the recipient's desk.

The functions consist of message composition, presentation services, address determination, enveloping, selecting transmission routes, physical transmission, and so on. In general, these same functions must be performed when transmitting a message between computers in a network. The OSI reference model explicitly identifies seven layers of functions that must be performed in network interconnections: application, presentation, session, transport, network, data link, and physical. Figure 1–12 represents the OSI layers in two network nodes, a sending and a receiving node.

In the letter-routing example, each functional layer on the sending side performed a specific set of functions, and each function was performed for a peer layer on the receiving side. Placing the correspondence in the interoffice envelope was done by the sending administrative assistant and undone by the receiving administrative assistant. In the OSI reference model, each layer in the sending network node is designed to

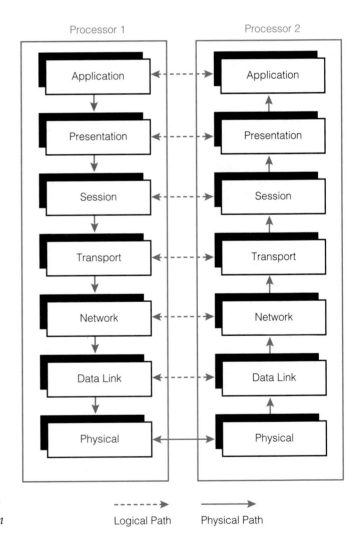

Figure 1–12
OSI Peer Layer
Communication

- - - - - ▶   Logical Path   ——▶   Physical Path

perform a particular set of functions for its corresponding (peer) layer in the receiving network node. The application layer in the sending node prepares the data for the application layer in the receiving node. The application layer then passes the message to the presentation layer. The presentation layer formats the message properly for the presentation layer on the receiving node, passes the data to the session layer, and so on. In Figure 1–12 the solid line shows the physical route of the message, and the dotted lines show the logical route, from peer layer to peer layer. Also notice that each layer has a well-defined interface through which it communicates with adjacent layers.

Functions of OSI Layers

The functions of each OSI layer are briefly described below. More extensive explanations of several of these layers are given later as needed.

Application   The **application layer** is functionally defined by the user. Sometimes application programs must communicate with each other. The content and format of the data being exchanged are dictated by the needs of the organization. The application determines which data is to be transmitted, the message or record format for the data, and the transaction codes that identify the data to the receiver. Suppose an order entry transaction started on a sales node needs to pass product shipping information to a warehouse node. In this application, the message contains the ship-to address, part identifiers, quantities to be shipped, and a message code showing the action to be taken by the receiving application.

application layer One of the layers of the OSI reference model. The functions of this layer are application dependent.

Presentation   The **presentation layer** formats the data it receives from the application layer. If certain data preparation functions are common to several applications, they can be resolved by the presentation services rather than being embedded in each application. The types of functions performed at the presentation level are encryption, compression, terminal screen formatting, and conversion from one transmission code to another (such as EBCDIC to ASCII).

presentation layer One of the layers of the OSI reference model. The presentation layer addresses message formats.

Session   The **session layer** establishes the connection between applications, enforces the rules for carrying on the dialogue, and tries to reestablish the connection if a failure occurs. The dialogue rules specify both the order in which the applications are allowed to communicate and the pacing of information so as not to overload the recipient. If an application is sending data to a printer with a limited buffer size, the agreed-upon dialogue may be to send a buffer-size block to the printer, wait for the printer to signal that its buffer has been emptied, and then send the next block of data. The session layer must control this flow to avoid buffer overflow at the printer.

session layer One of the layers of the OSI reference model. The session layer is responsible for establishing a dialogue between applications.

Transport   The **transport layer** is the first layer concerned with the world external to its processor. It performs end-to-end delivery; that is, it ensures that all blocks or packets of data have been received by the destination computer, that there are no duplicate blocks, and that blocks are ordered in

transport layer One of the layers of the OSI reference model. The transport layer is responsible for end-to-end integrity of the receipt of message blocks.

the proper sequence. It does this by affixing sequence numbers to packets being transmitted.

Network   The **network layer** does message routing and collects billing and accounting information.

Data Link   The **data link layer** must establish and control the physical path of communication to the next node. This includes error detection and correction, defining the beginning and end of the data field, resolving competing requests for a shared communication link (deciding who can use the circuit and when), and ensuring that all forms of data can be sent across the circuit. The conventions used to accomplish these data link functions are known as **protocols.**

Physical   The **physical layer** specifies the electrical connections between the transmission medium and the computer system. It describes how many wires are used to carry the signals, which wires carry specific signals, the size and shape of the connectors or adapters between the transmission medium and the communication circuit, the speed at which data is transmitted, and whether data (represented by voltages on a line, modification of radio waves, or light pulses) is allowed to flow in both directions and, if so, whether the flow can be in both directions simultaneously.

OSI Reference Model Example

Let us look at an example of activities that might occur at each level of the reference model as an application on one network node transmits a message to an application on another network node. Consider a financial application running on the network illustrated in Figure 1–13. Suppose that a bank customer uses an ATM attached to node A and that the customer's account is located on node X. An application on node A sends a message to node X requesting that the customer's account record be updated by an application running at node X. To reach node X, the message must pass through node M.

Application Layer   The application on node A builds a record with a transaction identifier, the number of the account to be updated, the date and time of the transaction, and the amount to be deducted or added. The transaction identifier tells the message recipient what to do with the record: Insert it, update it, and so on. The message is illustrated in Figure 1–14(a). The application then invokes a procedure call to send the message to the recipient.

Presentation Layer   The application layer formatted each field in the record being transmitted according to its own format rules. The receiving application may have a different set of format conventions. For example, the sending application may view a date in one format, whereas the receiving application uses a different date format. The presentation layer is responsible for translating from one format to another. It can do this by changing to a standard transmission format, which is converted by its peer layer, or it can convert directly to the format expected by the receiving application. The

network layer One of the layers of the OSI reference model. The network layer is responsible for message routing.

data link layer One of the layers of the OSI reference model. The data link layer governs the establishment and control of the communication link between two directly connected computers.

protocol Convention used for establishing transmission rules. Protocols are used to establish rules for delineation of data, error detection, control sequences, message lengths, media access, and so on.

physical layer One of the layers of the OSI reference model. The physical layer specifies the electrical connections between the transmission medium and the computing system.

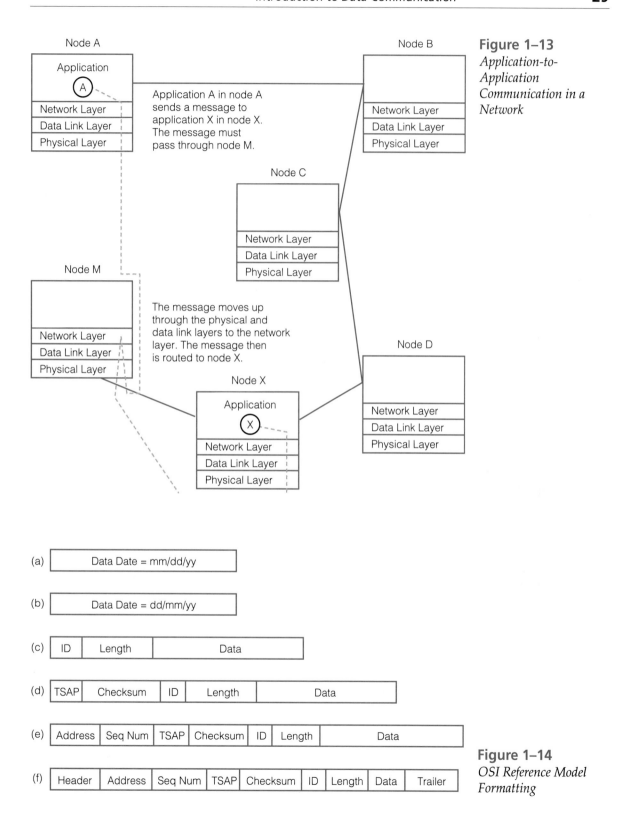

Figure 1–13
Application-to-Application Communication in a Network

Application A in node A sends a message to application X in node X. The message must pass through node M.

The message moves up through the physical and data link layers to the network layer. The message then is routed to node X.

(a) | Data Date = mm/dd/yy

(b) | Data Date = dd/mm/yy

(c) | ID | Length | Data

(d) | TSAP | Checksum | ID | Length | Data

(e) | Address | Seq Num | TSAP | Checksum | ID | Length | Data

(f) | Header | Address | Seq Num | TSAP | Checksum | ID | Length | Data | Trailer

Figure 1–14
OSI Reference Model Formatting

simplex transmission A mode of data transmission in which data flows in only one direction. One station is always a sender and another is always a receiver over a simplex link.

full-duplex mode A data transmission mode in which data is transmitted over a link in both directions simultaneously.

half-duplex mode A data transmission mode in which data can travel in both directions over a link but in only one direction at a time.

flow control Setting up how messages are transferred.

transport service access point (TSAP) An address used by the transport layer to uniquely identify session entities.

network routing table In the process of message transmission, a table in which the network layer looks up the destination address to find the next address along the path.

checksum A technique used to check for errors in data. The sending application generates the checksum from the data being transmitted. The receiving application computes the checksum and compares it to the value computed and sent by the sending station.

message after such translation has taken place appears in Figure 1–14(b). The presentation layer then sends the message down to the session layer by requesting the establishment of a session.

Session Layer   The session layer's major functions are to set up, and perhaps monitor, a set of dialogue rules by which the two applications communicate and to bring a session to an orderly conclusion. A session dialogue can be one-way (simplex) or bidirectional. In **simplex transmission,** one application sends messages to another but receives no messages in return. Bidirectional sessions can allow messages to flow in both directions simultaneously (**full-duplex** mode) or in both directions but in only one direction at a time (**half-duplex** mode). Setting up how messages are transferred is called **flow control.** Once the connection has been made, data transfer can occur. The session layer appends an identifier and length indicator at the beginning of the data block, as illustrated in Figure 1–14(c). These two fields are used to identify the function of the message, such as whether it contains user data as opposed to control functions such as session establishment or termination.

Transport Layer   The transport layer is the first OSI layer responsible for transmitting the data. The higher layers described above are oriented toward the data and application interfaces, not toward data transmission. The transport layer uses an address called a **transport service access point (TSAP)** to uniquely identify session entities. TSAPs of the source and destination session entity, together with a sequence number to detect errors, are appended to the message received from the session layer. If the sender and receiver's sequence numbers agree, the data is assumed to be correct. This step is shown in Figure 1–14(d). If the message is lengthy, the transport layer divides it into appropriate-sized transmission units.

Network Layer   The network layer provides accounting and routing functions. Upon receiving a message from the transport layer, the network layer logs the event to the accounting system and then prepares the message for transmission to the next node on the path to the destination (node M in our example). It looks up the destination address in its **network routing table** to find the next address along that path. (A routing table for a node in a small network is shown in Figure 1–15.) This is illustrated in Figure 1–14(e).

Data Link Layer   The data link layer is responsible for data delineation, error detection, and logical control of the link. Logical link control consists of determining how and when a station can transmit, connecting and disconnecting nodes on the link, and controlling flow between data link entities. Thus, the data link layer facilitates flow control between nodes A and M and between nodes M and X. Note that data link flow control is for a link, whereas session flow control is end-to-end (between source and destination applications). To fulfill its function, the data link layer appends a header and a trailer to the message. The header contains a flag that indicates the beginning of the message, the address of the recipient, message

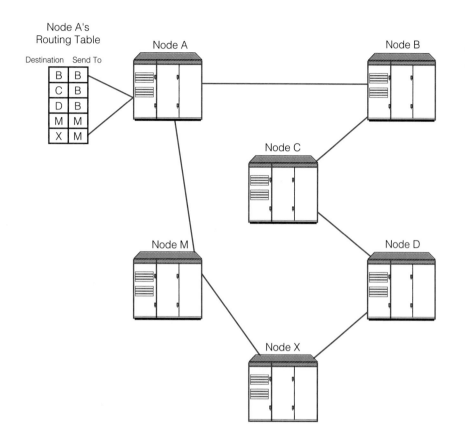

Figure 1–15
*Network Showing a
Network Routing Table*

sequence numbers, and the message type (data or control). The trailer contains a checksum for the data link block and a frame-ending flag. A **checksum** is used to help detect data errors. Headers and trailers are illustrated in Figure 1–14(f).

Physical Layer   The physical layer does not append anything to the message. It simply accepts the message from the data link layer and translates the bits into signals on the medium.

In the example, the message arrives at node M and percolates up to the network layer. The network layer services recognize that the message is destined for node X and send the message down to the data link layer for delivery to the next (and final) node. This is illustrated in Figure 1–13. The discussion in subsequent chapters starts from the bottom up, beginning with the physical layer (together with hardware components used in configuring a data communication network).

THE SOFTWARE ENVIRONMENT

Before beginning the technical discussion of the data communication system, an explanation of how it supports applications is worthwhile. Let us take a brief look at the application environment of a data communication system. Within the central processing system resides an operating system, together with data communication, database, and application software. This is illustrated in Figure 1–16. These software subsystems perform the following functions.

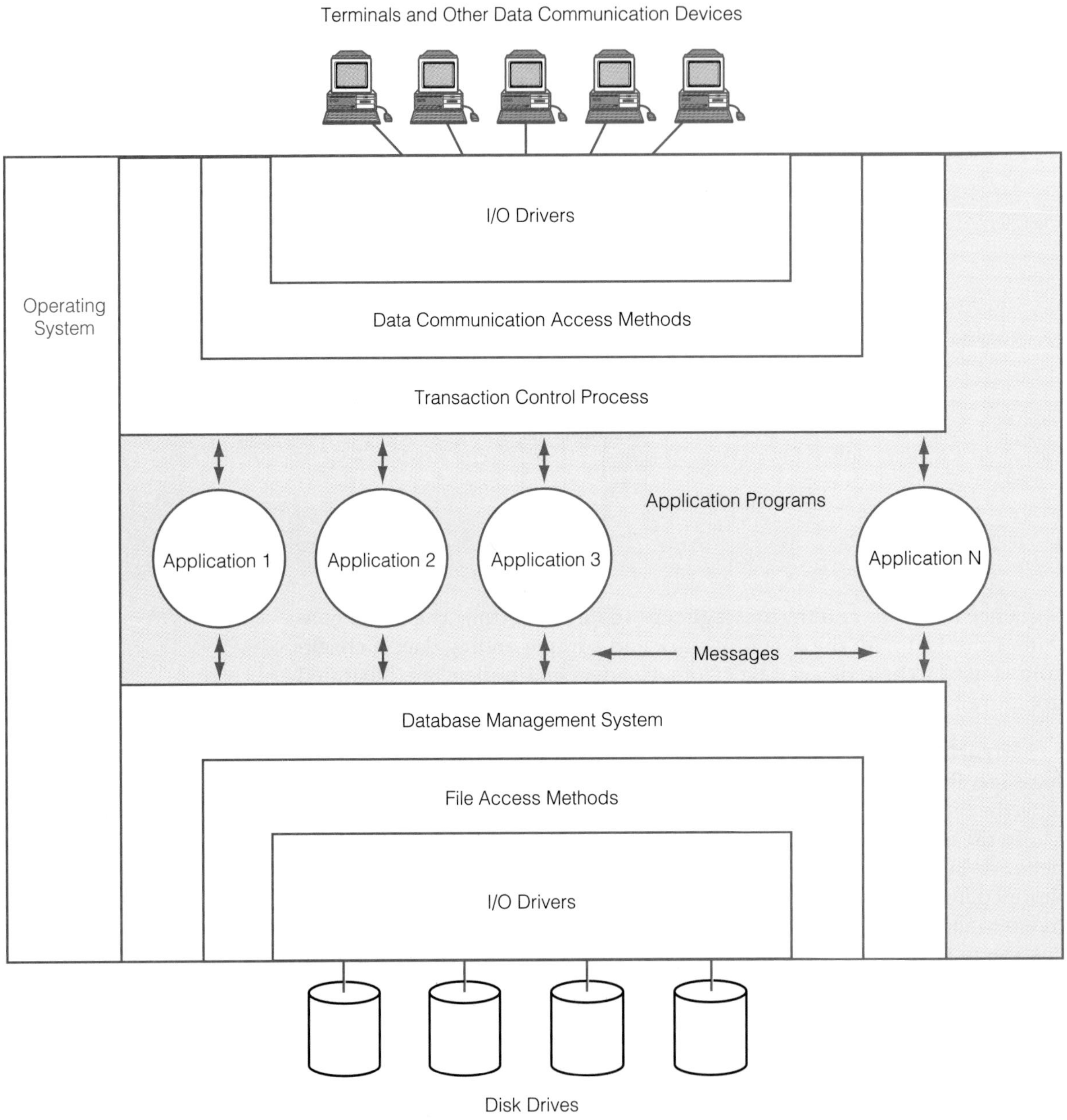

Terminals and Other Data Communication Devices

I/O Drivers

Operating System

Data Communication Access Methods

Transaction Control Process

Application Programs

Application 1

Application 2

Application 3

Application N

Messages

Database Management System

File Access Methods

I/O Drivers

Disk Drives

Figure 1–16
Application Environment

Application Programs

Application programs are the heart of the system. They are the sole reason for having a computer and associated software and hardware. Application software may be purchased from the computer vendor or a third party or developed locally. There are many varieties of application programs. For example, an inventory system has many programs, each of which performs one or more inventory functions, such as inventory update, inventory listings, and printing packing lists. A banking system consists of many programs that provide functions such as creating new accounts, deleting accounts, updating accounts, and reporting account statuses.

To make the development process efficient, programmers should not have to concern themselves with the intricacies of data communication and storage. This is why application support software, such as the operating system, data communication system, and database system, is used. The purpose of these systems is to allow application developers to concentrate on solving business problems rather than on the specifics of devices such as terminals and disk drives. By isolating applications at this level of detail, a company can also introduce devices into a system with minimal or no impact on existing application programs.

For example, it is typical to have a variety of terminals within a computer network. The way data is displayed on these devices often differs from one terminal to the next. The capabilities supported by the devices also may differ. One terminal may have a color display, and another, a monochrome display. Requiring each application to keep track of these differences would place a heavy, unnecessary burden on the application programmer. The data communication system accommodates device differences and provides a standard interface that allows an application to deal with any type of terminal.

Operating System

The operating system manages the resources of the computer. It manages memory, controls access to the processor(s), and provides interfaces to users, the input/output (I/O) subsystems, and the file system.

Data Communication

The data communication subsystem is responsible for interfacing to terminals and other devices that are attached via communication lines. These devices are distinguished from locally attached peripherals such as disk drives, printers, and tape drives. In addition to the function defined above, the data communication system provides a bridge between applications and the devices with which they must communicate. In this capacity, it switches messages between terminals and applications and becomes involved in recovery in the event of a system failure. The data communication component that provides this service is called a **transaction control process (TCP).**

transaction control process (TCP) A process that receives inputs from terminals and routes them to the proper application processes. TCPs also may edit input data, format data to and from a terminal, log messages, and provide terminal job sequencing. Examples include IBM's CICS and Tandem's Pathway. Also called a teleprocessing monitor or message control system.

Database Management System

The database management system (DBMS) serves as an interface between the application programs and the data they need to resolve business problems. The functions provided by the DBMS are data definition, data manipulation, and data management and control. Data definition provides the ability to define fields, combine fields into records, and define files, data access methods, and associations. Data manipulation allows users to retrieve, insert, delete, and modify data in the database. Data management and control allows the database administrator and operations personnel to start, stop, monitor, and reorganize the database.

transaction A user-specified group of processing activities that either are entirely completed or, if not completed, leave the database and processing system in a consistent state.

We can see how these software components work together by tracing a transaction through the system. A **transaction** is a user-defined piece of work that, from the perspective of the database, performs a series of operations that leaves the database in a consistent state. Either the entire transaction must be completed or the database must be left in the state it was in before the transaction started. For a transaction that transfers money between two accounts, there are three database states: (1) at the start of the transaction, (2) after taking money from one account, and (3) after placing the money in the second account, or the end of the transaction. The database is inconsistent in the second state.

Transaction Processing

A particular example of a transaction would be adding a new employee to the database. This process consists of inserting two records into the database, an employee record and a payroll record. The transaction starts at a terminal in the personnel department; the activity is shown in Table 1–4.

From an opening menu displayed on the terminal, the operator selects an option for adding a new employee. This selection is transmitted to the data communication system, which determines that an employee input form is

Table 1–4   User Interaction

TCP displays menu on terminal.
User selects "add employee" activity and sends to TCP.
TCP responds to terminal with data entry screen.
User fills out screen and sends to TCP.
TCP checks data for consistency and writes data to transaction log.
TCP begins transaction.
TCP sends message to application to process transaction.
Application formats data and calls DBMS routine to add employee record
   to database.
DBMS processes application request and returns completion status to application.
Application formats data and calls DBMS routine to add payroll record to database.
DBMS processes application request and returns completion status to application.
Application sends completion status to TCP.
TCP ends transaction.
TCP sends completion status to user at terminal.

required. This screen template or input form is transmitted to the terminal, where the operator enters the required information. The terminal access method is responsible for ensuring that the proper control characters are inserted to format the data for the type of terminal being used. The lower levels of the data communication system provide the logic to properly place the data on the communication line, detect transmission errors, and provide the proper electrical signals for transmission.

The operator enters the data pertaining to the new employee and transmits it back to the computer, where it is received by the data communication system. The TCP checks the message for transmission errors, logs the message to a transaction log file, and determines the transaction type. Because this transaction updates the database, the TCP formally begins a transaction for recovery purposes. The TCP recognizes that it is a message for an application, determines which application should process the transaction, and sends the message to the proper application.

The application program receives the message—to insert two new records into the database—from the data communication system and begins to process it. It formats the records and makes the DBMS request to insert them.

The DBMS accepts the records and inserts them into the database. Before inserting the records, however, the DBMS logs the record images, both before and after making the changes. These before and after images can be used for recovery if a failure occurs. All necessary associations and access methods are established as well. Upon successful completion of the record insertions, the DBMS returns a successful completion status to the application program. The application program then responds to the data communication system that the transaction has been successfully processed. The TCP ends the transaction and sends the completion status back to the terminal operator.

Throughout the transaction the operating system is actively involved, transferring control from one software subsystem to another, interfacing with the peripheral devices, and managing memory. Through the interaction of all the software systems, the transaction is completed. The operating system, the data communication system, and the DBMS support the application process in performing its work.

The preceding example was presented in the context of a network using a single host processor. With only minor modifications the discussion may also be applied to a LAN configuration or a WAN. Let us briefly look at the way in which these activities would occur on a LAN.

A user at a LAN workstation may begin by running a database program located on the file server. The database program is transferred over the LAN medium into the workstation's memory. From the user's perspective the file server appears to be a disk drive because the application issues a read or write request for a record, and the request is handled by the file server. The database processing logic is thus carried out by the workstation's processor. The database application periodically needs access to records stored in a shared database on the file server. A request is sent from the workstation to the file server asking the file server to access the desired record. The file server accepts the request, accesses the records from its disks, and transmits the records to the requesting workstation. In this example, the file server responds to requests by simply providing the workstation with the requested records. The file server does not participate in processing database records. In a different LAN scenario we may find a **database server** that cooperates with the workstation in carrying out database requests. With this alternative the workstation sends the database server a request for database processing rather than a request for individual records. The request might be something like "Give me the total sales for the Northwest Region." The database server acts on the request and returns the single figure answer rather than the set of records essential to deriving the answer. In this scenario the database server cooperates with the workstation in processing the data.

There is a common thread in each of the above examples: A user or program made a request that was acted on by one or more other processes. In one example, all of the cooperating processes were running in one processor. In the LAN examples the software was resident in two different processors. The networking trend, particularly for LANs, is to distribute the processing for a single application over two or more network nodes. An application at one node makes requests that software on other nodes process. The requester is called a client process and the processes that act on those requests are called server processes. This general concept is called client/server computing. With client/server computing, the network is called upon to solve application problems rather than having a single node responsible for all application requirements. In essence, then, the network becomes the computer! We discuss client/server computing more extensively in Chapter 5.

database server A computer that allows microcomputers on a network to request database processing of records, returning a single-figure answer rather than the set of records needed to determine the answer.

CASE STUDY

To make the discussions more understandable and relevant, examples are cited throughout this book. A common case study is carried from chapter to chapter, where applicable. This case study is adapted from actual situations. Syncrasy Corporation is a startup company in Kansas City, Missouri. The president and two founders decided to capitalize on the boom in the microcomputer marketplace by becoming a mail-order discount outlet for microcomputer hardware, software, and supplies. They have just opened their offices and warehouse and have begun taking orders. All their data processing requirements are met by a microcomputer and there is no need for data communication. As subsequent chapters illustrate, Syncrasy will become a high-growth company whose needs for computing power and data communication change rapidly as they grow and extend the enterprise.

SUMMARY

Data communication is the electronic transmission of computer-readable data. For two entities to communicate, four essential elements—message, sender, receiver, and medium—must be present. The message also must be understood by the receiver and there ought to be a means for detecting transmission errors.

The data communication industry experienced tremendous expansion during the 1970s and 1980s, largely as the result of lower prices for both equipment and transmission media. During these two decades network hardware and software became faster and more sophisticated to meet the requirements of an online system: performance, consistency, reliability, flexibility, recovery, availability, and security.

As networks proliferated, so did the ways in which they were built. In many cases this resulted in the inability of computers on one network to communicate with computers on another network. The ISO developed the OSI reference model to remedy this. The OSI reference model describes seven functional layers—application, presentation, session, transport, network, data link, and physical—for moving data from an application in one network node to an application in another node. Many standards have been developed based on the OSI reference model. The key to the model is that the interfaces and protocols are open to all, and networks designed around the model and standards can be more easily interconnected.

KEY TERMS

application layer
Arpanet
availability
batch applications
Carterphone case
checksum
common carrier
consistency
database server
data communication
data entry applications
data link layer
data link protocol
distributed applications
enterprise network
fault tolerance
fiber optic cable
file server
flexibility
flow control
full duplex
half duplex
Hush-a-Phone case
inquiry/response applications

interactive application
International Standards
    Organization (ISO)
Internet
intranet
local area network (LAN)
mean time between failure (MTBF)
mean time to repair (MTTR)
medium
network layer
network routing table
office automation systems
open architecture
Open Systems Interconnection (OSI)
    reference model
physical layer
presentation layer
protocols
recovery
reliability
remote job entry (RJE)
response time
security
sensor-based applications

session layer	transistor
simplex transmission	transport layer
Telecommunications Act of 1996	transport service access point
throughput	(TSAP)
transaction	twisted-pair wires
transaction control process (TCP)	wide area network (WAN)

REVIEW QUESTIONS

1. What is the distinction between telecommunication and data communication?

2. Why did the data communication industry grow so rapidly during the 1970s and 1980s?

3. Explain the significance to the data processing industry of each of the following:
   a. the Hush-a-Phone decision
   b. the Carterphone decision
   c. MCI
   d. the Internet
   e. the Telecommunications Act of 1996

4. Characterize each of the following types of application:
   a. interactive
   b. inquiry/response
   c. batch
   d. data entry
   e. distributed
   f. sensor based

5. What are the requirements of an online system?

6. What is a fault-tolerant data communication network? How does fault tolerance improve the reliability of a network?

7. List the seven layers of the OSI reference model.

8. List two functions of each layer in the OSI reference model.

9. What is a(n)
   a. intranet
   b. enterprise network
   c. LAN
   d. WAN

PROBLEMS AND EXERCISES

1. How does the history of data communication differ from that of database development?

2. Investigate in detail two data communication applications. Note specifically the hardware used. Determine the categories of data communication into which the applications fall.

3. Select a specific application of data communication and identify the functions that would be required in the application, presentation, and session layers of the OSI reference model.

4. Discuss the history of telephone companies in the United States or your country as that history relates to the data communication industry.

5. How do U.S. telephone companies differ from their counterparts in Great Britain, France, Germany, Japan, and Australia? In what respects are they the same?

6. How might data communication systems be used in the home?

7. Which components (if any) can be deleted from Table 1–4? Support your answer.

8. Do all transactions require database services? Give an example to support your answer.

9. In the section on performance (see "Requirements of an Online System"), two different definitions were given for response time. Using each definition, calculate the response time for a response of 2000 characters transmitted over a 2800-character per second (28,000 bps) data communication line.

10. Syncrasy has only one microcomputer and the company does not use data communication. Explain how Syncrasy could use data communication to help run its business. For example, how could Syncrasy use information resources such as the Internet, America Online, or other remote facilities?

11. Suppose Syncrasy has several microcomputers rather than just one. Can Syncrasy use data communication effectively? Explain your answer.

CHAPTER 2

Physical Aspects of Data Communication: Media

CHAPTER OBJECTIVES

After studying this chapter you should be able to

- Describe the major data communication media
- Compare selected data communication media
- Select media appropriate to a specific application
- Describe how signals are represented
- Explain the functions of a modem and CSU/DSU

In Chapter 1 we examined the essential features of communication, one of which was a medium. We also briefly discussed the OSI reference model, including the physical layer. In this chapter we examine the various media available for transmitting information, the strengths and weaknesses of each medium, and the ways to represent data during its transmission.

The transmission media commonly used in today's data communication networks can be broken down into two major classes: conducted and radiated. **Conducted media** use a conductor such as a wire or a fiber optic cable to move the signal from sender to receiver. Conducted media include telephone and telegraph wires, private wires, coaxial cables, and fiber optic cables. **Radiated media** use radio waves of different frequencies or infrared light broadcast through the air or space and therefore do not need a wire or cable conductor to transmit signals. Radiated media include broadcast radio, microwave radio, satellite radio, spread-spectrum radio, and infrared light. These options are listed in Table 2–1. Each medium, together with its necessary transmission facilities, is discussed below. The discussion focuses on the characteristics that make each medium desirable or undesirable, including

conducted media Media that use a conductor such as a wire or fiber optic cable to move a signal from sender to receiver.

radiated media Media that use radio waves of different frequencies or infrared light to broadcast through air or space and accordingly do not need a wire or cable conductor to transmit signals.

Table 2–1   Transmission Media

Conducted Media	Radiated Media
Electrical conductors	Radio frequency
Wires	Broadcast
Coaxial cable	Microwave
	Satellite
Light conductors	Spread spectrum
Fiber optics	Cellular
	Light frequency
	Infrared

speed, security, distance, susceptibility to error, and cost. These attributes form the basis of the selection criteria discussed later in the chapter.

CONDUCTED MEDIA

Wires

Wires are the earliest and currently the most commonly used data transmission medium. Much of the terminology and technology regarding this communication medium derives from telephony and telegraphy because, in setting up its own data communication networks, the computer industry used the existing network of telephone and telegraph lines. The advantages of wires are their availability and low cost. Their disadvantages include susceptibility to signal distortion or error and the low transmission rates they provide for long-distance links.

Private Versus Public Lines

Wires used in data communication are either private or public. Private lines are those deployed by the user, and public lines are those provided by a common carrier such as a telephone company. Public lines are generally in use where distances are great or the terrain or other environmental factors prohibit the use of private wires.

Transmission Speed and Frequency Range

The maximum transmission speed along wire links depends on the thickness of the wire, the number of wire conductors used, and the distance covered. Some wire media can support speeds up to 1 billion bits per second (Gbps) by using several conducting wires over short distances; some single-conductor wires covering long distances are restricted to speed under 10 thousand bits per second (Kbps). Local or private wire links typically operate at speeds up to 80 Kbps and long-distance switched telephone connections operate at 56 Kbps using analog modems and up to 9 Mbps using one of several digital switched technologies generically called **digital subscriber lines (DSLs).** DSL technology is covered in

digital subscriber lines (DSLs) An emerging service that provides much faster transmission rates than analog modems and ISDN.

Chapter 4. Higher-speed long-distance circuits are also available for applications with high-volume data transfer requirements. LAN implementations run at speeds up to 1 Gbps over copper wires enable people to use low-cost wires for very-high-speed LANs.

Cable Cost, Gauge, and Types

Private cable ranges in cost from 4¢ per foot to more than $1 per foot, depending on the shielding, gauge, and number of conducting wires in the cable. The type of wire most commonly used for private lines is copper, of American wire gauges 19, 22, 24, 26, and 28. Figure 2–1(a) shows a single-conductor wire. Private wires are usually bundled, providing multiple conductors inside one insulating sheath. The number of conducting strands in such a cable varies, with 4, 7, 8, 10, 12, 15, and 25 conductors being the most common. Figure 2–1(c) shows a wire bundle with multiple conductors.

Ordinary telephone wire consists of a twisted pair of wires. Bundles of these wire pairs from telephones in a given area are sheathed together. Each pair of wires is twisted together to minimize signal distortion from adjacent wire pairs in the sheath. Figure 2–1(b) depicts an individual twisted-pair wire. Twisted-pair wires are one of the most common media in LANs. The two basic types of twisted-pair wires are unshielded (UTP) and shielded (STP). STP wires have an extra foil cladding that protects the wires from external interference. When used in LANs, twisted-pair wires commonly operate at speeds of 1, 10, 16, and 100, and 1000 Mbps.

Switched Connections Versus Leased Lines

Data communication over long distances can use either switched or leased line connections. **Switched connections** use the same equipment as a standard voice telephone call. One device dials the telephone number of another device's line. Because the telephone company cannot guarantee exactly which path or switching equipment such a connection will use, the speed and quality of the switched connection are limited by the equipment used to set up the circuit. Low-quality equipment may be used to establish the call because the circuit may be routed in a variety of ways. Today most switched, analog telephone connections operate at speeds of 28.8, 33.6, or 56 Kbps. Higher speeds are possible, but the potential for error and the cost of

switched connection A communication link established when one station dials a telephone number to connect to another station. A switched connection uses voice circuits. The circuit exists for the duration of the session.

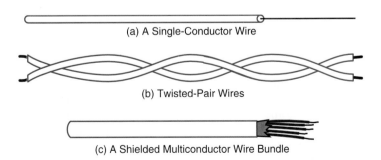

(a) A Single-Conductor Wire

(b) Twisted-Pair Wires

(c) A Shielded Multiconductor Wire Bundle

Figure 2–1
Types of Wires

the extra equipment necessary make such speeds cost prohibitive for most users. This limit on speed is being increased in certain areas as telephone companies implement digital data transmission technology, which allows speeds of up to 9 Mbps with switched connections. In Chapter 3 you will read about digital data transmission; common carrier options are discussed in Chapter 4.

Because they are more expensive for dedicated use than leased lines, switched lines are used when the amount of transmitted data is small or when many locations must be contacted for short periods. Two examples are a team of salespeople entering information on their portable terminals and a central host computer for a retail organization that contacts each retail outlet at the close of the business day to collect sales and inventory data. In both these situations the amount of data to be transferred is small, and the number of locations may be large or variable. Switched lines become more expensive as the connection time increases, and their cost-effectiveness may depend on their location, the time of transmission, and the number of required connections. Chapter 4 discusses an alternative to switched lines: packet distribution networks.

Leased lines are used if the connection time between locations is long enough to cover the cost of leasing or if speeds higher than those available with switched lines must be attained. The cost of a leased line is a function of the distance covered, the transmission speed of the line, and the line's susceptibility to error. Common carriers provide a wide variety of options to satisfy diverse needs. For example, a leased line would enable users in a sales office in Seattle to communicate with a host computer in San Francisco. For this application the data volume is low and a low transmission speed is sufficient but the connection is maintained throughout the day, which makes the leased line cost-effective. An application in which a leased line would be used for both economy and speed is when two distant computers—in Chicago and Los Angeles, for example—must exchange high volumes of information in a timely manner and for interregional traffic on the Internet. (For now, only the medium of wires is being considered, and alternatives are being ignored.)

Telephone companies can provide **conditioning** for leased telephone lines to reduce error rates and increase transmission speeds. One example of conditioning is the use of special equipment that equalizes the signal delay for all frequencies. The five levels of conditioning are C1 through C5, with level C3 not commercially available. Conditioned leased lines typically operate at speeds up to 64 Kbps. Again, digital data transmission may be considerably faster.

Very-high-speed connections are also available. Although such high-speed links may use other media, such as fiber optics and microwaves, they are included in this discussion of wires because of their association with telephone lines. These high-speed services are designated T-1, T-2, T-3, and T-4 and offer transmission rates of 1.5, 6.3, 46, and 281 Mbps, respectively. T-2 service is not commonly available. More detail about common carrier services may be found in Chapter 4. The cost of leased lines has continually changed as a result of new technologies and industry competition.

leased lines Lines leased from common carriers. Lines are leased if the connection time between locations is long enough to cover the cost of leasing or if speeds higher than those available with switched lines must be attained.

conditioning A service provided by telephone companies for leased lines. It reduces the amount of noise on the line, providing lower error rates and increased speed.

Twisted-Pair Wires

Twisted-pair wiring consists of a bundle of color-coded wires, usually 4 or 8 wires. Two of these wires with matching color codes form a pair that are twisted about each other, as illustrated in Figure 2–2(a). One such color scheme uses a solid color and a solid color with a white stripe as a pair; for example, a solid blue wire and a blue and white striped wire form one pair and an orange and orange-white striped wire form another pair. One pair may be used to transmit data and the other is used to receive data. Twisted-pair wires are classified in several ways:

- by American wire gauge (AWG) rating
- by shielding (either UTP or STP)
- by categories that define the wire's rated acceptable speed and error characteristics

AWG Rating   The AWG is a measure of the thickness of the copper conductor in the cable. The higher the AWG rating, the smaller the diameter of the wire; that is, a wire with an AWG rating of 12 is thicker than one with an AWG rating of 24. Twisted-pair wires for LANs have an AWG rating of 22–26. Standard telephone wires may be smaller, with an AWG rating of 26. When selecting LAN wiring, you ordinarily do not need to consider the AWG rating of the wires because it is included in the specifications used to define wire categories.

UTP and STP   You might have been wondering about the significance of twisted wires as opposed to straight wires. When electrical signals are transmitted over wires, an electromagnetic field is created along the axis of the wire. This electromagnetic field may affect the signals being transmitted along adjacent wires. When the wires are twisted about each other with at least two twists per foot, the effect of the electromagnetic field is minimized.

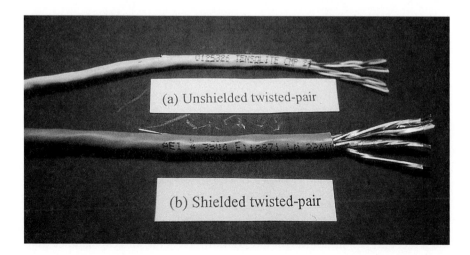

(a) Unshielded twisted-pair

(b) Shielded twisted-pair

Figure 2–2
Twisted-Pair Wires

This type of interference, called crosstalk, is measured in decibels and is discussed later in the section on error sources. Straight wires are more susceptible to crosstalk than are twisted-pair wires.

Even though twisting pairs of wires together minimizes crosstalk, it does not eliminate it and there are other sources of transmission errors. Some of these errors can be reduced by shielding the wires. STP wires have a metal foil or wire mesh wrapped around individual wire pairs, with a metal braided shield around the twisted-pair wire bundle itself; the entire bundle is enclosed in a polyvinyl chloride (PVC) jacket. The STP wire bundle is illustrated in Figure 2–2(b). Twisting pairs of wires helps eliminate interference from neighboring wires; the metal shielding helps prevent ambient distortion from heavy-duty motors, electrical or magnetic fields, and fluorescent lights. UTP wires, as the name implies, have no protective metal covering. Consequently, UTP wires are more susceptible to environmental noise that can disrupt the signal. When the signal is disrupted, transmission errors are likely to occur. When errors are detected, the data must be retransmitted and the efficiency of the network is reduced. Companies use UTP because it is cheaper than STP. UTP may safely be used in environments where external disruptions are rare.

In addition to being classified as UTP or STP, twisted-pair wires are classified by categories. Several different rating classifications exist. One of the principal classifications was developed by the Electronics Industries Association (EIA) and the Telecommunications Industries Association (TIA). This classification, EIA/TIA-568, defines five categories of wires. In general, the distinctions between categories are the thickness of the wire, as defined by the AWG standard, and the error characteristics. Also included in the specification are connector types to be used in making the connection of the wires to wiring hubs and wiring closet punchdown blocks. A **punchdown block** is used as a terminal point for multiple-wire cables. Figure 2–3 shows a wall block connection panel.

punchdown block A connector used as a terminal point for multiple-wire cables.

Category 1 Wire   Category 1 wire is the traditional telephone wire. It uses thin copper conductors and is not rated for LAN speeds.

Category 2 Wire   Category 2 wire is certified for speeds up to 4 Mbps. This type of wiring has been used in older networks that operated at or below this speed. Because most of today's LAN implementations operate at 10 Mbps or higher, category 2 wires should be avoided.

Category 3 Wire   The specifications for category 3 wires are more stringent than those for categories 1 and 2. Category 3 wire must have at least 3 twists per every foot of wire and no two pairs should have the same number of twists per foot. This configuration provides better protection from crosstalk and provides more error-free transmissions than categories 1 and 2. Category 3 wire is common in LANs operating at 10 Mbps, and some 100-Mbps implementations allow category 3 wires over short distances.

Category 4 Wire   Category 4 wire is common in 16 Mbps LANs. It must meet higher standards for attenuation, crosstalk, and capacitance than

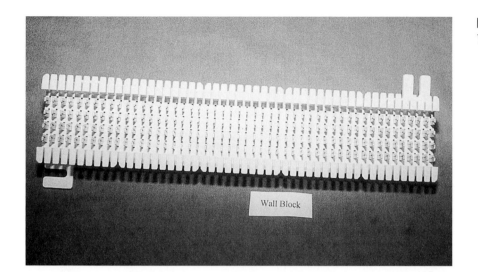

Wall Block

Figure 2–3
Wire Connection Panel

lower categories. **Attenuation** is signal loss over distance. Signals transmitted over LAN media fade according to the distance they travel, just as your voice transmission fades as more distance is placed between you and the person you are talking to. Capacitance is a measure of the energy stored by the cable. If the stored energy is high, transmission errors are more likely than if the energy level is low.

attenuation Weakening of a signal as a result of distance and characteristics of the medium.

Category 5 Wire   Category 5 wire is the best of the five categories. It is certified for speeds up to 1 Gbps, and as the speed threshold for twisted-pair wires increases, category 5 (or new categories) will probably be the only wire category supported. The attenuation and crosstalk characteristics of category 5 wires are better than those of category 4 wires.

Connectors   Two connectors for twisted-pair wires are defined by the EIA/TIA-568 standard. An 8-pin modular connector, typically a telephone-like RJ-45 jack, as illustrated in Figure 2–4, is used to connect to a LAN adapter and to a wiring hub or wall outlet as well as other connectors.

Table 2–2 summarizes the characteristics of the five wire categories, and Figure 2–5 illustrates a generic twisted-pair wiring layout. Other wire classifications other than those just described exist. For example, the IBM Corporation established a wiring classification and cable layout plan using four wire classification types: type 1, type 2, type 6, and type 9. Like the EIA/TIA classification, these classifications specify different AWG specifications and error characteristics. The relative cost column in Table 2–2 indicates wire cost differentials. For example, if category 1 cable costs 5¢ per foot, category 3 cable is approximately 10¢ per foot and category 5 cable is 20¢ per foot. Thus, category 5 cable costs approximately 1.33 times as much as category 4 cable. Cable costs can vary by as much as 15 or 20¢ per foot for category 5 cable. As of this writing, category 1 cable costs begin at about 4¢ per foot.

Figure 2–4
RJ-45 Telephone Jack

An additional configuration for twisted-pair wires is plenum cables. Normal cables are insulated with PVC. In the case of fire, PVC cables may emit a hazardous gas and building codes may prohibit the use of such cable in certain areas. Plenum space is defined as the air space between the ceiling and the next floor, and ordinances may require that cables in plenum areas be enclosed by metal conduits or be plenum rated. Plenum cables are coated with a coating such as Teflon, which does not emit noxious gases during fires. Plenum cables are somewhat more expensive than nonplenum cables.

Twisted-pair wires, particularly category 5, are commonly used as the medium for LANs. The advantage of twisted-pair wires is their ability to support high speeds at a low cost. Their disadvantages include susceptibility to signal distortion or error and lower transmission speeds when they are deployed over longer distances (compared to other types

Table 2–2   Twisted-Pair Wire Category Characteristics

Category	Maximum Data Rate	Typical Use	Cost (relative to category 1)
1	1 Mbps	Telephones, low-speed LANs	1
2	4 Mbps	Token-ring LANs	1.5
3	10 Mbps	Ethernet LANs	2
4	16 Mbps	Token-ring LANs	3
5	100 Mbps and 1 Gbps	Ethernet and fast Ethernet LANs, CDDI LANs, and asynchronous transfer mode	4

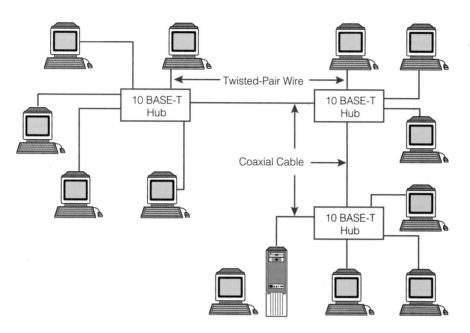

Figure 2–5
Generic Twisted-Pair Wiring Layout

of media). For example, in one LAN standard, the maximum wire distance between a workstation and the wiring hub is 100 m. Longer cable distances for this same technology are possible for coaxial cable and fiber optic cable.

Coaxial Cable

Coaxial cable is primarily used in LANs or over short distances, generally fewer than 10 mi (except for use by common carriers). Most LANs are privately owned and are restricted to a small geographical area such as an office building or complex of buildings. LANs are discussed in more detail in Chapters 6–9. Coaxial cable is also used to connect terminals with terminal controller units (see Chapter 10 for information about communication controllers). Data transmission rates of up to 100 Mbps are not uncommon, and the theoretical bit rate is more than 400 Mbps.

Technology

Coaxial cable comes packaged in a variety of ways, but essentially it consists of one or two central data transmission wires surrounded by an insulating layer, a shielding layer, and an outer jacket, as depicted in Figure 2–6. Coaxial cable transmission involves two basic techniques: baseband and broadband. In **broadband transmission** the data is carried on high-frequency carrier waves; thus, several channels may be transmitted over a single cable. Frequency separation, using **guardbands,** helps keep one signal from interfering with another. Broadband technology allows one medium to be used for a variety of transmission needs, so that voice, video, and multiple data

broadband transmission A form of data transmission in which data is carried on high-frequency carrier waves; the carrying capacity of the medium is divided into a number of sub-channels, such as video, low-speed data, high-speed data, and voice, allowing the medium to satisfy several communication needs.

guardband Frequency separation that helps to keep one signal from interfering with another.

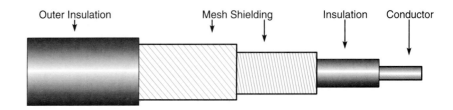

channels of varying transmission speeds can all exist on one cable. A subchannel with frequencies between 200 and 250 million hertz (MHz) might be used to carry video data, a subchannel operating between 175 and 200 MHz could be used for a LAN, voice data could be carried on a subchannel operating between 50 and 75 MHz, and so on.

baseband transmission
Sends the data along
the channel by means
of voltage fluctuations.
The entire bandwidth
of the cable is used to
carry data.

    Baseband transmission, on the other hand, does not use a carrier wave but sends the data along the channel by voltage fluctuations. Baseband technology cannot transmit multiple channels on one cable, but it is less expensive than broadband because it can use less expensive cable and connectors. Some coaxial cable can be used for either baseband or broadband. Baseband and broadband transmission are illustrated in Figure 2–7.

Advantages and Disadvantages

The television industry has helped develop coaxial cable technology, including the ability to add stations or tap into a line without interrupting existing service. In an environment where workstations are regularly added, moved, or deleted, the ability to alter the equipment configuration without disruption to existing users is significant. However, the ability to tap into the cable without disrupting service is a disadvantage if a high degree of security is required. Coaxial cable shielding provides a high degree of immunity to externally caused signal distortion. In LANs of less than a half-mile range (the distance varies with specific implementations), signal loss or attenua-

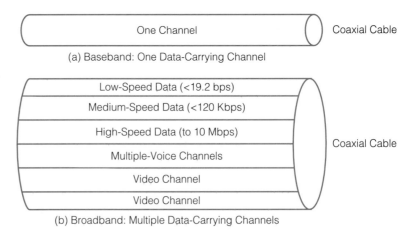

tion is not a concern; for longer distances, repeaters that enhance the signals are necessary.

Security may be considered both an advantage and a disadvantage of coaxial cable. If a very secure medium is required, with taps being difficult to make and easy to detect, coaxial cable presents a serious problem. Whenever distances are great, attenuation becomes a problem, as does the cost of the greater amount of cable and the repeaters that must be installed to enhance the signals over long distances. The advantages of coaxial cable include its high data transmission rates, its immunity to noise or signal distortion (compared with twisted-pair wires), its capability for adding stations, and its reasonable cost over short distances.

Coaxial cable was once the primary LAN medium. It is used less often in today's LANs for several reasons: high speeds over cheaper twisted-pair wires, reduced costs for fiber optic cables, and ease of maintenance for fiber optic cables. Coaxial cable is heavy, bulky, and harder to deploy than twisted-pair wires and fiber optic cable.

Fiber Optic Cable

Fiber optic cable is used by telephone companies in place of long-distance wires and by private companies in implementing local data communication networks.

Technology

Fiber optic cables come in three varieties, each with a different way of guiding the light pulses from source to destination. All three have the same basic form and characteristics. One or more glass or plastic fibers are woven together to form the core of the cable. This core is surrounded by a glass or plastic layer called the cladding. The cladding is covered with plastic or some other material for protection. Figure 2–8 shows a side

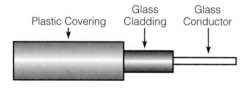

(a) Side View of a Fiber Optic Cable

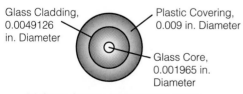

(b) Cross-Section of Fiber Optic Cable

Figure 2–8
Views of a Fiber Optic Cable

Figure 2–9
Fiber Optic Multimode Step Index

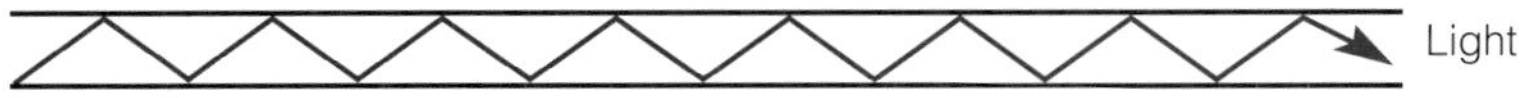

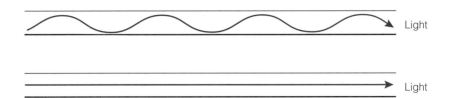

view and a cross-section of a fiber optic cable. All three cable varieties require a light source; laser and light-emitting diodes (LEDs) are most commonly used.

The oldest of the three fiber optic technologies is **multimode step-index fiber.** The conduction core of this cable is the largest of the three, approximately 100 microns for the core and 140 microns for the cladding. With multimode step index the reflective walls of the fiber move the light pulses to the receiver, as illustrated in Figure 2–9. The light pulses traveling straight through the core arrive at the end of the fiber slightly ahead of those being reflected off the walls. This limits the transmission speed, and this form of fiber is the slowest of the three. In **multimode graded-index fiber,** light is refracted toward the center of the fiber by variations in the density of the core. The diameters of the core and cladding for multimode graded index are approximately 50 and 125 microns, respectively. Multimode graded-index fiber is commonly used in LANs. Figure 2–10 depicts the movement of light in a multimode graded-index fiber. The third and fastest fiber optic technique is **single-mode transmission.** With single-mode transmission the core is very small, approximately 10 microns, and the light is guided down the center of this extremely narrow core. Single-mode fiber is commonly used for longer-distance communication links and very-high-speed LANs. Single-mode transmission is depicted in Figure 2–11. A comparison of the diameters of the three types of fiber optic cable is given in Figure 2–12. Fiber optic transmission rates currently available range up to approximately 2 Gbps, and speeds greater than that are possible.

multimode step-index fiber The oldest fiber optic technology, in which the reflective walls of the fiber move the light pulses to the receiver.

multimode graded-index fiber Fiber in which light is refracted toward the center by variations in the density of the core.

single-mode transmission The fastest fiber optic technique, in which the light is guided down the center of an extremely narrow core.

Benefits and Cost

One shortcoming of fiber optics is the inability to add new nodes while other nodes are active. Although it is now easy to splice the fiber optic cable and add new stations, the network or a portion of the network must be down while the splice is being prepared. Fiber optic links for very short distances cost more than wires, but as distance or the required transmission rate increases, fiber optics becomes cost-effective. The breakeven point generally occurs when the distance is so great that coaxial cable or wires would require expensive signal-enhancing equipment. A significant advantage of fiber optic cable over copper wire is its lower size and weight; it is about

Figure 2–10
Fiber Optic Multimode Graded Index

Figure 2–11
Fiber Optic Single Mode

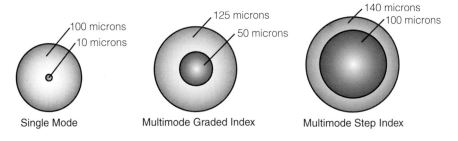

Figure 2–12
Diameter Comparison of Fiber Optic Cable

one-twentieth as heavy and one-fifth as thick as equivalent copper wire (either coaxial or twisted-pair). Very low error rates and immunity to environmental interference are additional benefits.

RADIATED MEDIA

Broadcast Radio

Broadcast radio uses not only the radio frequencies typical of AM and FM radio stations, but short-wave or short-distance radio frequencies as well, with a total frequency range from 500,000 Hz to 108 MHz. Broadcast radio's primary applications are in paging devices, cellular radio telephones, and wireless LANs. A good example of an early use of radio broadcast for data communication is the AlohaNet at the University of Hawaii. Broadcast radio was chosen to overcome the difficulty of setting up wire links in the islands, and it proved quite effective when the number of stations was small. As more stations were added, however, contention between broadcast stations increased, collisions and interference became more common, and effective use dropped. The medium also proved to be susceptible to interference from other radio broadcast sources. The AlohaNet transmission rate was 9600 bps. When broadcast radio is used with LANs, cables connecting each microcomputer are eliminated. The elimination of cables makes installation and changing of workstations easier and reduces the problems of loose connections that can occur as a result of people walking or pulling on cables; however, wireless LANs cannot match the speed of LANs using conducted media.

Mobile computing has expanded the role of broadcast radio in data communication. The importance of mobile computing and communication is such that major evaluation and reallocation of the available radio frequencies may result. Mobile computing, of course, requires a wireless medium and broadcast radio is being increasingly used in this manner. This new application of radio transmission is placing ever higher demands on a limited range of broadcast frequencies. The demand is reaching the point at which some experts suggest that countries need to reevaluate the use of the entire frequency spectrum and use radio-frequency transmission only for mobile communication. Nonmobile communication such as television would be delivered exclusively by conducted media, thus freeing those frequencies for mobile communication devices such as portable computers and personal communicators.

broadcast radio Uses AM, FM, and shortwave radio frequencies, with a total frequency range of 500,000 to 108 MHz. Its primary applications include paging terminals, cellular radio telephones, and wireless LANs.

mobile computing Has expanded the role of broadcast radio in data communication. It requires a wireless medium such as cellular radio, radio nets, and low-orbit satellites. It makes installing and changing workstations easier.

The most common media for mobile computing communication are cellular radio, radio nets, and low-orbit satellites. Cellular radio, as currently implemented, tends to be costly and operates at low speeds, typically 28.8 Kbps or lower. This makes cellular radio suitable primarily for transfers of small amounts of data such as electronic mail messages. Cellular radio transmission for data is also subject to high error rates.

Radio nets using dedicated frequencies over large areas are also used for mobile computing. These networks require the use of a radio modem to send and receive data. Currently radio nets operate at speeds up to 28.8 Kbps, but higher speeds are likely as this technology expands. Low-orbiting satellites offer another communication alternative. Unlike geosynchronous satellites, low-orbit satellites do not remain in a fixed position relative to the earth. However, using several low-orbit satellites ensures that at least one is always in position to accept and relay signals. Use of this technology for commercial mobile computing is still in its infancy. Each of these three technologies has the disadvantages of low speed, possibility of signal interference, and lack of security.

Microwave Radio

microwave radio A method of transmitting data using high-frequency radio waves. It requires a line of sight between sending and receiving stations. Capable of high data rates, microwave is used for WANs and wireless LANs.

It was MCI's proposal for a **microwave radio** linkage between Chicago and St. Louis that first stimulated competition for long-distance telephone service. The first commercially implemented digital microwave radio system was installed in Japan by Nippon Electric Company in 1968.

Microwaves are being used as a medium for wireless LANs. For networks where installation of conducted media is difficult or too expensive, microwaves provide a high-speed alternative. The microwaves are generated at a low power to minimize the effects on humans, but the waves are able to penetrate through thin walls. Microwaves as a LAN medium provide transmission speeds of 10 Mbps, and higher speeds are inevitable.

Technology

Microwave transmission rates range up to 45 Mbps. Because microwave signals travel in a straight line, both transmitter and receiver must be in each other's line of sight (there can be no obstructions between them, except as noted above for LANs). The curvature of the earth therefore requires that microwave stations be approximately 30 mi apart on level ground. The difference between the highest and lowest possible frequencies, also called the limiting frequencies, of a microwave channel is called the channel's bandwidth. Bandwidth is an indicator of a medium's speed. The bandwidth of a microwave channel can be subdivided into many subchannels, similar to the multiple channels in broadband transmission. The subchannels may be used for voice-grade transmission, high-speed data links, or both. Bandwidth and other measures of carrying capacity are discussed later in this chapter.

Advantages and Disadvantages

Microwave transmission offers speed, cost-effectiveness, and ease of implementation; however, it is susceptible to interference from other radio waves.

It also is limited by line-of-sight considerations, and commercial transmissions are insecure because they can be intercepted by anyone with a receiver in the line of transmission. Microwaves can also be affected by environmental conditions. Transmissions at the same or nearly the same frequencies can interfere with each other, and some atmospheric conditions, such as high humidity, can affect the signal. Figure 2–13 shows a microwave relay station.

Satellite Radio

Satellite radio transmission, like microwave radio transmission, transmits data via very-high-frequency (VHF) radio waves; both media require line-of-sight transmission between stations. The primary difference between the two media is station location. Microwave makes use of land-based stations only, whereas satellite uses both land-based stations and orbiting stations. Commercial communication satellites are placed in an equatorial, geosynchronous orbit at an altitude of 22,300 mi. A **geosynchronous orbit** means that the satellite remains stationary relative to a given position on the earth,

satellite radio transmission Transmits data via very-high-frequency (VHF) radio waves and requires line-of-sight transmission between stations.

geosynchronous orbit A satellite orbit in which the satellite is stationary with respect to the earth. The satellite is always positioned over the same location.

Figure 2–13
Microwave Relay Station

Figure 2–14
Geosynchronous Satellite Orbit

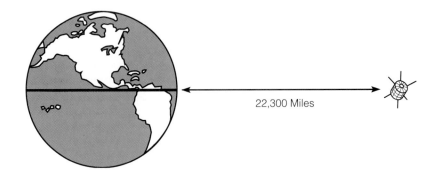

Figure 2–14
Geosynchronous Satellite Orbit

as illustrated in Figure 2–14. At this altitude, only three satellites are required to cover all points on the earth, as shown in Figure 2–15. Because there is limited room for geosynchronous orbiting satellites, a variation called inclined orbit satellites is being used more often. Inclined orbit satellites are also positioned 22,300 mi above the equator; however, inclined orbit satellites move slightly north and south of the equator, as illustrated in Figure 2–16. This movement requires that the earth stations track the movement of the satellites. Typically, tracking antennas are smaller (1.2 to 2.5 m in diameter) than the more traditional earth stations (7 m in diameter or larger). These smaller antennas are called very small aperture terminals (VSATs). The added expense of having a tracking antenna is typically offset by lower transmission costs.

Low-orbit satellites are also beginning to be used more extensively. Several companies are implementing networks of low-orbit satellites (approximately 400 to 1000 mi high). These satellite networks can be used to provide low-speed data services. Potential uses include paging, mobile telephones,

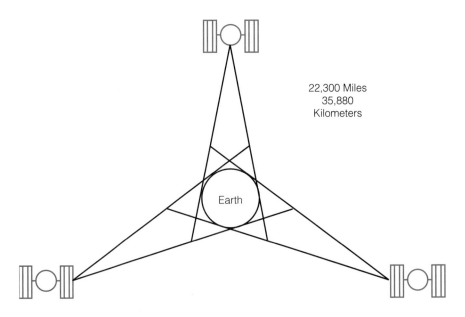

Figure 2–15
Geosynchronous Satellite Positioning

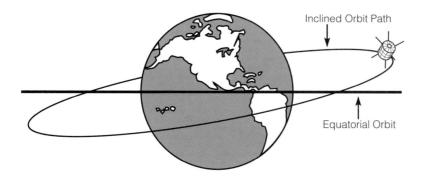

Figure 2–16
Inclined Orbit Satellite

communication with vending machines (the machine can report low stock levels), and video conferencing. Some of these networks will eventually have enough satellites in place to provide worldwide coverage. An example of how a message would be routed from New York to Paris by such a system is shown in Figure 2–17.

Technology

The basic components of satellite transmission are the earth stations and the satellite component called a **transponder.** The transponder receives the transmission from earth (uplink), amplifies the signal, changes the frequency, and transmits the data to a receiving earth station (downlink). The uplink frequency differs from the downlink frequency so that the weaker incoming signals are not interfered with by the stronger outgoing signals. Satellite frequencies are spoken of in pairs, such as 12/14 GHz. The first number represents the downlink frequency and the second the uplink frequency. Thus, 12/14 GHz means a downlink transmission frequency of 12 GHz and an uplink transmission frequency of 14 GHz. To avoid interference, geosynchronous communication satellites must be separated by an arc of at least 4 degrees, as depicted in Figure 2–18. (This has led to concern, especially among countries currently incapable of launching satellites, that only a limited amount of space is available for these satellites and that the space will be allocated without them obtaining a slot.) Low-orbit and inclined-orbit satellites provide alternatives to geosynchronous satellites, but there are still space limitations. Each transponder has a transmission rate of approximately 50 Mbps, which can be divided into 16 1.5-Mbps channels, 400 64-Kbps channels, or 600 40-Kbps channels. Although this transmission rate is high, there still is a significant delay because the signals must travel a long distance from source to destination.

transponder In satellite communication, a transponder receives a transmission from earth (uplink), amplifies the signal, changes frequency, and retransmits the data to a receiving earth station (downlink).

Propagation Delay

The amount of time it takes for a signal to travel from its source to its destination is called **propagation delay.** Because most data communication signals travel at nearly the speed of light, propagation delay on earth is insignificant (about 5 ms for a 1000-mi journey). Actual terrestrial transmission speeds are somewhat slower due to characteristics of the medium and

propagation delay The amount of time it takes for a signal to travel from its source to its destination.

Figure 2–17
Transmission with Low-Orbit Satellites

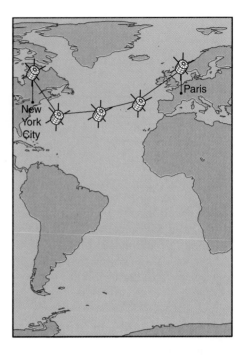

the characteristics of transmission equipment; however, the propagation delay is barely noticeable in response times. Across the extremely long distances of space, however, propagation delay can be noticeable. The delay includes travel time as well as the time required to accept, enhance, and retransmit the signal. Propagation delay becomes significant for applications that have sending times of less than a quarter-second or response times of a half-second or less. Propagation delay is ordinarily ignored for terrestrial links, but satellite transmission system designers must be aware of this

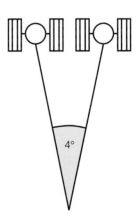

Figure 2–18
Satellite Separation

factor. Table 2–3 gives an example of how propagation delay is computed for a transaction in which a remote terminal sends a message to a host computer and receives a reply from it.

Satellite Providers

The several providers of transponders for satellite communication include Hughes Network Systems, Comsat, AT&T Tridom, GTE Spacenet, and Scientific Atlanta, as well as broadcast agencies in Canada, Japan, Europe, and the former Soviet Union. The number of transponders per satellite is typically between 12 and 24. Providers of satellite time usually lease a whole transponder, but it is also possible to sublease transponder subchannels from another user. Satellites make expansion of a data communication network easy. All that is required is to add earth stations (except when the area being served is outside the area served by the satellites being used). Satellite networks can present security problems, however, because transmission can be intercepted by anyone with proper receiving equipment.

Spread-Spectrum Radio

The primary application of **spread-spectrum radio (SSR)** for data communication is wireless LANs. SSR has long been used by the military to provide reliable radio communication in battlefield environments where signal jamming can be expected. One characteristic of SSR is reliability in environments where signal interference is likely.

Two methods, frequency hopping and direct sequencing, are used to provide SSR signals. With **frequency hopping,** data is transmitted at one frequency, then the frequency is changed and data is transmitted at the new frequency, and so on. Each piece of data is transmitted over several frequencies to increase the probability that it will be successfully received. **Direct sequencing** sends data over several different frequencies simultaneously. When used in wireless LANs, SSR distances are limited to approximately 1000 feet, making it useful for small LANs or as the medium for small segments of larger LANs. Examples of SSR being used in a large LAN include the use of portable computers and LAN connections in an area in which it is difficult or expensive to install conducted media. SSR signals can penetrate normal office walls but signal strength is reduced considerably by concrete

spread-spectrum radio (SSR) The primary application for data communication is for use with wireless LANs. It has a characteristic reliability in environments where signal interference is likely.

frequency hopping Data is transmitted at one frequency, the frequency changes, and the data is transmitted at the new frequency. Each piece of data is transmitted over several frequencies to increase the probability that the data will be received successfully.

direct sequencing Sends data out over several different frequencies simultaneously to increase the probability of success.

Table 2–3   Satellite Propagation Delay

Remote–satellite input uplink	22,300 mi
Satellite–host input downlink	22,300
Host–satellite response uplink	22,300
Satellite–remote response downlink	22,300
Total distance	89,200 mi
Travel time = 89,200 mi / 186,000 mi/s = 0.48 s	

Table 2–4 Frequency Spectrum Classification

Frequency (Hz)	Wavelength
10^{16}	X rays, gamma rays
10^{15}	Ultraviolet light
10^{14}	Visible light
10^{13}	Infrared light
10^{12}	Millimeter waves
10^{11}	Microwaves
10^{10}	UHF television
10^{9}	VHF television
10^{8}	VHF TV (high band) FM radio
10^{7}	VHF TV (low band) Shortwave radio
10^{6}	AM radio
10^{5}	Very low frequency
10^{4}	Very low frequency
10^{3}	Very low frequency
10^{2}	Very low frequency
10^{1}	Very low frequency

and metal walls. Like most radiated media, SSR is susceptible to signal interference and interception. The speed of data transmission (2 Mbps) also is lower than that of many of today's LANs using conducted media.

Infrared Transmission

infrared transmission Uses electromagnetic radiation of wavelengths between visible light and radio waves. It is a line-of-sight technology used to provide local area connections between buildings and is also used in some wireless LANs.

Infrared transmission uses electromagnetic radiation of wavelengths between those of visible light and radio waves. Infrared transmission is another line-of-sight technology. It is used to provide local area connections between buildings and is used in some wireless LANs. Data transmission rates are typically on the order of 4 Mbps or less.

Radiated Media Frequencies

The frequencies of various radiated media are given in Table 2–4.

MEDIA SELECTION CRITERIA

Several factors (Table 2–5) influence the choice of a medium for a data communication network. Because every configuration has its own set of constraints, not all factors apply in every situation; in some situations, there may be only a single viable alternative. However, system designers must consider each criterion, either implicitly or explicitly. The factors also may influence one another. For example, a strong correlation often exists between a

Table 2–5   Media Selection Criteria

Cost	Security
Speed or capacity	Distance
Availability	Environment
Expandability	Application
Error rates	Maintenance

medium's application and its required speed, so that the application usually dictates a minimum acceptable transmission speed (although other factors such as cost and expandability can also pertain).

Cost

A dramatic expansion in the application of data communication began during the 1970s, influenced strongly by improvements in technology and lower costs. Cost reductions were the result of improved technology and competition among the common carriers providing transmission services. The technological advances included communication equipment capable of supporting higher data transmission rates at lower costs, as well as the commercial availability of fiber optics and satellite transmission.

The costs associated with a given transmission medium include not only the costs of the medium but also ancillary fees, such as the costs of additional hardware and software that might be required. A deferred ancillary cost that is important to consider when making an initial selection is the cost of expansion. An emerging marketing organization located in Houston, Texas, might initially select the specific market areas of New York City, Chicago, Houston, and Los Angeles. The logical choice for connecting the remote offices to the host computer in Houston is to lease a line from a common carrier. As the corporation expands into other cities, however, a satellite link could be more economical because the expense of adding new locations might be less than that of leasing more land lines.

Speed

A tremendous range of transmission speeds is available. Low-speed circuits transmit at rates less than 100 bps, high-speed circuits at more than 1 Gbps. Within a given medium, higher speeds mean higher costs, although this is not necessarily attributable to the medium itself. Higher data transmission rates require more sophisticated (expensive) communication equipment. Two factors dictate the required speed of a medium: response time and aggregate data rate. Design goals for an online application should include the expected response time for each type of transaction. The **aggregate data rate** is the amount of information that can be transmitted per unit of time. Medium speeds are summarized in Table 2–6.

aggregate data rate
The amount of information that can be transmitted per unit of time.

Response Time

Response time has two components—transmission time and processing time—and each of these can be broken down into subcomponents. Suppose

Table 2–6 Media and Their Common Transmission Speeds (bps)

Private line	300, 1200, 2400, 4800, 9600, 19,200, 38,400, 56,000, 64,000, 80,000
Switched line (analog)	300, 1200, 2400, 4800, 9600, 19,200, 38,400, 56,000
Switched line (digital)	64 K, 128 K, 1 M, 6 M
Leased telephone line	2400, 4800, 9600, 19,200, 56,000, 64,000, 80,000
T1, T2, T3, T4	1.5 M, 6.3 M, 46 M, 281 M
Unshielded/shielded twisted pair	1 M, 10 M, 16 M, 100 M, 1 G
Coaxial cable	1 M, 2 M, 10 M, 50 M, 100 M (over 400 M potential)
Fiber optics	Over 2 G
Microwave	To 45 M
Broadcast radio	9600, 19,200, 28,800
Spread-spectrum radio	2 M
Infrared light	1 M, 4 M
Satellite	To 50 M

the design objective is a response time of 3 s for 95% of one type of transaction. If processing takes 1 s, transmission must take 2 s or less. If the transaction involves the exchange of 500 characters of information, then the speed of the medium must be at least 250 characters per second (500 characters divided by 2 s), which represents approximately 2400 bps. This assumes that there is no sharing of the communication link. If the line is shared, allowances must be made for the amount of time that the line might be unavailable to a specific user. Chapter 10 discusses several ways in which one communication line can be shared among several users.

Aggregate Data Rate

In applications such as bulk data transfers, aggregate data rate may dictate line speed. Suppose the application just discussed required that the line be available to office personnel during the day for inquiries and updates and that within an hour of closing time a file of 2 million characters had to be transmitted to a host computer. The business day requirements for response time could be satisfied with a 2400-bps channel, but the file transfer would require an aggregate data rate of about 555 characters per second (2 million characters per hour divided by 3600 seconds per hour), which is a 7200-bps channel. (Note: These examples do not allow for any overhead or retransmissions due to errors.)

Availability

Availability has two aspects: availability when needed and sufficient carrying capacity to handle the volume of data. An operation that uses a switched telephone line would be at a disadvantage when phone lines are busy, as on certain holidays. Imagine a fast-food chain with stores throughout the United States that maintains a central file of sales and inventory data. Each store's terminals record the daily receipts and foods dispensed. At the end of the business day the central location dials the phone number of each store's computer, transfers and processes the data collected during the day, and then orders supplies for each restaurant. On Mother's Day the phone circuits are extremely busy, which interferes with the chain's ability to contact all of its locations. This lack of availability would not be catastrophic for this application, but for a process control or factory control application, lack of availability could produce disastrous results.

Shared Lines   Shared lines also can create problems of availability. One user may monopolize the line, thus making it unavailable to others. Suppose two terminals share a line, and one user is attempting interactive queries into a database while the other attempts to copy a lengthy file to an attached printer. The line's capacity may be taken up with the file transfer, making the line unavailable to the other user.

Control Messages   Some of a line's capacity must be reserved for control messages. For instance, error detection requires additional bits of information to be appended to the data. A long message that must be broken down into segments for transmission requires extra information to delimit the message's beginning, end, and segments. Acknowledging receipt of transmitted data creates additional line congestion. When erroneous messages are received, then the last message, and perhaps several previous messages, must be retransmitted. Multiple devices per line requires that addresses be appended to messages; in many instances, control sequences must be transmitted to establish when each device can use the medium and receive data. Finally, idle time may occur on the circuit because there is no data to send or because the state of the circuit is being changed, as with a control message to disconnect from a switched connection. These types of control functions can take up a considerable amount of the carrying capacity of a circuit—as much as 30%, excluding idle time. Figure 2–19 illustrates some of the extra fields appended to a message for transmission and for segmenting a long message.

Expandability

Often it becomes necessary to expand the scope of a data communication configuration, either by adding more devices at a given location or by adding new locations. Some media—such as coaxial cable and satellites—make expansion into new locations easy, whereas others—such as leased telephone lines—make expansion more difficult or more costly. It is important that communication networks be designed for the future as well as for immediate needs. Suppose a rapidly growing computer company used private wires to attach terminals for some employees in the head office. The initial applications were extremely successful, and new applications and employees were quickly added. This created a need for more terminals, which required additional communication circuits. The company had to go

Figure 2–19
Message Transmission

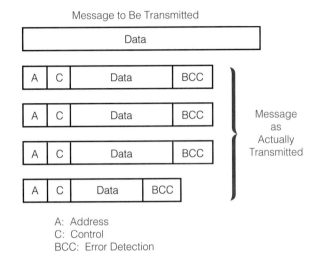

through the time-consuming and expensive process of stringing additional wires throughout the facility. Had they anticipated their growth correctly, the additional wires could have been installed with the initial set.

Several alternatives are available in such situations. Instead of supplying additional circuits, the company could have added new hardware, such as concentrators, multiplexers, or addressable terminals. Such solutions are the subject of Chapter 10. Expandability is a problem not just of media availability but also of hardware. When a system has reached its maximum capacity with respect to the available number of devices and communication circuits, a larger machine or additional machines must be added. The airline industry's reservation systems have faced this problem several times as more subscribers were added to the network.

Error Rates

All transmission media are subject to signal distortion, which can produce errors in the data. The propensity for error influences not only the quality of transmission but also its speed. For example, switched telephone lines are subject to noise from switching equipment and other sources, which typically limits the speed to 56 Kbps or less. Such errors pose no problem in voice communication because humans are adept at detecting errors and recovering from them; either a person does not understand what is being said or the context is incorrect, and recovery is simple because a person can usually ask that a message be repeated. Computers, on the other hand, do not understand context, and therefore are unable to detect a corrupted data bit. The impact of even one undetected inverted bit can be significant. Suppose that a bank must use data communication to transfer several million dollars to another bank. If just one of the high-order bits in the money field is changed, a difference of several million dollars can result. Detecting transmission errors in data communication environments requires that redundant information be included with the transferred data. This technique reduces the efficiency of the link and still cannot ensure absolute accuracy of the data. The common methods for detecting errors are discussed in Chapter 3.

Security

The lack of security in data communication networks was made clear by several widely publicized incidents of hackers or espionage agents penetrating several major networks. To read about these incidents, read the following:

> *Approaching Zero* by Paul Mungo, Random House, 1992
>
> *Cyberpunk* by Katie Hafner, Simon & Schuster, 1991
>
> *The Fugitive Game* by Jonathan Littman, Little, Brown & Company, 1996
>
> *Takedown* by Tsutomu Shimomura, Hyperion, 1996
>
> *The Cuckoo's Egg* by Clifford Stoll, Doubleday, 1989

Personal computers equipped with a modem provide a low-cost way to connect to computer networks. With this equipment all an intruder needs is sufficient network connect time to find and exploit the network's security weaknesses. The above references show that costs for connect time can be avoided or minimized through the use of toll-free numbers, local calls to installations in the hacker's calling area, use of an established low-cost access network such as the Internet, use of stolen telephone credit cards, or illegally bypassing a common carrier's toll system.

Providing complete security, like providing an error-free medium, is impossible. However, some media, such as fiber optics, are more difficult to penetrate than others such as microwave and satellite. Microwave and satellite transmissions are easy to intercept because they are broadcast and anyone with the proper receiver can pick up the signals. The conducted medium most vulnerable to the average hacker is switched telephone lines. Most companies providing data communication have switched telephone line access. In some instances computer vendors insist on such an access capability for emergency maintenance and diagnostic purposes. To avoid misuse of these lines, they should be deactivated when not needed and protected by security devices such as a call-back unit when operational. Call-back units and other security devices are described in Chapter 10.

Distance

Distance includes not only transmission distance but also the number of locations served. If the distances are short (within one building or complex of buildings), private media such as wires, coaxial cable, or fiber optics may be feasible. With greater distance or number of locations, it usually becomes necessary to obtain media from a common carrier. As the number of locations to be reached becomes very great, or when it is necessary to communicate with remote locations, a broadcast medium such as a satellite may be the only viable solution.

Environment

The constraints of environment can eliminate certain types of media. Even when the distance between two buildings to be connected in a data communication network is small enough to make private lines feasible, local ordinances may prohibit the user from installing such lines. If a locale prohibits the stringing of wire over or under a public street, the user might have to pick a medium other than private wires. Direct satellite links in leased office facilities might be impossible because the lease prohibits installing earth stations on the premises. Private lines that must be strung through areas with considerable electrical or magnetic interference might be impractical because of the potential for inducing error in transmission. Environment clearly plays a critical role in the selection of a transmission medium.

Application

Certain applications (such as environmental monitoring) use devices designed to connect to a system in a very specific way and at specific speeds. In such applications, the characteristics of the required equipment may dictate the type of medium and interfaces to be used. As noted above, the particulars of an application also help determine other required characteristics of the medium, such as speed, security, and availability. For instance, the most obvious media for a high-speed LAN are twisted-pair wires, coaxial cable, and fiber optics, whereas the private branch exchange (PBX) telephone system would be a lower-speed alternative.

Maintenance

Just as all media are subject to error, all are subject to failure. In some cases repair or replacement is simple: A telephone cable severed in an excavation accident can be repaired within days, and while repairs are being made an alternative path might be made available. Repair or replacement of a defective satellite, however, is a lengthy process, which is why communication companies often have a backup transponder available. Maintenance concerns do not have a high priority because such failures are rare. Nonetheless, system designers must consider the impact of medium failures and their probable duration and must prepare a backup or contingency plan so communication can continue while repairs are being made. Consider a major bank in Australia that depended heavily on its computer center. The bank established multiple computer centers, each served by different telecommunication trunk lines. It also made provisions for switching lines from one center to another in case the communication links to one of the centers were severed. As a result, no failure at a single point was able to disrupt the bank's ability to process data.

A comparison of the principal data communication media is provided in Table 2–7. In some instances it is difficult to separate one criterion from another. Consider the expandability of a network that uses wires. It can be expanded in several ways. One expansion option may be to add new hardware instead of new lines. Suppose a company needs to add two more terminals in a location that currently has only one. Instead of adding two new

Table 2–7   Media Comparison Table

	Wires	Coaxial Cable	Fiber Optics	Microwave	Broadcast Radio	Satellite
Availability	Good	Good	Good	Good	Possible contention	Fair to good
Expandability	Fair	Good in local area	Good	Good	Good	Good
Errors	Fair	Good	Good	Fair	Fair	Fair
Security	Fair	Fair	Good	Poor	Poor	Poor
Distance	Good	Poor	Good	Good	Good	Good
Environment	Fair	Good	Good	Fair	Fair	Fair

communication lines, a hardware device called a multiplexer can be installed at each end of the connection. A multiplexer will allow all three terminals to share the same line. Multiplexers are covered in Chapter 10. Another expansion option is to allow the three terminals to share the same line using a technique called polling. Polling is also discussed in Chapter 10. Another alternative is to add two new communication lines. If this last alternative is chosen, there is usually no problem in obtaining the circuit. Unfortunately, the cost may be high, which is why this cell in the table is assigned a rating of fair. This table should be used in conjunction with Table 2–6, on transmission speeds, because it is important that each device communicating on a medium have sufficient access and speed to perform its task. Configurations such as the line-sharing ones just mentioned reduces the availability of the medium to individual attached devices. This means that with one type of multiplexer on a 56-Kbps line with four devices, the available speed to an individual device is only 14 Kbps.

SIGNAL REPRESENTATION AND MODULATION

As noted above, each medium has individual characteristics that determine how and where it might be used. The medium serves as a conduit for data. It is also important to understand how data can be represented on the medium. The two basic classes of data representation are analog and digital. We now look at how data are transmitted.

Bit Rates, Baud Rates, and Bandwidth

Up to this point, data transmission speed has been discussed exclusively in bits per second, or **bit rate.** This is the most appropriate unit for system analysis; however, two other terms also are commonly used: bandwidth and baud rate.

bit rate One method of measuring data transmission speed, in bits per second.

Bandwidth   The **bandwidth** of a channel is the difference between the minimum and maximum frequencies allowed. A voice-grade channel that can transmit frequencies between 300 and 3400 Hz has a bandwidth of 3100

bandwidth The difference between the minimum and the maximum frequencies allowed.

Hz. Bandwidth is a measure of the amount of data that can be transmitted per unit of time and is directly proportional to the maximum data transmission speed of a medium. The higher the bandwidth, the greater the data-carrying capacity.

Baud Rate   The **baud rate** is a measure of the number of discrete signals that can be observed per unit of time. Only in the binary situation is the baud rate exactly the same as the bit rate. Unfortunately, the two terms are often used interchangeably. But the bit rate is higher than the baud rate when a baud represents more than one bit of information. In the binary amplitude modulation situation, two different signal levels can represent the bits 0 and 1. If the signal changed 7200 times a second, the baud rate would be 7200 and the bit rate would be 7200 bps. Suppose, instead, that four different amplitudes were represented—1, 2, 3, and 4 per unit of time—as in Figure 2–20. Each level could then be used to represent two bits. This technique is called **dibits.**

Now suppose a signaling rate of 7200 changes per second is maintained. The baud rate remains at 7200, but the bit rate doubles to 14,400 bps because each signal represents two bits. Figure 2–21 shows the transmission of the bit pattern 1001001 using dibits (with one bit added to make the number of bits even). Similarly, eight signal levels could represent three bits with each signal, a technique called **tribits.** If 16 different signaling levels were used, four bits per signal could be represented, a technique called **quadbits.** Therefore, with current technology the bit rate equals the baud rate or a multiple thereof (two, three, or four times the baud rate). **Phase shift keying (PSK)** or a derivative is the most common method of achieving dibit and tribit transfer; **quadrature amplitude modulation (QAM)** is the most common method for quadbit transfer. Later in this chapter we explain how PSK and QAM are implemented.

Digital Versus Analog Representation

All the computers we are considering store data in digital form and transmit this data in analog or digital form. In **digital transmission,** data is repre-

baud rate A measure of the number of discrete signals that can be observed per unit of time.

dibits A transmission mode in which each signal conveys 2 bits of data.

tribits A method of modulation that allows 3 bits to be represented by each signal.

quadbits A technique in which each signal carries 4 bits of data. Requires 16 different signals.

phase shift keying (PSK) A form of phase modulation.

quadrature amplitude modulation (QAM) A modulation technique using both phase and amplitude modulation.

digital transmission A transmission mode in which data is represented by binary digits rather than by an analog signal.

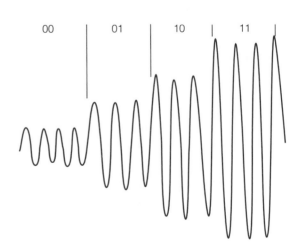

Figure 2–20
Dibits Using Amplitude Modulation

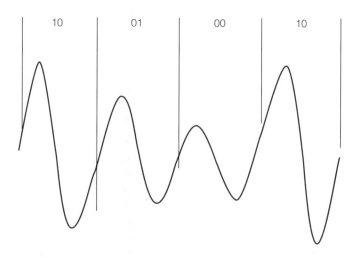

Figure 2–21
Example of Dibits Using Amplitude Modulation

analog transmission
Refers to measurable physical quantities, which in data communication take the form of voltage and variations in the properties of waves. Data is represented in analog form by varying the amplitude, frequency, or phase of a wave or by changing current on a line.

sented by a series of distinct entities. In data communication equipment this series is almost always a binary digit, or bit, either 0 or 1. **Analog transmission** refers to measurable physical quantities, which in data communication take the form of voltages and variations in the properties of waves. Data is represented in analog form by varying the amplitude (height), frequency (period), or phase (relative starting point) of a wave. Translation from digital format to analog format and back to digital format is accomplished by a device known as a **data set** or **modem** (an acronym for modulator–demodulator). A modem accepts digital data (a string of bits), transforms the data into an analog signal, and passes the signal along a medium to another modem. The receiving modem translates the analog signal back into digital data. Because the telephone companies' original communication systems transmit information in analog form, these systems must change the data to analog form to meet the requirements of data communication transmission facilities. For digital lines, another device, a channel service unit and data service unit (CSU/DSU), provides the line interface. In a later section we discuss modem capabilities. First, we look at a method for representing data in an analog format.

modem (data set) Short for modulator–demodulator. A device that changes digital signals to analog signals for transmitting data over telephone circuits. Also used for some fiber optic transmission (digital fiber optics do not require a modem) and any transmission mode requiring a change from one form of signal to another.

Carrier Signals

One of the trigonometric relationships between angles in a right triangle is called the sine of the angle. The values for the sine of an angle vary from 1 to -1 and a continuous curve of this function can be plotted. Figure 2–22 depicts a simple sine wave. A wave of this form has the potential for carrying information. If the wave continues without change, as depicted, no information can be discerned. Such an unmodulated signal is called a **carrier signal.** The purpose of a modem is to change, or modulate, the characteristics of the carrier wave so a receiver can interpret information. The simple sine wave has several properties that can be altered to represent data: amplitude (height), frequency (period), and phase (relative starting point). Modems alter one or more of these characteristics to represent data.

carrier signal A wave that continues without change, carrying information that cannot be discerned but can be modulated by a modem so a receiver can interpret the information.

Figure 2–22
Simple Sine Wave

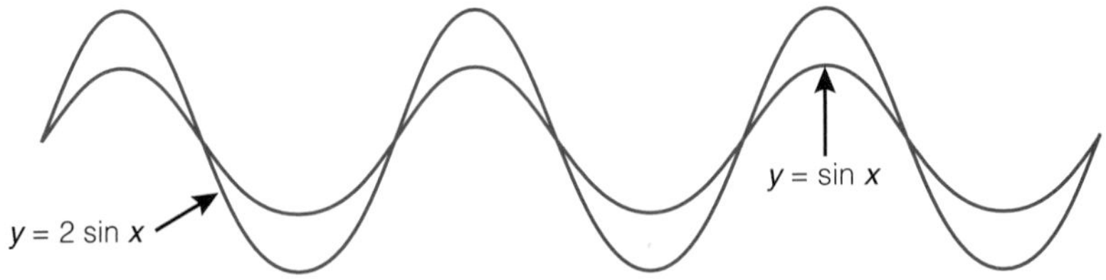

$y = \sin x$

Figure 2–23
Superimposed Sine Waves, Example 1

$y = \sin x$

$y = 2 \sin x$

Amplitude Modulation

amplitude modulation (AM) One method of changing the properties of a wave to represent data.

The simplest characteristic to visualize is **amplitude modulation (AM).** Figure 2–23 represents two sine waves superimposed on one another. One curve represents sin x and the other represents 2 sin x. Note that the 2 sin x curve has twice the amplitude of the sin x curve. (Varying the amplitude of a curve is similar to changing the voltage on a line.) How is this variation used to convey information? Suppose the bit pattern 1001001 is to be transmitted. If a 1 bit is represented by the curve of 2 sin x and a 0 bit by the curve traced by sin x, the bit pattern would be represented by the modulated sine curve depicted in Figure 2–24.

Frequency Modulation

Hertz (Hz) The term used to denote frequency; 1 Hertz is one cycle per second.

Frequency modulation (FM) (frequency shift keying (FSK)) One method of changing the characteristics of a signal to represent data. The frequency of the carrier signal is changed. Often used by lower-speed modems.

The period, or frequency, of a sine curve is the interval required for the curve to complete one entire cycle. In the simple sine curve the period is 2 π (pi), where pi is approximately 3.14159. In data transmission such intervals are only seconds, so the period is the number of seconds required for the wave to complete one cycle. The mathematical function that alters the period is sin nx. Figure 2–25 shows the curve of sin 2x. When the horizontal axis represents time, the period is frequency (oscillations) per unit of time. **Hertz (Hz)** is the term used to denote frequency; 1 Hz is one cycle per second. The human ear can detect sound waves with frequencies between 20 and 20,000 Hz. Telephone systems use the much smaller frequency range between 300 and 3400 Hz, which is satisfactory for carrying voice transmission.

To convey information by **frequency modulation (FM),** or **frequency shift keying (FSK),** is to vary the frequency of the transmission. To transmit the

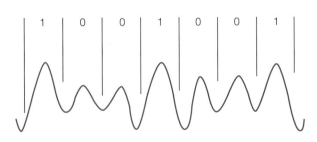

Figure 2–24
Amplitude Modulation

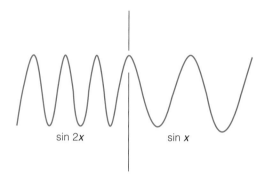

Figure 2–25
Curve of sin 2x

sin 2*x*   sin *x*

binary pattern 1001001 by frequency modulation on a voice-grade line, a frequency of 1300 Hz can represent the 1 bit and a frequency of 2100 Hz can represent the 0 bit (one of the values used by some modems). The signal received must be within 10 Hz of these values to be acceptable, which means the range for a 1 bit is 1290–1310 Hz. These frequency values must be different enough to minimize the possibility of signal distortion altering the values transmitted. Thus, if the 1 bit were represented by 1500 Hz and the 0 bit by 1510 Hz, a decrease of only 10 Hz would change a 0 bit into a 1 bit. Figure 2–26 shows an example of frequency modulation for our selected bit pattern 1001001.

Phase Modulation

A third modulation technique is **phase modulation** (phase shifting). If the simple sine curve is represented by sin x, then a change of phase is represented by sin $(x + n)$. Figure 2–27 shows the curve of sin x, Figure 2–28 shows the curve of sin $(x + \pi)$, and Figure 2–29 shows the two curves superimposed on one another. Transmitting the bit pattern of 1001001 using phase modulation, where a 1 bit is represented by no phase change and a 0 bit by a change in phase of pi radians, yields the curve in Figure 2–30.

Phase modulation is often used for high-speed modems because it lends itself well to the implementation of dibits, tribits, and quadbits. Figure 2–31(a) shows 8 different angles in a full circle. Suppose each angle is used as a phase shift in phase modulation. Thus, with 8 different signals we can represent 3 bits of information per signal, or tribits. In Figure 2–31(b) the 8 angles are combined with two levels (amplitudes) of signal, providing 16 different signals, each of which can represent 4 bits. This

phase modulation A change in the phase of a carrier signal. Commonly used alone or in conjunction with amplitude modulation to provide high-speed transmission (4800 bps and higher).

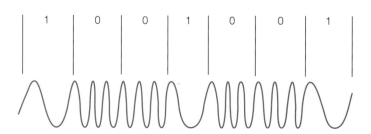

| 1 | 0 | 0 | 1 | 0 | 0 | 1 |

Figure 2–26
Frequency Modulation

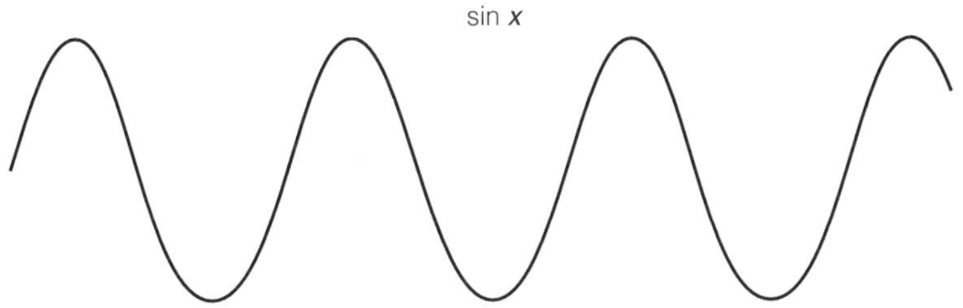

Figure 2–27

Curve of sin x

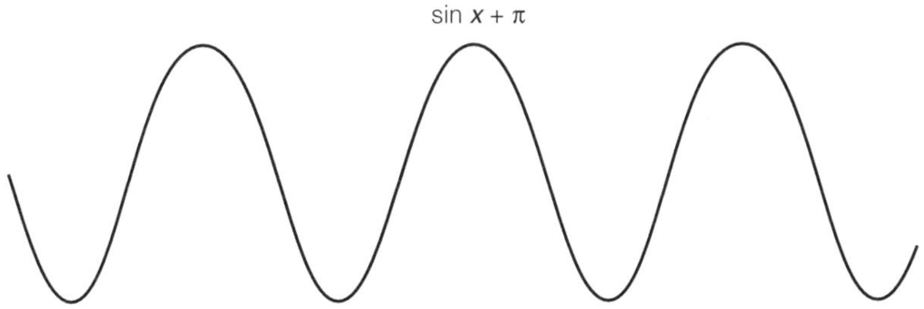

sin *x*

Figure 2–28

Curve of sin x + π

sin *x* + π

combination provides a quadbit capability known as quadrature amplitude modulation (QAM). QAM on a 1200-baud line can provide transmission of 9600 bps. The most common modulation techniques in data communication are frequency modulation (frequency shift keying) and phase modulation, also known as phase shift keying (PSK). Also available are a variation known as **differential phase shift keying (DPSK)** and QAM.

differential phase shift keying (DPSK) A modulation technique that uses phase modulation. DPSK changes phase each time a 1 bit is transmitted and does not change phase for 0 bits.

Modems and Their Capabilities

Modems fall into three basic categories: copper-based, radio frequency, and fiber optic. Copper-based modems are used to interface to twisted-pair wires, radio-frequency modems are used for wireless communication, and fiber optic modems are used with fiber optic cable. The principle of each type of modem is essentially the same: changing signals from one format to another and then back again. Copper-based modems change a device's digital signals to analog or digital electrical signals, radio-frequency modems change digital signals to radio frequencies, and fiber optic modems change a device's digital signals to optical digital signals. When the supplier of fiber optic cable is a common carrier, the common carrier is responsible for signal generation. A company that installs its own fiber optic cables may need to purchase its own fiber optic modems.

When modems are used to transmit data over communication links, they are always used in pairs. The modems in a pair must be configured alike. Most modems have a variety of available options. Figure 2–32 shows a modem. Some modem capabilities are presented in Table 2–8, and a terminal–computer connection using modems is illustrated in Figure 2–33. Most modems on the market do not offer all of these capabilities. Some options are explained here; the remainder are discussed in Chapters 4, 10, and 11.

Speed All modems are designed to operate at a specific speed or range of discrete speeds. A variable-speed modem can be set via switches

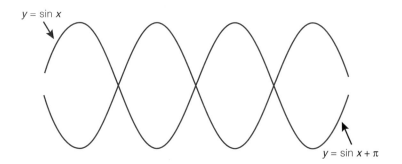

Figure 2–29
*Superimposed Sine
Waves, Example 2*

on the modem, via program control, or by automatic adjustment of the transmission speed.

Telephone Options Auto-answer, manual answer, auto-dial, auto-disconnect, automatic redialing, and keyboard dialing features are available with switched telephone lines. Most newer modems can react to the ring indicator on the line and automatically answer a call. For a manual-answer modem, someone must help in making the connection. This "inconvenience" promotes security. Auto-dialing means that the modem can dial a number itself. Many modems can remember frequently called numbers. Each memory location can usually be associated with a code name, making dialing even easier. For example, the code name "school" can be used to represent the telephone number for the school's computer center. The user can then direct the modem to dial school rather than selecting the specific number. With auto-disconnect a modem terminates a call automatically when the other party hangs up or a disconnect message is received. Automatic redialing modems automatically redial a call that resulted in a busy signal or no connection. Finally, keyboard or programmable dialing means that the number can be dialed using the keyboard of a terminal or via program control. For mobile computing, cellular radio, broadcast radio, and pocket modems are available. Pocket modems are small modems used primarily for portable computers. Modems conforming to the Personal Computer Memory Card International Association (PCMCIA) standards are available for notebook computers. Pocket, PCMCIA, and radio-frequency modems are new technologies and show that

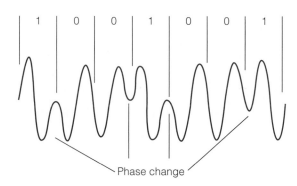

Figure 2–30
Phase Modulation

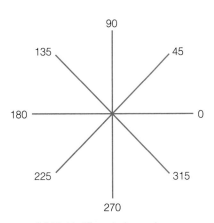

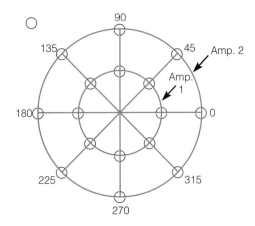

(a) Eight different phase changes suitable for tribits.

(b) Eight phase changes plus two amplitudes yields 16 different signals for quadbits. The 16 different signals are represented by circles.

Figure 2–31
Phase Modulation Angles and Amplitudes

mobile computing is becoming an important segment of the data communication market.

Self-Testing Most new modems, and many older models, have some type of self-testing mode. These include a loop-back test, in which the modem's outgoing signal is looped back to itself; memory diagnostic checks; and modem-to-modem test transmissions. These self-tests are quite valuable in isolating problems in the communication equipment.

Voice-Over Voice-over data capability allows voice communication over the same circuit as the data, as voice or data or as voice and data simultaneously. This arrangement is beneficial when the data transmission application requires a dedicated circuit to a remote location. Suppose a company requires voice telephone communication between offices already linked by leased lines. Every such call can be dialed, incurring a toll for each, or voice-over data modems can be used, occupying a portion of the line ca-

Figure 2–32
High-Speed Modem

Table 2–8 Some Modem Capabilities

Speed and variable speed	
Manual answer	Auto-answer
Manual dial	Auto-dial
Manual disconnect	Auto-disconnect
Automatic redial	Programmable control (e.g., computer-controlled dialing and setting of data rate)
Speaker (to monitor dialing and connection)	Keyboard dial
Full or half duplex	Synchronous or asynchronous
Secondary channel	Reverse channel
Line conditioning capabilities (equalization)	Multiport
	Self-testing mode
Voice-over data	Compatibility with Bell modems
Compatibility with Hayes modems	MNP 4 error correction
MNP 5 data compression	ITU (CCITT) standards
Electronic Industries Association (EIA) standards	U.S. government standards

pacity already leased. The only additional costs of voice transmission, then, are the price of the modems and the reduced data capacity on the line.

   Compatibility A variety of modem standards exist, and adherence to widely accepted standards helps establish modem compatibility. One of the references for compatibility is the modems supplied by AT&T; more recently, compatibility with modems manufactured by the Hayes Corporation is often cited. Two other entities involved in modem standards are the **Consultative Committee for International Telegraph and Telephony (CCITT),** a

Consultative Committee on International Telegraph and Telephony (CCITT) A committee of the International Telecommunications Union.

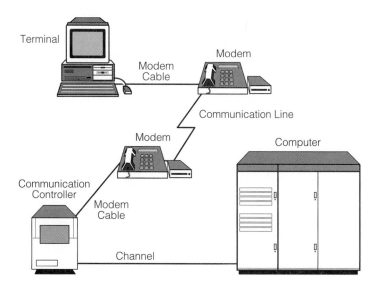

Figure 2–33
Terminal Computer Connection Using Modems

International Telecommunications Union (ITU) An international standards organization.

microcomputer network protocols (MNP) A set of modem protocols providing for data compression and error checking, such as MNP Level 4 and MNP Level

committee of the **International Telecommunications Union (ITU),** and Microcom, Inc. Microcom has established or helped to establish a series of standards called **microcomputer network protocols (MNP).** ITU standards used to be called CCITT standards; however, today's practice is to call them ITU standards. Some of the standards to which modems might adhere include the following:

- ITU V.32, modulation specifications for high-speed modems commonly operating at 9600 bps, with speeds of more than 38,400 bps possible with data compression.
- ITU V.32bis, 14,400 bps.
- ITU V.34 (formerly called V.fast), a 28,800-bps modem standard. If the V.42bis standard for data compression is added to a V.34 modem, the effective speed can be 115 Kbps or higher.
- ITU V.34bis, standard for 33,600 bps.
- ITU V.42, error correction.
- ITU V.42bis, data compression. Data compression can significantly increase the apparent speed of a modem by reducing the number of bits transferred. Compression ratios of 4:1 or higher may be attained depending on the data being transmitted. A modem rated at 9600 bps may attain transmission speeds of 38,400 bps via compression.
- ITU V.56, 56,000-bps downlink, 33,600-bps uplink over analog lines.
- MNP 1, 2, 3, and 4, error correction.
- MNP 5, data compression.
- K56Plus, a Rockwell standard for 56,000-bps downlink and 30,000-bps uplink.
- K56Flex, a Lucent Technologies modem similar to K56Plus.
- X2, a U.S. Robotics implementation offering 56,000-bps downlink and 28,800-bps uplink.

Multiport modems are discussed in Chapter 10; reverse and secondary channels, full- and half-duplex operations, and conditioning are covered in

Table 2–9   Representative Modem Costs

Speed in bps (speed is typically higher if compression is used)	Cost	Speed
33,600	$ 125	33.6 Kbps
56,000	200	56/28.8 Kbps
HDSL	1200	1.5 to 2 Mbps
Cable	400	10 Mbps
ISDN	200	128 Kbps
Fiber optic (multimode)	275	1 Mbps

Chapter 3; and synchronous and asynchronous transmission are addressed in Chapter 11.

Cost

The price of modems is much like that of media: constantly changing and, in general, dropping as a result of new technology and competition. As summarized in Table 2–9, the price also varies according to the capabilities offered, with speed being the most influential factor.

Short-Haul Modems

For short distances, short-haul modems can be used. These allow for transmission distances up to about 20 mi, at varying speeds. As distance increases, speed decreases. Table 2–10 presents the relationship between distance and speed with short-haul modems. Strictly speaking, distance is a function of the resistance of the conductor, and speed is a function of the capacitance and resistance of the conductor. For practical purposes, distance and speed are functions of the thickness or gauge of the conductor. Table 2–10 holds for 24-gauge wire; greater speeds or distances are possible with 19-gauge wire, and lower speeds or distances would result from the use of 26-gauge wire. The advantage of short-haul modems is a significant reduction in cost; 90% savings or better are possible.

Modem Eliminators

For very short distances, **modem eliminators** provide additional savings and very high data transmission rates. Modem eliminators, also called line drivers or null modems, can connect two devices that are in close proximity. A modem eliminator provides clocking and interface functions between two devices. One modem eliminator can replace two modems, as illustrated in Figure 2–34. The spannable distances are covered by interface specifications such as the RS-232-C standard, which recommends a distance of 50 ft for standard wires, or the RS-449 standard, which specifies 200 ft. Although manufacturers usually certify their modem eliminators at these standard distances, longer distances are possible. One use of modem eliminators is high-speed, computer-to-computer

modem eliminator A device that allows data transmission over short distances without a modem. Provides for signal timing as well as data transmission.

Table 2–10   Short-Haul Modems: Speed vs. Distance

Distance (mi)	Maximum Speed (Kbps)*
3.0	128
4.6	64
4.8	56
5.0	48
5.5	32

* Using AWG 24 wires.

Figure 2–34

Modem Eliminator

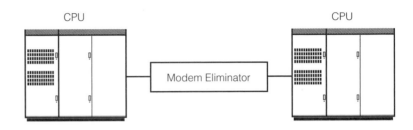

communication links. Data transmission rates up to 1 Mbps can be supported by modem eliminators.

The previously described modems are connected directly to communication wires. An **acoustic coupler** allows for data transmission across telephone lines, using the telephone handset to pass the data. Acoustic couplers have a send-and-receive receptacle into which the handset is placed. Transmission rates for acoustic couplers are usually either 300 or 1200 bps. Acoustic couplers are often used with portable terminals, some of which even incorporate the acoustic coupler as an integral part of the terminal.

acoustic coupler An acoustic coupler converts digital signals to analog and analog to digital. It is used mostly in switched communication and uses the telephone handset to pass data between a terminal or computer and the acoustic coupler.

CSU/DSU

The CSU connects to a digital line and terminates the digital signal. The DSU transmits digital signals onto the digital line. A CSU/DSU may be separate units, or their functions may be integrated into a single unit. CSU/DSUs provide a variety of interface options, such as T-1, fractional T-1, and frame relay interfaces. Some have integrated modems to allow network support staff to remotely operate the unit.

Fiber Optic Modems

Modems are also used for fiber optic transmission at speeds ranging from 1200 bps up to 50 Mbps, with popular intermediate speeds of 56 Kbps, 100 Kbps, 250 Kbps, 1.544 Mbps, 5 Mbps, and 10 Mbps.

Switched Digital Lines

Widespread use of the Internet (see Chapters 13 and 14) has created a demand for high-speed switched data transfers. With each of the last two analog modem speed increases, experts have predicted that higher speeds over plain old telephone system (POTS) wires were unlikely. Technology advances will probably improve analog POTS speeds, but for very high speeds, we need to look at other technologies. The leading candidates at this time are digital services such as integrated services digital network (ISDN), digital subscriber line (DSL), and **cable modems.** Each of these services can provide speeds greater than 100 Kbps; some exceed 1 Mbps. Each requires a different interface equivalent to a modem. We describe each of these services in Chapter 4.

cable modem A device that allows data transmission and Internet access via cable television lines.

B usiness at the Syncrasy Corporation has been progressing. President Ima Overseer and the other two founders report that business has been excellent and expansion is in order. The first phase of expansion will include a larger computer system and two new locations in New York City and Los Angeles. Each remote office will have ten terminals connected to the host computer in the Kansas City office, where all inventory, pricing, and customer information is stored. It is expected that sales activity will occur throughout the day in both remote locations. The average order consists of 500 input characters and 100 response characters. The company's objective is to provide 5-s response time for each order; it has been determined that processing time per order averages 2.5 s. Thus far, each terminal operator enters 20 orders per hour on the average, with peak loads of 30 transactions per hour. Ms. Overseer wants to know which medium will best serve Syncrasy's immediate needs. Determining this requires some basic calculations, the first of which is to figure the necessary speed of the lines.

LINE SPEED

Usually a system is configured to meet the peak transaction load; if it can handle the peaks, it can definitely handle the valleys. Although configuring for peak loads is not absolutely necessary, it is undesirable to have the system bog down when it is needed the most. Configuring to the peak workload also provides latitude for expanding work during off-peak periods, including development activities such as program compiling and batch operations such as payroll and periodic reports.

Line speed is based on response time and throughput. Syncrasy has decided to use the conservative response time definition, which requires all response characters to be received. It is assumed that two or more terminals might share a communication path (Chapter 10 discusses how this is done). First, the needs of a single terminal are considered. Five hundred input characters and 100 output characters equal 600 characters transmitted per average transaction. The expected response time is 5 s, of which 2.5 s is communication time (estimated processing time was 2.5 s). Thus, one terminal will require a path with a speed of 600/2.5 = 240 characters per second. Assuming 10 bits per character, a line speed of 2400 bps is required. A standard speed that meets this requirement is a 2400-bps line. However, actual line use is usually less than the rated line speed. If we assume an effective data rate of 70%, a 2400-bps line will provide 1680 bps. Therefore, a line speed of 4800 bps or higher might be necessary.

NUMBER OF TERMINALS PER LINE

Determining how many terminals could effectively share a line demands some intuition: A peak rate of 30 transactions per hour per terminal translates to 300 transactions per hour, or 5 transactions per minute. This rate is

Table 2–11   Transaction Activity

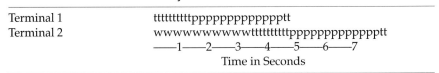

Terminal 1	ttttttttttppppppppppppppptt
Terminal 2	wwwwwwwwwwwttttttttttttppppppppppppppptt
	——1——2——3——4——5——6——7
	Time in Seconds

not excessive, and all ten terminals could conceivably use the same 2400-bps line. The only problem would be if two users were to enter data at exactly the same time; one response time would be the expected 5 s, whereas the other would be approximately 7 s. The logic behind this is provided in Table 2–11, in which t represents transmission time, p represents processing time, and w represents wait. Terminal 2 sees a slower response time because it must hold off transmitting until terminal 1 has sent its data. If the line speed were twice as fast (4800 bps), two concurrent terminals could be handled within the 2-s response time.

If three users enter information at exactly the same time, one of them, of course, will have a lower response time. However, the chances of that happening with ten terminals on a line is slight. Assuming a random arrival rate, the probability of three transactions arriving in a 2-s interval is less than one in a thousand (0.00065) (see Exercise 4). A 4800-bps line should be satisfactory for all ten terminals.

ADDITIONAL CRITERIA

There are no special environmental, security, expansion, maintenance, or error rate concerns to resolve in this system, and the application issues have already been addressed. The calculations show that a high-speed path is not necessary. Distance is a factor in the remote connections, and transmission facilities should therefore be acquired from a common carrier. Private wires are best for the local terminals in the Kansas City offices because the offices are free of environmental disturbances and there are no distance problems to overcome. Private wires also are far more cost-effective than other solutions, and their speed can be greater than that of leased lines. Fiber optics and coaxial cable are possibilities, but they would be more costly if privately implemented, and such high data transmission rates are not required.

SUMMARY

A wide variety of transmission media are available to the network designer, and many networks use several of them. If the telephone companies' use of fiber optics, microwave, and satellite channels is considered, most long-distance networks are a combination of media. Numerous factors influence the selection of transmission media. Each medium has information carrying capacity, which carries from a few characters per second to millions of characters per second. The terms *bit rate, baud rate,* and *bandwidth* are used to describe a medium's carrying capacity, and these measures are interrelated. Other important characteristics of a medium are its susceptibility to errors, cost, distance, availability, expandability, environment, application, maintenance, and security.

In transmitting data between devices in a computer network, it is often necessary to convert a device's digital signals to analog format. There are several ways to do this; frequency modulation, phase modulation, and phase modulation plus amplitude modulation are the most common. The device that translates digital signals to analog signals and then back again is known as a modem or data set. Modems differ greatly in the bit rate provided as well as the options available.

A computing device's digital signals may be transmitted over a medium in digital format. A device called a channel service unit and data service unit (CSU/DSU) provides the line interface. The CSU connects to a digital line and terminates the digital signal. The DSU transmits digital signals onto the digital line.

KEY TERMS

acoustic coupler
aggregate data rate
amplitude modulation (AM)
analog transmission
attenuation
bandwidth
baseband transmission
baud rate
bit rate
broadband transmission
broadcast radio
cable modem
carrier signal
conditioning
conducted media
Consultative Committee on International Telegraph and Telephony (CCITT)
data set
dibits
differential phase shift keying (DPSK)
digital subscriber line (DSL)
digital transmission
direct sequencing
frequency hopping
frequency modulation (FM)
frequency shift keying (FSK)
geosynchronous orbit

guardband
Hertz (Hz)
infrared transmission
International Telecommunications Union (ITU)
leased lines
microcomputer network protocols (MNP)
microwave radio
mobile computing
modem
modem eliminator
multimode graded-index fiber
multimode step-index fiber
phase modulation
phase shift keying (PSK)
propagation delay
punchdown block
quadbits
quadrature amplitude modulation (QAM)
radiated media
satellite radio transmission
single-mode transmission
spread-spectrum radio (SSR)
switched connections
transponder
tribits

REVIEW QUESTIONS

1. What are the advantages and disadvantages of private lines?

2. Distinguish between switched lines and leased lines.

3. Compare broadband and baseband transmission.

4. Rank wires, coaxial cable, and fiber optics with respect to speed, cost, and resistance to noise. Which is fastest? Which is least expensive? Which is least error prone?

5. Describe the effects of propagation delay on satellite transmission.

6. Describe
   a. Amplitude modulation
   b. Frequency modulation
   c. Phase modulation

7. Compare broadcast, microwave, and satellite radio.

8. How does spread-spectrum radio work? What is its primary data communication application?

9. Why do some experts believe that television signals should be transmitted by conducted media rather than by radiated media? Do you agree or disagree?

10. Explain how the terms *baud rate, bit rate,* and *bandwidth* are used to describe the speed of a communication link.

11. Describe what a modem does.

12. What are the three basic types of modems?

PROBLEMS AND EXERCISES

1. Given the different modes of communication—private lines, switched lines, leased lines, coaxial cable, fiber optic cable, microwave, satellite, and wireless LAN media—which would be the most suitable for the following applications? Why?
   a. A U.S. marketing organization must transmit large amounts of product information, sales data, facsimiles, and electronic mail to 40 cities. Each of the 40 locations has computers and sends volumes of sales data, facsimiles, and electronic mail. Response time is not critical.
   b. A manufacturing plant has multiple computers, data processing workstations, and terminals, all spread throughout six buildings. All facilities are located within 1 km of each other and all rights of way are controlled by the company. The data being transmitted includes small files, memos, electronic mail, and online transactions. Response time is critical for the online transactions.
   c. A hospital has automated its patient care system. Terminals have been placed in all administrative offices, laboratory facilities, doctors' and nurses' offices, and nursing stations. The online transactions include data entry, inquiries, and short reports. Rapid response time is important.
   d. A research corporation is evaluating solar energy systems. It has data collection devices attached to several experimental wind and solar collectors. A large, continuous volume of data is transmitted to the computer center, which is 10 mi from the test grounds. The computer center can be seen from the test grounds.
   e. A major fast-food chain has chosen to centralize its inventory and sales data. Each restaurant maintains its sales and inventory data on a small computer located in the store. This computer is attached to point-of-sale terminals that serve as data entry devices. Every time an item is sold, the inventory and

sales data on the local computer are updated. Every evening the central office must retrieve the information from each store. The amount of information to be transmitted is approximately 10,000 characters per restaurant.

f. A major car rental agency has decided to regionalize its inventory and reservation system. Approximately 75% of the reservation requests are resolved by the regional center, and the remaining 25% must be forwarded to another regional processing center. The peak amount of data to be transmitted to another center is approximately 10,000 characters per minute. This also means that each regional center will receive approximately 10,000 characters per minute.

g. A research corporation must exchange data among three computers located in different departments within one building. The data is highly sensitive, so security is a major concern. The data consists of text, research results, graphics, and electronic mail. Response time is not critical. A communication speed of 9600 bps would be adequate. The optimum path for private wires would require the wires to pass through research areas with a considerable amount of electrical or magnetic activity.

2. A small insurance company wants to connect its ten microcomputers in a LAN. The company is situated in an old house that has been renovated. Speeds must be at least 2 Mbps but will not exceed 16 Mbps. There are no devices that have potential for disrupting signals on radiated or conducted media. What medium would you recommend? Justify your answer.

3. A corporate office needs to connect several departmental LANs. The interconnection will be made using a LAN to which the departmental LANs are connected. The interconnection LAN must operate at 100 Mbps. The medium will be run through elevator shafts and a machine room, so signal distortion is a concern. What medium would you recommend? Justify your answer.

4. The probability of k random arrivals in an interval of length T is given by the formula

$$P_k(T) = \frac{(LT)^k}{k!} \times e^{-LT} \text{ for } K = 0, 1, 2, 3, \ldots$$

where

$P_k(T)$ is the probability that k transactions will arrive in time interval T

k is the number of arrivals

T is the time interval being considered

e is the natural base for logarithms

L is the average number of transactions per unit of time

$!$ is the factorial function

If the arrival rate of transactions per second is 0.25, the probability that two transactions will arrive in 5 s is given by

$$P_2(5) = \frac{(0.25 \times 5)^2}{2!} \times e^{-(0.25 \times 5)} = 0.22$$

Using this formula, verify that the probability of three transactions arriving in a 2-s interval is approximately 0.00065 when the number of transactions arriving per hour is 300. In making your calculations, make sure that your time units match.

5. Suppose Syncrasy wanted a 1.5-s response time. What is the lowest common transmission speed that will satisfy this requirement for a single terminal? Assume 70% line use.

Physical Aspects of Data Communication: Data Transmission

CHAPTER OBJECTIVES

After studying this chapter you should be able to

- Describe the three basic flow control protocols used in data communication
- Discuss the characteristics of major data codes
- Explain the types and sources of errors that can affect data transmission
- Describe how errors are detected and corrected
- Compare digital and analog data transmission

This chapter continues the discussion of physical transmission of data and data transmission utilities. Setting up and managing today's communication networks is more complex than ever. More vendors are providing communication services at a wider variety of speeds. Different forms of communication also are increasingly being integrated onto one transmission medium. As a result, the sphere of responsibility for the modern data communication manager is expanding. In addition to selecting communication facilities for data transmission, the communication manager may also be responsible for selecting hardware and software that can meet the corporate needs for data, voice, video, facsimile, and other forms of electronic communication.

DATA FLOW

Every data communication network must have some mechanism of control over the flow of data. This is accomplished at two levels. The first level provides for contention control, which determines which stations may transmit, the conditions under which transmission of data is allowed, and the pacing of data transmission. Contention control is discussed in later chapters. The more basic level of data flow relates to the transmission equipment used: lines, modems, and devices. The three elementary types of data flow are simplex, half duplex, and full duplex.

Simplex Transmission

In simplex transmissions data may flow in only one direction, like traffic on a one-way street. Radio and television transmissions, illustrated in Figure 3–1(a), are examples. In simplex transmission one station assumes the role of transmitter and the other station is the receiver; these roles may not be reversed. Although this may appear rather limiting, simplex transmission has numerous applications. Devices such as keyboards, microcomputer monitors, and optical character recognition (OCR) scanners involve simplex communication. Communication with printers that are capable of transmitting status information back to the host is not classified as simplex, but data collection devices that serve as input devices only do use simplex communication. In solar energy research installations, heat sensors, solar monitors, and flow meters are used to monitor the environment and transmit samples of data via a simplex line. A building environmental monitoring system also operates in this mode, sending temperature and humidity readings to a computer that controls the heating and cooling of the building. Simplex

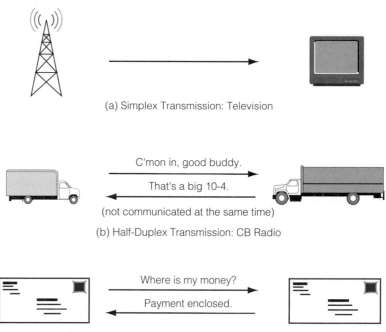

(a) Simplex Transmission: Television

C'mon in, good buddy.

That's a big 10-4.

(not communicated at the same time)

(b) Half-Duplex Transmission: CB Radio

Where is my money?

Payment enclosed.

(communicating in both directions at the same time)

(c) Full-Duplex Transmission: Mail System

Figure 3–1
Examples of Data Flow

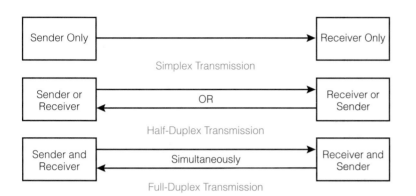

Figure 3–2
Data Flow Alternatives

lines are less common in business applications than half-duplex or full-duplex lines. Simplex lines are used for some printers, for monitoring devices in environment and process control applications, for transmitting stock exchange data (stock tickers), and for most radio and cable television data transmissions.

Half-Duplex Transmission

In half-duplex transmission, data may travel in both directions, although only in one direction at a time, like traffic on a one-lane bridge. Figure 3–1(b) shows the example of citizens' band (CB) radio, where radio operators on the same frequency may be either sender or receiver but not both at the same time. Half-duplex transmission is a common method of flow control in LANs.

Full-Duplex Transmission

In full-duplex mode, data can be transmitted in both directions simultaneously, like traffic on a two-way street. An example of data transmission using full-duplex capabilities is the postal service: Letters can be transmitted in both directions simultaneously, as illustrated in Figure 3–1(c). Figure 3–2 shows full-duplex communication. Full-duplex operations are effected in radio-wave transmissions by using two different frequencies, one for each direction. With coaxial cable, full-duplex operations require broadband transmission. Switched telephone connections commonly use full-duplex flow control.

DATA CODES

As already mentioned, data is stored in digital computers as sequences of binary digits (bits), each with a value of either 0 or 1. To provide meaning to a sequence of bits, you must set up the number of bits that are grouped to form a data character and create an encoding scheme, or translation table, by which the system translates each group of bits into a character. In the encoding scheme of telegraphy, Morse code, each character is represented as a combination of dots and dashes. Although these could be also interpreted as bits, Morse code is not suitable for data communication because characters are represented by a different number of bits (the letter A is represented by dot-dash and the letter S by dot-dot-dot). Telegraphers distinguish one letter grouping from another by the time delay between characters. Such a scheme is not practical for computer-based systems. As a result, virtually all computer codes use a fixed number of bits per character. The number of bits that makes up the characters also determines the number of distinct characters that can be represented. Table 3–1 lists several data encoding schemes as well as the number of bits per character and the number of characters that can be represented by those codes.

ASCII

American Standard Code for Information Interchange (ASCII) A code that uses 7 or 8 bits to represent characters. One of the two common computer codes (see also EBCDIC).

American Standard Code for Information Interchange (ASCII) and EBCDIC (see next section) are the codes most commonly used. ASCII (also known as USASCII) is implemented primarily as a 7-bit code, although an extended 8-bit version also exists. With 7 bits, 128 characters can be represented; with 8 bits, 256 characters are available. As an alternative to the 8-bit code, the 7-bit form can be extended by using reserved control characters to shift from one character set to another. Extending the number of characters provides additional character sets for graphics and for foreign languages such as Katakana. The 7-bit ASCII code is presented in Table 3–2.

EBCDIC

Extended Binary-Coded Decimal Interchange Code (EBCDIC) A code that uses 8 bits to represent a character of information. One of the most common computer codes (see also ASCII).

Extended Binary-Coded Decimal Interchange Code (EBCDIC) uses 8 bits to form a character; 256 characters can be represented. The EBCDIC code is presented in Table 3–3. As Tables 3–2 and 3–3 show, both ASCII and EBCDIC have some codes (such as ASCII 0000000 and 0000011) with mnemonic names such as NUL and ETX. These special characters, which are discussed in more detail in Chapter 11, are used to provide control information to nodes on the network as well as to represent binary data.

The EBCDIC tables show gaps following the letters i, r, z, I, R, and Z. The gaps represent unassigned bit values. This is a disadvantage because the unassigned bit values fall within the letter sequence; the ASCII tables have no such gaps. If these values are ever assigned, it may interrupt the collating sequence of the letters. The gaps also make arithmetic operations on the characters more difficult. In ASCII, we can obtain the numeric value of an ASCII character and manipulate it arithmetically, such as by adding 15 to the numeric representation of the letter A to obtain the letter 15 characters down the alphabet from A. Another disadvantage of EBCDIC is that some charac-

Table 3–1   Common Data Codes

Coding Scheme	Number of Bits	Characters Representable
Standard ASCII	7	128
Extended ASCII	8	256
EBCDIC	8	256
Touch-tone telephone		12 frequencies

Table 3–2   The USACSII 7-Bit Code

		High-Order Bits						
	000	001	010	011	100	101	110	111
0000	NUL	DLE	SPACE	0	@	P	`	p
0001	SOH	DC1	!	1	A	Q	a	q
0010	STX	DC2	"	2	B	R	b	r
0011	ETX	DC3	#	3	C	S	c	s
0100	EOT	DC4	$	4	D	T	d	t
0101	ENQ	NAK	%	5	E	U	e	u
0010	ACK	SYN	&	6	F	V	f	v
0111	BEL	ETB	'	7	G	W	g	w
1000	BS	CAN	(	8	H	X	h	x
1001	HT	EM	)	9	I	Y	i	y
1010	LF	SUB	*	:	J	Z	j	z
1011	VT	ESC	+	;	K	[	k	{
1100	FF	FS	,	<	L	\	l		
1101	CR	GS	-	=	M	]	m	}
1110	SO	RS	.	>	N	^	n	~
1111	SI	US	/	?	O	—	o	DEL

(Low-Order Bits — row labels at left)

ters—such as [and]—have not been defined. Omission of these characters raises problems in programming languages such as Pascal and C, which use these symbols.

Touch-Tone Telephone

The touch-tone telephone code turns a touch-tone telephone into a data communication terminal. Some banks allow customers to pay bills and transfer money between accounts using touch-tone telephones. Many colleges

Table 3–3 (a)   The EBCDIC 8-Bit Code

		High-Order Bits						
	0000	0001	0010	0011	0100	0101	0110	0111
0000	NUL	DLE	DS		SPACE	@	-	
0001	SOH	DC1	SOS					
0010	STX	DC2	FS	SYN				
0011	ETX	DC3						
0100	PF	RES	BYP	PN				
0101	HT	NL	LF	RS				
0110	LC	BS	ETB	UC				
0111	DEL	IL	ESC	EOT				
1000		CAN						
1001	RLF	EM						\
1010	SMN	CC	SM		¢	!			:
1011					.	$	'	#
1100	FF	IFS		DC4	<	*	%	@
1101	CR	IGS	ENQ	NAK	(	)	-	'
1110	SO	IRS	ACK		+	;	>	=
1111	SI	IUS	BEL	SUB			?	"

(Low-Order Bits — row labels at left)

Table 3–3 (b)   The EBCDIC 8-Bit Code

				High-Order Bits				
	1000	1001	1010	1011	1100	1101	1110	1111
0000					{	}	\	0
0001	a	j	~		A	J		1
0010	b	k	s		B	K	S	2
0011	c	l	t		C	L	T	3
0100	d	m	u		D	M	U	4
0101	e	n	v		E	N	V	5
0110	f	o	w		F	O	W	6
0111	g	p	x		G	P	X	7
1000	h	q	y		H	Q	Y	8
1001	i	r	z		I	R	Z	9
1010								
1011								
1100								
1101								
1110								
1111								

Low-Order Bits

and universities allow students to register for classes using touch-tone telephones. Telephones have 12 keys, so 12 different codes can be transmitted. Each key on the telephone keypad transmits a high frequency and a low frequency. The combination of the two frequencies uniquely defines which key has been pressed. Figure 3–3 shows the relationship between the telephone keypad and the frequencies each transmits. If a user presses the 9 key, the frequencies 852 Hz and 1447 Hz are transmitted. Because only 12 key codes are available, the telephone is limited in its use as a data communication input device.

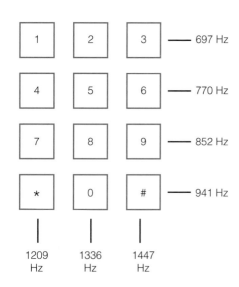

Figure 3–3
Touch-Tone Telephone Code

Data Code Size

The transition from 5-bit and 6-bit codes to 7-bit and 8-bit codes was necessary to increase the number of unique code sequences that could be represented. The two most common data communication codes are 7-bit and 8-bit codes, which are able to represent 128 and 256 unique symbols, respectively. Is this a sufficient number of symbols? An 8-bit code can represent the 26-letter Roman alphabet (both uppercase and lowercase), the 10 Arabic numerals (0 through 9), and punctuation, totaling approximately 100 characters and symbols. Additional bit patterns may be required for line control, so perhaps up to 128 characters can be used. What are the rest used for?

For one thing, there may be a need to accommodate other alphabets, such as Greek and Cyrillic (Russian), and their accompanying diacritical marks, such as the tilde, umlaut, and accents. Still, 256 bits can accommodate the Roman alphabet and one other alphabet, with characters left over—until we look at Asian and Middle Eastern languages. The Kanji character set used for written communication in Japan and China contains more than 30,000 ideograms and symbols. Clearly, 256 unique symbols do not go very far. In addition to accommodating various alphabets, a data code may need to transmit, store, manipulate, and display graphic information, thus requiring additional characters. Line drawing characters can easily exceed 100 different symbols. Several microcomputers use an extended ASCII code to permit use of business graphics symbols. It is also likely that some of the newer technologies, such as videotex (in which text and images are transmitted together), will require a large number of characters. The data communication codes in current use have proved to be inadequate in meeting the communication demands among different cultures and languages, as well as the anticipated demands for extended services such as videotex. Now that the limitations of 8-bit codes are apparent, perhaps an international code using 16 bits will emerge. In Japan this has already been addressed by several standards.

To be effective a good communication code also must provide three other capabilities: It must be standardized, it must be nonsequential, and it must provide for error detection. Being standardized means that the bit representations are sanctioned by a recognized standards group. Being nonsequential means the sequence in which characters are detected is immaterial. The 7-bit ASCII code when used with upshift and downshift characters is sequential, as the upshift and downshift characters are critical to the meaning of characters received. If an upshift or downshift character is missed in the transmission, the message text following the missed shift character is incorrectly interpreted. An error detection capability inherent in the code allows detection of transmission errors. A parity bit is often appended to 7-bit ASCII to detect errors. Parity is less commonly used with 8-bit codes such as EBCDIC. In the next section we discuss how errors are caused and how they can be detected.

ERROR SOURCES

All data transmissions are subject to error, although some media are more susceptible than others. Contextual recognition of errors is usually impossible in data communication systems. If the data transmitter and receiver are computers, it is virtually impossible for editing routines to determine whether 1 or more bits have been changed; even if data is displayed on a terminal, the operator may be unable to discern all the errors. If a bank teller interrogates a customer's account balance, as illustrated in Figure 3–4, it is unlikely that the teller would recognize that a 1-bit error had changed the balance from $100 to $228. Errors can be induced during data transmission in a number of ways. The most common are attenuation, impulse noise, crosstalk, echo, phase jitter, envelope delay distortion, and white noise.

Attenuation

Attenuation, the weakening of a signal as a result of distance and characteristics of the medium, can produce a significant number of data errors. For a given gauge of wire and bit rate, a signal can be carried for a certain distance without enhancement. Beyond that distance a signal repeater or amplifier must be included to ensure that the receiving station can properly recognize the data.

Impulse Noise

impulse noise A noise characterized by signal spikes. In telephone circuits it can be caused by switching equipment or by lightning strikes and in other situations by transient electrical impulses such as those occurring on a shop floor. Impulse noise is a common cause of transmission errors.

Impulse noise is characterized by signal spikes. In telephone circuits it can be caused by switching equipment or lightning strikes, and in other situations, by transient electrical impulses such as those occurring on a shop floor. The various pieces of equipment on a shop floor require large amounts of electricity. This equipment also often cycles up and down, drawing more and less power. Setting an electrical charge in motion generates a magnetic field, and magnetic fields can affect signals transmitted through unshielded data communication wires. Impulse noise, the primary cause of data errors in telephone circuits, is heard as a clicking or crackling sound. It usually is short (several milliseconds), with varying levels of magnitude.

Crosstalk

crosstalk When the signals from one channel distort or interfere with the signals of a different channel.

Crosstalk occurs when signals from one channel distort or interfere with the signals of a different channel. In telephone connections, crosstalk sometimes appears in the form of another party's conversation heard in the background. Crosstalk is also present in radio-frequency and multiplexed trans-

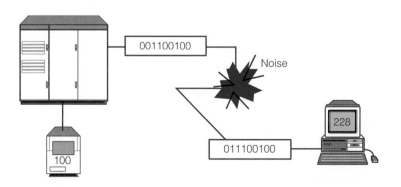

Figure 3–4
Transmission Error

missions (see Chapter 10) when the frequency ranges are too close together. Crosstalk in wire pair transmission occurs when wire pairs interfere with each other as a result of strong signals, improper shielding, or both. Another common cause of crosstalk is interference between receivers and transmitters when a strong outgoing signal interferes with a weaker incoming signal. Crosstalk is directly proportional to distance, bandwidth, signal strength, and proximity to other transmission channels; it is inversely proportional to shielding or channel separation. Crosstalk is not usually a significant factor in data communication errors.

One special form of crosstalk is intermodulation noise, which is the result of two or more signals combining to produce a signal outside the limits of the communication channel. Suppose one mode of frequency shift keying (FSK) modulation represents a 1 bit as a frequency of 1300 Hz and a 0 bit as a frequency of 2100 Hz, with a variation of 10 Hz. Intermodulation noise might result in two acceptable signals, such as 1305 Hz and 2105 Hz, combining to form a signal of 3410 Hz (1305 + 2105 = 3410). This signal is out of the accepted frequency range of voice communication over telephone lines (300–3400 Hz).

Echo

Echo is essentially the reflection or reversal of the signal being transmitted. This is most likely to occur at junctions where wires are interconnected or at the end of a line in a LAN. Telephone companies have installed **echo suppressors** on their networks to minimize this echo effect. The echo suppressor works by allowing the signal to pass in one direction only. In voice transmission, the suppressor continually reverses itself to match the direction of conversation. Obviously this would impede data transmission in full-duplex mode, so echo suppressors are disengaged when full-duplex transmission is required.

Phase Jitter

Phase jitter is a variation in the phase of a continuous signal from cycle to cycle; it is especially significant when the modulation mode involves phase shifting.

Envelope Delay Distortion

Envelope delay distortion occurs when signals that have been weakened or subjected to outside interference by transmission over long distances are enhanced by being passed through filters. Passing the signals through a filter delays them a certain amount, depending on the frequency of the signal.

White Noise

White noise, also called **thermal noise** or **Gaussian noise,** results from the normal movements of electrons and is present in all transmission media at temperatures above absolute zero. The amount of white noise is directly proportional to the temperature of the medium (hence the term *thermal noise*).

echo The reflection or reversal of the signal being transmitted. Also used to define a transmission convention in which the receiver of data sends the data back to the sender to assist in error detection.

echo suppressor A device that allows a transmitted signal to pass in one direction only, thus minimizing the echo effect.

phase jitter A variation in the phase of a continuous signal from cycle to cycle.

white noise One source of data communication errors. It results from the normal movements of electrons and is present in all transmission media at temperatures above absolute zero. Also known as thermal noise or Gaussian noise.

Figure 3–5

Impact of Noise on a Data Signal

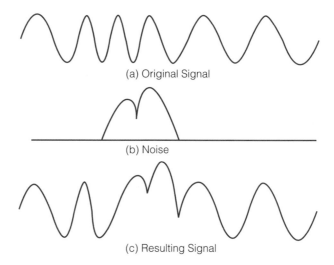

(a) Original Signal

(b) Noise

(c) Resulting Signal

White noise also is distributed randomly throughout a medium (hence the term *Gaussian noise*). White noise in telephone circuits is sometimes heard as static or hissing on the line. The magnitude of white noise usually is not sufficient to create data loss in wire circuits, but it can become significant in radio-frequency links such as microwave and satellite. Because white noise is proportional to bandwidth as well as temperature, improperly focused antennas (such as those directed toward the sun) can create enough disturbance to produce errors. Figure 3–5 illustrates the impact of noise on a data communication signal.

Impact of Data Errors

Table 3–4 shows the possible effects of impulse noise of various durations, for different line speeds. It is significant that fewer bits are subject to error when transmission is at lower rather than higher speeds. Although the figure applies to any type of noise for the same durations, impulse noise was chosen because it is one of the most common types of noise affecting telephone wires. The most significant thing shown by Table 3–4 is that the potential number of bit errors increases with both duration of the noise and line speed. Although the ideal is to eliminate all errors, a rate below 1

Table 3–4   Potential Number of Corrupted Data Bits

Line Speed (bps)	Impulse Noise Duration (ms)				
	0.2	0.4	0.6	0.8	1.0
300	0.06	0.12	0.18	0.24	0.30
1200	0.24	0.48	0.72	0.96	1.20
2400	0.48	0.96	1.44	1.92	2.40
4800	0.96	1.92	2.88	3.84	4.80
9600	1.92	3.84	5.76	7.68	9.60
19,200	3.84	7.68	11.52	15.36	19.20

error per 100,000 bits is considered satisfactory. (Most line media and radio-wave transmission systems are designed for fewer than 1 error per 1 million bits transmitted.)

PREVENTION

The best method to guard against data errors is to correct their source. Eliminating all noise is impossible, but error prevention techniques can reduce the probability of error corruption in the data. Such techniques include telephone line conditioning, reducing transmission speed, shielding, line drivers, and using better equipment.

Telephone Line Conditioning

When a line is leased from a telephone company, conditioning, sometimes called equalization, can be included for an additional charge. The two classes of conditioning are class C and class D, with four commercial levels of class C conditioning: C1, C2, C4, and C5. Each level of class C conditioning provides increasingly stringent constraints on the amplitude and phase distortion permitted on the line. A line with C5 conditioning should be more error-free than a line with C1 conditioning. One useful aspect of class D conditioning—a new service—is that the telephone company will inspect the circuits available between the desired communication points to select the one with the least amount of noise. Users can also obtain equipment, such as certain modems, that aids in the conditioning of lines.

Lower Transmission Speed

A bit error is much less likely to occur at lower transmission speeds. Some modems adjust their speed automatically or via program control to accommodate noisy lines. With a high-quality line, such a modem will operate at 56 Kbps; if the quality of the line deteriorates, the modem can switch to a lower speed, say 28.8 Kbps.

Shielding

Although additional shielding of leased telephone cables is not a user option, shielding can be provided for private lines to reduce the amount of crosstalk and impulse noise from the environment. Media shielding in the form of coaxial cable or shielded twisted-pair wires is often used for LAN media.

Line Drivers (Repeaters)

Line drivers, or repeaters, can be placed at intervals along a communication line to amplify and forward the signal. Digital signal noise can usually be eliminated because the signal is being regenerated. For analog signals, however, it is difficult to separate most noise from the signal; noise that is picked up also is amplified by the repeaters. The function of repeaters is to restore signals to their full strength and overcome signal loss due to attenuation.

line drivers Devices placed at intervals along a communication line to amplify and forward the signal in order to restore signals to their full strength and overcome signal loss due to attenuation.

Better Equipment

Because some older mechanical equipment and some older transformers and power supplies are more likely to produce noise than newer equipment (such as electronic switches), replacing older components with better equipment can reduce the amount of noise.

ERROR DETECTION

Unfortunately, the remedies just cited to minimize the number of errors may be impractical from either a cost or a feasibility standpoint. Because error elimination is impossible, it is also necessary to determine whether a transmission error has occurred and, if errors have occurred, to return the data to its proper form. Error detection algorithms in data communication networks are based on the transmission of redundant information. In telegraphy, one way to ensure correctness of data is to transmit each character twice. This is not entirely error-proof, so it could be taken one or more steps further by sending each character three or more times. Although this might increase the reliability of the transmission, line capacity drops dramatically. As the error rate approaches zero, so does the effective use of the medium. Some middle-ground approach clearly is required that can detect almost all errors without significantly reducing the data-carrying capacity of the medium.

Parity Check

parity check/vertical redundancy check (VRC) The same as parity error checking. For each character transmitted, an additional bit is attached to help detect errors. The bit is chosen so that the number of 1 bits is even (even parity) or odd (odd parity).

One of the simplest and most widely used forms of error detection is known as a **parity check** or **vertical redundancy check (VRC).** A parity check involves adding a bit, known as the parity bit, to each character during transmission. The parity bit is selected so the total number of 1 bits in the code representation of each character adds up to either an even number (even parity) or an odd number (odd parity). Each character is checked upon receipt to see whether the number of 1 bits is even or odd. Consider the string of characters DATA COMM, as coded in 7-bit ASCII with odd parity. The representations of these characters plus the parity bit for odd parity are given in Table 3–5. It can be seen that the number of 1 bits in each 8-bit sequence (octet) is always odd (either one, three, five, or seven); the parity bit ensures

Table 3–5   Parity Bit Generation

Letter	ASCII	Parity Bit	Transmitted Bits
D	1000100	1	10001001
A	1000001	1	10000011
T	1010100	0	10101000
A	1000001	1	10000011
Space	0100000	0	01000000
C	1000011	0	10000110
O	1001111	0	10011110
M	1001101	1	10011011
M	1001101	1	10011011

this. If even parity were chosen, the parity bit would be selected so the number of 1 bits would always be an even number.

Besides even and odd parity, you can have no parity, a parity bit with no parity checking, mark parity, or space parity. If there is no parity bit or if the parity bit is not checked (called no parity check), the ability to detect errors using this method is lost (although other methods, described later, could be used). Mark parity means that the parity bit is always transmitted as a 1 bit, and space parity means the parity bit is always transmitted as a 0 bit. Clearly, mark and space parity are ineffective as error detection schemes. If two stations attempting to communicate disagree on the parity scheme, all messages will be seen as being in error and will be rejected.

In the odd parity example in Table 3–5, each character transmitted consists of 8 bits: 7 for data and 1 for parity. Parity enables the user to detect whether 1, 3, 5, or 7 bits have been altered in transmission, but it will not catch whether an even number (2, 4, 6, or 8 bits) has been altered. One common error situation involves burst errors, or a grouping of errors (recall the possible effect of impulse noise during high transmission rates). The likelihood of detecting errors of this nature with a parity check is approximately 50%. At higher transmission speeds this limitation becomes significant. (A burst error for the duration of 2 bits does not necessarily result in two bit errors. Zero, 1, or 2 bits could be affected.)

Longitudinal Redundancy Check

We can increase the probability of error detection beyond that provided by parity by making, in addition, a longitudinal redundancy check (LRC). With LRC, which is similar to VRC, an additional, redundant character called the **block check character (BCC)** is appended to a block of transmitted characters, typically at the end of the block. The first bit of the BCC serves as a parity check for all of the first bits of the characters in the block, the second bit of the BCC serves as parity for all of the second bits in the block, and so on. Table 3–6 is an example of LRC. An odd parity scheme has been chosen to perform the redundancy check, so each column has an odd number of 1 bits.

LRC combined with VRC is still not sufficient to detect all errors (no scheme is completely dependable). Table 3–7 presents the same DATA COMM message transmission, with errors introduced in rows and columns marked by an asterisk. Although both LRC and VRC appear correct, the data received is not the same as that transmitted. Adding LRC to VRC brings a greater probability of detecting errors in transmission.

block check character (BCC) In the error detection methods of longitudinal redundancy check or cyclic redundancy check, an error detection character or characters, called the BCC, is appended to a block of transmitted characters, typically at the end of the block.

Cyclic Redundancy Check

A **cyclic redundancy check (CRC)** can detect bit errors better than VRC, LRC, or both. A CRC is computed for a block of transmitted data. The transmitting station generates the CRC and transmits it with the data. The receiving station computes the CRC for the data received and compares it to the CRC transmitted by the sender. If the two are equal, then the block is assumed to be error-free. The mathematics behind CRC requires the use of a generating polynomial and is beyond the scope of this book.

cyclic redundancy check (CRC) An error detection algorithm that uses a polynomial function to generate the block check characters. CRC is a very efficient error detection method.

Table 3–6   LRC Generation

Letter	ASCII	Parity Bit	Transmitted Bits
D	1000100	1	10001001
A	1000001	1	10000011
T	1010100	0	10101000
A	1000001	1	10000011
Space	0100000	0	01000000
C	1000011	0	10000110
O	1001111	0	10011110
M	1001101	1	10011011
M	1001101	1	10011011
BBC	1000011	0	10000110

If the CRC generator polynomial is chosen with care and is of sufficient degree, more than 99% of multiple-bit errors can be detected. Several standards—CRC-12, CRC-16, and CRC-CCITT—define both the degree of the generating polynomial and the generating polynomial itself. Because CRC-12 specifies a polynomial of degree 12 and the last two standards specify a polynomial of degree 16, the BCC will have 12 or 16 bits. CRC-16 and CRC-CCITT can detect

- all single-bit and double-bit errors
- all errors in cases in which an odd number of bits is erroneous
- two pairs of adjacent errors
- all burst errors of 16 bits or fewer
- more than 99.998% of all burst errors greater than 16 bits

Because of its reliability, CRC is becoming the standard method of error detection for block data transmission (as opposed to transmission of one char-

Table 3–7   LRC Transmission Errors

Letter	ASCII	Parity Bit	Transmitted Bits
D	**1000100	1	10001001
A	1000001	1	10000011
T	*1100100	0	10101000
A	*1110001	1	10000011
Space	0100000	0	01000000
C	1000011	0	10000110
O	1001111	0	10011110
M	1001101	1	10011011
M	1001101	1	10011011
BBC	1000011	0	10000110

acter at a time). Chapters 7 and 11 discuss different data transmission protocols and their associated error detection schemes.

Sequence Checks

If sending and receiving nodes are connected directly, the receiving station receives all transmissions without the intercession of other nodes. However, large communication networks may have one or more intermediate nodes responsible for forwarding a message to its final destination, and one complete message may be divided into a number of transmission blocks. These blocks also may not all be routed along the same path and could be received out of order. In such a case, it is important to assign sequence numbers to each block so the ultimate receiver can determine that all blocks have indeed arrived and can put the blocks back into proper sequence.

Message Sequence Numbers

Suppose you send someone one letter per day for 5 days through the postal system. There is no guarantee that the letters will be received in the order sent. Several might arrive on the same day (and out of order), one might be lost, or all five might arrive at the same time. If the letters are intended to be read in order, you can number them sequentially (1/5, 2/5, 3/5, and so on). This alerts the recipient to the order and allows him or her to detect missing messages. A similar scheme can be used for data communication messages.

One sequencing technique appends a message sequence number to each data block transmitted between two stations. If a processor is communicating with two different stations, each link would have its own sequence number. Every time a message is transmitted, the sequence number is sent along with the message. The receiving station compares the received sequence number with a number maintained in its memory. If the message numbers agree, no messages have been lost; if the received message number disagrees with the expected message number, an error condition is created and the receiver requests that the sender retransmit the missing messages.

Packet Sequence Numbers

In some networks, messages are segmented into smaller transmission groups, or packets. If there are multiple communication paths between sender and receiver, the packet routing strategy may use several of the paths simultaneously to speed delivery of the entire message; the packets could arrive out of order. To ensure that such a message can be reassembled in proper sequence, packet sequence numbers are appended to each packet. These sequence numbers also allow for error control. The transport layer is responsible for sequence numbers between the source and destination nodes, and some data link layer protocols use sequence numbers to add reliability and efficiency over a link connecting two devices (see HDLC in Chapter 11).

In any of the situations just discussed, if a data block arrives and an error is detected, or if some of the blocks in a sequence have not been received, the recovery method is to ask the sending station to retransmit the erroneous or lost data. An acknowledgment usually is sent for all blocks received correctly; if a block is not positively acknowledged, the transmitter must resend it. This obligates the transmitting node to retain all transmitted blocks until they have been acknowledged. Being able to request that a message be retransmitted implies that the flow control is either half duplex or full duplex. If an error is detected on a simplex line, the recipient cannot send a request for retransmission. The only recourse in this case is to ignore the message or to use the message as received.

Error Correction Codes

Some error-detecting schemes allow the receiving station not only to detect errors but also to correct some of them. Such codes are called forward error-correcting codes, the most common being Hamming codes. As with straight error detection codes, additional, redundant information is transmitted with the data. Error-correcting codes are convenient for situations in which single-bit errors occur, but for multiple-bit errors the amount of redundant information that must be sent is cumbersome. The effectiveness of forward error-correcting codes is reduced by transmission noise that often creates bursts of errors, so these codes are not used as commonly as are error detection schemes. Error-correcting codes have good applications in other areas, such as memory error detection and correction, where the probability of single-bit errors is higher. Some semiconductor memories use a 6-bit Hamming code for each 16 bits of data to allow for single-bit error correction and double-bit error detection.

Miscellaneous Error Detection Techniques

Several other methods increase the probability of detecting data errors.

Check Digits   Check digits or check numbers are one or more characters (often simply the sum of fields being checked) that are appended to the data being transmitted. They are usually generated by the sending application or device and checked by the receiving application or device.

Hash Totals   One technique that validates operator input as well as augmenting an error detection scheme involves appending a hash total, which is the sum of a group of items. For a batch of credit card authorizations, the sum of all charges can be computed separately or by the input device. Computing separately before operator input provides an accuracy check of data entry as well as transmission. The receiving computer sums the number of fields transmitted and compares its total with the transmitted hash total. If the totals agree, it is assumed that there are no errors; if the hash totals do not agree, the data must be retransmitted.

Byte Counts   A byte count field can be added to a message. When an entire block of data is sent at one time (synchronous transmission), the loss of a character would ordinarily be detected either by LRC with VRC or by CRC. When every character is transmitted individually with its own error detection scheme (asynchronous transmission using parity checking), a lost character can go undetected. Transmitting one or more characters that indicate the total number of characters in the message helps detect transmission errors in which entire characters may be lost.

Character Echoing In some systems, especially with asynchronous transmission, the characters transmitted are echoed to the user as a check. Because of the additional line time required, this technique is less often used in synchronous transmissions. Consider an operator at an asynchronous terminal: When a key is struck the character is transmitted to the host computer, which echoes (resends) the received character to the terminal. If the character displayed at the originating terminal is incorrect, the operator backs up the cursor to the character position and enters the correct character. With a high-speed communication line it appears to the operator as though the character is locally displayed as well as being transmitted to the host; with low-speed communication links, or when communicating with a busy processor, the echoing may become somewhat apparent. Echoing has the disadvantage of doubling the chances of obtaining an error, as the message must be transmitted twice. The original message may be received correctly, but if the echoed message has been corrupted, the original sender will detect an error.

Error Correction

Whenever an error is detected, it must be corrected. If an error-correcting code is used, the transmitted data can be corrected by the receiver. This is seldom the case in data communication. The most common error correction mechanism is to retransmit the data. In asynchronous transmission, individual characters are retransmitted, whereas in synchronous transmissions, one or more blocks may need to be retransmitted. This type of correction is known as automatic request for retransmission or automatic request for repetition (ARQ).

Message Acknowledgment The mechanism used to effect retransmission is the positive or negative acknowledgment, often called ACK and NAK, respectively. When a station receives a message, it computes the number of error detection bits or characters and compares the result with the check number received. If the two are equal, the message is assumed to be error-free and the receiver returns a positive acknowledgment to the sender; if the two are unequal, a negative acknowledgment is returned and the sending station retransmits the message. Of course, the sending station must retain all messages until they have been positively acknowledged.

Retry Limit In some instances the second message is also received in error, perhaps due to an error-prone communication link or faulty hardware or software. To cut down on continual retransmission of messages, a retry limit—typically between 3 and 100—can be set. A retry limit of 5 means that a message received in error will be retransmitted five times; if the message is not successfully received by the fifth try, the receiving station either disables the link or disables the sending station itself. The objective of a retry limit is to avoid the unproductive work of continually processing corrupted messages. Once the cause of the problem has been corrected, the communication path is reinstated.

DIGITAL DATA TRANSMISSION

All communication media are capable of transmitting information in either digital or analog form; despite the fact that computer data is represented in digital form, originally computer data was transmitted mostly in analog form. The primary reason for this is that the providers of communication transmission facilities had established analog facilities for voice transmission. However, advances in digital technology and lower prices for digital transmission electronics are bringing about a change to digital transmission. Within several decades most major metropolitan areas will have made the transition; were it not for the considerable existing investment in analog transmission facilities, the changeover might come even sooner. If telephone companies were to begin today, it is likely that their transmission facilities would be digital rather than analog. There are four primary reasons for this.

Advantages of Digital Transmission

The advantages of digital transmission for data communication are lower error rates, higher transmission rates, elimination of the need to convert from digital format to analog and back to digital, and better security.

Lower Error Rates   Current telephone networks transmit signals over wires or via radio broadcast, continually amplifying the signals to overcome attenuation. Long-distance transmission demands that the signals be amplified multiple times to overcome attenuation. Because any frequency within the bandwidth is acceptable, it is difficult to filter out introduced noise or distortion, so both are amplified and propagated along with the original signals.

Like analog signals, digital signals also attenuate. Figure 3–6(a) shows a digital signal as it is originated. Figure 3–6(b) illustrates a possible effect of attenuation on that signal. A digital signal represents only two discrete values, so it is possible to completely regenerate the signal. Restored to its original state and strength, the data can be forwarded to the next regeneration point or to the final destination without any associated noise. This is accomplished by a digital regenerator. Figure 3–6(c) shows a regenerated signal.

Higher Transmission Rates   Another benefit of digital transmission is increased transmission speed. With digital transmission, switched connections commonly operate at speeds of 128 Kbps and with digital subscriber line technology speeds of 6 Mbps and higher are possible. The current limit is 56 Kbps for switched analog circuits and approximately 64 Kbps for leased analog telephone lines.

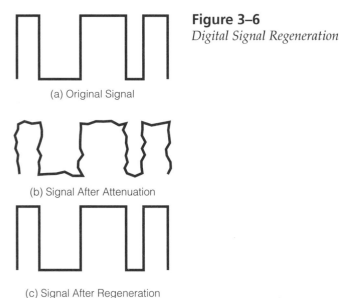

Figure 3–6
Digital Signal Regeneration

(a) Original Signal

(b) Signal After Attenuation

(c) Signal After Regeneration

No Digital–Analog Conversion   Digital transmission theoretically avoids the need for conversion between formats. Unfortunately, not all locations are served by digital networks, whose implementation has been restricted thus far to highly populated urban centers. In addition, the connection from a given location to the digital transmission and switching equipment is still an analog link in many cases. This makes it necessary to convert a signal from digital to analog and back to digital for transmission to the message's destination. The device that converts the analog signal to digital is known as a codec, an acronym for coder–decoder.

Security   Companies are becoming increasingly concerned about security of data and voice transmissions. One method for protecting these transmissions is encryption. You may be familiar with this concept as voice scramblers used on secure telephone lines. Although encryption algorithms exist for both analog and digital formats, digital encryption algorithms are more advanced and hence more secure and difficult to crack. Therefore, digital transmissions have the potential for greater security.

Digital Voice Using Pulse Code Modulation

In converting from analog to digital transmission lines, telephone companies are faced with the opposite problem faced by the data communication industry: On a digital line it becomes necessary to transform analog voice patterns into digital representation and then convert the digital

Analog Signal   Digital Transmission Line

Figure 3–7
*Codec Converting
Analog and Digital
Signals*

Figure 3–8
Pulse Code Modulation

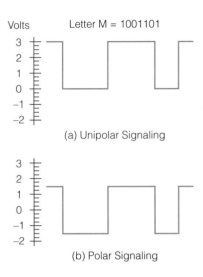

(a) Unipolar Signaling

(b) Polar Signaling

patterns back to analog format. This is illustrated in Figure 3–7. A variety of conversion techniques exist, but the most commonly used is known as **pulse code modulation (PCM).** On a communication wire, PCM is represented as pulses of current. A pulse of 3 volts could represent a 1 bit, and 0 voltage could represent a 0 bit. In some schemes a 1 bit would be represented by a voltage of +1.5, and the 0 bit by a voltage of -1.5. The first technique is called unipolar signaling; the latter is polar signaling. These techniques are illustrated in Figure 3–8.

pulse code modulation (PCM) A method for transmitting data in digital format.

INTERFACE

Once a medium has been selected, it is necessary to connect it to the computer equipment. The two classes of equipment in data communication are **data communication equipment (DCE)** (modems, media, and media support facilities such as telephone switching equipment, microwave relay stations, and transponders) and **data terminal** (or terminating) **equipment (DTE)** (including terminals, computers, concentrators, and multiplexers, all of which are covered in Chapter 10). The physical interface is the manner in which these two classes of equipment are joined together. Figure 3–9 depicts a data communication linkage, with the DCE and DTE components identified.

data communication equipment (DCE) One class of equipment in data communication, including modems, media, and media support facilities.

data terminal equipment (DTE) The second class of equipment in data communication, including terminals, computers, concentrators, and multiplexers.

The interface between DCE and DTE can be divided into four aspects: mechanical, electrical, functional, and procedural. The mechanical portion includes the type of connectors to be used, the number of pin connections in the connectors, and the maximum allowable cable lengths. The electrical characteristics include the allowable line voltages and the representations for the various voltage levels. The functional interface specifies which signals—timing, control, data, or ground leads—are to be carried by each pin in the connector. Table 3–8 lists the signals assigned to each of the 25 pins in an RS-232-C interface.

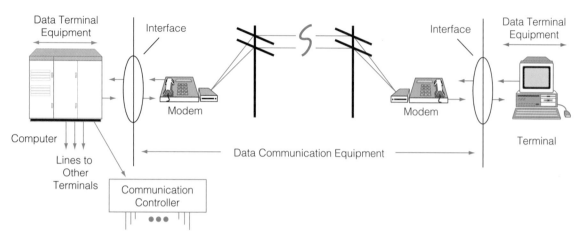

Figure 3–9
DTE and DCE Components

Procedural characteristics define how signals are exchanged and delineate the environment necessary to transmit and receive data. One pin or conducting wire in the connector might represent the ability of a terminal to accept a transmission; when the terminal is ready to receive data, a signal is raised on that lead. When no signal is raised on that circuit, transmission to the terminal is not valid. Table 3–9 shows a procedural interface to transmit from a processor to a terminal.

Interface Standards

Numerous standards are adhered to in establishing an interface between DCE and DTE. The following brief descriptions familiarize you with these standards and what they generally cover.

RS-232-C   Currently in the United States the predominant interface standard is the Electronic Industries Association (EIA) **RS-232-C standard,** established in October 1969 and reaffirmed in June 1981. RS-232-C encompasses serial binary data interchange at rates up to 20,000 bps and a recommended distance of up to 50 ft; longer distances are possible for shielded wires. (Shielded wire is certified by the manufacturer as capable of spanning 500 ft at 9600 bps.) Because of the speed limitations, RS-232-C has its greatest application in interfacing to wire media, where this bit transmission rate is most common. It covers private, switched, and leased connections, with provisions for auto-answer switched connections. In **serial binary transmission** (or bit serial transmission), bits are transmitted in single file. This is contrasted with **bit parallel transmission,** wherein bits are transmitted in parallel. Figure 3–10 illustrates the difference between these two techniques.

The RS-232-C standard does not specify size or type of connectors to be used in the interface. It does define 25 signal leads, 3 of them unassigned,

RS-232-C standard An Electronic Industries Association (EIA) standard for asynchronous transmission.

serial binary transmission The successive transmission of bits over a wire medium.

bit parallel transmission The simultaneous transmission of bits over a wire medium.

Table 3–8   Interface Connector Pin Assignments

Pin Number	Circuit	Description
1	AA	Protective ground
2	BA	Transmitted data
3	BB	Received data
4	CA	Request to send
5	CB	Clear to send
6	CC	Data set ready
7	AB	Signal ground (common return)
8	CF	Received line signal detector
9	—	(Reserved for modem testing)
10	—	(Reserved for modem testing)
11		Unassigned
12	SCF	Secondary for pin 8
13	SCB	Secondary clear to send
14	SBA	Secondary transmitted data
15	DB	Transmission signal timing
16	SBB	Secondary received data
17	DD	Receiver signal timing
18		Unassigned
19	SCA	Secondary request to send
20	CD	Data terminal ready
21	CG	Signal quality detector
22	CE	Ring indicator
23	CH/CI	Data signal rate selector
24	DA	Transmit signal element timing
25		Unassigned

Table 3–9   Procedural Interface Between Processor and Terminal

1. Processor and terminal raise data terminal ready signal to modem.
2. Modems raise data set ready signal.
3. Processor raises RTS (request to send) signal.
4. Processor's modem sends a carrier signal.
5. Terminal's modem detects carrier and raises CD (carrier detect) signal to processor's modem.
6. Processor sends data on transmit data.
7. Processor's modem modulates data onto the carrier wave.
8. Terminal's modem demodulates data onto received data.
9. Processor lowers RTS signal.
10. Processor's modem drops CTS and carrier wave.
11. Terminal's modem drops CD.
12. Transmission is complete.

**Message to Be Transmitted: LINE
Representation: ASCII**

L	1001100
I	1001001
N	1001110
E	1000101

Figure 3–10

Serial vs. Parallel Transmission

```
1001100   1001001   1001110   1000101
L         I         N         E
```
(a) Bit Serial Transmission

```
1 1 1 1
0 0 0 0
0 0 0 0
1 1 1 0
1 1 0 1
0 0 1 0
0 1 0 1
L I N E
```
(b) Bit Parallel Transmission

2 reserved for testing, and the remaining 20 used for grounding, data, control, and timing. In the absence of a standard, one connector—a 25-pin connector—has become common in implementing RS-232-C connections. Figure 3–11 depicts this type of connector. Actual transmissions typically use fewer than 25 signal leads. A simple modem interface can require that only 7 pins be active, yet on occasion connectors supporting 15, 9, and 7 pins are used to interface with these devices. A 15-pin connector and a 9-pin connector are also illustrated in Figure 3–11(b) and 3.11(c). The RS-232-C standard covers all four aspects of the interface: mechanical, electrical, functional, and procedural. This is significant because other interface specifications treat them separately, which means two or three standards may be cited that together form the equivalent of what is specified by RS-232-C.

RS-449   Because of the speed and distance constraints of the RS-232-C standard, the EIA **RS-449 standard** was adopted. It provides for a 37-pin connection, cable lengths up to 200 ft, and data transmission rates up to 2 Mbps. RS-449 equates with the functional and procedural portions of RS-232-C (the electrical and mechanical specifications are covered by RS-422 and RS-423). Because of RS-449's enhanced capabilities over RS-232-C, it should eventually replace RS-232-C as the predominant interface in the United States.

RS-366   EIA has also adopted an **RS-366 standard,** a 25-pin connection with enhanced capabilities for automatic calling equipment. RS-366 covers interface details such as what signals must be present when the dial tone is

RS-449 standard An Electronic Industries Association (EIA) standard that improves on the capabilities of RS-232-C.

RS-366 standard An Electronic Industries Association (EIA) standard for automatic call unit interfaces.

Figure 3–11
Cable Connectors

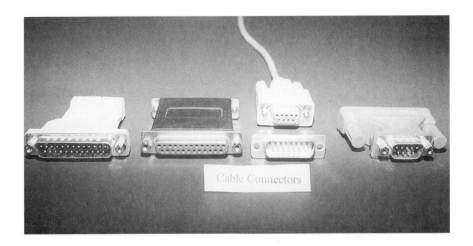

Cable Connectors

ISO-2110 A functional interface standard similar to the functional portion of RS-232-C that describes which signals will be carried on specific pins.

ITU V.10 and V.11 Electrical interfaces similar to those specified by RS-422 and RS-423.

ITU V.24 Covers both the functional and the procedural aspects of a 25-pin interface similar to that specified by RS-232-C.

ITU V.25 Covers the procedural aspects of establishing and terminating automatic calling unit connections over switched lines.

ITU V.28 Covers the electrical interface in a manner similar to that of RS-232-C.

ITU V.35 Defines a 34-pin connection for interfaces with speeds of 48,000 bps.

detected, when dialing, and so on. (The electrical portion of the interface is covered by the RS-423 standard.)

ISO and ITU Standards The International Standards Organization (ISO) and the Consultative Committee on International Telegraph and Telephony (CCITT), a subcommittee of the International Telecommunications Union (ITU), also have adopted standards that are widely adhered to. The most significant of these international standards for interfaces are briefly described below.

- **ISO-2110:** A functional interface standard similar to the functional portion of RS-232-C. It describes which signals will be carried on specific pins.
- **ITU V.10** and **V.11:** Electrical interfaces similar to those specified by RS-422 and RS-423.
- **ITU V.24:** Covers both the functional and the procedural aspects of a 25-pin interface similar to that specified by RS-232-C.
- **ITU V.25:** Covers the procedural aspects of establishing and terminating automatic calling unit connections over switched lines.
- **ITU V.28:** Covers the electrical interface in a manner similar to that of RS-232-C.
- **ITU V.35:** Defines a 34-pin connection for interfaces with speeds of 48,000 bps.
- **ITU X.20** and **X.21:** Cover the interface between DCE and DTE for packet distribution networks (PDNs). (PDNs are discussed in detail in Chapter 4.)
- **ITU X.24:** Covers the functional aspects of interface for PDNs.

Other Standards The U.S. government and U.S. military have their own interface standards. Specifically, MIL-STD-188-114 and U.S. government standards 1020 and 1030 provide for electrical interfaces similar to those of RS-422 and RS-423.

ITU X.20 and X.21 Cover the interface between DCE and DTE for packet distribution networks.

ITU X.24 Covers the functional aspects of interface for PDNs.

SUMMARY

The three basic types of data flow are simplex, half duplex, and full duplex. Most business data communication systems use either full or half duplex. Several different communication codes are used in data communication, the most common being ASCII and EBCDIC.

All media are subject to error. Detecting errors requires that redundant information be transmitted with the data. The three most common error detection schemes in data communication are vertical redundancy check (VRC), longitudinal redundancy check (LRC), and cyclic redundancy check (CRC). The most effective is CRC. In some protocols, sequence checking is also used to improve the reliability of transmission.

Digital data transmission provides both higher transmission speeds and fewer errors. Common carriers are gradually making the conversion from analog to digital transmission equipment. Digital transmission has led to new transmission capabilities, specifically the integration of different services over one medium. It is now common for both data and voice to be transmitted over the same circuits. One of the technologies rapidly being implemented to provide this capability is the integrated services digital network (ISDN).

Interface standards exist regarding connections between data terminal equipment (DTE) and data communication equipment (DCE). Both domestic and international standards address mechanical, functional, procedural, and electrical interfaces; unfortunately, these standards do not always agree.

KEY TERMS

American Standard Code for Information Interchange (ASCII)
bit parallel transmission
block check character (BCC)
crosstalk
cyclic redundancy check (CRC)
data communication equipment (DCE)
data terminal equipment (DTE)
echo
echo suppressor
Extended Binary-Coded Decimal Interchange Code (EBCDIC)
Gaussian noise
impulse noise

ISO-2110
ITU V.10, V.11, V.24, V.25, V.28, V.35, X.20, X.21, and X.24 standards
line drivers (repeaters)
longitudinal redundancy check (LRC)
parity check
phase jitter
pulse code modulation (PCM)
RS-232-C standard
RS-366 standard
RS-449 standard
serial binary transmission
thermal noise
vertical redundancy check (VRC)
white noise

REVIEW QUESTIONS

1. Define
   a. simplex transmission
   b. half-duplex transmission
   c. full-duplex transmission

2. What are the limitations of a 6-bit data code?

3. What are the limitations of an 8-bit data code?

4. Describe
   a. white noise
   b. impulse noise
   c. echo
   d. attenuation

5. Which of the four types of noise is most likely to cause an error in data transmission?

6. Describe four ways to prevent transmission errors.

7. Describe how parity checking works. If even parity is used, what will the parity bit be for the ASCII characters P, A, R, I, T, and Y?

8. Explain why CRC is a better error detection scheme than parity or longitudinal redundancy checks.

9. Explain how sequence checks can increase the integrity of data transmission.

10. What are the advantages of digital data transmission?

11. Explain how digital data transmission can obtain higher speeds than analog and at the same time have fewer errors.

12. Why are interface standards important?

PROBLEMS AND EXERCISES

1. Label each of the following items as simplex, half duplex, or full duplex.
   a. commercial radio
   b. CB radio
   c. television
   d. smoke signals
   e. classroom discussion
   f. family arguments
   g. ocean tides
   h. shortwave radio communication

2. Calculate the line time required for the following transaction. Assume a line speed of 28,800 bps, and 10 bits per character.
   a. Operator enters 10-character employee ID.
   b. System returns 500-character employee record.
   c. Operator changes zip code and retransmits only the 5-character zip code back to the system.
   d. System acknowledges receipt and positive action by sending operator 20-character message.

3. Identify instances other than those mentioned in the chapter in which a code with 256 different characters may be insufficient.

4. Obtain and examine the Japanese Industrial Standard (JIS) for data codes that contain a portion of the Kanji character set. What other characters are allowed? How many bits are required to support this standard? What special features are included, if any?

5. Why is Morse code not a viable alternative for computers?

6. If the speed of transmission on a line is 7200 bps and that line is hit by lightning that causes an impulse distortion of 3.5 ms, what is the maximum number of bits that could be in error?

7. Assuming the worst case in Exercise 6, what percentage of the errors incurred would be caught by VRC?

CHAPTER 4

Common Carrier Services

CHAPTER OBJECTIVES

After studying this chapter you should be able to

- Describe the history and current status of the telephone industry in the United States
- Compare the transmission services provided by common carriers
- Match one or more common carrier services to system requirements
- Describe the common carrier services available for mobile computing
- Discuss the characteristics of high-speed switched communication

This chapter continues the discussion of physical transmission of data and data transmission utilities. Setting up and managing today's communication networks is more complex than ever. More vendors are providing communication services over a wider variety of speeds. Different forms of communication also are increasingly being integrated onto one transmission medium. As a result, the sphere of responsibility for the modern data communication manager is expanding. In addition to selecting communication facilities for data transmission, the communication manager may also be responsible for selecting hardware and software that can meet the corporate needs for data, voice, video, facsimile, and other forms of electronic communication. In this chapter you will learn about data transmission facilities and other common communication facilities.

THE U.S. TELEPHONE INDUSTRY

Each country has one or more entities responsible for providing telephone and telecommunication systems. Some countries have federal or quasi-federal agencies responsible for this. For example, several countries have a postal, telephone, and telegraph (PTT) agency that operates under the auspices of the government and is a protected, regulated monopoly responsible for providing such services. In some instances, these regulated agencies have been deregulated and operate as nongovernment companies with competitors. It is unrealistic to discuss the telecommunication industries of all countries; therefore, we will concentrate on the telecommunication industry in the United States. First we look at the organization of the common carrier communication network. We consider how the network was organized in the United States both before and after the **AT&T divestiture** and the consequences of deregulation.

Predivestiture Organization

Before the divestiture AT&T dominated the telephone service industry. Other general service providers included GTE, and competition for long-distance service had begun to appear. The AT&T network is described here. Figure 4–1 illustrates the organization of the AT&T network. Note that there is a hierarchy of switching stations through which a call can be forwarded. A telephone subscriber is connected to a local switching office called a class 5 office. Class 5 offices are also called **end offices** because they are at the extremities of the telephone switching network. If the subscriber calls another subscriber who is also attached to the same local office, the call is switched through that single end office. This is illustrated in Figure 4–1 by subscriber A's connection to subscriber B. It is also possible for subscriber C to call subscriber D, whose telephone is connected to another class 5 office in the same general area. C's call goes directly from C's end office to D's end office and then to D's local line. Both calls are local calls and will incur no long-distance fee.

If the call is not local, like subscriber E's connection to subscriber F, the call is routed from the class 5 station to a class 4 station called a **toll center.** This initiates the billing process for the call. From the class 4 station, the call goes to a class 3 station called a **primary center.** At this point, if the call is destined for a regional high-use area, the class 3 station might route the call directly to the recipient's class 5 local switch. Alternatively, the call is routed up through the class 2 station, termed a **sectional center,** to a class 1 station, called a **regional center.** The class 1 station then passes the call to another class 1 station. A class 1 station might then send the call to another class 1 center. Class 1 centers form a backbone transmission network. When the call reaches the class 1 station closest to the call's recipient, the connection is switched down through the hierarchy until it reaches the recipient's class 5 end office. At the end office, the call is switched to the recipient's local line.

Postdivestiture Network

The divestiture in 1984 broke up AT&T into independent **regional Bell operating companies (RBOCs)** and a separate AT&T company. The divestiture not only ended the regulated monopoly AT&T had enjoyed but also freed AT&T and the RBOCs to enter into business areas formerly denied them, such as the computer industry. RBOCs are responsible for handling

---

AT&T divestiture In 1984 AT&T was broken up into independent regional Bell operating companies (RBOCs) and a separate AT&T company. The divestiture ended the regulated monopoly of AT&T and freed AT&T and the RBOCs to enter into business areas previously denied to them.

end office A telephone company office to which a subscriber is connected. Also called a class 5 office.

toll center In the telephone network, a toll center is a class 4 switching office. Also called a class 4 station.

primary center A telephone company class 3 station. A primary center is one station higher than a toll center.

sectional center In the telephone network, a class 2 station.

regional center A class 1 telephone station.

regional Bell operating company (RBOC) The AT&T divestiture resulted in the formation of RBOCs and a separate AT&T company. An RBOC is responsible for local telephone services within a region of the United States.

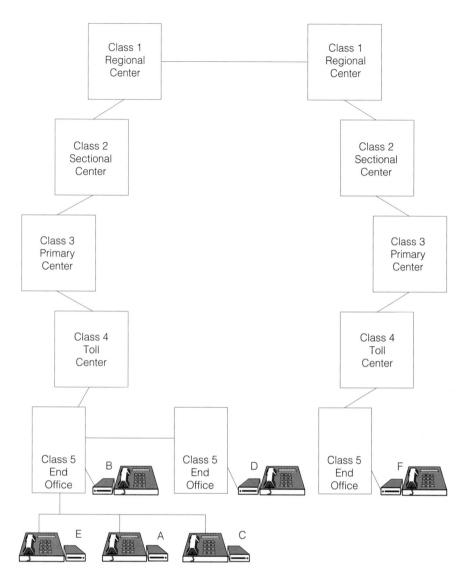

Figure 4–1
Predivestiture Telephone Switching Network

subscriber services within their area; one of the functions of AT&T is to provide long-distance services. The divestiture resulted in a revamping of how long-distance calls are handled.

Local calls are handled in much the same way as in the predivestiture era. However, the regions served by RBOCs were divided into **local access and transport areas (LATAs).** A LATA corresponds to a common calling area. In areas of high population density, such as the San Francisco Bay area, several area codes may fall within the same LATA. All calls originating and terminating within a LATA are handled exclusively by the RBOC. Any call that crosses a LATA boundary becomes the responsibility of a long-distance carrier, such as AT&T, MCI, or Sprint.

Each telephone subscriber is free to choose a long-distance carrier, and long-distance carriers are required to have equal access to subscribers. To

local access and transport area (LATA) The region served by an RBOC is divided into LATAs. LATAs are not rigidly defined, but calls within a LATA are handled exclusively by the RBOC (the call is not handled by a long-distance carrier but still may be a toll call).

point of presence (POP)
In the U.S. public telephone network, a POP is a point at which a transfer is made from a local telephone company to the long-distance carrier.

provide equal access, each LATA has a designated interchange **point of presence (POP).** An inter-LATA call is routed to the POP, where it is accepted by the designated long-distance carrier. The long-distance carrier routes the call to the POP in the recipient's LATA and the call is switched to the recipient's end office and telephone. This is illustrated in Figure 4–2.

The Telecommunications Reform Act of 1996

The basic telecommunication act under which the United States operated before 1996 was passed in 1934, before computers, television, and cellular telephones. A change was long overdue. The AT&T divestiture had a significant impact on telephone and data communication services, but it did not address the broad scope of telecommunication. After the divestiture, the RBOCs provided local telephone service and AT&T, MCI, Sprint, and other companies provided long-distance services. Other companies were involved in cable television and other broadcast services. The Telecommunications Reform Act of 1996 is a broad reform of the spectrum of telecommunication that reduces government regulation and widens competition. We will focus only on the areas that significantly affect data communication.

Before the Reform Act, long-distance carriers could not provide local service and vice versa, and cable TV companies could not provide services typically assigned to the telephone carriers, such as data transmission. The Reform Act changed the rules for service providers and extended competition

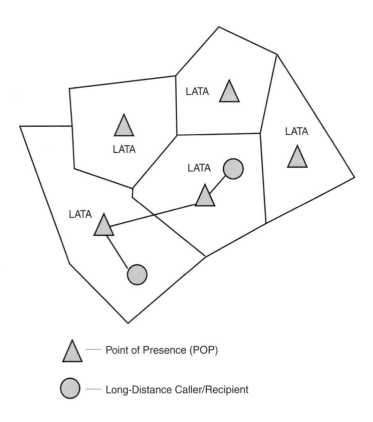

Figure 4–2
Postdivestiture Long-Distance Switching

for local and long-distance services. Long-distance carriers can compete on the local level and the RBOCs can enter the long-distance market. The Reform Act does not require companies to build the cable infrastructure to provide local or long-distance services. Two capabilities, interconnect and wholesaling, are stipulated in the act to give companies access to the existing telephone networks.

Wholesaling means that the owners of a telephone network must allow any organization to acquire and resell their existing services. Thus, if you wanted to go into the telephone business, you could lease lines from an existing carrier and resell services over those lines at a profit under these provisions. Thus, a long-distance carrier can provide the entire communication package, local and long-distance, to its customers; similarly, local carriers can do the same by acquiring long-distance lines.

The interconnect provision prohibits a common carrier from charging unreasonable rates for services terminating in their cable network. Without this provision, a local carrier could charge high termination rates and essentially prohibit competition.

The Telecommunications Reform Act of 1996 is too new to allow us to determine its full implications. However, we can review what has already occurred and make some conjectures about the future. Thus far, the advertising companies and merger brokers are definitely the winners in the Reform Act. Media providers have staged campaigns to generate support for their services and several companies have merged with or acquired companies that are compatible with their objectives for expanded services. Thus, a number of television, cable TV, movie, and telephone companies have merged to position themselves for the future. Data is being transmitted over wires that previously were used only for television programming, and before long, telephone calls will use the same medium. Users of this medium can take advantage of the higher data rates to get 10 Mbps access to the Internet without disrupting their TV programming. Soon, companies will be able to use one-stop shopping when acquiring their telephone and data communication services because one company will be able to handle local telephone, long-distance telephone, data communication, and video conferencing services tailored to their needs and for lower prices.

AVAILABLE SERVICES

Common carriers provide a broad range of services. The primary services are discussed in the following sections.

Switched Lines

Switched lines, as defined in Chapter 2, simply make use of the existing telephone circuits and switching equipment to establish a connection between sender and receiver. This facility is available wherever telephone wires exist. The speed of the lines depends on the quality of telephone equipment and the modem used. Plain old telephone service (POTS) using the standard analog format currently supports up to 56 Kbps. Digital switched services, described later, provide much higher data rates.

Leased Telegraph-Grade Lines

Leased telegraph-grade lines provide lower transmission rates than the voice-grade lines described below. They are used for very low transmission rates and are seldom used for data communication.

Leased Voice-Grade Lines

Leased lines also were discussed in Chapter 2. Leased lines may be conditioned to reduce error rates, which allows higher transmission speeds.

Wide Band Transmission

Wide band transmission allows very high data transmission rates. Transmission rates in this category are in the range of 48 to 80 Kbps. Most wide band services available today are digital rather than analog.

T-*n* Service

T1/DS1 through T4/DS4 High-speed data transmission circuits from a common carrier.

T-*n* is a general term for several classes of high-speed services, such as T-1, T-3, and T-4. **T-1 service,** also called **DS-1 signaling,** provides digital transmission rates of 1.544 Mbps. A T-1 communication link is created by multiplexing (combining) a number of lower-speed lines. Although the implementation may vary, generally a T-1 circuit is created by multiplexing 24 64-Kbps services. The product of 24 and 64,000 is 1.536 million. The additional 8000 bps are control bits. The 8000 bps derives from the PCM algorithm discussed earlier.

Higher speeds are available with T-3 and T-4 services, also called **DS-3** and **DS-4 signaling,** respectively. **T-3 service** provides a data rate of 45 Mbps and is derived from multiplexing 672 64-Kbps services. **T-4 service** provides transmission at 274 Mbps and is derived from multiplexing 4032 64-Kbps services. T-1 is the most common option; however, as the need for speed increases and the rates for T-3 and T-4 services decline, higher-speed services such as T-3 are likely to become more common. The Internet uses T-3 lines for high-speed backbone links. One use for higher data rates may be full-motion video and audio. With current technology, T-1 and T-3 speeds are insufficient for full-motion video transmission.

Fractional T-*n*

fractional T-1 A T-1 service that fills the void of high-speed transmission options between 64 Kbps and 1.5 Mbps by providing a portion of a T-1 line to customers.

A T-1 service that began to appear in the late 1980s is known as **fractional T-1** service. Before fractional T-1, high-speed transmission options were 56 or 64 Kbps or 1.544 Mbps, with few options in between. Fractional T-1 is intended to fill this void by providing a portion of a T-1 line to customers. Organizations needing data rates higher than 64 Kbps but less than the 1.544 Mbps of a T-1 line can subscribe to fractional T-1 service. For speeds between T-1 and T-3, fractional T-3 services are available. Fractional T-*n* service allows a user to share a T-*n* line with another subscriber by using only a portion of the 64 Kbps lines that are multiplexed together to form the T-*n* circuit. A fractional T-1 subscriber could subscribe to 64, 128, 192, 256 Kbps and up. Some common carriers limit the available increments by allowing multiples of 1, 2, 4,

6, 8, and 12 channels for speeds of 64, 128, 256, 384, 512, and 768 Kbps. Fractional T-*n* services allow the subscriber to optimize the line speed and the cost of the service.

Switched Multimegabit Data Service

Switched multimegabit data service (SMDS) is a high-speed connectionless digital transmission service. *Connectionless* means that the sender and receiver do not need to be connected via a dedicated link. In SMDS, the common carrier provides the user with access points for both sender and receiver. With SMDS, data is broken down into transmission packets. The common carrier provides high-speed switching equipment that routes these packets to their destination address. SMDS speeds are 1.54 Mbps (T-1) and 44 Mbps (T-3), but 155 Mbps services probably will be available soon. SMDS can be used for high-speed data transmissions such as the long-distance interconnection of LANs.

PACKET DISTRIBUTION NETWORKS

The concept of a packet distribution network (PDN) was first introduced in 1964 by Paul Baran of the Rand Corporation as a process of segmenting a message into specific-size packets, routing the packets to their destination, and reassembling the packets to re-create the message. In 1966, Donald Davies of the National Physics Laboratory in Great Britain published details of a store-and-forward packet distribution network. In 1967 plans were formulated for what is believed to be the first packet distribution network, Arpanet, which became operational in 1969 with four nodes. The Arpanet has since expanded to more than 125 nodes and generally evolved into the NSFNet. NSFNet and several other regional networks are integrated into one supernetwork called the Internet. The Internet is discussed later in Chapters 13 and 14.

A PDN is sometimes called an X.25 network, a packet switching network, a value-added network (VAN), or a public data network. *Packet distribution* and *packet switching* both refer to how data is transmitted: as one or more packets with a fixed length. The X.25 designation stems from ITU's recommendation X.25, which defines the interface between data terminal equipment (DTE) and data circuit–terminating equipment (DCE) for terminals operating in the packet mode on public data networks. The term *public data network,* which derives from the X.25 recommendation, is somewhat of a misnomer because packet switching networks also have been implemented in the private sector. When the network is public, users subscribe to the network services much as they subscribe to telephone services. The term *value-added network* is used because the network proprietor adds not only a communication link but also message routing, packet control, store-and-forward capability, network management, compatibility among devices, and error recovery. These are the services associated with the OSI physical, data link, and network layers.

Packet distribution networks specify a selection of different packet sizes, with sizes of 128, 256, 512, and 1024 bytes being most common. All packets transmitted must conform to one of the available packet lengths; individual users subscribe to a service providing one of the available packet sizes. Limiting the number of variations in packet size makes managing message buffers easier and evens out message traffic patterns.

PDNs and the OSI Layers

Only three OSI layers have been described for PDNs because a PDN is only responsible for message delivery. The three layers of the OSI reference model responsible for message delivery are the physical, data link, and network layers. From the PDN user's perspective all seven OSI layers exist; the application, presentation, session, and transport layer functions are implemented in the user's segment of the network.

Current PDN Implementations

The use of PDNs has increased significantly since the first PDN was established, and most computerized countries currently have access to at least one. In addition to the privately implemented NSFNet, public networks in the United States include those offered by AT&T, CompuServe, GE Information Services, Infonet Services, MCI Communications, and the Sprint Corporation, to name a few. Implementations outside the United States include Datapac in Canada, Transpac in France, EuroNet in Europe (essentially an extension of Transpac), Britain's Packet Switching Service (PSS), Germany's DATEX-P, and Japan's Nippon Telephone and Telegraph (NTT) DDX-2 system. Interconnections exist among these networks, providing international networking capabilities at a reasonable cost. Several ITU recommendations, covering different aspects of PDN access and use, are listed in Figure 4–3 where applicable.

Connection Options

switched virtual circuit (SVC) One of three types of circuits in a packet distribution network. When a session is required between two users, an end-to-end circuit is determined and allocated for the duration of the session. Similar to a switched connection.

permanent virtual circuit (PVC) One of three types of connection for a packet distribution network. A PVC provides a permanent link (like a leased line) between two nodes. It is usually selected when two nodes require continual transmission.

A PDN provides up to three types of connection options: switched virtual circuit, permanent virtual circuit, and datagram service. A virtual circuit is a communication path established between the sending and receiving nodes.

Switched Virtual Circuit   A **switched virtual circuit (SVC)** is similar to a switched communication link in that both are established when needed by a session and dissolved when the session ends. When an SVC session is established between two users, an end-to-end circuit is allocated for the duration of the session. This is accomplished via a call setup request that is initiated by the user. On receiving a call setup request, the X.25 network establishes a transmission link for the session. The switched virtual circuit is dissolved at the end of the session, a process known as call clearing.

Permanent Virtual Circuit   A **permanent virtual circuit (PVC)** is usually selected when two nodes require almost continuous connection. A PVC is similar to a leased communication link, as described in Chapter 2. With a PVC a circuit is permanently allocated between two nodes, so no call setup is required.

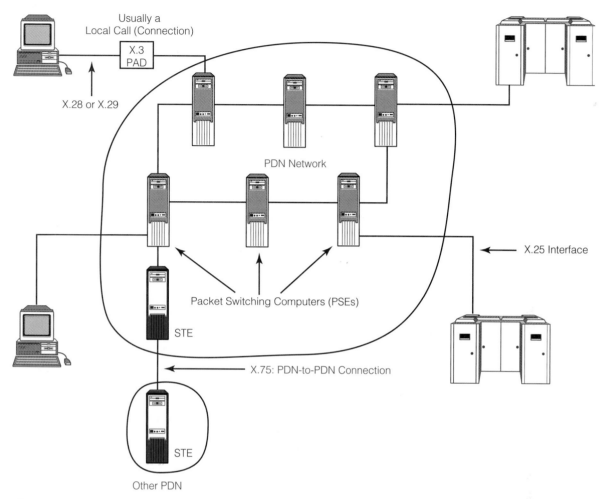

Figure 4–3
PDN General Configuration

Datagram Service   The third type of connection option is a **datagram,** which is a message that fits completely into the data field of one packet. Because a temporary path is established for each datagram, two datagrams from the same source can have two different circuits established. This type of circuit allocation is called connectionless because a dedicated connection is not established. Datagram service has the potential of fast service for short, unrelated messages. Although they have lower overhead because they do not require a virtual circuit, certain features of datagrams make them undesirable for many applications. First, the arrival order of datagrams is not guaranteed, as each datagram sent by a particular node may take a different route. Second, and more important, arrival itself is not guaranteed because the PDN establishes datagram arrival queue depths, and a datagram is discarded if the queue is full when the datagram arrives. This

datagram A connection option for a PDN. The message fits into the data field of one packet. There is less accountability for packet delivery than for other connection types.

problem is compounded by the fact that recovery of lost datagrams is the responsibility of the user, not the PDN, making datagrams best suited to messages of low importance and messages where speed is more critical than the possibility of lost data (such as in process control environments and certain military situations).

Example of a PDN

To see how a PDN functions, we follow a message as it proceeds from the starting terminal to its destination address, using a switched virtual circuit connection.

Establishing the Virtual Circuit   The user connects to the PDN by dialing the nearest PDN access port (a local telephone call in most large cities). After a logon procedure, the address of the other node is supplied. The PDN then goes through the process of establishing the virtual circuit. The call sequence is as follows:

1. A call request packet is sent from the sending node to the receiver. The call request is delivered to the receiver as an incoming call packet. The receiver may accept or reject the call.

2. If the receiver wishes to accept the connection, it transmits a call accepted packet that is presented to the sender as a call connected message. This establishes the connection, and data exchange may begin.

3. To terminate the connection, either node can transmit a clear request to the other. The recipient of the clear request acknowledges the disconnect with a clear confirmation control packet.

Data Exchange   Data exchange can begin once the virtual circuit has been established. The recommended data link protocol is link access procedure balanced (LAPB), an HDLC-type protocol (see Chapter 11). Other data link protocols also have been specified for use on an interim basis because many pieces of data terminal equipment do not support LAPB. The data portion of the frame is restricted to a specific maximum length (128 octets recommended, with 16, 32, 64, 256, 512, and 1024 specified as options). The Ns and Nr subfields (see Chapter 11) are defaulted to 3 bits each, but they also may be expanded to 7 bits. In the defaulted situation, up to seven frames can go unacknowledged, although the X.25 specification recommends that no more than three frames be sent before acknowledgment. This acknowledgment limit can be altered at the discretion of the implementer and would almost always be increased when the Ns and Nr subfields are expanded to 7 bits. The PDN uses a portion of the data field for control information: circuit addressing, packet sequence numbers, and packet confirmation. Three or four octets are used in information packets for this purpose, four when the sequence numbers are 7-bit entities. Figure 4–4 illustrates the format of a PDN packet.

Octet

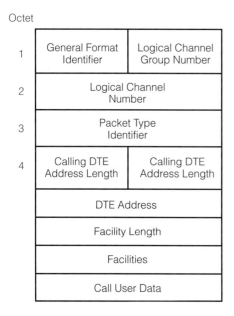

Figure 4–4
Call Request and Incoming Call Packet Format

Packet Assembly/Disassembly   The first step in sending the data is to assemble the packets, a function performed by a packet assembly/disassembly (PAD) module. The PAD function is not considered a part of the PDN; rather, it is the responsibility of the data terminal equipment. However, because many terminals used in PDNs lack the intelligence to perform this function, most PDNs still provide this capability. PAD functions are specified in the ITU X.3 standard. The PAD acts on one end to transform a message into one or more packets of the required length and then reassembles the message at the other end. The PAD is also responsible for generating and monitoring control signals such as call setup and clearing.

Once the message has been transformed into packets, the packets are passed to the PDN in accordance with the X.25 interface. The PDN then moves the data through the network for delivery to the destination. The standards do not discuss the internal workings within the PDN, such as routing and congestion control. The receiving PAD takes the information from the data portion of the packet and reassembles the message.

PDN Equipment   Two types of machines have been defined for use within a PDN: packet switching equipment (PSE), which accepts and forwards messages, and signaling terminal equipment (STE), which is used to interface two different PDNs according to ITU standard X.75. The standards for a packet switching network specify interfaces and functions of the PSEs and STEs, but not the nature of the equipment itself. Figure 4–5 illustrates the connections between users' equipment and the PSE.

Advantages and Disadvantages of a PDN   PDNs have several advantages. First, the user is charged for the amount of data transmitted rather than for connect time. Applications that send low volumes of data

Figure 4–5

*Connections in an X.25
Network*

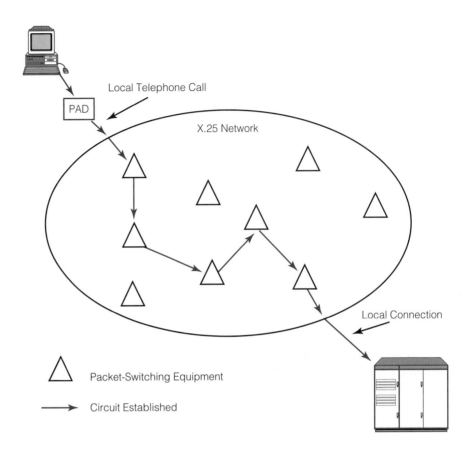

over a long period of time will find the charges for a PDN lower than those for leased lines or switched lines. The PDN also gives access to many different locations without the cost of switched connections, which usually involve a charge for the initial connection plus a per minute use fee. Access to the PDN is most often via a local telephone call, which also reduces costs. Maintenance of the network and error recovery are the responsibilities of the PDN.

There are also disadvantages to using a PDN. Because the PDN is usually shared, users must compete with each other for circuits. Thus, it is possible for message traffic from other users to impede the delivery of a message. In the extreme case, a switched virtual circuit to the intended destination may be unobtainable. This is also true for a switched connection from a common carrier. If the number of data packets to be transferred is great, the cost of using a PDN can exceed that of using leased facilities. Because the PDN is controlled by its proprietor, the individual user is unable to make changes that might benefit an individual application, such as longer messages or larger packets, longer message acknowledgment intervals, and higher transmission speeds, all of which are set by the PDN administrators.

OTHER SERVICES

Frame Relay

Frame relay is an outgrowth of the X.25 network. X.25 was developed when the quality of telecommunication lines was much worse than today and communication errors were more common. To compensate for the larger number of errors, extensive error checking was implemented in X.25. An example of the error checks that were made is illustrated in Figure 4–6(a). Frame relay reduces the number of error checks to that shown in Figure 4–6(b).

Frame relay services are provided by several common carriers, such as MCI Communications, Sprint Corporation, and LDDS Worldcom. International connections to other providers are available. Frame relay speeds are typically between 56 Kbps and 1.54 Mbps. Frame relay was originally used to provide data paths for nodes on WANs. The high speeds that are now supported by frame relay make it an attractive alternative to leased T-1

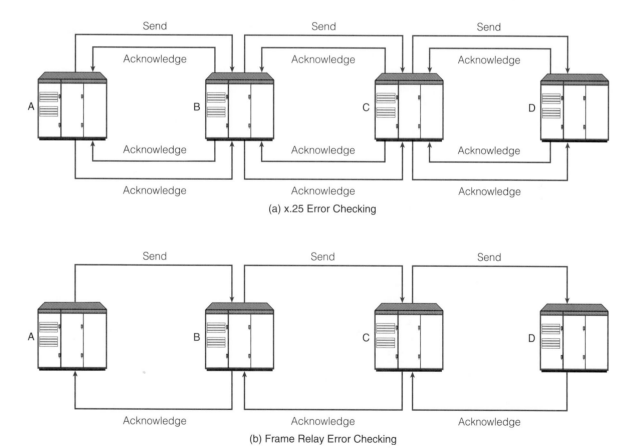

Figure 4–6
X.25 and Frame Relay Error Checking

connections and significantly expand the number of applications that can take advantage of the service. For example, at the higher speeds, frame relay services can provide a high-speed connection between geographically distributed LANs or high-speed Internet access through the frame relay service provider's connection, or can be used to transmit voice as well as data. Frame relay providers are increasing their capacity to accommodate the increased usage. It is anticipated that the number of ports serviced by frame relay technologies will grow by as much as 50% per year. A frame relay configuration is illustrated in Figure 4–7.

Asynchronous Transfer Mode

asynchronous transfer mode (ATM) A high-speed transmission protocol in which data blocks are broken into small cells that are transmitted individually, possibly via different routes, in a manner similar to packet switching technology.

Asynchronous transfer mode (ATM) and frame relay are similar services that provide high-speed switching of data packets. Both provide high-speed data transfers ranging into the hundreds of megabits per second. There are also differences between the two. In ATM a user starts the transmission process by sending a block of data addressed to the recipient. The data is broken into 48-byte data packets for transmission. Five bytes of control data are appended to the 48-byte data packets, forming a 53-byte transmission frame. These frames are then transmitted to the recipient via an ATM switch, where the 5-byte control data is stripped and the message is reassembled.

A variety of ATM speeds are available. Originally speeds of 155 and 622 Mbps were specified; however, switches based on ATM technology operating at lower speeds of 25 and 100 Mbps exist. The size of the ATM cell was a compromise between two interests: video/voice and data transmission. The video/voice advocates wanted short cells to minimize delay and provide better quality of service, whereas the data transfer interests were more interested in throughput and thus wanted larger packets to reduce overhead. ATM media is fiber optic cable for the highest data rates and category 5 UTP is used for lower speeds and distances.

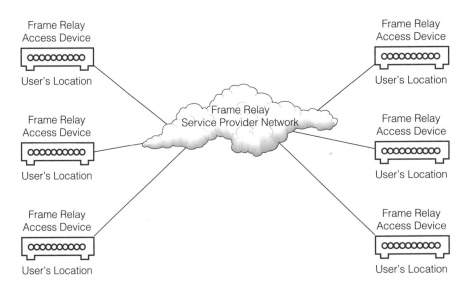

Figure 4–7
Frame Relay Configuration

To accommodate different types of ATM traffic—whether time sensitive or not—five different levels of service, called quality of service levels, were specified. Only four are typically implemented because two of the levels were not sufficiently distinct. The levels of service are called ATM adaptation layers (AAL). The basic provisions of each layer are given in Table 4–1.

WATS

Wide area telecommunications (or telephone) **service (WATS)** includes both inbound and outbound services. The inbound WATS service is the familiar toll-free 800 and 888-prefix numbers. A customer may subscribe to an inbound service, an outbound service, or both. The common carrier charges a flat monthly fee for the service, which covers a specific number of hours of connect time to designated regions. The cost of the service is based on both the number of hours of connect time and the distance to be covered by the service. When WATS service is used for data transmission, the effect is the same as using switched lines, but the cost of the call differs.

> **wide area telecommunications (or telephone) service (WATS)** An inbound or outbound telephone service that allows long-distance telephone service. In the United States the inbound service is associated with 800 and 888 area code toll-free numbers.

Satellite Service

Users may rent satellite transponder time from a number of common carriers. Satellite transmission was described in Chapter 2.

Integrated Services Digital Networks

Increased use of common carrier facilities for data communication has prompted providers of such services to evaluate their networks. One conclusion that has been drawn is the need for one network capable of transmitting data in various forms. These forms could include digital data, voice, facsimile, graphics, and video. The benefits to the user community of this type of network are higher transmission speed and potential cost reductions for communication services resulting from the ability to combine multiple data forms onto one network. One objective of an **integrated services digital network (ISDN)** is to allow international data exchange. This requires interfaces between a number of national and regional providers of such services. The first mission of the ISDN program has been to define the functions and characteristics of the network and to establish

> **integrated services digital network (ISDN)** The integration of voice and data transmission (and other formats such as video and graphics images) over a digital transmission network. This network configuration is proposed by numerous common carriers.

Table 4–1   ATM Adaptation Layers

Adaptation Layer	Type of service	Applications
AAL-1	Constant bit rate	Voice and video
AAL-2	Time sensitive but variable bit rate	Packetized voice
AAL-3/4	Bursty, connection-oriented service needing extra error checking	Applications where delays can be tolerated (e.g., file transfer)
AAL-5	Similar to AAL-3/4	Applications desiring less overhead for error checking

implementation standards. In 1984, the ITU produced the first of what is likely to become several standards for ISDN implementations. This standard provides for several different types of service.

The ISDN system specifies three basic types of channels, designated as B, D, and H types. Within the type H channel several options are available. These options are shown in Table 4–2. ISDNs will initially provide two interface structures designated as basic service and primary service. The basic service is designated as $2B_{64} + D_{16}$, which indicates that it consists of two type B channels and one 16-Kbps type D channel, for an aggregate speed of 144 Kbps. The primary service has a different configuration for North America and Japan than for Europe. The North American and Japanese specification is designated as $23B_{64} + D_{64}$, for an aggregate speed of 1.544 Mbps. This is the same speed as the T-1 service. In Europe, the primary service is designated as $30B_{64} + D_{64}$, for an aggregate speed of 2.048 Mbps, equivalent to E-1, the European version of T-1 transmission.

ISDN was the first high-speed alternative to switched analog connections for Internet access. ISDN used for Internet access usually provides speeds of 128 Kbps. Furthermore, with the right interfaces, the ISDN line can provide voice telephone service while also providing data transmission; however, in this mode the data transfer rate is typically reduced to 64 Kbps. ISDN line interfaces are called network termination (NT) devices. The NT provides terminal connection on the customer side and line connection on the common carrier's side. It is important when forming an ISDN connection that you consult with your service provider because complete standardization is lacking in some areas. ISDN has other uses than Internet access, some of which are

- digital voice transmission
- LANs (see Chapter 9 for additional information about this use of ISDNs)
- office automation (routing and access to documents)

Table 4–2   ISDN Channel Types and Options

ISDN channel types
  B: 64 Kbps
  H0: 384 Kbps (= 6B)
  H11: 1.544 Mbps (= 23B + $1D_{64}$), North America and Japan
  H12: 2.048 Mbps (= 30B + $1D_{64}$), Europe

Control data
  D: Both 16 and 64 Kbps

Basic service options
  $2B_{64} + D_{16}$ = 144 Kbps

Primary service
  $23B_{64} + D_{64}$ = 1.544 Mbps, North America and Japan
  $30B_{64} + D_{64}$ = 2.048 Mbps, Europe

- security via transmission of graphic images, such as signatures for check cashing verification or freeze-frame images to security guards
- video telephone service
- concurrent transfer of voice and data (for example, two users can be engaged in a telephone conversation while simultaneously transmitting data between their workstations)

PBX and Centrex Services

Private branch exchange (PBX) is discussed in more detail in Chapter 9 as a delivery mechanism for a LAN. Centrex service is essentially a PBX service provided by a common carrier. Instead of the switching equipment being located on the customer's premises, the common carrier provides the switching equipment on the common carrier's site. This allows several locations in a city to share the same switch and use the same calling prefix and allows extension dialing as though the telephones were located in one building and served by an on-site PBX. Like a PBX, Centrex service can be used to transmit data as well as voice.

private branch exchange (PBX) Telephone switching equipment located on corporate premises and owned by the corporation. A PBX allows telephone calls within an office to be connected locally without using the telephone company's end office or transmission circuits.

Mobile Services

Mobile services untether a user from telephone lines. Mobile services are used for telephone services, pagers, facsimile transmissions, and data transmissions. Currently the limitation of all available services is low data rates, generally 28,800 bps or lower; however, some metropolitan areas will soon have services of 56 and 100 Kbps. The available services include circuit switched cellular (CSC) radio telephone, cellular digital packet data (CDPD), mobile radio data, and personal communication services (PCS). Use of these services requires the proper interfaces, such as radio-frequency modems. Furthermore, the interface for one service will typically not work with the other services. Therefore, a user planning to use two or more of these services will probably need an interface for each.

Circuit Switched Cellular Radio Telephone

Circuit switched cellular (CSC) radio telephone provides mobile telephone connections. Currently cellular telephones are available only in major metropolitan areas because it is not economical to establish the facilities in areas of low population density. It is likely that satellite transmission will be added to existing systems and thereby overcome this limitation.

Circuit switched cellular (CSC) radio telephone A system of mobile telephone connections, currently available only in major metropolitan areas.

Figure 4–8 shows a diagram of a cellular system. Transmission is via FM radio broadcast. Before cellular technology, signals for a major metropolitan area were broadcast from a central site like ordinary radio station signals. Because of the limited available channels (dictated by the assigned frequencies), only a limited number of calls could be in progress at one time. With cellular technology, the calling area is divided into cells, each of which is served by a transmitting station. The transmissions are low power and thus serve only that cell, allowing the same frequency to be used concurrently by

Figure 4–8

Cellular Radio Telephone System

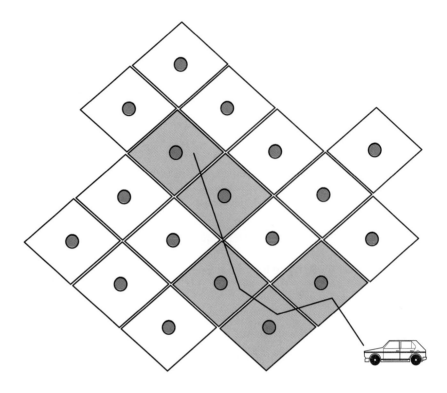

nonadjacent cells. As a mobile user moves from one cell to another, the responsibility for transmission is passed from the cell being exited to the cell being entered. Because cellular technology provides connection to line-based telephone networks, the full range of data transmission capabilities that exists for regular telephone service is available. Some cars are now equipped with facsimile machines for mobile fax transfers, and it is possible to connect portable computers in mobile stations to computer networks. The data rate for CSC is currently 14,400 bps.

Cellular Digital Packet Data

cellular digital packet data (CDPD) An enhancement to CSC in which data is transmitted in digital format using protocols like those used on the Internet.

Cellular digital packet data (CDPD) is an enhancement to CSC. Data is transmitted in digital format using protocols like those used on the Internet. Currently, the data is transmitted over idle CSC voice channels at speeds up to 28,800 bps.

Mobile Radio Data

Mobile radio services for data transmission are available from two primary sources. Bell South Mobile and RAM Broadcasting offer RAM Mobile Data and Motorola and IBM provide a service called Ardis. Both are available in most metropolitan areas. Speeds up to 28,800 bps are possible.

Personal Communication Service

personal communication service (PCS) Originally used for paging devices, PCS has expanded to include digital transmission for telephone and portable computers. Like cellular radio telephones, PCS technology uses multiple fixed stations to communicate with users in a local area or cell.

Personal communication service (PCS) was originally used for paging devices. The PCS market has expanded to include digital transmission for telephone and portable computers. Like cellular radio telephones, PCS technology uses multiple fixed stations to communicate with users in a local area or cell. As a user moves from one cell to another, control is transferred to the new cell. Currently, transmission speeds are equivalent to those of cellular telephone speeds. Because several competing transmission technologies are being used for PCS services, communication devices may not interoperate among service providers.

Digital Subscriber Lines

Digital subscriber lines (DSLs) are an emerging service that provides much faster transmission rates than analog modems and ISDN. A variety of DSL services are proposed, to include **asymmetric DSL (ADSL), rate adaptive DSL, high data rate DSL (HDSL), single-line DSL (SDSL), very-high-speed DSL (VDSL or BDSL),** and **very high speed ADSL (VADSL).**

ADSL The *asymmetric* in *ADSL* refers to the difference in data rates between upstream and downstream transmissions. In typical Internet access, the number of bits transmitted from a user's node to the Internet is much smaller than the number of bits the user's node receives. Consequently, asymmetric transmissions (like those used in the high-speed switched analog modems) provide faster service to a user. The upstream rates for ADSL will vary from 16 Kbps to 640 Kbps and the downstream rates will vary from 1.5 Mbps to 9 Mbps. The speeds depend on the gauge of the wires being used and the distance between the subscriber's location and the telephone company end office. Early implementations will probably use the lower speeds. The maximum distance between the subscriber's equipment and the telephone end office for ADSL is approximately 5.5 km (18,000 ft); currently T-1 speeds can be attained at this distance over 24-gauge wires. Higher-speed transmissions are available when the distance is lower. ADSL has been standardized by ANSI and the European Telecommunications Standards Institute.

RADSL RADSL adapts the transmission speed depending on the length of the loop and the quality of the lines being used. Otherwise, it is similar in distance and speeds to ADSL. Both ADSL and RADSL are well suited to applications in which more data flows in one direction than in the other, as in Internet access.

HDSL HDSL will provide speeds equivalent to T-1 (1.5 Mbps) or E-1 (2 Mbps) lines. E-1 is the European equivalent of T-1. The T-1 speed will require a user to have two telephone lines and three lines are required for E-1 speeds. As technology improves, the number of lines required may decrease or the speed will increase. The transmission is symmetric, meaning that the upstream and downstream data rates are the same. Symmetric transmission is useful for applications in which the upstream and downstream data rates are approximately the same, such as computer-to-computer transfers and video conferencing. The maximum distance between the user's premises and the telephone exchange is approximately 3.7 km (12,000 ft) over 24-gauge UTP.

digital subscriber lines (DSLs) An emerging service that provides much faster transmission rates than analog modems and ISDN.

SDSL   SDSL was developed by a company, not a standards group. The benefit of SDSL is that it operates on a single telephone line. This type of service is well suited for individual users who do not want to incur the expense of an additional telephone line yet want higher-speed network access. SDSL speeds are T-1 or E-1, with a maximum distance between the subscriber and telephone end office of approximately 3 km (10,000 ft) over 24-gauge UTP.

VDSL   VDSL provides very high data rates of 12.9 to 52.8 Mbps downstream and 1.5 to 2.3 Mbps upstream. The transmission is therefore asymmetric. With the higher speeds, the distance is much shorter, approximately 1.35 km (4500 feet) over 24-gauge UTP.

All of the DSL technologies require an xDSL modem/voice splitter at the subscriber end and compatible equipment at the common carrier end. The common carrier will terminate the DSL lines with DSL access multiplexers (DSLAMs). A DSLAM splits the traffic on the DSL line into a data switch or a voice switch, depending on the type of data being transmitted. This is illustrated in Figure 4–9.

cable modem A device that allows data transmission and Internet access via cable television lines.

Cable Modems

Cable television providers are beginning to move into the data communication business, primarily to provide Internet access. With a **cable modem**

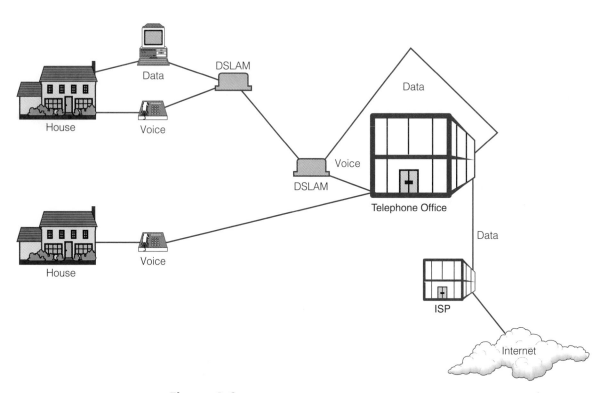

Figure 4–9
DSLAM Voice and Data Switching

attached to a cable TV line, a user can realize speeds of 10 Mbps. Other advantages of cable access include availability and interoperability with television programming. For many households, the cable is already in place and using the cable for Internet access does not tie up a telephone line. Cable modem technology allows simultaneous transmission of television and Internet data so one person could be surfing the Internet while others are using the same medium for television programming.

Service Providers

In the United States the following companies provide some or all of the above capabilities.

Aliant Communications	GTE
Alltel	MCI
Ameritech	NYNEX
AT&T	Pacific Telesis Group
Bell Atlantic	SBC Communications
Bell South	U.S. West
Centel	Wiltel
Citizens Utilities	WorldCom

SUMMARY

Common carriers provide the communication infrastructure for local and long-distance data communication. A wide variety of services are available. These services cover switched, leased, and public packet switching technologies operating at a variety of speeds. The trend has been for faster transmission capabilities and the integration of voice, video, and data.

Historically, national and local governments have regulated telecommunication companies. The regulations typically provide protection for both the consumer and the telecommunication company. Today, this is changing. In many countries, telecommunication providers are evolving to meet the changing demands of international communication. Often, this evolution involves deregulating the communication providers. An example of such deregulation is the U.S. Telecommunications Reform Act of 1996, which widens competition for local and long-distance services.

Today, a company or individual needing communication services can typically choose from several vendors and classes of services. Switched services range from slow analog services up to 56 Kbps to multimegabit digital services such as xDSL. Dedicated services such as T-1, T-3, and T-4 and fractional T-n services provide various combinations of speed and cost.

Packet distribution networks provide users the ability to interconnect communication equipment in a variety of locations. PDNs have the benefit of charging only for the packets transferred. For users needing to connect equipment in many locations with a moderate amount of data to be transferred on a regular basis, a PDN can be a compromise between switched and leased services. In the right applications the cost can be lower than those of switched or leased connections.

Mobile communication is a rapidly expanding sector in data communication. Common carriers are increasing the options and speeds of wireless technology. Digital cellular, mobile radio data, and digital personal communication services are readily available in urban locations. Emerging satellite services will further expand both the availability and speed of mobile communication.

KEY TERMS

asymmetric digital subscriber line (ADSL)
asynchronous transfer mode (ATM)
AT&T divestiture
cable modem
cellular digital packet data (CDPD)
circuit switched cellular (CSC) radio telephone
datagram
digital subscriber line (DSL)
DS-1 signaling
DS-3 signaling
DS-4 signaling
end office
fractional T-1
high data rate digital subscriber line (HDSL)
integrated services digital network (ISDN)
local access and transport area (LATA)
permanent virtual circuit (PVC)

personal communication services (PCS)
point of presence (POP)
primary center
private branch exchange (PBX)
rate adaptive digital subscriber line (RADSL)
regional Bell operating company (RBOC)
regional center
sectional center
single-line DSL (SDSL)
switched virtual circuit (SVC)
T-1 service
T-3 service
T-4 service
toll center
very-high-speed ADSL (VADSL)
very-high-speed DSL (VDSL or BDSL)
wide area telephone service (WATS)

REVIEW QUESTIONS

1. Describe the pre–AT&T divestiture telephone system in the United States.

2. What effect did the AT&T divestiture have on the U.S. telephone industry?

3. What is the general nature of the U.S. Telecommunications Reform Act of 1996?

4. Describe
   a. ADSL
   b. RADSL
   c. HDSL
   d. VDSL

5. What are ISDNs? Give two examples where ISDNs might be used for data transmission.

6. How does a cellular radio telephone system work?

7. Briefly describe
   a. Switched multimegabit data service
   b. Asynchronous transfer mode
   c. Fractional T-*n*

PROBLEMS AND EXERCISES

1. ISDN services are widely written about in data communication magazines and journals. Research the literature and describe four different applications that use this technology.

2. Interfaces are being defined for attaching microcomputers to ISDNs. Research the literature and find the cost and capabilities of one such interface.

3. Determine the types and providers of cellular radio telephone service in your area. What are the distance limitations of the service? What is the cost?

4. Obtain the costs for subscribing to a PDN. What are the monthly charges and what are the packet charges?

CHAPTER 5

Introduction to Networks

CHAPTER OBJECTIVES

After studying this chapter you should be able to

- Define the characteristics of local area networks (LANs), metropolitan area networks (MANs), and wide area networks (WANs)
- Compare LANs, MANs, and WANs
- Discuss the rationale behind LANs, MANs, and WANs
- Describe major LAN, MAN, and WAN applications
- Explain the concepts of client/server computing
- Compare and contrast LAN administration and stand-alone microcomputer administration

As noted in the discussion of data communication history in Chapter 1, the 1970s brought a significant growth in WAN technology, and one of the biggest growth segments of the communication industry during the 1980s was LAN technology. The LAN boom has resulted from lower hardware costs, availability of network and application software, and the integration of microcomputers into the workplace. This is not to say that all LANs use microcomputers as workstations. LANs were in operation before microcomputers became common, and high-speed LANs are still used to connect large computing systems. The next few years are likely to be characterized by the continued growth of LANs; the widespread interconnection of networks of all types; mobile networking; expansion of the use of multimedia over networks; expanded business use of the Internet; integration of telecommunication networks such as telephone, computer, radio, and television networks; and a significant increase in network speeds. In a few years the differences between WANs, MANs, and LANs may be slight and we will be able to once again just talk about networks. Until that time, we need to recognize the existence of the three basic network types and where each fits in the world of data communication.

In this chapter we first define LANs, MANs, and WANs, including the reasons for having them and applications that lend themselves to these network types. We also introduce common network terms. Some of these terms are generic to all network types and some are specific to either a LAN or a WAN. This chapter also introduces the concept of network management and specifically addresses the differences between LAN administration and the management of stand-alone microcomputers. An understanding of this material will aid in your understanding of the details of network hardware, topologies, media access control, system software, and network implementations, which are covered in Chapters 6–9 for LANs and Chapters 10–15 for WANs. We start by comparing WANs, MANs, and LANs.

DEFINITIONS

WAN

A WAN is the oldest of the three networks. It typically

- spans a wide geographical area
- uses transmission media supplied by a common carrier
- operates at transmission speeds lower than those for LANs and MANs
- uses data link protocols different from those of LANs and MANs

It is possible for a WAN to be confined to a local area and to use all private transmission media.

MAN

metropolitan area network (MAN) A network serving an area approximately the size of a city. The media distance limitations are on the order of 200 km (125 mi). MAN speeds are similar to those of LANs.

A **metropolitan area network (MAN)** serves an area approximately the size of a city. The media distance limitations are on the order of 200 km (125 mi). The area that can be served is thus much smaller than that of a WAN but considerably larger than those of most LANs. MAN media may be private or obtained from a common carrier. MAN speeds are similar to those of LANs. The most commonly implemented MAN, the fiber distributed data interface (FDDI), operates at 100 Mbps. The data link protocols used by MANs are similar to those used in LANs. The major difference between MANs and LANs is the distance spanned.

LAN

A LAN serves a local area. The media limitations for LANs are on the order of several kilometers. Often the LAN medium is privately owned. LAN speeds typically range up to 1 Gbps.

Because MANs and LANs are similar in many respects and because MANs are less commonly implemented, we will discuss primarily WANs and LANs. The distance factor aside, most of what we say about LANs is also true of MANs. We will make distinctions between the two whenever necessary.

THE RATIONALE BEHIND NETWORKS

The first type of network to be developed was the WAN. The major motivations for WANs were to overcome distance, to overcome the computational limitations of a single computer, and to provide departmental computing. Companies that are national or international often have multiple computing sites. Networks are used to connect these geographically dispersed sites and provide for the exchange of data and software. In some instances, the computing needs at one location exceeded the capacity of a single computer. In these instances multiple computers were installed at one location and then networked to provide resource sharing as well as greater computing capacity. Resources that were shared included hardware and data. As computers became smaller and less expensive with the introduction of minicomputers, some departments purchased computers to better control their computing environment. The department-level computers usually were networked with corporate computers and other department-level computers.

The last two motivations for WAN networking resulted in several computers being located in a small geographical area. The mode of interconnection, however, was basically the same as that being used to connect computers over long distances. LAN and MAN technology developed to overcome the speed limitations of this type of network. Originally LANs were installed to connect mainframe and minicomputers, and most LANs were implemented for two reasons: high-speed data transfer and resource sharing in a local area. Today there are several additional reasons, including use of group-oriented software, communication among workers, management control, cost-effectiveness, and downsizing, in which large computer systems are replaced by LANs. We consider each of these reasons here.

Large Data Transfers

In a large data processing installation with a variety of processors, moving data from one system to another once was accomplished by magnetic tape or low-speed communication links (less than 100 Kbps). Magnetic tapes provide high data transfer rates but have two disadvantages. First, manual intervention is required to effect data transfers. Operators are required to mount and dismount tapes. This not only tends to slow down the transfer but also often means that the transfer must be scheduled, reducing the potential for as-needed transfers. Second, incompatibilities between tape formats on different systems must be accommodated when tapes are used as a transfer medium. When using communication links slower than 100 Kbps, large file transfers are very time-consuming. If we consider a speed of 56 Kbps in transferring 1 million records of 100 bytes each, the transfer requires

$$(1,000,000 \text{ records})(100 \text{ bytes per record})(8 \text{ bits per byte})/56,000 \text{ bps} =$$
$$14,286 \text{ s} = 238 \text{ min} = 3.97 \text{ hr}$$

The above figures assume that the line is operating at 100% capacity and there is no protocol overhead, both unrealistic assumptions. The actual transfer time would probably be more than 6 hr. The corresponding time for a 100-Mbps LAN is 8 s.

A LAN can provide the best attributes of each of the above solutions: high speed coupled with operator-free implementation. LANs operating at speeds of 10–100 Mbps are approximately 200–2000 times faster than the 56-Kbps link. A caveat is required at this point: Although the medium can transmit data at a rate of 100 Mbps, actual transfer between two systems is often considerably slower because of the CPU and memory transfer time necessary to send and receive the message. Still, the transfers are time-efficient and can be initiated under program or user control without operator intervention.

Resource Sharing

print server A computer that allows several users to direct their printed output to the same printer.

Resource sharing is best exemplified by microcomputer LANs. Early microcomputer LAN systems were oriented primarily toward printer and file sharing (**print server** and file server technology). Printer sharing allows several users to direct their printed output to the same printer. In Chapter 8 we explain how this is done. With file sharing, two or more users can share a single file. The file can be an application program, a database file, or a work file such as a spreadsheet or word processing document. In Chapter 6 we consider server technology and ways in which files can be shared. LANs now are used to share more than printers, disks, and data. Other hardware shared on a LAN includes facsimile (fax) machines, modems, and terminals.

Groupware

groupware Workgroup productivity tools that allow a group of users to communicate and to coordinate activities.

LANs have expanded the potential of the microcomputer from individual productivity to workgroup productivity; however, workgroup software is not exclusively a microcomputer technology. Workgroup productivity tools, collectively called **groupware,** have their roots in WANs. Groupware allows a group of users to communicate and coordinate activities. Basic groupware capabilities such as e-mail and project management systems were common WAN applications before the introduction of microcomputers. Some workgroup productivity tools are described below.

e-mail Electronic mail.

Electronic Mail (E-Mail)   One of the earliest workgroup applications was **electronic mail (e-mail).** An e-mail system has many of the capabilities of a conventional postal system, such as collecting and distributing correspondence of various sizes and types and routing the correspondence to recipients in a timely manner. However, we have come to expect many more capabilities from an e-mail system than from a conventional postal system. Today's e-mail systems allow correspondents to exchange communication containing text, graphics, and voice images in batch or real-time mode. For many companies, e-mail has become a primary mode of communication, and because of its importance, we discuss its characteristics in some detail in Chapter 19.

Electronic Appointment Calendars **Electronic appointment calendars** are stored on the network. One user can consult other users' appointment calendars to find a time at which each user is available for a meeting. The electronic calendar system can then schedule the meeting for each participant.

electronic appointment calendar A workgroup productivity tool that is stored on the network so that users can consult each other's appointment calendars.

Electronic Filing Cabinets E-mail and other machine-readable documents can be stored in disk folders that are equivalent to file folders in conventional filing cabinets. Messages and documents in the folder can later be retrieved, modified, or deleted. Most filing systems maintain an index of the folders and their contents.

File Exchange Utilities **File exchange utilities** allow files to be easily copied from one network node to another.

file exchange utilities Workgroup productivity tools that allow files to be easily copied from one network node to another.

Project Management Systems **Project management systems** assist in planning projects and allocating resources. The introduction of LAN implementations has allowed these systems to be integrated more completely into the workgroup. A manager and team member can agree on the parameters of a task, the team member can update his or her progress, and the manager can monitor the progress. Projects can therefore be managed more effectively.

project management system A management tool that assists in planning projects and allocating resources.

Group Decision Support Systems **Group decision support systems (GDSSs)** assist individuals and groups in the decision-making process and help them set objectives. There are two levels of GDSSs. A lower-level GDSS does not have an underlying decision support system, but simply serves as a bulletin board for the exchange and development of ideas. A higher-level GDSS includes a decision support system that provides more tools for group users than a lower-level GDSS.

group decision support system (GDSS) System that assists individuals and groups in the decision-making process and helps them set objectives.

Electronic Meeting Systems **Electronic meeting systems** go beyond simple teleconferencing. The inclusion of networks allows participants to exchange machine-readable information in the form of graphics, text, audio, and full-motion video. If electronic meeting systems are combined with decision support system software, meeting participants can work in parallel to reach solutions.

electronic meeting system Network that allows participants to exchange machine-readable information in the form of graphics, text, audio, and full-motion video.

Document Management Systems **Document management systems** help an organization manage and control its documents. Capabilities include indexing documents, finding documents based on keywords contained in the document, controlling document changes, and allowing several users to collaborate on document editing.

document management system System that helps an organization manage and control its documents.

The motivation for using microcomputer LANs has evolved from that of simple hardware resource sharing, to data and application sharing, to idea sharing and personnel coordination. Although LANs are still used to share hardware, software, and data, the biggest benefit of LANs may lie in groupware applications. We discuss groupware in more detail in Chapter 19.

Communication

Most of us view telephone networks as a way to allow people to communicate. We use data communication networks for the same reason. However, in a data communication network, the entities that communicate with each other are not necessarily people. The network depicted in Figure 5–1 represents a variety of users and applications communicating: a person-to-person communication, a person-to-application communication, and an application-to-application communication.

The messages being exchanged can also differ. The person-to-person communication may be an electronic conversation, with the two parties exchanging messages in real time, as illustrated in Figure 5–1. User A types a message on the terminal and presses the Enter key, and the message is immediately displayed on user B's workstation. The person-to-application communication may be a user making an inquiry into the corporate database. In Figure 5–1, the user communicating with the application might be checking on a shipment for a customer. The application-to-application communication may be the transfer of a file from one node to another.

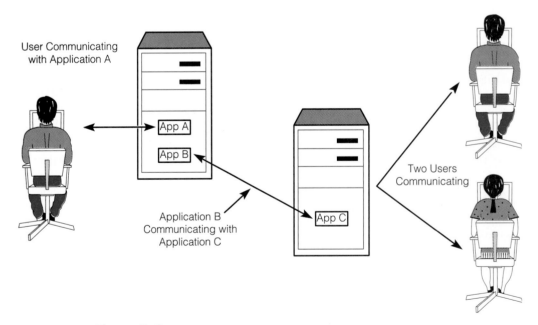

Figure 5–1
Applications and Users Communicating in a Network

Management Control

Another reason for using a LAN is management control. A LAN can help a company standardize the microcomputer environment. Application standards can be set up more easily in a network because most application programs can be installed on one or more network nodes called servers. In general, a **server** provides a service commonly needed by applications. Some common server classes are file, database, print, terminal, and modem. Servers in these classes allow applications to share the hardware and capabilities that the servers provide. Users access these services over the network. In a small network, all users may run the same word processing program that is located on a specific network node. All users will use the same version of the same word processor, making document interchange a simple matter. Contrast this with two or more users having different versions of the same word processor or, worse yet, completely different word processing software. In this case, documents created under one system would probably need to be converted and possibly reformatted before being used by the other word processing system.

LANs can also help control one of the most unsettling problems facing computer users: computer viruses. A computer virus is a segment of code that attaches itself to a file (usually a program), to memory, or to system portions of a disk. A computer virus is intended to replicate itself and to disrupt the normal functioning of the computer. With diskless workstations and virus detection software, management can reduce the risk of viral infections. **Virus detection software** analyzes a system and attempts to discover any viruses that have infected the system. Once a virus is detected, the virus detection software or another software utility can be used to remove the virus. A **diskless workstation** has no local disk drives, which reduces the ways in which a virus can be introduced. An added security benefit of diskless workstations is that a company's workers are unable to copy software or corporate data for personal gain. The disadvantage of diskless workstations is the complete dependence on the network. They cannot be used in a stand-alone mode or in a location that does not have access to the network.

server The routine, process, or node that provides a common service for one or more other entities. In one configuration for online transaction processing, application programs act as servers for users' requests. This is called a requester server environment.

virus detection software Software that analyzes a system and attempts to discover and remove any viruses that have infected the system.

diskless workstation A workstation that has no local disk drives, reducing the ways in which a virus can be introduced.

Cost-Effectiveness

Communicating, sharing, and management control are three benefits of using networks. However, the primary reason for using a network is cost-effectiveness. The ability to share resources has a direct impact on an organization's expenses. If users can share hardware, less hardware is needed. If a network were used only for resource sharing, it would be cost-effective when installing and operating the network is less expensive than or equal to the hardware, software, data preparation, and other costs in a non-networked environment. Less obviously, cost-effectiveness may derive from the ability of users to communicate and thus improve their productivity. One direct benefit is the reduction of paperwork. Electronic data exchange is converting paper offices to electronic offices.

Downsizing

In some companies, LANs have been used to downsize the data processing hardware, software, and personnel requirements. Downsizing means using smaller computer platforms in place of large computers or choosing the correct size computer for the job. Some companies have replaced their mainframe computers with one or more microcomputer LANs. These companies found that they could provide better data processing services for their users. The better services were obtained at lower hardware, software, and personnel costs; however, reduced costs are not always the result of downsizing. Other companies that have downsized have not saved money or have found the downsized system less effective than the conventional system it replaced. As an example of one downsizing success story, one company was able to cut its annual system budget from $10 million to $2 million and reduce its programming staff from 70 to 20. Overall the company realized an 80% cost savings. Diagrams of that company's computer configuration before and after downsizing are shown in Figure 5–2.

Client/Server Computing: A Network Application Architecture

client/server (C/S) computing A data processing architecture in which one or more processes called servers provide processing services for other processes called clients. The server and client can be running in the same network node or in different network nodes.

Networks are changing the way we view computing and how we design application systems. Data processing has evolved from batch-oriented systems on stand-alone computers, to online transaction processing with terminals and a host computer, to distributed application processing using several computers in a network. One of the distributed software architectures on networks is called **client/server computing.** Client/server (C/S) computing divides the work an application performs among several computers. In C/S computing one application, called the client, requests processing services from another application, called the server. In LAN systems, the client and the server processes typically run in different computers. Some of the more common server functions are database services, in which a database server processes database requests, and mail services that route and store mail messages. A client process may use the services of several different server applications in carrying out its work.

The concept of C/S computing was not developed for networking; however, networks in general and LANs specifically have created an environment amenable to C/S technology. Perhaps looking at the precursors of today's C/S environment will make it easier to understand the LAN implementations. Figure 5–3 depicts a large computer to which many terminals are connected. Terminal users each have a set of applications and transactions they are allowed to run, and different users may have different sets of capabilities. A person's job needs determine which applications and transactions may be used. Figure 5–3 shows three classes of software components in the host processor: a transaction control process (TCP), applications, and a database management system (DBMS).

Consider the needs of Kim, a specific terminal user. Kim works in the personnel department. Some of the functions she can do are adding employees, updating employee records, and deleting the records of employees who left the company more than 3 years ago. The add-employee transaction

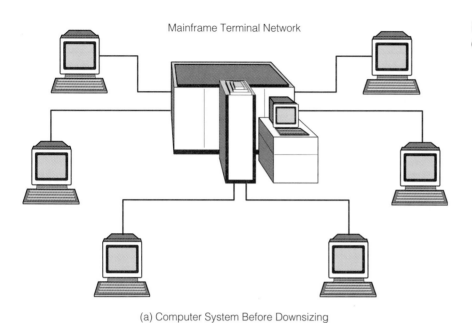

Figure 5–2
Computer Configuration

Mainframe Terminal Network

(a) Computer System Before Downsizing

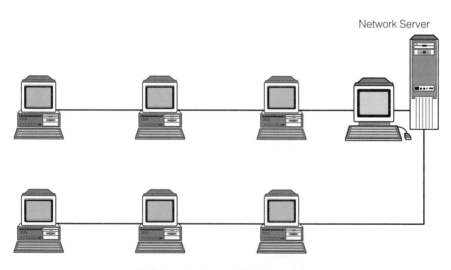

Network Server

(b) Computer System After Downsizing

requires the services of three different applications, one each for employee, insurance, and payroll updates. When Kim requests that a certain transaction, such as adding an employee, be run, her request is received by the TCP. The TCP is responsible for routing the transaction to the appropriate applications. In this case, three applications must work on the transaction,

Figure 5–3

C/S Computing in a Mainframe Computer

A Processor

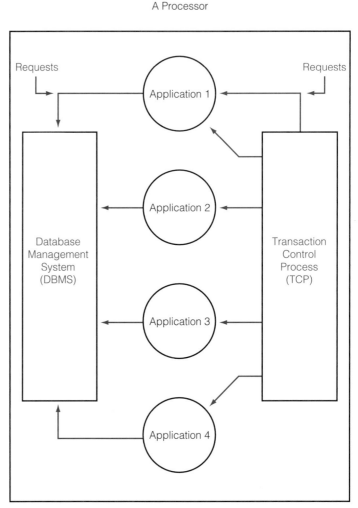

TCP has a role as a client with applications as servers.
Applications have roles as clients with DBMS as a server.

a capability called cooperative computing. In this scenario, the TCP requests each application to perform a service. In some systems the TCP is called a requester and the applications are called servers. In today's terminology the TCP could be called a client. The client makes requests that are carried out in whole or in part by other processes, called servers. In this example the applications in turn make requests of the DBMS and the operating system for services they perform. Thus, a server can also become a client.

In WANs, some companies have extended this type of C/S technology by allowing the server processes to be on nodes different from the one on which the client is running. This provides a distributed processing environment in which the hardware, software, and data resources of several computers combine to solve a problem. In essence, with C/S computing the network becomes the computer. We can also talk about server classes. A server class is represented by one or more applications, all of which can carry out certain tasks. With server classes, a client does not need the services of a particular server process because any process in the class can perform the requested service.

A C/S LAN configuration is illustrated in Figure 5–4. This figure shows two instances of C/S computing: a database or SQL server and an e-mail server. (SQL is an abbreviation for structured query language, a standard database language.) Earlier we described how a database server works. An

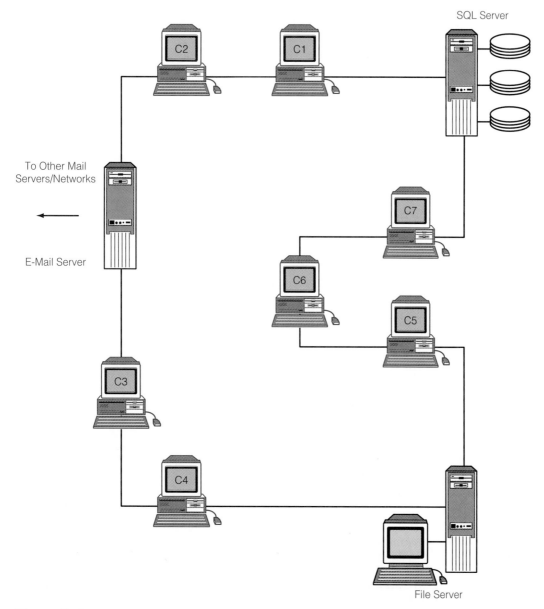

Figure 5–4
LAN C/S Computing Environment

e-mail server operates like a post office for its clients. An e-mail server performs functions such as supplying mail addresses given a user's name, distributing mail, and providing mail agent functions. There are several types of mail agents, one of which is a vacation agent. An e-mail vacation agent can provide services such as collecting incoming mail in an electronic folder or rerouting mail to another designated user while the original recipient is away.

In LAN C/S technology, clients typically run in workstations and request services from microcomputer, minicomputer, or mainframe nodes that operate exclusively as servers. Alternatively, C/S computing can be implemented in a peer-to-peer LAN. In a peer-to-peer C/S environment, server and client processes can be running in the same node. In Figure 5–5, both client A and server 1 are running in node 1.

Advantages of C/S Computing

System Expansion   Growth is one objective of many companies, and it is often accompanied by the need for additional computing power. With C/S computing the computing power is distributed over multiple processors. Because the computer is the network, in C/S computing we can expand the

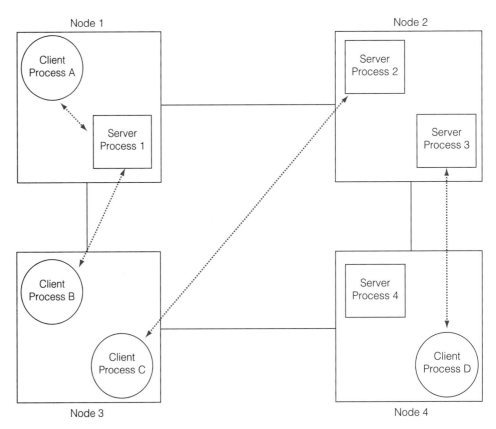

Figure 5–5
Peer-to-Peer C/S Environment

computer by adding hardware and software components to the network. Adding to the network can be done in small, manageable increments. This means that the computer can be scaled up (or down) without incurring large expenses and major hardware upgrades. Applications also can be easily expanded. Once the C/S environment is set up, new applications can be quickly installed and can immediately take advantage of the services available. This growth is made easier because the application functions provided by the server processes are already in place, and the work of application programmers is reduced.

Modular Applications C/S applications are generally improved because applications are modular. Modularity can reduce the memory required for client applications and optimize server processes. Part of the application logic is contained in the servers and therefore does not need to be replicated in the client portion of the code. An analogy may be helpful here. If you are building a house, you would probably not do all of the jobs yourself because it would be difficult for you to learn all of the necessary carpentry, plumbing, electrical, and landscaping skills. However, if you become a client and use the services of those who already know how to do these things, you will probably get the job done faster and better. This analogy applies directly to the concept of C/S computing. Server modules are optimized to perform their function on behalf of their clients, and the clients do not need to be burdened with the logic essential to performing those tasks.

Portability Some computer systems are better able to perform certain jobs than others. For example, some platforms are noted for their ability to do high-resolution graphics applications, such as computer-aided design and drafting (CAD), whereas other hardware and software combinations are well suited for office automation applications. The combination of hardware and software of an SQL server also makes the server able to manage data more effectively than a general-purpose computer and operating system. As new technologies emerge, the C/S environment provides an easy way to integrate such technologies into the network. A company can switch among hardware and software vendors to find its ideal computing system. Ordinarily, these changes will not affect the remaining components. Using an SQL server as an example, if a new, more powerful server engine becomes available, it should be easy to install the new engine in place of existing SQL servers or to simply add the new server to augment existing servers.

Standards As C/S develops we will probably see new standards for the way in which clients and servers communicate. Some of these are already being developed by leaders in C/S technology. With interface standards available, software and hardware from many vendors can be integrated to create a modular, flexible, extendable computing environment.

Disadvantages of C/S Computing

One disadvantage of C/S technology on WANs is reduced performance because of the slowness of the communication links. With high-speed LANs, the communication link does not become an obstacle to performance. Another disadvantage of C/S computing on networks is the complexity of creating the optimum C/S environment. This disadvantage is common to WAN and LAN implementations. Once these problems are overcome, several advantages are afforded by C/S computing.

C/S Technology

C/S technology on LANs is in its infancy, but its direction has already begun to take shape. In this section we look at some of the technology that underlies C/S computing, the interfaces that exist between clients and servers, and standards that are being developed.

Clients and servers must have a way to communicate with each other. There are two basic ways in which this is done: remote procedure calls and messages. You may be familiar with programming languages that support local procedure calls. With local procedure calls, one segment of a program invokes logic in another program segment called a procedure. The procedure does its work, and then the results and processing control are passed back to the point in the program from which the procedure was called. You can think of the procedure as performing a service for the program. Remote procedure calls extend this concept to allow an application on one computer to call on the services of another process. The process being called could be running in the same computer or, as is typically the case in C/S computing, the process being called could be running in another computer. Moreover, the process being called may not be running at the time of the call. The remote procedure call in this instance initiates the server process on the other computer.

Message exchange is a more flexible method of communication. The client and the server enter into a session (recall the OSI session layer) and exchange information. The client sends a request and the server responds with the answer to the request.

One issue to be resolved with C/S computing is how to find the server or servers that perform the needed functions. Today, we are looking primarily at clients and servers that are attached to the same LAN. It is logical to extend this to having servers and clients on different LANs. To maintain the modularity and flexibility of C/S computing, we would like to be able to add servers, delete existing ones, and perhaps move an existing server from one LAN to another. Changes of this nature also should be transparent to the clients, which means the clients should not have to be reprogrammed. This problem can be solved by having servers "advertise" themselves. For example, they might place an entry into a network directory or send messages to all nodes registering their presence.

Clients communicate with servers through an application program interface, as illustrated in Figure 5–6. Standards are being developed that will make forming C/S interfaces easier. Having many different C/S interfaces should be avoided to maintain flexibility. It is better to have one or a few standard interfaces so a company can develop client applications that can access servers created by other companies. These interfaces have come to be called **middleware.** The objective of middleware

middleware A software interface that functions as an intermediary between clients and servers.

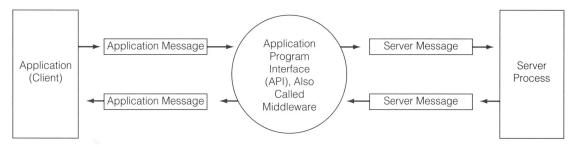

Figure 5–6
C/S Application Program Interface

is to serve as an intermediary between clients and servers, which means that the middleware is responsible for making the connection between clients and servers.

One example of middleware and its standardization efforts is the Distributed Computing Environment (DCE) specifications established by the Open Software Foundation. DCE addresses the use of remote procedure calls, security, name services, and messages for C/S computing. Another example is the Object Request Broker (ORB) established by the Object Management Group. A client communicates with a server through the services of the ORB. The ORB receives a client's request, finds a server capable of satisfying that request, sends the message to that server, and returns the response to the client. The ORB thus provides client and server independence. Any client that can communicate with the ORB is then able to communicate with any server that can communicate with the ORB. This provides both hardware and software independence.

We can use three models to represent the distribution of functions in a C/S environment. First, the majority of the application logic can reside in the client system, with only the specialized server logic residing in the server system, as illustrated in Figure 5–7(a). In this model, the server is less burdened and can be more responsive to volumes of client requests. This is usually the model used for database servers. In a database server, the server responds to a client's request for data and data meeting the constraints of the request are returned to the client for processing. This model is sometimes called the data management model.

A second model uses the client primarily to display or print data, and the data management and application logic are resident on the server, as illustrated in Figure 5–7(b). This approach could be used for graphics applications wherein a high-speed server processor is used to generate the drawing details and the workstation is responsible for displaying the details on the monitor. This model can be called the presentation model.

The third possibility embeds application logic in both the client and the server, as illustrated in Figure 5–7(c). This model might be used in a transaction processing system in which the application contains logic about customers and the server contains the application logic for banking accounts.

Figure 5–7
C/S Application Models

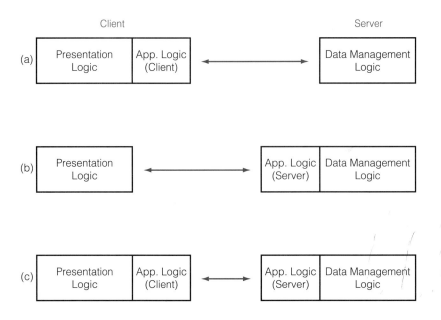

LAN AND WAN CHARACTERISTICS

The applications described above have several things in common:

- communication between a variety of devices in a limited geographical area
- use of several different applications
- high-speed data transfer
- high reliability
- device and data sharing
- transparent interface to shared resources
- adaptability to meet changing hardware and software requirements
- potential access to other networks such as a WAN, a PDN, or another LAN
- potential access to a multiuser host system such as a minicomputer or a mainframe
- security from interference from other users, either accidental or intentional
- ease of management
- private ownership

This, then, is the basis for a LAN: multiple devices of different types and capabilities providing transparent access to diverse applications in a limited geographical area, all requiring reliability and rapid response for common services needed by the devices. The network must be manageable, able to accommodate changing requirements and devices, and able to interface to other communication networks. Most important, the LAN must contribute to the solution of business problems.

High speeds over limited distance make LANs very suitable for joining computers in a building or building complex. Typically, LAN speeds are 1 Mbps or faster, and speeds of more than 2 Gbps have been attained. The distance spanned depends on the specific implementation. Usually workstations are not dispersed over a distance of more than a few miles; MAN implementations support distances of 100 mi or more.

The LAN itself consists of communication software, a communication medium, nodes, connectors that attach the nodes to the medium, and network software. In contrast, a WAN usually consists of data terminal equipment owned or controlled by the user and data communication equipment provided by a common carrier; however, some WANs are implemented as totally private networks without using the services of a common carrier. It also is common for LANs and WANs to be connected to a larger enterprise network, and the distinction between the two regarding speed and distance is decreasing. Perhaps in several years we will just talk about networks without making distinctions between the two.

ADDED RESPONSIBILITIES OF NETWORKS

Thus far, we have mentioned several problems that networks can help solve and the potential benefits of implementing a LAN or a WAN. Networks also mean additional responsibilities. With stand-alone computer systems, whether microcomputers, minicomputers, or mainframes, each individual microcomputer user or individual data processing organization is responsible for computer operations. These single entities are principally responsible for their own management tasks such as making backups, keeping the system running, reporting problems, and replacing paper in the printer. A network provides sharing of many resources, but the responsibility for network management should not be shared. When management is everyone's responsibility it is also no one's responsibility. Thus, a network must be managed and someone must be given that responsibility and authority. Computer system management for large systems is the rule; although some new technical skills may have been required, management of networks was a natural extension of computer system management. Formal management of stand-alone microcomputers is the exception. A significant change must take place when a company converts from stand-alone microcomputers to a LAN. Effectively managing a LAN requires additional skills to those usually required for individual microcomputer users. Depending on the number of users and applications, LAN management ranges in scope from a part-time responsibility to a full-time job for one or more employees.

Now it is time to get into some details of how networks work. We start the discussion of implementation details by introducing some networking terms.

NETWORK TERMINOLOGY

Network and Node

network Two or more computers connected by a communication medium, together with all communication, hardware, and software components. Alternatively, a host processor together with its attached terminals, workstations, and communication equipment, such as transmission media and modems.

The term *network,* as used in Chapters 5–15, means a group or set of computer systems and their attached communication devices, such as terminals and multiplexers. Each computer system is called a network **node.** *Computer system* is the term used rather than *processor* or *computer* because of the existence of multiple processor systems. Thus, a node is one or more processors that collectively serve as a termination point for a communication link with another node.

node Processor in a network, either a LAN or a WAN.

Link, Path, and Circuit

path A group of links that allows a message to move from its point of origin to its destination.

In Chapter 1 you read about the data link layer and how it helps move data from one node to another. We can also talk about the path a message takes to get from the sender to the receiver. There is often a difference between a link and a path: A **path** represents end-to-end message routing, whereas a **link** connects one node to an adjacent node or one node to a terminal. A link is also known as a **circuit** because a circuit is a conduit for data and in some instances multiple lower-speed connections are combined to form a single higher-speed connection through a technique called multiplexing. In Figure 5–8, the lines represent communication links connecting nodes. Figure 5–8 shows two paths available for communication between node A and node C (the path A ⟶ B, B ⟶ C and the path A ⟶ D, D ⟶ C), with two links on each path. We sometimes also refer to a **virtual circuit,** which is a connection established between

link The circuit established between two adjacent nodes, with no intervening nodes.

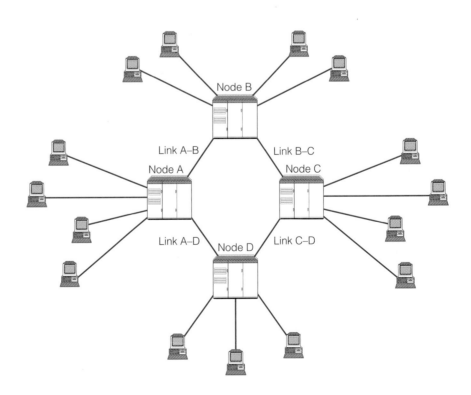

Figure 5–8

Links and Paths in a Network

a sender and a receiver upon setting up a communication session. In a virtual circuit, all messages are sent over the same path.

Routing

Routing is a function of the OSI network layer and refers to how the path from sending node to receiving node is determined. In general, routing in a LAN is simple: The message is broadcast to all nodes. This can be done efficiently because of the speed of data transmission. In WANs routing is usually more selective in that a single optimum path is selected for sending data, or several paths may be used concurrently. It is seldom the case, however, that a message is sent to all nodes as in a LAN.

Session and User

Session refers to a communication dialogue between two users of a network and is a function of the OSI session layer. A user can be a terminal operator, an application, or any other originator of messages. In some systems, sessions are quite formal, with well-defined conventions for establishing, continuing, and terminating the dialogue.

Packet Switching, Packet Distribution Network, and Circuit Switching

Packet switching is the technology of transmitting a message in one or more fixed-length data packets. A packet switching network is also sometimes called a **packet distribution network (PDN), public data network** (also **PDN), X.25 network** (X.25 is a standard designation), or **value-added network (VAN).** Henceforth, the abbreviation PDN is used. A PDN generally connects a user and the nearest node in the PDN. The PDN routes the data packets to their final destination by finding the best route for each packet (packet switching).

Store-and-Forward

In a **store-and-forward system,** messages may be stored at nodes along the transmission path before these nodes deliver the messages to the next node. There are several reasons for using store-and-forward. First, there is the responsibility for being able to resend the message. If node A is transmitting a message to node Z, the path between the two may pass through several intermediate nodes. To ensure delivery, either node A must keep the message until it is delivered or an intermediate node that has received the message must assume this responsibility. In a store-and-forward system, a node that receives the message will write it to disk or store it in memory and then acknowledge to the sender that the message has been received. This relieves the sender of accountability for the message. Store-and-forward is attractive for financial transactions because it provides a trace of the progress of the transaction.

Second, store-and-forward algorithms are used for time-staged delivery systems. These systems allow users not only to send messages but also to specify a required delivery time, providing several benefits. Corporations with offices in various time zones can assign a delivery time for their mail

circuit Either the medium connecting two communicating devices or a path between a sender and a receiver in which there may be one or more intermediary nodes. The exact meaning depends on the context.

virtual circuit A connection, established when setting up a communication session, between a sender and a receiver in which all messages are sent over the same path.

routing An algorithm used to determine how to move a message from its source to its destination.

packet switching The transmission of a message by dividing the message into fixed-length packets and then routing the packets to the recipient. Packets may be sent over different paths and arrive out of order. At the receiving end, the packets are reordered. Routing is determined during transmission of the packet. Also known as a packet distribution network (PDN), public data network, X.25 network, or value-added network.

store-and-forward system When transmitting data between two nodes, the messages are logged at intermediate nodes, which then forward them to the next node.

messages. If the delivery time is not immediate, the system can process the message during a period of low activity. Suppose that a mail message is posted at 2:00 P.M. for delivery to a time zone that is 4 hr later, where it is 6:00 P.M. If the delivery time is set as 9:00 A.M. the next day, the message can be stored locally and sent at midnight, when both the sending and receiving systems are less busy. Time-staged delivery of large files can also allow their transmission to be paced over time, making the communication links more available for other transmissions.

Third, store-and-forward systems may be used if no path to the destination is available. If a link fails during the process of sending the message and the message cannot be delivered, the node at the point of failure can store the message. When the link is restored, the message is forwarded to the next node in the path. This practice relieves the message originator from the responsibility of saving the message until it reaches its destination.

Finally, store-and-forward techniques can be used in systems in which messages have different priorities. Low-priority messages may be stored for later delivery to give higher-priority messages better access to a link during periods of congestion.

Network Architecture and Topology

network topology A model for the way in which network nodes are connected. Network topologies include bus, ring, and star.

network architecture The way in which media, hardware, and software are integrated to form a network.

The physical layout of a network, which is the way that nodes are attached to the medium, is called the **network topology.** The **network architecture** is the way in which the media, hardware, and software are integrated to form the network.

SUMMARY

A LAN is a high-speed network serving a limited geographic area. Originally, LANs were used primarily for sharing hardware and software and high-speed data transfers. Recent reasons for using a LAN include the ability to use workgroup software or groupware, serving as a communication vehicle among workers, downsizing applications, and management control of computing resources.

One of the application architectures used in computing systems is the client/server (C/S) model. In C/S computing one process, the client, makes requests from another process, the server. This architecture lends itself well to networks in which the client may reside in one node, such as a desktop system, while the server resides in another node. C/S computing provides an environment for controlled, incremental growth, modular applications, and application portability.

LANs extend the capabilities of stand-alone computers. LANs also mean additional responsibilities. Stand-alone microcomputers are managed by those who use them. A LAN requires more centralized management and control. This is a part-time responsibility for small LANs but is a full-time responsibility for one or more employees for medium to large-scale LANs. Poor management can ruin the effectiveness of even the best configured LANs.

KEY TERMS

circuit
client/server computing
diskless workstation
document management system
electronic appointment calendar
electronic mail (e-mail)
electronic meeting system
file exchange utilities
group decision support system (GDSS)
groupware
link
metropolitan area network (MAN)
middleware
network
network architecture

network topology
node
packet distribution network (PDN)
packet switching
path
print server
project management system
public data network (PDN)
routing
server
store-and-forward system
value-added network (VAN)
virtual circuit
virus detection software
X.25 network

REVIEW QUESTIONS

1. What is the difference between a link and a path?

2. What is a store-and-forward system?

3. What were the motivating factors for the development of LANs?

4. What are the distinguishing features of a LAN? What are those of a WAN?

5. What is a computer virus?

6. Describe three LAN applications.

7. What is client/server computing? How does it differ from traditional application architectures?

8. What is middleware? What functions does it provide?

9. What are the advantages and disadvantages of client/server computing?

10. Explain the differences between managing a LAN and managing stand-alone computers.

PROBLEMS AND EXERCISES

1. Your company has decided to implement multimedia applications on a LAN with 100 users. The speed of the LAN is 10 Mbps and it is estimated that as many as 30 users will be using multimedia applications at the same time. Suggest a configuration that will support the additional load on the network.

2. Investigate the literature and describe the behavior of four different computer viruses.

3. Choose a specific LAN installation. Describe the hardware, software, and vendor details. Cover such items as maintenance policies, support fees, cost of adding a station, number of stations that can be supported by the system, system management procedures and costs, and the type of work accomplished by workstations.

CHAPTER 6

LAN Hardware

CHAPTER OBJECTIVES

After studying this chapter you should be able to

- Identify the major classes of LAN servers
- Compare file and database servers
- Identify the principal hardware components of a LAN
- Discuss LAN hardware needs
- Design the hardware components of a LAN for a specific application
- Recognize the tradeoffs made in designing LAN hardware

When selecting and installing a LAN you have several important decisions to make. You must choose the medium, media access control protocol, topology, hardware, and software. We discussed media in Chapters 2 and 3. Chapter 7 discusses the topology and media access control, and Chapter 8 covers LAN software. In this chapter we look at the principal hardware components of a LAN. A wide variety of components are available—servers, workstations, adapters, and so on—but the key to success is choosing components that can be integrated to form an effective system. In this chapter you will read about servers, backup devices, workstation hardware, LAN adapters, printers, and miscellaneous hardware devices.

SERVER PLATFORMS

To make an informed decision regarding server hardware, you must understand what the server does. Services provided by a server include disk, file, database, printer, terminal, modem, facsimile (fax), and remote access.

Disk servers allow a disk to be logically segmented into individual user disks; this older technology has been replaced by file servers that manage disk storage more efficiently. A terminal server allows terminals to be attached to a LAN; the terminal server provides the necessary computation capabilities. Modem and fax servers allow users to share modems and fax machines. A remote access server provides LAN services to users who access the LAN via telephone lines or mobile services. File, database, application, and printer servers are the most common server types and are the focus of this chapter. We begin by comparing file and database servers.

File Services

File services is one of the primary jobs of a server. The purpose of a file server is to provide users access to data, programs, and other files stored on the server's disk drives. It should be transparent to the user that the data or files he or she is using are located on the server's disk drives rather than on a local disk drive. Over time several technologies have been developed to provide file services. File and database servers are the most commonly used today.

File Servers   A file server allows users to share files. If several LAN users need access to an application such as word processing, only one copy of the application software resides on the file server. Individual users can share this application if the users' company has observed the product's license agreement. In this case, one copy of the program files can satisfy the needs of all application users. When a user enters a command to start an application, that application is downloaded into the user's workstation. Consider the disk space savings in a company having 100 users for a product that requires 50 MB of disk storage. Storage on a file server requires only 50 MB of disk space for all users. Storing the same application on 100 users' local disk drives requires 5000 MB of disk space. File server technology is illustrated in Figure 6–1.

When a user needs data from the file server, that data is transferred to the user's workstation. This is suitable for small files, but consider the impact of such technology when one is accessing a large database. If a user enters a request that requires looking at thousands of records, each record must be transferred over the LAN to the user's workstation.

Suppose you want to determine the average grade point average (GPA) for all students in your school and that there are 40,000 records in the student file. With file server technology the database application runs on your workstation; it is downloaded to your workstation when you start the application. When you make your request to find the average GPA, each student record is transferred over the network to your workstation, where the GPA data is extracted and computations are made. This is how the application would operate if the database were stored locally. Transferring all 40,000 database records over the network can place a heavy load on the medium and reduce its performance. In a case like this it is more efficient to have the server do the calculations and pass only the response over the network. A database server performs this function.

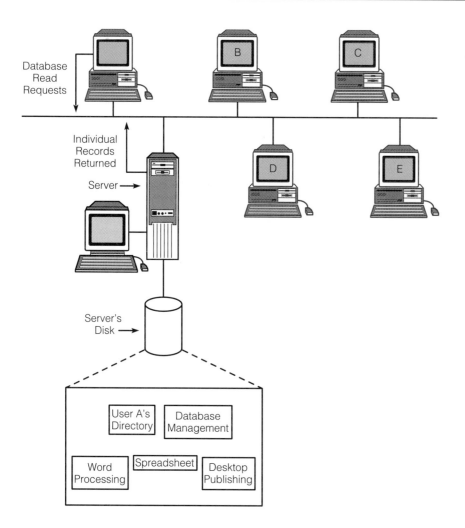

Figure 6–1
File Server Technology

Database Servers The database server was developed to solve the problem of passing an entire file, several files, or large portions thereof over the medium. The most common example of a database server is the SQL server. **Structured Query Language (SQL)** is a standard database definition, access, and update language for relational databases. An SQL server accepts a database request, accesses all necessary records locally, and then sends only the results back to the requester. In the GPA example, all 40,000 student records still must be read, but the computation is done by the SQL server. Only one record containing the average GPA is sent back over the network to the requester. This reduces the load on the network medium, but it does place an extra load on the server. The server must not only access the records, but also perform some database processing. This can affect other users who are also requesting SQL services. The SQL server must be powerful enough to provide services effectively for all users and avoid becoming a performance bottleneck.

An interface also must exist between the application software making the database request and the SQL server. The interface must be capable of

Structured Query Language (SQL) A relational database language developed by IBM and later standardized by ANSI.

Figure 6–2
SQL Server Technology

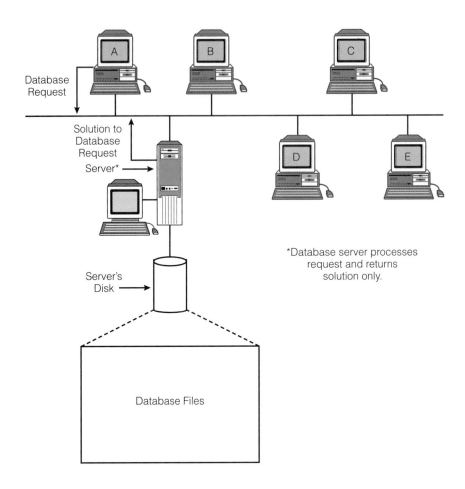

translating an application's data needs into an SQL statement. This means that an SQL server cannot work unless the application or an application interface exists that can generate the SQL syntax. SQL server technology is illustrated in Figure 6–2.

Application Servers

In Chapter 5 we presented the concept of client/server (C/S) computing. In this application architecture, processing may be accomplished on several network nodes. An **application server** is a node that provides application-oriented processing on the server side of C/S computing. Application servers should be able to run standard programs to allow distribution of an application over a network. A standard program is one that can be easily created with standard programming tools such as a C++ compiler, JAVA, and Visual Basic. Although this may sound simple, some network operating systems (the operating systems that control servers) are not well adapted to application services. For example, Novell's NetWare 3.x and 4.x network operating systems require that modules run on the server be network loadable modules (NLMs). NLMs must be written using NetWare application pro-

application server A node that provides application-oriented processing on the server side of C/S computing.

gram interfaces and it is more complicated for the typical programmer to create NLMs than standard executables. Programs that can run under the Windows or UNIX operating systems do not run under those versions of NetWare. Thus, NetWare 3.x and 4.x are not well suited to be application servers. In contrast, Microsoft's Windows NT Server can run standard Windows applications and is better suited to the role of application server.

Server Disk Drives

File and database servers share the need to access data efficiently. When choosing a file or database server, you should carefully select the server's disk subsystem, which consists of the disk drives and the disk controllers. Two factors are critical when choosing a disk drive: storage capacity and average access time.

Server disk drives are typically high-capacity units, which means that they have fast access times and can store large amounts of data. The capacity to store large amounts of data is important because the server must store many data and program files. A file server is essentially each user's hard disk. Individual data storage, together with the shared storage needed for application software, databases, several versions of operating system software, utility programs, print files, and electronic mail messages, can easily require several gigabytes. Some network operating systems require approximately 90 MB of disk storage. An SQL server holds database files as well as the SQL server software. Organizations adopting SQL server technology usually have large databases and require high-volume storage.

The need for large amounts of data storage might be satisfied by one high-capacity drive or several lower-capacity drives; both alternatives offer benefits. Having fewer disk drives provides a configuration that is easier to manage. Having several smaller-capacity drives is beneficial because several disks can be working simultaneously to satisfy user requests, and the impact of a disk failure can be lessened. Suppose you need 5 GB of storage. You could select one 6-GB drive or three 2-GB drives. With one drive it is simple to determine file allocation: All files are placed on that drive. With three drives your objective should be to spread the files over the three drives to provide equal access and to ensure equal activity.

If an application requires 45 disk accesses per second, a single fast disk drive may have difficulty keeping up with this load. With three drives and a good distribution of files, you would have only 15 requests per drive per second. This configuration may be more expensive but it provides better performance. Remember, for file or SQL server disk drives, you should select those with sufficient storage capacity and speed to meet your performance objectives. A powerful processor with a slow disk subsystem can cripple your network. This point cannot be emphasized enough.

A second factor to consider when choosing a disk drive is the **access time** of the disk itself. The three components of disk access are seek time, latency, and transfer time. The **seek time** is the time required to move the read/write heads to the proper cylinder. Once the heads are positioned, you must wait until the data revolves under the read/write heads; this is

access time The total time required in accessing a disk, including seek time, latency, and transfer time.

seek time In disk accessing, the time it takes to move the read/write heads to the proper cylinder.

latency On disk drives, the average time required for the data being read to revolve under the read/write heads.

transfer time In disk accessing, the amount of time required for the data to be moved from the disk to the processor's memory. In data communication, the amount of time required for a message to move from the sender to the receiver.

disk drive interface/controller Sets the standards for connecting the disk drive to the microprocessor and the software commands used to access the drive.

called **latency.** The average latency is one-half the time required for the disk to make a complete revolution. **Transfer time** is the time required to move the data from the disk to the computer's memory. Fast disks have average access times of approximately 10 ms. In contrast, many floppy disk drives have access times of approximately 200 ms. In general, your file server should have disks with fast average access times.

Finally, you also need to consider the **disk drive interface,** or the **controller.** The disk drive interface sets the standards for connecting the disk drive to the microprocessor and the software commands used to access the drive. There are a variety of disk drive interfaces. Some are well suited to server operations and some are too slow for most LANs. You must choose an interface supported by your LAN operating system. The two interfaces most commonly used for microcomputer-based servers are the small computer system interface (SCSI, pronounced "scuzzy") and the integrated drive electronics (IDE) or enhanced IDE (EIDE) interface. Both interfaces provide high-speed data transfers and large-capacity disk drives. SCSI generally is more efficient and is currently the interface of choice.

SCSI drives are generally preferred for LAN servers. The maximum capacity of SCSI drives has historically been greater than for EIDE drives. However, capacity is not the most critical factor. All SCSI interfaces allow eight devices to be attached, one of which is the host adapter. This allows seven devices such as disks, tapes, and optical drives to be attached to one interface. In contrast, only two drives can be attached to an EIDE interface. SCSI-3 supports up to 32 devices. With an EIDE interface, only one of the disk drives can be working. Thus, if two drive requests are pending, one for each drive, one request is held until the first is completed. In contrast, SCSI drives can be working simultaneously. This allows for parallelism in the input/output (I/O) process. To attain parallelism with EIDE drives, two controllers would be required, one for each drive. Finally, it is possible for one SCSI device to communicate directly with another device on the same SCSI interface. This feature could be used to back up data from a disk directly to a tape drive. Because servers often have multiple disk drives and the need to optimize I/O, SCSI interfaces are usually preferred.

Server Memory

A server is a combination of hardware and software. The software should be designed to take full advantage of the hardware, and in Chapter 7 you will learn techniques for ensuring this compatibility. Memory is often a good hardware investment because many software systems can take advantage of available memory to provide better performance. High-speed **cache memory** can significantly improve a computer's performance. Today, microcomputer memories operate at speeds of 60–70 ns. High-speed cache memory operates at speeds of approximately 15 ns, and is thus 4–5 times faster than RAM. Obviously, it is faster to fetch instructions from cache memory than from RAM. The processor first looks for the instruction in cache memory. If it is found in cache, the fetch is very efficient. If the instruction is not in cache, it and a block of the following instructions are transferred from lower-speed RAM into cache. This increases the chances that the next instruction will be found efficiently in cache

cache memory High-speed memory that improves a computer's performance.

memory. Another form of caching is called **disk caching.** Disk caching is similar in function to cache memory except that main memory serves as a high-speed buffer for slower disk drives. In both types of cache, memory is used as a buffer for lower-speed hardware.

When choosing a LAN operating system that provides disk caching, you need to configure the server with sufficient memory to make caching effective. The fundamental premise of disk caching is that a memory access is faster than a disk access (nanoseconds versus milliseconds). A disk cache therefore attempts to keep frequently accessed data in memory. Caching works as follows: If a user's request for data is received, cache memory is searched before the data is physically read from the disk. If the data is found in cache memory—a process known as a logical read—then the data is made available almost instantly. If the data is not found in cache memory, then it is read from the disk, which is called a physical access. As data is read from the disk, it is also placed into cache memory so that any subsequent read for that data might be a logical read.

Disk caching taken to the fullest extent results in all data residing in memory and all reads being logical reads. This is rarely the case. However, it should be clear that effective use of cache memory can improve performance. Because disk caching requires memory, sufficient memory must be available to provide a large percentage of cache hits, in which the data being read is found in cache memory. Consider the following example, which illustrates the effects of having too little memory.

Suppose that LAN data requests cycle through four records, A, B, C, and D, and that you have only enough cache memory for three records. When additional space is needed, the cache-management scheme typically replaces the record that has been dormant the longest with a new record. Records A, B, and C have been read in that order and are in cache memory, as illustrated in Figure 6–3(a). A request is issued for Record D, but it is not in cache memory, so a physical read is required. Record D is read and must be inserted into cache memory. Because Record A is the least recently used, Record D replaces Record A, as illustrated in Figure 6–3(b). Next, a request is received for Record A. Because it is not in cache memory, a physical read is issued and Record A replaces the least recently used record, Record B. Cache memory now looks like Figure 6–3(c). Next, a request is made for Record B, which is also not in cache memory, as illustrated in Figure 6–3(d). Record B is read and replaces Record C. Unfortunately, Record C is the next record to be read and again requires a physical read. It is read into cache memory, replacing Record D. Then the cycle repeats again. In this simple example, the cache is one record too small and is totally ineffective. In fact, it is counterproductive, as the processor must search cache memory for records that are not cache resident, incurring extra overhead.

The problem of insufficient cache memory can be corrected by expanding the cache memory. In the example, just one more record slot results in 100% cache hits after the four initial reads. Of course, this example is contrived, and 100% cache hit rates are rarely attainable. The example demonstrates that there is a critical threshold for cache memory. If the available memory is under this threshold, cache can be ineffective. When the available

disk caching Similar in function to cache memory except that main memory serves as a high-speed buffer for slower disk drives.

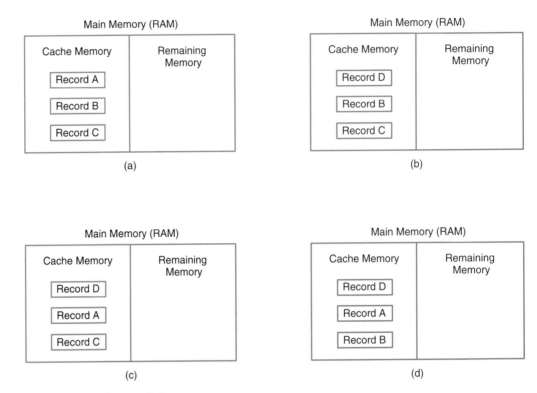

Figure 6–3
Example of Disk Cache Memory

cache memory is over this threshold, cache can be very effective. Some users have experienced cache hits as high as 80 to 90%. The hit rate depends on the access patterns, so this figure does not hold true for all systems.

An ample amount of memory is important for reasons other than disk caching. You also should have sufficient memory to avoid disk swapping. Most of today's memory management schemes are based on **virtual memory management,** which uses the disk as an extension of memory so each program has virtually all the memory it needs. Virtual memory management allows the real memory of a system to be less than the aggregate memory required by all the applications. To do this, application code and data are swapped back and forth between the disk and memory. The swap rate goes up if the available memory is too small. When the swap rate increases, the operating system is spending extra time managing memory and less time is available for doing application work. The amount of application work done per unit of time decreases as the swap rate increases. Today, server memories begin at 32 MB, with many servers configured at 64 MB or above.

Processors and Processor Speed

The processing power of the server is also a critical factor. It seldom makes sense to select a server that has fast disks and sufficient memory but a slow

virtual memory management A memory management scheme that uses the disk as an extension of memory so each program has virtually all the memory it needs.

CPU. In general, the server ought to be one of the fastest (if not the fastest) computers on the network. One exception to this generalization is a server providing small amounts of data to graphics workstations. Most graphics applications require high-speed processors to create and print graphic images. In these networks the workstation computing power may equal or exceed that of the server.

For additional processing power in one server, multiple-CPU systems are available. Multiple-CPU systems can be **symmetrical multiprocessing (SMP)** or asymmetrical multiprocessing systems. An SMP system has CPUs that are alike and that share memory, processing responsibility, and I/O paths. In asymmetrical systems the processors may be of different types and one processor may be dedicated to I/O operations while another is dedicated to application processing. SMP systems allow for load balancing, whereas asymmetric systems do not. Thus, in an asymmetrical multiprocessing system, one processor can be extremely busy while another has little to do. Most multiprocessor servers are SMP servers. SMP hardware must be supported by the network operating system to take advantage of the additional processors.

symmetrical multiprocessing (SMP) An SMP system has CPUs that are alike and that share memory, processing responsibility, and I/O paths.

Expansion and Power

A server should have sufficient expansion capability and the power to use the expansion slots effectively. Network server capacity can be expanded by adding hardware to the existing server or by adding servers. Expanding the capabilities of an existing server is less expensive than adding a new server, so the server you choose should support expansion. This allows you to add more memory, disks, printers, or other hardware devices that users can share, such as modems, fax machines, tape drives, and optical disk drives.

System Bus

A computer's bus provides the connection among system components such as the CPU, memory, and device controllers. The size, speed, and type of bus affect the computer's performance. The bus size determines how many data bits can be transferred among system components at one time. A server with a 16-bit bus takes twice as many transfers for 1000 bytes of data as a system with a 32-bit bus, and the operation takes approximately twice as long to perform; a 64-bit bus provides better performance than a 32-bit bus. The speed of the bus determines how fast data is transferred along the bus. A faster bus provides better performance than a slower one. The type of the bus refers to the interface standard the bus supports. Microcomputers use three main bus architectures: industry standard architecture (ISA), extended industry standard architecture (EISA), and peripheral component interconnect (PCI). The ISA bus is the one on which the original IBM PC was based, and is still widely used. The EISA bus is an improvement over the original ISA bus and is better suited for high-capacity servers. The PCI bus provides rapid data transfer rates and is usually configured with an ISA or EISA bus. PCI can provide 64-bit data paths and up to 264 million bytes per second transfer rates. Some systems have more than one bus, such as a separate bus for the monitor and for disk drives. Having two or more buses allows multiple data paths between devices and can further improve performance.

WORKSTATIONS

Some LANs are homogeneous, which means that all the workstations are of the same basic type, all are running the same level of the same operating system, and all use essentially the same applications. It is easier to configure this type of network than one that is heterogeneous, but homogeneous networks are less common. Often a network is assembled from workstations acquired over time. These workstations usually represent different levels of technology and perhaps use different versions of operating systems. Consider a network with the following workstations:

- IBM or compatible with an ISA bus
- IBM or compatible with an EISA bus
- IBM or compatible with an ISA and PCI bus
- Apple Macintosh or compatible
- Sun workstation

If you are selecting components for a heterogeneous network, your hardware and software options are more limited than for a homogeneous network. You may be limited in your choice of network operating systems (see Chapter 7) or LAN adapters. The limitations arise from the inability of some LAN software to support different workstations or from the limited availability of required hardware, such as a LAN adapter. You will find many options for a LAN with only IBM-compatible workstations and several for LANs with only Apple workstations, but some of these options do not support both types of microcomputers. Fortunately, interoperability of different hardware platforms on a single LAN is becoming more common.

Diskless Workstations

diskless workstation A workstation that has no local disk drives, reducing the ways in which a virus can be introduced.

When configuring your LAN, you may want to consider **diskless workstations.** As the name implies, a diskless workstation has no local disk drives. Instead, a diskless workstation has its boot logic in a read-only memory (ROM) chip. This chip contains the logic to connect to the network and download the operating system from the server. Thus, a diskless workstation cannot be used in a stand-alone mode; it is fully dependent on the server for all of its software, and it cannot function if the network or server is not operating. This is the disadvantage of a diskless system. Its advantages are cost, security, and control.

Because diskless workstations have no disk drives, they are less expensive than those with disks. Moreover, the maintenance costs for diskless systems are less than for systems with disk drives. Diskless systems provide extra security because users are unable to copy the organization's data onto local hard or floppy disk drives. This is important because an organization's primary security risk is its employees. Diskless systems also provide a greater measure of control because employees cannot introduce their own software into the system. This not only ensures that standard software and data are used but also reduces the chances of computer viruses being introduced into the network.

Workstation Memory and Speed

Like servers, workstation memory configurations are important. If you have stand-alone microcomputer systems, each with the minimum application memory configuration, you may need to add more memory to those systems to run the same applications on a network, because LAN software must also run in the workstations. Moreover, LAN software stays memory resident. Suppose you have an old microcomputer with 2 MB of memory and that this is just sufficient to load the operating system and your database management system. Placing that same microcomputer on a network requires that some of the memory be allocated to the LAN interface; thus, you may be unable to run your database management system because of insufficient memory. The solution is to expand the computer's memory. The amount of memory required for LAN software varies from one LAN to another. Some require less than 20 KB, and some require over 70 KB of resident memory.

The speed of the workstation's processor must be compatible with the type of work for which it is being used. If you use the workstation for word processing, a low-speed processor probably is satisfactory. However, a workstation used for graphics work requires a high-speed processor. Basically, it is the application, not the LAN, that determines the power of the workstations.

BACKUP DEVICES

No LAN is complete without a backup device. One of the LAN administrator's most important duties is to make periodic file backups. A **backup** is a copy of files made at a specific time; it is used to restore the system to a workable state following a system failure or an event that damages the data, or to restore data that is needed only on a periodic basis. For example, research data that is needed only once or twice a month and year-end payroll data that is needed temporarily to file workers' tax notices can be backed up and then replaced on disk on an as-needed basis.

The principal backup device is a magnetic tape drive, and a variety of these are available. Removable disk drives and optical disk drives are alternatives. The primary backup technologies are described below and listed in Table 6–1.

backup A copy of files made at a specific time, used to restore the system to a workable state following a system failure or an event that damages the data, or to restore data that is needed only on a periodic basis.

Floppy Diskette Drives

You can use floppy diskettes as the backup medium. The diskette drives may be server or workstation drives. The major disadvantage of this backup method is the low capacity and speed. Typical diskette capacities of IBM-compatible systems are 360 KB, 720 KB, 1.2 MB, 1.44 MB, and 2.88 MB.

Table 6–1   Primary Backup Technologies

Diskette backup	1.44 MB, 2.88 MB, 20 MB
Hard drive, fixed	Multiple capacities
Hard drive, removable cartridge	40 MB to over 1 GB
Tape backup, 4 mm or 1/4 in.	To 15 GB, 60 MB, 150 MB, 160 MB, 500 MB, 1.2 GB, 2.2 GB, 15 GB, 30 GB (compressed)
Tape backup, 8 mm or VCR	To 2.2 GB
Tape backup, 9-track	To 100 MB
Optical drives, WORM	To 4 GB
Optical drives, rewritable	To 4 GB
Digital Versatile Disks	10–14 GB

Diskettes with capacities of up to 20 MB are also available. Often the capacity of server drives is 1 GB or more. A large LAN may have tens of billions of bytes of disk storage. Backing up this amount of data to 1-MB (or even 20-MB) diskettes is cumbersome. The advantages of diskette backup are high availability on workstations and servers and low cost. Diskette backup for LANs with small disk requirements or for backing up a few small files can be practical, but for large-disk systems, the number of diskettes needed to store all the data is high. This process is slow and subject to errors, and requires handling many diskettes.

Hard Disk Drives

A hard disk drive on a server or a workstation may also be used for backup. The arguments for and against this alternative are much the same as those for diskettes. The major difference is that the capacity of hard disk drives is greater than that of diskettes. If the hard disk is not removable, it is difficult to keep multiple generations of backups, a procedure that is important for a comprehensive backup plan. For example, you should have at least three generations of backups, which means that if you make a backup weekly, three weeks' worth of backups are always available. Some hard drives have removable disk cartridges, which are an excellent backup alternative because they provide high capacity (1 GB or more per cartridge) and rapid access.

Optical Disk Drives

Optical disk drives are gaining popularity as backup devices. The reasons for this are their decreasing costs and large storage capacity, and the recently introduced ability to erase and write to optical disks. There are two classes of optical disk drives: WORM (write once, read many) and erasable drives. As the name implies, WORM technology allows you to write to the medium only once. You cannot erase a WORM disk. This can make the cost of backups expensive because the cost of cartridges for many such drives on microcomputers is over $100. An advantage of WORM technology is that the data cannot be changed, so the backup cannot be destroyed accidentally. Erasable optical drives have generally replaced WORM drives as the preferred optical technology. The costs of erasable drives and CD media now start at under $1000 and $10 respectively, with 650 MB of storage per CD. Emerging CD standards promise to provide several gigabytes of storage per CD. The **digital versatile disk (DVD)** format provides double-side/double-density recording and holds approximately 14 GB per diskette.

digital versatile disk (DVD) An optical format that provides double-side/double-density recording and holds approximately 14 GB per diskette.

Magnetic Tape Drives

As mentioned earlier, a magnetic tape drive is the usual choice for a backup device. Magnetic tapes are less expensive than the other options. They hold large volumes of data, are easy to use and store, and generally provide good performance. A variety of tape backup devices are available. The drives themselves are less expensive than disk or optical drives with comparable storage characteristics, and you can choose from a wide range of data capacities. Tape drives vary in the size of the tape and recording method. If more than one tape drive is to be used in one organization, it is best to establish a standard tape configuration so the tapes can be exchanged among the different drives. The main magnetic tape options are summarized in Table 6–2.

Like other hardware discussed in this chapter, the tape drive must be compatible with the server or workstation on which it is installed. A drive usually has a controller that must be installed in the computer, so you must select a drive that has a controller compatible with your equipment. Also, you need backup software and procedures to make backups. The most common server tape drive controller interface is SCSI.

Table 6–2　Magnetic Tape Backup Functions

Back up all files
Back up all files modified since a particular date
Back up by directory
Back up by list of files
Back up all but a list of files to be excluded
Back up by index
Back up by interface to a database
Back up using wildcard characters in file names
Create new index on tape and disk
Maintain cross-reference of tape serial numbers and backup
Back up manually
Back up automatically by time or calendar
Start backup from workstation or server
Compress data
Back up many volumes
Generate reports

LAN ADAPTERS

LAN adapters provide the connection between the medium and the bus of the workstation or server. LAN adapters are designed to support a specific protocol using a specific medium, although a few can support two different medium types. One type of Ethernet card supports twisted-pair wires and another type supports coaxial cable. After you match medium and protocol, there are additional choices to make regarding vendor and architecture. We discuss protocols in Chapter 7.

The choice of a LAN adapter vendor determines the support, quality, and price of the LAN adapter. Just as you should be careful when selecting a LAN vendor, you should also be careful in choosing the vendor of individual components such as a LAN adapter. The LAN adapter that is initially the least expensive may prove to be more costly in the long run if it is of inferior quality, if it does not have a good vendor support policy, or if the vendor goes out of business, making replacement LAN adapters difficult to obtain.

LAN adapters are installed in each workstation and server. Naturally, the LAN adapter must be compatible with the hardware architecture of each computer into which it is installed. You also need to ensure that a LAN adapter is available for each type of network node you anticipate having. Certain combinations of equipment may not be supported. You may have difficulty finding ARCnet cards for each node in a network consisting of a Digital Equipment Corporation VAX server and Apple Macintosh, Sun, and IBM workstations. LAN adapters also must be compatible with the bus of the host computer. For IBM and Apple microcomputer-based LANs, you may need cards compatible with ISA, EISA, PCI, Personal Computer Memory Card International Association (PCMCIA), and NuBus components.

LAN adapters also have their own architecture. LAN adapters for IBM or compatible systems often come in 8-bit, 16-bit, and 32-bit architectures. The 32-bit adapters are almost always more expensive and faster than the corresponding 16-bit and 8-bit adapters. By faster we mean that a 32-bit adapter can transfer data between the computer and the medium faster than a 16-bit adapter, which is faster than an 8-bit adapter; the architecture does not affect the speed at which data is transferred over the network medium. A 32-bit adapter is faster than a 16-bit adapter because it transfers data between the adapter and memory 32 bits at a time, whereas the 16-bit adapter transfers data in 16-bit groups.

PRINTERS

One major factor that affects the success of a LAN is printer support. Although a printer is technically not LAN hardware, printers are an integral part of a LAN. Some LANs have restrictions regarding the distribution of printers and the number of printers that can be supported by one server. Suppose that network printers must be attached to a server and that each server can support a maximum of 5 printers. An organization that needs 20 printers therefore must have at least four servers.

You must be concerned not only with the number of printers but also with the type of printers supported and the way in which they are supported. A **printer driver** is a software module that determines how to format data for proper printing on a specific type of printer. The printers you intend to use must be supported by the software drivers provided by the vendor. You may find that a laser printer you attach to the LAN can operate in text mode but is restricted in its graphic mode operation or in its ability to download fonts. Be sure to consider interoperability of hardware and software components to ensure that they meet your needs. Some LAN systems provide a utility program that allows you to tailor a generic printer driver to work with a specific printer you want to use. This utility allows you to define printer functions and the command sequences essential to invoking those functions. Because new printer technologies are constantly appearing, this utility is quite useful.

printer driver A software module that determines how to format data for proper printing on a specific type of printer.

HUBS AND SWITCHES

Some LAN architectures use **wiring hubs** to provide device interconnection. A wiring hub is a concentrator that connects workstations on some LANs. Specifically, it is used to connect nodes in an Ethernet LAN using twisted-pair wires and in token-ring LANs. A token-ring LAN may use a MAU to provide the connection between a node and the ring. Ethernet LANs using twisted-pair wires use wiring hubs for the same purpose. ARCnet LANs use both active and passive hubs for connectivity. Naturally, hubs designed for one architecture, such as Ethernet, will not work in another architecture, so it is essential to choose a wiring hub of the proper architecture. Beyond that, you have a variety of options.

wiring hubs Devices used by some LAN implementations to provide node-to-node connection.

Hubs vary in the number of ports available. A very common configuration is 8 ports, but 12- and 16-port hubs are common alternatives. Hubs may be stand-alone or stackable. A stand-alone hub is usually enclosed in a chassis and has two or more ports that allow wire-based connections to other hubs. Stackable hubs are modular hubs that can be stacked on top of each other or mounted in a wiring rack. Stackable hubs share a backplane, so multiple hubs can be treated as a single hub. (A backplane is a board that holds the bus interface in modular devices, allowing new modules to be added easily when needed. The modules plug into the backplane, which contains a bus over which signals are transmitted. A backplane is similar to the buses found in a computer.) The common backplane provides a high-speed interconnection between the hubs. By concentrating the hub connections into a stackable unit, the network administrator creates one central location for resolving wiring problems.

Some hubs have reliability and maintenance features that help minimize the possibility of failure and streamline the repair process. Dual power supplies with shared power enhance reliability. During normal operation the hub draws power from both power supplies; if one power supply fails, the remaining one can provide power for the entire hub. Hot-swappable components simplify maintenance; *hot-swappable* means that the hub can be repaired while it is functioning, which minimizes or eliminates downtime. For example, a failed power supply can be replaced while the hub is operating, without interrupting network operations.

It is important to have the ability to manage wiring hubs. Some hubs collect data about network traffic and make this data available through one of several available network management standards. The principal network management standards are the Simple Network Management Protocol (SNMP) and the Common Management Information Protocol (CMIP). SNMP is part of the Transmission Control Protocol/Internet Protocol (TCP/IP) protocol suite and CMIP is an ISO OSI standard. More information on these two network management protocols is provided in Chapter 18.

switches A LAN device that examines a transmitted packet and finds the address of the recipient.

LAN **switches** physically resemble wiring hubs but their function is quite different. For example, consider an Ethernet hub like the 8-port hub shown in Figure 6–4. When a node transmits a packet, the hub sends the packet out on all other ports so each node receives the packet. In contrast, a switch examines the packet and finds the address of the recipient. A connection between the sender and recipient is established and the packet is sent directly to the recipient. While that connection is being used, two other nodes can also be communicating over a different connection. Switches therefore increase the aggregated data rate on the network. Switches also have additional capabilities in LAN interconnections, and we will look at those capabilities and specific types of switches in Chapter 16.

Some switches provide LAN administrators an additional configuration alternative: that of creating virtual LANs. In a nonvirtual LAN, all nodes connected together via hubs or a common medium are on the same physical

Figure 6–4
Ethernet Hub

LAN. Switches allow the network administrator to group a set of workstations connected to a switch into one virtual LAN and another group of workstations into a different virtual LAN. The virtual LANs thus created function as though they were separate physical LANs. The switch provides the ability to provide these logical groupings. The advantages of virtual LANs are as follows:

- A user on a virtual LAN can move physically to a different switch connection or node and still be included on the same virtual LAN.
- The administrator can easily change a user from one workgroup to another by assigning the user's workstation to a different virtual LAN.
- Virtual LANs reduce the costs associated with physically adding, moving, and changing a node from one physical LAN to another.

The disadvantage of virtual LANs is that currently there are no standards defining how nodes on a virtual LAN are identified. Thus, one vendor may allow the administrator to group nodes by their network addresses whereas another may allow grouping by an identifier such as a node name. Because of these differences, one vendor's switch may not interoperate with another vendor's switch in setting up virtual LANs.

Switches also perform additional functions in LAN interconnections; we will look at those functions and specific types of switches in Chapter 16.

UNINTERRUPTIBLE POWER SUPPLY

As mentioned earlier, dual power supplies and hot-swappable components improve reliability, but this works only if power is available. There are many ways to improve the reliability of network components, particularly network servers. However, if there is a power outage, those reliability capabilities may not work. Fortunately, there is a reliability option that covers this problem. An **uninterruptible power supply (UPS)** is a hardware device that provides power to devices in the event of a power outage. Every server and related components should be protected by a UPS because the cost of a UPS is small relative to the cost of servers crashing because of power loss. An unexpected server crash can result in a time-consuming recovery. Recall the discussion of disk cache. A server keeps a considerable amount of data memory resident, such as end-of-file locations for open files, changes to user accounts, and the last updates to files. A server crash can cause this data to be lost. Furthermore, the crash may occur in the midst of a related set of file operations and result in inconsistent file data. For example, a related set of updates for index tables for a database access method may be in progress at the time of failure. If an entry is made in one index table and the corresponding update in another index is nullified by a server failure, data pointed out by the index tables may be unable to be located.

A UPS uses batteries as a source of power when a power outage occurs. During normal operation, power is available from the main power supply. This power is passed through the UPS and maintains the charge on the batteries. If the main power source fails, the UPS battery takes

uninterruptible power supply (UPS) A backup power unit that continues to provide power to a computer system during the failure of the normal power supply. A UPS is often used to protect LAN servers from power failures.

over and continues to supply power to the connected devices. The duration of UPS power varies depending on the power load drawn from the equipment and the capacity of the UPS itself. The power load drawn relies on the total ratings of the equipment being sustained by the UPS, so different configurations consume different amounts of power. UPSs come in different sizes, and the size is usually measured in volt-amps (VA), but wattage is another measure sometimes used to describe the power rating. The higher the VA rating is, the more power available. Generally, LAN administrators configure the power of the UPS to sustain the equipment it powers for approximately 1 hour. UPS sizes run the gamut from the ability to provide power for a small microcomputer for a few minutes to supplying power for large mainframe systems for several hours. Other capabilities of a UPS include

- surge protection
- power smoothing
- battery level indicators
- brown-out protection

Some UPS systems are combined with software to provide management capabilities. The UPS typically communicates with the computer via a serial connection. Software in the computer can interrogate statistics maintained by the UPS and report on those statistics. Information that might be reported includes high and low power levels supplied by the main power source, battery condition, power consumption over time, and temperature. Software features also include some management capabilities such as automatically shutting the system down and starting the system at certain times and initiating alarms for out-of-tolerance situations such as low battery or overload situations.

ADDITIONAL LAN HARDWARE

Other hardware components you may find in a LAN are

- Terminal servers, which allow terminals to access the network. However, a terminal attached to a LAN does not have the same functionality as a microcomputer attached to a LAN.
- Modem servers, which allow users to share one or more modems.
- Fax machines, which may be attached to a server and shared by network users, or fax servers, which include the fax mechanisms within the server itself.
- Remote access servers, which allow remote users dial-in access to the network.

These services are important but are less common than file, database, or printer services, so we do not devote more coverage to them.

MAKING CONNECTIONS

Thus far we have discussed the medium, the network nodes, and the LAN adapter. All that remains is to connect the nodes to the medium. Connections can be made in a variety of ways. You have already learned that you must pick a LAN adapter that is compatible with the medium you choose. Therefore, it is the medium that primarily influences the way in which physical connections are made. Let us look at the problem from a generic perspective.

The objective of network connection—connecting a computer to the LAN medium—is to provide a data path between the medium and the computer's memory. To accomplish this there must be a connection to the medium and a connection to the computer's bus or channel. The interface or connection to the medium is called the **communication interface unit (CIU)** and the interface or connection to the computer's bus is called the **bus interface unit (BIU).** These functions, illustrated in Figure 6–5, are provided by the LAN adapter.

A key component of the network connection is a **transceiver,** which establishes the connection to the medium and implements the transmit and receive portion of the protocol. In a few Ethernet LANs, the transceiver is connected directly to the medium. Most of today's Ethernet implementations have a transceiver that is located on the LAN adapter, as illustrated in Figure 6–6.

The physical connection between the computer and the medium is established through **connectors.** Many different types of connectors are used, but the principal ones are

- BNC-, TNC-, or N-type connectors for coaxial cable
- RJ-11, RJ-45, or DB-n (DB-25 or DB-15) connectors for wires
- SMA, ST, SC, and FSD connectors for fiber optic cable
- DIN connectors

The type of connector you need is determined by your LAN adapter. A wide variety of connector adapters allow you to change connector types.

communication interface unit (CIU) In a LAN, the communication interface unit provides the physical connection to the transmission medium.

bus interface unit (BIU) In a LAN, the bus interface unit provides the physical connection to the computer's I/O bus.

transceiver A device that receives and sends signals. A transceiver helps form the interface between a network node and the medium.

connector Establishes the physical connection between the computer and the medium.

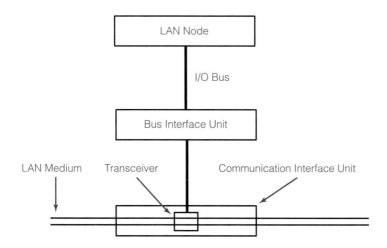

Figure 6–5
Bus/Communication Interface Units and Transceiver

Figure 6–6

Transceiver on a LAN Adapter

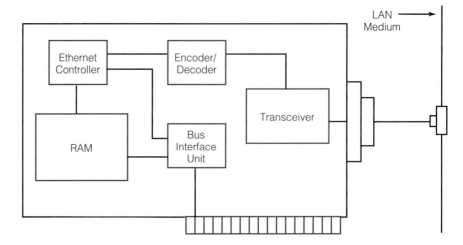

baluns Adapters that change coaxial cable connectors into twisted-pair wire connectors, allowing transfer from one medium to another or from a connector for one medium to a different medium.

multistation access unit (MAU) In an IBM token-ring LAN, a MAU is used to interconnect workstations.

active hub A node connection hub used in an ARCnet LAN that provides signal regeneration and allows nodes to be located up to 2000 feet from the hub.

One adapter can change a bayonet nut connector (BNC) to a TNC-type connector. **Baluns** are adapters that change coaxial cable connectors to twisted-pair wire connectors. These adapters allow you to transfer from one medium to another or from a connector for one medium to a different medium. Several connectors are illustrated in Figure 6–7.

In some networks, connecting a computer to the medium is sufficient for making that computer active on the network. Some LAN implementations use wiring hubs to provide node-to-node connection. Several kinds of connection hubs are commonly used. In an IBM token-ring LAN, individual stations are connected to a wiring hub called a **multistation access unit (MAU).** The ring is established via internal connections within the MAU, as illustrated in Figure 6–8. An ARCnet LAN may use active and passive hubs for node connections, as illustrated in Figure 6–9. An **active hub** provides signal regeneration and allows nodes to be located at distances up to 2000 ft

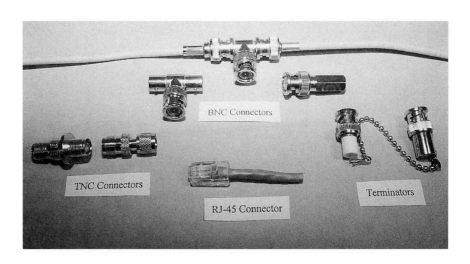

Figure 6–7

Use of Connectors and Terminators

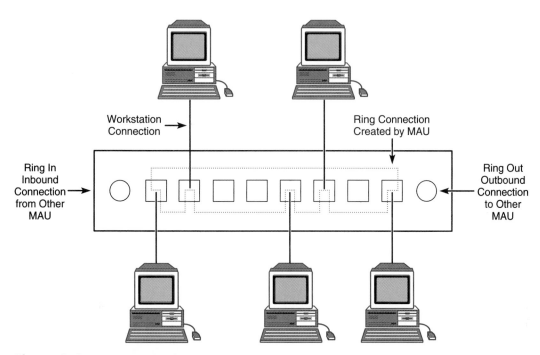

Figure 6–8
Multistation Access Unit

from the hub. A **passive hub** does not provide signal regeneration, so nodes can be located no more than 100 ft from the hub.

A variety of other hardware components are sometimes needed to make the network function. On bus networks or networks using wiring hubs, **terminators** are often needed to prevent signal loss. Terminators are used at the ends of a bus to prevent echo and are required on unused passive hub ports in an ARCnet network for the same reason. The location of terminators in a LAN configuration is shown in Figure 6–7.

Sometimes LAN connections go further than simply connecting a node to the medium. You may also need to connect one LAN to another or connect a LAN to a WAN. We discuss this subject in detail in Chapter 16.

passive hub A node connection hub used in an ARCnet LAN that does not provide signal regeneration, so nodes can be located no farther than 100 feet from the hub.

terminator A resistor at a cable end that absorbs the signal and prevents echo or other signal noise.

SUMMARY

LAN hardware consists mainly of server platforms, workstations, LAN adapters, printers, a medium, and connectors. The hardware combines with software to provide the LAN services. LAN adapters are protocol and medium oriented. Servers must be properly configured to provide the performance and backup services required by an efficient LAN. The keys to meeting this requirement are sufficient memory, a powerful processor,

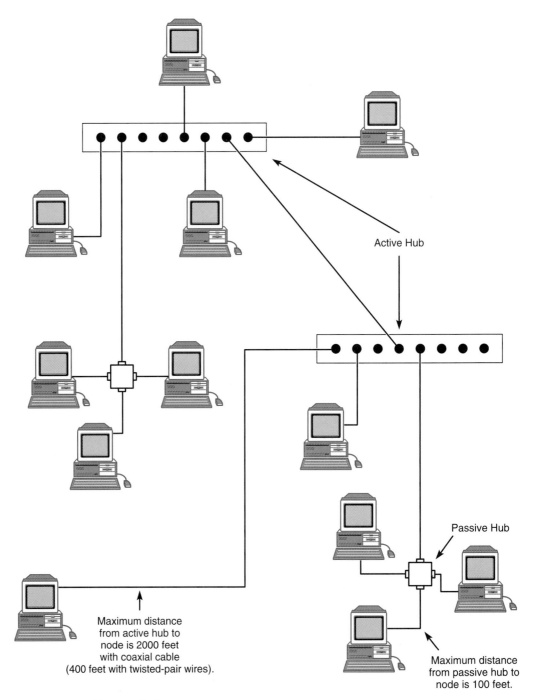

Active Hub

Passive Hub

Maximum distance
from active hub to
node is 2000 feet
with coaxial cable
(400 feet with twisted-pair wires).

Maximum distance
from passive hub to
node is 100 feet.

Figure 6–9
ARCnet LAN with Active and Passive Hubs

high-performance disk drives, and a file backup unit. Naturally, the software also must be available to exploit the hardware configuration.

You can choose from many combinations of hardware and software when building a LAN. The key to success is combining the alternatives so that the hardware and the software form an effective team.

KEY TERMS

access time	latency
active hub	multistation access unit (MAU)
application server	passive hub
backup	printer driver
baluns	seek time
bus interface unit (BIU)	Structured Query Language (SQL)
cache memory	switches
communication interface unit (CIU)	symmetrical multiprocessing (SMP)
connectors	terminator
controller	transceiver
digital versatile disk (DVD)	transfer time
disk caching	uninterruptible power supply (UPS)
disk drive interface	virtual memory management
diskless workstations	wiring hubs

REVIEW QUESTIONS

1. What are the generic functions of a server?

2. Distinguish between file and SQL server technology.

3. What must you take into consideration when you select a server disk drive?

4. How do servers use memory to improve performance?

5. Explain how disk caching works. What is its benefit?

6. Why should servers have high processor speeds?

7. How do diskless systems work? What advantages do they have over disk systems? What are the disadvantages of a diskless system?

8. What is data backup? What devices are used to effect backup?

9. Why are floppy disks usually ineffective as a backup device?

10. What options must be considered in selecting a LAN adapter?

11. What are wiring hubs, baluns, and terminators? What function does each perform?

12. What does a switching hub do? What is the advantage of a switching hub over a standard hub?

13. What does a UPS do?

PROBLEMS AND EXERCISES

1. Suppose you need to establish a small network with 1 server and 15 workstations. Describe a hardware configuration for the server and the workstations. Make all workstation configurations the same. Consult one or more recent

magazines to help you determine the hardware costs for your LAN. Include the server, workstations, LAN adapters, a backup tape device, three laser printers, and three ink jet printers in your cost estimates. Configure the server with at least 10 GB of disk storage, 64 MB of memory, and a UPS.

2. You have a file server with 600 MB of data. If you use 1.4-MB disks to back up this data, how many disks are necessary? Your backup utility provides a data compression ratio of 1.8:1 for your files, which means that on average, 1.8 bytes can be compressed into 1 byte. Using this compression ratio, how many disks are required? List the advantages and cost of a more suitable backup medium.

3. Examine current literature and give an example of how each of the following is used:
   a. a terminal server
   b. a modem server
   c. a fax server
   d. a UPS

4. A company has an IBM-compatible microcomputer with an 80486/66 processor, 8 MB of memory, and a 300-MB disk drive. The company wants to know whether this computer will work as a file server for a 25-node network. The primary applications are word processing, spreadsheets, and desktop publishing. Will it work? Justify your response.

5. Assuming that you decided that the microcomputer in Problem 4 could handle the job if it were upgraded, what upgrades would you recommend?

CHAPTER 7

LAN Topologies and Media Access Control

CHAPTER OBJECTIVES

After studying this chapter you should be able to

- Describe several important LAN standards
- Identify the three major LAN topologies
- Compare the three major LAN topologies
- Describe the LAN media access control protocols
- Recognize the advantages and disadvantages of each media access control protocol
- Discuss the ways in which topologies and media access control protocols are combined
- Compare the major LAN architectures

When you build a LAN, you will probably investigate the capabilities provided by a variety of vendors. You will discover several ways in which to build a LAN, and you also might hear conflicting statements about the merits of each. In this chapter you will learn about the network layouts that vendors most commonly propose. You will also read about LAN topologies, media access control protocols, common ways in which topologies and media access control protocols are combined, and the strengths and weaknesses of several LAN configurations. The LAN components covered in this chapter exist at the OSI physical and data link layers.

THE LAN SYSTEM

If you evaluate vendor proposals during a LAN selection process, you may first read statements intended to give you a general idea of the type of solution proposed. Here are some examples:

> "We are happy to propose a Novell IEEE 802.3 network for your consideration."
>
> "We believe a Banyan Vines token-ring network will best suit your purposes."
>
> "Our solution uses Microsoft's Windows NT software and Ethernet."

media access control (MAC) protocol A sublayer of the OSI reference model's data link layer. The MAC protocol defines station access to the media and data transmission. Common MAC protocols are carrier sense with multiple access and collision detection (CSMA/CD) and token passing.

network topology A model for the way in which network nodes are connected.

These statements encapsulate three major LAN components: the LAN software, the topology, and the **media access control (MAC) protocol.** A **network topology** is the model used to lay out the LAN medium and connect computers to the medium. A MAC protocol operates at the OSI data link layer and describes the way in which a network node gains access to the medium and transmits data. The combination of these three components is what we call the LAN architecture and provides much of the uniqueness of a LAN. In general, you will be considering three basic topologies—ring, bus, and star—and two basic MAC protocols—contention and token passing. The major distinctions between one token ring, contention bus, or token bus and another are in the network operating system, the hardware, and the medium. A number of vendors, such as Apple, Artisoft, Banyan, IBM, Microsoft, and Novell, provide networking software.

When you are selecting a LAN, one idea is paramount: You are selecting a system. The system has many components, and the overall success of the LAN is how well these components can be integrated to form a system. Interoperability is the key, not the efficiency of a single component. For example, you must be able to attach workstations to the LAN and support each workstation's operating systems. The LAN might have IBM or IBM-compatible workstations together with Apple Macintosh or compatible systems, all with a variety of operating systems and printers. In this case the system you choose must support all of these components; some networks cannot do this.

LAN TOPOLOGIES AND STANDARDS

What do we mean when we talk about a LAN topology? First, the term *topology* derives from a mathematics field that deals with points and surfaces in space—that is, with the layout of objects in space. Thus, LAN topology is the physical layout of the network. Another way you can look at a topology is as a model for the way in which you configure the medium and attach the nodes to that medium. In general, LAN topologies correspond to the OSI physical layer described in Chapter 1.

LANs have three basic topologies: bus, ring, and star. Each configuration is illustrated in Figure 7–1. Let's take a closer look at each topology.

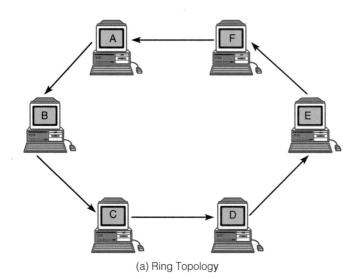

(a) Ring Topology

Figure 7–1
Basic LAN Topologies

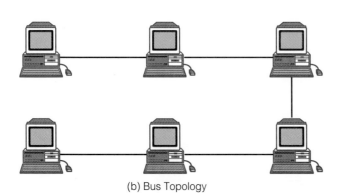

(b) Bus Topology

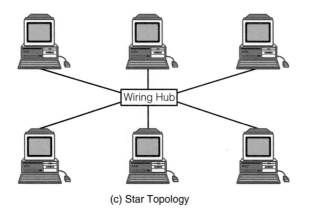

(c) Star Topology

bus topology A communication medium for transmitting data or power. A LAN topology.

Ethernet A LAN implementation using the CSMA/CD protocol on a bus. The IEEE 802.3 standard is based on Ethernet. One of the popular LAN implementations.

Institute of Electrical and Electronics Engineers (IEEE) A professional society that establishes and publishes documents and standards for data communication. IEEE has established several standards for LANs, including the IEEE 802.3 and IEEE 802.5 standards for LAN technology.

Bus Topology

In a **bus topology,** illustrated in Figure 7–1(b), the medium consists of a single wire or cable to which nodes are attached. The ends of the bus are not connected. Instead, they are terminated by a hardware device called a terminator, as discussed in Chapter 6. A variation of a bus topology has spurs to the primary bus formed by interconnected minibuses (see Figure 7–2). This variation of the bus topology is quite common.

As with ring topologies, several standards describe a bus implementation. The most common of these is an implementation originally known as **Ethernet.** Ethernet LAN specifications were originally proposed by Xerox Corporation in 1972. Soon thereafter Xerox was joined in establishing the Ethernet standard by Digital Equipment Corporation (DEC) and Intel Corporation. The **Institute of Electrical and Electronics Engineers (IEEE)** 802 Committee then developed the **IEEE 802.3 standard,** which encompasses most of the premises of the original Ethernet specification. Thus, the IEEE 802.3 standard is sometimes called an Ethernet implementation. The **IEEE 802.4 standard** also proposes a bus technology. The primary difference between the two is the MAC protocol. The IEEE 802.3 standard specifies a contention protocol, and the 802.4 standard uses a token-passing protocol. Again, these protocols are covered later in this chapter.

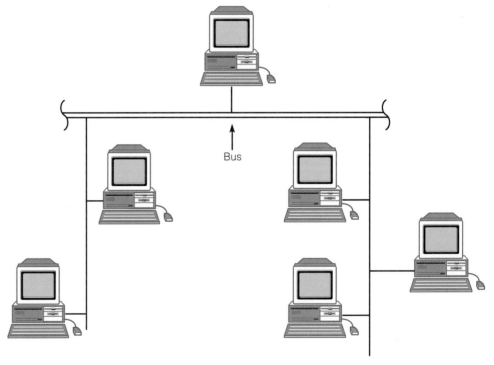

Figure 7–2
Bus Topology with Spurs

The common speeds of bus LANs are 1, 2.5, 5, 10, 100, and 1000 Mbps. Versions of the IEEE 802.3 and 802.4 standards specify each of these speeds. Currently, 100-Mbps LANs are in fairly common use and 1-Gbps LANs began emerging in 1997. IEEE 802.3 and 802.4 media are either twisted-pair wires or coaxial cables. Very-high-speed bus architectures use twisted-pair wires, coaxial cables, or fiber optic cables as media. Fiber optic cables are also used for 802.3 LANs. Ethernet technology has also been implemented using microwave radio as the medium.

IEEE 802.3 standard A standard that covers a variety of CSMA/CD architectures that are generally based on Ethernet.

IEEE 802.4 standard A subcommittee that sets standards for token bus networks.

Ring Topology

In a **ring topology** the medium forms a closed loop, and all stations are connected to the loop or ring. We first look at the basics of a ring and then at some specifics of two implementations.

On a ring, data is transmitted from node to node in one direction. Thus if node A in Figure 7–3 wants to send a message to node F, the message is sent from A to B, from B to C, from C to D, and so on, until it reaches node F. Usually node F then sends an acknowledgment that the message was successfully received back to node A, the originator of the message. The acknowledgment is sent from node F to G, and then from G to A, completing one journey around the loop.

Nodes attached to the ring may be active or inactive. An **active node** is capable of sending or receiving network messages. An **inactive node** is incapable of sending or receiving network messages; for example, an inactive node may be powered down. Naturally, nodes may go from inactive to active and from active to inactive. For example, when a worker leaves at night,

ring topology A network configuration commonly used to implement LANs. The medium forms a loop to which workstations are attached. Data is transmitted from one station to the next around the ring. Generally the access protocol is token passing.

active node A node capable of sending or receiving network messages.

inactive node A node that may be powered down and is incapable of sending or receiving messages.

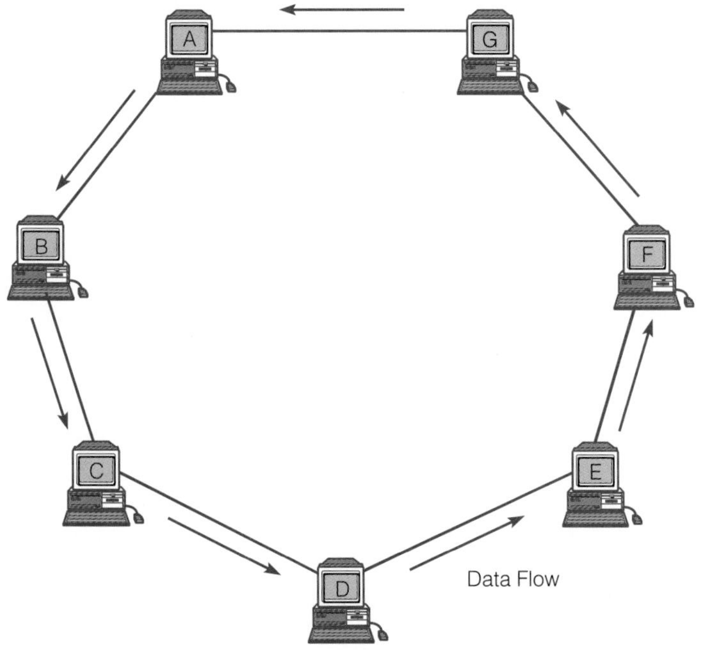

Data Flow

Figure 7–3
Token-Passing Ring Configuration

she might turn her workstation off, placing the workstation in an inactive state. In the morning she powers up her system and brings it into the active state. A failed or inactive network node must not cause the network to fail; an overview of how such a network failure can be prevented is included later in this chapter.

The most commonly used microcomputer ring network is a token-passing ring. IBM's LAN approach has been widely adopted and conforms to the **IEEE 802.5 standard,** so we describe it here. Realize, however, that we are discussing only the topology and MAC protocol. The token-passing ring we are describing can be implemented using a variety of different network operating systems, including Novell NetWare, Banyan Vines, and Microsoft Windows NT Server.

As pointed out in Chapter 6 (Figure 6–7), in IBM's token-passing ring network, stations (nodes) are connected to a multistation access unit (MAU). You can see that this configuration looks somewhat like the star configuration of Figure 7–1(c): The MAU forms the ring internally. Figure 7–4 shows the connection of two MAUs. IBM token-passing ring speeds are 4, 16, and 100 Mbps using twisted-pair wires or fiber optic cable as the medium.

Another network that uses a ring topology is a high-speed MAN, which is designed to cover a wider geographical area than a typical LAN. The **American National Standards Institute (ANSI)** standard for this type of network is called the **fiber distributed data interface (FDDI)** standard and is discussed later.

Star Topology

Figure 7–5 shows a **star topology,** which for LANs consists of interconnected wiring hubs or a wiring closet to which all other nodes are directly connected. This type of topology is common in microcomputer LAN networks. Common star-wired LAN architectures are ARCnet and Ethernet using twisted-pair wires.

ARCnet technology was developed in the 1970s by Datapoint Corporation to form networks of their minicomputers. The technology was well developed when microcomputer LANs were evolving, and the technology was readily adopted. Because it has been so widely used, ARCnet has become a de facto microcomputer LAN standard. An ARCnet configuration, illustrated in Figure 7–6, is a token-passing bus but does not conform to the IEEE 802.4 standard. As discussed in Chapter 6, ARCnet uses both active and passive hubs to connect network nodes. ARCnet speeds are 2.5 Mbps and 20 Mbps, and both speeds can be used in the same network. ARCnet media are usually either twisted-pair wires or coaxial cables. Fiber optic cables are also used for ARCnet LANs, primarily in higher-speed implementations. ARCnet was a common LAN implementation during the early days of microcomputer LANs because it provided proven technology at a low price. Few new LANs are being implemented using this architecture, so we will not discuss it further.

An Ethernet **star-wired LAN** configuration is similar to the basic star topology (Figure 7–1(c)) in that each workstation is connected to a wiring

---

IEEE 802.5 standard A subcommittee that sets standards for token-ring networks.

American National Standards Institute (ANSI) A U.S. standard-making agency.

fiber distributed data interface (FDDI) An ANSI LAN standard for fiber optic LANs spanning a distance of approximately 200 km and providing speeds of 100 Mbps.

star topology A network topology using a central system to which all other nodes are connected. All data are transmitted to or through the central system.

ARCnet LAN implementation based on Datapoint's attached resource computer network.

star-wired LAN A variation of star topology in which a wiring hub is used to form the connection between network nodes.

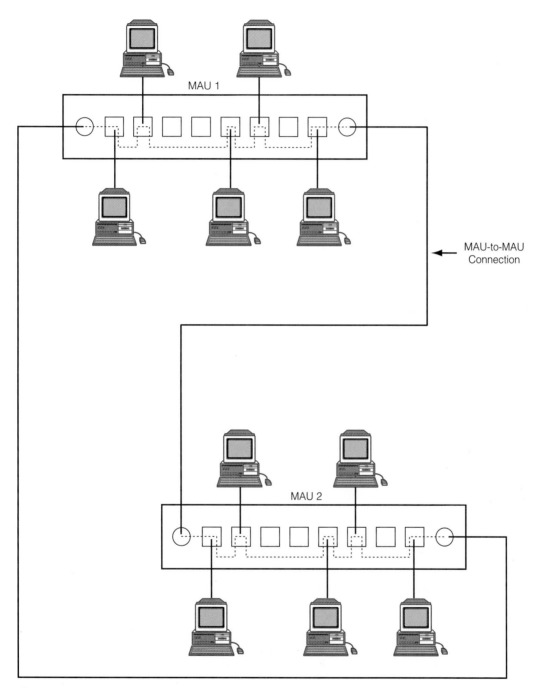

Figure 7–4
MAU-to-MAU Connection

Figure 7–5
Star Topology

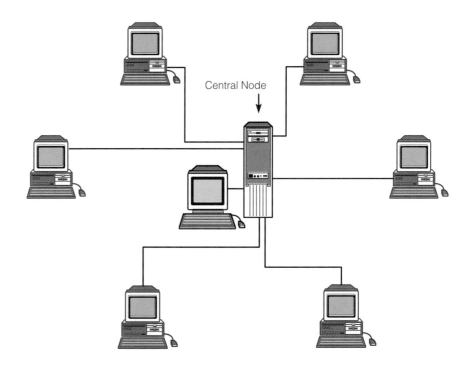

Central Node

hub. Note that the configuration is also similar to that of the ARCnet configuration (Figure 7–6).

IEEE Project 802 Subcommittees

The IEEE established a standards group called the 802 committee. This group is divided into subcommittees, each of which addresses specific LAN issues and architectures. The subcommittees and their objectives are described here.

802.1: High-Level Interface   The high-level interface subcommittee addresses matters relating to network architecture, network management, network interconnection, and all other issues related to the OSI layers above the data link layer, which are the network, transport, session, presentation, and application layers.

logical link control (LLC)
A sublayer of the OSI reference model data link layer. The logical link control forms the interface between the network layer and the media access control protocols.

802.2: Logical Link Control   IEEE has divided the OSI data link layer into two sublayers: **logical link control (LLC)** and MAC. The MAC sublayer implements protocols such as token passing or CSMA/CD. Figure 7–7 illustrates the relationship between the LLC and the MAC sublayers. The objective of the LLC is to provide a consistent, transparent interface to the MAC layer, so the network layers above the data link layer are able to function correctly regardless of the MAC protocol.

802.3: CSMA/CD   The IEEE 802.3 standard covers a variety of CSMA/CD architectures that are generally based on Ethernet. Several alternatives are available under this standard. Some of these are given in Table 7–1.

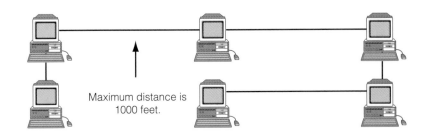

Figure 7–6 (a)
ARCnet Bus
Configuration

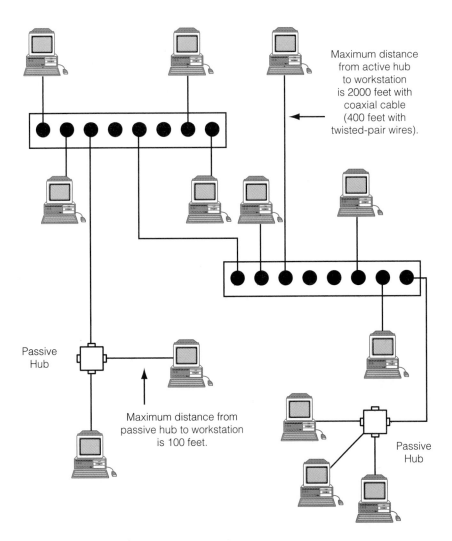

Figure 7–6 (b)
ARCnet with Active and
Passive Hubs

802.4: Token Bus The IEEE 802.4 standard subcommittee sets standards for token bus networks. The standard describes how the network is initialized, how new stations can insert themselves into the set of nodes receiving the token, how to recover if the token is lost, and how node priority can be established. The standard also describes the format of the message frames.

Figure 7–7
LLC and MAC Sublayers of the OSI Data Link Layer

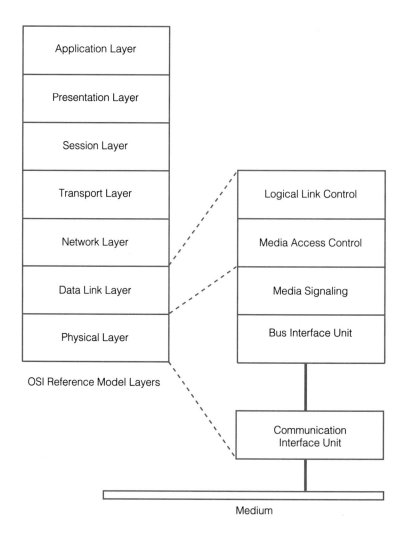

OSI Reference Model Layers

Medium

802.5: Token Ring The IEEE 802.5 standard subcommittee sets standards for token-ring networks. The standard describes essentially the same functions as those described by the token bus network.

802.6: MANs The FDDI family of technologies is not the only MAN proposal. The IEEE 802 LAN standards committee has also developed specifications, IEEE 802.6, for a MAN. The IEEE 802.6 standard has also been adopted by ANSI. The standard is also called the distributed queue dual bus (DQDB) standard.

As the name *DQDB* indicates, the architecture uses two buses. Each bus is unidirectional, meaning that data is transmitted in one direction on one bus and in the other direction on the second bus, as illustrated in Figure 7–8. Each node must therefore be attached to both buses. The specification also allows for a variation called a looped bus. The looped bus still uses two one-direction buses; however, each bus forms a

Table 7–1   IEEE 802.3 Alternatives

1Base5	1-Mbps baseband medium with a maximum segment length of 500 m (a baseband medium is one that carries only one signal at a time, as opposed to a broadband medium that can carry multiple signals simultaneously). The segment length is the length of cable that can be used without repeaters to amplify the signal. This standard encompasses implementations commonly known as StarLAN.
10Base5	10-Mbps baseband medium with a maximum segment length of 500 m.
10Base2	10-Mbps baseband medium with a maximum segment length of 185 m. The cable used in this implementation is commonly called Thinnet or Cheapernet.
10Base-T	10-Mbps baseband medium with twisted-pair wires as the medium.
10Broad36	10-Mbps broadband medium with a 3600-m segment length.
100Base-TX	100-Mbps baseband medium with twisted-pair wires as the medium.
100Base-FX	100-Mbps baseband medium using fiber optic cable.
100VG-AnyLAN	A specification of the IEEE 802.12 subcommittee. This specification competes with 100Base-T for the 100 Mbps Ethernet market. The specification calls for twisted-pair wires and can support either CSMA/CD or token-passing technologies.
1000Base-Sx	1000-Mbps baseband medium using fiber optic cable.

You may infer from this nomenclature that, in general, the initial number represents the speed of the medium in millions of bits per second. The "base" or "broad" designator represents baseband or broadband, respectively. With five exceptions, 10Base-T, 100Base-TX, 100Base-FX, 100VG-AnyLAN, and 1000Base-Sx, the last number represents the segment length of the medium in hundreds of meters.

closed loop, as illustrated in Figure 7–9. Several speeds are defined in the standard. Speeds depend on the medium used. With coaxial cable the speed is 45 Mbps; the speed is 156 Mbps over fiber optic cable. Distances up to 200 mi are supported. This subcommittee sets standards for networks that can cover a wide area and operate at high speed. Distances of up to 200 mi and speeds on the order of 100 Mbps are being considered for MANs. A MAN could transmit voice and video in addition to data.

802.7: Broadband Technical Advisory Group   This group provides guidance and technical expertise to other groups that are establishing broadband LAN standards, such as the 802.3 subcommittee for 10Broad36.

802.8: Fiber Optic Technical Advisory Group   This group provides guidance and technical expertise to other groups that are establishing standards for LANs using fiber optic cable.

802.9: Integrated Data and Voice Networks   This committee sets standards for networks that carry both voice and data. Specifically, it is setting standards for interfaces to integrated services digital networks (ISDNs).

802.10: LAN Security   This committee addresses the implementation of security capabilities such as encryption, network management, and the transfer of data.

Figure 7–8
ANSI Distributed
Queue Dual Bus LAN

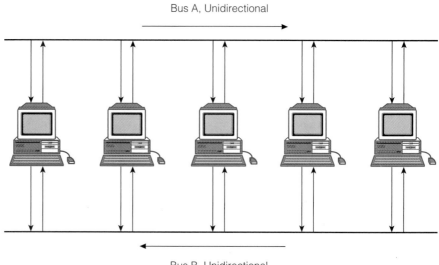

Bus A, Unidirectional

Bus B, Unidirectional

802.11: Wireless LANs   These standards cover multiple transmission methods to include infrared light, as well as a variety of broadcast frequencies to include spread-spectrum radio waves and microwaves. Thus, many of the existing wireless implementations are covered under the standards proposed.

802.12: Demand Priority Access Method   This subgroup developed the specifications for the 100VG-AnyLAN protocol. The protocol specifies 100-Mbps speeds over twisted-pair wires.

The ANSI FDDI Standard

Two major uses have been suggested for high-speed LANs. The obvious one is the high-speed exchange of data among computers located within a large urban area. Often, companies have several offices distributed throughout a large metropolitan area, and a MAN allows computers in these locations to exchange large amounts of data almost instantly. The second purpose is as a **backbone network** to interconnect distributed LANs, as illustrated in Figure 7–10.

ANSI originally established the FDDI for a high-speed LAN using fiber optic cable. The **copper distributed data interface (CDDI)** extension uses twisted-pair wires as the medium. The FDDI is similar to the MAN being proposed by the IEEE.

The FDDI specifications call for a token-ring LAN operating at a speed of 100 Mbps over distances up to 200 km. As the name implies, the medium is fiber optic cable. The maximum cable segment allowed without repeaters

backbone network A network used to interconnect other networks or to connect a cluster of network nodes.

copper distributed data interface (CDDI) An ANSI LAN standard for twisted-pair-wire LANs providing speeds of 100 Mbps. An extension of the FDDI LAN.

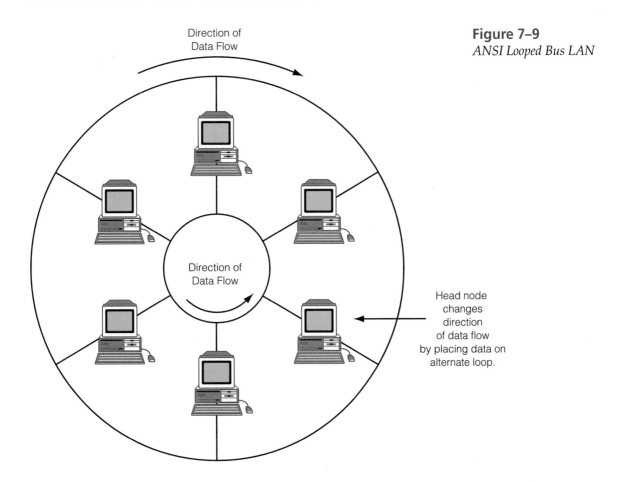

Direction of
Data Flow

Direction of
Data Flow

Head node
changes
direction
of data flow
by placing data on
alternate loop.

Figure 7–9
ANSI Looped Bus LAN

is 2 km. The 200-km distance can be attained by connecting 100 such segments. Up to 1000 nodes can be connected to the ring. With a LAN spanning
this distance, it is not efficient to have only one message on the ring at one
time. Multiple messages may be circulating at a given time. The protocol for
doing this is as follows: Only one token circulates around the line. When a
station receives the token, such as node A in Figure 7–11(a), it removes the
token from the ring and transmits its message. At the end of its message, A
appends the token, as illustrated in Figure 7–11(b). The next node, node B,
sees the token and can piggyback a message onto the existing message.
Node B then appends the token onto the message, as illustrated in Figure
7–11(c). A's message continues to circulate around the ring until it gets to
the recipient, node X. X returns the message to A as an acknowledgment,
and A removes its message from the ring, as illustrated in Figure 7–11(d).
The specification also allows a node to transmit multiple messages in suc-
cession. A transmit time limit is established during which a node is allowed to send multiple messages while it holds the token.

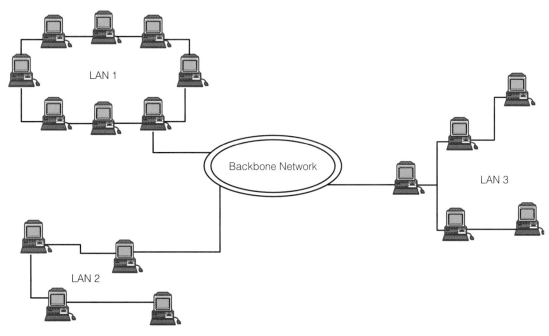

Figure 7–10
Backbone Network Connecting LANs

Two addressing modes are allowed in an FDDI network. One mode uses a 15-bit address and the other uses a 46-bit address. However, the standard does not stipulate the exact format of addresses. The FDDI LAN can be used as a backbone network to connect multiple LANs, as a high-speed LAN connecting large computing systems, and as a high-speed document delivery system for office automation and graphics applications.

DATA LINK AND MAC PROTOCOLS

The physical layer of the OSI reference model describes the medium, the connectors required to attach workstations and servers to the medium, and the representation of signals using the medium, such as voltage levels for baseband transmission or frequencies for broadband transmission.

Once connected to the medium, a network node must have the ability to send and receive network messages. This function is described by the data link layer of the OSI reference mode. A convention, or protocol, must exist to define how this function is accomplished. The method by which a LAN workstation is able to gain control of the medium and transmit a message is a MAC protocol. The MAC protocol is implemented in LANs as one of two sublayers of the OSI reference model's data link layer. The other sublayer is the LLC sublayer. We first look more closely at the functions provided by a data link protocol.

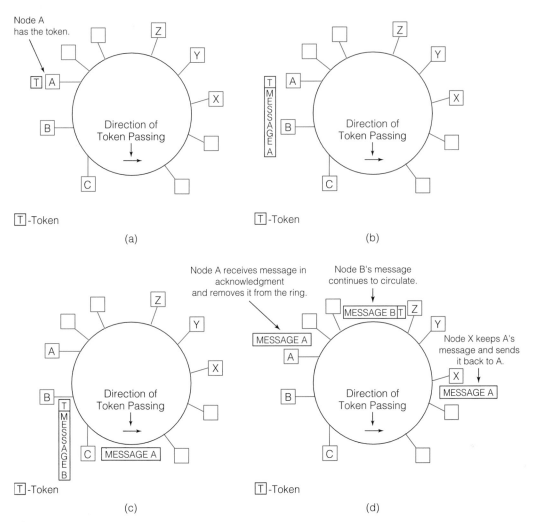

Figure 7–11
Message Passing in an FDDI LAN

Data Link Protocols

In general, a data link protocol establishes the rules for gaining access to the medium and for exchanging messages. To do this the protocol describes several aspects of the message exchange process. Six of the most important aspects are

- delineation of data
- error control
- addressing
- transparency
- code independence
- media access

Delineation of Data   A data link protocol must define or delineate where the data portion of the transmitted message begins and ends. You may recall from the discussion of the OSI reference model in Chapter 1 that each layer may add data to the message it receives from the layers above it. The data link layer is no exception. Some of the characters or bits it adds to the message may include line control information, error detection data, and so on. When these fields are added, a data link protocol must provide a way to distinguish among the various pieces of data. This can be accomplished in two basic ways: by framing the data with certain control characters or by using a standard message format wherein a data segment is identified by its position within the message.

The framing technique is used in two types of data link protocols: asynchronous transmission and binary synchronous transmission. These protocols are common to WANs and are discussed in Chapter 11.

Many of today's LANs use a standard message format for sending data. For example, an Ethernet message has several distinct parts, as illustrated in Figure 7–12. (Note: There are several different formats for Ethernet frames.) The message frame begins with a 64-bit synchronization pattern. The synchronization bits give the receiving node an opportunity to sense the incoming message and establish time or synchronization with the sending node. The message is a stream of continuous bits, so it is important that the receiving node be able to clock the bits in as they arrive. The IEEE 802.3 standard uses a 64-bit synchronization pattern; however, the standard divides this into a 56-bit group and an 8-bit group. The first 56 bits are for synchronization, and the 8 bits that follow signal the start of the frame and

Preamble	Destination Address	Source Address	Type Field	Data Field	32-Bit CRC

(a) Original Ethernet_II Frame

Preamble	Start Frame Delimeter	Destination Address	Source Address	Length Field	Data Field	32-Bit CRC

(b) IEEE 802.3 Frame

Preamble	Start Frame Delimeter	Destination Address	Source Address	Length Field	IEEE 802.2 Control	Data Field	32-Bit CRC

(c) IEEE 802.2 Frame

Preamble	Destination Address	Source Address	Length Field	DSAP	SSAP	CTRL	Data Field	32-Bit CRC

(d) Ethernet_SNAP (an 802.2 variant)

Figure 7–12
Ethernet Message Formats

thus indicate where the first bit of the remaining frame can be found. The next two fields are the addresses of the destination node and the sending node. Each address is 48 bits long.

The 16-bit field type is a control field. In the IEEE 802.3 standard, this represents the length of the data field that follows. The length is expressed as the number of 8-bit groups, or **octets.** If the message is short, extra bits may be added to make the entire message long enough to allow the message to clear the length of the network before the sending node stops transmitting. This is essential to ensure correct transmission. The frame check sequence, a 32-bit cyclic redundancy check (CRC) field, as illustrated in Figure 7–12, provides for error detection.

octet A group of 8 bits used in bit synchronous protocols. Data, regardless of its code, is treated as octets.

Error Control Error control is used to detect transmission errors. Common error detection techniques are parity and cyclic redundancy checks. These techniques are discussed in Chapter 3.

Addressing Communication between two network nodes is accomplished through an addressing scheme. Network addressing is similar to addressing used for postal mail. A postal address is a hierarchical addressing scheme, with the hierarchy being individual recipient, street address, city, state, country, and zip code. Networks also use a hierarchical addressing scheme, with the hierarchy being application, network node, and network. Like postal addresses, network addresses must be unique; otherwise, ambiguity arises as to which node is the recipient. At this point, we are concerned only with network node addressing, not network or application addressing.

Each network has a specific way in which it forms station addresses. In Ethernet and the IBM token ring, each address is 48 bits long. Each Ethernet or IBM token-ring LAN adapter card has its address set by the manufacturer. This ensures that all nodes, regardless of location, have a unique address. (Note: Many Ethernet adapters store their addresses in an updatable chip. Because these addresses may be changed by software utilities, they are not guaranteed to be unique once changes have been made). In ARCnet a node address is an 8-bit entity, and the LAN administrator typically sets the node address through switches on the LAN adapter. On a LAN, node source and destination addresses are included in the MAC headers of messages being transmitted.

Transparency In data link protocols, **transparency** is the ability of the data link to transmit any bit combination. In the binary synchronous data link protocol (shown in Figure 7–13) the start-of-text and end-of-text framing characters have special meaning. These characters can be sent as part of the data only when special considerations are made. Without these special considerations, the protocol is not transparent. We want protocols to be transparent because they can be used to transfer binary data such as object programs as well as text data. The Ethernet message illustrated in Figure 7–12 does provide transparency: No bit patterns in the data field can cause confusion in the message.

transparency The ability to send any bit string as data in a message. The data bits are not interpreted as control characters.

Figure 7–13

Framing in the Binary Synchronous Data Link Protocol

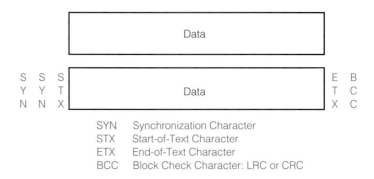

SYN   Synchronization Character
STX   Start-of-Text Character
ETX   End-of-Text Character
BCC   Block Check Character: LRC or CRC

code independence
The ability to successfully transmit data regardless of the data code, such as ASCII or EBCDIC.

Code Independence   **Code independence** means that any data code, such as ASCII or EBCDIC, can be transmitted. These codes use different bit patterns to represent many of the characters. Code independence is important because often you must communicate with or through computers having a data code different from that of your computer. In the Ethernet protocol this is accomplished by sending data in octets. The octets are not tied to any particular code, so any code can be used. If your computer uses a 7-bit code, such as one of the two ASCII codes, the only requirement is that the total number of bits transmitted be divisible by 8. Thus, if you are sending 100 7-bit characters, the total number of bits in the data portion must be 704. The last 4 bits are added to pad out to an integral number of octets (700/8 = 87.5; 704 bits are necessary because 704 is a multiple of 8).

Media Access   Media access is the way in which a device gains access to the medium—that is, the protocol by which a device gains the right to transmit data on the medium. This convention is covered next.

MAC Protocols

LAN technology adheres to two primary data link protocols: token passing and contention. In the IEEE 802 standards, the data link layer is divided into the two sublayers: LLC and MAC. The LLC provides the functions of flow control, message sequencing, message acknowledgment, and error checking. The MAC layer describes token passing and contention.

Contention

contention   A convention whereby devices obtain control of a communication link. In contention mode, devices compete for control of the line either by transmitting directly on an idle line or by issuing a request for line control.

In a true **contention** MAC protocol, each network node has equal access to the medium. Although variations of this protocol exist, essentially it works like this:

1. Each node monitors the medium to see whether a message is being transmitted.
2. If no message is detected, any node can begin a transmission.

The act of listening to the medium for a message is called carrier sensing because when a message is being transmitted, a carrier signal is present.

Several nodes can have messages to send. Each of them may detect a quiet medium, and each may begin to transmit at one time. The ability of several nodes to access a medium that is not carrying a message is called **multiple access.**

If two or more nodes begin to transmit at the same time, a **collision** is said to occur. Multiple simultaneous transmissions cause the messages to interfere with each other and become garbled. It is imperative that collisions be detected and that recovery be effected. When a collision occurs, the messages are not transmitted successfully. On detecting a collision, the sending nodes must resend their messages. If both nodes immediately attempt to retransmit their messages, another collision might occur. Therefore, each node waits a small, randomly selected interval before attempting to retransmit. This reduces the probability of another collision.

There is only a small time interval during which a collision can occur. For example, suppose that two nodes at the extremities of a 1000-m bus network have a message to send and that the medium is not being used. The collision interval is the time it takes for a signal to travel the length of the cable. Because the signal travels at nearly the speed of light, the collision window is the time it takes for the signal to travel 1000 m, the signal's propagation delay. The propagation delay is approximately 5 ns per meter. For a 1000-m segment, the maximum propagation delay is therefore approximately 5 microseconds (5 millionths of a second). Although this interval is small, collisions can still occur.

The media access control technique just described is known as **carrier sense with multiple access and collision detection (CSMA/CD).** It is the most common of the access strategies for bus architectures and is the MAC protocol used in Ethernet LANs. The CSMA/CD MAC protocol, sometimes called listen-before-talk, is summarized in Table 7–2. You should note that the CSMA/CD protocol is a broadcast protocol. All workstations on the network listen to the medium and accept the message. Each message has a destination address. Only a workstation having an address equal to the destination address can use the message. Using a broadcast technique makes it easy for new workstations to be added to and removed from the network.

CSMA/CD is known as a **fair protocol,** meaning that each node has equal access to the medium. In a pure CSMA/CD scheme, no one node has priority over another. Variations of this protocol exist that give one workstation priority over another and minimize the likelihood of collisions. One of these protocol variations divides time into transmission slots. The length

multiple access The ability for several nodes to access a medium that is not carrying a message.

collision In a CSMA/CD MAC protocol, a collision occurs when two stations attempt to send a message at the same time. The messages interfere with each other, so correct communication is not possible.

carrier sense with multiple access and collision detection (CSMA/CD) A MAC technique that attempts to detect collisions and is the most common access strategy for bus architectures.

fair protocol A protocol in which each node has equal access to the medium.

Table 7–2 CSMA/CD Media Access Control Protocol

1. Listen to the medium to see whether a message is being transmitted.
2. If the medium is quiet, transmit message. If the medium is busy, wait for the signal to clear and then transmit.
3. If a collision occurs, wait for the signal to clear, wait a random interval, and then retransmit.

of a slot is the time it takes a message to travel the length of the medium. Nodes on the network are synchronized, and each node can begin a transmission only at the beginning of its allocated time slot. This protocol has proven to be more efficient for networks with lots of message traffic.

carrier sense with multiple access and collision avoidance (CSMA/CA) A MAC technique that attempts to avoid collisions.

A variation of CSMA/CD is **carrier sense with multiple access and collision avoidance (CSMA/CA).** This protocol attempts to avoid collisions that are possible with the CSMA/CD protocol. Collisions are avoided because each node is given a wait time before it can begin transmitting. For example, suppose there are 100 nodes on the network and the propagation delay time for the network is 1 ms. Node 1 can transmit after the medium has been idle for 1 ms. Node 2 must wait 2 ms before attempting to transmit, node 3 must wait 3 ms, and so on. Each node therefore has a specific time slot during which it can transmit, and no collisions will occur. However, the node with the lowest-priority time slot may experience long delays in getting access to the medium.

Token Passing

token passing A MAC protocol in which a string of bits called the token is distributed among the network nodes. A computer that receives the token is allowed to transmit data onto the network. Only the stations receiving a token can transmit. Token passing is implemented on ring and bus LANs.

The second major MAC protocol is token passing. It is used on both bus and ring topologies. **Token passing** is a round-robin protocol in which each node gets an equal opportunity to transmit. An overview of the token-passing protocol is given in Table 7–3. With token passing, the right to transmit is granted by a token that is passed from one node to the next. Remember that a token is a predefined bit pattern that is recognized by each node. In a ring topology, the token is passed from one node to the adjacent node. On a token-passing bus, the order of token passing is determined by the address of each node. The token is passed in either ascending or descending address order. If it is passed in descending order, the station with the lowest address passes the token to the node with the highest address. The routing of a token from high to low addresses in a token-passing bus is illustrated in Figure 7–14.

When a node obtains the token, it has two options: It can transmit a message or, if it has no message to send, it can pass the token to the next node. If the node has a message to transmit, it keeps the token by changing the format of the message header from "token" to "transmit" and sends the message. The message recipient keeps the message and then transmits it back

Table 7–3   Token-Passing Media Access Control Protocol

1. Wait for transmit token.
2. If transmit token is received and there is no message to send, send the token to the next node.
3. If transmit token is received and there is a message to send, then
   a. Transmit message.
   b. Wait for acknowledgment.
   c. When acknowledgment is received, pass token to the next node.

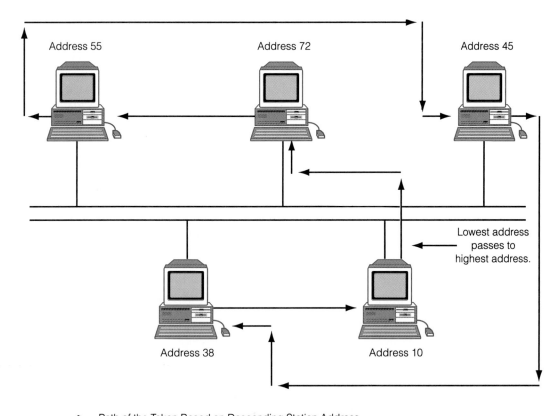

Path of the Token Based on Descending Station Address

Figure 7–14
Token-Passing Bus

onto the network. The message eventually arrives back at the sending node. When a node receives the message it sent, it accepts the message as an acknowledgment that the message was successfully received. The transmitting node then activates the token by sending it to the next node. The token-passing protocol does not allow a node to monopolize the token and the network. Note that, unlike the CSMA/CD protocol, the token-passing protocol does not allow collisions to occur.

Token-Passing Ring   In a **token-passing ring,** the token can become lost if a node holding the token fails or if transmission errors occur. To allow recovery from this, one node is designated as the active monitor. Other nodes are designated as standby monitors. The active monitor periodically issues a message indicating that it is active. The standby monitors accept this status and remain in standby mode. If the active monitor message fails to appear on time, a standby monitor assumes the active monitor role. A major function of the active monitor is to ensure that the token is circulating. If the token does not arrive within a certain amount of time, the active monitor generates a new token. This technique is guaranteed to work because the token circulation time is very predictable.

token-passing ring A LAN architecture using a ring topology and token passing media access control protocol.

Token-Passing Bus   Token passing is slightly different on a **token-passing bus.** On a bus, the token is passed from one workstation to another based on station addresses. As mentioned earlier, the token can be passed in ascending or descending address order. Let us assume that the token is passed in descending address order, so the station with the lowest address forwards the token to the station with the highest address. This token-passing scheme is illustrated in Figure 7–14. Such a protocol must allow for new workstations to be inserted and active ones deactivated.

Suppose a station attempts to send the token to the next station, and the next station has been shut down. Recovery must be possible when a station goes from active to inactive status. For example, when a sending station does not receive the token back in a prescribed interval, the sending station transmits the token to its neighbor again. If a second failure occurs, the sending station assumes that the neighboring station is inactive and issues a message, asking for the address of the next station. The "who is next" message contains the address of the unresponsive station. The successor of the failed station recognizes the address in the "who is next" message as its predecessor station and responds. If the successor node has also failed, another "who is next" message is then sent out with the entire address range of the LAN. If any other stations are active, they respond.

Allowance also is made in the token-passing bus protocol for new stations to enter the LAN. Periodically stations issue a "solicit successor" message. This message contains the sending station's address and the address of that station's current successor node. Stations receiving this message inspect the addresses of the sender and the successor. If a station has an address that falls between these two addresses, it responds to the message. Two stations can respond at the same time, in which case a collision occurs as in CSMA/CD, and collision resolution is effected. This allows an orderly process for insertion of new stations.

MAKING THE DECISIONS

Without even considering the network operating system software alternatives, the number of alternatives available in choosing a LAN can be overwhelming. You have three basic conducted media choices or three choices in wireless medium technology, three major topology choices, two primary media access control choices, and a wide variety of vendor choices. The issue then becomes which is the best configuration for your company and applications. If one clear option were superior for all applications and for all users, the choice would be easy. However, applications vary significantly with respect to the number of nodes, number of concurrent users, data access needs, distance spanned, and budget. Next, we explore tradeoffs you can consider when making LAN choices.

Token Passing and CSMA/CD Compared

The pros and cons of the token-passing and CSMA/CD protocols are summarized in Table 7–4. Note that each protocol has advantages and disadvantages. In practice both have been noted to have good performance.

Table 7–4   MAC Protocol Comparison

Token Passing	CSMA/CD
Access is equal for all nodes.	Access is equal for all nodes.
Access window is predictable.	Access window can be unpredictable.
Maximum wait time to transmit is token circulation time.	Maximum wait time to transmit is unpredictable and depends on collisions.
Average wait time to transmit is predictable: half the maximum circulation time.	Average wait time to transmit is unpredictable.
Network congestion does not adversely affect network efficiency.	Network congestion may result in collisions and reduce network efficiency.
A node must wait for the token before being able to transmit.	A node may be able to transmit immediately.
One node cannot monopolize the network.	One node may be able to monopolize the network.
Large rings can result in long delays before a node obtains a token.	A node can transmit when the network is quiet.
Performance is consistent for large, busy networks.	Performance is unpredictable for large, busy networks because of possibility of collisions.

Topology and Protocol Tradeoffs

We consider the three primary combinations of topology and protocol: CSMA/CD bus, token bus, and token ring. The **StarLAN** model LAN is covered under the IEEE 802.3 standard, and its characteristics are similar to those of the CSMA/CD bus. As of this writing, wireless LANs are so new that tradeoff data regarding their use is not readily available. When specifics are required, we will use popular implementations as examples: Ethernet or an IEEE 802.3 implementation for CSMA/CD buses and IEEE 802.5 token ring. Table 7–5 summarizes the topologies and protocols, which are described in the following sections.

StarLAN A configuration similar to the basic star topology in that each workstation is connected to a wiring hub. The primary medium used for implementations is twisted-pair wires.

CSMA/CD Buses   Most CSMA/CD bus implementations use either twisted-pair wires or coaxial cable. Less often, fiber optic cable and microwave radio are used. Common speeds for these LANs are 1, 10, 100, and 1000 Mbps, with 10 and 100 Mbps being the most common. The distances spanned by these networks vary, but the IEEE 802.3 standard, which covers several implementations, specifies 925, 2500, and 3600 m. The number of supported nodes also varies. In the IEEE standard, one implementation allows 150 nodes and another allows 500. The number of nodes allowed is a hardware-based limit and addresses the issue of connectivity. The network operating system and performance needs also may limit the number of network nodes. Some network operating systems restrict the number of network nodes. We discuss network operating systems in Chapter 8.

A network's performance is a critical factor in its productivity. Performance depends on both the hardware and the software. There are many different combinations of hardware and software, so we consider the general

Table 7–5   LAN Topology and Protocol Summary

	IEEE 802.3 or Ethernet	IEEE 802.5 Token Ring	ARCnet	StarLAN
Speed	10, 100, 1000 Mbps	4, 16, or 100 Mbps	2.5 or 20 Mbps	1 Mbps
Medium	Twisted-pair wires, coaxial cable, or fiber optic cable	Twisted-pair wires	Twisted-pair wires or coaxial cable	Twisted-pair wires
Distance	500 m for thick cable, 185 m for thinnet cable segments; 5 segments can be connected with repeaters to give maximum lengths of 2500 and 925 m	366 m for the main ring; can be extended to 750 m with repeaters and to 4000 m with fiber optic cable	6110 m; maximum distance between active hubs is 620 m and between passive hubs is 31 m	500 m
Number of stations	802.3–100 per thick cable segment, 30 per thinnet segment Ethernet-1024	260	255	Not stated by 1Base5 standard (early StarLANs set limit at 50)
Standards	IEEE 802.3	IEEE 802.5	De facto (submitted for approval as an ANSI standard)	IEEE 802.3 1Base5
Cost for NIC and connectors only	Low (approx. $50 per station)	High (approx. $225 per station)	Low (approx. $50 per station)	Low (approx. $50 per station)

outlook for CSMA/CD bus systems. The major concern people have voiced regarding CSMA/CD bus performance is its capacity under load. As the number of users and the number of messages being sent increase, so does the probability of collisions. If the collision rate is high, the effectiveness of the LAN decreases. When the LAN is busy, the efficiency may drop, and you might lose effectiveness just when you need it most. LAN vendors and researchers have run numerous tests to gauge the effect of high collision rates. Under these tests the performance characteristics did not drop appreciably. However, the true test of performance comes from actual use. Under light load conditions, access to the medium and the ability to transmit are good; there is little waiting time to transmit. Performance under heavy loads can be unpredictable.

Token Buses and Token Rings   We discuss these two implementations together because their MAC characteristics are similar.

Token rings operate at 4, 16, or 100 Mbps. Stations on the LAN connect to a MAU. A typical MAU contains ports for eight workstations plus an input and output connector to another MAU. Like all LANs, a token-passing ring has limitations on distance and number of stations. The maximum distance spanned by a ring is 770 m and the maximum number of nodes allowed is 260. These limitations can be extended by setting up two or more token-ring LANs and connecting them with a device called a bridge. When

LANs are connected in this way, a user on one ring can communicate with users or devices on another connected ring; from the user's perspective the interconnected rings appear as a single LAN.

Predictability is the key to token LAN performance. Because the medium is accessed through the possession of a token, and because each station is assured of receiving the token, you can predict the maximum and average times needed for a station to transmit its message. The problem of collision, inherent in contention LANs, does not exist in a token-passing LAN. When network traffic is light, a station may need to wait longer than a station on a contention bus; however, when network traffic is heavy, the token-passing station may wait less time. Regardless of the wait time, a station is assured that it can transmit in a predictable amount of time. The maximum time a station must wait is given by

$$T_{Max} = (\text{Number of stations} - 1)$$
$$\times (\text{Message transmit time} + \text{Token-passing time})$$

Thus, a station that has just passed the token to its neighbor may become ready to send a message. That station must wait until the token comes back around. The worst-case scenario would be that every other station has a message to transmit. Thus, the station must wait on all other stations in the ring to transmit their messages and pass the token. On average, a station ready to transmit must wait for half the other stations.

Ethernet LANs usually have a lower per station cost than token rings operating at comparable speeds. This statement is based on the cost of the hardware (LAN adapters, MAUs, wiring hubs, cables, connectors, and wiring). Because prices fluctuate over time and from one vendor to another, you should verify these costs.

SUMMARY

A LAN topology is the pattern used to lay out the LAN. The main LAN topologies are bus, ring, and star. The medium access control protocol is the way in which a station interfaces with the medium. The main media access control protocols for LANs are carrier sense with multiple access and collision detection (CSMA/CD) and token passing. CSMA/CD is used on bus topologies and star topologies. Token passing is used on bus and ring topologies.

A variety of standards covering medium access control, LAN topology, medium distances, and the maximum number of LAN nodes have been developed. The two principal standards organizations for LANs are IEEE and ANSI. Standards have resulted in open architectures. With open architectures, a variety of manufacturers can develop products that will interoperate on a LAN. As a consequence LAN administrators usually have several product choices, and competition among product developers leads to product innovation and lower prices.

KEY TERMS

active node
American National Standards Insti-
    tute (ANSI)
ARCnet
backbone network
bus topology
carrier sense with multiple access
    and collision avoidance
    (CSMA/CA)
carrier sense with multiple access
    and collision detection
    (CSMA/CD)
code independence
collision
contention
copper distributed data interface
    (CDDI)
Ethernet
fair protocol
fiber distributed data interface (FDDI)

IEEE 802.3 standard
IEEE 802.4 standard
IEEE 802.5 standard
inactive node
Institute of Electrical and Electronics
    Engineers (IEEE)
logical link control (LLC)
media access control (MAC)
    protocol
multiple access
network topology
octet
ring topology
StarLAN
star topology
star-wired LAN
token passing
token-passing bus
token-passing ring
transparency

REVIEW QUESTIONS

1. What is a topology?

2. What are the primary LAN topologies?

3. What is a MAC protocol?

4. What are the primary LAN MAC protocols?

5. What are the IEEE 802.3, 802.4, and 802.5 standards?

6. What is the ANSI FDDI? How does it differ from the CDDI?

7. What function is performed by a MAU?

8. List four items that are specified in the IEEE LAN standards.

9. Compare ARCnet and Ethernet.

10. Compare Ethernet and token-passing ring LANs.

PROBLEMS AND EXERCISES

1. The ALOHAnet, an early example of a LAN, was developed by the University of Hawaii. Research the literature to find the details of this network's architecture.

2. What are some of the uses of a MAN such as the fiber distributed data interface?

3. What are the advantages and disadvantages of LAN standards?

4. Suppose you had a LAN application in which guaranteed access to the medium within a specified time was essential. Which MAC protocol would you choose? Justify your choice.

CHAPTER 8

LAN System Software

CHAPTER OBJECTIVES

After studying this chapter you should be able to

- Describe the functions of LAN system software
- Discuss the functions performed by LAN workstation software
- Explain important characteristics of LAN server software
- Describe how a spooler works
- Explain the importance of making backups
- List backup options and elements of backup procedures
- Discuss the software requirements for shared data and application use
- Describe several types of software licenses

In Chapter 6 you examined the details of the LAN hardware system. In this chapter you will learn about the software system that drives the hardware. We separate LAN software into two classes: workstation system software and server system software. The success of the LAN depends on how these two software classes and the application software interact in setting up the communication capability.

GENERIC FUNCTIONS OF LAN SYSTEM SOFTWARE

Application software is designed to solve business problems. It is assisted in this goal by supporting system software such as the operating system (OS), database management systems (DBMSs), and data communication systems. Like all system software, LAN system software is essentially an extension of the OS. It carries out hardware-oriented LAN tasks, such as interfacing to the medium, and input/output (I/O) oriented tasks, such as directing print jobs and disk read and write requests to a server. A few OSs are designed specifically to carry out LAN server tasks and have these functions integrated with other OS tasks such as the user interface and job, file, and memory management. Other LAN system software implementations operate in partnership with a general-purpose OS such as UNIX or OS/2. The general-purpose OS is responsible for providing much of the user interface and job, file, and memory management. The LAN extensions are responsible for implementing the LAN-oriented tasks such as the LAN interface and file and printer server functions.

System software is designed to insulate applications from hardware details such as I/O and memory management. System software provides an interface through which the applications can request hardware services. The applications make requests for services, and system software contains the logic to carry out those requests for a specific type of hardware. For example, an application makes disk access requests independent of the type of disk drive being used. A disk driver is a component of the OS that fulfills the request for a specific type of disk drive.

LAN system software resides both in the application's workstation and in the server, as illustrated in Figure 8–1. The workstation's LAN system software includes the redirector and the medium interface software. We use the example of a workstation environment to examine the interaction between workstation and server software components.

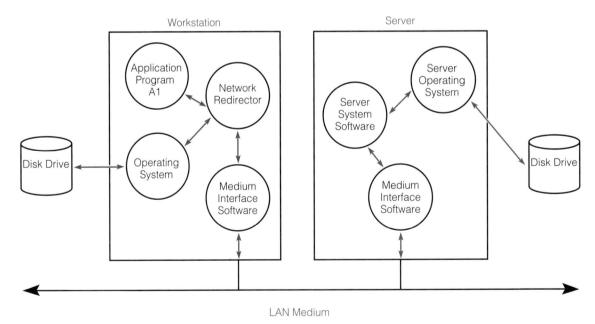

Figure 8–1
LAN System Software in Server and Workstation

Consider a workstation in which the server provides file and printer services. The workstation has local disk drives A, B, and C. The file server's disk drives are known to the workstation as drives F and G. The workstation's local printer ports are LPT1 and LPT2. A local dot-matrix printer is attached to LPT1; output to LPT2 is directed to a network laser printer. The key to making this environment work is transparent access to all devices. From the user's perspective, printing to a network printer and accessing a network disk drive are transparent. Thus, the workstation user accesses remote drives F and G in exactly the same way as he or she accesses local drives A, B, and C. The user also prints to the laser printer as though it were locally attached. This transparency is accomplished by the LAN system software. To see how, we consider an application that issues a read for a record located on the file server.

System Software Functions

You learned in Chapters 5 and 6 that the hardware provides the physical connection between a workstation and a server. The software forms the logical connection by using the hardware to carry on sessions between applications on a workstation and the server. The first function of the LAN software is to set up these logical connections. For now, we assume that this is done by the user issuing a server logon request. If the logon is successful, the user can use the server in accordance with his or her security controls.

The OS running in the workstation is aware only of the devices physically attached to that workstation. In our example, the OS is capable of handling requests to drives A, B, and C and to LPT1 on its own. However, it cannot handle I/O requests to drives F and G or direct output to the network printer at LPT2. Ordinarily, when an application issues a file or print request, the request is accepted and carried out by the OS. If a request is made to access a device not attached to the workstation, the OS returns the error message "device not found." To prevent this error message from being returned in a LAN situation, the requests for drives F and G must be intercepted before they get to the OS. The software that reroutes I/O requests is generically called a **redirector.**

redirector A software module that intercepts and reroutes network application I/O requests before they get to the workstation's OS.

The redirector is a software module that intercepts all application I/O requests before they get to the workstation's OS. If the request is for a local device, the redirector passes the request to the computer's OS. Thus, local device access requests are carried out as usual. If the redirector gets a request for a remote access to a LAN server, it sends the request over the network to the server. This is illustrated in Figure 8–2.

The server receives a request for file or print service, in this case, a request for a database record. Many workstations are attached to the network, and any of them can make server requests at any time. The server may receive several requests simultaneously, and efficiency requires that the server be able to work on multiple requests at once. This capability is known as **multithreading** because the server can have multiple transactions in progress at the same time. The server software must keep track of the progress of each transaction.

multithreading The capacity of a server to work on multiple requests at once.

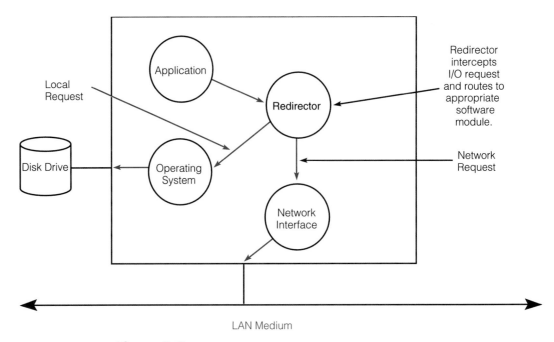

Figure 8–2
Redirector Software

client/server protocol
An application framework in which the processing load is divided among several processes called clients and servers. Clients issue requests to servers, which provide specialized services such as database processing and mail distribution. Within this framework, clients are able to concentrate on business logic while servers can use specialized hardware and software that allows them to provide their services more efficiently. When clients and servers are located in different computers, application processing is distributed over multiple computers and, in effect, the network becomes the computer.

Suppose the server simultaneously receives two requests for a database record, three requests to write to a network printer, and one request to download an application program. These requests arrive in single file, as illustrated in Figure 8–3. The server accepts the first request, a database record read, and searches disk cache memory. If the record is not in cache memory, the server issues a disk read to satisfy the request. It also remembers the address of the workstation that requested the read. While the disk is working to find the requested record, the server takes the next request, a printer write request, and issues a write to the print file. The server then accepts the next request, one for downloading an application program, and issues a read request for the first segment of the program.

At this point the server is notified that its read for the first database record has been completed. The server recalls the address of the workstation making the request and sends the record back to that workstation. Then the server takes the next request, a database read, and issues the read that satisfies the request. Thus the server software spends most of its time changing between accepting requests, issuing reads or writes to satisfy them, reacting to completions of those reads and writes, and sending the results back to the requester.

The application/server protocol just described is the **client/server protocol** discussed in Chapter 5. To understand the importance of the multithreading capability of the server, consider the following example of single-threading versus multithreading. Suppose you went to a restaurant and your waitperson could wait on you only when all tables ahead of you

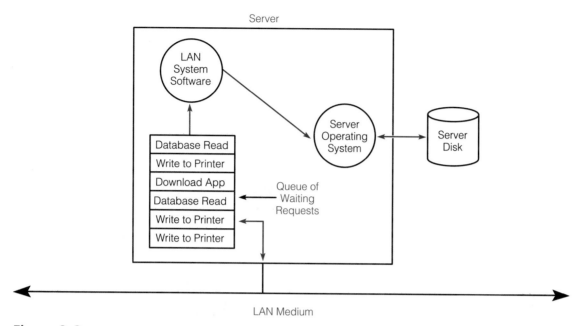

Figure 8–3
Server Request Queue

were done. You would end up waiting a long time before getting service, but the service would be great when you finally got it. However, the wait-person would have large amounts of idle time waiting for the food to be cooked. In a fast-food restaurant, you may be willing to wait for the person ahead of you in line to be served before placing your order. Likewise, in a small LAN such a service protocol might work well; however, a larger LAN may have multiple concurrent requests, so the use of multithreading becomes essential.

We now look at the LAN system software in more detail. We discuss the software components and explore how each component becomes involved in handling a server request.

LAN WORKSTATION SOFTWARE

LAN workstation software can also be divided into three classes: application software, workstation system software, and LAN system software. LAN workstation software is simple compared to server software, but do not expect this to continue. The simplicity of today's environment results from workstations being primarily single-application, single-user systems in which the workstation is doing only one thing at a time. This means that the LAN workstation software can be single-threaded. As workstations become more powerful, you can expect the associated software to also become more powerful to fully exploit the hardware. We limit our discussion to the current workstation environment.

Workstation Software Interface

We use computers as tools to solve problems. Application software has the logic necessary for solving specific problems, but it does not do all the work essential to the problem solution; instead it relies on system software to perform hardware-oriented tasks such as interfacing with disk drives and printers. Applications make requests to system software, which then assists the applications in carrying out their work. System software support may come from workstation system software or LAN system software, depending on the application's needs. Workstation system software assists with local requests and LAN system software assists with requests needing LAN services.

If you have experience with a programming language, you may be familiar with procedures that contain the logic to perform a certain kind of processing. You pass input to a procedure, and it carries out the necessary processing on the input and returns output. For example, a procedure called FINDMAXIMUM accepts a list of numbers as input and returns the largest value in the list. When you invoke the procedure, you are making a request. The procedure acts on your request and returns the results. It is not important that you know how the procedure arrived at its conclusion, only that the conclusion is correct. Similarly, when you make a read or write request to a disk drive, you do not write directly to the disk. Instead, you pass data to the OS, which carries out this activity on your behalf.

interrupt A signal issued by hardware or an application requesting a service from the operating system.

When an application requests a service from the OS, it does so by issuing a signal called an **interrupt.** A computer's OS recognizes many interrupts, some generated by application software and some generated by the hardware. Each interrupt reflects a different class of service. The LAN system software reacts to the interrupt and decides whether it is a LAN request or a local request. Thus, the interrupt generated by the application must match those that are expected by the LAN software.

Today, most widely used software packages can run on a LAN; however, some applications operate correctly on one LAN implementation but not on a different one. This can happen because some application software is written specifically for one type of LAN and generates the proper interrupts only for that LAN's software. When selecting software that is compatible with your hardware and LAN software, you also must determine whether the software will run on the LAN you will be using and whether it will support concurrent users.

Workstation System Software

The LAN system software basically consists of two parts: One part interfaces with the applications and the OS, and one part interfaces with the network hardware.

The portion of the software that interfaces with the applications, the redirector, is responsible for handling the application's interrupts. The application generally is not aware that the device it is reading from or writing to is a LAN device. This means that each potential LAN service interrupt must be acted on. The LAN redirector therefore accepts all such interrupts, whether they are for local or remote requests. Local requests are sent to the OS, and network requests are passed to the medium-oriented portion of the LAN system software.

Workstations connected to the LAN may use different versions of OSs. In one LAN system, some workstations may use a version of Microsoft Windows, some may use DOS, some may use OS/2, some may use Apple DOS, and some may use a version of UNIX. The software for a heterogeneous system must be able to accommodate each of these versions and the interrupts they expect. Inability to do so limits the OSs that can be used and thus limits which workstations can be used.

The medium-interface portion of the LAN workstation software has two basic functions: placing data onto the network and receiving data from the network. This portion of the software is responsible for formatting a message block for transmission over the network. It is closely tied to the LAN server software because it must format message blocks so they are compatible with what is expected by the server, and the workstation software must be able to recognize the format of messages received from the server. The data communication software also interfaces directly to the LAN adapter card.

SPECIFICS OF SERVER SOFTWARE

As previously stated, server software is more complex than workstation software, because server software is usually multithreaded and because the software must work well with the hardware to provide efficient service. We have already discussed the benefits and general strategy of multithreading. Now we consider several other functions that might be found in LAN server system software.

Server Operating Systems

Two basic approaches are taken in creating server software. One approach is to integrate the server and OS functions into one complete software package. The other approach is to write LAN functions that run under an existing OS, such as UNIX or OS/2. Each approach has advantages and disadvantages. Table 8–1 lists several leading LAN OSs.

Table 8–1 Leading LAN Operating Systems

LAN OS	Vendor	Topology	Protocol(s)
NetWare	Novell	Bus, ring, star	CSMA/CD or token passing
Warp Server	IBM	Ring, bus	CSMA/CD or token passing
Windows NT	Microsoft	Ring, bus, star	CSMA/CD or token passing
Apple Talk	Apple	Bus	CSMA/CA
LANtastic	Artisoft	Bus, star	CSMA/CD
TOPS	Sun Microsystems	Bus, star	CSMA/CD
VMS	Digital Equipment Corp.	Bus, star	CSMA/CD
Vines	Banyan Systems	Bus, ring, star	CSMA/CD or token passing

Novell's NetWare and Microsoft's Windows NT are leading examples of the integrated software approach. The primary advantage of this approach is that the designers can optimize the software for LAN operation. The system is designed specifically to provide server functions and can be custom-tailored for that purpose. The disadvantage is that this approach requires writing complex software that may already be provided by an existing OS. This makes the development effort longer and the maintenance more complex.

Creating LAN software that runs under an existing OS overcomes the disadvantages cited for the integrated approach. Examples of LAN software that run under an existing OS are Banyan Vines, which runs under UNIX, and IBM's Warp Server, which runs under OS/2. The disadvantages are that a general-purpose OS may be less efficient than one designed to carry out only the special functions required for LAN services.

Some OSs, such as MS-DOS, are not well suited for hosting a LAN, primarily because of their inherent memory limitations, single-user orientation, and lack of security provisions. Despite these limitations, some LAN software runs under DOS and is successful in supporting LANs with few workstations or with limited server requirements. The OSs that most often host LAN software are UNIX and OS/2.

First we look at some functions you might find in a LAN OS. Then we look briefly at specific LAN OSs by Novell, IBM, and Banyan. The other OS options listed in Table 8–1 are competitive with those systems, although we do not discuss them in detail here.

LAN OS Functions

A LAN OS provides a variety of special capabilities. Among these are I/O optimization and fault tolerance.

I/O optimization A variety of ways to optimize the task of file access, which improves the performance of the server.

Optimized I/O   A primary service provided by a server is file access. Optimizing this task, or **I/O optimization,** increases the performance of the server. Some optimization methods are hardware oriented and some are software oriented. One commonly used technique is called disk caching, which we discussed in Chapter 6.

disk seek enhancement An I/O optimization technique that reduces the head movement during seeks and improves performance.

Another I/O optimization technique is **disk seek enhancement.** A disk read requires that the read/write heads be positioned to the proper disk location. The act of moving the read/write heads is called a seek. The place to which the heads are moved is called a cylinder or track. Disk requests typically arrive in random order. Disk seek enhancement arranges the requests in order so the read/write heads move methodically over the disk, reading data from the nearest location, as illustrated in Table 8–2. In Table 8–2(a) you can see the order in which several disk requests are received. Table 8–2(b) shows the optimum way to access those records and the savings in number of cylinders when processing the requests in the optimum order. Reducing the number of seeks improves performance.

Fault Tolerance   Some network operating systems (NOSs) provide increased reliability through a feature called fault tolerance. If you have only

Table 8–2 Disk Seek Enhancement

(a) Disk read requests (cylinder or track) in order of arrival 50, 250, 25, 300, 250, 50, 300	Number of cylinders moved (assume a starting position of cylinder 0) 50 + 200 + 225 + 275 + 50 + 200 + 250 =1250
(b) Disk read requests (cylinder or track) in optimal order 25, 50, 50, 250, 250, 300, 300	25 + 25 + 0 + 200 + 0+ 50 + 0 = 300
Savings = 950 cylinders	

one server and it fails, the network is down. A LAN with fault tolerance allows the server to survive some failures that ordinarily would be disabling. Fault tolerance is usually provided by a combination of backup hardware components and software capable of using the backup hardware.

The lowest level of fault tolerance is the ability to recover quickly from a failure. This means that a failure that shuts the server down may occur, but the system can quickly be recovered to an operational state. One technique that makes this possible involves writing backup copies of critical disk information—disk directories, file allocation tables, and so on—to an alternative disk drive. Another helpful technique is called **read-after-write.** After writing data to a disk, the system reads the data again to ensure that no disk write errors occurred. If the data cannot be read again, the area of the disk containing that data is removed from future use and the data is written to a good area of the disk.

Fault tolerance can also be provided by **mirrored disks,** which are two disks that contain the same data. Whenever a disk write occurs, the data is written to both disk drives. If one disk fails, the other is available and processing continues. Mirrored disks have an additional benefit: Two disk drives are available so both disks can work simultaneously on behalf of two different requests. For added support some LAN servers also allow duplexed disk controllers. In this configuration, if a controller fails, another is available to continue working. Thus, you can survive a controller failure and a disk failure.

Mirrored disk reliability can be extended using **redundant arrays of independent disks (RAID).** RAID technology spreads data over three or more disk drives. The stored data consists of the actual data plus **parity data** (additional data that provides the ability to reconstruct data that has been corrupted). If one drive fails, the data stored on that drive can be reconstructed from data stored on the remaining drives. Parity data can be reconstructed because the remaining parts of the file are still available. If a section of the file is lost, it can be reconstructed from the parity data and the remaining parts of the file. The advantage of RAID over mirroring is that fewer disk drives are required for redundancy. With mirroring, two drives of data require four disk drives; with RAID, the same information can be stored on three drives with the same level of reliability. Disk mirroring and RAID technology,

read-after-write A fault tolerance technique in which the system reads the data again after it has been written to a disk to ensure that no disk write errors occurred.

mirrored disks A fault tolerance technique in which two disks containing the same data are provided so that if one fails, the other is available, allowing processing to continue.

redundant arrays of independent disks (RAID) A fault-tolerant disk storage technique that spreads one file plus the file's checksum information over several disk drives. If any single disk drive fails, the data stored thereon can be reconstructed from data stored on the remaining drives.

parity data In RAID technology, additional data that provides the ability to reconstruct data that has been corrupted.

illustrated in Figure 8–4, can provide more efficient data access because multiple disk drives are available for reading and writing.

duplexed servers The fault tolerance technique in which one server can fail and another is available to continue working.

The best fault tolerance is provided by **duplexed servers.** With this configuration one server can fail and another is available to continue working. Even though it appears that this fault tolerance capability is primarily hardware oriented, the software must be able to take advantage of the duplexed hardware. A duplexed server is illustrated in Figure 8–5. Fault tolerance has been provided commercially by large systems since 1977. Fault tolerance features are currently available in most leading NOSs.

clustering A fault tolerance technique in which multiple servers assume the workload of a failed server.

A new fault-tolerant capability is **clustering.** Fault-tolerant clustering has been implemented using Microsoft's Windows NT. If one server in a cluster of servers fails, the remaining servers assume the workload of the failed server. The ultimate goal of server clustering is to provide load balancing and failover capability. Failover is the ability of remaining cluster servers to assume the workload of a failed server in the cluster.

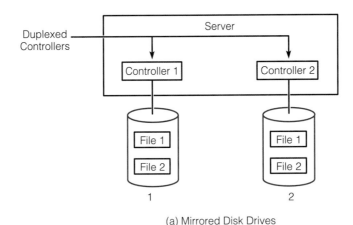

(a) Mirrored Disk Drives

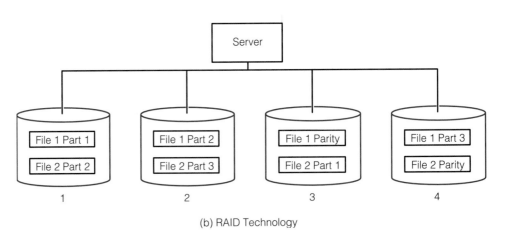

(b) RAID Technology

Figure 8–4
Mirrored Disk Drives and RAID Technology

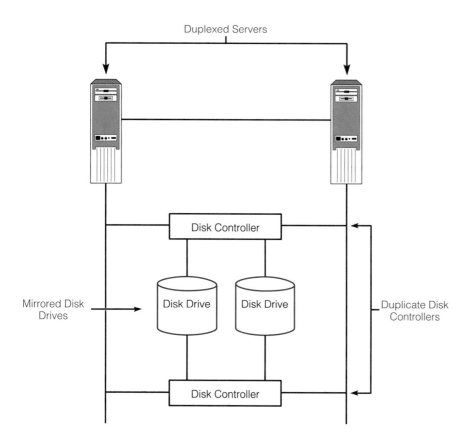

Figure 8–5
Duplexed Servers

PRINT SPOOLER

LAN users share LAN printers. It may be obvious that only one user can be physically printing to a printer at one time, yet several users may need to logically write to one printer at the same time. Logically writing to a printer means the user has opened a printer and has written to that printer; however, the printed output may not be physically written to the printer at that time. The output is first written to a disk file and is printed after the complete output has been collected. The software subsystem that allows several users to logically write to one printer at the same time is called a **spooler.** The operation of a spooler is shown in Figure 8–6. Let us trace the activity of a print job through the spooler.

A user at one workstation is using a word processing program to create a report, and a user at another workstation is using a spreadsheet program to prepare a budget. At nearly the same time, each user prints the document he or she is working on. The output is directed to LPT2 on each system. On each system, LPT2 is mapped by the network software to a laser printer attached to the server. Before writing to the printer, each application first opens the printer. The redirector at each system directs the open request to the server. When the server receives the printer open request, it is passed to the spooler software. The spooler software prepares to receive

spooler A software system that collects printer output (typically on disk) and schedules the data for printing. *Spool* is an acronym for *simultaneous peripheral operation online.*

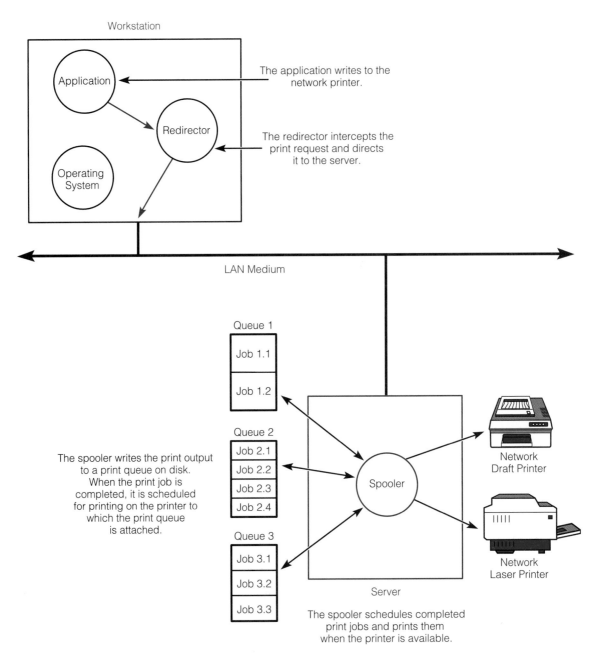

Figure 8–6
Spooler Operation

each workstation's printed output into a disk file. When each application receives an acknowledgment that the printer has been successfully opened, it begins to send output to the printer.

The spooler receives the output from each workstation and stores the output in that workstation's print file on disk. This process continues until

Table 8–3   Spooler Options

Collect printed output	Attach/detach printers from print queue
Direct print jobs to designated printers	Set/change job priorities
Hold jobs in disk queue after printing	Add/delete printers
Hold jobs in disk queue before printing	Start/stop printers
View jobs on hold in print queue	Start/stop spooler process
Set number of print copies	Print banners
Set print job priorities	Close print jobs based on timeout interval
Delete jobs from print queue	Print statistical reports

each workstation is finished. When the application closes the printer file, the print job is ready to be physically written to the printer.

Be aware that some applications, such as some versions of Lotus 1-2-3, do not close the print file until the user explicitly chooses a close printer option or until the application terminates. If this occurs, a user may not get a printout when expected. Suppose Maria is working on a spreadsheet and prints a portion of it. If the printing had been sent to a locally attached printer, it would print immediately. With a spooler, however, the spreadsheet program does not close the printer, and the job is left open. This allows another portion of the spreadsheet to be printed directly after the first print range. The spreadsheet program continues to hold the file open until Maria exits from the spreadsheet. Her job is then scheduled for printing. In this case, printing on a LAN differs from printing to a local printer and may not be what Maria needs. She may want the range to be printed immediately so she can use that information for further work. For such instances, some spoolers also allow the print job to be closed if a certain time elapses before they receive additional print data. This feature allows the user to obtain the printed results without exiting from the application.

When a print job has been closed, the spooler schedules the job for printing. Spoolers have a priority scheme by which they decide which job prints next. Some spoolers print the jobs in the order in which they became ready to print (first in, first out); some print the smallest available job; others print jobs according to user-assigned priorities. When the job has been printed, it may be removed from the disk to make room for other print jobs. Alternatively, the job may be held on disk for printing at a later time, for printing to a different device, or for perusal from a workstation. Spooler systems provide a variety of options regarding the association of logical print devices with physical printers and the treatment of jobs captured in the spooler files. Some of these options are listed in Table 8–3.

BACKUP SOFTWARE

In Chapter 6 we discussed backup hardware. The software used to perform the backups is as important as the hardware. **Backup software** is responsible for reading the files being backed up and writing them to the backup device. During recovery, a restoration module reads the backup medium and writes the data back to disk. Several backup software options are available.

backup software Software that is responsible for reading the files being backed up and writing them to the backup device.

Table 8–4 Backup Software Capabilities

Back up all files	Create new index on tape and disk
Back up all files modified since a particular date	Maintain cross-reference of serial numbers and backup
Back up by directory	Manual backup
Back up by list of files	Automatic backup by time or calendar
Back up all but a list of files to be excluded	Start backup from workstation or server
Back up by index	Data compression
Back up by interface to a database	Multivolume backup
Back up using wildcard characters in filenames	Generate reports

They all provide the basic functions of backing up and restoring data. However, they differ with respect to backup and restoration procedure, including the options they provide, the devices they support, and their ease of use. Backup devices often come with a backup/restore program (both capabilities are contained on one program), and most LAN system software includes a backup/restore module. Novell's backup/restore program for one version of their network software is NBACKUP. Some LAN administrators choose to purchase a separate, more functional backup system than the LAN or backup device version. Table 8–4 lists some features supported by backup software.

SOFTWARE REQUIREMENTS FOR SHARED USAGE

Most early microcomputer applications were written for single-user systems, which means that software developers could make certain simplifying design decisions. To use these applications in a shared LAN system, accommodations must be made by the LAN administrators, the LAN system software, or the application itself. Let us now consider the required changes.

Hardware Configuration

Software written for a single user need not be concerned with problems of computer configuration. You are probably aware that microcomputers may be configured with a variety of options. The primary variations are in memory, disk configuration, printer configuration, and monitor support. In a stand-alone system the application software is set up to match the configuration of that system. However, a LAN might have many different workstation configurations, and application software should support each configuration as much as possible.

Some applications support only one configuration. The hardware settings of such applications are stored in a single file. One way to use this type of application is to configure the application for the lowest common denominator of hardware and have each user get essentially the same configuration. Users with high-resolution color graphics monitors might have images displayed in monochrome at low resolution, or a user with a hard disk drive might have to use a floppy disk drive rather than the hard disk for some files. Usually LAN administrators can avoid this type of configuration by storing multiple versions of the application in different disk directories. Users can then use the configuration that most closely matches their computer's profile.

Some applications allow several configuration files and decide which to use by a run-time parameter or by making a default choice if the startup parameter is not specified. LAN administrators can provide each user with a tailored environment using a batch startup file.

Applications designed for LAN use usually have a user-oriented configuration file. Each LAN user has his or her personal configuration that is custom-tailored for the specific user and the specific hardware. This provides users with the most flexibility and requires little or no customization by the LAN administrator. These options are listed in Table 8–5.

Application Settings

The software equivalents to hardware configurations are application settings. Ideally, users tailor application settings to meet personal preferences. One user may prefer his or her word processor application to display green characters on a black background with tabs at every five character positions. Another user might prefer white characters on a blue background with tabs at every four character positions. Each user should receive these settings as the default. Application settings can be defined in a way similar to setting hardware options.

Contention

You learned a little about contention in Chapters 3 and 7. Remember that whenever two users can access the same resource at the same time, contention for that resource can occur. Similar problems occur when accessing files.

A classic contention problem is illustrated by two users working on one document at the same time. The same type of problem can occur when two users access and update the same database record. A primitive way to handle contention is simply to avoid it by scheduling user activities so they do not interfere with each other. On small LANs this may be possible, but as the

Table 8–5   User Configuration Options

Default disk drive	Disk drive/directory search paths
Default disk directory	Printer mappings
Disk drive mappings	Initial program/menu

exclusive open mode A mode in which an open request is granted only if no other user has the file opened already.

protected open mode A mode that is granted only if no other user has already been granted exclusive or protected mode.

shared open mode A mode that allows several users to have a file open concurrently.

lock Record- or file-level control that overcomes the problem with file open contention.

number of concurrent users increases, this method becomes clumsy. Rather than avoiding contention, an application or LAN software should prevent contention problems by exerting controls over files or records.

One prevention mechanism is activated when an application opens a file. The three basic file open modes are exclusive, protected, and shared. In **exclusive open mode,** an open request is granted only if no other user already has the file open. File open requests from other users also are denied until the application having an exclusive open closes the file.

Exclusive opens may be too restrictive for some applications. Suppose two users, Alice and Tom, are both working on the same word processing document. Alice needs to update the document, and Tom only needs to read it. In this case Tom will not interfere with Alice's work. A **protected open mode** can satisfy both users' needs. Protected open mode is granted only if no other user has already been granted exclusive or protected mode. Once a file is open in protected mode, only the application with protected open can update the document. **Shared open mode** allows several users to have the file open concurrently. In shared update mode, all users can update the file. In shared read-only mode, all users can read the file but cannot write to it. If Alice opens the document in protected mode and Tom opens the document in shared read-only mode, Alice can read and update the document but Tom can only read it. Furthermore, Tom cannot open the document in exclusive, protected, or shared update mode while a protected open exists.

Sometimes a read-only application must be protected against file updates. An application that is doing a trial balance of an accounting file must prohibit updates during the reading and calculations. If another application makes changes while the file is being read, the figures may not balance. The trial-balance application can protect against this by opening the accounts file in protected read-only mode. This prevents other processes from opening the file in update mode while allowing them to open the file in shared read-only mode. Table 8–6 shows the combinations of exclusive, protected, and shared open modes.

Exclusive and protected open modes are sufficient for meeting some contention problems, such as our word processing example. However, they are overly restrictive for other applications, such as database processing. One objective of database applications is to help several users share data. Exclusive opens allow only one user at a time to use the data. The problem with file-open contention resolution is overcome by exerting controls at a lower level, the record level. Record level controls are called **locks.**

Table 8–6 Comparison of Open Modes

Open Mode Requested	Currently Opened As			
	Exclusive	*Protected*	*Shared Update*	*Shared Read-Only*
Exclusive	Denied	Denied	Denied	Denied
Protected	Denied	Denied	Denied	Granted
Shared update	Denied	Denied	Granted	Granted
Shared read-only	Denied	Granted	Granted	Granted

Suppose Alice and Tom want to update a database. As long as they are using different records, they will not interfere with each other. However, suppose that at some time both Alice and Tom need to access and update the same record, leading to contention problems. If Alice locks the record when accessing it, Tom's read request will be denied until Alice unlocks the record. This process is illustrated in Figure 8–7. Note that Tom must wait until the record has been unlocked before being allowed to proceed.

Record locking can cause another problem: deadlock, or deadly embrace. Suppose that Alice and Tom are accessing the database. Alice's application reads and locks record A and, at nearly the same time, Tom's application reads and locks record B. After reading record A, Alice attempts to read record B and, of course, waits because the record is locked. If Tom then attempts to read record A, deadlock occurs: Alice and Tom are waiting for each other, and neither can continue until the record they are waiting for is unlocked, which can never happen because there is a circular chain of users waiting on each other. Three or more users can also be involved in this circular chain of events. The deadlock problem is illustrated in Figure 8–8. Deadlock avoidance or resolution methods exist but are beyond the scope of this text. You can read about these methods in many database texts.

Some database systems take care of contention for users. These systems recognize when contention is occurring and prevent the problems associated with it. One convention used to do this is outlined as follows:

1. User A reads record X.
2. User B reads record X (and the read is allowed).
3. User A updates record X (and the update is allowed).
4. User B attempts to update record X.
5. The DBMS recognizes that the record has been changed since user B read it.

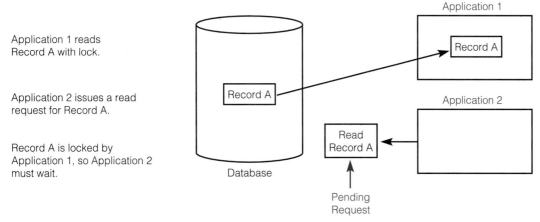

Figure 8–7
Record Locking and Accessibility

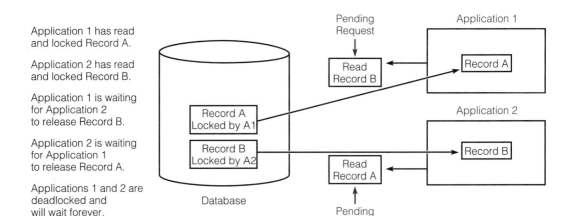

Application 1 has read and locked Record A.

Application 2 has read and locked Record B.

Application 1 is waiting for Application 2 to release Record B.

Application 2 is waiting for Application 1 to release Record A.

Applications 1 and 2 are deadlocked and will wait forever.

Figure 8–8
Deadlock

6. The DBMS sends the revised copy of record X to user B and notifies the user that the update was rejected because the record was changed by another user.

7. User B reissues the update or takes another course of action.

In selecting LAN software, it is critical that you understand the problems of configuration and contention. If these issues are not resolved the effectiveness of the system is reduced or, worse yet, the data becomes corrupted. Sharing data has another side effect that must be addressed: security.

Access Security

access security Security that controls a user's access to data. The controls may regulate a user's ability to read and update data, to delete files, and to run programs.

Early OSs, and many current ones for stand-alone microcomputers, do not provide file security. Even though only one user can use a microcomputer at one time, several users might use one system. Without **access security** these users not only have access to another user's sensitive data, but also might accidentally (or intentionally) remove another user's files. Access to the computer essentially provides access to all data stored on that computer. Users might store sensitive data on a stand-alone microcomputer's disks, but those users are limited with respect to their ability to protect that data from unauthorized reading, changes, or destruction. Instead, a user could store data on a removable disk and store it in a secure place when it is not being used. Another alternative is buying an application that provides password security or allows hiding or encrypting data to protect it from misuse. When you install a LAN, data that must be shared and was once stored as private data on one or more stand-alone systems is likely to be placed in a database on a server. Without security, all data on the servers can be accessed, updated, and deleted by any LAN user. For most applications this is not acceptable. Therefore, the LAN system software must provide protection through security.

Other security concerns include protecting against software piracy and preventing the introduction of computer viruses. We discuss security in more detail in Chapter 19.

SOFTWARE LICENSE AGREEMENTS

One of the most important things to know about your software is its **license agreement.** Virtually all software you buy is covered by a license agreement. This is true for both system and application software. The license agreement covers the rules under which you are allowed to use the product. It is a way of protecting both the manufacturer and the user of the product. To better understand the need for license agreements, we first look at an analogy.

license agreement An agreement that covers the rules under which you are allowed to use a product.

Consider the books you purchased for school, which probably were rather expensive. Of course, the publisher does not pay nearly that much to print the book. Part of your book price goes to profit, but the publisher also incurs other expenses. One or more authors worked many hours to write the material, editors worked many hours with the authors to develop the format and content, designers laid out the style (graphics and page formats), marketing analysts determined a marketing strategy and created advertising brochures, and the sales force was told about the book, its target markets, and key selling points. All of this activity required a considerable investment. Some books never become popular and the publishing company loses money on them. Others become very popular and the publishing company makes a profit. Some of that profit is used to offset losses on other projects. Now, suppose someone decides to illegally reprint a text and sell the successful books. With today's technology, it does not cost much just to print these copies. This person can sell the copies for much less than the publisher because he or she has not had to make the investment of developing the work, paying the salaries of editors and production workers, the royalties to the developers, and so on.

Patent and copyright laws are intended to protect the investment of designers, artists, filmmakers, authors, publishing companies, and so on. Software companies also make a sizable investment in creating application or system software. System analysts design the product, programmers write and debug the code, marketing analysts create a marketing plan, advertising campaigns are developed and implemented, manuals are created, a support organization is staffed and trained, and the product is brought to market.

Several years probably elapsed from the time the product was conceived to the point at which it was ready to sell and make a profit. Thousands of dollars were probably spent before there was any opportunity to sell the software. In addition, once a software product is released, expenses continue. Support staff must be paid and new enhancements designed. As with illegal book printing, the gain from all this effort can be eroded by illegal copying. To give you an idea of the magnitude of this problem, at the end of the 1980s several software piracy shops in Hong Kong were raided. Some estimated the annual loss of revenues to software companies resulting from software piracy in one building alone to be hundreds of millions of dollars.

Software vendors must therefore take steps to protect their investment. Like books, pictures, films, and fashion designs, software can be illegally copied and sold. Software is protected in six basic ways:

- The code is kept secret so other software houses cannot use special algorithms developed by the company to write a competing system.
- The code is copyrighted to prevent another company from copying the code and writing a competing system.
- The software is copy protected to deter the making of illegal copies.
- The software requires a special hardware device to run.
- License agreements are used to establish the terms of ownership and use.
- Legislation penalizing those who do not adhere to the copyright and license restrictions is enacted.

The first two of these measures protect the source code from being used by someone else. During development, it is common to keep the source code of software secret. However, after the product has been released, it is always possible to derive the source code, even if the software is released only in object code format. Deriving the source code from object code is done through reverse engineering. To protect themselves from reverse engineering, software manufacturers usually copyright their software. Copyright laws, originally intended to cover writing, films, and works of art, have been extended to include software. New legislation also has been enacted to further define the restrictions and penalties for unauthorized software copying.

Each of these measures is rather clear; most people understand and observe the rules. However, the remaining two issues—copy protection and license agreements—are less standard and directly involve how the software is used. Software piracy has always been a problem, even before the introduction of microcomputers. With minicomputers and mainframe systems, software piracy is easier to detect and hence its incidence is negligible compared to its occurrence on microcomputers. There are two good reasons for easier detection of large system software piracy. First, large computers are used by large organizations with professional data processing departments. Software piracy is difficult to hide in such organizations, and ordinarily anyone found using pirated software is subject to dismissal and the company is subject to lawsuits. Second, large computer sites typically work closely with the software vendor's personnel. The vendor's employees are aware of the software its customers are authorized to use, and it is easy to detect the presence of unauthorized software. Easy piracy detection is not the case with microcomputer software.

A few software companies protect their software by requiring the use of a special hardware device that attaches to a serial or parallel port. The device and an application work together to provide application security. When started, the application attempts to read data encoded in the device. If the device is not attached, the application terminates. One disadvantage to this approach is that a user may have several applications, each of which need a different device. Because the number of serial or parallel ports is limited, changing from one application to another may require changing the device. Other companies have accomplished somewhat the same effect by requiring a key disk. The **key disk** is usually a floppy disk that must be in a disk drive when the application is run. The application uses the key disk only to verify the disk's presence. This technique is seldom used today and, of course, cannot be used with diskless systems.

key disk A security system in which a flexible disk must be in the disk drive when the application is run.

Originally many microcomputer software vendors used copy protection to deter software piracy. The software diskette was encoded to prevent copying using standard OS copy facilities such as DOS's COPY or DISKCOPY commands. In general, copy protection only gave rise to a new software industry; software to allow copying of copy-protected software. Of course, vendors of such software were careful to point out that the sole purpose of their software was to make a backup copy and not to make illegal duplicate copies. Many companies that once used copy protection have abandoned that means because it proved ineffective. Instead of or in addition to copy protection, software vendors now rely on copyright protection together with software license agreements.

When you buy software, both application software and LAN system software, often the diskettes that hold the software are sealed in an envelope. Written on or attached to the envelope is text regarding the license agreement and a message that opening and using the software is a commitment to adhere to the stipulations of that license agreement. The license agreement states the conditions under which you are allowed to use the product.

In essence, when you buy software, you do not get ownership of that product; you are simply given the right to use the product. An attorney might quibble with this statement, but the basic premise is correct. Some license agreements explicitly state that you own the diskette but not the contents of the diskette. This means that you cannot make copies of the software to give to your friends, you may not be able to run it on several workstations at the same time, you may not reverse engineer it to produce source code for modification or resale, and so on. Your rights to the software are limited to using the software in the intended manner. If you like, you can destroy the software, cease to use it, sell it, or give it as a gift. In the last two cases you also transfer the license agreement to the recipient. Some software vendors go so far as to state that transferring the software must be approved by the software vendor. In some cases the software license covers the use of the accompanying documentation as well.

One of the problems with license agreements is that there are no standards. If you buy two different applications, you are liable to find two different license agreements. To protect yourself and your organization from civil and criminal suits, you must understand the provisions of each agreement. Several companies and a major state university have been investigated for illegally copying software, have been found guilty of the offense, and have been heavily fined. It is important that users respect license agreements. We look at some general licensing provisions, namely

- single user, single workstation
- restricted number of concurrent users
- site license
- single user, multiple workstation
- server license
- corporate license

Single User, Single Workstation

Single-user, single-workstation license agreements are the most restrictive. They specify that the software is to be used on one workstation only and by only one person at a time. If you have a multiuser microcomputer, only one user can run the software at any time. In most instances, restricting the software to only one machine also implies a single user.

This license agreement also means that if an office has two or more computers, a separate copy of the software must be purchased for each machine on which the software is to be used. If you have two employees, one on a day shift and one on a night shift, using the same software but on different workstations, each needs a licensed copy of the software. In this situation, the software is never used concurrently, yet two copies are required. One of the ways in which software vendors enforce this policy is through the software installation procedure. The install process counts the number of installations. When you install the product the counter is decremented to zero and you are not able to install the program on another system. To move the software to another system you must uninstall the software. The uninstall process removes the application from the computer's disks and increments the installation count. Another method used to enforce a single-user, single-workstation license is the requirement for a key disk described earlier.

Single User, Multiple Workstation

This type of license agreement relaxes the constraints of the single-user, single-workstation agreement. It usually also relies on the honor system for enforcement. Software vendors that use this agreement recognize that different people may want to use the software and at different workstations, such as in the office and on a portable computer. The purchase of a single copy of the software allows the owner to install it on several systems. However, the license restricts use of the software to one user at a time per software copy. Suppose an office with ten workstations must do word processing. Each of ten employees can use the word processor, but only five employees can use the product concurrently. With this license agreement, the company can buy five copies of the software and install them on ten different systems. As long as five or fewer employees use the word processing application at any one time, the company has lived up to the license provisions. Note that it is possible for six users to inadvertently use the application at the same time, in violation of the license agreement.

Restricted Number of Concurrent Users

On a LAN it is common for several users to run an application concurrently. Three employees may be doing word processing, 10 may be using the spreadsheet software, and 25 may be using the database software. With file or database server technology, only one copy of each application is on the server's disks. Most LAN-compatible software is inherently designed for multiple users; however, some software vendors place restrictions on the number of concurrent users. The main idea behind this strategy is to charge by the number of users.

Consider the database needs of the company just mentioned, where the maximum number of concurrent database users is 25. The database vendor has a license agreement that allows 10 concurrent users for a certain fee. The company also has an expansion policy that allows additional concurrent users to be added in groups of 10 with an additional fee for each such group. The company must purchase three modules to satisfy its need for 25 concurrent users. This type of license is typically enforced by a meter program that controls the concurrent use of the application. When a user starts the application, the meter program increments a counter by 1. When a user exits the application, the counter is decremented by 1. If the license agreement is for 30 users, a user can run the application as long as the counter is 29 or fewer. If the counter is 30, a user requesting the application receives an error message indicating that the application is not available.

Server License

A **server license** allows an application to be installed on one server. All users attached to that server may use the application. If a company has three servers and wants to use the application on each of them, the company must purchase three licenses or three copies of the software.

server license A license that allows an application to be installed on one server.

Site License

A **site license** gives the user unlimited rights to use the software at a given site. The site may be a single LAN or multiple LANs at one location.

site license A license that gives the user unlimited rights to use the software at a given site.

Corporate License

A **corporate license** gives a corporation unlimited use of the software at all locations. Some companies restrict a corporate license to all locations within one country. Sometimes the right to reproduce documentation is also granted.

corporate license A license that gives a corporation unlimited use of software at all locations.

The license agreement is intended primarily to protect the rights of the manufacturer. However, the holder of a license agreement also has certain rights, which may include the following:

- The owner can transfer or assign the license to another user.
- The owner can get a refund if the product is defective or does not work as stated.
- Legal rights may be granted by certain states or countries regarding the exclusion of liability for losses or damage resulting from the use of the software.
- The user can terminate the license by destroying the software and documentation.

When selecting your application and system software, you must take care to understand fully all the conditions of the license agreements. You want each user to have the necessary software services available. Different license and pricing policies among competing products can result in substantial differences in availability to you or cost to your company.

NOVELL OPERATING SYSTEMS

Over time Novell has offered several versions of NOSs. Today, Novell offers three basic systems with a variety of configuration options for two of the versions. For high-end networks Novell offers NetWare 3.x and NetWare 4.x. For small networks using peer-to-peer workstations, Novell offers Personal NetWare.

peer-to-peer LAN A LAN in which any or all nodes can operate as servers.

In a **peer-to-peer LAN,** any or all nodes can operate as servers. If five microcomputers are networked in a peer-to-peer LAN, the network administrator can designate which computer resources are shareable and which are not. On one computer, a laser printer may be shared but a dot-matrix printer may be private to the user of that system. The computer's hard disk drive and one floppy disk drive may be shared but a second floppy disk drive may be private. All of the computers in this network are primary workstations for a user. Thus, the activities of a user can directly affect other users. If a user powers down the computer, its resources are not available to other users, and if a user's program gets caught in a loop, that computer's resources are not available to other users. Some peer-to-peer NOSs allow you to designate each node as client only, server only, or both. A peer-to-peer LAN is used primarily when there are few LAN workstations. The main benefit of peer-to-peer networks is the low cost per node, usually less than $200 for both hardware and software. Two disadvantages of peer-to-peer LANs are that centralized network management is more difficult and fewer capabilities are provided for linking to other networks than are typically found in server-based LANs.

Personal NetWare (PNW) An NOS for small workgroups who simply want to share applications and printers.

Personal NetWare (PNW) debuted as NetWare Lite. Its primary attributes are simplicity, reasonable flexibility, and the ability to share files, printers, modems, and CD-ROMs. For small workgroups who simply want to share applications and printers, PNW is a good low-cost option. On the other hand, PNW lacks security capabilities, fault tolerance, management tools, and some of the capabilities we have come to expect of NOSs.

NetWare 3.x

NetWare 3.x (formerly known as NetWare 386) and **NetWare 4.x** are Novell's server-based NOS offerings. NetWare 4.x is newer than 3.x, but NetWare 4.x at the outset was not marketed as a direct replacement for NetWare 3.x. Both products are actively marketed and supported. The primary difference between the two NOSs is the way in which network information is stored. NetWare 3.x uses a server-oriented bindery and 4.x uses a network-oriented directory. Eventually, NetWare 3.x will probably be phased out.

The NetWare 3.x network information database is called the bindery. The bindery consists of three files that contain the names of objects (such as users, print queues, and groups), properties of objects, and values associated with those properties. For example, for a group object we might have a property called *members* and multiple values for members of that group. The bindery is server-centric. This means that it primarily contains data specific to that server. Thus, if a user needed to have access to two servers, that user would have a user entry in the bindery of each server; furthermore, on each server would be values for the properties of that user, such as passwords. The information stored on the different servers is not synchronized. This can result in unnecessary duplication and inconsistency in the user's stored data. Also, if a user were allowed to use 10 servers, 10 separate entries would need to be made, one for each server. In contrast, in a network directory, only one entry would be required. NetWare 3.x is well suited to LANs with one or two servers. As the number of servers increases, the effectiveness of NetWare 3.x decreases.

Lack of a network directory makes NetWare 3.x less suitable for large networks; however, for smaller networks, it provides a robust set of capabilities enhanced by a vast collection of third-party hardware and software. Let us now look at some of the specifics of NetWare 3.x.

A single server can support up to 16 printers in a variety of configurations. The print server process that runs in the NetWare 3.x server can support at most 16 printer definitions, and only one print server can be running on a server at a time. Printers may be directly attached to the server, attached to dedicated printer server systems, or attached to a nondedicated print server. A dedicated print server system does nothing but control printers and interface to the server's print server software module. For example, some installations use outmoded computers such as 286 CPU systems as dedicated print servers. Nondedicated print servers allow printers attached to client machines to be shared among network users. The disadvantage of nondedicated printers is the ability of a user to disable network printing by turning his or her computer off or by running a program that causes the system to hang. The printer alternatives are illustrated in Figure 8–9.

The security capabilities in NetWare 3.x are superior to those provided in the previous version, NetWare 2.x. Installations that upgraded from 2.x to

NetWare 3.x and 4.x
Leading examples of the integrated LAN operating system software approach by Novell.

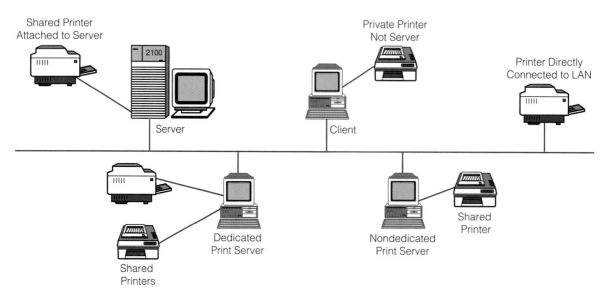

Figure 8–9
Printer Alternatives

3.x found a significant increase in security capabilities. Security provisions address file access, printer access, user requirements, and intruder detection.

When we think of security, we usually think first of controlling unauthorized users and unauthorized access to files. Every user on the system has a user ID. Security-conscious network administrators can make passwords mandatory rather than having passwords a user option. Passwords can be set up so they must be changed periodically and must have a minimum number of characters. A password history can be used to ensure that new passwords are created when the password expiration time arrives or whenever the user changes their password. File access security is based on a user, groups to which a user belongs, inherited rights, and rights given explicitly to a user. The scheme is both comprehensive and complicated.

As in many network systems, network management tools are severely lacking in NetWare 3.x but improvements in this situation are constantly being made. A variety of Novell and third-party network management utilities are available, but there is no comprehensive, coordinated management capability. Network administrators must therefore assemble a set of tools from a variety of sources to provide adequate diagnostic and monitoring capabilities. Backup and restore software are included with the system, but many installations prefer to purchase more comprehensive backup software.

NetWare 3.x allows for disk mirroring, disk duplexing, and RAID drives. It also provides read-after-write capabilities and the ability to move bad areas of the disk to another part of the disk. Disk mirroring and duplexed disks are supported. In addition, NetWare 3.x supports a transaction tracking system (TTS) that is able to restore the integrity of data files by reversing work done on transactions that do not complete successfully. Using

TTS helps avoid inconsistent data following a failure. System fault tolerance (SFT) level III, which allows server duplexing, is also available.

I/O optimization features include disk caching and elevator seeking. With elevator seeking, disk access requests are ordered according to their location on the disk. Elevator seeking allows the read/write heads to move systematically over the disk from the inner tracks to the outer tracks and back again. This prevents excessive disk seeking. Faster access to files on disk is provided via directory hashing. Hashing allows a file's location to be determined more quickly than is possible with a sequential search.

A rudimentary accounting facility is available but is generally not widely used. Accounting allows an installation to track such events as connect time, disk space used, disk reads, disk writes, and service requests. The information reported by the accounting system allows an installation to apportion costs among users or to perform basic capacity planning.

Starting with NetWare version 3.11, Novell included message handling services (MHS), which provides delivery of messages among servers. Also included as part of MHS is a basic e-mail system.

NetWare 4.x

IntraNetWare 4.11 is currently the flagship of the Novell NOS line. Naturally, the next version is already on the drawing board and should be released by the time you are reading this text. NetWare 4.x provides nearly all the capabilities of 3.x versions, although the user interfaces have changed considerably in some areas. Version 4.x also includes several important new features. As mentioned in the discussion of NetWare 3.x, the major feature that distinguishes NetWare 4.x from NetWare 3.x is the network directory called **Novell Directory Services (NDS).** In NetWare 4.0 and 4.1, NDS was called NetWare Directory Services (also NDS). Novell has made NDS available for NOSs other than NetWare, so the name change was appropriate. By making NDS available to other OSs, Novell can position its product at the heart of the network, the repository of information on the enterprise network. IntraNetWare 4.11 provided a significant extension to NetWare 4.10; these changes are discussed at the end of this section.

NDS is a global, hierarchical directory that allows replication and distribution. A sample directory tree is shown in Figure 8–10. In the sample directory tree, some objects are subordinate to other objects. Objects that can have subordinate items are called container objects. Some of the container objects defined in NetWare include Country, Organization, and Organizational Unit. Objects that cannot have subordinate objects are called leaf objects. Some of the leaf objects available in the directory are Computer, Group, Server, Print Queue, Print Server, Printer, User, and Volume. Each directory tree has a unique top-level object called the Root object or the Top. Distributed portions of the directory are called partitions. The directory uses a hierarchical naming convention, with the naming hierarchy up to 15 levels deep. Thus, a generic four-level object name in the directory might be

company-name.region-name.department-name.user-name

IntraNetWare 4.11 The current flagship of the Novell NOS line.

Novell Directory Services (NDS) The network directory that distinguishes NetWare 4.x from NetWare 3.x. In NetWare 4.0 and 4.1, NDS was called NetWare Directory Services (also NDS).

Figure 8–10
Sample Directory Tree

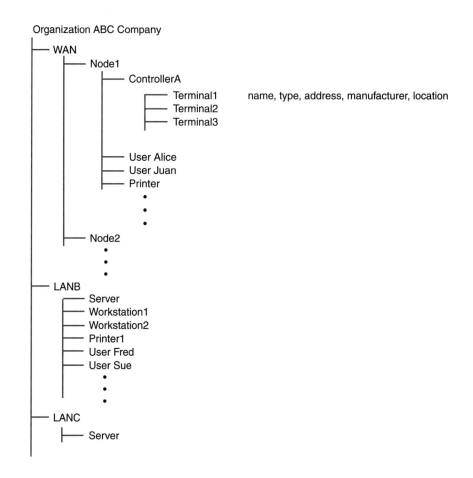

NDS is a global directory because it can span the entire enterprise network. As you will see later, some directory services are restricted to network segments. We will discuss the issues of replication and distribution in Chapter 20. The ITU X.500 standard served as a model for the implementation of NDS; however, NDS is not X.500 compliant.

Defining the directory tree is accomplished via two utilities: NWADMIN, which is a Windows application, and NETADMIN, which is a DOS-based menu application. The template for the directory definition is called the schema. The schema contains the definitions of the objects that can be included in the directory and the properties of those objects. Developers are able to extend the schema by adding new objects or new properties to existing objects. This is accomplished via **application program interface (API)** procedures available in a developers' toolkit. Some of the available objects and a partial list of the properties for each is given in Table 8–7.

There are other differences between 3.x and 4.x. One of the shortcomings of NetWare 3.x is that it is not well suited to LANs with hundreds of users. NetWare 3.x generally can support up to 250 users. A design objective of 4.x was to support LANs of up to 1000 users. The user interface in 4.x has been upgraded. Although there are still some menuing and

application program interface (API) In LANs, the interface between application programs and the network software.

Table 8–7   Sample NDS Objects and Properties

Object	Some Properties	
Computer	Network address Serial number Operator	Server Status Owner
Country (container)	Name	Description
Group	Common name Description E-mail address	Full name Members
NetWare server	Network address Operator	Status Version
Organization	Name Description Postal address	Postal code State/province Telephone number
Print server	Network address Operator	Status
Printer	Default queue Host device Network address	Operator Status
Queue	Device Network address Operator	Server Volume

User	Account balance
	Address
	E-mail address
	FAX number
	Groups
	Home directory
	Telephone number
		Language
		Last login time
		Login script
		Password expiration
		   time, change allowed,
		   unique required,
		   required, minimum
		   length
		User ID

Volume	Host server	Status

command line utilities, some graphical user interfaces (GUI) are available. GUIs make working with the network easier. Another key difference is that 4.x provides disk compression utilities that are not available with 3.x. Finally, with 4.x, Novell has provided support for symmetric multiprocessing (SMP) architectures. SMP systems have two or more CPUs that allow parallel processing and greater throughput.

The distribution CD-ROM includes a complete set of documents and document viewer. This allows the entire set of documents to be installed online. Unlike 3.x, NetWare 4.x comes with only a few manuals oriented to installation, upgrading from previous versions of NetWare, and explanation of NDS. Hard-copy documentation is available for an added cost. Navigating the online documents is easy and users can print portions of the document as needed.

NetWare 3.x's support for only 16 network printers on a network with 250 users can be a problem. In 4.x, each server can support up to 256 printers. Installing the print system in 4.x is easier than in 3.x.

NetWare 4.x generally provides all the security capabilities mentioned for NetWare 3.x, and 4.x extends those capabilities. Two significant enhancements have been provided. Perhaps the most significant is the ability to audit network activities. Users with administration privileges can disrupt the system and make unauthorized modification to files. NetWare 4.x provides an audit facility that allows a user independent of LAN administrators to monitor selected activities. A wide range of events can be selected to audit. Some of these are listed in Table 8–8. The key to the audit capability is the independence of auditing and administration. A LAN administrator is unable to see what events the auditor is monitoring and the audit data itself. Furthermore, the LAN administrator cannot delete the audit files unless the administrator is able to obtain the auditor's password. A second important security capability is the extension of security to NDS attributes. That is, a user may be given the ability to change the telephone number of a user object but be unable to view or change other attributes.

Like NetWare 3.12, the management software an installation needs will probably come from several sources. Included with NetWare 4.x are utilities for remote management that let administrators control a server from any network node. The remote management facility (RMF) allows an administrator to execute console commands, load and unload NetWare loadable modules (NLMs), and reboot a file server. An NLM is an application-oriented software module that runs in the server. Both Novell and third-party software vendors provide NLMs that are dynamically bound to or unbound from the NetWare OS while the server is operational. For example, the print server application runs as an NLM. NDS maintenance can be effected via both Microsoft Windows GUI and DOS menu interfaces. Beyond that, you need to purchase additional software, some of which is available from Novell. Novell and Intel have combined resources to provide ManageWise. ManageWise allows administrators to monitor server operations by recording information such as memory, CPU, and disk usage. It also provides information on the printing environment. Novell also sells NetWare LANalyzer, an NLM that monitors packets sent to and transmitted by a server. With LANalyzer, a network administrator can identify the type and source of protocol problems. Because the NDS is fundamental to the operation of 4.x, it is essential that tools be available for managing, maintaining, and recovering the NDS system. NDS tools are available that allow administrators to manipulate the NDS tree. Branches of the tree can be replicated and distributed and distributed branches can be merged.

Table 8–8 Sample Audit Events

Create/delete directory	File open/close/create/delete	File read/write
File rename/move	User logon/logoff	User creation/deletion
Print queue create/delete	Server down/restart	Volume mount/demount

For customers who have used or are also using NetWare 3.x servers, version 4.x provides interoperability features. Version 3.x servers use the bindery files and many software modules interface only to this form of directory. NetWare 4.x provides bindery emulation to support bindery-oriented interfaces.

NetWare 4.x provides interfaces to a variety of other networks and protocols. Included among these are

- IBM system network architecture (SNA) gateway
- X.25 gateway
- LAN-to-LAN interconnection via X.25 or T-1 lines
- structured query language (SQL) server
- Transmission Control Protocol/Internet Protocol (TCP/IP)
- remote access services
- World Wide Web server

IntraNetWare 4.11 expands on the capabilities just discussed by providing Internet protocols and capabilities. The Internet has become an important business forum and Internet tools such as browsers, hypertext documents, and the World Wide Web provide Internet with a wide array of information and services (see Chapters 13 and 14). Because of their ease of use, many companies have begun using Internet tools and protocols on private networks; such private networks are called **intranets.** With IntraNetWare 4.11, a company can use Novell servers to provide services to both the Internet and an intranet. IntraNetWare expands Novell server capabilities to include Web server functions. This extra function is integrated with the NDS, allowing users to access the directory to locate network information or resources.

intranet A private network that incorporates Internet tools and protocols.

Entering the domain of the Internet is a major step for Novell because the transport and network layer protocols of the Internet, TCP/IP, are different from the native NetWare protocol, SPX/IPX. IntraNetWare allows both protocols to coexist.

MICROSOFT'S NETWORK OPERATING SYSTEMS

Microsoft has had several NOS products. OS/2 LAN Manager was an NOS based on OS/2. It was similar to an IBM product called OS/2 LAN Server, which has evolved into OS/2 Warp Server. Microsoft also provided peer-to-peer networking with its Windows for Workgroups product and enhanced version of Windows 3.1. Both products have been replaced by Windows 95 and Windows NT Server for peer-to-peer and server-based networks respectively.

Windows 95

Windows 95's LAN capabilities are bundled with the software so there is no additional software cost to set up a network. A Network Neighborhood icon is established on the desktop to assist users in identifying the available servers and printers. Windows 95 allows users to connect to server-based networks such as NetWare and Windows NT Server as well as to other computers in a peer-to-peer mode. A user can provide security capabilities by password protecting resources. To gain access to those resources, users need to provide the correct password. Under this mechanism, if you have 10 shared directories (called folders in Windows 95), there will be 10 passwords involved, one for each folder. Of course, this could be a problem if one user needs access to all 10 folders. That user would need to remember 10 passwords and the folders to which they pertained. Security can be resolved on a name basis if a NetWare or Windows NT server is available. With user-level control, this user could provide a user ID and a single password to the server. This user would then be allowed to access all resources for which she has been granted access without supplying an individual password for each. Sharing can be on a read-only basis or full access basis. Peer-to-peer sharing can be done between Windows 95, Windows for Workgroups, and Windows NT client machines.

Windows NT Server

Windows NT Server (NTS) Microsoft's integrated LAN OS software, which functions as an application server.

Windows NT Server (NTS) is enjoying considerably more success than its predecessor, OS/2 LAN Manager. NTS has gained market share and acceptance since its initial release. A portion of NTS's acceptance comes from its capabilities as an application server. At the beginning of this text we mentioned that a variety of services can be provided by a server. In the past, the principal ones were file and print services. A server role that has been expanding is application services. An application server does more than deliver files or records and handle printing. Application servers participate in the processing of the data. Thus, an application server allows the processing work to be divided between the client and the server. NTS has gained popularity as an application server because of the NT operating system. Because it is a 32-bit OS, it can directly access up to 4 GB of main memory. NT supports preemptive multitasking and multithreading, which means that it can run several tasks concurrently and switch between them efficiently. Preemption means that a running process can be suspended by the OS to allow another process access to the CPU. Finally, NTS has good support for servers with multiple processors, allowing for parallel processing.

As of this writing, NTS does not have a global, distributed network directory; however, one has been announced and may be available in 1998. Instead, NTS provides a limited directory service called a domain. In a single-server network, a user logs onto the server and the user's capabilities are limited to that server. In a network with multiple servers, a user can do the same thing: log onto a given server and use that server's resources. As an alternative, a user could log onto a domain server and gain access to the resources of multiple servers within that domain. A domain server contains the security database for all servers in the domain. Domain servers can be primary or secondary. A secondary domain server has a backup role in case the primary server is not available. Domains generally are oriented around networks in limited geographical area. Because the domain database cannot be replicated, long-distance access is required for remotely located nodes and that access would ordinarily be quite time-consuming. For controlling access in department or campus environments, domain service is as effective as a global directory. Interdomain sharing is possible via a mechanism known as trusting. A trust relationship may be established between two domains and as long as this relationship is maintained, users in one domain can access resources in the other trusted domain. Companies that are geographically distributed or have completely separate networks have several distinct domains, each of which is administered individually; therefore, in the trusted domain situation, each domain database is maintained separately. Contrast this with the single-database concept of a global directory.

In the fault tolerance area, NTS supports disk mirroring and RAID disk arrays. NTS can be installed in DOS-formatted disk drives (FAT format), High Performance File system formats (HPFS), or Windows NT file systems (NTFS). With FAT formats, installations lose some of the file security capabilities because the DOS file format does not support many file attributes. The benefit of this format is that NTS can be installed in disks that are currently in use and that disk can be used for DOS applications, Windows applications, and the NT server. This may be of benefit in small installations, in which the server may also be needed as a desktop system. The HPFS format allows OS/2 disk access. The NTFS is preferred because it provides all the benefits of NTS security and performance. The management utilities are Windows based, making the management tasks easier.

BANYAN VINES

Banyan Vines is recognized for its support for large networks and network interconnections. Banyan Vines runs on UNIX-based servers, a distinct advantage because many WANs contain nodes running the UNIX OS. This makes it easier for Vines systems to connect to those nodes. A server based on UNIX also can be used effectively as an application system in addition to providing LAN services, which means that the server platform can function not only as a server but also as a platform for running application programs. OS/2 OSs allow multitasking but not multiuser capabilities and thus cannot match UNIX-based machines, which allow several users to run applications.

One major strength of Vines is a global naming strategy called **StreetTalk.** StreetTalk is a database that provides **network directory services** such as identifying network resources (users, files, hardware, and so on). This database is replicated on each server in the network, providing a measure of fault tolerance as well as making resource lookup more efficient. Applications use StreetTalk to locate needed resources: A mail application can use it to find the location of mail recipients. LAN managers use StreetTalk to assist in controlling the network and network users: The access rights of each user can be placed in the StreetTalk database. A unique feature of StreetTalk, particularly for international networks, is the ability to store information such as status and error messages in several languages.

Banyan Vines An example of LAN software that runs under an existing OS, UNIX.

StreetTalk (Banyan) A database that provides network directory services.

network directory services A database that contains the names, types, and network addresses of network resources. Examples of resource types include users, printers, and servers. The directory database may be replicated on several network nodes, thus allowing users and processes to locate resources they need to complete their work.

Table 8–9 Possible Complications of Having Two Network Operating Systems in One LAN

Compatibility of user identifiers and passwords
Synchronization of user identifiers and passwords across servers
Ability to simultaneously access data on two servers
Ability to access data on one server and print to spooler on another
Applications that can run from both servers
Support for common application program interfaces
Support for common protocols at the OSI network and transport layers
Ability to use/have two redirector processes

INTEROPERABILITY OF SERVER SOFTWARE

A large LAN may need more than one file server; the point at which a second server is needed varies according to the number of active, concurrent users and their server access profiles. If two or more servers are required, you must ensure that they operate correctly. If all servers are using the same hardware and software platforms, they often can operate correctly in concert. It is not always true, however, that two different server software packages can interoperate correctly.

interoperability The ability of all network components to connect to the network and to communicate with shared network resources.

Interoperability is the ability of all network components to connect to the network and to communicate with shared network resources. With a global view, this means the ability to interconnect different networks so that nodes on one network are able to communicate with nodes on the same network or on another network. On a single network, it means that any node can access resources to which it has appropriate security. Interoperability is usually easy in a homogeneous network, in which only one NOS version is used and the workstations are all the same type and use the same OS. Networks using a mixture of NOSs and workstation platforms make interoperability more complex.

We now look at interoperability in a single network. Consider a network that has two servers with different NOSs, such as Novell's NetWare and Microsoft's Windows NT. If users were to use only one or the other server, it would probably be easier to divide the network into a Novell network and a Windows NT network. If both servers are available on one network, we may assume that some users must have access to both servers. Table 8–9 lists complications that may exist as a result. How well the server OSs handle these issues affects the interoperability of the network.

The Syncrasy Corporation has installed two separate LANs in the home office. Two LANs were chosen for several reasons, two of which are separation of department functions and the number of users. The two LANs are connected but the connection is used primarily to allow users to exchange e-mail messages. The intention is for all users to access applications located on a server attached to their LAN, so that a user on LAN A does not access applications located on a LAN B server. To meet most users' application needs, Syncrasy has chosen four core microcomputer products—word processing, spreadsheet, database management, and presentation graphics—that are to be available to all LAN users in the home office. It was decided to use individual software packages for these core products rather than purchasing one of the combined office program packages. A consequence of using multiple software vendors is having to understand and adhere to several different license agreements. The license agreement provisions of each of the core products are as follows.

WORD PROCESSING

Basic network licenses on one server for 25 and 50 users are $2500 and $4500, respectively. A 25-user license includes 5 sets of manuals and a 50-user license has 10 sets. Additional sets of documentation are available for $20 each. Additional user licenses come in 25-user increments and cost $2000. The 25- and 50-user licenses for an additional server are $2000 and $4000, respectively.

SPREADSHEET

A basic network license for 25 users is $2000. This includes two sets of documentation. Additional licenses are available in 10-user increments for $750. Additional copies of manuals are available for $20 each. No additional costs are charged per server at the same location.

DATABASE MANAGEMENT

A site license is available for $6000. This allows an unlimited number of users and installation on multiple servers. The cost includes two sets of documentation. Additional manual sets are available for $25 sets.

PRESENTATION GRAPHICS

A single-server license covering 25 users costs $2500 and allows installation on one server only. Additional server licenses for 25 users cost $2500. Additional users on a single server can be added in increments of 25 at a cost of $2000. Each server license includes five sets of documents, and additional sets of documents can be purchased for $30 each.

Once the software selection was made, it was necessary to order the proper number of licenses to ensure that Syncrasy was compliant with each vendor's license provisions. Determining the cost for each product required an understanding of the license provisions for the product and the parameters under which the product would be used at Syncrasy. Table 8–10 shows the factors that were gathered to complete the cost analysis. Some of the data in Table 8–10 may not need to be applied in the license analysis for

Table 8–10   Software License Cost Analysis

Product	LAN A Server Maximum Concurrent Users	LAN B Server Maximum Concurrent Users	Maximum Concurrent Users on Both Servers	Document Sets Required
Word processing	60	25	75	50
Spreadsheet	60	20	70	50
Database management	40	30	60	50
Presentation graphics	25	20	40	50

a specific product. We consider the analysis that was conducted to determine the product costs for the word processing and spreadsheet applications. Analysis for the three remaining products is left as an exercise.

WORD PROCESSING LICENSE AND MANUAL COSTS

For the LAN A server (server A), Syncrasy needs a 50-user license and a 25-user extension to cover 60 concurrent users. This will cost $4500 + $2000, for a total of $6500. For LAN B's server (server B) an additional server license for 25 users must be purchased for $2000. The total license cost is therefore $6500 + $2000, or $8500. A 50-user license includes 10 manual sets and a 25-user license includes 5 sets. From the license costs, 20 manual sets are available, 15 on server A and 5 on server B. Syncrasy must purchase an additional 30 manual sets to have 50 sets of manuals available. Each manual set costs $20, so the manual cost will be $600. The total software license and manual costs for word processing are therefore $8500 + $600, or $9100.

SPREADSHEET LICENSE AND MANUAL COSTS

The cost of the spreadsheet software must be calculated differently from the cost for word processing because the license provisions are different. Syncrasy must be able to accommodate 70 concurrent users on both LANs. This is accomplished by purchasing the basic 25-user license and adding 5 extensions of 10 users each. The costs for this is $2000 + (5)($750), or $5750. The license fees include 2 manual sets, so 48 additional sets at a cost of $20 each are needed; the additional manuals will cost $960. The total software and manual costs for the spreadsheet are $5750 + $960, or $6710.

SUMMARY

LAN software can be separated into system software and application software. LAN system software in the servers and workstations is responsible for carrying out the LAN functions. Application software solves business problems. LAN system software is found on servers and workstations.

Workstation system software is responsible for intercepting application I/O requests and deciding whether the request is local or network. If the request is local, the workstation LAN software passes it along to the workstation OS. If the request is for a network resource, the workstation LAN software formats a network message and sends the request over the network for processing. The workstation LAN software is also responsible for accepting LAN messages and passing them along to the proper application. Because LAN workstation software must remain resident in the workstation memory, a stand-alone workstation may need a memory upgrade to run some LAN applications.

LAN server software is more complex than workstation software. Some functions it may provide are

- I/O optimization
- fault tolerance
- printer services
- utility and administrative support
- access security
- file backup and restore
- contention resolution

These functions help to make performance better, to improve reliability, or to protect data from accidental or intentional damage.

When choosing LAN software, you need to consider how that software will interoperate with other software, other networks, and your hardware. Poor interoperability increases the complexity of using a LAN and decreases its usability.

A major difference between stand-alone microcomputers and microcomputers attached to a LAN is resource sharing. Sharing hardware and data may lead to contention problems, and mechanisms must be available to arbitrate resource contention. Spoolers manage contention for network printers. Open modes and file or record locks are commonly used to resolve data contention. These forms of data contention resolution may lead to another problem called deadlock. If two or more processes are involved in a deadlock, none of the processes is able to proceed until one of them releases the resources it has locked. Resolving contention and deadlock problems is essential to preserving the integrity of data and ensuring the progress of applications.

Purchased software is covered by a license agreement that describes the manner in which the software may be used. In using the software, an organization agrees to abide by the licensing provisions, which typically limit the number of concurrent users and the hardware platforms on which the software may be installed. License agreements protect the software vendor's investment in manufacturing and distributing the software and give the user rights to use and upgrade a product. System administrators must ensure that the licensing provisions are adhered to. Numerous organizations that have ignored licensing provisions have been assessed large fines and were required to pay for additional licenses to cover the way in which the software was being used.

KEY TERMS

access security	mirrored disks
application program interface (API)	multithreading
backup software	NetWare 3.x and NetWare 4.x
Banyan Vines	network directory services
client/server protocol	Novell Directory Services (NDS)
clustering	parity data
corporate license	peer-to-peer LAN
deadlock	Personal NetWare (PNW)
disk seek enhancement	protected open mode
duplexed servers	read-after-write
exclusive open mode	redirector
interoperability	redundant arrays of independent
interrupt	disks (RAID)
intranet	server license
IntraNetWare 4.11	shared open mode
I/O optimization	site license
key disk	spooler
license agreement	StreetTalk
lock	Windows NT Server (NTS)

REVIEW QUESTIONS

1. Explain the functions of workstation redirector software.

2. Explain how an application's network request is processed by both the workstation and the server.

3. Why may a stand-alone workstation need a memory upgrade when added to a LAN?

4. Explain why multithreaded server operation is important.

5. What is a client/server or requester server protocol? Give an example.

6. What is an application program interface?

7. What is the purpose of I/O optimization? Give two examples.

8. What is the benefit of fault-tolerant servers?

9. Describe three fault tolerance capabilities.

10. Explain how a print spooler works.

11. Explain two ways application software can be tailored to individual users.

12. Describe two ways data contention can be avoided.

13. What is deadlock? Give an example.

14. What is a software license? Why are software licenses necessary?

PROBLEMS AND EXERCISES

1. Use the literature to identify and briefly describe five capabilities of fault tolerance systems, such as Novell's SFT or Tandem's NonStop systems. The following magazine sources may prove helpful: *Network Management*, *LAN Times*, *LAN Technology*, *LAN*, and *Network Computing*. You also may use CD-ROM sources, such as Computer Select.

2. Evaluate a LAN-compatible DBMS to determine how it resolves contention. Is contention resolution the responsibility of the user or the database management system? Systems you may want to examine include dBase IV, Access, Paradox, Oracle, and Sybase.

3. Research the literature for references to a LAN server that runs under DOS. How many users does the system support? Attempt to determine the expected level of performance.

4. Investigate one of the backup/restore software packages available. What functions does it provide?

5. You have been asked to configure the hardware for a LAN to provide office automation capabilities for a small office. The office manager wants you to provide a LAN that will make use of four IBM compatibles with 4 MB of memory, two IBM compatibles with 8 MB of memory, two IBM compatibles with 16 MB of memory, one laser printer, and two ink-jet printers that the office currently owns. Draw a network diagram of your proposed LAN using a bus topology. Label all hardware components in your diagram. Prepare a report to accompany your diagram that gives the following details:
   a. the equipment, software, and cabling that will be needed to connect each device to the LAN
   b. necessary upgrades to any of the existing hardware to make it LAN usable

6. Consider the office LAN described in Problem 5. Some employees want to access the LAN from their homes to transfer files and do remote printing. Configure the hardware, software, and communication capabilities required at the LAN and user ends of the connection.

7. The office described in Problem 5 wants to add fax capabilities to the network. The capabilities needed include the ability to send and receive fax transmissions and to store fax images on disk. Images sent and received may be in either hard copy or disk image format. Describe the hardware, software, and communication equipment necessary to create this capability.

8. Investigate several LAN software systems and describe the type of license agreement each uses.

9. The Software Publishers Association is an organization funded by many software firms. The charter of the association includes protecting against software piracy and the violation of software license agreements. Research the literature and find three instances of actions taken against companies or universities for violation of software license agreements.

10. Complete the Case Study in this chapter by calculating the license and manual costs for database management and presentation graphics. What are the total software and manual costs for all four products?

CHAPTER 9

LAN Considerations

CHAPTER OBJECTIVES

After studying this chapter you should be able to

- Describe several LAN alternatives
- List several LAN selection criteria
- Discuss how a specific criterion influences the selection process
- Evaluate a company's needs and develop a basic LAN strategy that meets those needs

Although originally designed to connect minicomputers, mainframes, and supercomputers, most LANs being installed today are used to link microcomputers. In this chapter, you will learn about the selection, implementation, and use of microcomputer-oriented LANs and alternatives to microcomputer LANs.

LAN ALTERNATIVES

We can look at LAN alternatives from two perspectives: different types of LAN implementations or hardware and software alternatives to LANs. In this section we discuss both. We start by looking at the ways LANs can be implemented.

LAN Implementation Alternatives

A LAN can be implemented using dedicated servers, using nondedicated servers, and as a peer-to-peer implementation.

dedicated server One or more computers that operate only as designated file, database, or other types of servers.

Dedicated Servers   In a **dedicated server** LAN, one or more computers are designated as file or database servers and these computers serve only in that capacity. They do not double as user computers. Many current LANs use client/server technology with dedicated server nodes. This is certainly true of most large LANs. However, the average number of nodes per microcomputer LAN is 6.3, so many LANs have six or fewer nodes. For these small LANs, dedicating an expensive server machine (which will probably be underused) reduces the cost-effectiveness of the network. Two other technologies, nondedicated servers and peer-to-peer LANs, provide an alternative to dedicated servers. Peer-to-peer LANs were defined in Chapter 8.

nondedicated server A computer that can operate as both a server and a workstation.

Nondedicated Server   A few LAN operating systems allow nondedicated servers. A **nondedicated server** works as both a server and a workstation. A nondedicated server usually is the workstation with the most resources. For example, it is hard to imagine four users in a typical office keeping a dedicated server busy most of the time. If the server is allowed to also function as a workstation, it can be used more effectively.

The advantage of nondedicated servers is more effective use of resources. There are also some disadvantages. A nondedicated server must divide its workload between its application work and its server work. Sometimes it might be very busy in both roles. In these instances, both those using the server as a server and those using the server as a workstation will experience service degradation. If these conflicts occur too often, the LAN administrator should think of making the server dedicated. Another disadvantage of nondedicated servers is the increased likelihood of server failures. Simply running both applications and server software increases the possibility of failures because the server is doing more and the environment is more complicated. However, the most probable source of a nondedicated server failure is the user's application or the user him- or herself. If the application gets locked, the server may be unable to attend to its server duties. If the user powers the server down or unintentionally formats the server disk, the server function will also be disrupted.

Other Implementations

Alternative implementations to a LAN include large, centralized computer systems; service bureaus; sub-LANs; and zero-slot LANs.

Large, Central Computer Systems   For years the traditional approach to computing was to have a central host computer, as shown in Figure 9–1. These large, central computers are still the mainstay of many data processing operations. They are the primary means for processing large volumes of data, producing big reports, supporting special-purpose hardware devices such as check reader/sorters, and so on. It is unlikely that a large bank would be able to process its daily closing work with a microcomputer or a network of microcomputers. However, most companies augment their processing capabilities with microcomputers for personal productivity applications, and as noted earlier, downsizing from large computer systems to LANs is more common than replacing LANs with large systems.

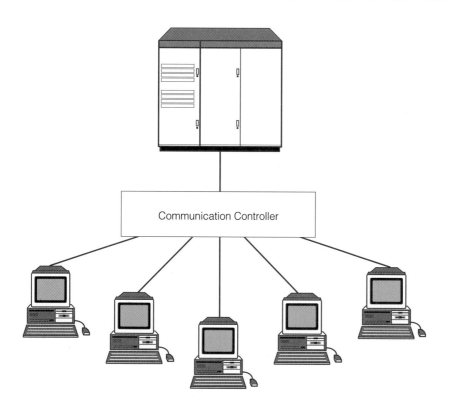

Figure 9–1
Central Host Computer

Service Bureaus   Another alternative that a potential LAN user might consider is contracting with a computer **service bureau.** This alternative provides the same computing and connectivity capabilities as the large, central host alternative but without the high initial costs. The subscriber pays for the amount of computing resources (disk storage, processing time, and printed output) used. Subscribers also pay for custom software modifications and possibly a monthly subscription fee. This pricing structure is similar to that offered by telephone systems, with a monthly connection charge regardless of usage and a second charge based on the amount of use. If usage is high, costs can be significant.

Zero-Slot LANs   Some low-speed LANs use "standard" microcomputer components such as a serial or a parallel port for connecting one node to another. These LAN implementations are sometimes called **zero-slot LANs** because they do not require an additional slot on the motherboard for a LAN adapter. When a LAN adapter is used, each station is assigned a unique address, which is set on the LAN adapter at the factory or through dual inline package (DIP) switch settings. Thus, the cost of implementing this type of LAN is typically lower because the costs are limited to cables, LAN software, and perhaps server hardware.

Sub-LANs   **Sub-LANs** provide a subset of LAN capabilities, primarily peripheral sharing and file transfer. They differ from a LAN in two ways: A sub-LAN's data transfer rates and costs are lower than those of a LAN, and

service bureau A subscription service in which the customer commissions disk storage, processing time, and printed output services of a large central host system based on usage.

zero-slot LAN A low-speed LAN using standard microcomputer components that do not require an additional slot on the motherboard for a LAN adapter.

sub-LAN A network that provides a subset of LAN capabilities, primarily peripheral sharing and file transfer, but has lower data transfer rates and diminished transparency than a LAN.

file transfer capabilities are typically less transparent than on a LAN. On most sub-LANs, if a user needs to transfer a file to another workstation, the sender must first call the person operating the receiving workstation to manually establish the setting for data transfer. Sub-LANs are implemented with data switches. **Data switches** provide connection between microcomputers in much the same way a telephone company provides connections between callers. A switch configuration is shown in Figure 9–2. If device A must connect with device B, the switch establishes the connection, as illustrated in Figure 9–3. Many data switches are designed specifically for sharing peripheral devices, such as printers and plotters, and use manual switching. This means that a user must turn a switch selector knob on the switch box to make the proper connection. With keyboard command switching, a user can enter the address of a desired device. If the device is not already in use, the connection is made; otherwise, the user must wait until the device is available. The connection remains active until one of the two stations requests a disconnect; alternatively, a disconnect may occur after a specified time of inactivity. Keyboard command switching does not solve the file transfer problem described above. Operators at the sending and receiving computers still must coordinate file transfer by starting the file transfer software at each end of the connection.

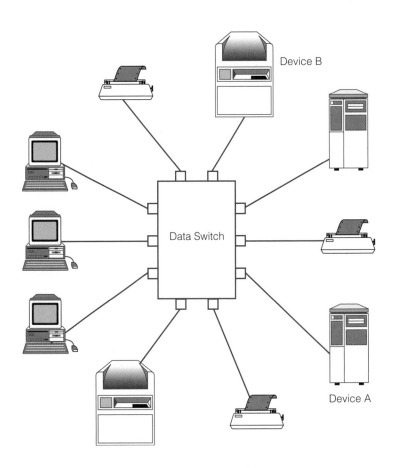

Figure 9–2
Switch Configuration

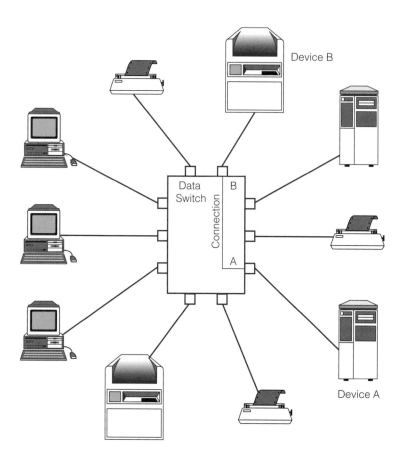

Figure 9–3
Connecting Hardware with a Switch

Sub-LANs are inexpensive. A serial or parallel interface is used between the microcomputers and the switch. Because serial and parallel ports are either standard or low-cost options, the cost for the microcomputer components is limited to those ports and a cable. A switch that can support eight devices together with the essential operating software can be purchased for less than $2500, making the cost per connection about $325.

The disadvantages of a data switch are the low speed of the communication link; lack of user transparency, expandability, and ability to interface to other networks; and contention. The line speeds supported are typically 19.2 Kbps or slower. This speed is adequate for small file transfers and individual database records but not for large data transfers such as downloading program files, large documents, or large portions of a database. The ability to connect to other networks is generally poor. Although one of the switch ports might be connected to a terminal port on a large system, making the connection is not simple. The number of such connection ports is also limited.

Contention can also occur when using a data switch. If two users want to connect to a device such as a printer, only one of the connections can be made. The first request received is granted, and the second user must wait until the first connection is severed. Some data switches have on-board

Table 9–1 Rating of LAN Alternatives and a Conventional LAN

	A	B	C	D	E
Number of workstations	1	2	3	3	1
Initial cost	5	4	1	1	3
Personnel costs	5	1	1	1	2
Operations/maintenance costs	5	4	1	3	3
Expandability	1	2	3	3	1
Microcomputer workstation support	4	3	2	1	1
User transparency	3	3	4	1	1
Accommodation for multiple users	1	1	4	3	2
Ease of use	3	4	4	2	1
Ease of management	3	1	2	4	3
Interface to other networks	1	5	5	4	1

A = large, centralized computer systems; B = use of a service bureau; C = sub-LANs;
D = Zero-slot and low-cost LANs; E = conventional LAN, such as Ethernet or token ring.

random access memory (RAM) to alleviate this contention problem. If multiple outputs for the same printer are received, one can be held in the switch's RAM until the printer becomes available. In the above situation, both users would perceive that their connection request was honored. Data switches are an effective, low-cost way to share peripherals and accomplish infrequent transfers of small files. They are not well suited for downloading software programs or large data files or for frequent file exchanges.

Comparison of Alternatives

Table 9–1 compares the LAN alternatives just discussed. The evaluation rates several criteria on a scale of 1 to 5, with 1 being best. As an example of how to interpret Table 9–1, consider the first line, which rates the number of workstations. A large, conventional LAN and a mainframe or minicomputer will allow hundreds or thousands of workstations or terminals; therefore, these two alternatives receive the highest rating. A service bureau will also provide access to a large number of terminals but generally at a higher cost, so this alternative is rated below the mainframe and large, conventional LAN alternatives. Sub-LANs and zero-slot or low-cost LANs are usually quite restrictive regarding the number of workstations allowed and thus tie for the lowest rating in this category.

LAN SELECTION CRITERIA

In preceding chapters we discussed LAN hardware, software, topologies, media, and media access control protocols. This material provides the foundation for evaluating a company's LAN needs and for selecting the components necessary to build an effective LAN system. We now look at the major factors influencing LAN selection. These criteria are summarized in Table 9–2.

Table 9–2 Major Factors Influencing LAN Selection

Cost	Number of workstations	Type of workstations
Number of concurrent users	Type of use	Number of printers
Medium and distance	Speed	Applications
Expandability	Device connectivity	Connectivity with other networks
LAN software and hardware	Vendor	Adherence to established standards
Vendor support	Manageability	Security

Cost

If cost were not a consideration, LAN selection would be easier. You could buy the fastest, biggest workstations and servers available and use the most comprehensive LAN software available. Deciding which hardware and software modules fit this description would not be simple, but lack of price constraints would make selection much easier. However, cost often is an overriding constraint, and you must choose the best solution within your budget. In the final analysis the LAN must be a cost-effective solution for your situation.

Hardware and software are not the only costs you will incur. Other costs you must plan for include the immediate and recurring costs shown in Table 9–3. Immediate costs are those you incur when installing a LAN. Recurring costs are the costs of operating and updating the LAN and training LAN users and administrators.

Number of Workstations

The effect the number of workstations has on the immediate costs of attaching a node to a LAN has already been discussed. The number of workstations is also a key factor in network configuration. Each LAN is physically capable of supporting a specific maximum number of workstations. If you exceed that maximum, you must make some provision for extending the maximum number. A variety of techniques exist for doing this, and each increases the cost of the LAN. Other workstation costs can be incurred as well. If you intend to use existing microcomputers on the LAN, they may need to

Table 9–3 Immediate and Recurring LAN Costs

Immediate Costs	
Equipment upgrades	Training (users, operators, administrators)
Documentation	Installation of cabling
Site preparation	System software installation
Hardware installation	Creating user environments
Installing applications	Space required for new equipment
Testing	Supplies and spares

Recurring Costs	
LAN management: personnel costs	Hardware and software maintenance
Consumable supplies	Training (new users, administrators)

be upgraded. For example, because LAN software is resident in each workstation, the amount of memory available to applications is reduced. You therefore may need to add memory to some workstations.

Type of Workstations

The type of workstations you use will be a significant factor in your LAN choice. If your LAN will consist of Apple Macintoshes, a number of DOS-oriented LAN systems will be eliminated. If your workstations are IBM-compatible systems, Apple LANs will be eliminated. The same logic applies if your LAN consists of any of the other possible workstation platforms, such as those of Sun Microsystems. The LAN hardware and software must be compatible with the workstations used. If you need to mix the types of workstations on the LAN to allow both Apple and IBM-compatible workstations, you will again eliminate a number of LAN options and, perhaps, increase the cost.

Number of Concurrent Users

The number of concurrent users may differ from the number of workstations. Some networks have restrictions regarding the number of active users. One network operating system allows four concurrent users, but more than four workstations can be attached. An increase in the number of concurrent users also increases the LAN workload. As the LAN workload increases, you have two basic choices: You can allow system responsiveness to decrease, or you can increase the work potential of the system to maintain or improve the responsiveness. Naturally, the second option involves higher costs. Some ways to improve LAN responsiveness are to select a faster LAN (one with higher transmission speeds), to use additional or more powerful servers (which means more expensive computers), or to use more efficient (and typically more costly) LAN software. The number of concurrent users of an application also has an impact on the cost of the application. Software vendors vary in their user license provisions; in general, application costs are directly proportional to the number of concurrent users. As the number of concurrent users goes up, so do software costs.

Type of Use

You may have surmised that having more concurrent users increases the LAN workload. However, you need to understand more about the effect of concurrent users on LAN performance. To do so, we look at two very different ways of using a LAN.

Suppose that the primary LAN application is word processing, and the operating mode is as follows: LAN users access the word processing software on the file server at the beginning of their work shifts, they save their documents on a local disk drive, and they periodically print documents. What demands are there on the LAN? The demand is heavy when a user starts the word processing program. The program must be downloaded, or transferred from the server to the workstation. The user does not need LAN services again until he or she prints a document or, in some cases, requires an **overlay module** for the word processor. An example of an overlay module is a spelling checker. Current microcomputer software is so rich in capabilities that all the functions cannot always be included in one memory-resident module. An overlay module overcomes this constraint by sharing memory with other overlay modules. LAN requests are therefore infrequent, but the amount of data transferred is large. Adding users may not significantly increase the LAN workload if there is a considerable amount of idle time. If you have used a LAN in a classroom situation, you probably have experienced this type of usage. At the beginning of the class, LAN response is slow because many students are starting an application at nearly the same time, and the demand for LAN resources is high. After that, however, LAN responsiveness improves because the LAN usage becomes intermittent.

Suppose instead that the primary LAN activity is database access, with users continually accessing and updating a database. In this case the LAN is constantly busy transferring large and small amounts of data. Adding new users in this instance can have a noticeable impact on LAN performance.

overlay module Overlaying is a memory management technique that divides a program into one resident segment and multiple overlay segments or modules. The resident module resides permanently in memory. The overlay segments occupy a common memory area. When code or data in an overlay module is referenced, it is either in the overlay memory area or on disk. If on disk, the overlay module is read into the overlay memory area and replaces the current overlay module.

Number and Type of Printers

The number and distribution of printers can affect your LAN decision as well. Some LAN operating systems require that network printers be attached to file servers, and each file server can support only so many printers. With such systems, if you need a large number of printers, you may need to add server hardware and software simply to provide printing services. You also must ensure that the LAN you select is capable of supporting the types of printers you will be using. Each printer requires printer driver software to direct its operation. The driver software knows how to activate the special printer features needed to print special typefaces, underlining, graphics, and so on. Spooler software is responsible for writing printed output to shared printers. It follows that there must be an interface between the spooler and the printer drivers. Drivers are often included as part of the server software. When selecting a LAN you must ensure both that the printers you plan to use are supported and that they are supported in the manner in which you plan to use them. For example, a certain printer may be supported for printing text but not for printing graphics.

Distance and Medium

LANs serve a limited geographical area at high speeds. Distance and speed are related. Attaining high speed over long distances can be very expensive, and each LAN has a maximum distance it can cover. Different types of LANs also have different distance limitations. The distance is measured in wiring length. If you snake a cable back and forth through an office complex, you may not cover a wide geographical area, but the cable distance can be quite long. In general, as the distance your LAN needs to cover increases, your LAN options decrease. Distances for popular microcomputer LANs range from a few hundred meters to several thousand meters.

The type of medium also influences the selection process. If your facility already has wiring installed, you may select a LAN that can use that type of wiring. Each medium has speed and error characteristics. Earlier you read that twisted-pair wires support lower speeds and are more susceptible to errors than either coaxial cable or fiber optic cable. If your LAN wiring must pass through areas that can induce transmission errors (such as areas that produce electrical or magnetic interference), you may need to select a LAN that can use a more noise-resistant medium such as coaxial cable or fiber optic cable. One company came to this realization the hard way. In wiring the building with unshielded twisted-pair wires, the company ran the wiring through the shaft of a freight elevator. The freight elevator was seldom used; however, every time it was operated, the motor interfered with the data being transmitted on the LAN, causing numerous transmission errors. Replacing the cabling in the elevator shaft with more error-resistant wiring eliminated the periodic failures.

Speed

LAN speeds can be somewhat deceptive. A LAN speed quoted by the vendor is the speed at which data is transmitted over the medium. You cannot expect the LAN to maintain this speed at all times. Time is required to place data onto the medium and to clear data from the medium. This is done in a variety of ways, which you learned about in Chapter 7. It is important to select a LAN capable of meeting your performance goals. If you expect access to data on your LAN's file server to have a transfer rate comparable to that of a hard disk, such as 5 Mbps, this requirement eliminates a number of low-speed LANs. Common LAN speeds available for microcomputers are 1, 2.5, 4, 10, 16, 20, and 100 Mbps. The trend is toward higher speeds because of greater LAN use and because of the types of data now being used in LAN applications. Applications using graphics, audio, and full-motion video are becoming more common. These applications require the transfer of large amounts of data and place a heavy load on the media and servers.

Applications

Most major application software packages are now available in LAN-compatible versions. This does not mean that all applications can run on all LANs. Applications communicate with the network through interfaces called application program interfaces (APIs), and a variety of APIs are in use. If the application uses an interface not supported by a particular LAN, then the application probably will not work on that network. Some software simply is not LAN compatible. It either cannot run on a LAN at all or it does not support sharing on a LAN but can be used by one user at a time. Custom-written applications also may not be LAN compatible. It is important to determine whether software you need to use will work on the LAN you are considering.

Expandability

After installing a LAN you probably will need to add workstations to it or move workstations from one location to another. The ease of doing this varies among implementations. The ease may depend on the medium used and on the way in which the medium was installed. Adding new nodes to some systems using twisted-pair wires or coaxial cable is easy. Adding a new node to a fiber optic cable may require cable splicing, which means that you must cut the cable, add the connectors, and rejoin the cable so the light pulses can continue along the cable. Fiber optic cable splicing technology has improved and is not difficult; however, adding a new node is still more difficult than for twisted-pair wires or coaxial cable.

Device Connectivity

Some organizations need to attach special devices to the LAN, such as an optical disk. LAN interfaces for such devices may not be available on some LANs or LAN file servers. This, of course, reduces your choices to the LANs and servers that support the interface.

Connectivity to Other Networks

A LAN is often only one part of an organization's computing resources. Other facets may be a WAN, a large stand-alone computer, or other LANs. If there are other LANs, they may be of different types. When a variety of computing resources are available, it is often desirable to connect these resources. This allows a node on the LAN to communicate with a node on a WAN or to access data on a central mainframe system. A variety of connection capabilities exist, but a given LAN may not support all of them. If you have immediate connectivity needs or anticipate them in the future, you need to select a LAN that will support the connection protocols you expect to use.

LAN Software and Hardware

If you already have microcomputers and associated software and hardware, you probably want to preserve your investment in them. That means you need to select LAN software and hardware that will be compatible with your existing equipment. Notable differences between LAN software and hardware capabilities also may be important in making your LAN selection.

Adherence to Established Standards

Some LANs conform to the standards for LAN implementation, whereas others do not. Several nonstandard LANs have been adopted by many users and have thus become de facto standards. Other LANs are neither covered by standards nor very widely adopted. A LAN's adherence to a standard does not necessarily mean that it is superior to nonstandard LANs. However, there are benefits to choosing a LAN that conforms to a standard. Because standards are published, any company can design components that work on the LAN. This creates competition, gives users alternative sources of equipment, and usually drives down the cost of components. Adopting a standardized LAN also is often regarded as a safe decision because the community of users is often large. This generates a body of expertise that new users can tap for information or personnel. On the other hand, a nonstandard LAN may provide innovative features that are not yet covered by standards. Adopting such a LAN can place an organization ahead of competition that is using a more conventional system. You can read about more LAN standards in Chapter 7.

Vendor and Support

When you select a LAN, you are selecting much more than hardware and software. You also are selecting a vendor or vendors with whom you expect to have a long-term relationship. Your vendors ought to be available to help you in times of problems, provide you with maintenance and support, and supply you with spare parts, hardware and software upgrades, and new equipment. You can be more successful with a good vendor and a less capable LAN than with a poor vendor and a superior LAN, especially if your vendor can quickly resolve problems, obtain needed equipment, and so on. Evaluate prospective vendors and their support policies as carefully as you evaluate the equipment itself.

Manageability

Do not underestimate the time and effort required to operate and manage a LAN. Even a small, static LAN requires some management once it has been installed and set up. Occasionally a user might be added or deleted, applications may be added or updated, and so on. The major ongoing activities will be backing up files, taking care of printer problems, and solving occasional user problems. In a large LAN, management can be a full-time job, perhaps for more than one person. In Chapters 17 and 18 you will learn about network management. During the selection process you must ensure that your LAN will have the necessary management tools or that third-party tools are available. Third-party tools are those written by someone other than the LAN vendor. The tools you need depend on the size of the LAN and complexity of the users and applications involved. As a minimum you should be able to easily accomplish the tasks listed in Table 9–4.

Table 9–4   LAN Management Tasks

User/Group Oriented	
Add, delete users and groups	Set user/group security
Set user environment	Solve user problems
Printer Oriented	
Install/remove printers	Set up user/printer environment
Maintain printers	
Hardware/Software Oriented	
Add/change/delete software	Add/change/delete hardware
Diagnose problems	Establish connections with
Plan and implement changes	other networks
General	
Make backups	Maintain operating procedures
Carry out recovery as necessary	Educate users
Plan capacity needs	Monitor the network
Serve as liaison with other network	
administrators	

Security

With stand-alone microcomputers, security generally is not an issue because stand-alone microcomputer systems are usually single-user systems, so no security provisions were built into the operating systems or application software. As a result, access to the system is tantamount to access to all data stored on that system. By contrast, data in a LAN is shared. This does not imply that all users have unlimited access to all data. The LAN software must have the ability to control access to data. For each user you should at least be able to establish read, write, create, and purge rights for each file. Chapter 19 gives more comprehensive coverage of LAN security.

With these selection criteria in mind, we look in on the Syncrasy Corporation. Recall from Chapter 8 that Syncrasy has two interconnected LANs in the home office. The multiple-LAN configuration evolved from an original single LAN. As Syncrasy's business grew and as LAN software evolved, Syncrasy decided that splitting the original LAN into two department-oriented LANs would better meet the company's computing needs. In this case study we describe Syncrasy's original LAN acquisition analysis. As this analysis began, Syncrasy soon found that choosing a microcomputer LAN is no easy task. Of the two primary architectures—CSMA/CD bus and token ring—each has several variations, which may include speed and baseband or broadband transmission as well as hardware and software. It became apparent to Syncrasy that the most important aspect of choosing a LAN was to understand and define the problem they were attempting to solve.

LAN REQUIREMENTS

The following points were formulated as some of Syncrasy Corporation's LAN requirements.

Data Sharing

Data maintained on the host system must be available to be used on microcomputer workstations. This data includes data in the database, text files, and graphics images.

Security

User access to the network must be controlled. Users must log onto the network to use it and the logon procedure must support passwords. User access to files must also be controlled so that on a user-by-user basis a user can be

- prevented from detecting the existence of a file
- able to detect a file's presence but not be able to read from or write to it
- able to read a file but not write to it

- able to read and write to a file
- able to erase a file or not

These important issues, common to LANs and WANs, are covered as an aspect of network security in Chapter 19.

Software Downloading

Most of the software that is to be run on the microcomputers must reside on one or more file servers. A user needing access to a particular program will run it from one of the file servers. This requirement is subject to software licensing agreements.

Printers

Approximately 20 printers will be distributed throughout the work areas. These laser printers, high-speed dot matrix printers, and plotters must be accessible to all users, which means that they must be attached to printer servers.

Backup/Restore

A suitable backup device and associated software are mandatory.

User Access

Users must be able to easily access the resources of both file and printer servers.

Remote Access

Remote access to the network must be available. Users on the WAN already installed must be able to attach to the LAN and use its resources.

Compatibility

The LAN should support all the IBM-compatible microcomputers currently owned by Syncrasy. New workstation technology should also be able to attach to the LAN and coexist with the current technology.

Other Hardware

Other hardware, such as minicomputers and mainframe systems, should be able to be attached to the LAN.

Fault Tolerance

Some level of fault tolerance is required, either through hardware and software features or through multiple components such as file and print servers. A UPS is considered a server requirement.

Support of User Base

The LAN must have the ability to support the current user base of 150 workstations.

Expansion

The LAN must have the ability to expand in a modular fashion. Support of up to 250 workstations within 2 years is considered essential.

Vendor Requirements

Vendors are requested to provide system configuration and costs for hardware, software, cabling, education, manuals, maintenance, and installation for the system capable of supporting 150 workstations. They also are required to explain how the system could be expanded to accommodate 250 workstations and to estimate the cost required to effect this expansion.

To obtain the best information on obtaining and implementing a LAN, Syncrasy launched a three-pronged effort. A request for information (RFI) was drafted, asking LAN vendors to indicate how their systems would meet the above requirements. Application software vendors were contacted to determine whether their software was LAN compatible, which LAN implementations were certified, and their licensing agreements. Finally, the selection committee arranged to visit a variety of comparable LAN implementations.

HARDWARE EVALUATIONS

When the LAN vendors returned their responses, Syncrasy was amazed at the variations in suggested approaches. Twenty responses were received. LAN speeds of 1, 2, 4, 10, 16, and 100 Mbps were proposed. Implementations included token rings, token buses, and CSMA/CD buses. The number of file servers recommended to provide service for 150 workstations varied from 1 to 6. In addition, for the configuration proposing one file server, the apparent processing capacity of the file server was equivalent to that of one of the file servers in the configuration proposing six servers! The supporting operating systems included MS-DOS, OS/2, UNIX, and custom server-oriented ones. Equating capabilities among the alternatives was not an easy task. After reviewing all responses, Syncrasy decided to attempt to reduce the systems being considered to a more manageable size of five. The company established a set of criteria to provide a fair elimination process. A summary of the process used to do this follows.

Resolving Areas of Uncertainty

Some RFI responses were not clear on certain points. These vendors were contacted for clarification.

Cost

At the outset Syncrasy had estimated the cost for workstation LAN adapters, wiring hubs, cabling, servers, server software, installation, education, and manuals at $130,000. This estimate did not include the costs of workstations or application software. This cost was based on the following rough calculations:

- LAN adapters, 150 at $100 each: $15,000
- Twisted-pair wires, 2000 feet at $0.10 per foot: $200

- Wiring hubs (8), 24 port at $400 each: $3200
- Cable installation: $15,000
- Education: $20,000
- Three servers: $30,000
- LAN operating system, 3 copies, 100 users each: $12,000
- Manuals: $5000
- First-year maintenance: $5000
- Miscellaneous, including network management and so on: $23,000

The only figure in the entire original estimate in which there was a high degree of confidence was the LAN controller cards and wiring hubs. Syncrasy knew how many they needed and documentation was available indicating that the per unit cost was a reasonable approximation. The other figures were mostly speculation.

The variation among vendor responses was considerable. Some vendors did not propose a configuration or price. The lowest cost was approximately $100,000, and the highest was more than $500,000! Because several attractive proposals were less than $200,000, it was decided to table all proposals over that figure.

Speed

Syncrasy wanted to run file server software at close to hard disk speed. Some of the literature they had read indicated that they would be fortunate to realize 50% of the rated LAN speed. Syncrasy's calculations indicated that at least a 10-Mbps transfer rate for the LAN would be necessary.

Manageability

Network management consists of establishing user IDs, setting security on files, making backups, managing disk usage, monitoring performance, tuning, and so on. Without working with a system it is difficult to determine the management involvement. However, Syncrasy believed that the greater the number of components involved, the more difficult the management tasks. Several viable solutions that used three or fewer file servers were proposed. Therefore, Syncrasy decided that all solutions calling for more than three file servers would be tabled. It also turned out that some of the solutions that had the most file servers also were among the most costly.

Connectivity

One requirement Syncrasy had placed on the system was the ability to connect existing computers to the LAN. Although they did not have plans for this at the outset, it was an option they wanted to hold open for the future. Some of the LANs proposed were limited in this capability. Interfaces must exist on two sides (the LAN side and the equipment side) to make connections. Almost all proposals supported connections such as asynchronous interfaces, but Syncrasy wanted a direct LAN attachment that could operate at LAN speeds. Connectivity also pertains to the number of workstations that can be added, the configuration for workstations, and how many printer servers can be supported. All LANs have limits; however, these limits are encountered in different areas. Examples of limitations include a maximum of five shared printers and a maximum of 64 workstations per file server.

Adherence to Established Standards

Syncrasy decided to implement a LAN for which a standard existed. This meant adherence to one of the IEEE 802 standards or to the ANSI FDDI standard. It was Syncrasy's belief that a standardized implementation would protect them from future isolation regarding attaching equipment to the LAN and the ability to take advantage of new technology.

Vendor Reliability

One or two vendors were rejected because Syncrasy was skeptical of their reliability, ability to support the product, or the reliability of the manufacturer of the equipment they proposed.

Viability of Proposal

As mentioned above, there were considerable differences among the proposed solutions. A small number of proposals were rejected because they did not seem plausible.

Syncrasy drew two key conclusions from this research: Do not assume anything, and ask questions even if the answers seem obvious. We do not divulge Syncrasy's final selection; it is left as a reader exercise. There is another reason for not indicating the final selection. There are many LAN alternatives and all fulfill certain user needs. Picking one over another here could be erroneously construed as an endorsement of that technology. There are many good solutions to a given LAN problem, and different constraints and emphases will lead to different implementations.

SOFTWARE EVALUATIONS

Just as there were considerable differences in the hardware proposals, Syncrasy found considerable differences regarding how application software vendors approached site licensing. For an organization to use software, it must comply with the software vendor's licensing agreements. Most software for microcomputers is licensed to operate on one system only, or at least on only one system at a time. Networks have added a new dimension to software use. The software resides on a file server and is available for any LAN user to access. For leading software packages, Syncrasy encountered all the following variations.

- There was no such thing as a site license.
- Running the software on the LAN was a violation of the licensing agreement, even if the site purchased one package for each potential user.
- The site license required that an individual package be purchased for every workstation.

- The site license required that an individual package be purchased for each simultaneous user. A counter was used to control simultaneous access to the program.
- The site license was a one-time fee for the software, which allowed as many users as the site needed.
- The site license was based on a per-server charge. There were no restrictions regarding concurrent use.
- There was a license fee for each server and for each workstation that would have access to the software.

Some leading software packages also would not run on a LAN because of copy protection or because they were not capable of supporting multiple users. Some software would work on one LAN implementation and not another. Syncrasy decided to adopt a standardized set of software for common functions such as word processing, database management, graphics, spreadsheets, desktop publishing, and statistics. Before Syncrasy made the final selection, the vendor was required to demonstrate each of these programs running on the proposed network in a multiuser environment.

SUMMARY

Microcomputer LANs are increasing in number. You can expect to encounter them or a LAN alternative whenever two or more microcomputers are located near each other. LAN alternatives include large mainframe systems and service bureaus on the high end and multiuser microcomputers, sub-LANs, and zero-slot LANs on the low end. These alternatives ought to be considered before you implement a LAN.

A variety of factors must be considered when selecting a LAN. First, you should decide whether a LAN is required or whether a LAN alternative will suffice. If a LAN is required, factors to consider include cost-effectiveness, available system and application software, security, compatibility with existing hardware and software, LAN organization (dedicated server, nondedicated server, or peer-to-peer), adherence to established standards, number of concurrent users supported, ability to interconnect with other networks and computers, and vendor support and expertise. The weight associated with each selection criterion may differ among organizations. In making the right selections, you need to evaluate the alternatives from the perspective of your organization's immediate and future communication objectives.

KEY TERMS

data switch
dedicated server
nondedicated server
overlay module

service bureau
sub-LAN
zero-slot LAN

REVIEW QUESTIONS

1. Compare a dedicated and a nondedicated server.

2. What are the advantages and disadvantages of a large, central computer system over a LAN?

3. Compare a multiuser microcomputer with a multiuser mainframe computer.

4. Describe how a data switch works. What are its weaknesses as a LAN alternative?

5. What is a zero-slot LAN? What are the advantages and disadvantages of zero-slot LANs?

6. How do the number and type of workstations affect the LAN decision process?

7. How do the number of users and type of use affect the LAN decision process?

8. How do distance and speed affect the LAN decision process?

9. What types of connectivity issues might arise when implementing a LAN?

10. Describe the importance of the choice of vendors and support for a LAN implementation.

PROBLEMS AND EXERCISES

1. You have decided that a LAN alternative is the correct solution for your application. You want to connect five microcomputers in one 20- by 30-ft room of your office complex. You want to share printers extensively and do a limited amount of file sharing. Cost is a critical consideration in your implementation. What LAN alternative should you use? Explain how you reached your decision.

2. If user transparency were a critical issue in Exercise 1, which LAN alternative would be best? Which alternative would probably be unsuitable? Explain your decisions.

3. Consider the Case Study in this chapter. Using the material in the preceding chapters and current hardware and software references, configure a LAN for Syncrasy showing the hardware and software costs involved. Recall that Syncrasy already has the 150 workstations. Assume that no upgrades to any workstation will be necessary except for inclusion of the LAN adapter. You must include servers, server and workstation software, and LAN adapters in your configuration.

CHAPTER 10

WAN Hardware

CHAPTER OBJECTIVES

After studying this chapter you should be able to

- Define the differences between dumb, smart, and intelligent terminals
- Discuss a variety of terminal attributes
- Describe how two or more terminals can share the same communication line
- Apply considerations for choosing the best terminal for a given task
- Describe how multiplexers work
- Compare front-end processors and concentrators
- Define the use of several types of WAN hardware and diagnostic devices

In this chapter we discuss WAN hardware, starting with terminals attached to the end of a communication line. After describing the terminal equipment we move to the primary processors of a system: host computers. Along the way, we examine devices that make the use of a medium more efficient, more cost-effective, or both. One configuration of some of the hardware we discuss is illustrated in Figure 10–1.

TERMINALS

We define a **terminal** as an input or output device that may be connected to a local or remote computer, called a host computer. The terminal is at certain times dependent on the host for computation, data access, or both. The phrase *may be connected* allows for switched connections and devices that

terminal An input/output device that can be connected to a local or remote computer called a host computer.

269

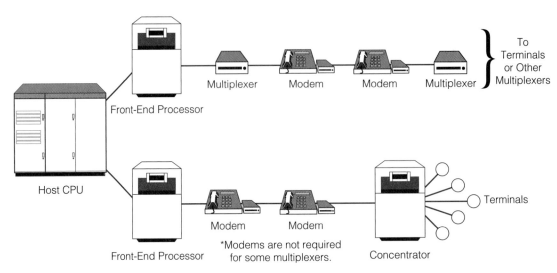

Figure 10–1
Hardware Configuration

have some degree of processing power and are connected to a host on a periodic basis, such as a microcomputer.

Terminal Types

Microcomputers   Microcomputers are an integral component of computer networks because they can augment the host by doing a portion of the processing. They may be grouped together in a LAN, connected as terminal devices to a host computer, or both. Some ways microcomputers are being used in networks include uploading processed data to the host, downloading host data for processing, and terminal emulation. **Uploading** happens when the terminal transfers files or programs to the host. **Downloading** is the act of transferring programs or data from a host to a terminal. With **terminal emulation,** a software program and a hardware interface allow one microcomputer to function as a variety of terminals in support of changing requirements.

Remote Job Entry Stations   Through remote job entry (RJE), a terminal can be used to forward recorded images to a host system and possibly to receive updated reports back from the host. Historically, input from such terminals has been card images and the resulting output has been printed reports or punched cards. Tape has also served as an input or output medium. This type of operation is sometimes called remote batch processing.

Data Entry and Display   A **video display unit (VDU)** or a hard-copy device such as a teletypewriter (TTY) can serve for data entry, data display, or both. Such devices can carry on a dialogue with the host(s) and get data from and provide data to the business's applications. A VDU is also sometimes called a video display terminal (VDT) or a cathode ray tube (CRT). A VDU terminal is shown in Figure 10–2.

uploading The transfer of files or programs from the terminal to the host.

downloading The transfer of files or programs from the host to the terminal.

terminal emulation A software program and a hardware interface that allow one microcomputer to function as a variety of terminals in support of changing requirements.

video display unit (VDU) A terminal that uses a technique such as a cathode ray tube or a liquid crystal display to represent data. Also called a video display terminal (VDT) or cathode ray tube (CRT).

Figure 10–2
VDU Terminal

Sensor Devices Sensor devices are used in laboratory, hospital, or data collection applications, often for input only. For example, many newer, large office buildings have computer-controlled environmental monitoring systems. Sensors located throughout the building alert the system to areas in which temperature is outside the comfort zone. The host responds by sending a message to an output-only terminal device that switches on heating or cooling.

Display-Only Devices A display-only device often serves as a receiver of data. The display monitors in stock market applications are display-only devices. Remote printers also fit in this class, although some also have the ability to transmit control information such as "out of paper" or "not ready to receive."

Point-of-Sale Terminals Point-of-sale (POS) terminals are used to help maintain inventory, record gross receipts, and in some instances participate in money transfers from a buyer's account to a merchant's account. The capabilities of POS terminals vary significantly.

Portable Terminals One application for portable terminals or microcomputers is in direct sales. Some marketing agencies provide their salespeople with portable terminals capable of storing information in memory.

The salesperson records customer orders during the day and can use a telephone link to transmit the orders to the home office for processing. Figure 10–3 features a portable microcomputer.

Touch-Tone Telephones   Touch-tone telephones can be used in bill paying, account inquiry or transfer applications, and student registration. Although not used extensively because of their limited input and output capabilities, they work well for certain applications.

Automatic Teller Machines   Most banks now have networks of automatic teller machines (ATMs) that enable the customer to personally handle simple banking transactions such as deposits, withdrawals, and account balance inquiries. ATMs have had a significant impact on the way people use banking services. Through the ATM, bank customers can get cash or make deposits 24 hours a day and without the assistance of a teller. The ATM provides convenience to the bank customer and reduces the number of personnel a bank needs to provide services, because the customer and the computer combine to accomplish services that formerly required the assistance of a bank teller.

Terminal Capabilities

Rather than discussing the wide variety of terminal types in depth, we focus our discussion on terminal capabilities and then present a list of attributes to be considered when selecting the proper terminal for a given

Figure 10–3
Portable Microcomputer

application. Terminals can be classified as dumb, smart, or intelligent, although no distinct lines separate these classes.

A **dumb terminal** passively serves for input or output and does no additional processing. Because dumb terminals usually have no memory to store data, each character entered must be transmitted immediately to the host, unsolicited, and the host must always be ready to accept data from the terminal. A dumb terminal generally operates in **conversational mode,** in which the terminal user and the host exchange messages in response to each other.

Smart terminals can do anything a dumb terminal can; however, smart terminals have memory. Data entered by the operator can be saved in the terminal's memory until an entire record or several screens of data have been entered. The terminal can then transmit all the entered data in one or more blocks, a capability called **block mode.** Often the screen can be divided into multiple windows, with each window representing a different object set. One window might represent text being written, one might contain notes about the text, another might contain a graphic image of an item being described in the text, and a fourth might contain a menu of tasks or commands that are valid in the current window. Most smart terminals are also addressable, which means that they can be given a name that both they and the host recognize. Thus, the host can transmit data addressed to that terminal, and the terminal will recognize that the data is intended for it and store the data in its memory. Smart terminals are subject to host control, which means that the host can specify when the terminal is allowed to

- send or receive data
- position the cursor on the display
- designate that certain fields, such as an employee's salary, are protected from alteration
- control the keyboard and disallow any data entry
- specify the display attributes of fields such as blink and half intensity
- read from or write to selected portions of the display

Addressing, memory, and host control capabilities enable several terminals to share the same medium and thereby reduce transmission costs.

Smart terminals may also support auxiliary data entry devices such as light pens, mice, and touch-screens. Many can have a printer attached, for printing a displayed page and for automatic logging of data received by the terminal. Many smart terminals have additional keys known as function keys, or program attention keys, that transmit specific character sequences to the host. Function keys allow the operator to indicate to the application what function is to be performed on the data provided. The number of function keys per terminal typically ranges from 4 to 32; some special-purpose terminals have 50 or more function keys.

An **intelligent terminal,** such as a microcomputer, has all or most of the capabilities of a smart terminal, but it can also participate in the data processing requirements of the system. In some situations the intelligent terminal is

dumb terminal A terminal that passively serves for input or output but performs no local processing.

conversational mode A mode in which the terminal and the host exchange messages.

smart terminal A terminal that can save data entered by the operator into memory.

block mode A mode in which data is entered and transmitted in one or more sets or blocks.

intelligent terminal A terminal that has both memory and data processing capabilities.

completely independent of the host; however, to satisfy our definition of terminal, at some point the intelligent terminal must be connected to a host processor for processing or data access. Because this terminal is programmable, it is also possible for an intelligent terminal to act as host for another terminal. Intelligent terminals may have secondary storage in the form of disk or tape, and an attached printer is a common option. If no auxiliary storage is available, programs can be downloaded to the terminal from the host computer. Like smart terminals, intelligent terminals can be controlled from the host and can operate in both conversational and block modes. Processing functions available on intelligent terminals include storage and display of screen formats, data editing, data formatting, compression/decompression, and possibly some local database access and validation.

Advantages of Dumb, Smart, and Intelligent Terminals

The advantage of smart terminals over dumb terminals is a certain amount of independence between the terminal operator and host. Once a data entry screen is displayed, the operator is free to enter data at his or her own pace, unrestricted by the transmission speed of the line. Any errors made by the operator can be corrected without the host's involvement. The operator can move the cursor to any field in the record and can correct any data before transmission to the host. The host then controls the terminal and solicits inputs and outputs according to its priorities rather than being periodically interrupted by unsolicited inputs, as is the case with dumb terminals. The advantages of intelligent terminals over smart terminals stem from the fact that control and processing are local. Some data, such as customer data, can be maintained locally where it is used frequently, and line time is not required for obtaining customer information, transmitting screen templates, or correcting edit errors.

Several terminal attributes are listed in Table 10–1. These attributes are among the criteria to consider when selecting a terminal for a given application.

Input and Output

Terminal output can be hard copy and soft copy. Hard-copy output leaves a permanent record of the data sent to the terminals, whereas soft-copy out-

Table 10–1   Some Terminal Attributes

Cost	Synchronous	Auxiliary storage	EBCDIC
Conversational	Batch	Protected fields	Protocol support
Block mode	Point-to-point	Graphics	Attached devices
TTY-compatible	Multipoint	Formatting	Duplex
Dumb	Function keys	Character sets	Screen size
Smart	Editing	Keyboard	Character size
Intelligent	Cursor control	Blink	Modified data tags
Printer	Host control	Half intensity	CPU
Speed	Color	Reverse video	Interface
Asynchronous	Programmable	ASCII	Portability

put leaves no record of the inputs or outputs. Hard copy uses some type of printed output, and soft copy uses a display monitor such as a CRT. The most common input mechanism is the keyboard, which can be configured in a variety of ways. Some configurations support foreign languages, whereas others have preprogrammed keys that support specific applications, such as specimen description keys for medical laboratories. Other input devices include various types of readers—badge readers and OCR readers—and light pens, mice, trackballs, joysticks, touch-screens, sensors, voice recognition and generation equipment, and digital image processing devices that scan graphic images and create digital images of them.

Cost

The cost of terminals varies dramatically, from several hundred dollars for a dumb terminal to tens of thousands of dollars for special terminals such as RJE or very-high-resolution graphics terminals with imaging devices. Cost analysis is difficult, as cost factors such as line use, operator acceptance, efficiency, and local processing ability are not always easy to quantify.

Speed

The speed at which a terminal accepts and transmits data depends on the terminal hardware, the type of line to which it is attached, and the types of modems used (if any). Any given terminal can receive and transmit information at a discrete set of rates. An unbuffered hard-copy terminal may have a maximum receive speed of 1200 bps because its print capacity is 120 characters per second. A CRT device, on the other hand, may be capable of receiving data at 56 Kbps or more. In addition to the maximum available speed, the intermediate speeds available should be considered. Some terminals have one or two speed settings, whereas others support several common speeds, such as 75, 300, 600, 1200, 2400, 4800, 9600, 19,200, 28,800, 33,600 and 56,000 bps.

Maintenance and Support

Some computer manufacturers sell terminals that are manufactured by other companies. These computer manufacturers usually provide the support for these terminals. Other computer vendors build their own terminals and design them to complement their computer systems. These terminals usually receive support consistent with the support for the rest of the system. An advantage of such vendor support is having only one organization to contact regardless of the problem. For instance, what appears to be a terminal problem may actually be an error in the software or hardware communicating with that terminal. Single-vendor support tends to eliminate the question of who is responsible for errors. Determining which vendor is responsible for a problem can become a difficult issue in multiple-vendor installations. Single-vendor support has one disadvantage for both terminals and computer equipment: Computer manufacturers sometimes charge more for their terminals than manufacturers who specialize in terminal equipment.

Display Attributes

Hard-copy devices have very few display attributes to select, with the possible exception of colored pens for plotters, graphics, italics, underline, type fonts, or overprint. Video display units have several display attributes to consider, including multiple colors, shading or intensity, reverse video, and highlighting such as blinking fields. Screen size and character size also should be taken into consideration because the number of characters per line and the number of lines per screen can vary significantly.

Data Link Protocol

Terminals communicate by a convention that transmits either a character at a time or a block at a time. In Chapter 7 we discussed LAN data link protocols. WANs also use data link protocols, but typically WAN data link protocols differ from LAN protocols. WAN data link protocols (discussed in more detail in Chapter 11) are a primary concern when purchasing a terminal. Many terminals communicate via only one of these conventions, such as an asynchronous protocol or one of several synchronous protocols.

Terminal Configurations

point-to-point connection A connection using a communication line to connect one terminal to a host computer.

On any communication channel, the two options for attaching terminals are point to point and multipoint. **Point-to-point connections** use a communication line to connect one terminal to the host computer. Point-to-point connections are common in computer-to-computer communication, local connections between a host and a terminal where the cost of the line is negligible, and remote connections with only one remote terminal. The method for controlling which station is allowed to use the communication link is sometimes called a line discipline. Data flow in a point-to-point configuration is usually determined by contention.

contention mode A mode in which the host and the terminal contend for control of the medium by issuing a bid for the channel.

In the **contention mode,** the host and the terminal contend for control of the medium, much like nodes on a CSMA/CD LAN. The terminal and the host are considered to have an equal right to transmit to the other. To transmit, one station issues a bid for the channel, asking the other party for control. If the other is ready to receive data, control is granted to the requester. Upon completion of the transfer, control is relinquished and the link goes into an idle state, awaiting the next bid for control. A collision can occur when both stations simultaneously bid for the line. If this occurs, either one station is granted the request based on some predetermined priority scheme or each station waits a while and then reattempts the bid. With the latter approach, the timeout intervals must not be the same, or another collision occurs. Conflicts for the use of the channel in a point-to-point configuration typically are few because only the host and the terminal are candidates for transmission.

multipoint connection A connection in which several terminals share one communication link.

For communication among several terminals over a long distance, true point-to-point connections would be quite expensive, as each terminal would require a separate line with a pair of modems. Several techniques have been developed to allow several terminals to share one communication link. One such technology is called a **multipoint connection.** The number of terminals allowed to share the medium depends on the speed of the medium and the aggregate transmission rate of the terminals. As the number of terminals on the line increases, the average time each terminal has access to the link decreases. With terminals, the most common approaches to multipoint connections are polling and multiplexing.

Polling   The process of asking terminals whether they have data to transmit is called **polling.** In polling, one station is designated as the supervisor or primary station. This role is almost always assumed by the host computer, although other pieces of equipment such as controllers or concentrators may be used instead. There is only one primary station per multipoint link; all other stations are called secondary stations. In the discussion that follows we assume that the host computer is the primary.

The primary station is in complete control of the link. Secondary stations may transmit data only when given permission by the primary station. Each secondary station is given a unique address, and each terminal must be able to recognize its own address. Although there are several distinct methods of polling, essentially the process works as follows. The primary is provided a list of addresses for terminals on a particular link. Several multipoint lines may be controlled by one primary, although addresses on a given line are unique. The primary picks an address from the list and sends a poll message across the link using that address. The poll message is very short, consisting of the poll address and a string of characters that has been designated as a poll message. All secondary stations receive the poll message, but only the addressee responds. The poll message is an inquiry to the secondary station as to whether it has any data to transmit to the primary. If it has data to transmit, the secondary responds either with the data or with a positive acknowledgment and then the data. If the secondary station has no data to send, it responds with a negative acknowledgment. Upon receipt of either the data or the negative acknowledgment, the primary selects another station's polling address and repeats the process.

Selection   When the primary has data to send to one or more secondary stations, it selects the station in much the same manner as with polling. Some terminals have two addresses, one for polling and one for selecting. In the selection process, the primary sends a selection message to the terminal. A selection message consists of the terminal's selection address and an inquiry to determine whether the terminal is ready to accept data. The terminal may respond positively or negatively. If the terminal's buffer is full, it cannot accept additional data and responds negatively. After a positive acknowledgment to the selection message, the primary transmits the data to the terminal. In some multipoint networks the primary can send a message to all stations simultaneously via a broadcast address, which is one address that all terminals recognize as their own.

Types of Polling   The two basic types of polling are roll call and hub polling. In roll-call polling the primary obtains a list of addresses for terminals on the line and then proceeds sequentially down the list, polling each terminal in turn. If one or more stations on the link are of higher priority or

polling The process of asking terminals whether they have data to transmit. One terminal, usually the host, is designated as the primary station and the rest are called secondary stations.

are more likely to have data to send, their address could be included in the list multiple times so they can be polled more often. Roll-call polling is illustrated in Figure 10–4.

Hub polling requires the terminals to become involved in the polling process. The primary sends a poll message to one station on the link. If that station has data to transmit, it does so. After transmitting its data or if it has no data to transmit, the secondary terminal passes the poll to an adjacent terminal. This process is repeated until all terminals have had the opportunity to transmit. The primary then starts the process again. Hub polling is illustrated in Figure 10–5. In the diagram, if T2 were not operational, T3 would pass the poll to T1.

Advantage of Multipoint Connections The advantage of multipoint lines is economic. First, only one communication link is required for a host to communicate with several terminals; second, if modems are required on the link, fewer modems are necessary. In a true point-to-point link, a pair of modems is often required for each terminal, one at the host end and one at the terminal end. For multipoint links, at most one modem per terminal and one at the host are required. In some instances a terminal cluster controller may be used at the terminal end, and if the terminals are sufficiently close to the controller, individual terminal modems are not necessary; only a host and cluster controller modem are required. If 10 terminals are to be located remotely, 10 point-to-point lines would require 20 modems. For a multipoint line, at most 11 modems would be required, and possibly 2 would be sufficient. Figure 10–6 presents multipoint configurations, together with their required modems.

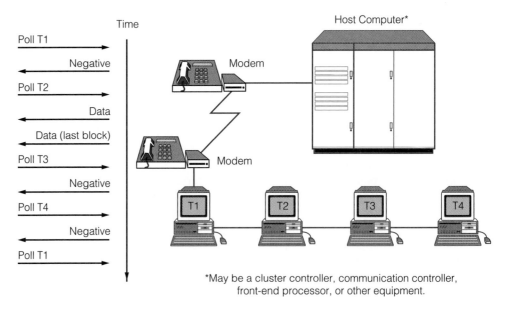

*May be a cluster controller, communication controller, front-end processor, or other equipment.

Figure 10–4
Roll-Call Polling

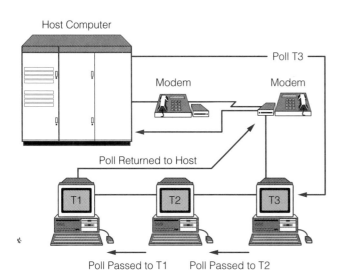

Figure 10–5
Hub Polling

Disadvantages of Multipoint Connections　There are also disadvantages to the multipoint configuration. First, terminals used in this environment must have some intelligence, making them more expensive than terminals in the point-to-point connection. This higher cost is usually negligible, however, when compared with the savings in medium and modems. Because the medium is shared among several terminals, a terminal may have to wait to transmit its information. If messages are short, the wait time should not be long; on the other hand, if messages are lengthy, as when a

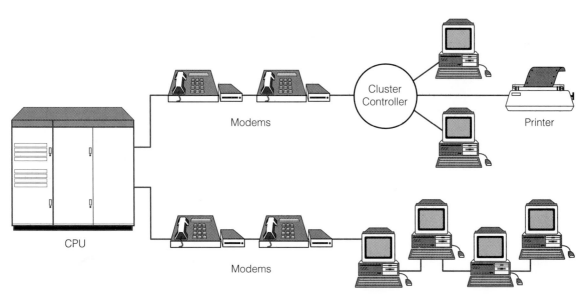

Figure 10–6
Multipoint Configurations

microcomputer transfers a file, the other terminals may have to wait an inordinate amount of time. Delays also have an impact on response times, and this delay should be factored into the response time calculations for a multipoint line.

MULTIPLEXERS

multiplexing A line-sharing technology that allows multiple signals to be transmitted over a single link.

Polling requires the use of smart terminals that are addressable and have memory. Another line-sharing technique, **multiplexing,** does not generally require the use of smart terminals. Multiplexing technology allows multiple signals to be transmitted over a single link. Multiplexing has been used by telephone companies for many years to combine multiple voice-grade circuits into a single high-speed circuit for long-distance communication. In data communication networks, multiplexers, or muxes, allow several devices to share a common circuit.

How Multiplexers Work

Remote locations often have multiple devices that must communicate with a host. Multiplexing provides an alternative to a point-to-point connection and polling. Figure 10–7 presents a general mux configuration. Several communication lines enter the mux from the host side. The mux combines the data from all incoming lines and transmits it via one line to a mux at the receiving end.

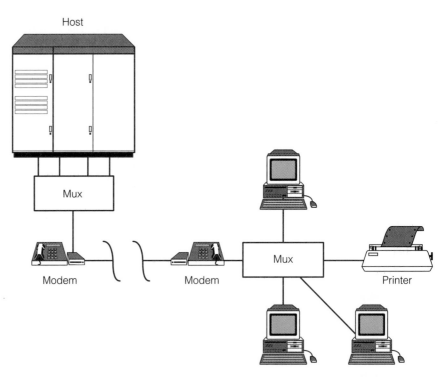

Figure 10–7
General Multiplexer Configuration

Four host lines combined with one long-distance line.
A modem is not required by all types of multiplexers.

This receiving mux separates the data and distributes it among the outgoing terminal lines. The number of lines going into the mux on the host side is the same as the number going out to terminals (or other muxes) on the remote side.

To the user, the multiplexer appears to function as though there were several physical lines rather than just one. The configuration of one high-speed link and a pair of multiplexers, however, costs less than that of several lower-speed links with a pair of modems for each. Applications written for a point-to-point terminal connection also can be used without change. The multiplexer makes the line sharing transparent to the user because the application essentially sees a point-to-point line.

Types of Multiplexers

A communication link is divided among several users in two basic ways. The first technique, known as **frequency division multiplexing (FDM),** separates the link by frequencies. The second technique, known as **time division multiplexing (TDM),** separates the link into time slots.

Frequency Division Multiplexing   In (FDM) the available bandwidth of the circuit is broken into subchannels, each of which has smaller bandwidths. Consider a telephone circuit with a bandwidth of 3100 Hz, a frequency range of 300 to 3400 Hz, and a line-carrying capacity of 1200 bps. On this line we could have one terminal operating at 1200 bps; however, instead of one terminal running at 1200 bps we want to have three terminals operating at 300 bps. Although arithmetically it appears possible to have four 300-bps terminals on the line, this is impossible because frequency separation of the subchannels must be maintained to avoid crosstalk. The recommended separation for a 300-bps circuit is 480 Hz. The subchannel separators are called **guardbands.** This situation requires two guardbands of 480 Hz each. Each of the three 300-bps subchannels therefore has a bandwidth of 713 Hz, derived as follows:

3100 Hz (total bandwidth of circuit)
        − 960 Hz (two guardbands at 480 Hz each)
                = 2140 Hz/3 channels = 713 Hz per channel

Similarly, a 9600-bps channel can be divided into four 1200-bps channels. The higher the speed of individual channels, the larger the guardbands must be. Figure 10–8 illustrates an FDM configuration and the division of the channel into several subchannels. There is no need for modems in this configuration because the FDM functions as a modem by accepting the signal from the data terminal equipment (DTE) and transforming it into a signal within a given frequency range. Thus, the modem is integrated into the FDM. Each line in the FDM is mapped onto one of the subchannels. The first line's signal is passed along the first subchannel, the second line's along the second subchannel, and so on. If terminals on that line are not busy, that portion of the carrying capacity goes unused.

Time Division Multiplexing   TDM is roughly equivalent to time-sharing systems. As with FDM, TDM has a group of lines entering the mux, one

frequency division multiplexing (FDM) A technique that divides the available bandwidth of the circuit into subchannels of different frequency ranges, each of which is assigned to one device.

Time Division Multiplexing (TDM) A technique that divides transmission time by allotting to each device a time slot during which it can send or receive data.

guardbands Subchannel separators that are implemented in frequency division multiplexing to avoid crosstalk.

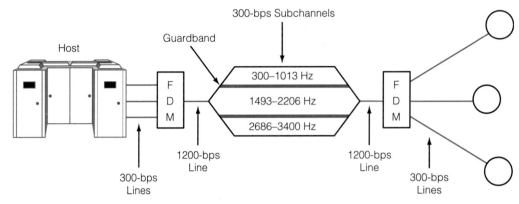

Figure 10–8
Frequency Division Multiplexer Configuration

circuit shared by all, and the same number of lines leaving the mux at the other end. Instead of splitting the frequency, however, TDM shares time: Each line is given a time slot for transmitting, which is accomplished by interleaving bits or characters. Bit interleaving is more common for synchronous (block at a time) transmissions and character interleaving is more common with asynchronous (character at a time) transmissions.

To understand how TDM operates, look at the four-port TDM in Figure 10–9. This mux combines signals from the four lines onto a single communication circuit. Data entering the TDM from the devices on the

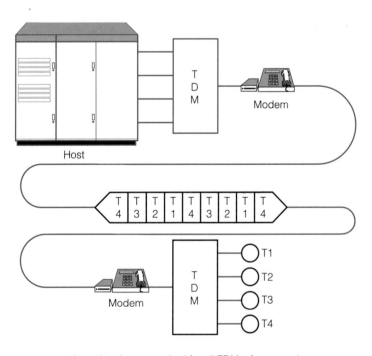

Figure 10–9
Time Division Multiplexer

*A modem is not required for all TDMs; for example, an in-house digital TDM may not require modems.

input line are placed in a buffer or register. With character interleaving, first a character from line 1 is transmitted, then a character from line 2, one from line 3, one from line 4, and back again to line 1 to repeat the process. Bit interleaving works in the same manner except that a bit instead of a character is taken from each line in turn to form a transmission block. The mux at the other end breaks the data back out and places it on the appropriate line.

As with FDM, each line gets a portion of the available transfer time. However, TDM requires no guardbands, so there is no loss of carrying capacity. Each line is given a portion of the circuit's carrying capacity even though there are no data to be transmitted. Still, the improvement is significant: Instead of only three 300-bps sublines on a 1200-bps line, there can be four lines, each capable of 300-bps transmission. A 9600-bps line can be multiplexed into eight 1200-bps lines or four 2400-bps lines, as illustrated in Figure 10–10.

Statistical Time Division Multiplexing **Statistical time division multiplexing (STDM or stat mux)** improves on the efficiency of TDM by transmitting data only for lines with data to send, so idle lines take up none of the carrying capacity of the communication circuit. Figure 10–11 illustrates STDM. Because neither time slot nor frequency is allocated to a specific terminal, an STDM must also transmit a terminal identification along with the data block. When all lines have data to transmit, an STDM looks just like a TDM; when only one line has data to send, the entire line capacity is devoted to that line.

Under good conditions, an STDM on a 9600-bps line can support five or six 2400-bps sublines, as illustrated in Figure 10–11, or three to four 4800-bps sublines. The reason for this apparent increase in carrying capacity stems from the probability that none of the incoming lines will be 100% busy. If each line is only 50% busy, then four 4800-bps lines could be placed on one 9600-bps link. STDMs also have internal buffers for holding data from a line in case all lines try to transmit at once. Newer stat muxes provide additional capabilities, including

- data compression
- digital data support
- line priorities

statistical time division multiplexing (STDM) A technique that provides improved time-sharing efficiency by transmitting data only for lines with data to send, rather than allowing idle lines to occupy carrying capacity of the communication circuit. Also known as a stat mux.

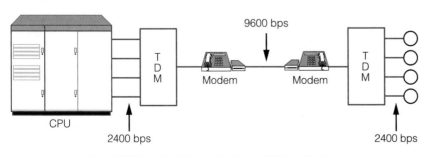

One 9600-bps Line Supporting Four 2400-bps Devices

Figure 10–10
Time Division Multiplexing

Figure 10–11
Statistical Time Division Multiplexing

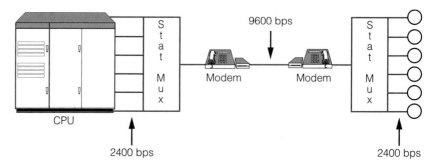

One 9600-bps Line Supporting Six 2400-bps Devices

- mixed-speed lines
- integrated modems
- network control ports for monitoring the multiplexed line
- host port sharing, in which two or more lines at the terminal end are mapped onto one line at the host end
- port switching, wherein a terminal can be switched from one port to another
- accumulation and reporting of performance statistics
- automatic speed detection
- memory expansion
- internal diagnostics

All of these features are not likely to be found in one mux. Different manufacturers offer one or more of these capabilities as standard or optional functions. A few of these features can also be found in TDMs. Most of the development and enhancements in the past several years have been devoted to stat muxes because of their higher performance capabilities.

Multiplexer Configurations

In addition to attaching terminals to muxes, other muxes can be added in **daisy-chain** fashion, a configuration illustrated in Figure 10–12. Daisy chaining, also called **cascading,** allows some circuits to be extended to another remote point, which is useful in a situation with two areas for data entry. With eight terminals in each area, a 16-port stat mux could provide linkage between the host and area A, and eight lines from area A could travel via an eight-port mux to area B. The number of ports on a mux can vary, but commonly there are 4, 8, 16, 32, 48, or 64 ports. Multiplexer prices vary according to the number of ports and features provided. For a plain four-port or eight-port stat mux, prices start at about $1000.

A less common mux known as an **inverse multiplexer** provides a high-speed data path between two devices, usually computers. An inverse mux accepts one line from a host and separates it into multiple lower-speed communication circuits. The multiple low-speed circuits are recom-

daisy chain A connection arrangement in which each device is connected directly to the next device. For example, a daisy chain of devices A, B, C, and D might have A connected to B, B connected to C, and C connected to D. Also known as cascading.

inverse multiplexer A mux that provides a high-speed data path between two devices by separating an incoming line into multiple lower-speed communication circuits.

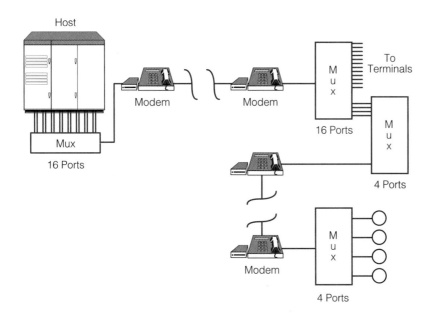

Figure 10–12
Cascading Multiplexers

bined at the other end into a high-speed link, as illustrated in Figure 10–13. A 56-Kbps link from a computer to an inverse mux can be split into six 9600-bps lines and then back to a 56-Kbps line at the remote end. Telephone companies use this type of multiplexing to provide high-speed communication lines.

CONCENTRATORS

A **concentrator** is also a line-sharing device. It functions similar to a mux, allowing multiple devices to share communication circuits. Because a concentrator is a computer, however, it can participate more actively than a mux in any application. In the early 1970s there was a marked distinction between a concentrator and a multiplexer. As multiplexers took on the additional functions just described, the difference between the two devices

concentrator A computer that provides line-sharing capabilities, data editing, polling, error handling, code conversion, compression, and encryption.

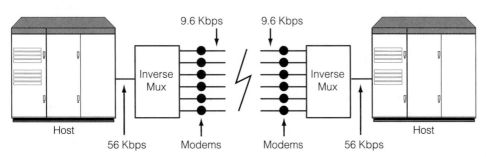

Figure 10–13
Inverse Multiplexer

Figure 10–14
Concentrator Configuration

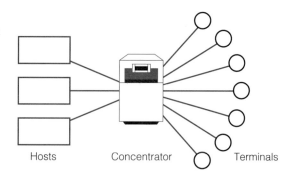

Hosts   Concentrator   Terminals

narrowed. Currently the principal differences between a mux and a concentrator are as follows:

- Concentrators are used one at a time; multiplexers are used in pairs.
- A concentrator may have multiple incoming and outgoing lines, with a different number of incoming lines than outgoing lines; a multiplexer takes a certain number of incoming lines onto one line and converts back to the same number of outgoing lines.
- A concentrator is a computer and may have auxiliary storage for use in support of an application.
- A concentrator may perform some data processing functions, such as device polling and data validation.

One possible concentrator configuration is illustrated in Figure 10–14.

Concentrators can further aid an application by providing data editing, polling, error handling, code conversion, compression, and encryption. Concentrators can also switch messages between terminals and hosts. In a banking ATM environment where three regional processing centers are responsible for authorizing transactions, each city with multiple ATMs could use a concentrator to handle ATM traffic. The concentrator would have three lines, one each for the three hosts in the three regional processing centers. There would also be one line for each ATM or cluster of ATMs. Based on the customer's ATM card number, the concentrator would switch each transaction to the processing center closest to the customer's home branch.

front-end processor (FEP) A communication component placed at the host end of a circuit to take over a portion of the line management work from the host. Also called a communication controller or message switch.

FRONT-END PROCESSORS

A **front-end processor (FEP),** sometimes called a communication controller or message switch, is used at the host end of the communication circuit, just as a concentrator is used at the remote end. The FEP takes over much of the line management work from the host; in many respects, FEPs and concentrators serve the same function. An FEP configuration is shown in Figure 10–15.

An FEP interface with a host system uses one or more high-speed links. The FEP is responsible for controlling the more numerous low-speed circuits. All functions of a concentrator can also be performed by an FEP, except, of course, concentrating message traffic for multiple remote terminals onto

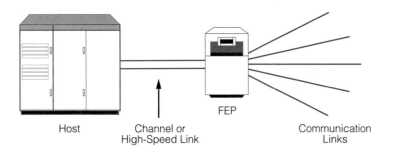

Figure 10–15
Front-End Processor Configuration

one communication line. FEPs may be either special purpose or general purpose. Special-purpose FEPs, such as IBM's communication controllers, are designed specifically for data communication. Their operating system and software are solely communication oriented. General-purpose computers, such as minicomputers, are also used as FEPs. When general-purpose computers are used in this way, their role is generally restricted to providing data communication functions.

PROTOCOL CONVERTERS

In Chapter 7 we discussed protocols, which are conventions for communication between devices. Protocols determine the sequences in which data exchanges may take place and the bit or character sequences required to provide device and line control. Each maker of terminals typically has its own proprietary protocols, which means that a Digital Equipment Corporation (DEC) VT420 terminal cannot directly communicate with an IBM system over a line configured for IBM 3270 terminals. To bridge these differences, companies have developed **protocol converters,** which are special-purpose devices that allow a terminal to look like a different type of terminal. A protocol converter also enables different computer systems to transmit to and receive from a given terminal model. Protocol conversion is accomplished by hardware or software. Figure 10–16 shows an example of protocol converters connecting several different devices. Many different types of protocol converters are available. Some of the more common types are

protocol converter A special-purpose device that allows a terminal to look like a different type of terminal in order to facilitate interconnection between different computer systems.

- asynchronous to synchronous
- TTY to IBM 3270

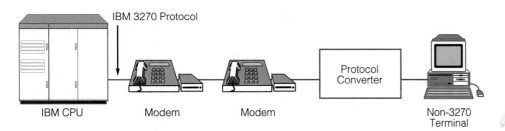

Figure 10–16
Protocol Conversion

- asynchronous to IBM SDLC
- IBM 3270 to IBM 2260 poll/select
- IBM 2780/3780 to IBM 3270
- PARS (airline reservation system protocol) to binary synchronous

DIAGNOSTIC AND MISCELLANEOUS EQUIPMENT

The hardware discussed thus far is involved in the transportation or receipt of data. Another set of hardware is often necessary to perform the following functions:

- provide security of transmission and facilities
- monitor data
- control the sequences being transmitted
- provide connections for switched communication lines
- provide other functions necessary to control and manage the communication network

Some of these devices are described below.

Security Hardware

Security of data transmission and storage is becoming increasingly important. Several types of hardware are available to assist in the protection of data.

call-back unit A security device for switched connections. It operates by receiving a call, verifying the user, severing the call, and calling the user back.

Call-Back Units   One simple but effective device is a **call-back unit,** which participates in making switched connections. A person trying to access a system using a switched connection must identify himself or herself with an ID and a password. The opening connection is severed after the ID and password are entered, and the call-back unit scans its tables for that user's number and calls the number to make the connection.

A call-back system has at least two problems. First, the host computer becomes responsible for the cost of the connection. Second, the call-back system prohibits portable terminal connections, such as that needed by a traveling salesperson or executive with a portable computer. However, some call-back units allow users with certain passwords to bypass the call-back. The bypass may be allowed at all times for certain users or may be programmed to allow bypass only during specific hours. This feature has the disadvantage of lowering security.

Encryption Equipment   Encryption equipment allows transmitted data to be scrambled at the sending location and reconstructed at the receiving end. The U.S. National Bureau of Standards (NBS) has approved a standard called the data encryption standard (DES), which uses a 64-bit pattern as the encryption key. The DES algorithm is available on a chip contained in commercially available encryption boxes. Figure 10–17 shows an encryption device installed on a communication link. Encryption is discussed in more detail in Chapter 19.

Line Monitors

Line monitors, also known as protocol analyzers, are used to diagnose problems on a communication link. Their basic function is to attach to a communication circuit so the bit patterns being transmitted over the link can be displayed for analysis and problem solving by a data communication expert. The two types of line monitors are digital and analog. Analog monitors are used primarily by common carrier personnel to analyze their lines. Digital monitors are used by data processing technicians to check for adherence to protocols. In this discussion we refer to digital monitors such as the one shown in Figure 10–18. Features commonly available on line monitors are

line monitor A device used to diagnose problems on a communication link. Also known as a protocol analyzer.

video display	memory
recording tape or disk	programmability
trap setting for selected bit patterns	multiple protocol support
variable character-length support	multiple interfaces
multiple speeds	function keys
graphics display	integrated breakout box
importing/exporting data	

If a corporation requires multiple line monitors to cover multiple locations, it is best to use models from one manufacturer. Each manufacturer usually has several models with varying capabilities, which allows the user to buy the minimum required capability for a specific location. There are two reasons for using equipment from only one manufacturer. First, personnel education is easier when there is only one manufacturer. Even

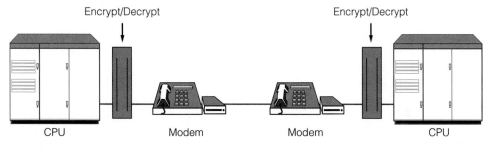

Figure 10–17
Data Encryption Box

Figure 10–18
Digital Line Monitor

though different models may be used, the operations are usually quite similar, especially for simple functions. Second, and more important, recordings made at one site may be shipped to another and analyzed; because there is no industry standard recording mode, a tape or disk recorded on Manufacturer A's machine is probably not readable on Manufacturer B's equipment.

Some microcomputers can be enhanced to provide line-monitoring capabilities. A microcomputer may be enhanced with an adapter board, connector, and software that will provide network and protocol analyzer capabilities. The price for this capability is usually less than that for a dedicated analyzer because some of the components of an analyzer—monitor, disk drives, and cabinetry—are already part of the microcomputer. Some of the necessary hardware and software to equip a microcomputer with this ability is priced under $1500.

Breakout Boxes

breakout box A passive, multipurpose diagnostic device that is patched or temporarily inserted into a circuit at an interface.

A **breakout box** is a passive, multipurpose device that is patched or temporarily inserted into a circuit at an interface. Figure 10–19 shows a programmable breakout box. Once the breakout box is installed, it is possible to monitor activity on each of the circuits, change circuit connections, isolate a circuit to prevent its signal from passing through to the receiver, and measure circuit voltage levels. Some breakout boxes are equipped with bit pattern generators and receivers, which allow for transmitting and receiving a small number of selected bit patterns. This beneficial feature allows the individual doing the testing to determine what effect a known data pattern has on the circuit.

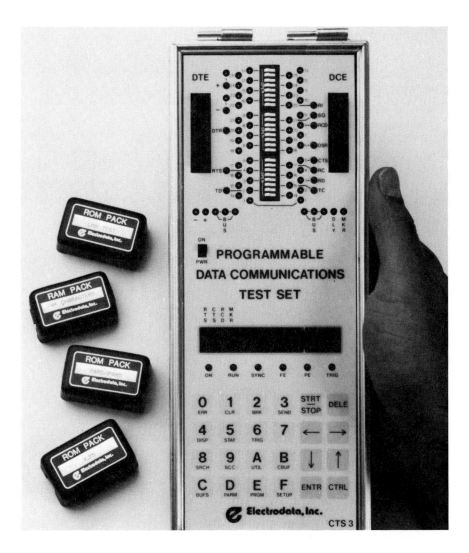

Figure 10–19
Programmable Breakout Box

Auto-Call Units

An **auto-call unit (ACU)** is used to place a telephone call without manual intervention. The ACU is able to open the line (equivalent to lifting the handset from its cradle), detect the dial tone, dial the number (through either pulse dialing or touch-tone dialing), detect the ring indicator or busy signal, and determine whether the call is complete or incomplete. Incomplete calls are usually the result of a busy signal, failure to answer, a busy circuit, or a number out of order. In the United States, ACUs could originally be sold only by the telephone companies. This policy changed with the Carterphone decision. The ACU and auto-answer functions are now common in modem equipment. The interface to ACU equipment in the United States is via the RS-232-C or RS-366 interface. The latter specifically addresses the electrical and functional interface for automatic calling equipment.

auto-call unit (ACU) A device used to place a telephone call automatically without manual intervention.

Port Concentrator

port concentrator A device that allows multiple input streams from a multiplexer to be passed to the host through a single communication port.

Multiplexers allow multiple terminals to share one communication link. However, for each terminal attached to a multiplexer there must be one communication port at the host end to receive the signal, which makes the multiplexer appear to be a point-to-point connection for both terminal and host. All systems have an upper limit to the number of communication ports that may be configured, and, of course, there is a cost to providing ports. A **port concentrator,** illustrated in Figure 10–20, allows multiple input streams from a multiplexer to be passed to the host through a single communication port. This is beneficial not only in reducing the hardware cost of the host but also in allowing for expansion beyond the port limitations of a particular processor. Port concentration requires that a software module be available in the host to receive the multiple terminal messages and then route them to the appropriate applications.

Port Selector or Data Switch

port selector A device that helps determine which users are granted access to applications when the number of potential terminal users far exceeds the number of available lines. Also known as a data switch.

A **port selector** helps determine which users are granted access to applications for which the number of potential terminal users far exceeds the number of available lines, as in reservation and library systems. If a particular system allows a total of 1000 terminals to communicate with a host at one time and there are 8000 potential users, obviously not all of these users can have access to the system at once. A port selector helps to determine which users are granted access. For switched lines the port selector can act as a rotary, allowing users to dial one number and connecting the incoming calls to any available switched port. It can also enable switched users to connect to an unused dedicated port. Port selectors can sometimes make connections to several hosts. Some port selectors give the user considerable control over how many ports will be used for switched calls, how many can be shared between dedicated and switched users, and how many can be routed to another host. Thus, the ports and the class of users who may select them can be configured to meet specific needs. Figure 10–21 shows how a port selector is used.

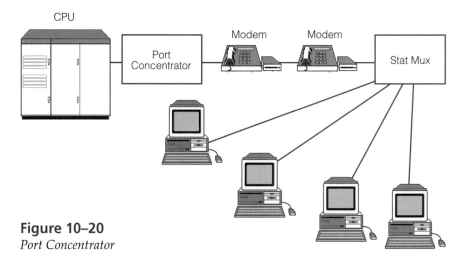

Figure 10–20
Port Concentrator

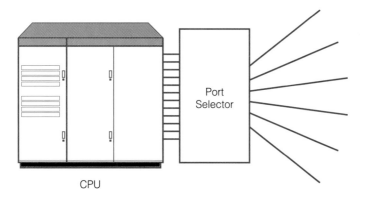

Figure 10–21
Port Selector Schematic

Cluster Controllers

A **cluster controller,** depicted in Figure 10–22, is designed to support several terminals. It manages the terminals, buffers data being transmitted to or from the terminals, performs error detection and correction, and polls. The controller may be attached to the host either locally or remotely. Although every terminal attached to a cluster controller usually uses the same communication protocol, the devices themselves may differ. The remote cluster controller in Figure 10–22 has VDUs and a printer attached.

cluster controller A device that manages multiple terminals by buffering data transmitted to and from the terminals and performing error detection and correction.

Private Branch Exchanges

A private branch exchange (PBX) is a private telephone switch. Within a company, some of the telephone calls are between employees in the same building complex. Rather than routing these calls through the telephone company's switch, a PBX switches the calls internally while routing external calls through the telephone company's system. In the past, private branch exchange (PBX) telephone switches were separate from data communication networks. More recently, PBXs have been integrated into networks, primarily to provide LAN capabilities. Using the PBX system as a LAN medium can be efficient because the wiring is already in place. The disadvantage of using PBX systems for LANs is lower transmission speed and competition between data and voice for available transmission capacity.

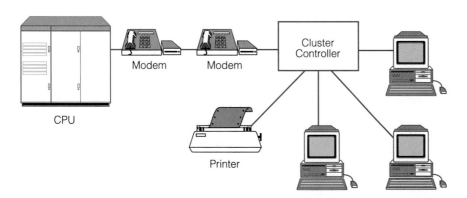

Figure 10–22
Cluster Controller

Figure 10–23
Matrix Switch
Hardware

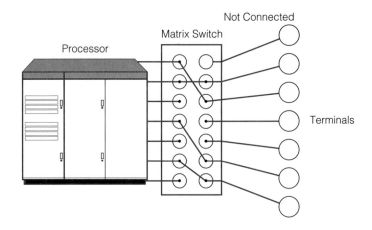

Matrix Switches

matrix switch A device that allows terminal connections to be switched among the available processors.

Some installations have multiple host processors, and terminal users may attach to a specific host in a variety of ways. One way is through a **matrix switch,** such as that shown in Figure 10–23. The switch allows terminal connections to be switched among the available processors. This is effected manually through a patch panel or automatically through program control. Matrix switches prevent the need to physically move communication lines between terminals and processors. Three ways a matrix switch may be used include the following:

- Users can be evenly distributed over several processors. If one processor in the system becomes saturated, some users can be quickly and efficiently transferred to another processor.

- If a failure occurs in one line, the terminals attached to that line are switched to a functional line.

- More terminals can be distributed than direct physical line attachment would permit. For example, it may be necessary to have terminals in conference rooms, demonstration areas, and unoccupied offices, where they are seldom used. For a system that supports 256 directly connected terminals, there may actually be 275 installed terminals. Using a matrix switch, terminals in low-use areas can easily be connected or disconnected from the system as needed.

The Syncrasy Corporation is considering expanding operations into several major marketing areas. A preliminary analysis has been initiated to determine the cost of expansion and a portion of the analysis has already been completed. System design objectives and system goals have been formulated. A feasibility study is under way to determine whether the design objectives can be met within the budget. One goal of this study is to determine the number of terminals required in each location, which necessitates first estimating transaction time.

TRANSACTION TIME

Syncrasy's preliminary analysis indicated that expansion needs will be met by a single host processor with multiple terminals at remote locations. For one location it has been determined that five types of transactions—order entry, credit check, customer maintenance, and send and receive mail—constitute the major transaction load. These transaction types are described in Table 10–2.

Think/Wait Time

Think/wait time is the amount of time the operator will wait or think while entering data for each transaction. A long think/wait time for a customer maintenance transaction (120 seconds) reflects the time the operator is obtaining the information from the telephone. Other possible sources of think/wait time are drinking coffee or tea, reading documents, rearranging papers, and so on.

think/wait time The amount of time an operator will wait or think while entering data for each transaction.

Data Entry (Input/Output) Time

The number of input characters represents the number of keystrokes the operator enters to complete a transaction. Depending on the type of data being entered, operators are capable of entering five or more characters per second. The following analysis assumes a more conservative keystroke rate of 1.5 characters per second. Number of output characters is the number of characters received in response to the transaction. We account for protocol overhead by assuming that each character transmitted requires 10 bits.

Disk/CPU/Queuing Time

Disk/CPU/queuing time is the amount of time the transaction is held by the processor and the time spent waiting in queues at different places in the system. For this analysis the cumulative times for these activities have been

Table 10–2 Projected Transactions for Syncrasy Corporation

	Transaction Type				
	Order Entry	Credit Check	Customer Maintenance	Send Mail	Receive Mail
Think/wait time (s)	10	5	120	60	180
No. of input characters	600	50	150	2000	50
No. of output characters	20	500	500	50	2000
Disk/CPU/queuing time (s)	1	0.5	0.5	1.5	1.5
Hourly peak	40	10	4	5	5

given. In reality, some of these times are difficult to determine. Disk access time is important because each transaction type requires records to be read from or written into the database. For order entry transactions, the inventory levels of each item ordered are adjusted by reading and writing the inventory record for each item, which might require that one or more index tables be accessed and searched. Database access times depend on the type of disk drive used and the organization of the database. There are usually three major components of disk access time: seek time, rotational delay or latency, and transfer time.

CPU time is the amount of time required for the CPU to execute the processing instructions, including those executed by the DBMS, the OS, the data communication software, and the application programs. CPU time is a function of the speed of the processor and memory, as well as of the number and type of instructions to be executed, and it is small compared to disk access time and data transmission time. Because most business transactions tend to be input/output (I/O) intensive, and because I/O time is usually much greater than CPU time, CPU time usually has little impact on the final calculations.

Queuing time is the amount of time the transaction must wait in queues for service. Queuing time, like CPU time, is difficult to determine accurately; unlike CPU time, it can represent a significant portion of overall transaction time. A transaction can wait in queues in various places within a system: at the terminal waiting to be polled, at an application or data communication activity waiting to be processed, and at the disk drive awaiting the completion of other disk requests. Transaction queues can be compared to lines at a grocery store, where a customer might wait in one line for a parking space, another line for check approval, and a third line for checkout. In the store situation, wait time is a function of line length or customer arrival rate, mean service time for customers in line, number of servers available, and the service convention, such as first-in-first-out (FIFO) or last-in-first-out (LIFO). The same is true of computer systems. The specifics of how to calculate the disk, CPU, and queuing times are quite complex. These times have been provided without derivation for this exercise.

Sidebar definitions:

CPU time The amount of time required for the CPU to execute the processing instructions, including those executed by the DBMS, OS, data communication software, and application programs.

queuing time The amount of time the transaction must wait in queues for service.

Number of Terminals

The amount of time required to completely process a single transaction is the total of operator think/wait time, data entry time, transmission time, and disk/CPU/queuing time, as seen in Table 10.2. The minimum number of terminals required can be found by determining the total time required to process all transactions in a given period, such as 1 hour. If 1200 transactions per hour were to be processed, each requiring 30 s (0.5 min) to complete, the number of terminals required would be

$$\frac{1200 \text{ transactions}}{\text{Hour}} \times \frac{0.5 \text{ terminal min}}{\text{Transactions}} \times \frac{1 \text{ hr}}{60 \text{ min}} = 10 \text{ terminals}$$

This is the minimum number of terminals required.

For several reasons, a user might decide to install additional terminals. There may be more potential operators than there are required terminals, such as in an office in which every employee is given a terminal even though each employee uses it only part of the day. To place ATMs more conveniently for customers, a bank might install more ATMs than required to meet transaction demand. Additional terminals might also be installed to accommodate expansion, to provide spares, and to provide a margin for calculation error.

It is assumed that all wait-time components are included in the transaction times. If this were not the case, the calculated number of terminals would be less than the minimum number required. Consider a polled communication line. Two types of messages are sent over the line: data and polling requests. If only the data transmission time were considered and the average wait time for polling were ignored, the results would not reflect the actual time of a given transaction. To determine the number of terminals required for Syncrasy Corporation, we calculate the transaction time for each type of transaction, multiply each transaction time by the number of transactions of that type per hour, and then total the results for each type of transaction. Shorter approaches could be taken, but they would be less instructive. Only the order entry transaction is computed in detail; the calculations for the remainder are left as an exercise.

Transaction time for the order entry transaction is given by

Transaction time = Think/wait time
  + Data entry time + Transmission time + Disk/CPU/queuing time

To determine transmission time, a transmission speed must be selected; for this exercise a speed of 4800 bps is assumed. Order entry transaction time is

$$10 + \frac{600}{1.5} + \frac{(620)(10)}{4800} + 1 = 412.3 \text{ s}$$

The transaction times required for credit check, customer maintenance, sending electronic mail, and receiving electronic mail are, respectively, 39.9, 221.9, 1399.1, and 219.1 seconds (perform the necessary calculations yourself to test your understanding). The total amount of time for all transactions in an hour is

$$(421.3)\,(40) + (39.9)\,(10) + (221.9)\,(4) + (1399.1)\,(5) + (219.1)(5) = 26{,}229.6 \text{ s}$$

In one hour, 26,229.6 s of terminal, communication link, and CPU/disk/wait time will be required, and the number of terminals needed is

$$\frac{29{,}229.6}{3600} = 7.29 \text{ terminals}$$

To provide for the total number of transactions from one location, eight terminals are needed.

SUMMARY

There is a wide variety of terminals, terminal capabilities, and terminal prices. The industry has been moving toward terminals with more intelligence, which provide functions that are simple to use and may also reduce overall communication cost and host processor work. Intelligent terminals in the form of microcomputers have replaced standard terminals in many networks. Their flexibility and local processing ability make them very effective in the modern communication network.

If several terminals are placed near each other in a remote location, it is impractical to have one line for each terminal, so the terminals must share one communication line. One way in which this is done is polling, which requires addressable terminals. In polling, a supervisor station asks each terminal in turn whether it has data to send. A terminal that is polled returns either data or a negative acknowledgment that indicates that it has no data to send. Selection is the procedure by which the supervisor sends data to a terminal. Line sharing is also accomplished with multiplexers and concentrators.

Many alternatives are available when configuring a data communication system. The hardware components—multiplexers, concentrators, and front-end processors—overlap in the functions they can provide. These components can reduce circuit costs significantly and make more efficient use of the circuits and reduce some of the processing load of the hosts. Configuration modeling tools, which have been designed for telephone company or similar common-carrier lines, are available to help system designers select the lowest-cost or most efficient communication lines. A wide variety of protocol conversion equipment is available to enable different manufacturers' terminals to interface with host equipment. Such conversion equipment can protect a user's investment in terminals. Diagnostic tools are necessary because errors can be encountered in connecting data terminal equipment to data communication networks. If properly used, these tools can reduce the time and effort needed to track down such problems.

KEY TERMS

auto-call unit (ACU)
block mode
breakout box
call-back unit
cascading
cluster controller
concentrator
contention mode
conversational mode
CPU time
daisy chain
downloading
dumb terminal
frequency division multiplexing (FDM)

front-end processor (FEP)
guardbands
intelligent terminal
inverse multiplexer
line monitor
matrix switch
multiplexing
multipoint connection
point-to-point connection
polling
port concentrator
port selector
protocol converter
queuing time
smart terminal

statistical time division multiplexing (STDM or stat mux)
terminal
terminal emulation
think/wait time

time division multiplexing (TDM)
uploading
video display unit (VDU)

REVIEW QUESTIONS

1. Describe each of the following types of terminals:
   a. microcomputer workstation
   b. remote job entry
   c. data entry and display
   d. point of sale
   e. portable terminal or microcomputer
   f. touch-tone telephone

2. Compare dumb, smart, and intelligent terminals.

3. Describe two terminal input devices and two terminal output devices.

4. Some applications have special terminal needs. Identify two such applications and the special keyboard options each needs.

5. Describe the poll/select protocol.

6. What are the advantages of multipoint connections? What are the disadvantages?

7. Why are microcomputers a good replacement for terminals?

8. In general, how does a multiplexer work?

9. Compare frequency division multiplexing (FDM), time division multiplexing (TDM), and statistical time division multiplexing (STDM).

10. Describe inverse multiplexing and give an example of its use.

11. Compare a multiplexer, a front-end processor, and a concentrator.

12. What functions are performed by a protocol converter? What are their advantages?

13. What does a digital line monitor do? What does a breakout box do?

PROBLEMS AND EXERCISES

1. Computer-aided design and computer-aided manufacturing (CAD/CAM) use terminals in the design process. Graphics capability is essential to these applications. What other terminal attributes would be beneficial in such applications?

2. Research the literature and find at least two cases in which employers are being sued as a result of terminal-related incidents.

3. Derive the transaction times for each transaction type described in the Case Study: credit check, customer maintenance, sending e-mail, and receiving e-mail.

4. A bank has decided to install ATMs in several locations. They have determined that the two major transactions at the ATMs will be withdrawals and requests for account balances. The characteristics for each transaction are given in Table 10–3. Determine the minimum number of ATMs required if the communication link speed is 2400 bps and each character transmitted requires 10 bits. Assume also that ATM users are able to enter 0.75 characters per second.

Table 10–3   Projected ATM Transactions

	Transaction Type	
	Withdrawal	Account Balance
Think/wait time (s)	15	15
No. of input characters	10	10
No. of output characters	100	100
Disk/CPU/queuing time (s)	2	1
Hourly peak	1000	100

5. Give examples in which multipoint configurations would be preferable to statistical multiplexing. Give an example in which the opposite is true.

6. What line speed would be required to provide a 5-s response time for a transaction that transmits 600 characters of information and receives a response of 350 characters? Assume a processing time of 2 s and 10 bits per character.

CHAPTER 11

WAN Topologies and Transmission Services

CHAPTER OBJECTIVES

After studying this chapter you should be able to

- Compare WAN and LAN network topologies
- Describe the workings of the asynchronous transmission protocol
- Discuss the workings of the byte synchronous transmission protocol
- Describe the workings of the bit synchronous transmission protocol
- Compare asynchronous and synchronous protocols
- Compare WAN and LAN data link protocols
- Describe the functions of the OSI network and transport layers

In this chapter we move to the data link and network layers of the OSI reference model. We examine data link protocols common to WANs and describe the functions of the network layer. We also discuss common WAN topologies. At the conclusion of this chapter, you will be familiar with WAN topologies, the criteria used to evaluate the effectiveness of a data link protocol, various types of WAN data link protocols, and network layer functions. Before reading further, you may want to review the functions of the data link layer in Chapter 7.

WAN TOPOLOGIES

Network topologies come in several varieties, which are defined by how the nodes are connected: star, hierarchical, interconnected, ring, bus, or combinations of these.

Star Network

star network A network topology using a central system to which all other nodes are connected. All data is transmitted to or through the central system.

In a **star network,** the central or hub node serves as a message switch by accepting a message from the originating node and forwarding it to the destination node, as illustrated in Figure 11–1. A star configuration has several advantages. First, it provides a short path between any two nodes with a maximum of two links, or hops, to traverse. The time needed for the message to go from the central node to a peripheral node or vice versa is even shorter because only one hop is required to get from source to destination. On the other hand, having the central node involved in the transmission of every message can lead to congestion at the central site. This causes consequent message delays, and such congestion is exacerbated when the central node is functioning for more than just message switching. If the central node is also the central processing system, as is often the case, higher-priority processing requirements could make the processor temporarily unable to attend to communication functions. This problem is more likely to occur in a uniprocessor system than in a multiple-processor system.

A star configuration also provides the user with a high degree of network control. Because the central node is in direct contact with every other node and all messages flow through it, a centralized location exists for message logging, gathering of network statistics, and error diagnostics and recovery. However, this centralized control and dependence on a centralized system sometimes are considered a disadvantage rather than an advantage. In a corporate network, having a centralized system may be consistent with a centralized management control philosophy. Close control of all other data processing centers by a main data processing center may be consistent with

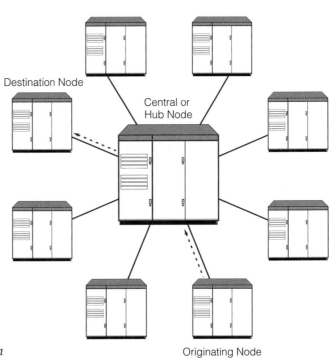

Figure 11–1
Star Configuration

corporate management objectives. In a network of peer organizations, having one organization act as a point of centralized control may be undesirable. Consider a network of major universities, where it may be difficult to reach agreement as to which university will serve as the centralized controller. Even after the decision is made, dependence on one data center for communication services may be undesirable for the other nodes.

Expanding a star network is a simple procedure because only the new node and the central node need to be involved. It simply requires obtaining the communication link, connecting the two, and updating the network tables in the other nodes. Some instances also require that a new system generation be performed for the other nodes. A new system generation is usually required if adding a new node exceeds the limits of memory allocated to the network routing tables. For dynamic networks it is common to allocate space for potential nodes to reduce the number of system generations that must be performed.

Star systems have a low reliability. The loss of the central node is equivalent to loss of the network. Failure of a peripheral node has little impact on the network as a whole, however, as only messages bound for that node are undeliverable. The best candidate for the central node is a fault-tolerant system that is almost immune to failure.

Star systems can have the disadvantage in a long-distance network of higher circuit costs. This is exemplified in the Case Study at the end of this chapter, in which the point-to-point configuration has a monthly circuit cost almost $1500 higher than that of the minimum media distance configuration. This is particularly true when the centralized node is not in the geographic center of the network. Other topologies are better able to configure the links between nodes so the distance spanned by the media is minimized.

Hierarchical Network

Hierarchical topology, shown in Figure 11–2, is also called a tree structure. Directly connected to the single root node (node A) are several nodes at the second level. Each of these can have several cascaded nodes attached. This type of network, often found in corporate computer networks, closely resembles corporate organization charts. With the corporate computer center as root node, division systems are attached directly to the root, regional systems to divisional systems, districts to regions, and so on. Corporate reports from a lower level are easily consolidated at the next higher level, and the network generally mirrors the information flow pattern in the corporation. Information flowing from a district in one division to a district in a different division would need to go through the root or corporate node. As with a star system, this allows for a great deal of network control.

Media costs for a hierarchical topology are likely to be lower than for a star topology, assuming that the lower-level nodes are closer to the next higher level than they are to the root. It is possible, of course, to devise configurations in which media costs are higher than for a centralized system. A hierarchical network can require quite a few hops for a message to reach its destination. If node F in Figure 11–2 needed to send a message to node Z, the message would have to pass through five intermediate nodes

hierarchical topology A network topology in which the nodes are arranged hierarchically. Also known as a tree structure.

Figure 11–2

Hierarchical
Configuration

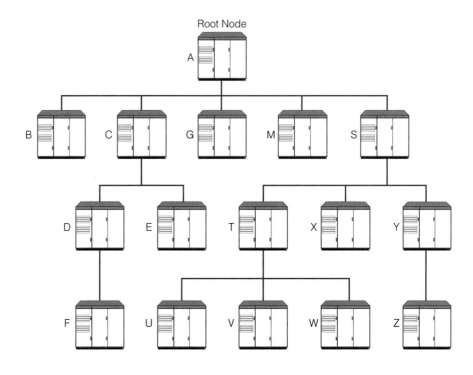

(F———→D———→C———→A———→S———→Y———→Z). In the hierarchical topology, nodes tend to communicate with neighboring nodes, so the need for a leaf node on one side of the hierarchy to communicate with a leaf node on the other side of the hierarchy is presumably small.

Expansion and reconfiguration of a hierarchical network can pose problems. In the configuration of Figure 11–2, splitting node C into nodes C and K, with D and F under C and E under K, would require more work than in the star configuration. Node K would have to be linked to node A, and node E would have to be unlinked from C and relinked to K. Although this may not sound difficult, it costs time and money to change circuits from one location to another, especially with circuits provided by a common carrier. As with most configuration changes, network routing tables must be updated, and a system or network regeneration may be needed. Failure of the root node in a hierarchical configuration is less costly than in a star configuration, but it does present a serious reliability problem. In fact, the failure of any node other than those at the extremities makes it impossible to reach that node or any of its subordinate nodes. Congestion at the root and high-level nodes is also a potential problem.

Interconnected (Plex) Network

interconnected (plex or mesh) network A network topology in which any node can be connected directly to any other node.

Two forms of an **interconnected (plex or mesh) network** are shown in Figure 11–3. In the fully interconnected network, Figure 11–3(a), every node is connected to every other node with which it must communicate. In the past, fully interconnected topology was required because the available network software was not sophisticated enough to perform the routing and for-

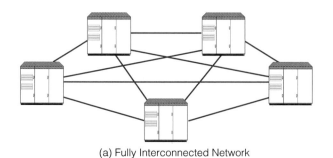

(a) Fully Interconnected Network

Figure 11–3
*Interconnected
Configuration*

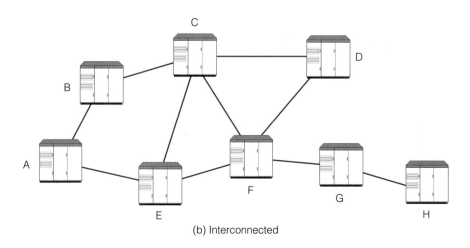

(b) Interconnected

warding functions. Current network software allows for but does not require fully interconnected nodes. Message traffic patterns are used to determine where links should be installed. As might be expected, the links in a fully interconnected network are quite costly. The number of links required for a fully interconnected network of n nodes is $n(n-1)/2$. The performance of an interconnected system is generally good, as direct links can be established between nodes with high amounts of data to exchange. Costs can also be controlled because interconnected topology is capable of the shortest or least expensive configuration. Any of the other topology types can be mimicked by an interconnected topology, although routing and control mechanisms would probably be different.

The expandability of interconnected configurations depends on the type of network and how the new node is to be connected. In the fully interconnected network, expansion is costly and time-consuming because a link must be established to every node with which the new node must communicate. In networks that do not require full interconnection, insertion of a new node can be simple. Adding node H in Figure 11–3(b) would be very simple, requiring only a link from node G to the new node H. Adding a node such as node C in Figure 11–3(b) would be more involved and costly. The impact of node failure depends on the specific configuration. Alternative paths around a failed node are sometimes available. If node C in Figure 11–3(b)

Table 11–1   Network Topology Characteristics

Topology Type	Cost	Control	Number of Hops	Reliability	Expandability
Star	Can be high	Very good	Maximum of two	Poor	Good
Hierarchical	Can be high	Good	Can be many	Fair	Fair to good
Interconnected, full	Highest	Distributed	One only	Good	Very poor
Interconnected, other	Can be lowest	Distributed	Can be many	Good	Good
Ring	Good	Distributed	Can be many	Good	Good
Bus	Good	Distributed	N/A	Good	Good

fails, all other nodes are still able to communicate. The loss of node F, however, would isolate nodes G and H. Because all nodes in an interconnected topology are equal, control is distributed rather than centralized.

Hybrid Networks

Combinations of the above topologies are sometimes integrated into one network. One such combination is a backbone network—such as a ring—with spurs attached. The backbone nodes can be dedicated to message transfer and data communication while the other nodes are used for both data processing and data communication. In widely distributed systems with many nodes, this helps reduce the number of hops, the length of the links, and congestion problems. If the backbone is implemented as a ring or with multiple paths available, reliability is also high. The cost of hybrid networks can be quite low because different topologies can be used for network segments. Table 11–1 summarizes the different types of topology with respect to cost, control, number of hops (speed), reliability, and expandability.

WAN DATA LINK PROTOCOLS

Most LANs use contention and token passing for data link control. WAN data link protocols are typically either asynchronous or a form of synchronous protocols. Asynchronous is most often used to connect hosts with terminals. Synchronous protocols are used between computers and between computers and terminals. We begin the discussion with asynchronous, the first WAN data link protocol.

Asynchronous Transmission

asynchronous transmission (async) The oldest and one of the most common data link protocols. Each character is transmitted individually with its own error detection scheme, usually a parity bit. The sender and receiver are not synchronized with each other. Also known as the start–stop protocol.

Asynchronous transmission (async) is the oldest and one of the most common data link protocols. Like many of the techniques used in data communication, it is derived from the telegraph and telephone industries. In asynchronous transmission, data is transmitted one character at a time, and sender and receiver are not synchronized with each other. The sender is thus able to transmit a character at any time. The receiver must be prepared to recognize that information is arriving, accept the data, possibly check for errors, and print, display, or store the data in memory. Individual characters also can be separated over different time intervals, meaning that no synchronization exists between individual transmitted characters.

Most dumb terminals are async devices, and many smart and intelligent terminals can also communicate asynchronously. Personal computers often use async transmission via their serial port to communicate with each other and with host systems. Async transmission is also called a start–stop protocol. This term and the terms *mark* (1 bit) and *space* (0 bit) are holdovers from telegraphy. It is called start–stop because each character is framed by a start bit and a stop bit, as illustrated in Figure 11–4.

Compatibility of Sending and Receiving Stations   A communication link is either idling or transmitting data. In the idle state, an async line is held in the mark condition, which is a continuous stream of 1 bits. The sending and receiving stations must agree on the number of bits per character before establishing the communication link. If parity is to be transmitted for error detection, both stations must agree on either even or odd parity and on whether the parity bit is to be checked (the parity bit could be transmitted but not checked by the data link software or hardware). The stations also must agree on a transmission speed because this determines the interval at which the line is sampled. Finally, there must be agreement as to what will terminate the message. A message terminator usually is a defined set of characters called **interrupt characters,** a count of a specific number of characters, or a timeout interval. For the following discussion we will assume that sending and receiving stations are the same with respect to the number of bits sent per character, parity, message termination, and maximum speed of the link (as detected by the receiving modem). The line is in the idle state, meaning that a continuous stream of 1 bits is being transmitted. There are 7 data bits and 1 parity bit, and odd parity will be checked.

interrupt characters A set of characters that terminate a message or cause an interruption in transmission to perform a special action, such as a backspace.

Transmitting a Character   A character's arrival is signaled by a start bit, which is a change in the state of the line from a mark to a space, or a 0 bit. The start bit is followed by 7 data bits, 1 parity bit, and a stop bit, which is a return to a 1 bit or mark condition. If parity does not check or if the tenth bit is not a 1, it is assumed that an error has occurred. Appendix A describes how checking for start, stop, data, and parity bits is physically accomplished. The ASCII representation for the character *F* is 1000110; the async representation for transmitting this character is given in Figure 11–4. After a character is transmitted, the line goes back to the idle state until the next start bit is encountered.

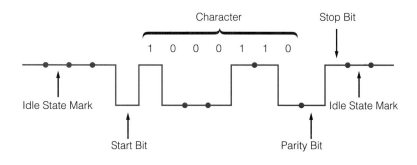

Figure 11–4
Asynchronous Transmission of the Letter F

Interrupt Characters   If interrupt characters are being used to end a transmission, each character received must be examined to determine whether it matches one of the interrupt characters. If they match, the message is considered complete and is delivered to the intended application. This is the usual way async communications are completed. On terminals, the character that is transmitted when the operator presses the Return key—usually a carriage-return character—is often one of these termination characters. Other interrupt characters can also be specified.

character-count termination A transmission termination technique wherein a transmission is complete when a specified number of characters have been received. Allows the computer to save the data in blocks and avoid buffer overflow.

Character Count   **Character-count termination** is used when the number of characters transmitted is large or when data are received from a device that transmits continuously without sending termination characters. Some news wire services send large amounts of text for a story without including message termination characters. The receiving computer must be capable of accepting the entire story regardless of its length. Because the message is received by the computer into a buffer that may be smaller than the entire message, a character-count termination allows the computer to save the data in blocks and avoid buffer overflow.

With character-count termination, a read is posted on the communication line for a specific number of characters. When that number of characters has been received, the transmission is considered completed, and the data is delivered to the application. It is the application's responsibility to make sense of the message, which includes determining the end of the transmission. On staffed terminals, character-count termination is usually used only for entering fixed-length data fields. Interactive questions with one-character answers often use this technique. Character-count termination may be used with the other termination methods. A continuous stream of data on the line as described above can cause another problem: buffer overflow.

buffer overflow/overrun A situation that arises when the buffer is either too small or too full to receive the transmitted data. In either case there is no place to store the arriving characters, and the data is lost.

Double Buffering   **Buffer overflow,** or **overrun,** can arise when the data block being transmitted is larger than the receiving buffer area or when data from a subsequent block is received before the previous block's data has been emptied from the buffer. In such cases, there is no place to store the arriving characters, and they are lost. Often in such instances the data link protocol uses a technique known as **double buffering** to avoid losing characters.

double buffering Used when buffer overflow/overrun occurs to avoid losing characters.

Double buffering means there are two (or more) input buffers capable of receiving data. The buffers are alternated: When one buffer is filled, new incoming characters are stored in the alternate buffer. While an alternate buffer is being used, data in the full buffer can be passed to the application, which makes that buffer available for receiving new data. Double buffering might be used when transmitting data from a microcomputer's disk to the host. Such data may form a continuous character stream that can arrive at any time at nearly maximum data link speed and in variable-length blocks. A receiving computer with single buffering may not be fast enough to empty its buffer and be ready to accept the next arriving characters.

timeout interval A period of time allowed for an event to occur. If the event does not happen, the timeout expires and the process initiating the event is notified.

Timeout Interval   Another termination mechanism is the **timeout interval.** This method is effective with a character count or when data is received from sensor-based or laboratory equipment. In conjunction with character count, the timeout interval is beneficial when the size of a message can vary. Suppose the termination character count is 100 and the message is 350 characters. If only character-count termination is used, the first 300 characters would be received routinely in three data groups, but the last 50 characters would be held in the buffer until it was filled, which would occur only when the next message is sent. A timeout termination prevents unnecessary delays in completing such a message. In the laboratory situation, a long interval between data arrival means that the entire data stream has arrived or the equipment is out of order. The timeout interval is not a good terminator for data being input by an operator, because if the operator should take a break in the midst of input, a timeout interval would prematurely terminate the message.

Effectiveness of Asynchronous Transmission

The following rating of asynchronous transmission, with respect to the data link objectives described earlier, uses a three-level grading system: poor, adequate, and good. The data delineation and contention control objectives are not rated because they are both essential functions; exactly how they are implemented, however, can influence the effectiveness rating. The ratings are based on the data link layer functions discussed in Chapter 7. The effectiveness of asynchronous protocols is summarized in Table 11–2.

Why Asynchronous Transmission Is So Popular

Despite the poor rating given to asynchronous transmission, it remains one of the most common data link protocols for several reasons. Async was the first protocol, and for several years it was the only way to transmit data. Many terminals and controller boards were designed for async operation. Thus, async technology is well developed, and a wide variety of hardware options are available at low prices. Async also is very well suited to many

Table 11–2   Effectiveness of Asynchronous Protocols

Capability	Comments	Rating
Error detection	Usually parity	Poor
Transparency	Not possible when interrupt characters are used	Poor
	Possible under other message termination options	Adequate
Addressing	No limitations	Good
Code independence	Number of bits per character established before communicating, and hence no code independence	Poor
Configurations	No inherent restrictions	Adequate
Efficiency	Protocol overhead 30%; character-at-a-time transmission slower than block-at-a-time transmission	Poor
Growth	Limited	Poor

types of applications. People performing data entry in a conversational mode or even in block mode operate at speeds compatible with async protocol. The primary drawback of async is its inefficient use of the circuit.

SYNCHRONOUS TRANSMISSION

synchronous A transmission protocol where the sender and receiver are synchronized. Data is generally transmitted in blocks, rather than a character at a time as in asynchronous transmission.

character synchronous protocol A type of synchronous protocol oriented toward specific data codes and specific characters within those codes.

positional protocol A type of synchronous protocol that delineates fields by the use of fixed-length fields on the message, by indicating the size of the message with a character count embedded in the message, or both.

framing protocol A type of synchronous protocol that uses reserved characters or bit patterns to delineate data and control fields within the message.

Synchronous data link protocols can be divided into three groups: character oriented, byte count oriented, and bit oriented. The last is the newest technology and the basis for many current data communication systems. Synchronous transmission allows sender and receiver to be synchronized with each other. Synchronous modems have internal clocks that are set in time with each other by a bit pattern, or sync pattern, transmitted at the beginning of a message. For long messages these sync patterns are periodically inserted within the text to ensure that the modem clocks remain synchronized. Synchronized clocks are one feature that separates asynchronous modems from synchronous ones; although there is a clocking function in async transmission, the clocks are not synchronized. The clocks on asynchronous modems are used to pace the bits on the line on the sending side and to sample the line when awaiting data on the receiving side. Once data starts arriving, the sampling rate is adjusted to the pace of the arriving characters so the characters can be recognized (see Appendix A).

Another difference between asynchronous and synchronous transmission is that instead of transmitting character by character, synchronous transmission involves sending a block of characters at a time. Failure to remain synchronized results in lost data. Figure 11–5 illustrates the differences between asynchronous and synchronous transmission.

CHARACTER SYNCHRONOUS PROTOCOLS

Data Delineation in Synchronous Protocols

One of the functions of a data link protocol is data delineation. With synchronous protocols, three methods are used to effect this. Some synchronous protocols are positional, some use a framing technique, and others use a byte count to delineate data. **Positional protocols** delineate fields by the use of fixed-length fields on the message (except perhaps on the data field), by indicating the size of the message with a character count embedded in the message, or both. **Framing protocols** use reserved characters or bit patterns

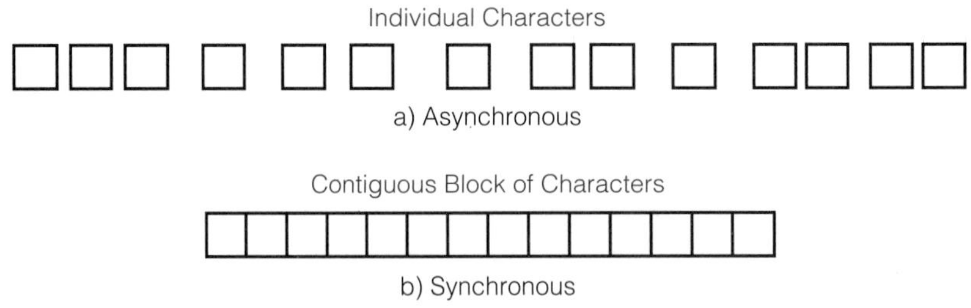

Figure 11–5
Asynchronous vs. Synchronous Transmission

Individual Characters

a) Asynchronous

Contiguous Block of Characters

b) Synchronous

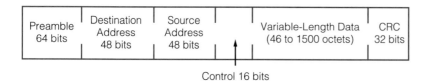

Control 16 bits

Figure 11–6
*CSMA/CD Message
Format*

to delineate data and control fields within the message. **Byte count protocols** delineate data by including the number of characters being transmitted within the message.

Positional Protocols   A fixed-message format used in the CSMA/CD LAN is illustrated in Figure 11–6. All fields except the data field are a specific length and at a specific location within the message. The end of the message is indicated by dropping the carrier signal on the medium. Neither framing characters nor character counts are used to define where address fields and data begin. The first 64 bits are always the preamble field, the next 48 are the destination address, and so on. All messages in Ethernet adhere to this fixed format.

Framing Protocols   A message may have several parts: a header, an address, data, and a block check character. If a message contains both a header and data fields, a framing protocol would use a special control character to indicate the start of the header, another control character to indicate the start of the data field, and a third control character to designate the end of the data field. This is illustrated in Figure 11–7. Other framed messages between the same sender and receiver could have different parts; for example, the header field could be omitted.

Byte Count Protocols   A byte count protocol includes the number of characters being transmitted in the message header. The recipient of the message reads the header and uses the message length stored there to determine the size of the message. Because the header is a fixed length, the remainder of the message can be delineated from the message size.

Standards for Character Synchronous Protocols

Both corporate and national standards specify how character synchronous protocols are to be implemented. National standards include American National Standards Institute (ANSI) standards X3.1, X3.24, X3.28, and X3.36, all of which pertain to various aspects of character synchronous transmission. The IBM **Binary Synchronous Communications (BISYNC or BSC) protocol**

byte count protocol A type of synchronous protocol that delineates data by including the number of characters being transmitted within the message.

Binary Synchronous Communications (BISYNC or BSC) protocol A transmission protocol introduced by IBM as the data link protocol for remote job entry. It later became a de facto standard for many types of data transmission, particularly between two computers. Data is transmitted a block at a time, and the sender and receiver must be in time with each other. Specific control characters are used to indicate beginning of text, end of text, start of header, and so on.

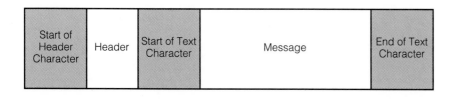

Figure 11–7
*Framing for a Character
Synchronous Message*

has become a de facto industry standard communication protocol supported by many manufacturers. Because it is so common, BISYNC is used as a model of character synchronous protocols in the following discussion.

BISYNC was introduced by IBM in 1967 as the data link protocol for remote job entry, using the 2780 workstation. Since that time its use has expanded to many other applications and with several other devices. Only two data codes are commonly used by BISYNC: ASCII and EBCDIC. One or more synchronization characters are transmitted at the beginning of each transmission block to synchronize sending and receiving modems. The receiving modem uses this bit pattern to establish timing and get in step with the sender. To maintain timing for long transmission blocks, additional sync characters are inserted at regular intervals. The number of sync characters required depends on the equipment being used, although two or three is the usual number. Figure 11–8 shows a message with BISYNC control characters for synchronization (SYN), the start of text (STX), and the end of text (ETX). BISYNC supports both point-to-point and multipoint configurations.

Message Control   Each transmitted block can have an optional header field for message control that designates such items as routing information, priority, and message type. The beginning and end of text are identified by framing the data with control characters. An STX character signals that the data portion of the text is starting. One of several characters—such as ETX, ETB, or EOT—can be used to identify the end of a block of data, depending on whether an intermediate or final block is being transmitted. The ETB control character designates the end of the transmission block, ETX signals the end of the text, and EOT means end of transmission. Lengthy messages are ordinarily broken down into segments or blocks. If a message were broken into four different transmission blocks, the first three blocks would terminate with the ETB control character and the last would terminate with the EOT character.

Transparency   Transparent transmission is a BISYNC configuration option involving the insertion of extra characters in the message, which can be rather cumbersome.

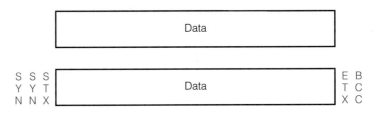

Figure 11–8
BISYNC Control Characters

SYN	Synchronization character
STX	Start of text character
ETX	End of text character
BCC	Block check character—LRC or CRC

Table 11-3 Effectiveness of Binary Synchronous Protocol

Capability	Comments	Rating
Error detection	With CRC	Good
	Without CRC	Adequate
Transparency	Possible, but design is clumsy	Adequate
Addressing	Wide range possible	Good
Code independence	None; only three codes supported	Poor
Configurations	Multipoint and point-to-point	Adequate
Efficiency	Fixed overhead per message; good for large messages, high for very short messages; inherent half-duplex nature restrictive	Good overall
Growth	Limited in supported configurations and lack of code independence	Adequate

Error Control   Error control is either parity or parity with LRC. Cyclic redundancy checks are used with EBCDIC and with ASCII when ASCII is configured for transparency. LRC and parity are used with non-transparent ASCII.

BISYNC's Half-Duplex Nature   One limitation of BISYNC is that it is essentially a half-duplex protocol, so each message transmitted must be acknowledged by the receiver before the next message can be sent. This is not a major concern for many applications, especially those involving terminal data entry, for which the amount of time required to acknowledge is short compared with the speed of data submission. For host-to-host communication, on the other hand, half duplex can be quite restrictive. Consider a file transmitted between two processors: It would be efficient for the sender to transmit several blocks before requiring an acknowledgment transmitted in parallel with the data, as would occur in full-duplex mode.

Effectiveness of the BISYNC Protocol   The effectiveness of BISYNC is summarized in Table 11-3.

Byte Count Synchronous Protocols

The difference between byte count synchronous protocols and BISYNC lies in how they signal the beginning and end of messages. They are called byte count protocols because the number of characters in the message is given in a required message header, as illustrated in Figure 11-9. The header is a fixed length, and the data field is of variable length. One advantage of byte count protocols is their transparency. With the byte count provided, it is clear

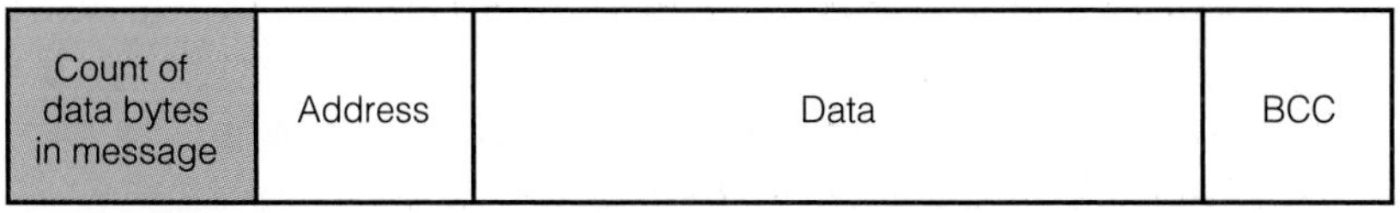

Count of data bytes in message	Address	Data	BCC

Figure 11-9
Byte Count Message Format

where the message begins and ends: The header is always x characters long. Therefore, the beginning of the data is x characters from the beginning of the message, the data span the byte count number of characters, and following that may be a block check character or CRC characters. Because there is no need to scan the input stream for termination characters, any bit pattern can be represented within the data stream.

Message Sequence Numbers   Some implementations of byte count protocols also include **message sequence numbers.** Each transmitted message is given a sequential number, allowing multiple messages to be transmitted without any acknowledgment. If three bits are used for sequencing messages, eight different sequence numbers (0 through 7) can be generated. When the count reaches 7, the next number assigned is 0. This allows up to eight messages to be transmitted before being acknowledged. The ability to send multiple messages without an acknowledgment can save a significant amount of time, especially on slower links or links with a high modem turnaround time.

Effectiveness of Byte Count Synchronous Protocols   The performance of byte count synchronous protocols is much the same as for BISYNC, the differences being in transparency and efficiency. Transparency is inherent in byte count protocols. Byte count protocols also have greater efficiency if message sequencing or true full-duplex operations are allowed. An example of a byte count synchronous protocol is Digital Equipment Corporation's Digital Data Communication Message Protocol (DDCMP). Its message sequencing allows 256 message numbers.

Bit Synchronous Protocols

Bit-oriented synchronous data link protocols use bits rather than bytes to delineate data and provide message control. The first bit-oriented synchronous data link protocol, Synchronous Data Link Control (SDLC), was introduced by IBM in 1972. Since then, numerous other bit-oriented data link controls have surfaced. The major bit synchronous protocols are

- **Synchronous Data Link Control (SDLC),** from IBM
- **Advanced Data Communications Control Procedure (ADCCP),** an ANSI standard data link protocol (ADCCP is often pronounced "addcap")
- **High-Level Data Link Control (HDLC),** a standard of the International Standards Organization (ISO)
- **Link Access Procedure, Balanced (LAPB),** designated as the data link protocol for the X.25 packet distribution networks (LAPB is an adaptation of HDLC)

All of these bit synchronous protocols operate similarly. Although there are both national and international standards, SDLC is used in the following discussion as the model for bit-oriented data link protocols because it is used in many IBM installations and represents many bit synchronous

---

message sequence numbers A system in which each transmitted message is given a sequential number, allowing multiple messages to be transmitted without acknowledgment.

bit-oriented synchronous data link protocol A data link protocol in which one or more bits are used to control the communication link. Bit synchronous protocols are commonly used on both LANs and WANs.

Synchronous Data Link Control (SDLC) An IBM positional synchronous protocol that operates in full-duplex or half-duplex mode in both point-to-point and multipoint configurations. Data is transmitted in fixed-format frames consisting of start flag, address, control information, block check character (BCC), and end-of-frame flag.

Advanced Data Communications Control Procedure (ADCCP) An ANSI standard bit-oriented data link control. Pronounced "addcap."

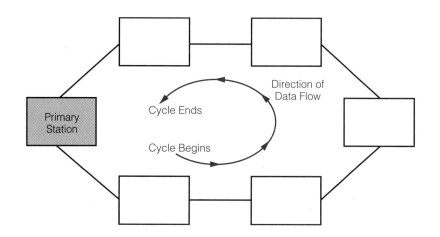

Figure 11–10
SDLC Loop Configuration

implementations. Many vendors also support SDLC as a connection to IBM networks and devices. More detailed information regarding SDLC may be found in Appendix B.

Synchronous Data Link Control

SDLC operates in full-duplex or half-duplex mode on nonswitched lines in both point-to-point and multipoint configurations. In half-duplex mode it also allows switched, point-to-point configurations. Under SDLC it is possible to configure stations in a loop, as depicted in Figure 11–10. Data are transmitted in one direction around the loop, as with hub polling. In all configurations, including point to point, one station is designated as the primary station and the others are secondary stations. The primary controls the link and determines which station is allowed to transmit.

The Frame   At the application level a given application transmits a message. At the transport layer the message may be broken down into packets. At the data link layer a packet may be broken down into frames. Thus, the basic unit of transmission in SDLC is the **frame,** presented in Figure 11–11. The flag field is used to indicate the beginning and end of the frame. The bit pattern for the flag, 01111110, is the only bit pattern in the protocol that is specifically reserved; all other bit patterns are acceptable. (This is discussed further in the SDLC section on transparency.) The second field within the frame, the address field, is 8 bits. A maximum of 256 unique addresses is possible. Other data link protocols, such as ADCCP and HDLC, allow the address field to be expanded in multiples of 8 bits, significantly increasing the number of addressable stations per link. The control field, also 8 bits, identifies the frame type as unnumbered, informational, or supervisory. Only the

High-Level Data Link Control (HDLC) A positional synchronous protocol that operates in full-duplex or half-duplex mode in both point-to-point and multipoint configurations. Data is transmitted in fixed-format frames consisting of start flag, address, control information, block check character (CRC), and end-of-frame flag. HDLC is an ISO standard similar to IBM's SDLC.

Link Access Procedure, Balanced (LAPB) A bit synchronous protocol similar to high-level data link control. LAPB is the protocol specified for X.25 networks.

frame A term used to describe a transmission packet in bit-oriented protocols.

8 bits	8 bits	8 bits	Variable	16 bits	8 bits
Flag 01111110	Address	Control	Data (Optional Octets)	Frame Check Sequence	Flag 01111110

Figure 11–11
SDLC Frame Format

first two of these three types are used to transmit data, with the primary data transport frame being the information frame.

The data field, always omitted for supervisory frames, is optional on unnumbered frames and is usually present on information frames. The only restriction on the data field is that the number of bits must be a multiple of eight, or an octet. This restriction does not mean an 8-bit code must be used; in fact, any code is acceptable. But if necessary, the data being transmitted must be padded with additional bits to maintain an integral number of octets (no partial octets). If the data being transmitted consists of 5 Baudot characters, at 5 bits each, only 25 bits would be required for the data and an additional 7 bits would be required to complete the last octet. Following the optional data field is a frame check sequence for error detection, which is 16 bits. The final field of the frame is the flag that signals the end of the message. The bit pattern for the ending flag is the same as that for the beginning flag. Thus, the ending flag for one frame may serve as the beginning flag for the next.

SDLC is a positional protocol, which means each field except the data field has a specific length and location relative to adjacent fields. No special control characters (except for the flag characters) are used to delimit the data or headings in the message. For control frames, which are either unnumbered or supervisory, the control function is encoded in the control field. Unnumbered frames have 5 bits available to identify the control function, so 32 different function types are possible. The supervisory frame has only 2 bits available, so a maximum of four functions can be defined.

number sent (Ns) subfield In bit synchronous transmission such as HDLC, a field on the transmission frame and on the sender's system used to represent the frame sequence number being transmitted.

number received (Nr) subfield In bit synchronous transmission such as HDLC, a field on the transmission frame and on the receiver's system used to represent the frame sequence number the receiving station expects to receive next.

Number Sent (Ns) and Number Received (Nr) Subfields In information frames, the control field contains two 3-bit fields known as the **number sent (Ns)** and **number received (Nr) subfields.** The Ns and Nr counts are used to sequence messages. Three bits allow for eight numbers, 0 through 7. When transmitting an information frame the sender increments the Ns field value. The Ns or Nr number following 7 is 0; thus, the number sequence cycles through those eight values. The Nr field is used to acknowledge receipt of messages. Every time a message is received, the receiver increments the Nr count, which represents the number of the frame expected next. An Nr count of 5 means message number 5 should arrive next. The Ns and Nr counts are compared every time a frame is received to make sure no messages have been lost. This scheme allows seven messages to be sent before an acknowledgment is required. The ability to receive up to seven frames without acknowledgment improves performance; however, it also places a burden on the sender, which must be ready to retransmit any unacknowledged frames. This requires that messages be saved in the sender's buffers until acknowledged, which can create problems for systems with small buffers or memory. Examples of how the Ns and Nr fields are used are found in Appendix B.

Both ADCCP and HDLC allow the control field to be expanded to provide for larger Ns and Nr counts, as illustrated in Figure 11–12. When the control field is expanded to 16 bits, the Ns and Nr fields can each be 7 bits, which allows 128 sequence numbers, and up to 127 messages can be

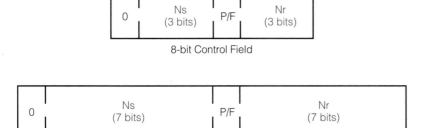

Figure 11–12
Control Fields for Information Frames

transmitted before being acknowledged. This arrangement is especially beneficial with satellite links because of the propagation delay for response, which can cause a small number of unacknowledged frames to create undesirable delays. Recall from Chapter 2 that satellite signals incur a one-way propagation delay of approximately a quarter of a second. If 10,000-bit blocks are being transmitted on a 1-Mbps satellite link, then 25 blocks theoretically could be transmitted every quarter of a second. With 3-bit Ns and Nr fields, only 7 blocks could be sent before waiting for an acknowledgment. In this case, transmission time for 18 blocks would be lost, limiting the available capacity.

Transparency   Transparency is implemented in SDLC by bit insertion, also known as **bit stuffing.** Because the beginning and ending flags use the only reserved bit sequence, their bit pattern, 01111110, must never appear in the data portion of the record. This is accomplished by inserting a 0 bit after five consecutive 1 bits are encountered in the data. After the control field, the receiver looks for two specific bit patterns: the ending flag and five consecutive 1 bits. If the ending flag is encountered the receiver knows that the preceding 16 bits are frame check characters and that all bits between the end of the control field and the start of the frame check are data. On the other hand, if five consecutive 1 bits arrive followed by a 0 bit, the receiver also knows that the 0 bit has been inserted for transparency. The inserted 0 bit is then stripped out and the receiver continues evaluating the input stream. An example of SDLC transparency is illustrated in Figure 11–13.

Effectiveness of the SDLC Protocol   The effectiveness of SDLC is summarized in Table 11–4.

bit stuffing The implementation of transparency in HDLC-like protocols through bit insertion.

CHOOSING A DATA LINK PROTOCOL

Although several other data link protocols exist, those described in this chapter are the most common. The question is, Which one is appropriate for which application? Table 11–5 compares synchronous and asynchronous protocols. When selecting the proper protocol, the network designer must first choose a protocol supported by the hardware vendor. Most vendors

Figure 11–13
SDLC Transparency

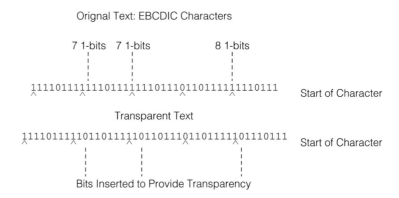

support some version of asynchronous, character synchronous, and bit synchronous protocols. CSMA/CD and token passing are found primarily in LANs. Second, the type of hardware used in an application partly dictates the data link protocol. Most terminals support one or possibly two protocols; the exception is intelligent terminals, which can support a wide variety of protocols. Third, the network support provided by the vendor affects the choice of data link protocol. Many newer network systems have been designed around a bit-oriented synchronous protocol. Because not all users have compatible terminals, accommodations are often made to support other protocols, such as BISYNC.

In practice, do not select a protocol and then gather the equipment to support it. Instead select a network design, a hardware vendor, and associated hardware, each of which dictates a particular protocol. Most current data link technology and development for WANs are based on bit-oriented synchronous protocols. There are several bit-oriented implementations and several standards exist. The industry trend is toward higher-speed transmission and efficient use of the data link, which definitely favor synchronous transmission protocols.

Table 11–4 Effectiveness of SDLC Bit Synchronous Protocol

Capability	Comments	Rating
Error detection	CRC	Good
Transparency	Designed in	Good
Addressing	8-bit address field	Fair
	Expandable address field	Good
Code independence	Inherent; only limit is that data must be in octets	Good
Configurations	Wide variety allowed	Good
Efficiency	Fixed overhead better for long messages; full duplex exchanges can enhance performance	Good
Growth	Designed for changing circumstances	Good

Table 11–5 Comparison of Asynchronous and Synchronous Protocols

Asynchronous	Synchronous
Character-at-a-time transmission.	Block transmission.
Modems are not synchronized.	Modems are synchronized.
Error detection commonly is parity.	Error detection commonly is CRC or parity plus LRC.
Fixed overhead per character.	Fixed overhead per block (may be less efficient for small messages but more efficient for large ones).
Less efficient use of communication link.	More efficient use of communication link.
Lower cost devices.	Higher cost devices.

THE OSI NETWORK LAYER

The OSI network layer performs four major functions: routing, network control, congestion control, and collection of accounting data. Whereas the data link layer is concerned with moving data between two adjacent nodes, the network layer is concerned with end-to-end routing, or getting data from the originating node to its ultimate destination. Data may take a variety of paths from the originating node to the destination node. The network layer must be aware of alternative paths in the network and choose the best one. Selection of the best path depends on several factors, including congestion, number of intervening nodes, and speed of links.

Network control involves sending node status information to other nodes and receiving status information from other nodes to determine the best routing for messages. The network layer must enforce the priority scheme when priorities are associated with messages. **Congestion control** means reducing transmission delays that might result from overuse of some circuits or because a particular node in the network is busy and unable to process messages in a timely fashion. The network layer should adapt to these transient conditions and attempt to route messages around such points of congestion. Not all systems can adapt to the changing characteristics of the communication links. In broadcast-type systems, very little can be done to overcome this problem.

network control Involves the sending and receiving of node status information to other nodes to determine the best routing for messages.

congestion control The reduction of transmission delays.

Message Routing

One function of the network layer, **routing,** is achievable through several algorithms used to direct messages from the point of origination to final destination. Determination of message routing can be either centralized or distributed. Routing itself can be either static, adaptive, or broadcast and is governed by a network routing table resident at each node. The network routing table is a matrix of other nodes with the link or path to that node. If a message destined for node X arrives at node K, the network routing table is consulted for the next node on the path from K to X. Network

routing An algorithm used to determine how to move a message from its source to its destination. Several algorithms are used.

routing tables can also contain more information than just the next link, such as congestion statistics. The following discussion covers a sample of routing techniques.

Centralized Routing Determination: The Network Routing Manager

In centralized determination of routing tables, one node is designated as the **network routing manager** to whom all nodes periodically forward such status information as queue lengths on outgoing and incoming lines and the number of messages processed within the most recent interval. The routing manager is thereby provided with an overview of network functioning, location of any bottlenecks, and location of underused facilities. The routing manager periodically recalculates the optimal paths between nodes and constructs and distributes new routing tables to all nodes.

This form of network routing has many disadvantages. The routing manager's ability to receive many messages from the other nodes increases the probability of congestion, a problem that can be exacerbated if the routing manager is itself a node used to accept and forward messages. Networks are sometimes subject to transient conditions, such as when the internode transfer of a file saturates a link for a short period of time. By the time this information is relayed to the routing manager and a new routing is calculated, the activity may have already ceased, making the newly calculated paths less than optimal. Some nodes also receive the newly calculated routing tables before others, leading to inconsistencies in how messages are to be routed. Figure 11–14 shows a change in the message path. Under the old routing mechanism the route was A ⟶ B ⟶ D ⟶ X, whereas the new path is A ⟶ C ⟶ D ⟶ X. Also, the new path from node B to node X is B ⟶ A ⟶ C ⟶ D ⟶ X. If node B receives its new routing chart while node A is still using the old chart, then for a message destined from A to X, A will route it to B and B will route it back to A, continuing until A receives the new routing table. Transmission of the routing tables themselves also may bias the statistics being gathered to compute the next routing algorithm.

An additional problem with centralized route calculations is the amount of CPU processing power needed. Reliability of the routing manager is another important factor. If this node fails, either the routing remains unchanged until the system is recovered or another routing manager must be

network routing manager A designated node that has an overview of network functioning, location of any bottlenecks, and location of facilities.

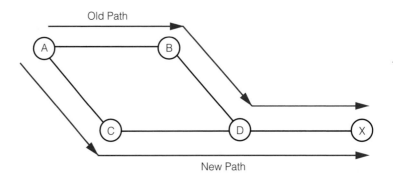

Figure 11–14

Change in the Message Path

selected. The best situation is to have alternative routing managers available in case the primary routing node fails. This is implemented most efficiently by having the routing manager send the alternatives "I'm alive" messages at predefined intervals; if the backup manager fails to receive this message within the prescribed interval, it assumes that the manager has failed and takes over. The backup manager's first responsibility is to broadcast that network status messages should now be routed to it.

Distributed Routing Determination

Distributed routing determination relies on each node to calculate its own best routing table, which requires each node to periodically transmit its status to its neighbors. As this information ripples through the network, each node updates its tables accordingly. This technique avoids the potential bottleneck at a centralized route manager, although the time required for changes to flow through all the nodes may be quite long.

distributed routing determination A routing algorithm in which each node calculates its own routing table based on status information periodically received from other nodes.

Static Routing

The purest form of **static routing** involves always using one particular path between two nodes; if a link in that path is down, communication between those nodes is impossible. Fully interconnected networks were sometimes used for this approach. The only path between any two nodes was the link between them. If that link was down, the available network software was incapable of using any alternative paths. This type of system has largely disappeared. Static routing generally now refers to the situation in which a selected path is used until some drastic condition makes that path unavailable. An alternative path is then selected and used, until the route is switched manually, a failure occurs on the alternative path, or the original path is restored.

static routing A form of routing in which one particular path between two nodes is always used.

When multiple paths exist, some implementations weight each path according to perceived use, which is called **weighted routing.** The path is then randomly selected from the weighted alternatives. Figure 11–15 shows three paths from node A to node X, via nodes B, C, and D. Suppose the network designers had determined that the path through node B would be best 50% of the time, the path through node C would be best 30% of the time, and the path through node D would be best 20% of the time. When a message is to be sent from node A to node X, a random number between 0 and

weighted routing When multiple paths exist, each is given a weight according to perceived use. A random number is generated to determine which of the available paths to use based on their weights.

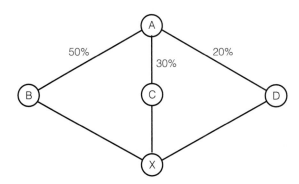

Figure 11–15
Weighted Routing

1 is generated. If the random number is 0.50 or less, the path through node B is traversed; if the random number is greater than 0.50 and less than or equal to 0.80, the path through node C is selected; otherwise, the path through node D selected. The path may alternate, but each path is used with the same frequency as in the routing tables. This type of routing can be changed only by altering the route weighting in the routing tables.

Adaptive Routing

adaptive routing A routing algorithm that evaluates the existing paths and chooses the one that will provide the best path for a message. Routes may change because of congestion and path failures.

Adaptive routing, occasionally called dynamic routing, attempts to select the best current route for the message or session. The best route may be determined by several different parameters, such as link congestion and link speed.

Quickest Link   The simplest adaptive routing algorithm is to have a node pass along the message as quickly as possible, with the only restriction being not to pass it back to the sending node. The receiving node looks at all potential outbound links, selects the one with the least amount of activity, and sends the message out on that line. There is no attempt to determine whether that path will bring the message closer to its destination. This type of algorithm is not very efficient and causes messages to be shuffled to more nodes than necessary, which adds to network congestion. The message could conceivably be shifted around the network for hours before arriving at its destination.

Best Route   The more intelligent adaptive routing techniques attempt to select the best route, as determined by one or more of the following parameters: the number of required hops, the speed of the links, the type of link, and congestion. Link congestion occurs when message traffic on a link is heavy, similar to freeway congestion during rush hours. Routing of this type requires current information on the status of the network. If a node is added to the network or if one is taken off the network, that information must be relayed to the nodes doing route calculation. Knowing the speed of the links as well as the number of hops is important. Traversing two links at 28.8 kbps is more costly than traversing one link at 14.4 kbps. The line time for both is the same, but some time is lost in receiving and forwarding the message. Avoiding congested areas prevents messages from being stuck on inbound and outbound queues. In Figure 11–16, if node A is transmitting a file to node C, the route from node A to node C through B is the shortest but probably not the quickest at that time. The route through nodes E and D would be more efficient because the link from B to C is congested.

Broadcast Routing

broadcast routing Routing in which the message is broadcast to all stations. Only the stations to which the message is addressed accept it.

Broadcast routing is exemplified by the CSMA/CD link protocol discussed in Chapter 7. Routing is quite easy, the message is broadcast to all stations, and only the station to which the message is addressed accepts it. The network layer of the OSI recommendation has fewer functions with broadcast routing.

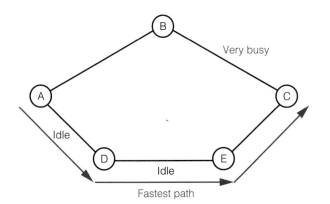

Figure 11–16
Routing Based on Congestion

THE OSI TRANSPORT LAYER

When a message moves from one node in a network to another node, it may pass through several intervening nodes along the path. The data link layer is responsible for detecting errors over a link from one node to an adjacent node, and the network layer routes the message to the next node on the path. However, neither the data link nor the network layers ensure the proper delivery of the complete transmission (which may involve multiple packets) to the destination node. The OSI **transport layer** is involved in end-to-end transmission services and assists the session layer in establishing the connections for a session. Functions that may be provided by the transport layer include

- end-to-end reliability
- packet sequencing
- flow control
- error control
- addressing
- security
- message segmentation
- connection management

transport layer One layer of the ISO open systems interconnection reference model. The transport layer is responsible for the end-to-end integrity of the receipt of message blocks.

End-to-End Reliability   Some network layer protocols, such as IP in the Internet and IPX on Novell LANs, do not guarantee delivery to the destination node. These network layer protocols use a time-to-live counter to determine the number of routing nodes through which a message has passed. The time-to-live counter protects the network from routing problems in which a packet could be endlessly transferred from node to node without reaching its destination. When the time-to-live counter reaches a predefined threshold, the packet is discarded by the network layer. The transport layer provides the **end-to-end reliability** by affixing sequence numbers to the transport layer header of each packet. This sequencing is

end-to-end reliability A mechanism in which a sequence number and acknowledgment number are included in the transport layer header, allowing the destination node to determine whether any packets are missing.

similar to mechanisms we use to ensure reliability in the sending of multiple packages in the mail. If we were sending five packages, we would probably label them 1/5, 2/5, 3/5, 4/5, and 5/5. This lets the recipient know how many packages to expect and allows her to determine which, if any, are missing. The transport layer sequence number allows the destination node to determine whether any packets are missing by including a sequence number and acknowledgment number in the transport layer header. The transport layer header used by the Internet's **Transmission Control Protocol (TCP)** is illustrated in Figure 11–17.

Reliability is typically accomplished by the destination node sending acknowledgments to the source node. The acknowledgments may be simple where each packet must be acknowledged before the next is sent. Alternatively, the transport layer may use a technique similar to that of the Ns and Nr counts in HDLC. With this technique multiple packets may be sent without waiting for an acknowledgment. If packets are found to be missing or received in error, the transport layer may request that the missing packets be sent or that all packets from the missing one be retransmitted. Typically, only the missing packet is resent.

Packet Sequencing In a connection-oriented session, all packets follow the same path and therefore arrive in the same order as they were sent. In a connectionless session, individual packets may take different paths depending on the routing algorithm. The transport layer is able to use the sequence numbers just described to reorder packets that arrive out of sequence.

Flow Control **Flow control** is used at the transport layer to provide buffer management. In full-duplex transmissions, the source node may send several messages without waiting for an acknowledgment. However, a limited number of messages may be sent before an acknowledgment is received. Therefore, the source may need to stop sending messages until a positive acknowledgment is received. Similarly, the receiving node may find that its buffer space is limited and will send the sender a message adjusting the number of outstanding unacknowledged messages it can send. In this way, the flow of packets between source and destination can be adjusted to the existing circumstances. Some newer transport layer protocols also consider rate control. Whereas flow control depends on buffer space, rate control depends on the ability of the source and destination nodes to process data. Rate control provides a pacing mechanism that accommodates vari-

Transmission Control Protocol An internetwork protocol developed by the U.S. Department of Defense.

flow control A type of buffer management in which the flow of packets between source and destination is adjusted to the existing circumstances.

Source Port			Destination Port
Sequence Number			
Acknowledgment Number			
Header Length	Reserved	Code Bits	Window (Buffer) Size
Checksum			Urgent Data Pointer
Options			Padding

Figure 11–17
TCP Header Format

ables such as different processing speeds and variations in the congestion at the source or destination nodes.

Error Control   In addition to the end-to-end reliability function, a transport layer may include a checksum in the header to detect transmission errors. Error detection is usually implemented at the data link layer and sometimes also at the network layer. A transport layer checksum gives another layer of protection from data corruption. Even if lower layer error detection is used, the message received by the transport layer could be corrupted. For example, suppose that error detection is implemented only at the data link and transport layer. When the message moves from the data link layer to the network layer (and possibly back down to the data link layer), the data might be altered. This type of error would not be detected by the data link layer because the error was introduced after data link error checking.

Addressing   A message is sent between a process in the source node and a process in the destination node. A network address consists of three basic components: a network address, a node address, and a process address. In an internet, all network addresses must be unique. In a single network, node addresses are unique. In a node, process addresses are unique. The three together therefore uniquely identify a single process in the internet. In Figure 11–17, the first two fields in the TCP header are the source and destination port addresses. These addresses correspond to processes in the source and destination nodes and are used to deliver the message to the receiving process.

Security   With the expanded use of the Internet and other networks, security has become a major concern. One of the places to coordinate security between the source and destination applications is at the transport layer. Originally, TCP did not have security functions, but this is changing. A variety of security mechanisms are being implemented to secure data transmissions. Naturally, the applications communicating with each other need to use the same mechanism. The transport layer is a natural place for this negotiation to occur and to exchange necessary security information such as encryption keys.

Message Segmentation   The source and destination nodes may have different sizes of buffers available. For example, a large WAN node may have buffers of several thousand bytes, whereas a desktop system may have buffers of a thousand bytes or less. The transport layers at the source and destination nodes can set a maximum segment size for message exchanges to accommodate buffer differences.

Connection Management   Connection management involves establishing a connection and dissolving it when the source and destination are done communicating. When establishing a connection, one transport layer initiates the request, and the other must be waiting for connection requests to arrive. When this occurs, the corresponding layers go through a handshake routine to establish connection parameters. Similarly, one end requests an end to the connection. Again, the two layers go through a routine to bring the connection to an orderly end.

Seymour Opportunity, vice-president of marketing for the Syncrasy Corporation, has convinced the other corporate executives that the future lies not only in mail-order operations but also in discount computer stores. Wanting to expand into several areas at once, Syncrasy is opening discount computer stores in Chicago, New York City, Atlanta, Houston, Los Angeles, San Francisco, and Kansas City. Penny Pincher, the comptroller, has exerted her influence by obtaining commitments that the cost of expansion will be held to a minimum. In this study, we have included prices for certain network components. Naturally, the cost of these items may change. You may want to make the case more up-to-date by doing some research and substituting current costs.

The computer stores in Chicago, New York, and Los Angeles will have five terminals each, and the other stores will have three each. Mail-order operations will continue, although on a diminished scale. The catalog stores in Kansas City, New York, and Los Angeles will be located 15, 20, and 40 mi from the discount stores, respectively.

COMPUTER STORE TRANSACTION TYPES

The two basic transactions at each computer store will be inventory and receipt transactions and parts and customer inquiries.

Inventory and Receipts

The first type of transaction deals with inventory control and receipts. Every time a sale is made, the part number, quantity sold, unit price, discount rate, and total amount of the sale are transmitted to the central computer. The line item for each part sold consists of 22 characters, and the total amount of the sale is a 10-character field. The usual response to the transaction is 10 characters. Orders that total more than $1000 are an exception and require a credit check. These transactions, which make up an estimated 30% of all inventory transactions, have 10 additional characters in the response portion of the message. Average processing time for normal orders is 0.5 s; for orders of more than $1000, it is 0.8 s. There is an average of 6 items per order and an average of 20 orders per terminal per hour, with peaks of 40 orders per terminal per hour. Peak transaction periods are from noon to 1:00 P.M. and from 5:00 P.M. to 6:00 P.M. It is required that 95% of all transactions of this type have a 3-s response time.

Parts and Customer Inquiries

The second type of store transaction is a parts or customer inquiry. Average input is 10 characters and average response is 500 characters. Average and peak rates for this transaction are both 10 per hour per terminal. A response time of 4 s is required. Processing time for these transactions is 1.5 s per order.

Catalog Store Activity

The third type of transaction will be in the catalog stores. Activity in the catalog store operations will decline as a result of having discount stores in the area. Catalog stores will have eight terminals each. The typical catalog store transaction has 500 characters of input data and a 100-character response. Each terminal averages 20 orders per hour, with a peak of 30 orders per hour; 5-s response time is required for these transactions. Processing time is 2.5 s per order.

PRICES, EQUIPMENT, AND MILEAGE

Only leased transmission lines from a common carrier are considered. Satellite transmission was considered by Syncrasy at the outset, but it was dismissed because of the light amount of traffic from the stores and the effect of propagation delay on response times. The following rates are used in this Case Study (and in the exercises at the end of this chapter).

Modems

The cost of modems has declined in recent years, so it is unlikely that modems will be leased. The following calculations are for monthly fees only, excluding modem costs. Syncrasy also has opted to buy statistical multiplexers with integrated modems.

Interstate Communication Lines

The line can handle speeds up to 38,400 bps. Line speed is governed by the modem.

First 100 miles	$2.52 per mile (including monthly fee)
101–1000 miles	$0.94 per mile
Each mile over 1000	$0.58 per mile

Local Communication Lines

The line can handle speeds up to 38,400 bps. Line speed is governed by the modem.

Each mile	$4.70

Statistical Multiplexer

Syncrasy chose stat muxes with additional memory and built-in modems. These muxes cost more than the $1000 entry-level muxes. Because the unit costs of these muxes are high, Syncrasy decided to lease them. The costs of the multiplexers Syncrasy has chosen are as follows:

Number of Channels	Purchase Price	Monthly Lease Price
4	$1700	$150
8	2600	225
16	4300	358
32	6500	540

Concentrators

The price of concentrators can vary enormously. This case uses two configurations. The first configuration will handle up to 32 output lines, which could be point-to-point terminals, multipoint communication lines, or lines to another concentrator or multiplexer. It sells for $30,000, with a monthly lease price of $1500. The second configuration must be large enough to handle all transactions. It sells for $40,000 and leases for $2000 per month. Each of these concentrators will be able to accommodate up to eight incoming lines from the host processor.

Front-End Processors

The price of the FEP, $40,000, is the same as that of the more expensive concentrator.

Terminals

Dumb terminals sell for $500, with a monthly lease price of $50. Smart terminals sell for $1200, with a monthly lease price of $95. Intelligent terminals sell for $1500, with a monthly lease price of $105.

Mileage

Airline miles are used for determining communication rates between cities. Table 11–6 lists the mileage between cities.

Table 11–6   Mileage Chart

	Chicago	Houston	Kansas City	L.A.	N.Y.C.	S.F.
Atlanta	708	791	822	2191	854	2483
Chicago		1091	542	2048	809	2173
Houston			743	1555	1610	1911
Kansas City				1547	1233	1861
Los Angeles					2794	387
New York City						2930

Preliminary Considerations

A simple Case Study has been constructed, with few locations and a centrally located computer center. Even so, the variation between media costs of the best and worst cases alone can be significant. Because of their extended capabilities, intelligent terminals have been selected.

MILEAGE COSTS

In practice, several common carriers would be consulted and their bids solicited for the best configuration. If there were many more locations, one of the network modeling systems would also be used to analyze all possible routes and provide a list of the best alternatives. Instead, this exercise uses the brute force method of hand calculations.

Long-Distance Line Costs

Although it is unusual to do so, point-to-point costs are calculated first. This allows comparison of the best- and worst-case line costs. The cost of the Kansas City–Los Angeles link is computed in detail; mileage and line costs for the remaining cities are simply listed. Because mileage rates are different for miles 0–100, 101–1000, and over 1000, the 1547 mi between Kansas City and Los Angeles must be broken down into these increments, yielding 100 + 900 + 547 mi. The cost for the Kansas City–Los Angeles link, then, is

$$(100)\,(2.52) + (900)\,(0.94) + (547)\,(0.58) = 1415.26$$

Monthly point-to-point link charges between the home city and all remote locations are as follows:

Kansas City to	
Atlanta	$ 930.68
Chicago	667.48
Houston	856.42
Los Angeles	1415.26
New York City	1233.14
San Francisco	1597.38
Total	$6700.36

Minimum-Distance Configuration Costs

Many combinations are available to find the lowest rate based on a minimum-distance configuration. The easiest way is to start with the shortest link—Kansas City to Chicago—and work outward until all locations are accounted for. A simple program could also be written to evaluate all combinations and pick the shortest route. A network configuration of the shortest routes is given in Figure 11–18. The costs of this network are as follows:

From	To	Distance (mi)	Cost
Kansas City	Houston	743	$ 856.42
Kansas City	Chicago	542	667.48
Chicago	New York City	809	918.46
Chicago	Atlanta	708	823.52
Kansas City	Los Angeles	1547	1415.26
Los Angeles	San Francisco	387	521.78
Total			$5202.92

Local Line Costs

The costs of local links between the mail-order and discount stores in Kansas City, New York City, and Los Angeles must be calculated in addition to the costs of long-distance lines. These charges are easier to compute because there is a flat rate per mile. The costs are as follows:

Location	Distance (mi)	Cost
Kansas City	15	$ 70.50
New York City	20	94.00
Los Angeles	40	188.00
Total		$352.50

The difference between the low-cost and high-cost configurations is $1497.44 per month ($6700.36 - $5202.92). This does not mean the configuration is finalized. Whether the capacity of the lines can support the application is yet to be determined. For instance, the link from Kansas City to Chicago must be capable of supporting all message traffic from Chicago, New York City, and Atlanta. If one 9600-bps line is not capable of this, another alternative will be required, such as linking Houston and Atlanta.

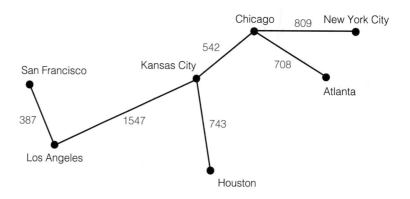

Figure 11–18
Network Configuration of the Shortest Route

CALCULATION OF LINE USE COSTS

Five items must be considered in calculating the costs of line use: overhead, response time, aggregate data rate, line contention, and configuration. The first line-speed calculation is for response time. Following that, the aggregate data rate for a given link is considered to ensure that there is sufficient capacity to meet all terminals' demands. Contention issues are then addressed, followed by an analysis of configuration.

Overhead

Overhead includes costs for several components: control messages, polling, and terminal access. Overhead reflects how efficiently the lines are used. As discussed earlier in this chapter, some of the purposes of data link protocols are to delimit data, provide error detection and line control, and allow for addressing. Each function requires that additional data be appended to the data message. In this case, control message overhead is approximated by using 10 bits per character rather than the actual 7 or 8 bits. Although not entirely accurate, this measure is adequate and certainly simplifies calculation.

A second overhead factor is polling costs, if a multipoint configuration is used. Determining polling overhead involves figuring the amount of time a terminal must wait to be polled. This averages out as follows:

Wait time = Polling interval × (Number of terminals − 1)/2

On average, a terminal will wait for half of the other terminals. Sometimes a terminal will wait for all of the other terminals, and at other times there will be no wait at all. Total wait time is the number of terminals that are waited for times the polling interval, or the amount of time required to send the poll message and wait for a reply. The amount of time required for a terminal to send data is not factored in because that is included in the contention calculations. Polling is ignored in this example because of the added complexity it requires.

The final component of overhead is the additional characters required for terminal access. Smart terminals using screen templates, protected fields, and video attributes require several characters to provide these capabilities. These include not only the characters needed for prompts, but also the control characters that position the cursor, allow for video attributes and protected fields, and so on. The number of additional characters required to support these capabilities varies from terminal to terminal. Although these additional characters are ignored in this case, the number of characters required for terminal access can be significant. Polling wait time can also be significant, especially with many terminals and half-duplex lines with slow modem turnaround times. These factors must not be ignored in a real-life situation.

Response Time: Inventory and Receipts

First, the inventory and receipts transaction is considered. The average number of line items per transaction is 6. Each line item consists of the part number, quantity, discount rate, and line item price, with a total of 22 characters per line item. For 6 line items, $6 \times 22 = 132$ characters are required, plus a 10-character total field, giving a total input record length of 142 characters. The response consists of 10 characters. The expected response time is 3 s. With 0.5 s required for processing, this leaves 2.5 s to transmit 152 characters, or $152/2.5 = 61$ characters per second. At 10 bits per character for overhead of the data link protocol, a 610-bps line will be required. Thus, a 1200-bps line will be sufficient for this transaction's response time, hereafter called transaction type 1.

Transactions of this type that are more than $1000 in total sales require the same response time but have an additional 10 characters in the response and 0.3 s of processing time. The system must be able to transmit 162 characters in 2.2 s, which is 74 characters per second, or a 740-bps capacity. A 1200-bps line will also satisfy the response time for this transaction, hereafter called transaction type 2.

Response Time: Parts and Customer Inquiries

The customer or inventory inquiry transaction requires 10 characters of input and generates a 500-character response, with 4-s response time and a 1.5-s processing time needed. The line time allowed is 2.5 s. The system must then transmit 510 characters in 2.5 s, or 204 characters per second. This equates to 2040 bps, which necessitates a 2400-bps line. This is hereafter called transaction type 3.

Response Time: Catalog Store Transactions

The catalog store transaction calculation was done in Chapter 2, where it was determined that 600 characters had to be transmitted in 2.5 s, for 240 characters per second or 2400 bps. This is hereafter called transaction type 4. Overall, considering individual terminal response time only, a 2400-bps line will be adequate.

Aggregate Data Transmission Rate

In determining the aggregate data rate for Syncrasy's lines, we can start with the line from Kansas City to Chicago, which must support five terminals in Chicago, eight catalog store terminals in New York City, five store terminals in New York City, and three store terminals in Atlanta. Computation of the aggregate data rate must also consider the peak transaction load. Table 11–7 contains all of the pertinent information for this analysis.

In Table 11–7, the Chicago type 1 transactions have been separated from the East Coast type 1 transactions. Because peak transaction rates occur during specific hours and the East Coast cities of New York City and Atlanta are in a different time zone from Chicago, the worst condition of peak traffic on the East Coast has been assumed, for 40 transactions per hour; average load has been assumed for Chicago. Also, of the 40 transactions, 30% are transaction type 2. Thus, there are 28 type 1 transactions and 12 type 2

Table 11–7   Transaction Analysis

Transaction Type (location)	Number of Transactions per Hour	Number of Characters per Transaction	Number of Terminals	Total Number of Characters per Hour
1 (East Coast)	28	152	8	34,048
1 (Chicago)	21	152	5	15,960
2 (East Coast)	12	162	8	15,552
2 (Chicago)	9	162	5	7,290
3 (both)	10	510	13	66,300
4 (mail order)	30	600	8	144,000
			Total	283,150

transactions per hour on the East Coast and 21 type 1 transactions and 9 type 2 transactions in Chicago. The total 283,150 characters transmitted per hour is the product of the number of terminals, the number of transactions per terminal, and the number of characters per transaction, as indicated in the last column of Table 11–7.

An aggregate data rate of 283,150 characters per hour equates to approximately 78 characters per second, which is derived by dividing the number of characters per hour by 3600 seconds per hour. These calculations indicate that a 1200-bps line is sufficient to support the aggregate data rate. Thus far, response time is the dominant factor with respect to line speed.

Line Contention

As discussed in Chapter 2, a 2400-bps line is adequate in a point-to-point environment, although not if two terminals attempt to start a transaction at the same time. If a random transaction arrival rate is assumed, the following formula (from queuing theory) may be used to determine the probability of several transactions arriving within the same interval.

$$P_k(T) = (LT)^k (k!)(e^{-LT})$$

where

$P_k(T)$ is the probability that k transactions will arrive in interval T

L is the average number of transactions per unit of time

T is the interval being considered

e is the natural base for logarithms

k is the number of arrivals

! is the factorial function

In this transaction environment there is a total of 840 transactions per hour, which is derived by summing the products of the number of transactions per hour and the number of terminals performing that transaction

Table 11–8   Transaction Arrival Probabilities

Number of Arrivals	Probability
2	0.21
3	0.08
4	0.02
5	0.005

rate, as shown in Table 11–7. This results in an average of 0.23 transactions per second (840 divided by 3600). Thus, L in the formula is 0.23. Assuming an interval T of 5 s, which is the time for the longest transaction, the probability of two transactions arriving within a given 5-s interval is

$$p_2(5) = (0.23 \times 5)^2(2!)(e^{-(0.23 \times 5)}) = (1.15^2)(2)(e^{-1.15}) = 0.21$$

The complete probability table is given in Table 11–8, from which it can be determined that the probability of two or more transactions arriving in any 5-s interval is

$$0.21 + 0.08 + 0.02 + 0.005 = 0.315$$

Thus, about 33% of the time two or more transactions will be active in a 5-s time span. Doubling the line speed will allow two transactions within 5 s to meet the expected response time. The probability then becomes only 0.10, or 10%, that transactions will contend with each other (the probability that three or more transactions will arrive within 5 s). A 5-s interval is quite conservative because it is not entirely devoted to line time—the element of interest. During the 5-s interval, for a given transaction, the line will be idle approximately 50% of the time at a speed of 2400 bps. Increasing the line speed to 4800 bps should adequately eliminate slow response time due to contention.

Configuring the System: East Coast

It would be most economical to use a short route line configuration with cascading statistical multiplexers. If the configuration follows a path from

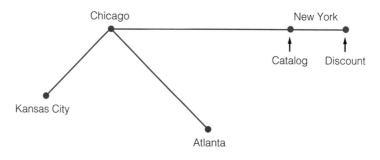

Figure 11–19
Syncrasy East Coast Network

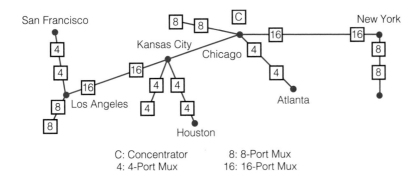

Figure 11–20
Syncrasy Configuration

Kansas City to Chicago, then from Chicago to New York City and Atlanta, and finally from New York City catalog store to New York City discount store, as shown in Figure 11–19, by the time the extremities have been reached, a stat mux is likely to have run out of capacity. Each time a line is dropped off, the speed generally steps down. In addition, cascading multiplexers down by five levels will probably result in performance problems. Another problem is the number of terminals in New York City that must be accounted for. A concentrator in Chicago will provide the following significant network capabilities:

- allows terminals to be polled from Chicago rather than Kansas City
- provides for later expansion
- allows for more local terminal and error handling
- can provide some local support if the path to Kansas City is malfunctioning
- makes for a more workable configuration than extensive cascading of muxes
- can support higher-speed circuits to the East Coast

Configuring the System: West Coast

A different configuration can be used for the West Coast link to Los Angeles and San Francisco: a direct link to Los Angeles and two separate drops (five terminals to the discount stores in Los Angeles and three to San Francisco). This contrasts with the link from Chicago to New York City, which involves 18 terminals. Cascading muxes are feasible for the West Coast. For the Houston link, a simple four-port statistical multiplexer on a 4800-bps line can be used. The final configuration is given in Figure 11–20.

FINAL COSTS

The final monthly costs, broken down by branches of the network, are summarized on the following page.

Monthly Equipment Cost for the Kansas City, Chicago, New York City, and Atlanta Branches of the Network

Multiplexers	2	16-port muxes at $358 each	$ 716
	4	8-port muxes at $225 each	900
	2	4-port muxes at $150 each	300
Modems		Purchased or integrated with muxes	
Terminals	11	Intelligent terminals at $105 each (two available from the mail-order store)	1155
Concentrator	1	$1500 each	1500
Subtotal			$4571

Monthly Equipment Cost for the Kansas City to Kansas City Branch of the Network

Multiplexers	2	4-port muxes at $150 each	$300
Modems		Purchased or integrated with muxes	
Terminals	1	Intelligent terminal at $105 each (two terminals available from mail-order store)	105
Subtotal			$405

Monthly Equipment Cost for the Kansas City to Houston Branch of the Network

Multiplexers	2	4-port muxes at $150 each	$300
Terminals	3	Intelligent terminals at $105 each	315
Subtotal			$615

Monthly Equipment Cost for the Kansas City to Los Angeles to San Francisco Branches of the Network

Multiplexers	2	16-port muxes at $358 each	$ 716
	2	8-port muxes at $225 each	450
	2	4-port muxes at $150 each	300
Modems		Purchased or integrated with muxes	
Terminals	6	Intelligent terminals at $105 each (two available from the mail-order store)	630
Subtotal			$2096

Total Monthly Costs for the Network

Total equipment	$ 7,687
Total long-distance line costs	5,203
Total local line costs	352
Total network costs	$13,242

Syncrasy will have to sell a lot of equipment to support this $13,242 per month configuration. However, there is the existing alternative of attaching to a packet distribution network (PDN). PDNs are discussed in Chapter 4. Because the amount of data being transmitted is small and PDNs charge by the number of packets and not by connect time, the overall cost could be lower.

SUMMARY

This chapter covered WAN topologies and the transmission services of the OSI data link, network, and transport layers. The principal WAN topologies are the star, hierarchical, and interconnected topologies. Rings or loops and buses are also used in WANs, but are most common in LANs.

The primary WAN data link protocols are asynchronous and synchronous. Asynchronous protocols were adapted from precomputer technologies such as telegraphy. Asynchronous transmission is widely used, particularly for connections between terminals and host computers and between microcomputers and other computers. There are several varieties of synchronous protocols. The preferred protocol today is a bit synchronous protocol such as SDLC, HDLC, LAPB, or ADCCP. Additional details of asynchronous and bit synchronous protocols can be found in Appendices A and B.

The OSI network and transport layers also provide transmission services. The OSI network layer performs four major functions: routing, network control, congestion control, and collection of accounting data. Several routing algorithms exist, and can be classified into two broad categories: static and adaptive. Static routing algorithms choose a path and continue using that path as long as it is available. Adaptive routing algorithms may vary the path used in an attempt to always use the best path. Thus, adaptive routing may be able to avoid congestion and more effectively use all available paths between a sender and receiver.

The OSI transport layer is involved in end-to-end transmission services and assists the session layer in establishing the connections for a session. One of the services performed by the transport layer is message accountability. Message sequence numbers are generated by the transport layer in the sending computer and checked by the transport layer in the recipient's computer, thus ensuring that the entire message was received. The transport layer also assists in finding the network address of the recipient.

KEY TERMS

adaptive routing
Advanced Data Communications
    Control Procedure (ADCCP)
asynchronous transmission (async)
Binary Synchronous Communica-
    tions (BISYNC or BSC) protocol
bit-oriented synchronous data link
    protocol

bit stuffing
broadcast routing
buffer overflow/overrun
byte count protocol
character-count termination
character synchronous protocol
congestion control
distributed routing determination

double buffering
end-to-end reliability
flow control
frame
framing protocol
hierarchical topology
High-Level Data Link Control
   (HDLC)
interconnected (plex or mesh) network
interrupt characters
Link Access Procedure, Balanced
   (LAPB)
message sequence numbers
network control

network routing manager
number received (Nr) subfield
number sent (Ns) subfield
positional protocol
routing
star network
static routing
synchronous
Synchronous Data Link Control
   (SDLC)
timeout interval
Transmission Control Protocol
   (TCP)
transport layer
weighted routing

REVIEW QUESTIONS

In answering some of the questions below, it may be helpful to refer to the material in Appendices A and B.

1. Explain why asynchronous protocols do not support code independence.

2. In asynchronous protocols, what function is provided by interrupt characters?

3. Why is double buffering necessary?

4. Explain the popularity of asynchronous protocols.

5. Distinguish between positional and framing synchronous protocols.

6. How does a byte count synchronous protocol work?

7. Name three implementations of bit-oriented synchronous data link controls. List the features indicated in the text that distinguish some of these from SDLC.

8. How do asynchronous and synchronous protocols differ? In what respects are they the same?

9. What advantages does SDLC have over BISYNC?

10. Which network topology provides the greatest amount of control? Which provides the lowest link costs? Which has the highest link costs?

11. What are the advantages and disadvantages of centralized routing calculations?

12. What are the advantages and disadvantages of local route determination?

13. Distinguish between static and adaptive routing.

14. What are the advantages and disadvantages of the quickest link routing algorithm?

15. Describe the weighted routing algorithm.

PROBLEMS AND EXERCISES

1. Make a chart that compares the overhead of asynchronous, BISYNC, and HDLC protocols. Make the chart for message sizes of 25, 50, 100, 500, and 1000

Table 11–9   Protocol Comparison Chart

Number of Text Characters	Number of Bits Transferred		
	ASYNC	BISYNC	SDLC
25			
50			
100			
500			
1000			

characters. The chart should look like Table 11–9. In filling out the chart, assume the following:

7-bit characters for asynchronous

a start, stop, and parity bit for asynchronous

8-bit characters for BISYNC and SDLC

six BISYNC control characters (SYN, SYN, STX, ETX, plus two for BCC) for message transfer

For BISYNC you should also include a point-to-point line bid (SYN SYN ENQ) and two acknowledgments (SYN SYN ACK0 and SYN SYN ACK1) of four characters each. One acknowledgment is for the line bid and one for the data.

For SDLC, a frame overhead of 48 bits

For SDLC count the acknowledgment as 16 bits, because ordinarily several frames will be acknowledged at once

Which is the most efficient protocol and under what conditions?

2. Diagram a sequence of message exchanges between two stations using SDLC that shows the changing of the Ns and Nr subfields.

3. Is transparency a requirement of code independence? Justify your answer.

4. Can there be a start–stop flag in the address or control field of an SDLC message? If not, why not? If so, why does it not terminate the message?

5. You need a WAN and want a topology that provides a low cost with good reliability and expandability. You also need good response times, which implies a limited number of hops. Which topology would you choose? Why?

Table 11–10   Mileage Chart

	Cleveland	Houston	Las Vegas	Phoenix	Portland	San Diego	Washington, D.C.
Boston	657	1830	2752	2670	3144	2984	448
Cleveland		1306	2093	2032	2432	2385	360
Houston			1467	1164	2243	1490	1365
Las Vegas				285	996	336	2420
Phoenix					1268	353	2300
Portland						1086	2784
San Diego							2602

6. Investigate three network implementations and answer the following questions.
   a. What topology does each use?
   b. What type of routing does each use?
   c. Are alternative paths available? If so, under what conditions are they used?

7. What is the lowest-cost communication configuration that will link each of the cities in the mileage chart in Table 11–10? Use the line costs presented in the Case Study.

8. If Houston is the central location, what is the cost of a network connecting Houston to each of the cities in Exercise 7 via point-to-point links?

9. Would a PDN be a suitable network for the Syncrasy Corporation's network of catalog and discount stores (see Chapter 5)? What would be the advantages and disadvantages of using a PDN for that application?

CHAPTER 12

WAN System Software

CHAPTER OBJECTIVES

After studying this chapter you should be able to

- Describe the functions of the OSI session layer
- Discuss the functions provided by an operating system and device drivers
- Compare database and telecommunication access methods
- Explain the capabilities of a teleprocessing monitor
- Trace the flow of a transaction through a system

In this chapter we discuss several major software components of a data communication network. In the OSI reference model, software exists at every layer from the data link level up. We have already looked at functions of the physical, data link, network, and transport layers. This chapter primarily addresses functions found in the OSI session layer. Consistent with prior approaches, the discussion moves from the level closest to the terminals and proceeds toward the host processor. In this chapter you will learn about system software functions. By system software, we mean software such as an operating system or data communication software that supports applications in carrying out their tasks.

THE OSI SESSION LAYER

Whenever two entities in a network communicate, a session is established between them. The major objectives of the session layer are to establish the dialogue rules between two entities, to manage the exchange of data between the entities, and to dissolve the session. The dialogue rules include the method of flow control, which can be either full duplex or half duplex. Simplex transmission is not supported in the OSI reference model.

Another aspect of the dialogue rules is establishing synchronization points. If a session is interrupted for any reason, the synchronization points help reestablish and recover the session. Other parameters that the session layer might stipulate for a session are message lengths and quality of service. Quality of service parameters include the ability to set priorities, security, and speed and quality of the communication link. When the entities involved in a session need to terminate the dialogue, the session must be dissolved. Dissolution may occur at the request of either session member. Before a session is dissolved, all data in transit must first be received and acknowledged. We now consider a generic software environment and two WAN software systems that provide session-level services.

SOFTWARE OVERVIEW

Application Software

A generic software configuration is depicted in Figure 12–1. At the heart of the system is the application software. The goal of **application software** is to solve a business or scientific problem, not to solve computer system problems. An example of a system problem is the details of how to display data on a terminal. In the early days of computer programming, an application program needed to contain logic to communicate with specific hardware devices. If a new terminal was introduced into the system, application programs had to be changed to support the differences between the new terminal and terminals the program already supported. If all currently supported terminals had monochrome screens and the new terminal had a color screen, the application program had to be modified to be able to display colors. When application software is responsible for device handling, the application programs take longer to create, test, and modify. The application programmer must have device interface skills as well as application design skills.

application software
Software that solves a business or scientific problem, as opposed to system software, which makes the system easier to use.

System Software

Most current systems provide system-level software that eliminates the need for hardware-dependent logic in application software. This allows programmers to focus their attention on business problems. To support this objective, software such as database management systems and teleprocessing monitors were developed to control and manage data and terminal devices, and access methods were added to provide easier access to data and terminals. These software capabilities provide functions common to most application programs and remove the details of file and device access from application software. This follows a trend of system-level software: making the system easier to program and use. Programs interface to devices via well-defined user interfaces. Just as the adjacent levels of the OSI reference model have interfaces that allow data to flow between layers, messages and

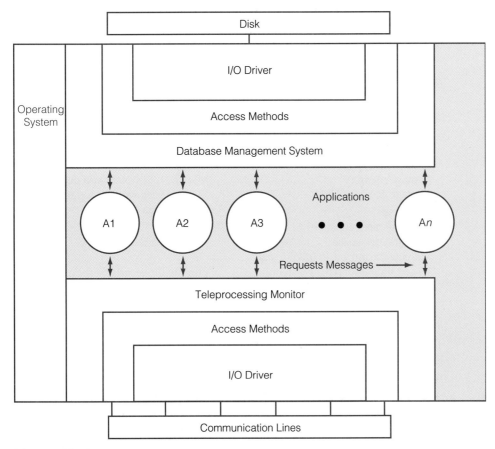

Figure 12–1
Generic Software Configuration

data flowing between application programs and the database or data communication system pass through interfaces to reach their destination. Perhaps the most important piece of software in effecting this is the operating system.

Operating System

The **operating system (OS)** helps applications by performing interface, process management, and file management functions, as listed in Table 12–1. The OS performs all of these functions in a manner largely transparent to the application program and the programmer. The OS also performs many functions for an executing program, but these functions are carried out without the programmer explicitly requesting them. The OS, the overall manager of the computing system, is loaded when the system is started and portions of the OS remain memory resident so it is always available to provide management and interface functions. One of the functions provided by the OS is managing the input/output (I/O) subsystem. The parts of the operating system that perform this task are called I/O drivers.

operating system (OS)
The overall manager of the computing system that performs all of its functions, transparent to the application program and the programmer.

Table 12–1   Operating System Functions

Interface Functions—Provide Interface To	
Users	I/O system
File system	
Process Functions	
Schedule processes for execution	Start/stop processes
Establish process environment	Enforce process priorities
Prevent processes from interfering with each other	Allow multiprocessing/multitasking
Management Functions	
Manage memory	Manage I/O system and devices
Manage access to CPU	Manage user access through security provisions
File Management Functions	
Allocate disk space	Maintain disk directories
Manage file attributes (owner, date and time updated, and so on)	Provide file security

I/O Drivers

I/O driver The part of the operating system that manages the input/output subsystem by providing low-level access to devices.

The **I/O drivers** in Figure 12–1 provide the low-level access to devices. On the database side the devices are tapes and disks, and on the data communication side they are communication lines. In data communication, low-level access involves implementing the data link protocols, such as asynchronous or HDLC, error detection, and buffer management. For disk drives the I/O driver issues seek, read, and write commands. The specifics of I/O drivers are system and device dependent.

Access Methods

access method A software subsystem that provides input and output services as interface between an application and its associated devices. It eliminates device dependencies for an application programmer.

Access methods exist for both database and data communication systems. Access methods generally separate the application from physical characteristics of the data or devices the application is accessing. An access method essentially functions as a black box to translate user read and write requests into lower-level requests tailored to the file or device being accessed. Database access methods allow users to retrieve data. Applications often need several data retrieval methods. With personnel files, for instance, an employee record might need to be accessed via employee name, employee number, and Social Security number. Access methods provide the ability to select a specific record from the database with a small number of disk accesses. Some access methods also allow records to be retrieved in order on a key, which provides a logical ordering to the records. Thus, one access method might be used to retrieve personnel records in employee name order and another access method might be used to retrieve personnel records in department order.

Data communication access methods allow users to display data on a terminal and to retrieve data that has been entered on the terminal. How data is displayed on terminals may vary from one terminal to another. In

Chapter 10, several terminal attributes were presented, including color, reverse video, and protected fields. Data communication access methods allow the user access to these attributes without knowing their implementation details. Access methods are covered in more detail later in this chapter.

Database and File Management Systems

A **database management system (DBMS)** organizes data into records, organizes records into files, and provides access to the data based on one or more access keys. A DBMS also provides a mechanism for relating one file to another. In a university database, records are maintained on students, classes, and teachers. File relationships allow users to answer questions such as, "What students are enrolled in section 4 of tapeworm taxonomy?" and "List the advisors for all students majoring in mathematics." Both requests require that data be extracted from at least two files via relationships that exist between the files (such as a teacher-advises-student relationship). A **file management system (FMS)** provides a subset of the capabilities found in a DBMS. An FMS is oriented toward one file and hence does not provide file relationships. Database and file management systems provide data services to application processes. Applications issue database requests to store, modify, retrieve, or delete data, and the DBMS carries out these requests.

database management system (DBMS) A system that organizes data into records, organizes records into files, provides access to the data based on one or more access keys, and provides the mechanism for relating one file to another.

file management system (FMS) A system that provides a subset of a database management system's capabilities. An FMS provides functions such as storage allocation and file access methods for a single file.

Transaction Control Process

Whereas the DBMS provides an application with access to data, application access to terminals or other nodes is provided by a transaction control process (TCP), also called a teleprocessing monitor or message control system (MCS). (Note that the term *TCP* as used in this chapter is different from the TCP of the Transmission Control Protocol/Internet Protocol, or TCP/IP.) A data communication access method can partially fulfill this function. Similar to the way in which a DBMS allows applications to share data, insulates the applications from the physical details of data storage, and provides data independence, the TCP enables different terminals to interface with multiple applications and removes an application from details such as the physical differences among terminals and among network nodes. Whereas the DBMS uses different data access methods to provide multiple paths to data, the TCP uses different terminal access methods to give access to multiple terminal types. A more detailed description of the TCP and its associated access methods can be found later in this chapter.

Example of Transaction Flow

With this brief overview of the application software environment, we now see how the software components cooperate in processing a transaction. The following example assumes that our system is configured to allow recovery from most system failures and that the transaction will be entered by a user at a terminal. For specifics, this discussion assumes a single-system environment; with only minor changes, this discussion could fit a client/server environment in which the client and server are in separate computers.

Preparation for a transaction begins before the user enters the information. The first step in a system startup, of course, is loading the operating system. Following that, the system and application software such as DBMS, TCP, spooler, and e-mail systems are started.

The application programs in Figure 12–1 receive their inputs from the TCP. Once the applications start, they must establish a session with the TCP. In some TCP systems, applications run directly under the control of the TCP. In other systems, applications are more independent of the TCP. In the first case the applications are tightly coupled to a single TCP, whereas in the second case applications can receive messages from one or more TCPs as well as from other sources.

Regardless of the implementation, a data path always exists or can be established between applications and a TCP. Once this path exists, the application issues a read request on its message file or otherwise indicates its readiness to accept a message for processing. The TCP displays an opening screen on each terminal under its control and then initiates a read for each terminal. Typical opening displays are a menu of available transactions or a user logon screen.

Multiple TCPs may be in operation concurrently, and each TCP exclusively controls several terminals. Terminals may be moved from one TCP to another, but may be attached only to a single TCP at any one time. However, not all terminals in the system need to connect to a TCP. Some terminals may be used outside the TCP for applications such as program development. Terminals may also alternate between use for transaction processing under TCP control and use for other applications outside TCP control.

At this point in the transaction environment, each application is awaiting a transaction from the TCP, and the TCPs are awaiting data from their terminals. We assume that a user has successfully logged onto the system, a menu of transactions has been displayed on the user's terminal by the TCP, and the user is ready to enter a transaction. When a terminal transmits a transaction (such as admitting a patient to a hospital), the following actions are taken.

1. The user selects the "admit patient" transaction from the menu. This selection is transmitted to the TCP.

2. The TCP responds to the user's selection by displaying a patient identification form on the terminal and issues a read request for that terminal. The user fills in the form and transmits it to the TCP.

3. The TCP receives the transaction from the terminal, completing the read the TCP has issued for that device. For each of the other terminals, the TCP also has an outstanding read. Thus, at any time, a terminal operator may complete a task and transmit data to the TCP. The TCP must be able to accept these messages when they arrive.

4. The TCP sends the patient's ID to an application with a request to find a patient record that matches the requested ID. The objective is to determine whether this patient already has a hospital record.

5. The application issues a database read request to obtain a patient record with the ID sent to it by the TCP. If the record exists, it is re-

turned to the application; otherwise, the application receives a message from the DBMS stating that the record does not exist.

6. The application returns the result to the TCP. In this case we assume that the patient does not have a record on file.

7. The TCP displays a patient registration form and posts a read on the terminal. The user enters data into the form and sends it back to the TCP. At this point the TCP has all the data necessary for admitting the patient.

8. Data edits are performed on all fields for which they have been specified. For example, the TCP determines whether the patient's name has been entered, whether the data entered for the patient's gender is M or F, whether the birth date entered is valid, and so on. If any of the fields are found to be in error, the TCP displays an error message on the terminal and highlights the field to be corrected. The user then corrects the mistake and the TCP rereads the data.

9. When all data edits have been successfully completed, the TCP writes the data received to a transaction log. The transaction log is used for recovering from failures and sometimes for system auditing.

10. Because this transaction will modify the database, the TCP starts a transaction for recovery purposes. A transaction that changes data in the database must leave the database in a consistent state, which means that the transaction must be completed in its entirety or leave the database as it was before the transaction started. Thus, a transaction is a unit of work as well as a unit of database recovery. Starting a transaction is typically not necessary for read-only transactions because they do not change the database and do not need to be recovered. If the admission clerk checks the database to see whether the patient already has a record on file, this activity does not require that a transaction be started.

11. The TCP examines the transaction and determines which application(s) should process it. Some transactions require the services of more than one application process. In this example, one application will create a patient record, another will locate a room and calculate room charges, and still another will generate a standard patient supply issue and build supply charge records. The TCP may send each participating application its work at the same time, or the TCP may wait until one application finishes before sending the second application its portion of the work.

12. An application receives its portion of the transaction and begins processing. We consider here only the activity performed by the application that creates the patient record. The application uses the data received from the TCP to create a database record for the patient. The application sends the record to the DBMS with a request to insert the new record.

13. The DBMS receives the request from the application and acts on it. Each time a record is updated or a new record inserted, images of

the records being changed are inserted into the DBMS recovery log. Images of the record before and after the changes are written to the log. This allows the transaction to be reversed if it cannot be completed and also allows it to be re-created at a later time if necessary.

14. After logging the before- and after-images, the DBMS inserts the patient record and returns a successful result status to the application.

15. When the application has performed all of its work, including the database requests, it formats a reply message and returns it to the TCP. In this case, the reply is a status code indicating the success of the transaction. If the database operation is unsuccessful, the response is an unsuccessful result code and a message or data to be returned to the terminal. This insert might have failed because the patient file was full.

16. The TCP determines whether another application process must become involved in the transaction. The other applications are given their work to accomplish, and they respond to the TCP with the results. When all applications have completed their work, the TCP posts a transaction completion message on the transaction log, formats a response, and sends the response back to the terminal.

17. The application process, having finished the transaction, posts another read request on the message file, which indicates its ability to accept another transaction (another transaction may already be queued on the application's input file). The TCP posts another read on the terminal, thus enabling additional transaction input.

While the above activity is being accomplished for this transaction, other transactions may also be in various states of completion. Examples of other transactions that may be in progress include the following:

- Another admission clerk may be admitting a different patient.
- A nurse may be reading a patient's record to find the patient's work telephone number.
- An accounting clerk may be consolidating the fees for a patient being dismissed.
- A clerk in the radiation laboratory may be entering a charge for a patient who has just been X-rayed.

We now consider the data communication software components in more detail, beginning with the access methods.

ACCESS METHODS

Data communication access methods give system users easier access to terminal devices. They make the device-specific attributes of terminals transparent to the user and provide connection, disconnection, and data transfer services to the applications. As with TCPs, the scope of access methods differs with the vendor and even within different access methods from a single vendor.

Application–Terminal Connection

Several approaches have been used to provide access methods, but we discuss only the most practical implementation. One function of an access method is to provide terminal–application connections. This may be accomplished by having a pool of applications and a pool of terminals available, as illustrated in Figure 12–2. The access method serves as a switch to connect terminal requests with the proper applications.

Accessing a Terminal

Because an access method separates the application program from the terminal access logic, access methods can be used with or without a TCP, depending on the environment. Figure 12–3 illustrates two situations: TCP present and TCP absent. The access method performs fewer functions when

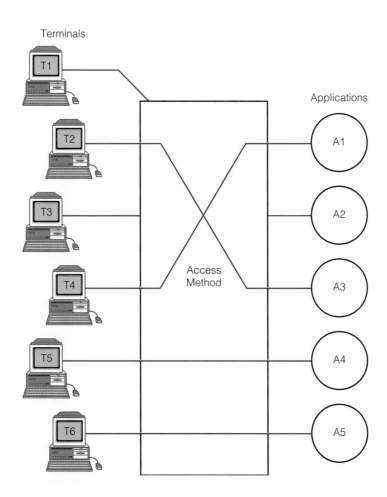

Figure 12–2
Access Method and Pooled Application– Terminal Connections

Figure 12–3
*Access Method with and
Without a TCP*

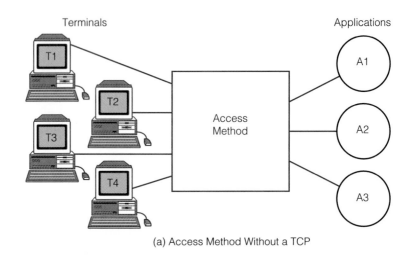

(a) Access Method Without a TCP

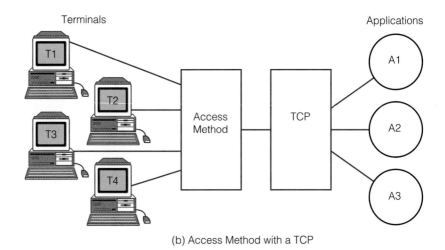

(b) Access Method with a TCP

the TCP is present because some functions, such as message routing and data editing, are performed by the TCP.

The first requirement of accessing a terminal from a program is to connect the two. The access method serves as an intermediary in this case. Either the application initiates a connection by issuing an open or connect request to the access method or the terminal initiates the action by issuing an application logon request through the access method. Once the connection is established, a communication path exists, and the terminal and application can exchange data. Connection requests can be denied for security reasons or because the application or device is already occupied.

Without a TCP, the access method makes the connection between an application program and a terminal. In some implementations the connection is static: The application and terminal are attached to each other and the terminal can run only the transactions provided by that particular application. For the terminal user to access another application process, the terminal must first be disconnected from its current access application and then reconnected to the new one. Other systems provide more flexibility in making the connection between a terminal and an application. For example, IBM's **Virtual Telecommunications Access Method (VTAM)** provides several methods for terminal–application connections.

Virtual Telecommunications Access Method (VTAM) One of IBM's telecommunication access methods.

TRANSACTION CONTROL PROCESS

TCP Configuration

The configuration of the TCP is depicted in Figure 12–4. Because the TCP serves as a switch between applications and terminals, it must be aware of the terminals attached to it, the transactions that can be submitted, and the applications responsible for processing those transactions. In this environment, any terminal can access any application known to the TCP. Implementation can be as a monolithic process, as in Figure 12–5(a), or as multiple processes, as in Figure 12–5(b).

Single Threading Versus Multithreading

The efficiency of the application environment depends on how quickly transactions can be processed. If multiple transactions can arrive at once, good performance requires that parallelism in transaction processing be provided. This means that the TCP may need to process several transactions concurrently, a concept known as **multithreading.** With **single threading,** a process

multithreading A technique that allows multiple operations to be processed concurrently.

single threading A technique in which only one operation is processed at a time.

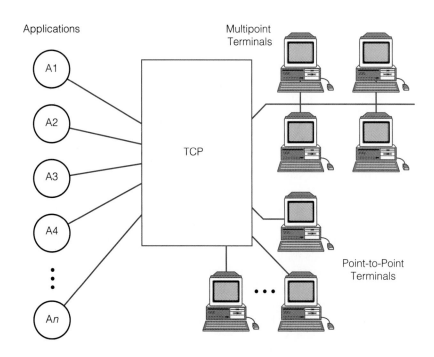

Applications

Multipoint Terminals

A1
A2
A3
A4
⋮
An

TCP

Point-to-Point Terminals

Figure 12–4
Generic TCP Configuration

Figure 12–5
TCPs

Applications

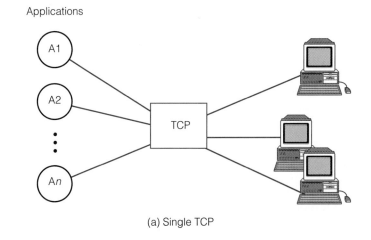

(a) Single TCP

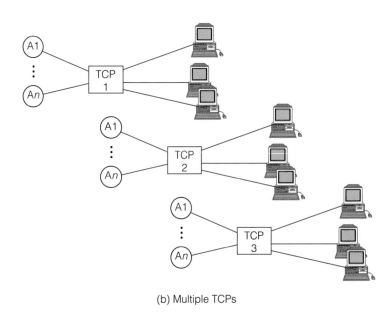

(b) Multiple TCPs

accepts an input, processes the input to completion, produces an output, and then is ready to accept another input for processing. A TCP operating in this manner would accept an input from one terminal, send the transaction to an application process, wait for the response, and send the result back to the terminal. Then, the TCP would accept another transaction and process it. Meanwhile, other terminals may be waiting for service. This processing method results in long delays for terminals with queued requests.

The difference between single threading and multithreading can be likened to what happens in a grocery store when people queue up at the checkout counter. The checkout clerk represents the TCP process, and the customers represent the terminals. The clerk ordinarily operates in a single-threaded manner, processing one customer and one customer only until the total order has been tabulated and the money collected before turning to the next customer. If an object does not scan correctly, everyone waits while an assistant checks the price. Looking up the price is analogous to accessing a disk, with the assistant as the DBMS. Everyone waits while the clerk scans each item, missing prices are checked, coupons are deducted, and the check is written and verified. To improve efficiency, the clerks could be multi-threaded: Everyone in the line would get attention as time allows. The clerks would maintain separate totals for each customer. While a missing price was being checked, the clerk could move on to the next customer's order. While a check is being written, another customer could be served. Of course, the multithreaded clerk must be much more flexible than the single-threaded clerk. Multiple totals are accumulated, items are taken from the correct basket and placed in the proper bag, and the totals are delivered to and collected from the proper customers. Multiple application threads are active simultaneously within a multithreaded process. A comparison of single-threaded and multithreaded processes is presented in Figure 12–6.

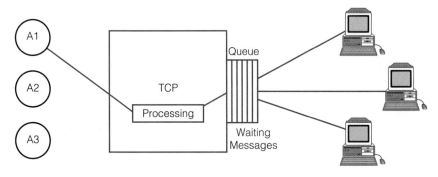

(a) Single Thread: Only One Transaction Active

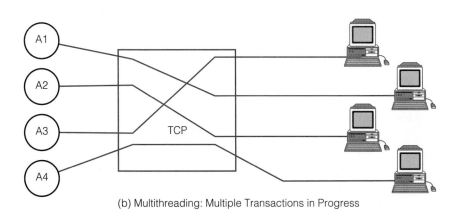

(b) Multithreading: Multiple Transactions in Progress

Figure 12–6
Single Threading vs. Multithreading

Maintaining Context

context data A require-
ment of multithreaded
processes that entails
unifying the work by
keeping track of the
completed parts as well
as the parts yet to be
worked on and ensur-
ing that an interrupted
transaction is restarted
at the correct point.

An additional requirement of multithreaded processes is maintaining **context data.** Each single-threaded transaction is completely self-contained. In a multithreaded process, a transaction might be separated into several parts, and each part might be acted on by a different program. To unify this work, one program must keep track of the completed parts and the parts yet to be worked on and ensure that an interrupted transaction is restarted at the correct point. The action to be performed also may be contingent on a previous activity. For instance, in searching a database for an employee named Smith, an application might select and display the first ten Smiths plus additional identifying information. If none of the ten names is correct, the next ten are displayed, and so on until the proper Smith is found. The search for the next ten names is contingent on where the previous search stopped.

Like the multithreaded grocery clerk, the TCP must handle multiple customers at once. Suppose a TCP controls four terminals (T1, T2, T3, and T4) and three applications (A1, A2, and A3). At the start of the system, all three applications request to open, or connect to the TCP. The TCP records this information and issues a command to open and display the first screen, and posts a read on each of the four terminals. At this point, the TCP is awaiting input from the terminals or a process. A chronological record of the TCP's activities is outlined in Table 12–2. This type of interleaved processing continues throughout the workday.

For the activities in Table 12–2, context was maintained in the TCP. It could also have been maintained within the application or the terminal. However, the application is not as logical a place as the TCP for maintaining context; multiple copies of one application may be used to increase efficiency, in which case the TCP would have to send the second part of a transaction to the same process that worked on the first part. Saving context in application programs also makes those application programs more complex. Some designers prefer to remove this type of complexity from the application. Because

Table 12–2   Multiple TCP Transaction Threads

Accept update transaction from T2	Receive A2's return message for T2
Write T2's transaction on audit log	End T2's transaction
Accept inquiry transaction from T4	Receive inquiry transaction from T1
Route T4's request to application A1	Receive request for next ten records from T4
Receive write complete on T2's audit log write	Send T1's request to A3
Begin transaction for T2	Receive notice that T2's transaction has ended
Route T2's transaction to A2	Send response to T2
Receive inquiry transaction from T3	Send T4's request together with stored context to A1
Route T3's transaction to A1	
Receive A1's return message for T4	
Write response to T4	

many TCP processes are supplied by software houses or computer vendors rather than being written by the end user, it benefits the user to have the multiuser complexity in the TCPs and not in the applications.

Memory Management

To manage context information and accept data from both terminals and applications, the TCP must provide **memory management** functions. At any time the TCP can receive a message from either terminals or applications, and multiple messages may be queued up simultaneously. The way in which TCPs manage memory varies. Essentially, the TCP must have sufficient memory available to provide storage for terminal and application messages as well as for context data. Sometimes this requires virtual memory algorithms similar to those used by some operating systems: The disk is treated as an extension of memory and data is swapped back and forth between real memory and disk.

memory management Functions provided by the TCP that manage context information and accept data from both terminals and applications.

Transaction Routing

The TCP also must provide **transaction routing,** which means routing the transaction received from a terminal to one or more application programs. Several techniques are used to determine how to route a transaction. One method uses a transaction code embedded within the data message itself. The terminal operator enters the transaction code in the text of the message, as illustrated in Figure 12–7. The TCP must recognize this code and route the transaction accordingly. Another method is based on context and a signal from the terminal. The signal is usually either a transaction code or the

transaction routing The routing of a transaction received from a terminal to one or more application programs.

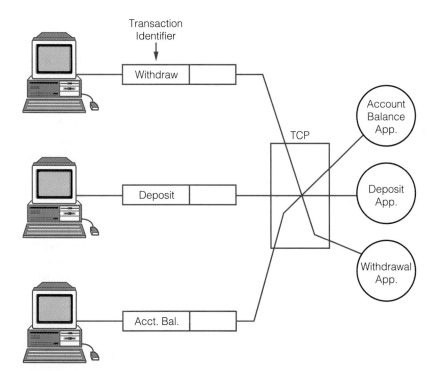

Figure 12–7
Transaction Routing in a TCP

operator pressing a designated function key. Other signals may be indicated by using a light pen, mouse, or touch-screen.

Transaction routing requires that the TCP know both which application handles a given transaction and the path or connection that leads to that application. Transaction routing could be table driven, in which case the TCP would look up the transaction ID in a table that provides directions to the proper application process. Alternatively, a procedural interface with a case statement or similar construct would result in a program call or a message being sent to that process.

Transaction Log

transaction log Records all of the data received and is used in recovering from failures and in system auditing.

The TCP is a logical place to implement transaction logging. A **transaction log** captures the transaction inputs, usually on tape or disk. Once inputs are captured, the system can assure the user that the transaction will be processed. This does not necessarily mean that the transaction will be successfully completed (errors could prevent that); it does mean that the transaction will not be lost should a system failure occur. In addition to its use in recovery, transaction logging is sometimes required by auditors, especially in financial transactions. Electronic data processing (EDP) auditors periodically check transaction sources and trace them through the system to determine whether they were correctly processed. If transaction logging is implemented, as soon as a transaction is received by the TCP, the transaction is written on the log file. Usually the TCP appends additional information to the message, such as a date/time stamp, transaction ID, or similar identifying information. Sometimes the completion of a transaction is also logged. In recovery situations this prevents a transaction from being processed twice.

In some systems the transaction log is synchronized with the database logging function to ensure that a message received by the system will be processed and that no duplicate transactions will be processed if a failure occurs. One system even guarantees that transactions requiring reprocessing in the event of a failure will be processed in the original order. This last is an important feature in banking applications. For instance, an account with an initial $100 balance receives a $500 deposit and then a $200 withdrawal. In the time-compressed recovery situation, the transaction could possibly be processed in reverse order, meaning that the withdrawal would be rejected for insufficient funds or the account would be overdrawn.

Security and Statistics

A TCP can be a focal point for online transactions entering the system, so it is a logical place to collect statistics and provide for security. Several statistics that are necessary to effectively manage a network system can be collected in the TCP, including the total number of transactions from all terminals, types of transactions, number of characters transmitted to and from a terminal, application processing time per transaction, and number of transactions per terminal. Security at the terminal and transaction levels could be enforced at the TCP. All online transactions for terminals managed by a TCP must be routed through the TCP, making the TCP a logical place to implement security.

Message Priorities

The TCP is in an ideal position to assist with implementing message priorities within the online system. Every message received could be examined for priority, or priorities could be assigned by the TCP. Priorities could be established according to the source and type of message. Priority messages could then be given service first and routed to special server applications to expedite message processing.

Application Development

It is necessary to establish test environments consisting of terminals, access methods, TCPs, applications, and a database when designing an online system. This environment is also used to develop and test enhancements and problem fixes after a system has been placed in operation. The TCP can provide features to make testing and debugging easier, including the ability to trace or examine transactions received by the TCP, to store transactions in a transaction file and pass them through the TCP as though they were entered at a terminal, and to vary the rate of transaction submission. The TCP should also allow concurrent running of production applications and test applications.

Operation Interface

An **operation interface** gives a network administrator the ability to monitor and control the TCP environment. Monitoring the TCP environment includes looking at statistics such as buffer use, number of transactions waiting in various queues for service, and busy rates for lines, devices, and the TCP. Controlling the TCP includes activities such as adding terminals and applications, starting or stopping devices, and reconfiguring the system. This may be accomplished through an operation interface program, illustrated in Figure 12–8. The operation interface provides some or all of the following capabilities:

operation interface An interface that gives a network administrator the ability to monitor and control the TCP environment. Monitoring the TCP environment includes looking at statistics such as buffer use, number of transactions waiting in various queues for service, and busy rates for lines, devices, and the TCP. Controlling the TCP includes activities such as adding terminals and applications, starting or stopping devices, and reconfiguring the system.

TCP startup	TCP shutdown
Defining lines, terminals, or applications	Starting lines, terminals, or applications
Stopping lines, terminals, or applications	Adding lines, terminals, or applications
Deleting lines, terminals, or applications	Enabling/disabling statistics gathering
Displaying statistics	Moving lines, terminals, or applications from one TCP to another

Other TCP Functions

Additional functions that a TCP might carry out include the following:

- If an application fails, the TCP should be able to automatically restart it. If a transaction arrives for a process that is not currently running, the TCP should be able to activate the process.

Figure 12–8
*TCP–Operation
Interface*

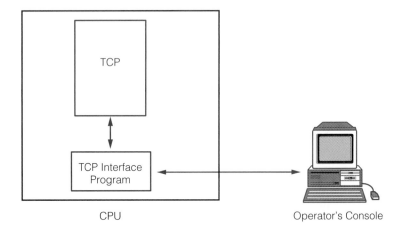

CPU   Operator's Console

- If one application receives so many requests that response times become degraded, the TCP should be able to initiate additional copies of that process to enhance performance.
- If a process has been inactive for a long time, the TCP should be able to optionally delete that process to free the resources the process is holding. Table 12–3 summarizes the activities of a TCP.

SUMMARY

Data communication software works closely with application, database, and operating system software to provide the functions required of today's systems. Two major components of networking software are access methods and transaction control processes (TCP). In some cases, access method software provides the linkage between application programs and terminal devices. Access methods always provide an interface with different terminal devices, providing terminal and application independence. TCPs also provide a link between application software and terminal equipment. A TCP will also use the access method software to interface with terminal devices. The functions provided by TCPs in interfacing applications and devices go

Table 12–3   TCP Activities

Provides a user interface with the TCP subsystem	Formats data for terminals and applications
Manages memory	Routes messages to server processes
Provides an interface between applications and terminals	Gathers statistics
Manages applications	Provides testing and debugging facilities
Logs messages	Assists in providing security
Participates in recovery	Assists in implementing a priority system
Provides transaction definition	
Edits data fields	

beyond those provided by the typical access method. These added capabilities include data edits, message switching, data formatting, and transaction definition and recovery.

KEY TERMS

access method
application software
context data
database management system
  (DBMS)
file management system (FMS)
I/O driver
memory management

multithreading
operating system (OS)
operation interface
single threading
transaction log
transaction routing
Virtual Telecommunications Access
  Method (VTAM)

REVIEW QUESTIONS

1. What functions are performed by the operating system? Explain how two of these functions support applications.

2. Describe how a database access method is used to access a record.

3. Describe the functions of a data communication access method.

4. Describe how a transaction flows through an online system.

5. Describe the functions of a TCP.

6. Compare the functions of a TCP and a data communication access method.

7. Compare the operations of a TCP and an operating system.

8. Why are audit (log) trails important?

9. Compare multithreading and single threading.

10. Why is multithreading of a TCP an attractive feature?

PROBLEMS AND EXERCISES

1. Other than the banking example given in the chapter, describe another transaction that could create inconsistencies in a database if it is not recovered in the same order in which it was originally processed.

2. Is the saving of context necessary for multithreading? Why or why not?

3. Is it necessary for all user transactions to be recoverable units? If so, why? If not, give an example of a transaction that would not have to be recovered if the system failed.

4. Some data processing professionals claim that a TCP uses a considerable amount of system resources and thus has a high overhead. This statement has some validity. How would you respond to such a statement in supporting the use of a TCP?

5. Research the literature to find an example of a TCP. What features does it provide?

6. Compare the functions of a LAN file server with those of a TCP.

Accessing and Using the Internet

CHAPTER OBJECTIVES

After studying this chapter you should be able to

- Distinguish between an internet, the Internet, and an intranet
- Trace the history of the Internet
- List the functions provided by Internet service providers
- Describe how a person can gain access to the Internet
- Identify common hardware and software components essential for Internet connection
- List common Internet services
- Discuss how business can be safely conducted on the Internet
- Describe how a company can benefit from an intranet

TERMINOLOGY: AN INTERNET, THE INTERNET, AND INTRANETS

If you read articles relating to internet technology, three terms will probably surface: an internet, *the* Internet, and an intranet. Let us begin by defining these terms, beginning with the word *internet*. The term *internet* is used in two contexts. If you have read the preceding chapters, you are aware that there are different types of networks, three of which are LANs, MANs, and WANs; furthermore, a single company may have several LANs and a WAN. When this is the case, it is typical that the various networks are combined or interconnected to form a single network or **internet**. In this context, an internet is the interconnection of two or more networks. Sometimes a company's internet is called an enterprise network.

internet The interconnection of two or more networks.

Internet A specific collection of interconnected networks encompassing most of the countries in the world.

The **Internet** (with a capital *I*) is a specific collection of interconnected networks reaching all but approximately 10 countries throughout the world (and these 10 will probably be attached soon). The Internet, or simply the Net, is a public network in the sense that private individuals are able to gain access to it and use its resources in a variety of ways. With today's technology, users typically "surf" the Internet using a software tool called a browser.

browser A program that allows users to contact a location on the Internet, access data there, and follow hypertext links to other information.

A **browser** is a program that allows you to contact a location on the Internet, access data there, and follow hypertext links to other information. The most common browsers in use today are Netscape's Navigator and Microsoft's Internet Explorer. Figure 13–1 shows a browser screen. However, other software interfaces can also be used. Some of these are yesterday's technologies that are still viable and others are emerging technologies. Today, these other interfaces would be used primarily by Internet nodes that do not have the processing power to support a browser, on nodes for which a browser has not yet been implemented or, in the case of newer technologies, by users wanting to take advantage of new capabilities.

hypertext Data that contains a link to other data.

Hypertext is data that contains a link to other data. For example, suppose this were a hypertext document. When you read the term *MAN* above, you might have wondered what a MAN was or wanted more information about it. Further information might be in this text or in another document, which could be located anywhere. In this book you would probably consult the index, find the link, go to those pages, and read the information. Then, you might want to follow another link there or return to this paragraph. In this case, you would have had to remember where you were before you followed the link. In a hypertext document, the presence of a link is indicated by some type of formatting, and with a browser you could simply use a pointing device such as a mouse to point to the link and click. Immediately, you are transferred to the reference, which on the Internet could be on the node you are accessing or halfway around the world. Later, you could click on a button and go back to previous pages or to the original page.

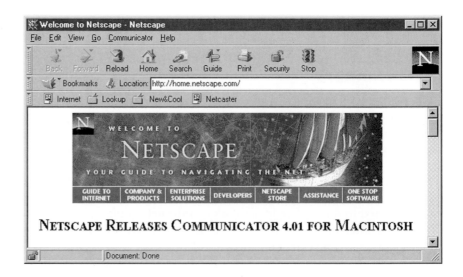

Figure 13–1
Browser Screen

Browsers are powerful yet simple to use. They are largely responsible for the large-scale use of the Internet by nontechnical users (some of the older tools have interfaces that are more easily mastered by computer professionals). Recognizing the ease with which information can be developed and accessed using Internet browsers and protocols, some businesses have begun using Internet technologies on their private networks. A private network that uses Internet technologies such as browsers and hypertext is called an **intranet.** Using an intranet, a company can make corporate information such as employee handbooks, price lists, and product information readily available to all users. Moreover, this information can be disseminated without large amounts of paper and the information can be kept current by updating it in only one location.

intranet A private network that uses Internet technologies such as browsers and hypertext.

Now that you know what intranets and internets are, let us begin our discussion of the Internet by reviewing its history.

INTERNET HISTORY

The Internet began as a concept in 1964 when the Rand Corporation introduced the idea of a **packet switching network (PSN).** A PSN divides a message into fixed-size packets and routes them to the destination. Individual packets may take different routes and they may arrive out of order. The receiving node is responsible for placing the packets in the proper order and for ensuring that all packets have been received (see X.25 networks in Chapter 4).

packet switching network (PSN) A network that divides a message into fixed-size packets and routes them to the destination.

The physical implementation of the Internet began in 1969 as a four-node network called the Arpanet. The **Arpanet** was named for and sponsored by the U.S. Defense Department's Advanced Research Project Agency (ARPA). The Defense Department was interested in a military network that would continue to function even if parts of it were destroyed. That is, if a portion of the network were lost because of a bomb or sabotage, other parts could continue to operate and packets would be rerouted around the inaccessible portions of the network. Naturally, resources on the failed portion would be unavailable but other nodes could continue to communicate. A PSN has these characteristics and the U.S. Department of Defense was one of the initial users of the Internet. The military portion of the Internet was named **MILNET.**

Arpanet A four-node network, named for and sponsored by the U.S. Defense Department's Advanced Research Project Agency (ARPA), that evolved into the Internet.

During the early years of the Internet, it was used as a communication medium not only for the military but also for researchers, many of whom were involved in defense-related projects. These early Internet nodes represented the military, research organizations, and colleges and universities, most of which were in North America and Europe. Until the 1990s, business was not conducted on the Internet, and any form of advertising or commercial use was discouraged (if not forbidden).

MILNET The military portion of the Internet.

In 1984 the Arpanet was shut down but the remaining nodes and subnets continued to function. In the 1980s several regional networks, such as BITNET and CSNET, joined the Internet and in 1983 the military network, MILNET, was taken off the Internet. As the number of nodes increased, a high-speed backbone network like that in Figure 13–2 was installed to speed communication between regions. In 1987 the National Science Foundation (NSF) assumed the responsibility for managing the backbone network and for administration of addresses and policy. NSF formed the NSFnet Network Service Center (NNSC) to carry out Internet management and the NNSC was the single point of contact for Internet information.

In 1993 the NSF replaced the NNSC with the InterNIC (Internet Network Information Center) and distributed the management functions among several companies. Network Solutions, Inc. was given the responsibility for Registration Services. Registration Services is responsible for controlling Internet addresses and domain names. The AT&T Corporation assumed management of the Directory and Database Services. Directory and Database Services is responsible for maintaining databases of Internet sites, information, and users. In 1995 the NSF quit all direct support, the backbone became commercially supported, and business use of the Net grew rapidly.

Since its four-node inception, the Internet has continued to grow, slowly at first and then rapidly in the 1990s. On average, it has more than doubled each year since its inception. In 1983 there were fewer than 500 hosts, by 1989 there were approximately 80,000, and by 1997 there were approximately 16 million hosts representing all but a few of the countries in the world. Much of the rapid growth in the 1990s can be attributed to three factors. First is the creation of the **World Wide Web (WWW)** in 1989 and browser products that made the Web easily accessible so that many new users could be accommodated. Second, microcomputer technology at low costs resulted in computers becoming a home appliance; this created a much larger market for the services provided by the Internet. Finally, the Internet became a tool for conducting business.

World Wide Web (WWW) A hypertext-based, distributed information system created by researchers at CERN in Switzerland.

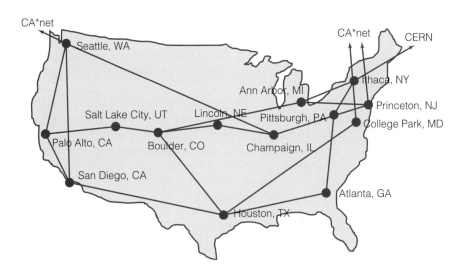

Figure 13–2
Internet High-Speed Backbone Network

GAINING ACCESS TO THE INTERNET

Individuals gain access to the Internet in a variety of ways, some of which are

- work
- school
- public services
- freenets
- individual paid subscription

When accessing the Internet from work, school, public services, and freenets, there is usually a policy regulating how you use the Net and consequences of misuse. At work the policy usually requires that access be work related and the consequences might be as severe as being fired. At school access is often restricted to course-related work and students may be restricted from printing large volumes of Internet documents or be charged for such printing. Students misusing the Internet may lose their Internet privileges or receive grade reductions. Before accessing the Internet from any source, you should first understand the policies covering Internet use and the consequences of not adhering to those policies.

Work

Many companies are connected to the Internet and employees of those companies may be able to access the Internet through their employers' connections. Ordinarily, this use of the Internet is intended to be work-related access; however, some studies indicate that employees use corporate Internet access for personal reasons such as planning vacations, reading magazines, and playing games. Before using your employer's Internet access for personal use, you should understand the corporate policy for such use and abide by that policy. The consequence of violating those policies may result in disciplinary action, perhaps even resulting in the employee being fired.

School

Almost all colleges and universities have Internet access and many public and private schools have access as well; thus, students may be able to gain Internet access through their school. In some schools, particularly those below the college level, Internet access is sometimes restricted to specific classes and the access is structured around the school's curriculum. Some colleges and universities also provide access only for students enrolled in specific courses; other institutions provide all interested students with Internet accounts, often for a nominal fee. Providing all students with Internet accounts is beneficial because the Internet is an outstanding research tool.

Public Services

A variety of public or government agencies provide Internet services. For example, many public libraries have Internet stations available for their patrons. Also, some government agencies allow people to access the Internet through their connection. In some instances, access may be restricted to nonworking hours.

Freenets

freenets Private, educational, or nonprofit organizations that provide Internet access for free.

Freenets are private, educational, or nonprofit organizations that provide Internet access for free. Some examples include Cleveland Free-Net, Dayton Free-Net, Erlangen Free-Net (Germany), Buffalo Free-Net, and Tallahassee Free-Net. Be aware that some freenets do not include the word *free* in their name. Some free access providers allow limited usage, such as Internet e-mail only.

Individual Paid Subscription

Finally, an individual may subscribe to Internet services. Let us look at how one goes about securing an individual subscription and the hardware and software necessary for making a connection.

Internet Hardware and Software

Before you obtain your Internet subscription, you need to have the correct hardware and software in place to make the connection. You have many options from which to choose. The most typical home connection is a personal computer (PC) equipped with a modem; however, there are lower-cost and higher-cost alternatives.

network computer (NC) A low-cost computer used primarily for Internet access.

One of the lower-cost alternatives is a **network computer (NC).** The concept behind the NC is simple:

- Large numbers of companies and private individuals access the Internet.
- Economical access is desirable for some of these users.
- A hardware platform designed specifically to access the Internet is more economical than a standard PC.

In the mid-1990s several companies, most notably Oracle, Microsoft, IBM, and Sun Microsystems, began to promote the idea of an NC and to develop such a product. An NC could conceivably be produced for approximately $500. Essentially, it might be a diskless PC or have small disk capacity. An NC might use a standard television or graphics display device as the monitor. The NC would support Java applications and provide high-resolution graphics and multimedia. **Java** is a platform-independent programming language that is used extensively to create Web applications. Many of these applications are small in size and are called applets. Applets may be quickly transferred to a user's computer to assist in processing the transaction. The NC would have an operating system optimized for Internet access and would not support standard PC applications and environments such as Windows. The target markets for NCs are businesses, schools, and individuals who want Internet access but are not interested in other personal

Java A platform-independent programming language used to create Web applications.

computer technologies. The low cost of the system provides considerable savings for organizations such as schools that buy large numbers of computers to provide Internet services. At this writing, NCs are beginning to be produced and it is not yet clear how well they will be accepted.

On the high-cost end, a user might use a top-of-the-line PC with an ISDN or xDSL connection. At present, the major cost component of this type of connection is likely to be the communication costs; however, the trend is for these costs to decrease as a consequence of competition. ISDN and xDSL technologies were discussed in Chapter 4.

Choosing a Service Provider

An individual who obtains a personal Internet connection does so through an **Internet service provider (ISP).** ISPs provide access to the Internet at three basic levels: national, regional, and local. National providers are commercial entities that sell access to the Internet in various cities. On a national scale you can access Internet services through providers such as America Online (AOL), Uunet, and regional or long-distance telephone providers. Regional providers sell access in a region. In the United States, a region might consist of several contiguous states and an ISP would possibly provide toll-free access numbers within the region. Examples of regional providers in the United States are the local and regional telephone providers and regional network companies. Local providers are proprietors of networks attached to the Internet and provide individual access to the network. Examples include companies such as the one the author subscribes to, Hometown Computing (www.htcomp.net). Hometown Computing provides Internet connections in several small towns in Central Texas. Most countries that are large Internet users also have ISPs. A representative list of U.S. ISPs is given in Table 13–1 and Table 13–2 lists some ISPs outside the United States.

ISPs vary considerably in the rates they charge and the services they provide. Some guidelines you should follow when selecting an ISP are given in Table 13–3 and discussed below.

Connection Type   Your Internet computer must be compatible with the equipment used by your ISP. The most common connection today is an analog, high-speed modem. We are currently reaching the upper speed

Internet service provider (ISP) ISPs provide access to the Internet on a national, regional, or local level.

Table 13–1   Some U.S. ISPs

aaaa.net	Netlimited
A.L.I.C.E. CompuSystems	Nighthawk Communications Corp.
CellularOne	
CompUnet, Inc.	SPRYNET
Fiberlink Communications Corporation	UUNET Technologies
	VIANET
jjj.net, Inc.	VPN Enterprises
MCI	Zocalo

Table 13–2   ISPs Serving Countries Outside the U.S.

Access One	Ocean Internet
ATS International	PSINet, Inc.
AUNET Corp.	SPRYNET
Crawford Communications	UUNET
EuroNet Internet	VIANET
Fiberlink Communications Corp.	VPM Enterprises
	WorldLink
iiNet	Zocalo
jjj.net, Inc.	

limit for this class of connection. Typically, when new technologies extend modem speeds, several competing technologies emerge. This was the case in 1996, when the first 56-Kbps modems were introduced. Two incompatible protocols were developed. If you purchased one of these modems and wanted to use it at its highest speeds, you would need to choose an ISP that had modems compatible with the model you chose. If you are using ISDN, cable modems, or xDSL technology, you need to ensure that your ISP supports those types of connections and that the ISP's hardware is compatible with yours.

The connection protocol you use is another consideration. You may connect to an Internet host using terminal emulation. With this type of connection, the host is providing the Internet access and processing and your computer is simply acting like a simple terminal, relaying keyboard and monitor information. Your computer is not "on" the Internet and does not have an Internet address. The host is the computer that is "on" the Net. Although this is the simplest type of connection to manage, it requires you to do extra work when transferring data to your computer or printer. By default, all data is stored on the host and you need to use file transfer protocols to download files to your computer. This type of connection is more typical of company connections than personal connections.

The two protocols most commonly used by individual subscribers using dial-up facilities to connect to their ISP are the **serial line Internet protocol (SLIP)** and **the point-to-point protocol (PPP).** The SLIP protocol is older and less desirable than the PPP protocol. A third potential protocol is the AppleTalk Remote Access (ARA) for Macintosh computers. With each of these protocols, your computer has an Internet address and is a node on the Internet. In the next chapter we will discuss Internet addressing and how an ISP subscriber obtains an address and lends it to a subscriber. SLIP and PPP

serial line Internet protocol (SLIP) One of the most common protocols used by individual subscribers to connect to ISPs.

point-to-point protocol (PPP) A protocol used by individual subscribers to connect to ISPs; newer and more desirable than the SLIP protocol.

Table 13–3   ISP Considerations

Connection type	Services
Cost	User-to-modem ratio
Support	Software

allow the use of the IP protocol over serial lines. However, SLIP was not based on established data link protocols. In contrast, PPP was developed by the Internet Engineering Task Force (IETF) with the intention of improving the ability to connect to the Internet via switched, serial lines. The PPP protocol is based on the HDLC data link protocol and is more robust than the more simple SLIP.

Services   All ISPs provide Internet access; beyond that there are differences in the additional services that may be available. Some ISPs provide each user with disk space on the ISP's Internet gateway node for a home page. Because individual users are not permanently connected, home pages should be on the Internet gateway computer, where they will be continuously available. Some ISPs go beyond simple Web hosting by assisting their clients with Web page design and content.

ISPs also vary with respect to the speed of connection to the Internet. There are two speeds to consider: the speed of the user connection to the ISP and the speed of the ISP host's connection to the Internet. Subscriber-to-ISP speeds are based on the type of line used, line interface (digital or analog), and the speed of the interface device. An ISP-to-Internet link should be at least T-1 speed unless the ISP has only a few concurrent users. For example, suppose that there are 100 concurrent users all connected at 56 Kbps. If all users are downloading files at the same time, the aggregate data rate could be as high as 56 Kbps × 100 = 5.6 Mbps. As you can see, a T-1 connection is not adequate for this task.

Another service the ISP should provide is continuity of operation. Although occasional short outages are to be expected, long periods of unavailability should not occur. One way they can be prevented is to have backup Internet servers. If one Internet host fails, another should be available to handle the network traffic. Naturally, some of the fault-tolerant features described in Chapter 8 should be in place. When choosing an ISP, particularly a smaller one, you should check to see whether backup systems are available to provide continuous operation (perhaps at lower performance levels) in the event of hardware or software failures.

Cost   Sometimes Internet access is free, but when it is not, you need to investigate the cost of the connection because costs can vary considerably. Many ISPs have adopted a flat rate for unlimited access, such as $20 per month. Some provide several pricing options, with the cost tied to the amount of connect time. Users who intend to be connected for long periods of time should find an ISP offering flat rate, unlimited access. If you live in a rural area, you may not have an ISP in your local calling area. If this is the case, and you intend to use your Internet connection extensively, you should look for an ISP that offers toll-free connections to avoid large long-distance bills.

Some ISPs provide users with free software essential to making the Internet connection, but others do not. Other costs you may incur include connection charges if you intend to use digital connections, such as ISDN or xDSL, and upgrades to your equipment, such as a faster modem. If you intend to be connected to the Internet for long periods of time, you may want to install a separate telephone line. Having an extra line allows you to receive telephone calls while you are online and the Internet line can be used for a fax machine or separate telephone line when you are not connected to the Internet. Recall from Chapter 4 that some ISDN connections provide simultaneous voice and data transfer; however, the data rate decreases during periods of concurrent voice/data transmission.

user-to-modem ratio
The user-to-modem ratio affects your ability to access a network; the lower the ratio, the more likely you are to get an Internet connection.

User-to-Modem Ratio   The essential service provided by an ISP is connectivity. The ISP installs a bank of modems for the subscribers and a high-speed connection to another node for the Internet connection. This configuration is illustrated in Figure 13–3. An ISP makes money from the number of subscribers it attracts. ISPs operate much like the telephone companies with respect to subscribers. That is, the system is not configured to provide one connection per subscriber. Some ISPs may have a **user-to-modem ratio** of 20 to 1 or more;

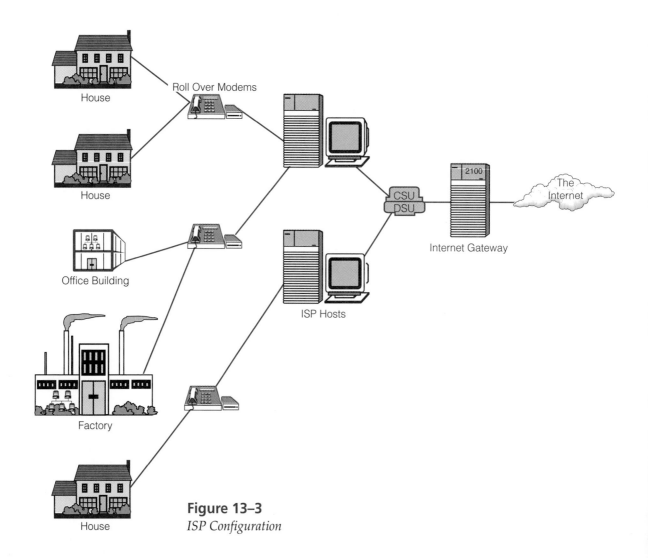

Figure 13–3
ISP Configuration

others have a smaller ratio of 8 or 10 to 1. The user-to-modem ratio affects your ability to access the network. The lower the ratio, the more likely you are to get an Internet connection. You may have read articles regarding a national Internet provider whose subscriber base grew much faster than its modem pool. Consequently, many users were unable to connect to the service because all the available lines were busy. When selecting your ISP, you should determine their objectives for this ratio. Over time, the ratio will fluctuate as new subscribers enroll and new equipment is installed. However, the ISP should be willing and able to upgrade their system to maintain the ratio within their objective range.

Support   The quantity and quality of support available can be the key to a user's ability to access the Internet effectively. New users particularly may depend on the ISP for support in setting up their hardware and software to make the Internet connection. Some of these users may benefit from elementary training by an instructor or a computer-based tutorial. The times at which the ISPs help desk is in operation are also important. Many individual users access the Net during the evenings and weekends when they are off work. A help desk that is available only from 9 to 5 Monday through Friday is of little benefit to them. Users who anticipate needing support should investigate the support hours, quality, and added cost (if any) when selecting an ISP.

Software and Hardware

In addition to a computer, you will need a modem or line adapter and Internet software to access the Net. The most common individual communication connection is an analog modem for use on standard telephone lines, although digital line connections are becoming more common. Speed and compatibility are the items to look for. Speed is important because it decreases your wait time while downloading files or Web pages. For example, downloading a 1-MB file over a 56-Kbps link requires approximately

$$\frac{1,000,000 \text{ bytes} \times 10 \frac{\text{bits}}{\text{byte}}}{56,000 \frac{\text{bits}}{\text{s}} \times 0.75} = \frac{10,000,000}{42,000} = 238 \text{ s} = 3.97 \text{ min}$$

The 0.75 in the denominator is an approximation of the actual line use. It is unrealistic to expect 100% use of any communication link and the 75% figure used is optimistic. In contrast, a 28.8-Kbps modem requires at least twice the time. ISDN speeds for a typical home connection are twice as fast as the 56-Kbps connection. For an asymmetric digital subscriber line (ADSL) connection, compatible transceivers must be installed at the subscriber's premises and at the telephone carrier's home office. ADSL downstream speeds may be 6 Mbps or higher. At that speed, the time to download the 1-MB file is approximately 3 s, or 107 times faster than the 56 Kbps connection. At that speed, the delaying factor will probably be on the Internet itself, not between your premises and the ISP.

Internet Software   The usual software interface is a Web browser. Some of these are free, but others are not. Naturally, today's pricing may change. The largest share of the browser market is divided between

hypertext markup language (HTML) A format that allows the user to create links, text highlighting, and graphic images within a Web document.

Microsoft and Netscape. Each company periodically releases new versions of the software with new features in an attempt to maintain technology leadership.

If you intend to design a Web page, you may want to invest in software that provides the proper formatting automatically. Originally, these products were self-contained; however, some word processing software now contains the capability to format a document as a **hypertext markup language (HTML)** document. For example, Microsoft Word version 7 allows you to edit a document and then save it as an HTML document. When you save the document in this format, Word provides the necessary format for links, text highlighting, and graphic images. An example of an HTML document is shown in Figure 14–7.

Most of us are interested in accessing the Internet as users. However, there is another aspect of Internet access, that of providing the service to users. Let us briefly look at what it takes to become an ISP.

GETTING STARTED AS AN ISP

As you might expect, there is more work involved in getting started as an ISP than there is in getting started as a subscriber to an ISP. The steps an ISP takes to begin operating are as follows:

- Create a business plan.
- Obtain financing.
- Obtain a place of business.
- Hire a staff or acquire working partners.
- Acquire hardware and software for the Internet host.
- Obtain a set of Internet addresses to make available to your customers.
- Acquire telephone connections to another Internet site.
- Acquire telephone connections for service subscribers.
- Install the hardware and software.
- Test the configuration.
- Solicit subscribers.
- Develop and implement a support strategy.
- Operate the business.

Create a Business Plan   If you plan to run a business, you need a business plan. The plan should describe the following:

- type of business
- market evaluation
- management history

- financing necessary to get started and operate until the business becomes profitable
- business goals
- competition
- pricing
- measurements of performance
- growth projections
- cost of growth
- personnel required and their salaries
- stock options (if applicable)

The business plan helps the owners to focus on the business objectives and costs and can be used as an aid for obtaining financing and partners. You can learn about formulating a business plan in management courses or get information over the Internet. In most urban areas people already have a choice of ISPs. If a new ISP is targeting such an area, the new ISP probably needs to provide better service or lower costs or have a target market. For example, the ISP might specialize in services for retirees or home schooling.

Obtain Financing   Most businesses do not start out making a profit. If you are starting out without any of the resources necessary for becoming an ISP, you can expect to spend thousands of dollars before beginning to realize a profit. You will need hardware, software, expertise, a business office, communication connections, and time to get the system configured and working, and you will need to draw a salary while doing so. For small businesses two of the most common sources of financing are loans and partnerships.

Obtain a Place of Business   You will need to obtain a place of business. It has been said that the three most important things to consider when starting a business are location, location, and location. Because an ISP business does not depend on drop-in customers, you do not need a highly visible location like a shopping mall; however, you will need one that has the communication facilities readily accessible. If you live in a rural area, it may be costly to have the necessary communication lines brought to your location. It is possible to run an ISP business from the home. If you do so, you should realize that there may be zoning restrictions that prohibit home businesses. Although this type of business does not generate a large amount of customer traffic, you must expect some subscribers, prospects, and suppliers to visit your place of business.

Hire a Staff or Acquire Working Partners   The ISP business is a 24 by 7 operation. That is, it runs 24 hours a day, 7 days a week. Availability is probably the most critical aspect of an ISP business's reputation. In your configuration you can build in fault tolerance, but fault tolerance does not prohibit all failures. A single individual is incapable of providing support for such an operation on a continuing basis.

Acquire Hardware and Software for the Internet Host   A high-powered system is necessary to handle multiple users. The most common operating system for Internet access is UNIX or a UNIX derivative such as Linux or FreeBSD, both of which are available in the public domain. Furthermore, you will need the software that runs on top of the operating system to provide the Internet services. The Internet server is responsible for implementing the hypertext transfer protocol (HTTP). HTTP allows clients to request information from the server and to send information to the server. A number of HTTP servers are available in the public domain, such as Apache, CERN HTTP Server, and NCSA HTTPD.

Obtain a Set of Internet Addresses to Make Available to Your Customers   When subscribers access a host in terminal emulation mode, they do not get an Internet address. When logging in using the SLIP or PPP protocols, they must have an Internet address for the duration of the Internet session and thus become an Internet node. Because each Internet node must have a unique address, an ISP must have a range of Internet addresses to assign to users when they request Internet connections. The details of addressing and how this is accomplished are discussed in Chapter 14. To ensure that Internet addresses are unique, a clearing house organization is responsible for assigning addresses. This task used to be performed by the NSF but is now performed by Network Solutions, the **InterNIC** Registrar. To obtain a **domain name** and a corresponding range of Internet addresses, you must pay a registration fee (currently $100) and an annual maintenance fee (currently $50) per domain name. A domain name is an organization name followed by the domain suffix of COM, ORG, NET, EDU, and GOV (as in ABC.COM). Currently, the NSF pays the fees for U.S. entities that qualify for the EDU or GOV domain designation.

Acquire Telephone Connections to Another Internet Site   An ISP may connect to another ISP's node, or to one of several nodes that have been officially designated as **network access points (NAPs).** A NAP map is shown in Figure 13–4. Some large ISPs provide connection services to smaller ISPs.

Acquire Telephone Connections for Service Subscribers   An ISP needs two classes of communication lines: a high-speed, dedicated line for the Internet connection and a bank of switched lines for subscriber connections. The Internet connection line should provide T-1 speeds (1.54 Mbps) or higher. The subscriber lines may be standard telephone lines as well as ISDN lines. The type of connectivity will probably change as higher-speed services such as xDSL become available.

Install the Hardware and Software   This step involves integrating the hardware platforms, software, and communication equipment. Exact details vary according to the type of equipment selected.

Test the Configuration   Once the hardware, software, and communication links are installed, they must be thoroughly tested to ensure that they operate correctly.

InterNIC A clearing house organization responsible for assigning Internet addresses.

domain name An organization name followed by the domain suffix of COM, ORG, NET, EDU, and GOV (as in ABC.COM).

network access point (NAP) An officially designated Internet node.

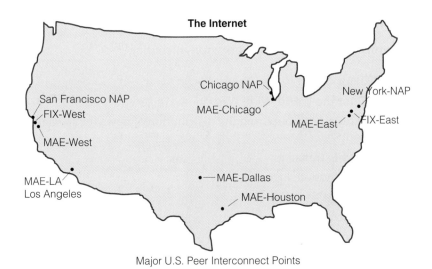

Figure 13–4
NAP Map

Major U.S. Peer Interconnect Points

Solicit Subscribers   This step will probably be done in parallel with the installation and testing. You may find some users who are willing to experience potential problems in exchange for an access point with few competing subscribers. This group of early users can provide beta testing of the installation as well.

Develop and Implement a Support Strategy   An ISP that caters to individual users will have subscribers with a wide range of computer skills. Some will be self-sufficient at the outset; others will need help getting connected and using the system at first but will become self-sufficient. A few will probably need ongoing support. The support strategy should cover all classes of users. Commonly found in ISP support programs are

- e-mail
- frequently asked question (FAQ) files
- how-to documents
- telephone support
- training classes

Note that e-mail and FAQ files assume that the subscriber is connected to the Net and has the ability to access these features.

Operate the Business   This step involves keeping the system running effectively, soliciting new subscribers, offering new services, establishing procedures, expanding the service area, and so on. Success in this area can be measured by how well the progress of the business adheres to the business plan.

Once you are connected to the Internet, a variety of services and capabilities are at your fingertips. It is impractical to attempt to cover all capabilities, so we shall briefly describe some of the major ones.

INTERNET SERVICES AND USES

The Internet provides a variety of services, including

- SMTP for e-mail
- HTTP for the World Wide Web
- NTTP for newsgroups and the distribution of news for special-interest groups
- FTP for file transfer
- Telnet for remote logon
- IRC for chat
- electronic journals
- miscellaneous services
- business services

E-mail   Although having an Internet e-mail address is not essential, most users have one. ISP subscribers do not need to be online for their mail to be accepted. Each e-mail user designates a mail server that accepts the user's mail when they are not online. Typically, the mail server is the ISP node, but another computer may be designated. When e-mail messages arrive at the mail server, they are stored in a file. When the user logs on, mail messages may be read and processed. Processing consists of a number of activities, such as responding, forwarding, saving, and deleting.

An Internet e-mail address has the general format of *User-name@computer/company-name.domain-name.* The user name is made up by the user and typically is a form of the user's name. For example, the author's e-mail name is *dstamper.* It could also have been *stamperd* or *daves.* The author's computer/company name is *htcomp* and the domain name is *net.* Thus, the author's e-mail address is *dstamper@htcomp.net.* We will look more closely at Internet addresses in Chapter 14.

A mail interface is essential for sending and receiving mail. There are some stand-alone mail interfaces, such as Pine and Eudora, but today most Internet users use the mail facility that is integrated with their browser software.

World Wide Web   We hear about the World Wide Web (also the Web, WWW, or W^3) from television, radio, newspapers, magazines, and so on. What is the Web and why do people want to explore it? There are a variety of reasons for using the Web, so I will give you my four primary reasons.

- *Research.* I used to spend extensive time in libraries and had to conform to their hours. I can get the same information and perhaps more current information on the Web whenever I want. However, you should be aware that just because things are published on the Web does not mean that they are true or accurate.

- *Communication.* I use e-mail to correspond with associates in distant places and for work-related matters. It is often easier to send e-mail to members of committees than to attempt to contact them individually via telephone or regular mail.
- *Business.* I can find low-cost air fares, make airline, car, and hotel reservations, and order merchandise over the Web.
- *Downloading files.* I can access a wealth of software and data and download them to my computer, getting instant access to items I think I need. Some of these files are free or available for a nominal cost, some are for examination for a limited time, and some must be paid for (I must agree to pay by credit card before downloading).

Naturally, my reasons differ from those of others. Some other reasons people use the Web are

- entertainment
- chatting socially with other Web users
- business (selling rather than buying, as in my list)
- browsing (just seeing what is out there)

A formal definition of the Web, obtained from the *Internet Users' Glossary* compiled by G. Malkin of Xylogics, is as follows:

> A hypertext-based, distributed information system created by researchers at CERN in Switzerland.

The Web is a superior integration of hardware, software, communication, and information technologies. From the hardware perspective, individuals and businesses can afford platforms necessary for Web access. The significant software capabilities are hypertext linkages and browsers that allow users to access locations and follow the links. The significant communication aspect is that large numbers of businesses, consumers, and users are connected to the Web. The hardware, software, and communication integration gives access to the wealth of text, graphics, video, and audio images that are stored on Web sites.

Usenet or Newsgroups **Usenet** is essentially a worldwide bulletin board on which any Internet user can post or read information. Usenet is organized into interest group categories, a few of which are computers (comp), business (biz), social issues (soc), recreation (rec), and teachers and students (K12). One of the largest of the interest categories is the alternative (alt) group. The alt group contains subgroupings that cover a wide range of subjects. In the alt category you can find fan club postings, humor, language, music, politics, religion, sex, and tv. Usenet access is through a news server that hosts the data and supports the Network News Transfer Protocol (NNTP). News servers vary according to the number and type of groups

Usenet A worldwide bulletin board on which any Internet user can post or read information.

supported and whether they allow public access. Some news servers support over 32,000 groups; others are more focused on specific issues, such as items for sale, and support only a few groups.

file transfer protocol (FTP) Part of the TCP/IP protocol suite that supports the ability to transfer files from one node to another.

File Transfer   Included in the TCP/IP protocol suite is the **file transfer protocol (FTP).** Because TCP/IP is the transport and network layer protocols of the Internet, the ability to transfer files from one node to another is supported. This may be accomplished with an FTP utility or through the services of a browser.

Electronic Journals   You can find a wide collection of electronic journals on the Internet. Included among these are newspapers, magazines, and research papers.

Garage Sales   Merchants are not the only entities that sell merchandise over the Internet. Individual users have several forums through which they can sell personal property. The term *garage sale* is used to describe this because the Internet provides a venue for selling items much like those found in a garage sale; the difference is that people from all over the world can participate. For example, suppose you want to sell your camera. You may have better success at getting the price you want if you advertise it on the Internet. For every seller, there must be a buyer, so people looking for a specific item or a bargain may browse for sale locations (virtual garage sales?) on the Internet.

chatting An activity in which a group of Internet users gathers at a virtual location to exchange ideas and comment on any subject.

chat room A virtual location on the Internet used for chatting.

Chatting   The Internet has spawned a unique activity, **chatting.** Chatting's inception can be found in the newsgroups. Through newsgroups, people carry on conversations that are focused on a specific topic of mutual interest. Chatting moves the conversation to a different level. A group of users can gather at a virtual location and exchange ideas and comments on any subject. A variety of **chat rooms** are available on the Internet. The visitor can sit on the sidelines and listen to the conversations (recommended for first-time visitors) or participate. A different type of chatting is available through Internet relay chat (IRC) servers. These chat forums are conducted in languages other than English. For example, a Spanish language student could use a Spanish IRC chat channel to improve her language skills.

In some instances Internet chatting has evolved to personal chatting, meetings, and in a few instances, marriage. Unfortunately, we must also issue a word of warning about chatting and personal contacts. Sometimes chatters are playing a role rather than representing their true persona. Some personal meetings arising out of chat room contacts have resulted in one of the parties being victimized.

Miscellaneous Uses   The Internet has uses other than those previously described and business. Some of these include

- meeting people
- exchanging ideas
- obtaining advice on a variety of subjects

- getting help with school work
- teaching classes
- listening to radio broadcasts unavailable in the user's locale

Some people have become acquainted on the Internet and have subsequently been married. The Internet has also been used in bad ways. Law enforcement agencies are concerned that criminals and terrorist organizations are using the Net to plan and coordinate activities. The Net has been used to disseminate pornography and as a mechanism for child molesters to find victims. Consequently, legislative bodies have made several attempts to make certain activities illegal. A 1997 U.S. Supreme Court decision struck down one such law because it was considered to be a violation of the freedom of speech.

Two other negative aspects of Internet usage are practices known as flaming and spamming. **Flaming** is an e-mail or newsgroup posting, sometimes insulting or even obscene, that publicly chastises a user for a breach of Internet etiquette or for a posting that the flamer disagrees with. **Spamming** consists of flooding e-mail with advertising or sending high volumes of mail to an individual. In the latter case the objective is to disrupt the user; this technique has been used as an electronic revenge mechanism. In both instances the anonymity of the participants precipitates actions that would probably not occur between people who have met face-to-face.

Business   The Internet provides companies with an alternative method for advertising, selling, and disseminating information to employees, customers, and prospective customers. Let us look at how business can be conducted via the Internet.

BUSINESS ON THE INTERNET

What began as a means of communication among military personnel and scientists has evolved to a mechanism for conducting business and personal communication. The Internet has become a marketplace, with millions of customers from around the world able to enter an electronic store and make purchases at any hour of the day. The type of commerce that can be conducted is extensive and demands new technologies to make transactions easier to conduct and to prevent electronic crime.

The U.S. Department of Commerce forecast that electronic commerce revenues will reach $600 billion by the year 2000. If this forecast holds, it means that large amounts of money will be exchanged via bits being transmitted over the Net. This digital representation of money will pass from the client's computer through several Internet nodes on its journey to the recipient. Where large amounts of money are involved, there are individuals and groups interested in taking a share illegally, in this case by diverting the funds or identifying cash equivalents such as credit card numbers. Consequently, Internet users need to take extra precautions when transferring cash equivalents over the network or when processing orders. The extra security involves the development and use of additional protocols. Furthermore,

flaming An e-mail or newsgroup posting, sometimes insulting or even obscene, that publicly chastises a user for a breach of Internet etiquette or for a posting that the flamer disagrees with.

spamming Flooding e-mail with advertising or sending high volumes of mail to an individual.

there are legal issues regarding conducting business on the Internet, such as collection of sales taxes and international issues. Let's start looking at these issues by looking at how a company can provide an electronic store, security capabilities that should be used, and the coining of digital money.

We have already covered one business application of Internet technology: an intranet. However, an intranet does not need to use the Internet—just its technology. In this section we will look at how the Internet is used to conduct business with the public. In a later section we will discuss the special features that need to be added to allow people to conduct Internet business safely.

Conducting business on the Internet is essentially the same as conducting business in a traditional store: The customer enters the premises, selects products or services, exchanges money, and receives goods. When a business transaction takes place in person, several activities occur. A cash transaction is the easiest to conduct because no verification is required to ensure the payment and the transaction may be conducted anonymously; that is, identifying information about the purchaser is not divulged to the merchant (with the exception of transactions such as the purchase of weapons that require identification). The same basic rules apply to Internet commerce, but the mechanisms for conducting a transaction differ.

Let us begin by looking at some of the business capabilities from the perspective of both merchants and consumers.

Internet Businesses

Virtually all classes of businesses can use the Internet in some way. The major uses are

- communicating via e-mail
- transferring documents via electronic data interchange
- advertising via Web pages and e-mail
- selling goods and services
- selling stocks or other financial instruments
- providing travel services
- providing reference materials

Communication via E-Mail   A company can use Internet e-mail capabilities for intracompany correspondence as well as communication with customers or prospects. Some companies periodically send e-mail messages announcing new products or pricing to customers willing to receive such notices. This use of e-mail is similar to bulk business mail except that delivery is almost instantaneous and postage is not required. As another example, an Internet auction company uses e-mail to advise a bidder that he has been outbid or has won the bid, and to advise him of upcoming auction items.

Electronic Data Interchange   **Electronic data interchange (EDI)** is used to transfer business documents within a company and between a company and its customers. Examples of documents that may be transferred are

electronic data interchange (EDI) The electronic transfer of business documents within a company and between a company and its customers.

orders, product information, and invoices. EDI provides rapid exchange of such information and is easier to process than hard-copy equivalents.

Advertising via Web Pages and E-Mail   **Web pages,** like that shown in Figure 13–5, are used by businesses of all sizes to advertise their goods and services. Web pages are easy to set up, have the potential to reach millions of customers, are available 24 hours a day, 7 days a week, are flexible to change so new products, services, and pricing can be kept current, and are inexpensive to maintain. The key to this form of advertising is attracting customers to the Web page. In a physical mall, large stores attract customers, who then may visit smaller stores in the mall. The Internet equivalent of this is having highly accessed locations on the Internet display links to other locations. To this end, some Internet services, such as search providers, sell reference services. For example, when an Internet user visits a search engine site, they will see one or more links to a merchant's Web site. Thus, the search provider receives revenues for advertising a merchant's Web site.

> **Web page** An Internet site used by businesses to advertise goods and services.

Selling Goods and Services   An extension to Internet advertising and product promotion is selling goods and services over the Internet. This application is similar to mail order with the exception that the entire transaction (except physical delivery of products) is conducted electronically. One term used to describe this capability is *the electronic mall*. A merchant can establish an electronic store via a Web page. Sometimes the company maintains its own store; an alternative is to house the Web page (electronic store) with a third party that sets up a virtual shopping mall housing multiple stores—a close counterpart to a shopping mall. Selling and buying on the Internet require special capabilities and protocols to ensure that customers and merchants are not defrauded. We will look at some of these later in this chapter.

Selling Stocks or Other Financial Instruments   One of the business activities conducted on the Internet is the sale of stocks, bonds, mutual funds,

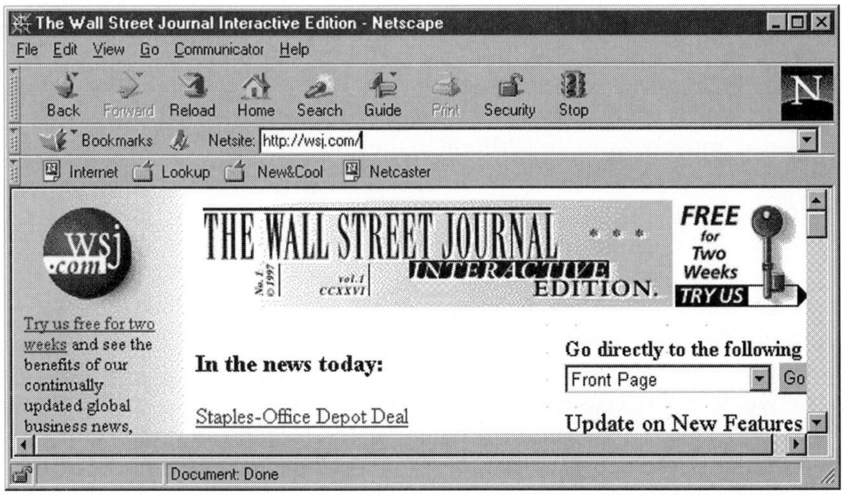

Figure 13–5
Commercial Web Page

and other investment instruments. This type of activity is a special case of selling of goods and services. Another use of the Internet is selling stocks to raise capital for a company. Recently, many startup companies have used the Internet to sell stock directly to investors, thus circumventing brokerage firms and registration with the Securities and Exchange Commission. Many of the companies attempting this have been successful at raising cash and have avoided paying the commission required by brokerage firms. These securities usually have not passed the scrutiny of a third party such as a brokerage firm or the Securities and Exchange Commission, so the buyer must beware!

Travel Services   An Internet user has many of the same capabilities as a travel agent. She can book airline, hotel, and car reservations. Some of the systems look for best fares and alternative routes. Most airlines have Web pages through which a user can book flights directly; alternatively, a user could use the services of a travel agent's Web pages to look at flights, hotels, and car rentals from a variety of airlines, hotels, and car rental agencies.

Providing Reference Materials   Providing reference materials is another special service, and some applications of this service deserve special mention. Currently, there are many Internet sites that you can visit for free; however, this may not be true in the future. For example, when you visit the site for a newspaper or magazine, you can read articles without charge. Other than advertising, there is no profit for the business. In the future, some merchants may begin charging for site visits. Thus, if you download a page from a newspaper or magazine you might incur a small charge for that activity—perhaps even a fraction of a cent. Furthermore, you might be able to set up a profile that will result in a virtual magazine or newspaper being created for you. For example, it may contain only articles you are interested in, such as business, world news, and sports. If you are in the market for a new car you might add advertisements for cars and automotive news until you purchase one (which also can be done via the Internet). Later in this chapter we discuss how small charges are collected.

Advantages and Disadvantages of Internet Use for Business

The Internet is good technology and many benefits may result from using it intelligently; however, good technologies sometimes are used in bad ways, so the user must beware. In addition to the potential problems arising out of personal Internet activities, there are potential problems in using the Internet for business.

When we engage in commercial transactions, money and goods are exchanged. Transmitting money and machine-readable goods over any network can result in loss. Our Internet money may be redirected to the wrong location. Machine-readable goods such as programs may be corrupted (damaged) during transmission, and the potential for fraud is great because we do not necessarily know with whom we are dealing and where they are located. Furthermore, when a business connects its computers to the Internet, there is a potential for outsiders to access the company's private network. It is important to understand how money and goods are exchanged over the Internet and some of the safeguards that can be used to protect the buyer, seller, and resources of computers and networks attached to the Internet.

Transaction Requirements

A business transaction requires the exchange of goods for equivalent value. The equivalent value is usually money or a representation thereof, such as a credit card number. Therefore, Internet transactions must provide a mechanism for such transfers. The following are desirable characteristics of Internet transactions:

- payment
- security and verification
- anonymity
- accountability/taxability

Payment

In the beginning of the Internet business era, access to information was mostly free. Information that was not free was usually made available through subscription and was protected by an access code. Goods that were sold were high-dollar items, typically costing $10 or more. Payment for these goods and services could be accomplished online by using a credit card.

Internet information proprietors have begun to realize that giving away valuable information is not profitable. For example, a user who accesses a magazine article online could be charged for reading that article; however, the charge would probably be quite low, say 10¢ or less. Some pieces of information, such as a single stock quote, might cost less, perhaps even a fraction of a cent. Other services, such as downloading a movie, might cost about $4. With low-cost transactions, payment by credit card is not feasible because the cost of processing the charge exceeds the charge itself. Therefore, new mechanisms are being developed to enable microcharges. The two primary technologies being proposed are smartcards and various forms of digital or electronic cash.

Smartcards   **Smartcards** are similar to credit cards, but there is a major distinction between the two: Smartcards have an embedded computer chip that is capable of storing and updating data. Using a smartcard for Internet trading will require a card reader/writer attached to the computer. Today these devices are somewhat costly, but if the technology expands to include Internet use, the cost may drop to $50 or less. A smartcard user would open an account with an institution that provides smartcards, such as a bank or perhaps an ISP. The smartcard would be encoded with the user's identifying information and a dollar amount. The user then can use the smartcard to pay for an Internet transaction by passing the card through the reader. The balance on the card would be decremented and the merchant's account would

smartcard A card with an embedded computer chip that is capable of storing and updating data; the card is used like a credit card for Internet trading.

be incremented accordingly. Payments could be made between a user and a merchant or directly between users. Thus, you could sell an item and receive immediate, verified payment rather than using collect on delivery (COD) mail service. Payments could be for amounts as small as 5¢. Internet Mondex is the leading developer of smartcard technology for the Internet.

Smartcards are currently used in Europe as an alternative to credit cards or other forms of payment. An Internet smartcard can also be used for transactions other than Internet transactions.

digital cash (d-cash) or electronic cash (e-cash) Potential Internet payment mechanisms suitable for micropayments.

Digital Cash   Another potential Internet payment mechanism suitable for micropayments is **digital cash (d-cash)** or **electronic cash (e-cash).** For many years we have represented money electronically. Banks transfer money from one place to another using electronic messages. With electronic shopping, people will be able to participate in electronic transfers of cash. Several possibilities exist for doing this.

One alternative is to write what is essentially an electronic check. This requires at least three parties to the transaction: the customer, merchant, and customer's bank or financial agent. With this technology, the business is not privy to customer information such as credit card number and the customer's account number is not transmitted over the network. Authorizing the transfer of money from the customer to the merchant is accomplished by the customer's financial agent. The money transfer is enabled by a digital signature. Unlike paper checks, the merchant receives the payment instantly and there are no insufficient fund or bad check losses.

Another form of e-cash is a money certificate that is obtained from a bank or other authorized distribution source. A customer can purchase such a certificate from a bank and money will be transferred from the customer's account. The digital certificate bears a unique serial number, just like regular cash. Like cash, the certificate is anonymous. That is, when a customer pays for goods with a credit card or check, she gives the merchant identifying information such as a credit card or checking account number. If she pays in cash, no such identifying information is given. When a customer makes a purchase using e-cash, she transfers the certificate to the merchant. As with currency, the merchant may use the digital certificate or deposit it in the bank. If a merchant believes the e-cash is counterfeit, he can contact the issuing bank and verify its accuracy.

A third form of cash that may come into existence represents money in very small denominations, as little as a fraction of a cent. Clearly, this type of currency is not in current use, so why is it necessary on the Internet? Between the extremes of free and expensive, some Internet nodes may begin charging for access to information they provide. For example, a magazine might charge a user a half cent when they access a page of their publication. After all, why would someone subscribe to a periodical if they could read it for free on the Net? If this type of charge becomes a reality, technology must support the ability to have large numbers of small-value transactions; furthermore, the cost of processing such transactions must be extremely low (paying two cents to recover 0.5 cents is hardly economical). Two organizations, Digital Equipment Corporation (DEC) and Carnegie Mellon University (CMU), have developed a way to define and process small currency amounts.

DEC's Millicent   DEC has named its approach to small denomination currency Millicent. Millicent is similar to digital check technology. The monetary units are called scrip and may be for values as low as fractions of a cent. The scrip is identified by a serial number and a value. A consumer purchases scrip from a bank or financial provider. The user also receives a key that is used to validate ownership of the scrip. The use of the key allows the user to conduct the transaction anonymously; that is, there is no (easy) way to attribute the scrip to a person. The recipient of scrip returns it to the provider for cash credit.

CMU's NetBill   NetBill is CMU's small-denomination system. The customer obtains a book of chits that can be exchanged for services. The chits are available from a NetBill provider and can be redeemed by a vendor through the same provider. Like Millicent, NetBill provides anonymous payments.

Other Potential E-Cash Providers   Other developers of e-cash systems are given in Table 13–4.

Why Digital Cash?   Because we already are conducting business using credit cards, why is there a movement toward e-cash? As we progress, more business activities will be conducted online. E-cash provides a simple way to pay for these goods. It eliminates sending credit card numbers and sending bills and payments via postal mail. Merchants receive their money immediately, and (with the exception of electronic fraud) there will be no bad checks. Through the Internet, small merchants may be able to compete with large, traditional merchants because they might be able to attract as many customers without the large overhead of buildings and staff. With e-cash, Internet customers can shop 24 hours a day, 7 days a week and will not need to leave their home or place of business to do so. Digital money is less prone to theft than hard currency. If you carry cash with you, you may lose it or have it stolen. E-cash can be backed up so it can be replaced if it is accidentally erased or destroyed. An e-cash thief will need to access your computer to steal your digital money and will also need to know your access key to make it available. If the e-cash is stolen, the serial numbers of the cash can be deactivated, much like a stop-payment on a check. With e-cash, your employer can pay you digitally and you will be able to monitor your expenses because they can be easily tracked and accounted for.

Table 13–4   Digital Cash Providers

Company	Product	Comments	Minimum payment
Newshare	Clickshare	Oriented toward newspapers and magazines	10 cents
CyberCash	CyberCoin	Netscape has adopted	25 cents
DigiCash	Ecash	Tested in smartcards and on Internet	1 cent
First Virtual Holdings	VirtualPIN	E-mail–based credit system	$1

Internet transactions require the transfer of monetary items over the network. If the Department of Commerce's prediction of $600 billion in sales by the year 2000 holds, $1.64 billion will be exchanged daily. Money in that amount will surely entice some people to attempt to illegally divert it. Consequently, security measures must be in place to protect against fraud and theft. Let us now look at some of these security measures.

Security and Verification

A transaction will be secure if

- The user gets the goods ordered.
- The merchant gets the money for the goods.
- No uninvolved parties have access to any of the transaction data.

We will look at these aspects of security from the perspective of credit card, smartcard, and e-cash transactions. Then we will see how a person's identity can be verified. We begin by looking at credit card transactions.

Credit Card Security

When a buyer uses a credit card, the credit card number must be transferred from the buyer to the seller and then to the credit card authorization center. An Internet credit card transaction essentially mirrors the activity of a credit card transaction in a store. Several standards have been developed to add security to electronic transactions. In all these standards, encryption is used to protect the credit card number and the transaction while they are being transmitted. This means that the software on the buyer's end and the software on the merchant's end must share encryption information.

secure socket layer (SSL)/Secure HTTP (S-HTTP) Two of the most commonly used protocols for securing electronic transactions. SSL is supported by Netscape and Microsoft browsers and S-HTTP was developed by Enterprise Integration Technologies and is used by Spyglass, Open Market, and several other software companies.

Secure Socket Layer Protocol   Two of the most commonly used protocols for securing electronic transactions are **secure socket layer (SSL) protocol** and **Secure HTTP (S-HTTP).** SSL is supported by Netscape and Microsoft browsers and S-HTTP was developed by Enterprise Integration Technologies and is used by Spyglass, Open Market, and several other software companies. It is possible to use both SSL and S-HTTP. The functional difference between the two is slight, so we shall discuss SSL as the example.

SSL is implemented at the presentation layer of the OSI reference model. It encrypts the Uniform Resource Locator (URL) and the message, including the credit card number. The SSL protocol is implemented in Web browsers and business software. Information exchanged between the customer and business is automatically encrypted before being transmitted and unencrypted by the recipient. As with all encryption methods, someone who intercepts the information can decrypt the messages, given sufficient time and energy. SSL uses a public key encryption algorithm (see Chapter 19).

SSL also provides authentication, which allows both parties to the transaction to verify the identity of the other. Authentication is accomplished via digital signatures. Several mechanisms—hashing, the U.S. Government's Digital Signature Standard (required for some government transactions), and public key encryption—are used to exchange digital signatures. Although the algorithms differ somewhat, the basic idea is the same. We use the public key encryption algorithm as an example. Public key encryption requires two keys: a public key and a private key. When someone wants to send me a secure message, they can use my public key to encrypt it. The private key is used to decrypt the message. Because I am the only person (presumably) who knows the private key, only I can decrypt the message. On the other hand, if I want to send my digital signature, I can encrypt the signature with my private key and the recipient will decrypt it with the public key. When the merchant decrypts the signature, it will yield my name only if it was encrypted with my private key. As an adjunct to this, we may add a certification to our signature. This is accomplished by receiving a certificate of authenticity from a clearing house. When transmitting signature data, the software encloses it in the certificate, which includes the public key. The vendor can then check with the clearing house to ensure that the certificate is valid and represents the proper individual.

Secure Electronic Transaction (SET) Another standard, **Secure Electronic Transaction (SET),** has been jointly developed by Visa, MasterCard, Netscape, Microsoft, IBM, and other companies. Like SSL, SET uses encryption to provide secure credit card transactions over the Internet. It includes features that ensure

- integrity (the packets being transmitted cannot be modified en route)
- confidentiality (only the transaction participants have knowledge of the transaction details)
- authenticity (a party to the transaction is assured of the identity of the other party)
- nonrepudiation (neither party can deny that the transaction took place)

In an SET transaction, the merchant does not have access to the credit card number because it is encrypted. The merchant forwards the encrypted credit card number to an authorization center, where it is decrypted and the purchase is authorized. This differs from the SSL approach, in which the merchant has access to the credit card number.

Digital Cash Transactions

E-cash transactions differ from credit card transactions in that the merchant is paid directly by the purchaser with a digital equivalent of money. The merchant is able to redeem the e-cash for hard currency. In this section, we look at how a consumer can get e-cash, how it is stored and safeguarded, and how it is exchanged and redeemed.

Obtaining Digital Cash E-cash is in circulation today. Digicash provides this capability in Europe, the United States, and Australia through several authorized banks. No doubt there will eventually be a variety of sources

Secure Electronic Transaction (SET) A standard jointly developed by Visa, MasterCard, Netscape, Microsoft, IBM, and other companies that uses encryption to provide secure credit card transactions over the Internet.

for e-cash and a variety of ways to obtain it. In general, the following will probably occur.

- The customer opens an account with the issuing authority, such as a bank.
- The bank issues e-cash certificates to the customer.
- E-cash certificates have serial numbers, just like hard currency.
- Encryption is used to transfer e-cash.
- The recipient of e-cash sends it to the issuer, where the digital certificates are authenticated.
- The recipient is credited with the funds.

As with the other security issues, encryption is essential to protect the integrity of the transaction as messages are exchanged between purchaser, merchant, and e-cash issuer.

Anonymity

There is a possible drawback to becoming a world of Internet traders: Governments and organizations can monitor our spending habits. This possibility already exists when we use credit cards. The identity of the card holder and the services or goods purchased become a matter of record with the credit card company. With Internet transactions, we can be tracked by our digital signatures and the serial numbers associated with our e-cash. This adds a new dimension to commerce. Today if we pay for merchandise with cash, our transaction can be anonymous because there is no link between our identity and the serial numbers on the currency we use. This linkage exists with e-cash. However, techniques have been developed that allow anonymity when using e-cash. The algorithms allow the consumer to obtain digital certificates in such a way that when the bank receives the certificates from a merchant, it is impossible to identify the certificates with an individual. Details of this algorithm are complex and are beyond the scope of this book; however, in simple terms, it involves both bank and consumer encryption keys applied to random serial numbers generated by the consumer.

Accountability and Taxability

There are other issues surrounding electronic commerce besides transaction security. These issues include who has an opportunity to participate, calculation and collection of sales taxes, and crime detection and prevention.

Opportunity to Use   Access to the Internet marketplace gives one a large, competitive merchant base from which to purchase. The competition may result in an Internet buyer being able to obtain lower prices for goods than someone without access to this resource. Those who are less affluent will probably end up paying more for goods and services because they lack the resources to establish Internet connections.

Sales Taxes   Most of the states in the United States use sales taxes as a major source of revenue. Even without the Internet, there is concern among some states regarding mail-order sales. If a Texas resident makes a mail-order purchase from a company doing business in another state, the company may not charge a sales tax for the purchase. Many Internet transactions may also avoid being taxed. Consequently, we may see some changes in state taxes.

Crime and Fraud   Despite the best efforts of merchants and Internet software and hardware developers, the amount of money at stake will be a temptation for some. We must anticipate attempts to defraud consumers and merchants, which will necessitate new legislation and policing authorities. The fingerprints of the Internet criminal will be on his keyboard, not at the crime scene, which will be somewhere in cyberspace. The Internet police will need new skills and tools to track down and apprehend the criminals of the future.

In the previous sections we have discussed several issues relating to Internet commerce. We now look at how they fit together in an Internet business transaction.

THE INTERNET STORE

Before Internet commerce begins, a business must establish an Internet presence and a way to conduct business. The first step is to establish a Web site that contains company information and product or service descriptions. There are several alternatives available for making transactions.

The simplest method is to use the Web as an advertisement medium only. For transactions, the customer would use conventional methods such as a personal visit or a telephone or fax message to place the order. The electronic commerce in this instance is advertising only. From an Internet purchaser's perspective, this is probably less satisfying than having the option to place the order and complete the transaction online. Some users prefer this method because they perceive that it allows them to avoid having their credit card information intercepted.

A second alternative is to have the entire transaction completed over the Internet. A company could implement the system to do this or could subscribe to the services of an Internet shopping service bureau. If the company handles the entire transaction, it must develop the necessary software and associated database to provide the Web page, an online catalog, and order taking and verification. A service bureau will provide these services for a fee. The tradeoff between these two is the cost of setting up a server and software internally versus the costs of having a service bureau provide a Web presence. Service bureaus of this type provide what is called an electronic mall and establish stores for their clients in the mall. There is typically a setup charge to establish a store and a monthly fee for processing orders. The monthly fees can be a flat rate, a rate based on transactions processed, a rate based on a percentage of the dollar amount processed, or a combination of these alternatives. In the following discussion we will focus on the issues of processing the order on the Net; we will assume that the business is providing the system for conducting business.

Today's Internet Transaction

Once the customer connects to the Net and accesses the business's Web page, the transaction can begin. Today, most business transactions use credit cards for payment. In the future, e-cash will become more common. Security should be inherent in all business transactions.

The general steps for making an electronic cash transaction are

- obtaining e-cash
- selecting items to purchase
- making payment
- receiving notification

Obtain Digital Cash   The consumer withdraws e-cash from the bank and stores the e-cash on her computer. In obtaining the e-cash, the consumer provides the bank with her public encryption key. The public key is embedded in the certificate so the recipient can decrypt it. Once stored on disk, the e-cash can be backed up to avoid loss; however, the e-cash can be used only once because it is validated when exchanged. Because each e-cash certificate has a unique serial number, once the e-cash has been spent, the serial numbers are invalidated. The e-cash can be used in any Internet store that has made arrangements to accept it. The e-cash is controlled by the consumer's software. For example, the amount of available cash can be displayed so the consumer knows how much is available for spending and the exchange of the e-cash is handled automatically.

Item Selection   The customer browses the online catalog and selects products or services. How this is accomplished depends on the design of the Web pages. Companies with large product lines typically provide indexes and links to subcategories or to the products themselves. The product display may consist of a photograph (perhaps with several perspectives), description, size, weight, colors, and so on. After viewing the product information, the consumer can select it for purchase or move on and continue browsing or exit from the merchant's page.

Payment   Once the item has been selected, the consumer may be given two options: The e-cash can be immediately transmitted or the consumer may be prompted to authorize the payment. Regardless, the e-cash certificates are transferred to the merchant. The merchant then sends the digital certificate to the issuing bank or a certification authority to check its authenticity. If the certificate is verified, the transaction continues.

Notification   The customer is notified of the order status. If the order has been accepted the customer usually receives a confirmation number and shipping information; if the order is not accepted, the customer is provided with a reason and, perhaps, additional steps to take.

If the transaction is a credit card or smartcard transaction, the payment step will differ somewhat. Credit card transactions require customer identification and authentication. When a customer connects to a merchant's Web site, the merchant may want to begin by identifying the user, gathering information during the user's first visit or transaction. Subsequent transactions may be easier to conduct because the merchant already has the relevant customer information on file. The customer information is usually protected by a password. Information collected about the customer may include the data given in Table 13–5.

When the credit card order is placed, the customer must provide credit card information, credit card number, type, and expiration date. This is typed into an entry screen and sent to the merchant. Alternatively, a repeat customer can use a credit card number on file with the merchant. Secure transactions use the SSL protocol to encrypt the data. If SSL is not used, some browsers notify the user that the transaction is not secure. When the merchant receives the credit card information, the transaction must be authorized. The merchant sends the credit card information together with the transaction amount to the authorization center's node. The authorization center transmits an acceptance number or a rejection number. If accepted, the order information is processed by the merchant's order entry software, which causes goods to be shipped, inventory records updated, accounting files to be updated, and so on.

One other payment option may soon become available: electronic checks. With electronic checks, a consumer essentially writes a check using a digital signature. The check is sent to the merchant, who forwards it to the customer's bank for validation. If the digital signature is correct, the purchase amount is transferred from the customer's account to the merchant's account.

Consequences of Internet Business

The Internet is already being used extensively as an electronic shopping mall, and experts predict that this use will grow rapidly over the next several years. In preceding sections we looked at the ways in which transactions are processed. Let us now look at another aspect of Internet business: the impact on existing businesses.

Many businesses exist to provide services to users. For example, the travel industry serves as a broker between airlines, cruise companies, hotels,

Table 13–5   Customer Information

Name	Address	Ship-to address
Telephone numbers (home, work)	Fax number	E-mail address
	Credit card number and type	Purchase history
Mother's maiden name		

and car rental agencies and travelers. Essentially, their job is to find accommodations suitable for clients' needs. The travel agent is able to fulfill those needs via computer connections to a variety of reservation systems. Now, consider the Internet travel alternative. From an Internet connection, a traveler has access to almost all the resources of the travel agent, and online travel agent software is available to assist in making reservations. Moreover, the traveler can view pictures of points of interest at their destination and contact local chambers of commerce and city home pages to find things to do at places on the itinerary. Through e-mail the traveler can solicit information from people living in the region being visited.

What impact will this capability have on existing travel agencies? Some will probably make their services available on the Internet and serve travelers throughout the world. Others will continue with business as usual by serving clients who do not have Internet connections or do not want to do their own research. If a significant number of Internet users make their own travel arrangements, some travel agencies will probably not survive. (Note the similarity between this and our telephone and banking transactions. We are all telephone operators with direct dialing and bank tellers when we use an ATM.)

The travel business is just one business that may need to adapt to the Internet. Others include newspapers, book publishers, magazines, stock brokerage firms, and retail stores. The laws of evolution may apply to some of these companies: Those that adapt will survive and those that cannot will become extinct. Jobs may be lost in many types of businesses because the customer and network software make the transaction without merchant employee support.

The impact of the Internet on businesses will be profound. Smaller businesses that do not have an Internet presence may see an impact similar to that of large department or discount stores on small retail shops: Some small businesses cannot compete and will eventually go out of business. On the other hand, a small business with an Internet presence has a worldwide customer base. Such businesses can compete with large businesses that have large capital investments and unwieldy corporate structures. Such large companies, even those having an Internet presence, may not be able to react as quickly to the changing global marketplace as their smaller competitors.

Conducting business on the Internet requires a variety of new security measures. In addition to securing transaction and payment information on the Internet, a company that has its networks connected to the Internet should also implement safeguards to prevent unauthorized access by outsiders.

SECURE ENTERPRISE NETWORKS

When a company connects its network to the Internet, its systems are susceptible to unauthorized access by outsiders. Most companies want Internet access without exposing all of their systems to public access. This is accomplished by erecting a barrier called a firewall. A firewall is a computer or software that sits between the Internet and the protected enterprise network and controls and monitors traffic between them. A firewall is illustrated in Figure 13–6.

Firewalls operate in a variety of ways. The essential idea is to restrict the data that flows between the Internet and the protected systems, which is done in two basic ways: defining the traffic (users, addresses, etc.) that is allowed and disallowing all other communication, or defining what is prohibited and allowing all other transmissions. A firewall may be set up using a router or a computer or both. A router is a device that connects networks together (see Chapter 16). On the Internet, routers use the IP protocol and determine the next node that is to receive the packet on its path to the destination node. A router-based firewall filters out packets from unauthorized source addresses. This type of firewall is called a screening router.

A second approach is to use a computer as a gateway to the private network. All packets are received by the gateway computer and transferred onto the protected system's network. Thus, the gateway system is the only one operating as an Internet node. This is illustrated in Figure 13–7. This type of firewall is called a screened-host gateway. This technique can be used in conjunction with a screening router.

A third firewall implementation possibility is a screened subnet, as illustrated in Figure 13–8. The subnet is available to the Internet and the protected systems can communicate with the Internet only through the protected subnet.

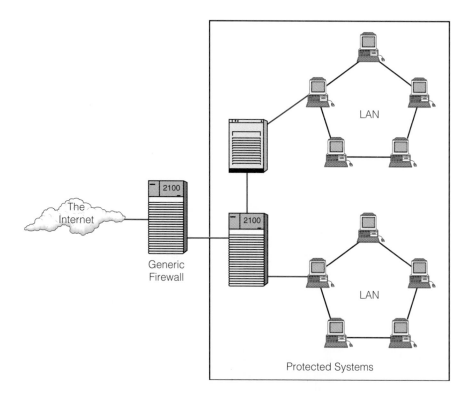

Figure 13–6
Generic Firewall

Figure 13–7
Gateway Firewall

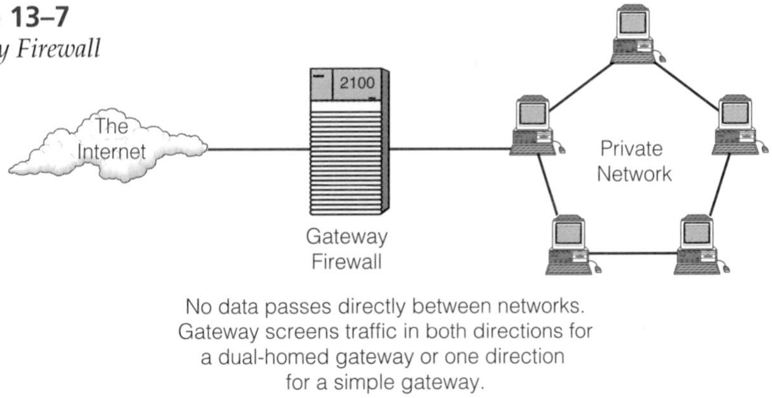

Gateway
Firewall

No data passes directly between networks.
Gateway screens traffic in both directions for
a dual-homed gateway or one direction
for a simple gateway.

A fourth approach is an application-level gateway. This type of firewall allows messages of certain types to pass between the Internet and the protected systems. Examples of messages that may be allowed to flow between the two networks are e-mail messages and business transactions.

virtual private network (VPN) A private network operated over a public network such as the Internet.

VIRTUAL PRIVATE NETWORKS

An outgrowth of firewalls and business use of the Internet is **virtual private networks (VPN).** A VPN is a private network operated over a public network

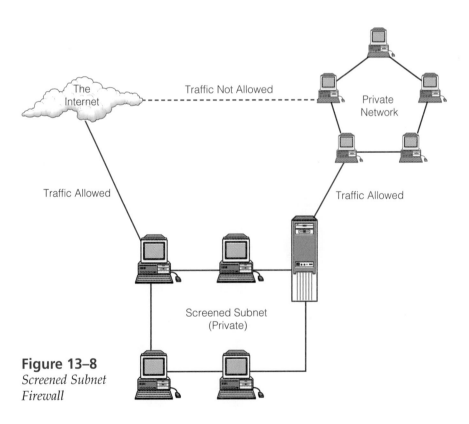

Figure 13–8
Screened Subnet Firewall

such as the Internet. A VPN does not need to be implemented over the Internet but we shall discuss VPNs in this context. This discussion could also apply to any public network such as the Concert Virtual Network Service, Worldsource VNS, and Fonselect VPN.

In the past, WANs were implemented largely by leasing transmission facilities from a common carrier. The transmission facilities were owned by the common carrier but dedicated to the lessor. The transmission media leasing expense was large for companies with big WANs. If a company has its systems connected to the Internet, the nodes are able to communicate over the Internet lines. The problems inherent in this are security and availability. We have already discussed the security issue. The Internet is a shared resource, so the bandwidth available to a single user or company varies. Companies that need guaranteed bandwidth for their applications may not be able to use the Internet as a circuit provider; however, the other public networks mentioned in the previous paragraph may be suitable. The obvious benefit of using the Internet as the foundation for a VPN is cost.

SUMMARY

The Internet started in 1969 as a U.S. government military project called the Arpanet. Since that time, it has grown exponentially and the Internet has become an important communication, research, and business tool. Businesses and individuals use the Internet in a variety of ways for work and recreation. Individuals gain access to the Internet for personal use primarily through Internet service providers. Large and small ISPs exist. When selecting an ISP, an individual should consider the user-to-modem ratio, connections supported, support, services, cost, and software and hardware.

The Internet provides a variety of services, including the World Wide Web, research, online journals, Usenet, file transfer, Telnet, business transactions, garage sales, and chatting. Business use requires additional safeguards for transaction security, user authentication, and user anonymity. Furthermore, new forms of currency, digital or electronic cash and electronic checks, have been developed to pay for Internet transactions. More traditional payment capabilities using credit cards and smartcards are also available.

Typically, companies that attach their enterprise networks to the Internet need to safeguard their private network from the public Internet. One of the ways to do this is a firewall. A firewall is a router that either allows only designated traffic to enter the private network or allows all traffic except messages from designated places or of a designated type. Firewalls and public networks have enabled companies to realize communication media savings by implementing virtual private networks. By allowing a network such as the Internet to provide the communication connection between geographically distributed areas, a company can avoid the cost of leasing communication lines.

KEY TERMS

Arpanet
browser
chat rooms
chatting
digital cash (d-cash)
domain
electronic cash (e-cash)
electronic data interchange (EDI)
file transfer protocol (FTP)
flaming
freenet
hypertext
hypertext markup language
   (HTML)
internet
Internet
Internet service provider (ISP)
InterNIC

intranet
Java
MILNET
network access point (NAP)
network computer (NC)
packet switching network (PSN)
point-to-point protocol (PPP)
secure electronic transaction (SET)
Secure HTTP (S-HTTP)
secure socket layer (SSL) protocol
serial line Internet protocol (SLIP)
smartcard
spamming
Usenet
user-to-modem ratio
virtual private network (VPN)
Web page
World Wide Web (WWW)

REVIEW QUESTIONS

1. Distinguish between an intranet, an internet, and the Internet.

2. Trace the history of the Internet.

3. What is an ISP? What services does an ISP provide?

4. List five ways in which an individual might gain access to the Internet.

5. Describe the hardware and software used to make an Internet connection.

6. List six guidelines an individual should consider when selecting an ISP.

7. List the 12 steps a company might follow to set up an ISP business. Identify the steps that could occur in parallel.

8. What is the World Wide Web? How is it used?

9. What is Usenet?

10. What is Internet chatting? What are the benefits and disadvantages of chatting?

11. What are flaming and spamming?

12. Describe three different ways of making payments for Internet business transactions.

13. What are the requirements for an Internet transaction and how can each requirement be satisfied?

14. What is the function of
   a. secure socket layer (SSL)
   b. secure electronic transaction (SET)

15. How can a person obtain e-cash? How is e-cash used in a transaction?

16. What is a virtual private network?

17. What is a firewall? What functions does it perform?

PROBLEMS AND EXERCISES

1. Compare the pricing policies of two ISPs in your area.

2. Choose an ISP and determine the types of user connections supported.

3. Use the Internet to find out which companies are using and providing e-cash.

4. Take a poll of ten Internet users to see
   a. how much time they spend accessing the Internet
   b. what Internet services they use
   c. what Internet providers they use
   d. what they like most about using the Internet
   e. what they like least about using the Internet

5. In some instances, chatting has led to personal meetings. Investigate the literature and find two positive and two negative consequences of chatting.

CHAPTER 14

Internet Technology

CHAPTER OBJECTIVES

In Chapter 13 we looked at how individuals and companies can use the Internet. In this chapter we look at some of the technology underlying the Internet. After studying this chapter you should be able to

- Describe the TCP/IP protocol
- Discuss Internet addressing
- Describe several protocols used on the Internet
- Define a subnet and describe how they are used
- List several components of the TCP/IP protocol suite

INTERNET ADDRESSES

The Internet is based largely on the Transmission Control Protocol and Internet Protocol (TCP/IP). TCP provides services at the OSI transport layer and IP is a network layer protocol. Internet addresses are represented in a variety of formats; however, all the formats are ultimately resolved to a 32-bit number known as an IP address. Figure 14–1 illustrates an IP header. Note that the header contains two addresses—the source address and the destination address—both of which are currently 32-bit entities. By the time you read this, IP addresses may be 128 bits long. Internet addresses must be unique, and the number of available 32-bit addresses is limited. The longer address will significantly enlarge the available address space. The 128-bit address is part of a new version of the IP protocol; this new version is called **IPng** and **IPv6** for next generation and version 6, respectively. The current version is version 4, or IPv4. In a later section we will look at the new features of IPv6 and why it is needed. Until that time, our discussion will be based on IPv4. A 32-bit number can range from 0 to approximately 4 billion.

IPng and IPv6 A new version of the Internet protocol; this new version is called IPng and IPv6 for next generation and version 6, respectively.

399

Figure 14–1
IP Header

| IP Version |
| Header Length |
| Service Type: throughput parameters |
| Total Length of Datagram |
| Identification, Flags, Fragment Offset |
| Time to Live |
| Protocol |
| Checksum |
| Source IP Address |
| Destination IP Address |
| IP Options |
| Padding |

You are probably wondering why there is a need for a larger address space. The answer lies in how Internet addresses are assigned and used.

Internet addresses are usually written as four separate numbers delineated by a period, or as an address name. Using the first convention, a node address might be written as 101.209.33.17. Each number in the group represents an 8-bit octet, that is, a range of numbers from 0 to 255 (2^8 - 1). In general, the first set of numbers represents the network identification of a node's network, called a subnetwork or **subnet,** and the last numbers identify a specific node on the subnet. The subnet address may consist of 1, 2, or 3 octets depending on the class of the node or subnet.

subnet A node's network, or subnetwork, identified by the first set of numbers in an Internet address.

Currently there are four address classes, A through D; class E is defined but reserved for future use. With the exception of class D, classes are based on the number of nodes on the subnet. As the number of nodes on the subnet increases, more bits of the address are needed to distinguish each node.

Class A addresses are used for networks with more than 2^{16} nodes. The first bit of the 32-bit address is 0, to distinguish this class from the others, which start with a 1 bit; the next 7 bits represent the network ID. There can be no more than 2^7 or 128 subnetworks in this class. The remaining 24 bits are used to distinguish among the subnet nodes; the 24 bits can provide up to 16 million distinct node addresses.

class A through class D The four currently used Internet address classes. With the exception of Class D, classes are based on the number of nodes on the subnet.

Class B addresses are used for subnets with 2^8 through 2^{16} or 64,000 nodes. The first two bits in this class start with a 1 followed by a 0, and 14 bits are used to represent the subnet address, leaving the last 16 bits available for node addresses within the subnet.

Class C addresses are used for subnets with fewer than 2^8 nodes; this class is distinguished by starting bits of 110. Class C addresses use 21 bits for the subnet address and 8 bits for subnet node addresses.

Class D nodes begin with bits of 1110 and designate host nodes that want to receive broadcast messages.

In conclusion, class A nodes use one octet to represent the subnet address, class B nodes use two octets, and class C nodes have three octets representing the subnet address. The class designator bits are included in the subnet portion of the address; the subnet portion of the address is followed by node addresses. All network addresses are assigned by the Network Information Center to avoid address duplication. Table 14–1 summarizes the Internet address classes.

Table 14–1   Internet Address Class Summary

Class	Subnets	Nodes	Comments
A	$2^7 = 128$	$2^{24} = 16$ million	Address begins with a 0 bit
B	$2^{14} = 16,000$	$2^{16} = 64,000$	Address begins with bits 10
C	$2^{21} = 2$ million	$2^8 = 256$	Address begins with bits 110
D			Address begins with 1110

Internet Naming Conventions

For most Internet users, the four-octet address representation, called a **dotted quad,** is too cumbersome. Therefore, most users substitute a naming convention called a **Universal Resource Locator (URL).** A URL uses names and abbreviations that are easier to use and remember than the dotted quad representation. A URL consists of two parts: the protocol used to access a resource followed by the resource name. However, a URL is simply a different representation of the 32-bit Internet address, and before a message is transmitted, the URL must be converted into a proper 32-bit IP address. We will see how this happens later.

The protocol in the URL is used to define how the resource will be accessed. It may be the hypertext transfer protocol (HTTP), the file transfer protocol (FTP), Gopher text reader, or another method such as mail or news readers. The resource may be a single article or file, a newsgroup, or a Web page located on an Internet host computer. In this case, the resource field may contain the name of a computer, an organization, and possibly a country designator, all of which make up what is called a **domain name.** Domain names are a hierarchical word-oriented representation of an Internet address. The hierarchy is similar to the notation used to address a letter. If you want to mail a letter to someone, you use the address hierarchy of

- recipient name
- street address
- city
- state
- zip code
- country (if the letter is international)

The combination of the address elements, which are ordered from the most specific (the recipient's name) to the most general (the country), uniquely identifies the recipient. Let us examine the sample domain name *frodo.mycompany.com.us* and explain its parts.

Like postal addresses, the domain naming hierarchy starts with the most specific part of the name and proceeds to the most general part. In the sample name, *frodo* (probably) represents the name of an Internet host computer owned by the company *mycompany.* The *com* term identifies the *mycompany* entity as a company. Other possible entity types are given in Table 14–2. The combination of these three terms nearly maps to an IP address. The *mycompany.com* portion is nearly the subnet and the computer name is the node on that subnet. The *us* term identifies the country in which the computer

dotted quad The four-octet address representation of an Internet address.

Universal Resource Locator (URL) A naming convention based on names and abbreviations that are easier to use and remember than the dotted quad representation. A URL consists of two parts: the protocol used to access a resource followed by the resource name.

domain name A hierarchical word-oriented representation of an Internet address.

Table 14–2   Root Level Domain Names

Name	Description
com	a for-profit company
edu	education (for example, a university)
gov	U.S. government
mil	U.S. military
net	network service
org	nonprofit organization
at	Austria
au	Australia
be	Belgium
ca	Canada
de	Denmark
es	Spain
fi	Finland
fr	France
il	Israel
it	Italy
jp	Japan
no	Norway
uk	United Kingdom
us	United States

Figure 14–2
Domain Name
Hierarchy

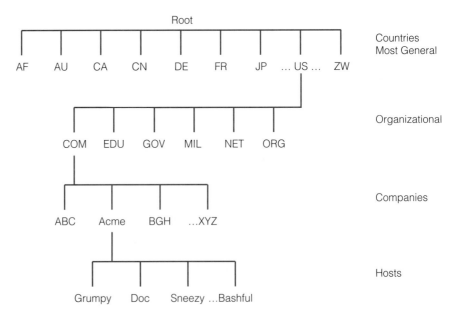

Table 14–3   Some URL protocols

Protocol	Explanation
http	Hypertext transfer protocol
ftp	File transfer protocol
file	File access
mailto	Send mail to a recipient
news	Access a newsgroup or news article
Gopher	Use the Gopher text-oriented access
Finger	Use utility to access information about a user

may be found, the United States in this example. Some other country designators are given in Table 14–2. Designators such as *.com* and *.us* are called root level or top level domains. It is conceivable that a resource called *frodo.mycompany.com.uk* also exists, so that is why we used the term *nearly* when saying that *frodo.mycompany.com* nearly represented an IP address.

When a business obtains an Internet address from the Internet Network Information Center (InterNIC), it also registers a unique domain name. The domain name is associated with the IP addresses assigned to that business. When a domain name is used as part of a URL, it must be resolved to the IP address. This is done automatically by the Internet Domain Name Service (DNS). Domain names and their IP addresses are stored in databases on a number of Internet nodes called **domain name servers.** Domain names are organized hierarchically from the most general to the specific, as illustrated in Figure 14–2. When a domain name must be resolved, the local host first looks to see whether it has the URL and associated IP address already available. If not, the host sends a message to a domain name server and obtains the necessary information. The host then places the IP address in the network layer IP header and transmits the message. To resolve the domain name *frodo.mycompany.com.us* the search would start at a local domain name server. If the domain name is not found there, the search would expand to the nearest available name server that contains all U.S. domain/IP address pairs.

Some of the possible URL protocols are listed in Table 14–3, and sample URLs are given in Table 14–4.

domain name server
An Internet node on which domain names and their IP addresses are stored.

Table 14–4   Sample URLs

URL	Explanation
http://www.mycompany.com	HTTP protocol accessing the web page of a company using the domain name mycompany.com
ftp://ftp.mycompany.com/pubs/usermanual.txt	Transfer a file called usermanual.txt in the pubs directory on the mycompany.com node
finger:jdoe@mycompany.com	Invoke the finger utility to get information on jdoe
gopher://frodo.abc.edu	Access the Gopher menu on node frodo at ABC University
mailto:jdoe@mycompany.com	Send mail to jdoe at mycompany
news:comp.newusers.announce	Access the newsgroup for announcements for new computer users

Table 14–5   Sample E-Mail Addresses

dstamper@frodo.abc.edu	User dstamper on node frodo at ABC University
jdoe@nasa.gov	User jdoe at NASA
comgen@usahq.mil	Commanding general at U.S. Army Headquarters
Sysmgr@xyz.com	System manager for the XYZ Corporation network

When sending e-mail to a user on the Internet, we use a slight variation of the domain name. In addition to identifying a node and subnet, we must also designate a user or recipient. The format of this type of address is *user@domain*. The @ symbol is used to separate the user name from the domain name. In this naming convention, the domain represents the mail server for that individual, and the user represents an e-mail post office box (user or function name) to whom the mail will be delivered. Sample e-mail addresses are given in Table 14–5.

Subnet Addressing

An Internet address is composed of three basic parts: the class type identifier, the subnet address, and the node addresses. An installation that has a class A address space has the potential for approximately 2^{24} node addresses (approximately 16 million). It is unlikely that the company would want all these nodes to be associated with a single network address. Consequently, a company can divide the node address range into two parts, a subnet address and a node address within the subnet. This is accomplished by placing a subnet mask over the local or node address part of the IP address.

For simplicity, consider a class C address. The local part of the address consists of 8 bits. Locally we could interpret this as having 256 node addresses or four subnets, each of which has 64 nodes, or two subnets, each of which has 128 nodes. Specifically, suppose we wanted to have four LANs obtain their addresses from this class C address. The addresses would be as shown in Table 14–6.

To create the above decomposition, a subnet mask is applied to the address. In the mask, a 1 bit designates the portion of the address that is to be interpreted as the network/subnet number. Therefore, the local segment just described would have a subnet mask of 11000000 for the last octet. The actual subnet mask is a 32-bit entity; we have just shown the rightmost portion of the mask. Bits in the mask set to a 1 bit are to be interpreted as the subnet portion of the address and bits set to 0 are to be interpreted as node addresses within the subnet. In the mask, all 1 bits are on the left and all 0 bits are on the right. The complete binary subnet mask for our example is therefore

11111111 11111111 11111111 11000000

Table 14–6   Four Subnet Addresses for Class C Address

Bit Range	Subnet Address First Two Bits	Node Address Range Bits 3 Through 8
00000000–00111111	00	000000–111111
01000000–01111111	01	000000–111111
10000000–10111111	10	000000–111111
11000000–11111111	11	000000–111111

Subnet address masks are often represented in the dotted quad notation, which in this instance would be 255.255.255.192.

In an IP network such as the Internet, addresses are unique. Let us now look at how a node obtains an Internet address.

subnet address mask A 32-bit mask used to subdivide an Internet address.

INTERNET NODE ADDRESSES

After obtaining a set of Internet addresses, say a class C address space, an organization must allocate the addresses in its subnet to nodes. An Internet node address is allocated in one of two ways: It is statically assigned or it is dynamically assigned. If a company has a class C address space and only 200 nodes that will be connecting to the Internet, each node may be permanently assigned one of the addresses. How this is accomplished depends somewhat on the system's software, but essentially the address is located in a startup file. When the node is started, it obtains its address from this file.

Dynamic Addressing

In **dynamic addressing,** a node is assigned an Internet address when one is needed. For example, consider an Internet service provider (ISP). As mentioned in Chapter 13, ISPs usually have modem-to-user ratios of 10 to 1 or more. Thus, an ISP with 200 Internet addresses could serve 2000 customers. When a customer connects to the ISP's host, it is assigned an Internet address that is not currently in use. The most common mechanism for dynamically assigning Internet addresses is the **dynamic host configuration protocol (DHCP).** An earlier protocol called BOOTP also provided dynamic addressing. BOOTP was developed for diskless workstations, and DHCP is more comprehensive.

dynamic addressing In dynamic addressing, a node is assigned an Internet address when one is needed.

dynamic host configuration protocol (DHCP) The most common mechanism for dynamically assigning Internet addresses.

A server is used to administer address assignments. A DHCP server can assign an address in one of three ways: automatic allocation, dynamic allocation, and manual allocation. With automatic allocation, the server attempts to always assign the same address to a given client. This is useful for clients that provide services to users, such as mail servers. This type of client needs the same address each time it boots because other nodes that use its services may have saved its Internet address. Manual allocation means that a network administrator has assigned the address. The ISP mentioned above will use static addresses for its Internet gateway host and dynamically assign addresses to most of its customers. With dynamic addressing, a node is given any address that is not currently in use.

An ISP node that wants to connect to the Internet starts by sending a broadcast message to locate a DHCP server. An installation may use several such servers to allow better access and to provide a level of fault tolerance. We will consider only the simple case in which there is only one DHCP server. For information about multiple DHCP servers, consult the Network Working Group's RFC 2131 standard document. When a server responds, the client requests an address. The server selects an address that is not in use and delivers it to the user. The client may also specify a time frame for use of the address. If this is the case, the DHCP server may allocate the address to another user when the requested time plus a margin-of-error interval has elapsed. A client can also renegotiate its allowed time. When the client is finished with the address, it notifies the DHCP server that it is releasing the address. Once released, the address may be assigned to another node.

You may be wondering how the DHCP server knows the address being provided is not being used. If it is the sole allocator of addresses, then it knows which addresses are in use and which are available. As an additional measure, the DHCP server should send out an echo request message using the Internet Control Message Protocol (ICMP) to determine whether the address is being used. If the address is in use, the server receives an echo reply response from the node using the address.

Another dynamic address assignment algorithm is used by some software systems. A node that needs an address chooses one from the address space and issues a message to determine whether the address is in use. If a node responds to the message, another address is chosen and the process repeats. If no response is received, the node assumes the address is not in use and adopts that address.

Internet Addressing on LANs

Sometimes, the node that needs to connect to the Internet is also a LAN node. In this instance an additional addressing consideration must be made. On a LAN, a message is delivered to a node based on its physical address, that is, the media access control (MAC) address of its network interface card. Therefore, if a LAN node also has an IP address, an IP message can be delivered only if the IP address is first translated into a MAC address. The protocol that performs this function is called the **address resolution protocol (ARP).**

address resolution protocol (ARP) The protocol that translates an IP address into a MAC address.

The ARP assumes that the node's IP address is known. For example, a LAN server may receive an IP message for a LAN node. The node's IP address is contained in the destination field of the IP header. The server will probably have an ARP table that contains IP addresses and the corresponding MAC addresses, as illustrated in Table 14–7. The first entry in the table is the ARP entry for the server itself, the second is a broadcast address used to search for an unknown address, and the remaining addresses are known IP/MAC addresses.

If the destination node's IP address is in the ARP table, the server extracts the corresponding MAC address, builds the MAC header, and sends the message to the node. If the destination node's IP address is not in the

Table 14–7   ARP Table

MAC Address	IP Address
03-A1-22-70-44-02	201.1.1.1
FF-FF-FF-FF-FF-FF	143.7.255.255
FF-FF-FF-FF-FF-FF	255.255.255.255
03-A1-22-70-44-07	201.1.1.8
03-A1-22-70-44-25	201.1.1.17
03-A1-22-70-44-B2	201.1.1.4

ARP table, the address must be discovered. The server broadcasts an ARP request packet on the network and any node that knows the IP/MAC address pair responds. When the node receives the proper entry, it stores the address in its ARP table and forwards the message to the node.

Obtaining a node's IP address is the first part of sending a message from one node to another. The second part is moving the message from source node to destination node, a process called routing. Let us look at how the IP protocol does this.

IP ROUTING

When an Internet node sends a message to another Internet node, it must know the destination node's IP address. The address may be resolved from a URL supplied by the user or obtained from a hypertext link or similar mechanism. At the heart of the routing algorithm is a **routing table** that contains network information essential to making intelligent routing decisions. In discussing how IP routing works, let us consider the network illustrated in Figure 14–3. In the figure, the clouds represent networks and the network addresses are shown within the clouds. Devices called **routers** (see Chapter 16) are responsible for internetwork message forwarding. Each router is connected to two (or more) networks (some routers have more than two ports), and each router port has an address on the attached subnet. Therefore, router A is connected to subnet 1 and has the address of 10.0.0.4 on that subnet and address 20.0.0.6 for the attachment to subnet 2.

Each router maintains a router table. Some of the information contained in those tables is given in Table 14–8, and the routing table for router A (based on the data in Table 14–8 and Figure 14–3) is given in Table 14–9. The

routing table An information source containing the node address and the identification of the LAN to which the receiving node is connected.

router A network interconnection device and associated software that links two networks. The networks being linked can be different, but they must use a common routing protocol.

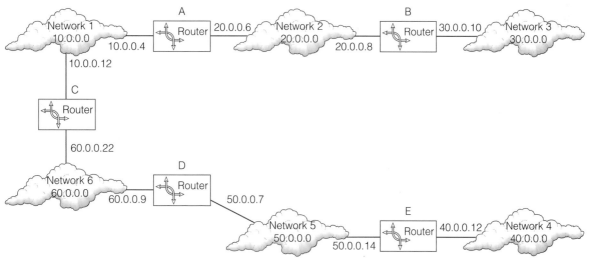

Figure 14–3
IP Network

Table 14–8 Some IP Routing Table Data

Network address	Next router
Hops to network	Port address

network address in the routing table is the subnet address. This data is contained in the first part of the IP address. The next router is the address of the router that should receive the packet next. The number of hops to the network is a measure of the distance to the destination network from the current router. The hop count is the number of routers or gateways through which the packet must travel to reach its destination. The hop count does not consider the speed of the networks through which the packet will travel. It may be faster to cover four hops through fast networks such as fast Ethernet LANs than to pass through two WANs using slower communication links. Other routing implementations use an additional distance measure called ticks, which represents the speed of transmission over a route. The port address is the address onto which the router will transmit the message to get it to the next router or to the subnet.

IP Routing Algorithm

The algorithm that the IP uses to route a message from source node to destination node is essentially as follows:

1. Source node obtains the destination node's IP address.
2. IP protocol builds the IP header and affixes it to the packet.
3. Source node sends the packet to the router.
4. Router determines the network address of the destination node.
5. If the network address is this network, use local delivery method and skip remaining steps. For example, use the ARP if this is a LAN and transmit using MAC address.
6. Router consults routing table for network address.
7. Router sends message out on port addressed to next router.
8. Receiving router decrements time-to-live field. The time-to-live field is a field in the IP header that indicates how long a packet will last before being discarded. The value of the time-to-live field is

Table 14–9 Router A's Routing Table

Net Address	Next Router	Hops	Port
10	None	Directly connected	10.0.0.4
20	None	Directly connected	20.0.0.6
30	B	1	20.0.0.6
40	C	3	10.0.0.4
50	C	2	10.0.0.4
60	C	1	10.0.0.4

the number of hops remaining. The time-to-live field is decremented by each router and the router setting the field to zero discards the packet.

9. If time-to-live field is 0, packet is discarded.

10. Return to step 4.

Note that in step 9, a packet may be discarded. The sending node sets the time-to-live counter to its initial value, and each time the packet passes through a router, the counter is decremented. The router that sets the counter to zero will not attempt to forward the packet. This keeps packets from circulating endlessly through the network, an event that could occur if routing tables were not consistent. If a packet is discarded, it is the responsibility of the TCP on the destination node to recognize the problem and request that the packet be resent. A flow chart of the routing process is shown in Figure 14–4.

OTHER INTERNET SERVICES

In Chapter 13 we discussed how to set up an Internet connection and use it for business purposes. The services discussed in that chapter were those used to create the business environment and Web browsers. The Internet has a variety of other services and tools available. Some of these services are a part of the TCP/IP protocol suite and others are tools that assist the user in using the Internet. Some of the more common tools and services are briefly described here.

Simple Mail Transfer Protocol

The **simple mail transfer protocol (SMTP)** provides a standard for the delivery of mail. Several mail user interfaces exist, such as browser mail, Eudora, PINE, and UNIX mail. Interoperability of the various interfaces is assured if all adhere to the SMTP standard. The SMTP describes the format of mail messages and describes how a mail message is to be handled by the recipient's software.

Simple Network Management Protocol

The **simple network management protocol (SNMP)** assists in collecting and reporting on data within a network. The SNMP is discussed in Chapter 18.

Telnet

Telnet is a program that allows a user at a computer to connect to another computer on the network. The computer from which the connection is made is called the local computer and the other is called the remote computer. When a Telnet connection is set up, keyboard data is transmitted to the remote computer and responses are displayed on the monitor of the local computer. A user may want to use Telnet to connect to her home computer

simple mail transfer protocol (SMTP) A standard for the delivery of mail.

Simple Network Management Protocol (SNMP) SNMP provides a guideline for creating network management software products. SNMP has four key components: the SNMP protocol, structure of management information (SMI), management information base (MIB), and the network management system (NMS).

Telnet A program that allows a user at a computer to connect to another computer on the network.

Figure 14–4
Routing Process

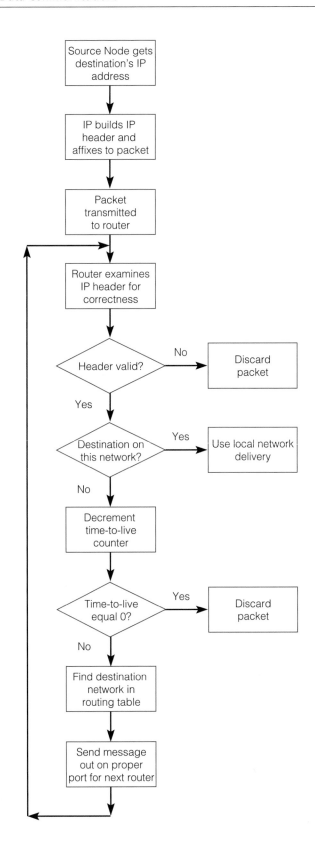

and access her mail messages or a user might want to connect to another system and run a program.

File Transfer Protocol

The **file transfer protocol (FTP)** is part of the TCP/IP protocol suite and provides a mechanism to transfer files between TCP/IP nodes. A user initiates the FTP from his system, which we will call the host. The FTP requires the user to identify a target system from which the files are to be transferred. For example, a user may enter *ftp archivedir.somesystem.edu* to establish himself in a directory on the target system. Naturally, a FTP user cannot access any file on any system; the user must have the proper privileges to transfer files. Therefore, the FTP connection requires a user logon. One common use of FTP is anonymous FTP. Anonymous FTP allows access to a user without a logon ID on the target system access. The user ID is anonymous and the usual practice is to enter a mail address as the password. Once properly logged on, the user can change directories, use directory commands to look at the available files, and transfer files to the host system. FTP capabilities are available through operating system command languages or via browsers.

Archie

Before browsers and search engines, Internet users had a way to search for files, a system called **Archie**. *Archie* is a derivation of *archive*. The Archie system consists of Archie servers and associated software. The servers house databases containing references to anonymous FTP documents stored on the Internet.

Gopher, Veronica, Jughead, and WAIS

Gopher is a menu-based system that allows you to access a variety of resources on a system. In many ways, it is the predecessor of today's browser software. **Veronica** and **Jughead** are Gopher add-ons that allow a user to search Gopher servers for menu items that contain specific terms in the menu titles. **WAIS** (wide area information server) is a search engine that allows users to look for documents by specifying keywords.

Search Engines

A variety of browser-oriented search engines have been developed that allow users to find resources on the Internet by supplying keywords. Through **search engines** a user can find links to almost any Internet location. Several commonly used search engines are listed in Table 14–10.

INTERNET TOOLS

A number of tools are available to allow users to access the Internet more effectively. Some of these tools are also available on systems not connected to the Internet.

file transfer protocol (FTP) Part of the TCP/IP protocol suite that provides a mechanism to transfer files between TCP/IP nodes.

Archie An early file searching system that consists of servers and associated software. The servers house databases containing references to anonymous FTP documents stored on the Internet.

Gopher A menu-based system that allows users to access a variety of resources on a system. In many ways, it is the predecessor of today's browser software.

Veronica and Jughead Gopher add-ons that allow a user to search Gopher servers for menu items that contain specific terms in the menu titles.

wide area information server (WAIS) A search engine that allows users to look for documents by specifying keywords.

search engines A variety of browser-oriented systems that allow users to find resources on the Internet by supplying keywords. Through search engines a user can find links to almost any Internet location.

Table 14–10   Common Search Engines

Name	Comments
Yahoo	Topic-based searches
Lycos	Full-text searches
Excite	Full-text searches
Bigbook	U.S. yellow pages
Switchboard	U.S. white pages
Infoseek	Full-text searches
Webcrawler	Full-text searches
AltaVista	Search engine from Digital Equipment Corporation

finger A utility that allows a user to gather information about other network users. Depending on the finger syntax, a user can find out who is logged onto a given network node or get detailed information about a selected user.

Finger

Finger is a utility that allows a user to gather information about other network users. Depending on the finger syntax, a user can find out who is logged onto a given network node or get detailed information about a selected user. For security reasons, some systems do not allow the use of this utility. An edited output of a finger request for logged on users is given in Table 14–11.

ping A tool that allows a user to determine whether a given system is active on the network.

Ping

Ping allows a user to determine whether a given system is active on the network. Some versions of ping also give performance information such as number of hops to the system and speed of the links if the system is available. The output from a ping command is shown in Figure 14–5.

Tracert A tool that allows a user to trace the round trip between the user's node and another node on the network.

Tracert

Tracert allows a user to trace the round trip between the user's node and another node on the network. The output of a Tracert command is given in Figure 14–6.

talk A UNIX utility that allows one user to communicate instantaneously with another user.

Internet relay chat (IRC) A tool that extends talk capability by allowing multiple users to communicate simultaneously.

Talk and Internet Relay Chat

Talk is a UNIX utility that allows one user to communicate instantaneously with another user. Through the talk utility, characters typed at one station are immediately displayed on the other participant's monitor. **Internet relay chat (IRC)** extends the talk capability by allowing multiple users to communicate simultaneously.

Table 14–11   Output of Finger Request

Login	Name	TTY	Date	Time
johnd	John Doe	4	Sep 5	12:12
alicet	Alice Trask	9	Sep 5	15:30
maryb	Mary Boggs	11	Sep 5	14:20

```
C:\WINDOWS>ping -a www.htcomp.net
Pinging www.htcomp.net [207.17.188.94] with 32 bytes of data:
Reply from 207.17.188.94: bytes=32 time=251ms TTL=125
Reply from 207.17.188.94: bytes=32 time=240ms TTL=125
Reply from 207.17.188.94: bytes=32 time=235ms TTL=125
Reply from 207.17.188.94: bytes=32 time=193ms TTL=125
```

Figure 14–5
Output of Ping Request

WHOIS Database

The **WHOIS database** is a repository of data about domains and users.

WHOIS database A repository of data about domains and users.

Web Page Design Tools

Web pages were originally designed by using a text editor to insert the hypertext markup language (HTML) control codes in a document. For example, the title of a page is denoted as *<TITLE>My Home Page<\TITLE>*. Similar control codes are used to provide effects such as bolding and font size, borders, and links.

Today many tools, including leading word processor programs, automatically provide the HTML constructs in a document. An example of a simple HTML document in Microsoft Word is shown in Figure 14–7(a) as a browser image and in Figure 14–7(b) as the text-oriented HTML version.

IPng or IPv6

The expansion of the Internet relative to the number of users, nodes, and types of uses has led to the need to extend the existing version of the IP. The new versions are IPng and IPv6.

The number of Internet nodes has grown exponentially, approximately doubling every year since its inception. Continued expansion is likely because more individuals and companies will connect to the Net, companies will expand their Net usage, and new technologies such as wireless connections coupled with hand-held wireless communicators

```
C:\WINDOWS>tracert 137.39.136.166
Tracing route to ms4-gw.customer.Alter.net [137.39.136.166] over a maximum of 30
hops:
1    188 ms    182 ms    176 ms    ppph101-110.htcomp.net [207.17.189.40]
2    175 ms    182 ms    177 ms    207.17.189.2
3    204 ms    205 ms    198 ms    hmltn-clb-T1.htcomp.net [207.17.189.1]
4    212 ms    206 ms    206 ms    Loopback0.GW1.DFW1.Alter.net [137.39.2.52]
5    254 ms    278 ms    217 ms    421.ATM11-0.CR2.DFW1.Alter.net [137.39.21.10]
6    356 ms    349 ms    358 ms    108.Hssi4-0.CR2.SEA1.Alter.net [137.39.58.129]
7    624 ms      *        627 ms    Fddi1-0.GW2.SEA1.Alter.net [137.39.42.194]
8    304 ms    334 ms    317 ms    ms4-gw.customer.Alter.net {137.39.136.166
Trace complete.
C:\WINDOWS>
```

Figure 14–6
Output of Tracert Command

Figure 14–7a
HTML Document

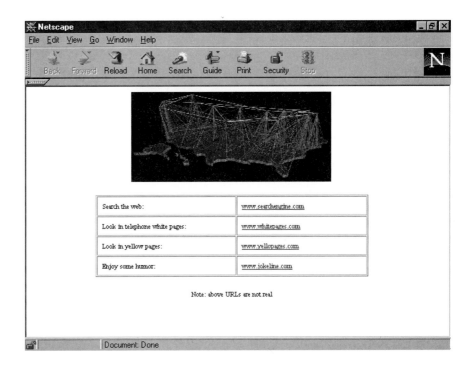

will allow people to connect to the Net from almost anywhere. Think about the number of people that you see using cellular telephones; each of these is a potential Internet user, and the number of cellular customers increases daily. Finally, the way in which the Internet is used will continue to change. One of the major changes is in the type of bits being transferred. The trend has been from text only data to graphics then to audio and video. Audio and video transmissions have needs not found in text and graphics; they must be timely. If a person is listening to a live radio transmission, delays in sending the data will distort the sound. The same is true of video transmission in real time. Couple all of this with the likely growth of the Internet in areas of low use and the Internet as we know it today will need upgrading.

Key Upgrades in IPv6

Expanded Address Space   Currently, Internet addresses are 32 bits long. This gives an address space of approximately 4 billion; however, the actual number of addresses available is less than that because some addresses are reserved (such as broadcast addresses) and some addresses in a class may not be used. IPv6 increases the size of the address field to 128 bits; this will allow up to 3×10^{38} addresses. The actual number of addresses will be smaller, of course.

Quality of Service   To accommodate time-sensitive transmissions such as audio and video, IPv6 will institute service categories to prioritize the flow of data. Transmissions declared as real-time will be provided

```
<HEAD>
<META HTTP-EQUIV="Content-Type" CONTENT="text/html;
charset=windows-1252">
<META NAME="Generator" CONTENT="Microsoft Word 97">
<META NAME="Template" CONTENT="C:\PROGRAM FILES\MICROSOFT
  OFFICE\OFFICE\html.dot">
</HEAD>

<IMG SRC="Image3.gif" WIDTH=299 HEIGHT=131>
<CENTER><TABLE BORDER CELLSPACING=1 CELLPADDING=7 WIDTH=408>
<TR><TD WIDTH="52%" VALIGN="TOP">
Search the web:&#9;&#9;</TD>
<TD WIDTH="48%" VALIGN="TOP">
www.searchengine.com</TD>
</TR>
<TR><TD WIDTH="52%" VALIGN="TOP">
Look in telephone white pages:&#9;</TD>
<TD WIDTH="48%" VALIGN="TOP">
www.whitepages.com</TD>
</TR>
<TR><TD WIDTH="52%" VALIGN="TOP">
Look in yellow pages:&#9;&#9;</TD>
<TD WIDTH="48%" VALIGN="TOP">
www.yellopages.com</TD>
</TR>
<TR><TD WIDTH="52%" VALIGN="TOP">
Enjoy some humor:&#9;&#9;</TD>
<TD WIDTH="48%" VALIGN="TOP">
www.jokeline.com</TD>
</TR>
</TABLE>
</CENTER>

Note: above URLs are not real
```

Figure 14–7b
HTML Document

with improved performance. Priority designations include classifications such as

- uncharacterized traffic
- filler traffic such as net news
- unattended data transfer such as e-mail
- bulk transfer such as file transfers
- interactive transfers
- real-time transfers

IP Header Changes The format of the IP header will change. Changes will be necessary to provide for the larger address space and **quality of service.** Header fields that are currently not used will be dropped. Header extensions are allowed, in essence providing variable-length headers. Extension headers

Table 14–12   IPv6 Header Format

Field	Size (bits)	Comments
Version	4	Contains protocol version 6 for IPv6
Priority	4	Message priority
Flow control	24	Quality of service identifier
Payload length	16	Size in octets of packet following the header
Next header	8	Type of header extension, if any
Hop limit	8	Number of hops allowed before datagram is discarded
Source address	128	Sender's IP address
Destination address	128	Recipient's IP address

can provide functions such as security and integrity, destination-specific information, and routing control. The new header format is given in Table 14–12.

Security and Privacy   To better accommodate secure transmissions, IPv6 will allow extensions to the header to provide security capabilities. The extensions will allow a variety of authentication algorithms and allow detection or elimination of known techniques by which one node can impersonate another node for sending or receiving packets.

Interoperability with IPv4   Naturally, it will be impossible for all Internet nodes to make the conversion to IPv6 at the same instant. Therefore, the new version will be backward compatible with the current version. Implementation of IPv6 may be accomplished in an incremental fashion, allowing nodes to be upgraded to the new version in piecemeal fashion.

We conclude our discussion of the Internet by looking at its relationship to a capability called the information superhighway, which is often mentioned in the press and by politicians.

THE INFORMATION SUPERHIGHWAY

information superhighway A national information system geared toward moving the raw materials (data) and finished goods (information and ideas) of information to their needed locations.

When the United States was primarily an industrial society, the federal government funded the building of a national highway system. This system, augmented by state and local roads, provided transportation for people, raw materials, and finished goods. The national highway system helped establish the strength of the U.S. economy. Today the United States is primarily an information society, with more than half the workforce engaged in the business of information. We now envision a new national highway system geared to moving the raw materials (data) and finished goods (information and ideas) of information to their needed locations. This new highway system is formally called the National Information Infrastructure (NII), but is commonly and most often called the **information superhighway.** If built and used correctly, the information superhighway will help maintain and extend the economic strength of the United States.

Building the Information Superhighway

The federal government was instrumental in funding and building the interstate highway system. In contrast, the information superhighway will be built largely by the private business sector. The role of the federal government will be to provide guidance, legislation, procedures, and prototype systems, and to fund research and development efforts for new technologies. After the information superhighway has been established, the federal government also may subsidize use of the system by public entities such as libraries, schools, and hospitals. In the areas of procedures and legislation, it has already been recognized that privacy and security issues must be addressed. Federal regulations will undoubtedly be required to help control access and set penalties for abuses, just as the Interstate Commerce Commission regulates commercial use of the interstate highways and roads. To provide this guidance the federal government has established an **Information Infrastructure Task Force (IITF)** to oversee information superhighway development.

Like the interstate highway system, the information superhighway will evolve over time. Many technologies needed for building the information superhighway are currently in place; still needed is the investment to integrate and install the technologies so they can be made available throughout the country. Different companies or consortiums may form regional segments of the information superhighway, and then the regional infrastructures will be integrated into a national or perhaps global supernetwork. This evolution will probably be similar to that of the Internet. The information superhighway also is likely to extend across national borders and become a global information superhighway. At this writing, no clear directions have been established and leadership roles have not materialized. However, activity is proceeding at a rapid pace, and the two key events thus far are as follows:

- The information superhighway is envisioned as an integration of communication networks, information and service providers, and computer hardware and software. To provide these components, mergers and alliances are being formed among common carriers, computer hardware and software companies, cable TV companies, and the entertainment industry.
- A cross-industry working team of 28 companies has been formed to design the information superhighway. The original members represent communication, computer, banking, publishing, and cable TV companies. The cross-industry working team has formed four subgroups: applications, services, architecture, and portability. The role of the first three is apparent from their names. The portability subgroup will address the needs of mobile communication.

The architecture of the information superhighway will probably resemble that of the Internet in that a high-speed backbone network of fiber optic and satellite links will speed data from one region to another. Local delivery

Information Infrastructure Task Force A federal government agency established to oversee information superhighway development.

will be established by regional providers over fiber optic cable, coaxial cable, and copper media. Businesses that make heavy use of the information superhighway will probably have the data delivered to their premises by fiber optic cable. Local distribution within the company will be over fiber optic cable, coaxial cable, or twisted-pair wires.

For personal use, it is unlikely that fiber optic cable will be brought into homes. Instead, fiber optic cable will bring the data to a local distribution point from which coaxial cable or twisted-pair wires will distribute the data to individual homes. There are several reasons for copper-based delivery to individual subscribers. In many locations cable TV companies have already installed this type of delivery mechanism and it can be used for the last-mile delivery system. The data speeds required for home use also will be much lower than those of many businesses, so the higher speed of fiber optic cable will not be necessary. Finally, the current cost of fiber optic cable and the difficulty of splicing and making new connections favor the use of copper-based end delivery. Figure 14–8 illustrates a potential information superhighway implementation.

Information Superhighway Uses

Several potential information superhighway uses are as follows:

- A business might use the information superhighway to conduct a conference among employees in different locations.
- A software company might use the information superhighway to distribute software directly to customers.
- A publishing company might distribute books or magazines directly to readers or perhaps to a local outlet for on-demand printing.
- Companies and individuals could subscribe to information utilities such as stock market and financial news and congressional records.
- Companies and individuals will be able to shop for merchandise via online catalogs and make airline, car, hotel, and entertainment reservations.
- Movies and games may be available on demand.
- Education classes at all levels may be available and allow people to learn new skills at their home or office.
- Some types of health care may be delivered remotely. A physician may be able to view patients at remote locations, coach paramedical personnel on procedures, and recommend treatment.
- E-mail and video images may be exchanged. Interactive use of such technologies may give rise to online discussion groups and conferencing.

From these few suggestions it is apparent that possible information superhighway uses are varied. The information superhighway will deliver far more that just data; it can deliver information in a variety of formats including data, voice, and video. At issue is how individuals and companies

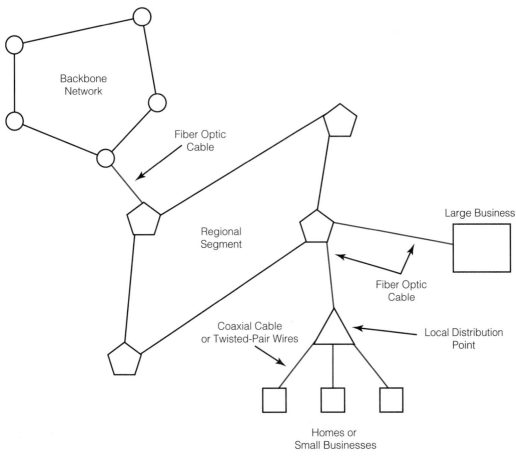

Figure 14–8
Potential Information Superhighway Implementation

will gain access to these resources and how much it will cost to use them. For some services, costs of more than $200 per connect hour are likely. Access to the information superhighway also will require the media connections and equipment necessary to send and receive the signals.

Social Implications

The information superhighway is likely to bring a profound change in the way businesses operate and in individuals' private lives. The costs required for information superhighway connection and services may also lead to new social issues. People who cannot afford these services will have fewer opportunities than those who have the services. Consequently, publicly funded access through schools, libraries, and civic centers may be needed to ensure that all members of society have access to the opportunities the information superhighway will provide.

SUMMARY

All nodes on the Internet must have a unique address. Currently, addresses are 32-bit entities but the next version of the IP protocol, IPv6, will use 128-bit addresses. An Internet address has several representations: the 32-bit number, a dotted quad, a fully qualified domain name, and a Universal Resource Locator (URL). The first portion of the 32-bit address represents a network number and the remaining bits represent node numbers within that subnet. Addresses fall into several classes: A, B, C, and D. The difference between the classes is the number of bits used to denote network addresses and node addresses.

A node may have its Internet address assigned statically or dynamically. A user who gains access to the Internet through an Internet service provider (ISP) will probably use dynamic address assignment. In this case, the ISP will have a range of addresses that can be used by its subscribers. When a user connects to the ISP's host, an available address will be assigned. The protocol used for dynamic address assignment is the dynamic host configuration protocol (DHCP).

For Internet nodes on LANs, the address resolution protocol (ARP) is used to transform an IP address into a MAC address. This translation is necessary because message delivery on a LAN occurs at the data link layer and an IP address is maintained at the network layer.

Routing between nodes and networks on the Internet is done by the IP protocol, which operates at the network layer. Routers are devices responsible for moving messages between networks. Each router maintains a routing table that contains information about paths to other networks. Through the information contained in the routing table, a router can move a message through the Internet toward its destination network.

In the United States the term *information superhighway* has been commonly used to describe the capabilities of the Internet. The U.S. government has established several organizations to monitor the progress of the information superhighway and to provide technical assistance for some research efforts. For the most part, the information superhighway will be funded by the public sector.

KEY TERMS

address resolution protocol (ARP)	finger
Archie	Gopher
class A address	Information Infrastructure Task
class B address	Force (IITF)
class C address	information superhighway
class D address	Internet relay chat (IRC)
domain name	IPng
domain name server	IPv6
dotted quad	Jughead
dynamic addressing	ping
dynamic host configuration proto-	quality of service
col (DHCP)	router
file transfer protocol (FTP)	routing table

search engine
simple mail transfer protocol (SMTP)
simple network management protocol (SNMP)
subnet
subnet address mask
talk

Telnet
Tracert
Universal Resource Locator (URL)
Veronica
WHOIS database
wide area information server
  (WAIS)

REVIEW QUESTIONS

1. Describe class A, B, C, and D Internet addresses.

2. Define and give an example of a(n)
   a. dotted quad
   b. URL
   c. Domain name

3. What is the hierarchy of an Internet domain address?

4. List five root level domain names that do not represent countries. List what each represents.

5. What does the InterNIC do?

6. Describe subnet masking. Why are subnet masks used?

7. Describe the operation of the dynamic host configuration protocol.

8. What is the address resolution protocol (ARP) and why is it necessary?

9. What information is contained in an IP routing table? What does each item represent?

10. What is anonymous FTP? What is the usual procedure for user ID and passwords when using anonymous FTP?

11. Describe the capabilities of
    a. finger
    b. ping
    c. WHOIS database
    d. Web page design tools

12. Describe the features of the key upgrades that will be available with IPv6.

13. What is the information superhighway?

14. What is the role of the U.S. government in setting up and operating the information superhighway?

PROBLEMS AND EXERCISES

1. A company has a class B address space and wants to define eight subnets using this address space. The dotted quad for the address is 131.10.0.0. What is the subnet mask for this? List the dotted quad representation for each subnet.

2. Access the Internet and search for IPv6 using three different search engines. What differences did you notice?

3. If you have finger and ping available, use each to see what information they provide.

4. What is the dotted quad representation of your Internet provider's URL?

CHAPTER 15

WAN Implementations

CHAPTER OBJECTIVES

After studying this chapter you should be able to

- Discuss the components and workings of IBM's Systems Network Architecture
- Describe the problems inherent in international networks

In this chapter you will learn about a specific WAN implementation, IBM's Systems Network Architecture (SNA), and some issues surrounding international networks. The chapter concludes with a Case Study that illustrates some considerations for implementing a WAN.

VENDOR WANS

Vendor offerings play a major role in network implementation and configuration, with almost every major computer vendor offering networking capabilities. Vendor networks compete with each other, with packet switching or X.25 networks, and with common carrier networks. The following section is devoted to IBM's SNA, which has become a de facto industry standard. Most networks currently being designed on IBM mainframe systems use SNA. If another vendor's equipment interfaces with an IBM network, it will probably do so via an SNA interface or TCP/IP. Many computer manufacturers have implemented or are implementing the ability to attach to an SNA network as a type of SNA node.

IBM'S SYSTEMS NETWORK ARCHITECTURE

Systems Network Architecture (SNA) IBM's architecture for building a computer network. Encompasses hardware and software components, establishing sessions between users, and capabilities such as message and file distribution services.

Systems Network Architecture (SNA), announced by IBM in 1974, provides the framework for implementing data communication networks using IBM or IBM-compatible equipment. SNA is not a product per se but a blueprint for how hardware, software, and users interact in exchanging data on IBM systems. A network based on SNA consists of a variety of hardware and software components in a well-defined configuration.

Why SNA?

Since the 1960s IBM has been the leader in computer sales and installations. The move to SNA was prompted not so much by competition from the outside but by competition from within IBM itself. Before 1974 the implementation of communication systems had been somewhat random: If a new terminal was developed, a new or modified access method and data link protocol were likely to accompany it. By 1974 IBM was offering more than 200 different models of communication hardware, 35 different device access methods, and more than a dozen data link protocols. Continuing this product proliferation would have created an enormous burden for IBM's support and maintenance. SNA was the result of integrating all these functions into one cohesive network architecture.

The objective of any network is to enable users to communicate with one another. Users in SNA are either people working at a terminal or operator's console or applications that provide services for other programs or terminal users. Thus, a user is an entity with some degree of intelligence. A terminal is not a user, although the terms *terminal operator* and *terminal* are often used synonymously. SNA was developed to provide communication paths and dialogue rules between users. This is accomplished via a layered network architecture similar to the OSI reference model.

half-session layer Represents a single layer (transmission control, flow control, and presentation service) in the four-layer definition of SNA functional layers.

physical unit (PU) In SNA, a hardware unit. Four physical units have been defined: Type 5, host processor; Type 4, communication controller; Type 2, cluster or programmable controller; and Type 1, a terminal or controller that is not programmable.

SNA Layers

The early releases of SNA referenced either six or four functional layers. The discrepancy between a six-layer and a four-layer definition is explained by the fact that layers three through five are sometimes called a single layer, known as the **half-session layer.** The lowest OSI reference model layer, the physical layer, is not usually specified in SNA, nor is the application layer included. However, both layers obviously must exist. The four-layer definition is given in Table 15–1. The six layers are identified in parentheses, where applicable. In the current version of SNA, the layering has been redefined. The presentation service layer is omitted and the service manager is now called the function management layer. Although the layering carries different names, the functions each performs are similar to those for the OSI reference model.

SNA also defines four distinct hardware groupings called **physical units (PUs).** The four physical units are numbered 1, 2, 4, and 5, with no PU currently assigned to number 3. These device types are listed in Table 15–2. The

Table 15–1   SNA Layers

Layer 1	Data link control
Layer 2	Path control

Layer 3	Half-session layer, consisting of
	    Transmission control (layer 3)
	    Flow control (layer 4)
	    Presentation service (layer 5)

Layer 4	Service manager (layer 6)

hardware configuration consists of IBM or IBM-compatible CPUs, communication controllers, terminal cluster controllers, and terminals, printers, or workstations. These are all connected by any of the media discussed in Chapter 2. Other vendors' equipment may also be included in the network if that equipment conforms to the SNA protocols. The preferred data link protocol is SDLC, but accommodations have been made for other protocols such as BSC and asynchronous.

Logical Units and Sessions

Users of SNA are represented in the system by entities known as **logical units (LUs).** An LU is usually implemented as a software function in a device with some intelligence, such as a CPU or controller. The dialogue between two system users is known as a **session.** Because a logical unit is the agent of a user, when one user wants to establish a session with another user, the LUs are involved in establishing the communication path between the two. A session involves two different LUs; the activities and resources used by one LU in a session are called a half-session. In the SNA layering in Table 15–1, the half-session layers represent the functions that would be performed by an LU for its user.

Session Types   Many different types of sessions can be requested, such as program to terminal, program to program, or terminal to terminal. Each category can be further stratified as to terminal type (interactive, batch, or printer) and application type (batch, interactive, word processing, or the like). One LU also can represent several different users, and a user can have multiple sessions in progress concurrently. If a terminal (operator) wants to

logical unit (LU) In IBM's SNA, a unit that represents a system user. Sessions exist between LUs or between an LU and the SSCP. Several types of LUs have been defined.

session A dialogue between two system users.

Table 15–2   SNA Physical Units

Physical Unit	Hardware Component
Type 1	A terminal device (e.g., 3278)
Type 2	A cluster controller (e.g., 3274)
Type 4	A communications controller (e.g., 3725)
Type 5	A host processor (e.g., 4381 or 3094)

retrieve a record from a database, the terminal must use the services of an application program to obtain the record. Each user—the terminal and the database application—is represented by an LU. The terminal LU issues a request to enter into a session with the database application LU. The application LU can either accept or reject the session request. The LU typically rejects transactions for security reasons (the requesting LU lacks authority to establish a session with the application LU) or because of congestion (the application LU has already entered into the maximum number of sessions it can support). If the session request is granted, a communication path is established between the terminal and the application. The two users continue to communicate until one of them terminates the session. Figure 15–1 shows several sessions between users communicating through their respective LUs.

LU Types Seven LU types have been defined within SNA. These are numbered from 0 to 7, with the definition for LU type 5 omitted. It is important to note that the LU types refer to session types, not to a specific LU. Thus, a specific LU can participate in a type 1 LU session with one LU and a type 4 LU session with another. For two LUs to communicate they must both support and use the same LU session type. Of the seven LU types, all

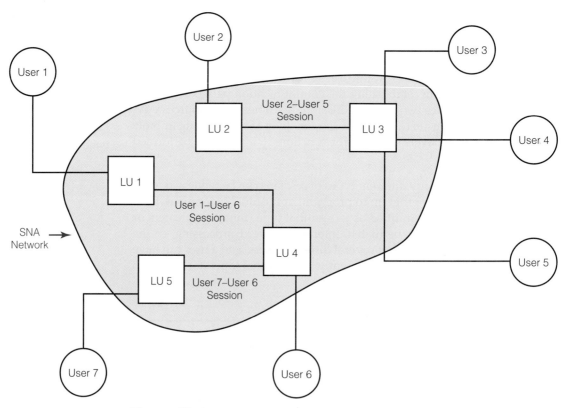

Figure 15–1
SNA Sessions and Logical Units

but types 0 and 6 address sessions with hardware devices such as printers and terminals. LU type 6 is defined for program-to-program communication. It has evolved through two definitions, LU 6.0 and LU 6.1, to its current definition, LU 6.2. LU 6.2 is a key SNA capability.

There are several significant aspects of LU 6.2. First, **LU 6.2** defines a protocol for program-to-program communication. Most of the other LU types are somewhat hardware oriented, involving sessions between 3270 devices, printers, and so on. A program-to-program communication interface is more general and can have wider uses than hardware-oriented interfaces. Second, program-to-program sessions provide a communication path for applications distributed over multiple nodes. Two applications communicating with each other are not required to be in the same node. This capability supports transaction processing systems with multiple processing nodes. For example, an inventory inquiry can start on a network node in a sales office and communicate with a warehouse node application to determine whether stock exists to cover a pending order. Finally, and perhaps most significantly, a program-to-program interface is more generic than a session type involving specific hardware devices. This means that other vendors' equipment can enter into SNA sessions with an application process running in an IBM processor as long as the communicating program in the vendor's processor adheres to the session rules. This allows an application on vendor A's hardware to enter into a transaction with a database application running on an IBM node.

Many vendors have implemented an LU 6.2 capability for their SNA interface because such an interface can be made device independent. Given the configuration illustrated in Figure 15–2, a program in vendor X's system can interface to its terminal device on one side and to an IBM application on the other. This logically provides the ability for a non-IBM terminal to interface to an IBM application system. Without LU 6.2, vendor X would need to appear to the IBM application as one of the supported hardware types, such as

LU 6.2 An SNA logical unit type representing a program-to-program session.

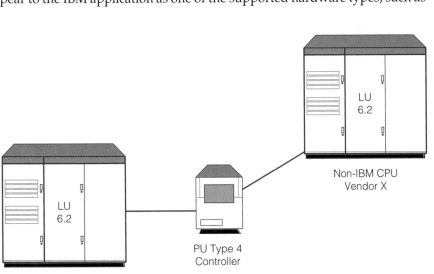

PU Type 5

PU Type 4
Controller

LU 6.2

Non-IBM CPU
Vendor X

Figure 15–2
Non-IBM Vendor in an LU 6.2 Session

a 3270 terminal or cluster controller. The International Standards Organization (ISO) also has agreed on a transaction interface that is compatible with IBM's LU 6.2 session.

Systems Services Control Point

As mentioned above, a dialogue between two users within the SNA environment is called a session. A supervisor or intermediary is involved in establishing a session. In SNA this extremely important entity is known as the **Systems Services Control Point (SSCP);** it resides in a host processor, which is a physical unit type 5. Not all PU type 5 devices house an SSCP. The SSCP is the software controlling its host's portion of the network. The devices controlled by the host and its SSCP represent a **domain.**

Networks implemented under early versions of SNA had only one SSCP and thus only one host computer. The entire network was controlled by this host. In 1979 SNA was enhanced to allow multiple-host systems, and hence multiple domains. This became necessary because large SNA networks were being implemented. Multiple SSCPs were better able to manage many devices and sessions. A two-domain SNA configuration is shown in Figure 15–3.

Within a given domain the SSCP is the controlling entity. It is responsible for the physical and logical units within its domain. In fulfilling this obligation, the SSCP manages its units, including unit initialization, maintaining the

Systems Services Control Point (SSCP) In IBM's SNA, the process that controls a domain. It is responsible for initiating network components, establishing sessions, and maintaining unit status.

domain In IBM's SNA, the network components managed by an SSCP.

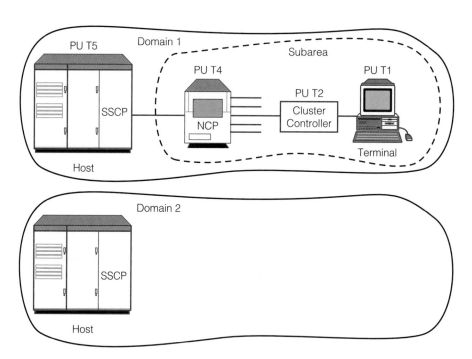

Figure 15–3
IBM SNA Network

status of individual units, placing units online and offline as necessary, and serving as mediator in the establishment of sessions. Physical units subordinate to an SSCP must be able to carry on a dialogue with the SSCP. To accomplish this, a subset of the SSCP functionality, called a **Physical Unit Control Point (PUCP)**, resides in SNA nodes that do not contain an SSCP. A PUCP is responsible for connecting the node to and disconnecting the node from the SNA network.

Addressing

For one user to communicate with another, an address is required because messages are sent to a specific unit using its address. Addressable components in SNA are called **Network Addressable Units (NAUs).** An NAU can be an SSCP, an LU, or a PU. Network addresses are hierarchical in nature. You have already learned that an SNA network consists of domains. Domains consist of subareas. A **subarea** consists of a communication controller (such as a 3745) and all its NAUs or of a host/SSCP together with all of the locally attached NAUs. Figure 15–4 shows two subareas. Each subarea has a unique address. NAUs within one subarea are known by a local address. An SNA address consists of two parts, a subarea address and a unit address. The combination of subarea address and unit address uniquely identifies an NAU in the network. In SNA, addresses may be either 16 or 23 bits. The longer address is known as **extended addressing,** which allows for a larger number of NAUs in a network.

In extended addressing mode, the first 8 bits represent the subarea and the last 15 bits represent the device within the subarea. The 16-bit address can be decomposed into a subarea and device address on a network-by-network

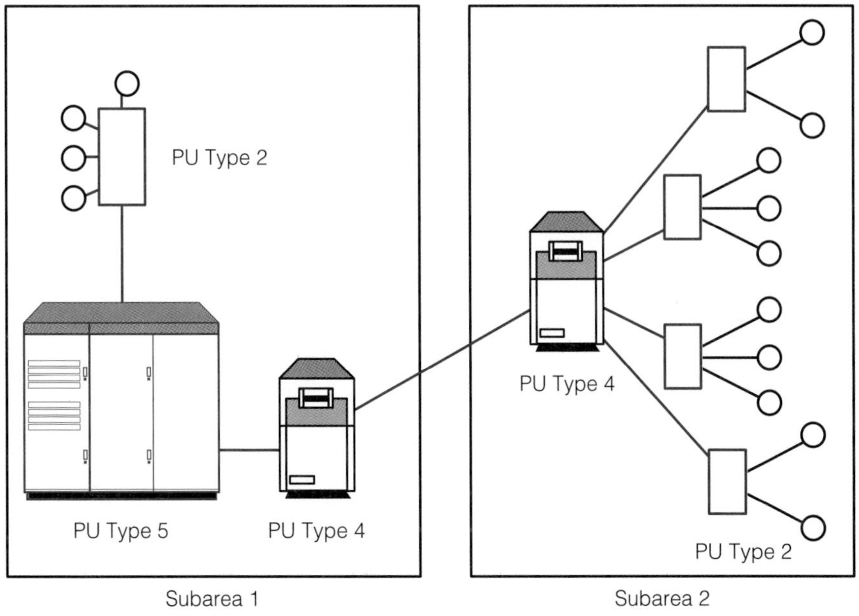

Physical Unit Control Point (PUCP) In IBM's SNA, a physical unit control point resides in nodes that do not contain an SSCP. The PUCP is responsible for connecting the node to and disconnecting the node from the network.

Network Addressable Unit (NAU) In IBM's SNA, any device that has a network address, such as logical units and physical units.

subarea The parts of a domain, consisting of a communication controller and all its NAUs or of a host/SSCP together with all locally attached NAUs.

extended addressing The 23-bit address representing the combination of subarea address and unit address that uniquely identifies an NAU and allows for a larger number of NAUs in a network.

PU Type 2

PU Type 4

PU Type 5   PU Type 4

PU Type 2

Subarea 1   Subarea 2

Figure 15–4
SNA Network with Two Subareas

end-to-end routing
Routing for which at
least one of the nodes
must be a type 5 physi-
cal unit or terminal and
the path is determined
and maintained through
the entire session.

virtual routing No permanently established
path exists; instead,
each node consults its
routing table to deter-
mine which node
should next receive the
message.

**Network Control Pro-
gram (NCP)** A data
communication pro-
gram that helps man-
age a communication
network. Specifically, a
program that runs in
IBM's 37xx line of com-
munication controllers.

**Advanced Communica-
tions Facility (ACF)** The
ACF provides interdo-
main communication,
improved error and
testing capabilities, and
dynamic device configu-
ration.

**Network Performance
Analyzer (NPA)** The
NPA provides perfor-
mance information for
the system, including in-
formation on lines,
buffers, errors, queue
lengths, and data trans-
mission rates.

**Network Problem De-
termination Aid (NPDA)**
The NPDA collects,
maintains, and reports
information on error
conditions within the
network. It also allows
for testing of the sys-
tem concurrent with
production operations.

basis; two networks can decompose the address in different ways. One network could have an 8-bit address for both subareas and devices, whereas another could adopt a split of 7 bits for subarea and 9 bits for devices.

Communication Between Users

If users A and B are in the same domain, communication between them is
established as follows. The LU representing user A sends a message to the
SSCP requesting a session with user B. On behalf of user A, the SSCP contacts the user B LU to request a session and also to provide information
about user A, including user A's access profile and type. User B either accepts or rejects the session request. If the session is rejected, user A is so notified. If user B accepts the invitation to enter into a session with A, a
communication path must be established. Communication between users in
different domains is established in a way similar to that for a single domain,
except that the SSCPs in both domains are involved: The request goes from
an LU to its SSCP to the SSCP in the other domain and then to its LU.

Path establishment was easy in early SNA implementations because
only one path existed between LUs. Currently, two routing methods are
supported: end-to-end routing and virtual routing. In **end-to-end routing,**
for which at least one of the nodes must be a Type 5 PU or terminal, the path
is determined and maintained through the entire session (unless the path is
broken). In **virtual routing** no permanently established path exists; instead,
each node consults its routing table to determine to which node the message
should be forwarded. The path control half-session layer is responsible for
path allocation. Each available path is given a weighting that assists in route
determination. A route might be selected based on best use according to
such factors as security, speed, and propagation delay (as for satellite links).
Up to five different paths between any two LUs can be described.

Additional SNA Elements and Capabilities

Network Control Program   The **Network Control Program (NCP),**
which resides in a communication controller such as the 3745, controls communication lines and the devices attached to them. It works with the Virtual
Terminal Access Method (VTAM) that resides in the host. VTAM serves as
the interface between application programs and the network.

Advanced Communications Facility   The **Advanced Communications
Facility (ACF)** was introduced in 1979. It provides such features as interdomain communication, improved error and testing capabilities, and dynamic
device configuration.

Network Performance Analyzer The **Network Performance
Analyzer (NPA)** provides performance information for the system, including information on lines, buffers, errors, queue lengths, and data transmission rates.

Network Problem Determination Aid The **Network Problem
Determination Aid (NPDA)** collects, maintains, and reports information on

error conditions within the network. It also allows for testing of the system concurrent with production operations.

Netview, Netview/PC, and Netview/6000 In 1986 IBM announced two network management packages for use in SNA systems. Netview runs on IBM hosts, and Netview/PC on microcomputers. With Netview, IBM has consolidated several previous network management facilities (including NPDA) and enhanced them to provide more comprehensive management capabilities. Netview/6000 was introduced in 1992 and is designed to provide network management functions for open systems, specifically non-SNA networks. The functions found in Netview are covered in Chapter 18, which addresses network management.

SNA Distribution Services **SNA Distribution Services (SNADS)** allow users to exchange documents using the SNA network. Document interchange differs from the typical SNA session. In a typical SNA session the sender and receiver are synchronized regarding information exchange. By *synchronized* we mean that the users communicate (through their LUs) and agree to carry on a conversation. In contrast, with document exchanges the users may not be synchronized. A sender may dispatch a document without first coordinating the transmission with the recipient. The recipient can then request access to the document at its convenience. SNADS provides the ability to distribute documents in such a manner. This is particularly helpful for office automation applications such as network mail and document distribution.

> **SNA Distribution Services (SNADS)** An SNA facility that provides asynchronous distribution of documents throughout a network.

Other SNA Capabilities SNA is being continually upgraded to meet changing communication needs. It has evolved from an IBM-only network architecture to include internetworking with other networks. Accommodations made in this regard include

- support for the TCP/IP protocol suite
- accommodations for LAN interfaces
- alterations that reduce the hierarchical nature of the network and provide support for peer-to-peer communication via advanced peer-to-peer networking
- support for distributed databases
- internetworking

Advanced Peer-to-Peer Networking

As we noted above, SNA is a proprietary network implementation. Proprietary networks were common in the 1960s and 1970s, but today open architectures are the norm. In a traditional SNA network, sessions are established when two entities need to communicate, and the session setup is mediated by the SSCP; this works well when all components and protocols are SNA compatible, but is a problem on open networks with a variety of components and protocols that are not SNA compatible. For example, today's networks typically consist of several LANs connected to a WAN, with computers ranging from desktop systems to mainframes. With the advent of open systems, it became necessary for IBM to extend SNA to enable communication between such objects in a peer-to-peer fashion. Advanced peer-to-peer networking (APPN) is a major part of this capability. It allows SNA users to retain their investment in SNA hardware, software, and personnel while opening the network to a multitude of devices.

APPN allows independent LUs to enter into sessions without the co-operation of the SSCP. APPN reduces the dependence on a host node and allows applications to specify session characteristics such as the type of path and security required. Non-IBM vendors have implemented APPN interfaces on their systems. This capability provides an easy way for programs to independently enter into a session and provides a way for applications that run on non-IBM computers to communicate via the services of SNA.

With APPN, LUs and a session are still required. What changes is the way the session is established. In the original version of SNA, LUs were given a network address, as described earlier, and hence were NAUs. APPN networks do not use the same type of addressing. A client may request to establish a session with a server somewhere in the network. APPN maintains directories of resources and establishes a route between the client and the server. A session between the two is established, and communication between the client and server is established. APPN allows any end user on the network to directly establish a connection with any other end user.

APPN provides several services in addition to peer-to-peer networking. Message traffic priorities can be set via a class-of-service capability. This reduces congestion delays for high-priority messages. High-performance routing provides the ability to route traffic around link failures and reconfigure routes to avoid congestion.

INTERNATIONAL NETWORKS

Data communication networks are not confined to national boundaries, and today many companies are international in scope. International computer networks help many of these companies manage their data and provide communication among employees. International networks are used by banks for money transfer and financial planning applications. With international networks, manufacturing companies can schedule production of parts in multiple locations for assembly at a central location. All international companies can use international networks and e-mail for immediate, timely communication. E-mail also helps eliminate the problems of time-zone differences. For example, working hours may not overlap between offices in England and Australia, but e-mail provides quick communication during an employee's normal working hours.

Designing and implementing international networks is more difficult than building a national network. The problems that may be encountered include politics, security, regulations, hardware, and language.

Politics

On occasion the problems to be resolved with international networks are political rather than technical. One company reported that it was given permission to install a microwave link in a particular country. However, that country's government suggested that the company double the capacity of the network. Upon completion, the microwave system was nationalized by the government, and the company that built it was "given" half of the carrying capacity of the network.[1]

Security

As messages pass from node to node in a network, it is possible for them to be captured and for someone to read or even change the contents of the message. Furthermore, if a company is using public networks such as the Internet, the possibility of message tampering is greater because the message flows through systems outside the control of the company. Consequently, for secure transmissions, messages should be encrypted with a strong encryption algorithm. We discuss encryption in Chapter 19.

Regulations

Networks require communication links. In many countries the communication networks are controlled by an agency we shall call the postal, telephone, and telegraph (PTT) authority. The PTT often is a government agency or government-regulated agency with exclusive rights to provide communication facilities. The regulations under which the PTTs operate generally were designed for their original mission of postal, telephone, and telegraph communication. These regulations sometimes impede the establishment of international data communication systems.

Sometimes regulations are established to protect or subsidize certain interests. In some countries, restrictions exist regarding which equipment can be connected to a network. A few countries require that hardware used in a network be manufactured in whole or in part within the country. Pricing regulations in some countries are structured so data communication services help subsidize individual telephone services. Regulations often prohibit competition in providing communication facilities. Thus, it is often difficult to set up a network using services provided by a single communication carrier. Many PTTs recognize that regulations must be changed to meet the needs of international networks; therefore, some countries have begun to deregulate their communication industries. Deregulation typically means opening competition regarding equipment that can be attached to the network and the cost and provision of communication facilities.

International networks sometimes conflict with other national interests. Some countries impose an import duty on software. Sometimes the duty is

---

[1] Jenkins, Avery. "Networks in a Strange Land." *Computerworld Focus: Critical Connections*, Volume 15, March 1986.

on the value of the carrying medium, such as a magnetic tape; other countries tax the value of the imported software. International networks provide the ability to import software over the network, making the collection of tariffs more difficult. Some countries view international networks as potential threats to national security. Data regarding national resources, the economy, and people can be more easily collected and transmitted to another country through international networks. Several nations are attempting to legislate solutions to these concerns.

Hardware

As mentioned earlier, in some countries restrictions exist regarding the source or type of equipment that can be attached to the communication facilities of a PTT. Several countries require that all or part of the equipment used within the country be locally manufactured. Some do not require the equipment to be manufactured in-country but still restrict the equipment that can be used to that manufactured by a selected group of companies. Most countries require that equipment attached to communication networks meet minimum technical specifications. Specifications also differ among countries. A communication controller that is certified for operation in the United States may not meet the tighter specifications for grounding that exist in Australia.

Another technical difference that must be accommodated is variations in power supplies among countries. When ordering equipment for a specific node, one must be sure that the equipment's power supply needs are consistent with the power available in that location. Many times new hardware also must be certified by a host country before it can be attached to the communication network. For example, a company that introduces a fax controller that connects to the common carrier's network must first undergo testing and evaluation by the host country. It is not unusual for certification to take several months and require that equipment and circuit schematics be provided for the evaluation process. Thus, introduction of new equipment into a network can incur substantial delays.

Language

Another problem needing resolution in international networks is language. Network managers at different locations must be able to communicate to resolve differences. Several different countries and hence several different languages may be involved in solving one problem. This makes it necessary to have not only technical expertise but also linguistic expertise in the network management organization. Data generated in one location may need to be translated when used in another country. Such translation may be manual or through language translation programs. Accompanying the need to translate from one language to another is the need to have hardware and software capable of displaying local character sets, such as Kanji in China and Japan, Hongul in Korea, and Farsi in Arab countries. Accommodations also must be made when the number of characters in a national character set exceeds the capacity of a particular code. For example,

7-bit ASCII codes can accommodate 128 distinct characters, but there are more than 30,000 Kanji characters.

Other Issues

An international network typically involves the coordination of several communication providers. One of the easier methods of creating an international network is to use the services of existing X.25 networks. The ease derives from the fact that most public X.25 network providers have established interconnections and the network implementer need not be concerned about PTT interfaces. If a company decides to procure exclusive links such as leased lines, creating the network may be more difficult. Responsibility for determining the correct interfaces and resolving problems must be assumed by the company. Problem resolution can be somewhat difficult in an international network. Consider a link from Australia to France. The end-to-end connection may use links from Australia to the United States, to England, and then to France. Thus, four PTTs, several protocols, a variety of vendor equipment, and several time zones may be involved. If a problem arises in transmitting data between the French and Australian nodes, the sheer number of vendors involved can cause delays. On more than one occasion a problem has been allowed to continue while two PTTs debated which was responsible for the problem.

Pricing an international network can present several difficulties. First, collecting tariff information can be time-consuming. When multiple nodes exist within a country, we typically must deal with local tariffs and international tariffs. In some cases, there may be multiple circuit providers, a variety of available rates, and variations between local and long-distance rates. In addition to tariffs for the use of lines, in some countries we also must determine the costs of taxes applied to the movement of data over a country's borders and taxes on imported software.

The International Telecommunications Union (ITU) and other international communication organizations realize the existing limitations and problems in implementing international connections and are addressing the issues. Standards such as OSI, X.25, and X.400 e-mail interface ease the burden of establishing international networks. Deregulation of the communication industries in some countries has allowed the introduction of new equipment and competition among providers of communication links. Issues such as the rights of communication facilities provided from a foreign country, such as a Canadian PTT operating circuits in the United States, are being discussed. All these efforts should make establishing international networks easier; however, the problems inherent in international networks will always be greater than those for domestic networks. Another international body, the **General Agreement on Trade and Tariffs (GATT),** an organization of 97 nations, has proposed a treaty that will ease the problems of international networks. Among the treaty provisions are stipulations regarding the use and cost of private lines.

General Agreement on Trade and Tariffs (GATT) An organization of 97 nations that has proposed an international treaty that includes stipulations regarding the use and cost of private lines.

The Syncrasy Corporation, once again expanding, intends to open retail outlets in several additional cities. A tentative list of these new cities is given in Table 15–3.

NETWORK REQUIREMENTS

Each city on the network will have at least one processor, and the existing network, discussed in Chapter 11, might be abandoned if a better configuration exists.

Reliability

The requirements of the new network include high reliability among the major centers in New York City, Chicago, Kansas City, and Los Angeles and among the European cities. For the Pacific area, however, it has been decided that distance and the related communication costs prohibit the redundant links required for reliability. Reliability for Syncrasy means that all nodes can continue to communicate should a link fail and that all remaining nodes can still communicate should a node fail.

Low Cost

The second design criterion is cost. Syncrasy wants the lowest-cost network that can provide the necessary functions.

U.S. NETWORK CONFIGURATION

The long-distance network in the United States must, of course, interface with the LAN designed in Chapter 9. The gateway function should be performed by a processor attached to both networks.

Backbone Network

The need for reliability in the four major U.S. cities demands a loop configuration, as depicted in Figure 15–5. At a minimum, the network routing algorithm must be able to switch paths if a node or link fails. This type of

Table 15–3   Expansion Cities

Seattle	Detroit	Rome	Phoenix
Denver	Oslo	Boston	Montreal
Hong Kong	Miami	Toronto	Sydney
Dallas	London	Tokyo	Washington, D.C.
Paris	Mexico City	Philadelphia	Frankfurt

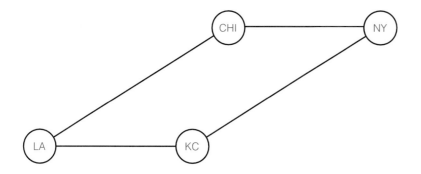

Figure 15–5
Backbone Network

configuration is sometimes called a backbone network, and the nodes are called backbone nodes. From the mileage chart given in Table 15–4, it can be determined that the backbone network in Figure 15–5 is the minimum-distance configuration.

One possible U.S. configuration is depicted in Figure 15–6. The backbone network serves as the delivery system for many of the nodes, such as from Seattle to Boston. However, a message sent from Seattle to San Francisco will not travel through the backbone system. Syncrasy has decided that the backbone nodes should be dedicated to the network task, so they will not be used for application processing. This decision was made because the amount of anticipated message traffic is high enough to allow dedicated backbone nodes. To increase the reliability of the backbone network, fault-tolerant computers were chosen.

REMAINING U.S. NETWORK

Three primary options were considered in configuring the remainder of the network: leased media, switched media, and public data network (PDN) (see Chapter 4). Which of these is most cost-effective is a function of distance and message traffic. Distance becomes a factor when determining the rates charged for leased and switched connections; it usually is not a factor with respect to PDN rates. Message traffic affects the connect time for switched connections and the packet charges for a PDN. For all U.S. nodes not in the backbone network, an analysis was performed to determine

Table 15–4   Mileage Chart

	Chicago	Houston	Kansas City	L.A.	N.Y.C.	S.F.
Atlanta	708	791	822	2191	854	2483
Chicago		1091	542	2048	809	2173
Houston			743	1555	1610	1911
Kansas City				1547	1233	1861
Los Angeles					2794	387
New York City						2930

Figure 15–6
Possible U.S. Network

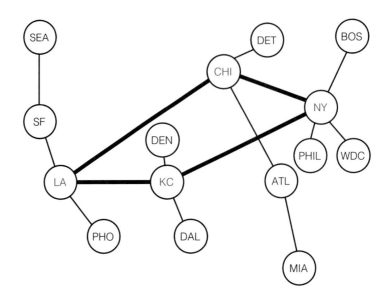

which of the three options would be most cost-effective. The analysis for the Seattle node follows.

Seattle–San Francisco Line Costs

The following rate information on the three options for connecting the Seattle node to the San Francisco node (the closest) is approximate and is intended for use only in this Case Study. Actual rates may vary. Leased line rates are given in Table 15–5, switched telephone rates in Table 15–6, and PDN rates in Table 15–7. Additional comparison information must be derived. To evaluate the switched connections, the number of connections per day and the total amount of connect time must be approximated. Seattle, a low-volume node at a network extremity, will not be involved in store and forward operations. In contrast, the San Francisco node will originate and receive its own messages and will forward messages to and from Seattle and other nodes. It is estimated that there will be three connections per day, requiring 250 min total connect time. A message traffic of 30,000 characters per day also is anticipated. A 23-day work month is assumed. The total distance between Seattle and San Francisco is 810 mi. Leased line charges are as follows:

First 100 mi @ $2.52/mi + 710 mi @ $0.94/mi = $252 + $667.40 = $919.40

Table 15–5 Leased Line Rates, Seattle to San Francisco

First 100 miles	$2.52 per mile (includes monthly service charge fee)
Next 900 miles (101–1000)	$0.94 per mile
Each mile over 1000	$0.58 per mile

Table 15–6　Switched Line Rates, Seattle to San Francisco

First minute of connect time	$0.60
Each additional minute	$0.40

Daily switched line costs are

3 connections @ $0.60/first minute
$$+ \text{247 remaining min @ } \$0.40/\text{min} = \$1.80 + \$98.80 = \$100.60$$

Monthly switched line costs are therefore

$$\text{23 days @ } \$100.60/\text{day} = \$2313.80$$

No additional telephone service charges are included in the analysis because telephones are already installed on the premises. If one or more telephones were dedicated to data communication, then their cost would have to be included.

PDN charges are derived as follows: Two stations must be connected at a fee of $400 each. There are 30,000 characters transmitted per day, which, at 128 characters per packet, is 235 packets. This assumes that all packets are full, which will not be the case. A message of 140 characters requires that two packets be sent. The 30,000 characters transmitted per day was approximated to include this variance. There is a charge of $1.50 per 1000 packets, and there are 23 workdays per month. Thus, the monthly PDN charges are

$$(2 \times \$400) + [(30,000/128) \times (\$1.50/1000) \times 23]$$
$$= \$800 + (235 \times \$0.0015 \times 23) = \$800 + \$8.11 = \$808.11$$

This analysis shows that PDN will be the most economical link between Seattle and San Francisco. This configuration has the added benefit of allowing the Seattle node to transmit directly to any node with a PDN port, meaning that such messages would not always need to be routed through San Francisco.

Breakeven Point

One more computation will complete the analysis of the link between Seattle and San Francisco. A breakeven figure will show the amount of message traffic necessary to make the cost of a leased link the same as that for a PDN.

Table 15–7　PDN Charges, Seattle to San Francisco

Connection charge per node	$400 per month
Packet charge	$1.50 per 1000 packets
Packet size	128 characters

(From the above analysis, it seems unlikely that a switched connection will ever be practical.) The breakeven number of characters per day, x, is given by

$$(2 \times \$400) + [(x/128) \times \$0.0015 \times 23] = \$919.40$$

$$x = 442{,}991 \text{ characters per day}$$

This is not a significant amount of message traffic; a 120-page typed document, at 80 characters per line and 55 lines per page, with no compression, exceeds this amount.

The above calculations assume that neither node has a PDN port and that there is one connection charge per node. If one of the nodes already has a PDN connection, the cost for that port either should not be included or should be distributed throughout the network. Thus, if San Francisco already had been configured with a PDN port, the PDN cost would decrease by $400, or the cost of that port should be apportioned among the nodes that must be connected to San Francisco.

San Francisco–Los Angeles Line

A similar analysis was performed for the San Francisco–Los Angeles connection. A switched line was not considered in this instance; a leased line was the most economical. The leased line rates between San Francisco and Los Angeles are different from those given in Table 15–5 because the link is intrastate. A leased line is available for $425. Because approximately 200,000 characters per day are transferred between the two cities, PDN charges are

$$\$400 + [(200{,}000/128) \times \$0.0015 \times 23] = \$400 + \$53.90 = \$453.90$$

International Lines

All the European cities will be connected by a backbone network. The connections between Europe, the United States, Canada, Mexico, Japan, Australia, and Hong Kong will be made via X.25 networks. The amount of message traffic between these entities does not warrant the use of leased facilities. Configuring the other parts of the network is left as an exercise.

SUMMARY

WANs are usually built around a particular vendor's network software. Although most major computer vendors offer network capabilities, the leader in proprietary network software is IBM's SNA. SNA provides an architecture for building networks, and many vendors support some type of connection to SNA networks. One of the ways vendors can communicate with an SNA network is via the LU 6.2 protocol. Microcomputers are increasingly found as WAN components. Their versatility makes them a cost-effective network tool.

SNA continues to evolve and mature as a network product. Internally, new network functions such as those provided by LU 6.2 and SNADS are being included in the architecture. Gateways to other networking products continue to be implemented, together with SNA interfaces between IBM SNA components and other manufacturers' equipment. Some vendors have gone so far as to implement PU type 4 and PU type 5 capabilities in their systems. SNA may be the most significant influence in WAN implementations today.

KEY TERMS

Advanced Communications Facility (ACF)
domain
end-to-end routing
extended addressing
General Agreement on Trade and Tariffs (GATT)
half-session layer
logical unit (LU)
LU 6.2
Network Addressable Unit (NAU)
Network Control Program (NCP)

Network Performance Analyzer (NPA)
Network Problem Determination Aid (NPDA)
physical unit (PU)
Physical Unit Control Point (PUCP)
session
SNA Distribution Services (SNADS)
subarea
Systems Network Architecture (SNA)
Systems Services Control Point (SSCP)
virtual routing

REVIEW QUESTIONS

1. What are the four types of physical units in SNA? What is the role of each in the network?

2. What is a half-session layer in SNA? What is its purpose?

3. Explain how a session is established in SNA.

4. Compare a WAN and a PDN.

5. Discuss the influence of SNA on other computer vendors.

6. How does SNA relate to the OSI reference model?

7. Describe three potential problem areas when setting up an international network.

PROBLEMS AND EXERCISES

1. Suppose message traffic between New York City and Boston is 600,000 characters per day. If the cost of a leased line is $650 per month, which will be more economical: a leased line or a PDN? Assume that New York City already has a PDN port. How many characters must be exchanged for a leased line to cost the same as a PDN? Use the costs included in the Case Study in your analysis.

CHAPTER 16

Network Interconnections

CHAPTER OBJECTIVES

After studying this chapter you should be able to

- List the ways networks can be interconnected
- Describe the principal methods for making network connections: repeaters, bridges, routers, and gateways
- List the capabilities of Transmission Control Protocol/Internet Protocol (TCP/IP)
- Describe the network interconnection capabilities of TCP/IP
- List capabilities of network interconnection utilities

The computing resources of organizations are diverse. They range from a single microcomputer to multiple LANs and WANs that connect hundreds of different types of computers: microcomputers, minicomputers, mainframes, and supercomputers. Today, a large organization may have several microcomputer LANs, a WAN, and perhaps connections to public computer networks. When one organization has a variety of computers and networks, those computers ordinarily must be interconnected to provide better use of hardware and software and to allow users to communicate easier. A LAN may need to be connected to another LAN, a large host computer, a WAN, remote workstations or terminals, or public networks, and it may be necessary to connect two or more different WANs. In this chapter we cover the principal ways these connections are made.

THE OSI REFERENCE MODEL REVISITED

Throughout this text, we have discussed the OSI reference model. Because network interconnections are established at the physical, data link, and network layers of the OSI reference model, at this time you may want to review the sections covering the functions of these three layers.

What do we mean when we say the connection interface is made at the physical, data link, or network layer? An interface that operates at the physical layer must be sensitive to signals on the medium, one that operates at the data link layer must be aware of data link protocol formats, and one that operates at the network layer must use a common network layer protocol and be able to route messages to the next node along the path to its destination. The interconnection at a specific layer must know the implementation details of that layer. We begin by looking at physical layer interconnections.

As signals are transmitted through a medium, the signals weaken. A signal eventually will become unintelligible unless it can be amplified or regenerated. To guard against this in the telephone system, repeaters are placed at regular intervals to amplify or regenerate the signal. If the transmission is analog, any frequency is allowed, so signals must be amplified. Amplification simply strengthens the signal and also amplifies any errors that have crept into the transmission. This is illustrated in Figure 16–1(a). A digital signal can be regenerated and restored to its original strength and values. Because a digital signal has only two states, a 0 or a 1, a regenerator can examine an incoming signal, decide which of the two states the signal represents, and restore the signal to its original value and strength, as illustrated in Figure 16–1(b).

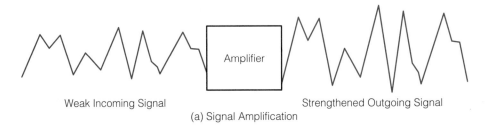

Weak Incoming Signal   Strengthened Outgoing Signal

(a) Signal Amplification

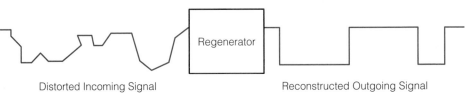

Distorted Incoming Signal   Reconstructed Outgoing Signal

(b) Signal Regeneration

Figure 16–1
Signal Amplification and Regeneration

A hardware device that amplifies or regenerates a signal at the physical layer is called a **repeater.** The function of a repeater is similar to that of some nonelectronic data transmission techniques. You may be familiar with communication techniques such as semaphore flags. Semaphores are line-of-sight transmissions. If the message must be transmitted over long distances, relay stations are necessary. If station A in Figure 16–2 needs to transmit a message to station D, the signaler at station B reads the signal sent from station A and resends the message to station C, where the message is repeated and sent to station D. At each relay station the signal is essentially amplified. If an error in transcribing or transmitting the message is made at any point, the error is propagated to subsequent stations.

In a similar manner, the length of the medium on a LAN can be extended by repeaters. A repeater is a physical layer device and hence must know and obey all the physical layer conventions regarding signaling and connections. Repeaters are commonly used in LANs to extend the distance

repeater A device used to amplify signals on a network. Repeaters allow the medium distance to be extended.

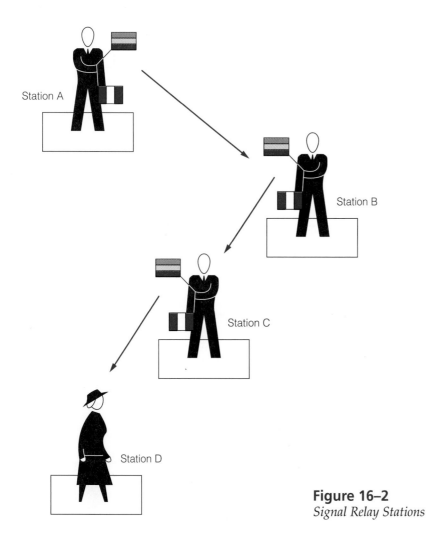

Station A

Station B

Station C

Station D

Figure 16–2
Signal Relay Stations

the signal can travel over the medium and still maintain signal strength. Unlike the telephone system, LAN standards limit the number of repeaters that can be used for a single LAN and hence limit the maximum length of the LAN medium. Figure 16–3 illustrates the relationship between a repeater and the OSI model.

Three functions of the data link layer of the OSI reference model are delineation of data, error detection, and address formatting. A data link protocol is concerned with getting data from the current node to the next node. A message may pass through several data link protocols on its path from the source node to the destination node, as illustrated in Figure 16–4. In this example, a message passes from a LAN data link protocol to a WAN data link protocol and back to another (possibly different) LAN data link protocol.

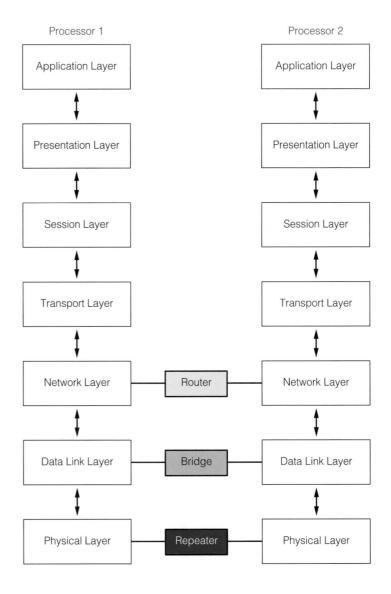

Figure 16–3
Repeater, Bridge, and Router in the OSI Reference Model

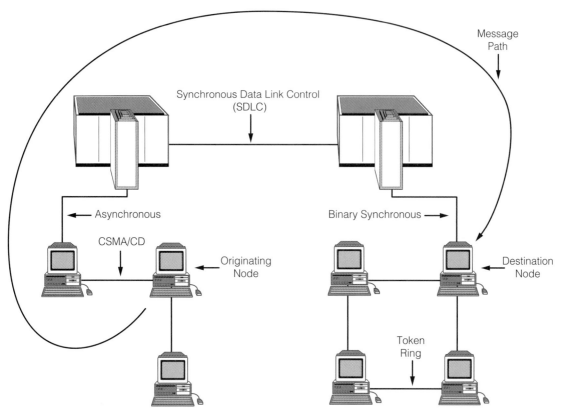

Figure 16–4
Message Passing Through Several Different Data Link Protocols

The data link protocol at each node is concerned only with moving the data to the next node.

An interface that operates at the data link or media access control (MAC) layer is called a **bridge.** Bridges are most commonly used in LANs to overcome limitations in distance or in number of workstations per LAN. A bridge is seldom necessary in WANs because they do not have distance limitations. WANs that limit the number of nodes per network usually use routers (see below) to interconnect two or more WANs.

Bridges originally connected LANs of the same type, such as two token-ring LANs or two IEEE 802.3 LANs. These early bridges indiscriminately forwarded all message traffic from one LAN onto the other LAN. Today's bridge technology is more sophisticated and can connect LANs using different data link protocols, such as bridging a token-ring LAN to a CSMA/CD bus LAN. Now, bridges selectively forward packets of data. Packets sent between two nodes on the same LAN are not acted on by the bridge; only internetwork packets are forwarded by a bridge, as illustrated in Figure 16–5. The relationship between a bridge and the OSI model is illustrated in Figure 16–3. Note that although the bridge is shown at the data

bridge The interface used to connect networks using similar data link protocols.

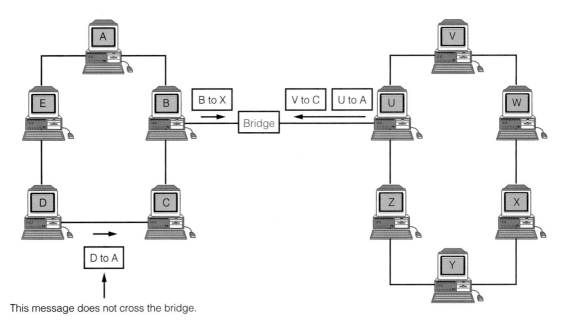

This message does not cross the bridge.

Figure 16–5
Bridge Packet Forwarding

link layer, the data is transmitted from the data link layer down to the physical layer, over the medium to a physical layer, and back up to the data link layer. When a bridge that has a physical connection to two LANs receives a message, the message passes from the bridge's physical layer to its data link layer. The bridge examines the destination address in the header attached as part of the data link protocol and determines the destination address of the packet. This address tells the bridge which of the two LANs has the message's recipient, and the bridge passes the message to the proper LAN using the services of the physical layer connection.

The network layer of the OSI reference model is responsible for packet routing and the collection of accounting information. Networks use a variety of routing algorithms. CSMA/CD and token-passing LANs send messages to each node using broadcast routing. WANs are more selective in their routing because broadcast routing in a WAN causes too much overhead and delay. You may want to refer back to Chapter 11 for a review of WAN routing algorithms. Several routing paths may be available in some networks, as illustrated in Figure 16–6. The network layer is responsible for routing an incoming message for another node onto an appropriate outbound path. Thus, a message for node X that arrives at node B in Figure 16–6 will arrive at the physical layer and be moved up through the data link layer to the network layer. If the packet is not intended for an application on node B, the network layer determines the outbound path for the message and sends it down to the data link layer, which formats the packet with the proper data link control data (perhaps a data link protocol different from that of the arriving message). The data link layer then passes the packet down to

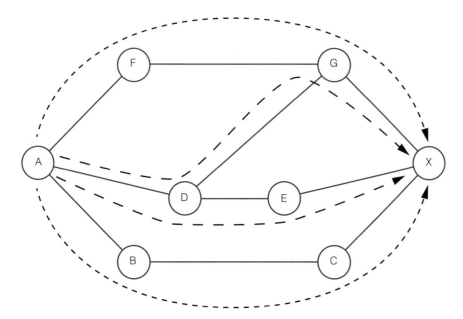

Figure 16–6
Several Routing Paths in a Network

the physical layer for transmission to the next node along the path to the final destination.

An interconnection interface that operates at the network layer is called a **router.** A router is not sensitive to the details of the data link and physical layers. Thus, a router can be used to connect different types of networks, such as a token-ring LAN to an IEEE 802.3 LAN or a LAN to a WAN. A router looks at the destination address of a message, determines a route the message should follow to reach that address, and provides the addressing required by the network and data link layers for delivery. This function is provided by **Transmission Control Protocol/Internet Protocol (TCP/IP)** in the Internet, whereas Novell networks typically use a protocol called Sequenced Packet Exchange/Internetwork Packet Exchange (SPX/IPX) to transfer packets between nodes. The TCP and SPX protocols operate at the transport layer, and IP and IPX protocols operate at the network layer. Some networks use a different type of protocol, such as the Xerox Network System (XNS). An SPX/IPX router cannot forward TCP/IP packets, and a router that knows only the XNS protocol cannot forward SPX/IPX packets. For two nodes to exchange data using a router, they must share a common network layer protocol. Figure 16–3 shows the relationship between a router and the OSI layers.

Network connections that operate at the network layer or above are generically called **gateways.** A gateway is used to connect dissimilar networks or systems by providing conversion from one network protocol to another. A gateway might be used to connect a LAN to a WAN, as illustrated in Figure 16–7. In making this interconnection, the gateway must accept packets from the LAN, extract the data from the packets, and format the data in a packet according to the WAN protocol, or vice versa.

router A network interconnection device and associated software that links two networks. The networks being linked can be different, but they must use a common routing protocol.

Transmission Control Protocol/Internet Protocol (TCP/IP) A suite of internetwork protocols developed by the U.S. Department of Defense for internetwork file transfers, e-mail transfer, remote logons, and terminal services.

gateway The interface used to connect two dissimilar networks or systems by providing conversion from one network protocol to another.

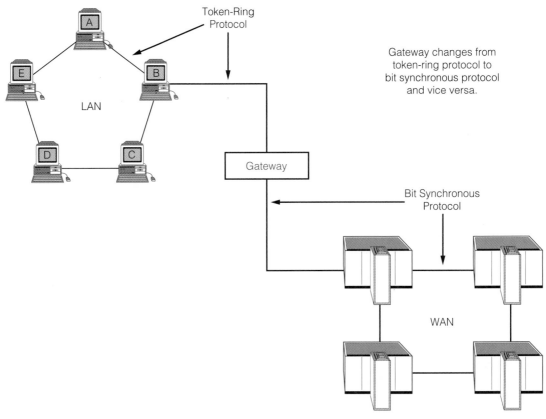

Figure 16–7
Gateway Connecting a LAN and a WAN

Now that we have introduced the basic types of network interconnections, we examine some of their details.

LAN-TO-LAN AND WAN-TO-WAN CONNECTIONS

By definition, a LAN serves a limited geographic area, and most LAN specifications place a limit on the length of the medium used. Companies that have LANs in geographically separated locations, or LANs that cover distances longer than the maximum allowed, often have a need for inter-LAN exchanges. Users on one LAN may want to exchange e-mail messages with users on the other LAN, or a user on one LAN may want to use resources located on another LAN.

Distance or geographic separation is not the only reason for having several LANs. Departmental computing is another rationale for having a multi-LAN environment. A company that is interested in department-level computing might implement a LAN for each department or for groups of departments. For example, a computer software manufacturer may go to great lengths to protect the integrity of their new products. Often details of new developments are not shared with employees who are not directly involved with a new product. Having separate LANs allows the company to separate functions and provides additional security of information. Among the software company's departments, there might be a LAN shared by software development and documentation, one for software support, one for accounting, one for personnel, and one for marketing. This separation reduces the likelihood that software being developed will inadvertently or intentionally be made available to customers through the support or marketing LAN. Likewise, personnel information can be more easily protected if it is on a separate LAN.

A third reason for LAN connections is to consolidate independent LANs that were formed in an ad hoc manner. Superficially this reason is similar to connecting departmental LANs. The difference is that department-oriented LANs are a planned separation whereas workgroup-oriented LANs were implemented as needed by individual departments or workgroups. This situation is common in many colleges and universities, where the departments or colleges of computer science, business, engineering, and nursing may have implemented LANs independently. Another reason for forming several small LANs rather than one large one is limitations on medium capacity. LANs supporting graphics and multimedia applications need to send high volumes of full-motion video and sound data in short amounts of time. Only a small number of multimedia workstations can be supported on media operating at 10 or 16 Mbps. Regardless of the original reasons for setting up several LANs, often a need arises for inter-LAN message exchanges and LAN interconnections to support them.

A fourth reason for having multiple LANs is the number of users per LAN. A LAN with hundreds of users might provide poorer performance than the same LAN with dozens of users. A LAN administrator attempts to maintain the responsiveness of a LAN even when more users are added. Responsiveness can be maintained by adding more resources to an existing LAN—more memory, more disks, or another server—or by splitting the LAN into two or more smaller LANs. When splitting a LAN, the administrator strives for a proper balance of users and resources; however, a perfect balance is not always attainable because of distance, physical location, or differences in workgroup sizes. Because inter-LAN communication involves more overhead than intra-LAN communication, an administrator must consider grouping of users and resources so the number of inter-LAN messages is reduced. Members of a department or workgroup often communicate with each other more than with members of other departments or workgroups. Thus, splitting a LAN because many users are being served often results in a configuration split along departmental or workgroup lines.

Companies may also have several WANs. One reason for having multiple WANs arises from corporate mergers and acquisitions. When two companies combine, each may have a WAN already in place. These WANs sometimes use different vendors' network architectures. After the merger, it is usually desirable to interconnect those networks; however, preexisting incompatibilities may make it necessary to retain separate WANs. Sometimes independent networks are started in regional areas and later need to be connected to form national and international networks. Finally, a company may want to connect its network to external networks such as the Internet. Different WANs also can arise from the need to support different work tasks. A bank might use one vendor's hardware and network architecture to set up a network of automatic teller machines and a different network to support its back office, platform, and administrative applications. Similarly, a manufacturing company may use one type of hardware and network to support research and development operations and another for sales and administrative purposes.

There are many good reasons for having several different networks in an organization. At some point, there is often a need to have these separate networks connected into one enterprise network. As a generic model for connecting separate networks, we use LANs as an example of both LAN-to-LAN and WAN-to-WAN connections. This is appropriate because the first two types of connections, repeaters and bridges, are most common in LANs. Routers are common to both network types.

Repeaters

Every LAN has a distance restriction. One of the IEEE 802.3 standards, 10Base5, specifies a maximum medium segment length of 500 m. To span longer distances, a repeater can be used to connect two segments. The standard allows for a maximum of four repeaters, for a total distance of 2500 m per LAN. Two repeaters connecting three segments in an IEEE 802.3 network is illustrated in Figure 16–8.

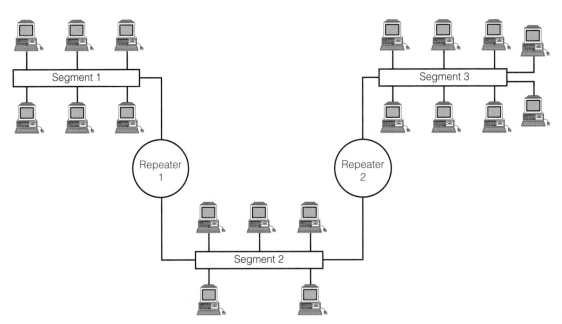

Figure 16–8
Repeaters Connecting Three LAN Segments

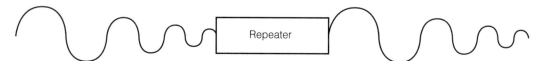

Figure 16–9
Repeater

As signals travel along the medium, they attenuate. Weak signals can result in transmission errors. A repeater is a simple hardware device that accepts a signal, regenerates or amplifies it, and passes it along at full strength. This is illustrated in Figure 16–9. A repeater does not buffer messages and does not know about MAC protocols or data packets. A repeater also does not separate one segment of the network from another. If a station in segment 1 and a station in segment 3 of the network in Figure 16–8 try to transmit at the same time, a collision will occur.

Table 16–1 is a list of repeater capabilities and characteristics. Note that one capability of some repeaters is media transfer. Although it is not commonly needed, this capability allows an administrator to change media from twisted-pair wires on one LAN segment to coaxial cable on another segment at a repeater junction; the MAC protocol remains the same even though the medium changes. The LAN administrator must also keep in mind that a change in the medium can result in a change in the overall maximum length of the LAN.

Bridges

Early bridges were used to connect two networks that used the same MAC protocol. Today, we have bridges that connect LANs having different MAC protocols. These newer bridges must be able to reformat packets from one data link protocol to another. Be aware that the use of the term *bridge* can vary. Sometimes a bridge is defined in the original sense: a device connecting two identical networks. Others use the broader definition of a device used to connect two networks at the data link layer. For example, you may encounter bridges that connect a token ring to an Ethernet LAN. Sometimes a device providing this capability is called a **brouter.** Figure 16–10 illustrates two LANs, LAN A and LAN B, using a token-ring protocol. These two rings may be configured around departments, with one ring per department, or around distance if the distance spanned by the workstations is greater than what can be supported by a single LAN. Regardless of the reason for

brouter A term used to describe new bridges that are able to connect two different LANs using the data link layer.

Table 16–1 Repeater Characteristics and Capabilities

Media transfer, such as coaxial cable to twisted-pair wires
Multiple ports allowing one repeater to connect three or more segments
Diagnostic and status indicators
Automatic partitioning and reconnection in the event of a segment failure
Manual partitioning
Backup power supply

having two rings, it is likely that an application on ring A will want to communicate with a server on ring B or that a user on ring A will want to send e-mail to a user on ring B. A bridge can provide this ability.

In Figure 16–10 the bridge's function is to move data packets between the two LANs. Unlike a repeater, a bridge is selective in what it does. It ac-

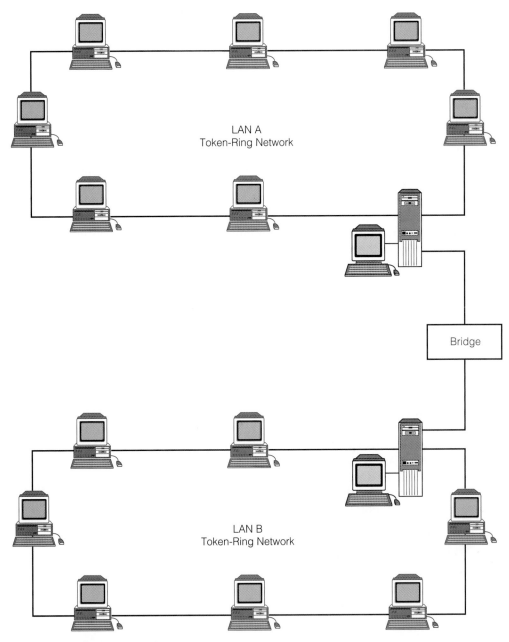

Figure 16–10
Token Rings Connected by a Bridge

cepts packets from both LANs and transfers LAN A packets addressed to nodes on LAN B and transfers LAN B packets addressed to nodes on LAN A. Some bridge functions are listed in Table 16–2.

A bridge must know about addresses on each network. Because the bridge knows the MAC protocol being used, the bridge can find the source and destination addresses in the packet and use those addresses for routing. (We use the *term* routing here to describe the process of the bridge deciding to which LAN the message must be transferred. In using this term we do not imply that the bridge is performing the functions of a router.) The only additional information the bridge must know is the LAN to which the destination node is connected. This is determined in several ways. Older bridges indiscriminately transferred each message onto both LANs or required network managers to provide a network routing table. A **routing table** contains node addresses and the LAN identifier for the LAN to which the node is connected. These older bridges are static regarding their ability to forward messages. If a new node is added to one of the networks, the routing tables in all bridges must be manually updated, and until that happens the new node will not receive inter-LAN messages. As shown in Figure 16–11, network interconnections using bridges can also be more complex than a single bridge connecting two networks. A network routing table for bridge B1 in Figure 16–11 is shown in Table 16–3.

Most bridges being sold today are called **learning bridges** or **transparent bridges.** Learning bridges build their routing tables from messages they receive. They do not need to be loaded with a predefined routing table. Essentially the network administrator need only connect the bridge to both LANs and the bridge is immediately operational. Two methods are commonly used for bridges to learn and build their routing table: spanning tree and source routing (both are described later). To understand how bridges of this type work, we start with a sample bridge configuration, as illustrated in Figure 16–11. Figure 16–11 shows four LANs (A, B, C, and D), four bridges (B1, B2, B3, and B4), and five nodes (N1, N2, N3, N4, and N5). In this figure, each bridge has two ports labeled P1 and P2. Bridge B2 has a third port, P3. Note that in this configuration, at least two paths exist between each pair of LANs.

routing table An information source containing the node address and the identification of the LAN to which the receiving node is connected.

learning bridge Bridge that builds its own routing table from the messages it receives, rather than having a predefined routing table. Also known as a transparent bridge.

Table 16–2   Basic Bridge Functions

Packet Routing Function

1. Accept packet from LAN A.
2. Examine address of packet.
3. If packet address is a LAN A address, allow the packet to continue to LAN A.
4. If packet address is a LAN B address, transmit the packet onto the LAN B medium.
5. Do the equivalent for LAN B packets.

Additional Functions

Media conversion	Remote connection	Speed connection
Learning	Signal conversion	Packet statistics
Token ring to Ethernet conversion		

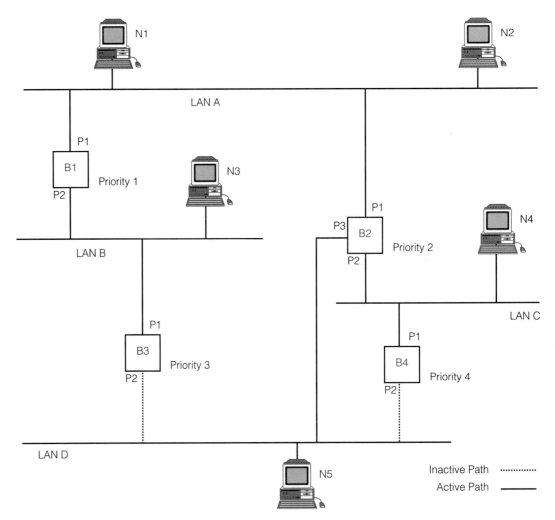

Figure 16–11
Network Interconnections Using Bridges

LAN A can get to LAN D via bridges B1 and B3 or directly via bridge B2; LAN D can get to LAN C directly through bridge B4 or bridge B2 or indirectly through bridges B3, B1, and B2. We start by explaining how a bridge works. In this example we assume each bridge has a fully developed routing table like the one shown for bridge B1 in Table 16–3. Note also that there is only one route for each node. If a route changes for some reason, the bridge will update its routing table to show the new route. Some networks use routing algorithms that allow multiple active paths between two nodes, but this is atypical of bridges. Following this example, we examine the two ways in which a bridge learns its routing information.

In Figure 16–11, suppose bridge B1 receives a packet from N1 destined for N2. Recall that each LAN packet contains the address of the sender, or

Table 16–3   Bridge B1's Network Routing Table

Node	Port	Comments
N1	P1	
N2	P1	
N3	P2	
N4	P1	Bridge B2 routes
N5	P1	Bridge B2 routes

source, and the recipient, or destination. The bridge examines its routing table for the destination address. In this case, the address is local because both the source and the destination addresses are on LAN A. Because the destination address is local, no further action is required; the bridge essentially does nothing. In a token-passing LAN, the bridge may need to forward the packet to the next node on the LAN. In a CSMA/CD LAN, the bridge will do nothing because packets are broadcast to all nodes.

Suppose bridge B1 receives a packet on port P2 from LAN B, with a source address of N3 and a destination address of N2 (LAN A). The bridge again consults its routing table for the destination address and finds the address to be a nonlocal node. The routing table shows the outbound port on which to send the packet, P1 in this instance. The bridge takes the packet as received and transmits through port P1 onto LAN A (if the LANs have a different MAC protocol, the bridge will format the packet to make the packet compatible with the receiving MAC protocol). Similarly, if bridge B3 receives a packet from node N5 with a destination of N2, B3 will consult its routing table, find that the path to N2 is port P1, and transmit the packet on LAN B. Bridge B1 on LAN B will receive this packet, consult its routing table, and forward the packet to LAN A through port P1. You may be wondering why bridge B4 did not also transmit the packet onto LAN C, or why bridge B2 did not also transmit the packet, causing a duplicate packet. The answer lies in how bridges operate and learn.

The Spanning Tree Algorithm

Spanning tree algorithms, in which bridges exchange routing information with each other, can be used on any type of LAN. The spanning tree algorithm has been evaluated by the IEEE 802.1 Media Access Control Bridge Standards Committee. The committee selected the spanning tree algorithm as the standard for all IEEE 802 LAN standards.

In developing the algorithm for spanning trees, let us first look at a simple case. You may wish to refer back to Figure 16–11 during this discussion. Recall that each LAN packet contains the source address and the destination address. If bridge B1 receives a packet on port P1, the bridge assumes that the source address is a node local to LAN A. Because a bridge receives all network traffic on a LAN to which the bridge is connected (bridge B1 gets all message traffic on LANs A and B), a bridge soon learns all of the local node

spanning tree algorithm A learning bridge algorithm in which bridges exchange routing information with one another. Based on the routing information thus received, each bridge maintains a routing table that shows how to route messages to other LANs.

addresses from the source addresses in these messages. If a source address is not found in the bridge's routing table, the address is added to the table.

Suppose node N3 in Figure 16–11 sends a message to node N2. If the destination address N2 is already in B1's routing table, the bridge forwards the packet accordingly. If the destination address is not already in the bridge's routing table, the bridge needs to locate the address. The bridge does this by sending the packet out on all ports other than the one on which it was received, which is called **flooding** (the packet will also be sent to all nodes on the LAN on which it was received). In this instance, the packet will be transmitted on port P1.

Flooding ensures that a packet will arrive at its destination by sending it along all possible paths. The bridge will eventually receive an acknowledgment that the packet was received or a message from the receiving station. The acknowledgment contains the address of the original recipient, N2 in this case. From this acknowledgment, the bridge can determine the direction in which the node lies, and it adds this information to its routing table.

Sometimes a path may become unavailable, or new bridges or paths may become operational, which may cause routing information to change. To keep routing as efficient as possible, each bridge sends status messages periodically to let other bridges know of its current state. Also, status messages are sent immediately if the topology changes.

Now we consider a more complex situation, in which multiple bridges are connected to the same network and there may be multiple paths between LANs and perhaps multiple ports per bridge, as illustrated in Figure 16–11. If node N5 sends a message to node N2, does the packet get sent via bridge B2 or via bridges B3 and B1 or even via bridge B4 and then bridge B2? To reconcile such decisions, each bridge is given a priority. If two or more bridges are available, the bridge with the highest priority is chosen. If the path along that route becomes disrupted, the path can change and the highest-priority alternative path is activated. We consider in more detail how this occurs.

A bridge has at least two ports. An **active port** accepts packets from the LAN end of the port; an **inactive port** blocks or does not accept packets from the LAN end of the port. An inactive port still can be used to transmit packets. However, these packets must originate from the bridge end of the port. Each bridge is assigned a priority by the administrator.

The bridge with the highest priority is designated as the **root bridge.** Each bridge has an active port in the direction of the root bridge. Other ports are active or inactive depending on the priority of the bridge and the configuration. Figure 16–11 also shows the priority of each bridge (with 1 representing the highest priority) and the active and inactive paths. A port is active if its path is active; otherwise it is inactive. All bridges have their port in the direction of the root bridge active. Therefore, packets from the root direction can be forwarded and received. For all other cases, the active port from a LAN is toward the bridge with the highest priority. Ports on the root bridge are always active. Thus, in Figure 16–11 LANs A and B will choose bridge B1's ports as the active ports. LAN C is connected to two bridges, B2 and B4. B2 will be chosen because it has the higher priority, and B2's port P2 will be active. B4's port P1 is also active because P1 is in the direction of the

flooding A technique used by a bridge to locate a destination address not present in the bridge's routing table by sending a packet out on all possible paths. An acknowledgment from the receiving station contains the destination address of the packet, which can then be added to the bridge's routing table.

active port The status of a port that will accept packets from the LAN end of the port.

inactive port The status of a port that will not accept packets from the LAN end of the port.

root bridge The bridge assigned the highest priority.

root bridge. LAN D is connected to three bridges, B2, B3, and B4. Because B2 has the highest priority, it will be chosen as the active bridge. Ports P2 on bridges B3 and B4 will be inactive and will not accept packets from LAN D.

The advantages of the spanning tree algorithm are that it is MAC layer independent, bridges can learn the topology of the network without manual intervention, and paths can change if an existing path becomes inoperable or if a better path is introduced. The algorithm overhead is the size of the routing table for networks with many communicating nodes, and the extra network traffic resulting from status messages and flooding.

Source Routing

In practice, spanning tree algorithms have been more commonly used for CSMA/CD LANs, and **source routing** is more common for token-passing LANs. Source routing is also being considered by an IEEE standards committee as a routing algorithm for token-passing networks.

Source routing relies on the sending station to designate the path for a packet. In Figure 16–11, suppose node N5 wants to send a packet to node N2. If N2 is in N5's routing table, the packet is sent along that route; otherwise, N5 must determine the best route to N2. N5 does this by sending a **discovery packet** on all routes available. In this case, the discovery packet is sent on port P2 of bridge B4, port P3 of bridge B2, and port P2 of bridge B3. Each bridge, in turn, transmits the packet on each port except the one on which the packet was received. Moreover, each bridge appends its information to the packet. Thus, node N2 receives several packets, each containing the identity of each bridge through which the packet traveled. All of these packets are returned to node N5. N5 selects the path from all the alternatives returned. In our example, node N5 will probably receive four discovery packets with paths B4–B2, B2, B3–B1, and B4–B2–B3–B1. Upon receiving the four responses from its discovery packets, node N5 will choose one. B2 would probably be the best route because there is only one bridge through which the message must pass. Realize, however, that path B3–B1 might be faster if B2's connections on ports P1 or P3 are slower than the connections for bridges B3 and B1.

After N5 discovers the path to node N2, whenever node N5 needs to transmit to node N2, it appends the selected routing information to its packet. Each bridge along the way investigates this information to determine by which route to send the packet.

You might have already noticed that the algorithm just explained has one possible fault. The discovery packet sent from bridge B4 will reach bridge B2, and B2 will send the packet out on all ports except the one on which it was received (ports P3 and P1). The packet on port P3 will be directed back to LAN D and will again reach bridges B4 and B3. A mechanism must be in place to prevent discovery packets from looping through the network. This is accomplished in one of two ways. First, a maximum number of hops is specified. If the maximum is set to ten, then a packet that has not reached its destination after traversing ten bridges is discarded. The second way to prevent a loop is to discard a packet that recirculates through the same bridge. For example, one of N5's discovery packets will go from B4 to

source routing A learning bridge algorithm in which the sending node is responsible for determining the route to the destination node. The routing information is appended to the message and the bridges along the route use the routing information to move the message from source to destination.

discovery packet A packet sent by the sending station on all available routes to determine the best route from the information collected by the packet.

B2 and then back to B4. When B4 finds that it has already handled that packet, it will discard the packet.

The advantage of the source routing algorithm is that bridges are not responsible for maintaining large routing tables for extensive networks. Each node is responsible for maintaining routing information only for the nodes with which it communicates. The disadvantages are the overhead of sending numerous packets during discovery and the extra routing data that must be appended to each message.

Other Bridge Capabilities

In the preceding discussion we did not consider the interconnected LANs' locations and media. Bridges are available that will accommodate media differences. Suppose LAN A in Figure 16–11 uses coaxial cable and LAN B uses twisted-pair wires as the medium. You could therefore select a bridge that has BNC connectors for coaxial cable on one port and RJ-45 connectors for twisted-pair wires on the other port.

There are also several interconnection options for connecting geographically distributed LANs. The most common of these are listed in Table 16–4. The speed of the connection between remote LANs usually is much slower than the speed within either LAN. This speed difference can cause the bridge to become saturated with messages if there are many inter-LAN packets. Bridges have memory that allows some messages to be buffered, which helps reconcile the differences in transmission speed. If too many messages arrive in a short period, the buffer will become full and newly arriving packets will be lost. Note that this condition can occur when two local LANs are connected. A bridge also must do some processing to determine where a packet must be routed. Except for very slow LANs, the processing time may exceed the arrival rate. Thus, bridges connecting LANs with high packet arrival rates can also become saturated.

Routers

Networks sometimes are connected at the network layer. This type of connection, called a router, is used to connect LANs to LANs, WANs to WANs, and LANs to WANs. As in any form of communication, a common language or protocol is needed. In a bridge the common protocol is the data link pro-

Table 16–4   Remote Bridge Connection Alternatives

RS–232 serial lines to 19.2 Kbps
RS–422 serial lines to 2 Mbps
xDSL switched connections
Internet connection
Synchronous transmission at 56 Kbps or 64 Kbps
T-1 line, 1.5 Mbps
Fractional T-1
X.25 or frame relay packet switching network
Integrated services digital network (ISDN)

tocol. Because the data link protocol may not be common for all links on networks connected with a router, the common internetwork protocol is formed at the network layer. Although the network interconnection is established at the network layer, data link and physical layer services are also involved.

A variety of network protocols are used for network interconnection. Novell's native network protocol is SPX/IPX. SPX/IPX can therefore be used to establish the common basis of communication between a Novell token-ring LAN and a Novell CSMA/CD LAN. However, SPX/IPX may not be implemented in WANs and in LANs provided by other network vendors, and SPX/IPX cannot be used as a routing protocol for these networks. Thus network administrators must find one network layer protocol supported by at least one node on each network. Several internetwork protocols have been developed, but the most common of these is TCP/IP. As a result, we use TCP/IP as our router example.

TCP/IP

TCP/IP was developed by the Advanced Research Projects Agency (ARPA) of the U.S. Department of Defense (DOD). Originated as an internetwork protocol, it has evolved over time into a suite of protocols addressing a variety of network communication needs, one of which is that of a router. Note that TCP/IP is not just a microcomputer protocol. On the contrary, it was developed on large systems and was later transported to microcomputers. Because TCP/IP runs on a wide variety of platforms, it is an ideal choice for a routing protocol. Other functions provided by the TCP/IP protocol suite include file transfer, e-mail, and logons to remote nodes.

Using TCP/IP's routing capabilities, users may be on either the same or different networks, networks that are directly connected by a bridge or router, or networks with one or more intermediate networks, as illustrated in Figure 16–12. In addition to providing network interconnection, TCP/IP also provides services for file transfers, e-mail, and provisions for a user on one network to log onto another network. Although these capabilities are important, we consider only the router functions of the protocol.

Figure 16–12 illustrates how networks might be connected using TCP/IP. Routing nodes are denoted by R and nonrouting nodes by WS (workstation). Note that internetwork connections are made through specific network nodes. Thus, node R1 on network A has a physical connection to node R2 on network B, and node R3 on network A has a physical connection to node R4 on network C. You should also realize that the networks we are discussing can be either LANs or WANs, and routing nodes that communicate with each other must share a common data link protocol and a physical link. Although we speak of routers operating at the network level, for messages to transmit from one node to another they must pass through the data link and physical layers of each computer. The key is that the information needed to determine how to forward the message is understood by the network layer's logic. In Figure 16–12, assume that network A is a CSMA/CD LAN, network B is a token-ring LAN, and network C is a WAN. Nodes R1 and R2 must share a common data link protocol over link L1, and nodes R3 and R4 must share a common data link protocol and medium

Figure 16–12
TCP/IP Routing in a Network

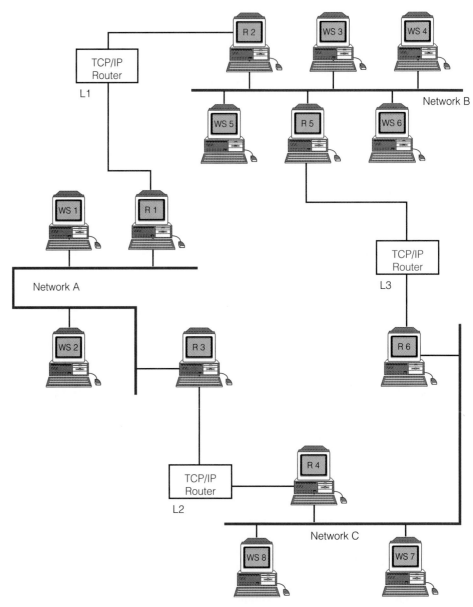

over link L2. The data link protocols at L1 and L2 may be different. A key concept for a router is that any data link protocol can be used.

As the abbreviation implies, TCP/IP consists of two distinct protocols, the Transmission Control Protocol (TCP) and the Internet Protocol (IP). The TCP operates at the transport layer and the IP operates at the network layer. Before tracing the flow of a message transfer using TCP/IP, let us first look at the functions of each protocol.

The IP provides two basic services: breaking the message up into transmission packets and addressing. Figure 16–12 shows several network interconnections, and each connection may use a different data link protocol.

Many data link protocols have a maximum size for transmission packets. For example, an Ethernet LAN packet contains at most 1500 characters. Some networks have a maximum packet size of 128 characters. An IP must be aware of these data link differences. The IP is also responsible for packet routing. On occasion this requires that the IP break a message into smaller packets of the appropriate size. To do this, the IP must determine the address of the next node on the path to the message's destination.

There are several functions an IP does not perform. The IP is not responsible for guaranteeing end-to-end message delivery. The TCP protocol is held accountable for message delivery. If a packet is lost during transmission, the TCP, not the IP, is responsible for resending the message. Also, the IP does not guarantee that individual packets will arrive in the correct order, a function that is also provided by the TCP. Thus, the primary functions of the TCP are to provide message integrity, to provide acknowledgment that a complete message has been received by a destination node, and to regulate the flow of messages between source and destination nodes. The TCP also may divide the message into smaller transmission segments. These segments usually correspond to an IP transmission packet.

We now consider how the TCP and IP cooperate in sending a message from one node to another. This example also serves as a model for the functions of a router. For this example we assume that node WS1 on network A needs to send a message to node WS5 on network B in Figure 16–12. TCP/IP uses the following procedure to carry out this transmission.

1. To start the process, the TCP in node WS1 receives a message from an application. The TCP attaches a header to the message and passes it down to the IP in node WS1. The message header contains the destination address and error detection fields such as a cyclic redundancy check (CRC) and a message sequence number. These are used to ensure that the message is received without errors and to ensure that messages are received in the proper sequence or can be reordered into the proper sequence.

2. Node WS1's IP determines whether the destination is an internetwork address. If the address is on the local network, such as node WS2, then the IP passes the message to the local network routing facility, which transports the message to the proper node. If the destination is a node on another network, the IP finds the best path to the destination and forwards the message to the next IP node along that path. In this case, the IP in node WS1 sends the message to node R1.

3. The IP at node R1 receives the message, examines the address, and determines the address of the next node, R2 in this example. The IP may break the message up into packets of the appropriate size. The IP adds a header to each packet and passes it down to the data link layer. The data link layer appends its transmission information and transmits the packets over link L1, between R1 and R2.

4. The data link layer at R2 receives a packet, strips off the data link layer control data, and passes the message to R2's IP. If the destination is local to that IP's network, as it is in this instance, the IP

delivers the message to the local network routing facility for delivery. If the destination is on another network, the IP determines the next node along the path and sends the message to it. If the node address were WS7, the packet would be routed to node R5 and then to node R6. Ultimately the message arrives at the destination node.

5. When the message arrives at the final destination node, it is passed up to the TCP, which then decodes the header attached by the sender's TCP. The receiving TCP checks for errors, such as message sequence errors or CRC errors. If no errors are detected, the TCP determines the destination program and sends the message to it.

On the path from source to destination, the message may pass through several IP nodes and traverse links with several different data link protocols. The router, TCP/IP in this example, is responsible for generating the destination address and intermediate addresses along the way, and for ensuring the correct delivery of the message.

TCP/IP is continually being extended to meet new communication needs. One extension, **Xpress Transfer Protocol (XTP)** enhances TCP/IP performance by reducing the amount of processing and allowing some functions to be worked on in parallel. One example of parallelism is the ability to transmit data while the CRC is being computed.

From the preceding discussion you should realize that a LAN node that must communicate with a node on another network must run both the TCP and the IP software. Most of today's LAN operating system vendors have TCP/IP software available in DOS, OS/2, and UNIX versions. You will also find this software and associated utilities available from independent software vendors. A variety of TCP/IP utilities can be found in the public domain and are thus available at no cost or at a minimal cost.

ISO Routing Standards

The International Standards Organization (ISO) has also developed standards for functions similar to those provided by TCP/IP. The counterpart to IP is the **Connectionless Network Protocol (CLNP).** In addition to forwarding messages, CLNP can provide message services such as message priorities, route selection parameters, and security parameters. The ISO has defined five classes of transport protocols, abbreviated TP0, TP1, TP2, TP3, and TP4. The classes are based on the error characteristics of the network. The lower classes assume better network error performance and hence provide less end-to-end support. TP4 makes no assumptions about the error characteristics of the network and provides the highest level of error detection and recovery. Combining the transport protocols with CLNP yields a service similar to that of TCP/IP. The ISO services are abbreviated TPn/CLNP, where n represents a number between 0 and 4.

Gateways

The interface between two dissimilar networks is called a gateway, which is basically a protocol converter. A gateway reconciles the differences between

Xpress Transfer Protocol (XTP) An extension of TCP/IP that enhances performance by reducing the amount of processing and allowing some functions to be worked on simultaneously.

Connectionless Network Protocol (CLNP) The ISO counterpart to the Internet Protocol (IP), this protocol provides message services such as message priorities, route selection parameters, and security parameters.

the networks it connects. With a repeater, a bridge, or a router, the communicating nodes share a common protocol at the physical, the data link, or the network layer, respectively. If it is necessary to connect two nodes that do not share a common protocol, a gateway or protocol converter can be used to make the connection. Naturally, the gateway must be able to understand the protocol of the two nodes being connected and also must be able to translate from one protocol to the other. The components of a gateway are the network interfaces and the logic that carries out the conversion necessary when moving messages between networks. The conversion must change the header and trailer of the packet to make it consistent with the protocol of the network or data link to which the message is being transferred. This may include accommodating differences in speed, packet sizes, and packet formats. If both a LAN and a WAN interface to a frame relay network, the frame relay network can serve as a gateway that allows stations on the LAN and the WAN to communicate; in this case, there are two gateways, one from the LAN to the frame relay network and one from the frame relay network to the WAN. This is illustrated in Figure 16–13.

Which Interface Is Right for You?

We have defined three network interconnection capabilities: repeaters, bridges, and routers. How do you choose the right one? In general, you should choose the connection at the lowest OSI level possible. Thus, a repeater is usually preferable to a bridge, and a bridge is usually preferable to a router. As you move up the OSI layers, your connection must be more intelligent, do more work, and have a lower packet exchange rate. These are not the only deciding factors, however.

A bridge can replace a repeater, and a router can replace a repeater or a bridge; however, the opposite is not always true. A repeater cannot always substitute for a bridge and a bridge cannot always substitute for a router. If you have the option of using a repeater, you might instead choose to use a bridge. This decision makes sense if the bridge can handle the message traffic and if you already have the bridge components. A bridge also allows some LAN isolation capability that a repeater does not provide. Thus, you might choose a bridge over a repeater to provide an extra level of network security.

LAN-TO-HOST CONNECTIONS

The preceding discussion explored ways of connecting networks—specifically, ways in which a LAN can be connected to another LAN or to a WAN. For many companies another LAN connection need is that of connecting a LAN to a stand-alone computer.

Many companies entered the microcomputer age with a large computer already installed. As these companies increased their use of microcomputers and then installed one or more LANs, the large computer continued to play an important role in their computing needs. For example, the large computer, often called a host, might be used for payroll or large database applications.

Figure 16–13
*LAN–WAN
Interconnection Using
Frame Relay*

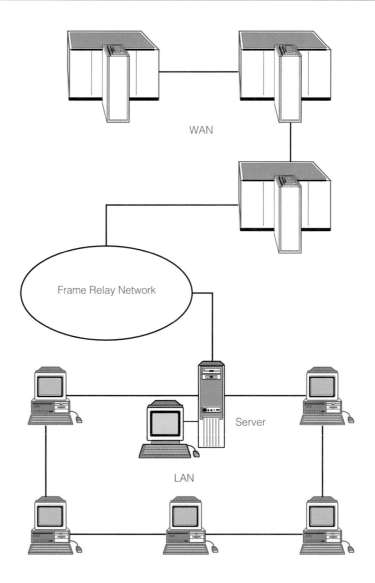

Even companies that replaced or are replacing the host with LAN technology go through a period when both computing environments exist. Companies that use hosts and LANs usually need to exchange data between the two environments. This can be done via media exchange: Data on the host can be copied onto a disk or tape and transferred to the LAN and vice versa. Often, a LAN–host direct connection is a more efficient way to accomplish data exchange. Figure 16–14 illustrates a host computer connected to a LAN. Before discussing the ways in which the LAN–host connection can be made, we look at several ways in which a LAN user can interact with a host.

In Figure 16–14, a user at node N1 might need to view, update, or evaluate data that is stored in the host's database. This user can do the work on the host or she can do the work on her LAN workstation. A user at node N2 might need to send an e-mail message to a user at terminal T1. A user at node N3 might need to run an application that exists only on the host. The

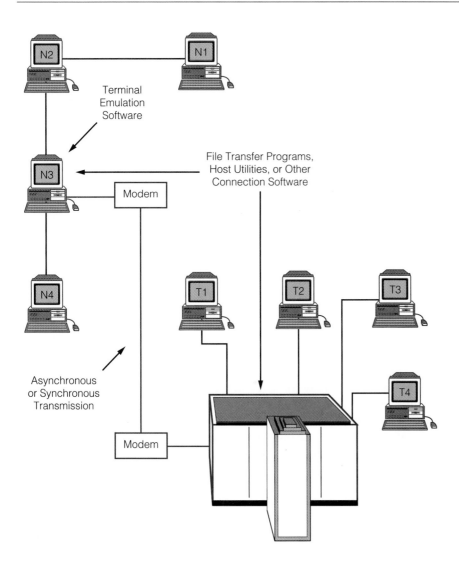

Figure 16–14
LAN-to-Host Connection

application may be available only on the host for a variety of reasons: It has not yet been implemented on the LAN, it needs special hardware available only on the host (such as a typesetting machine), or it requires computing power beyond that available on the LAN.

The three preceding examples cover most of the general connection needs of LAN users. These needs can be summarized as follows:

- using host data and applications
- transferring data from host to LAN or LAN to host
- using host hardware or software resources
- communicating with host users

A host user will probably have the same basic needs for LAN resources. You have already read about two ways in which a LAN–host connection can be made: routers and gateways. We now consider some other ways these connections can be made.

The Host as a LAN Node

Some hosts have the ability to connect to the LAN as a node. This is the most effective way of establishing the connection. The host can thus operate as a server, providing all of the above needs.

Asynchronous Connections

In Chapter 11 we discussed the asynchronous data link protocol. Virtually every computer has the ability to send and receive asynchronously. You are probably familiar with the term *serial port* on a microcomputer. The serial port is an asynchronous communication port. Because most computers support this protocol, it is sometimes used to link a microcomputer to a host. Usually a microcomputer attached to a host asynchronously operates in one of two modes: file transfer or terminal emulation.

Terminal Emulation   Terminal emulation software allows a microcomputer to imitate one or more types of terminals. This capability is commonly used when connecting to a host computer. For example, a user may connect to a mainframe and establish an IBM 3270 terminal session with an application or a user may connect to a bulletin board for information by emulating a standard teletypewriter (TTY) terminal or a Digital Equipment Corporation (DEC) VT100 terminal. Although in some instances the role of terminal emulation (and bulletin board systems) has been replaced by Internet connections wherein the microcomputer communicates with other computers using Internet protocols and software, terminal emulation remains a fundamental connection alternative.

Terminal emulation programs generally provide the ability to imitate a variety of terminal types. For example, the HyperTerminal emulation software in Windows 95 allows users to emulate the terminal types listed in Table 16–5; a cross-section of terminals emulated by a variety of other emulators is given in Table 16–6. Furthermore, terminal emulation packages usually provide capabilities beyond simple emulation. Some common functions include the following:

- File transfer protocols allow for uploading and downloading files. Common transfer protocols supported include XMODEM, YMODEM, ZMODEM, Kermit, BLAST, ASCII, IND$FILE, and CompuServe.
- Scripting allows command sequences to be placed in an executable script. Scripts can be used to provide unattended operation and to automate frequently used command sequences.

Table 16–5   HyperTerminal Emulation

ANSI Standard	TTY	Minitel (France)
DEC VT100	DEC VT 52	Viewdata (United Kingdom)

Table 16–6 Terminals Emulated by a Variety of Emulators

DEC VT 52 or VT 100, 200, 300, 600 series	AT&T 600 and 700 series
Tektronix 4000, 4100, 4200 series	Hewlett-Packard 700 series
ANSI	Wyse 50, 60
TTY	Televideo 900 series
IBM 3100, 3270, 5200 series	

- Buffer control allows the user to scroll the buffer to view forwards and backwards.

- Network support allows operation over networks such as LANs, SNA, and the Internet.

A summary of terminal emulation capabilities is given in Table 16–7.

Dedicated Connection per Microcomputer Host computers can usually accommodate many asynchronous connections. Small minicomputers usually support 32 or more, and large mainframes may accommodate hundreds. One way to connect a LAN node to a host is to provide a direct connection between a port on the host and each microcomputer needing a host connection. This is illustrated in Figure 16–15. In the figure, nodes N1, N2, N4, and N5 each have a dedicated connection to the host. Nodes N3 and N6 are not connected to the host.

A **dedicated connection** provides direct host access and the microcomputer does not use LAN resources for communicating with the host. In the typical connection, the microcomputer appears to the host as though the microcomputer were a host terminal. In addition to the serial port, the microcomputer needs terminal emulation software to establish the connection and carry on a host session. Terminal emulation software is available from many sources and can emulate a wide variety of terminals. With dedicated connections, the LAN administrator and data processing department can easily control which LAN nodes have access to the host. Nodes without a direct connection cannot make a host connection.

dedicated connection A connection providing direct access to the host using non-LAN resources for communication between the host and the microcomputer.

A dedicated connection has several disadvantages. First, as with all asynchronous connections, the speed of the link is slow. Asynchronous speeds can be faster than 100,000 bps, but typically for microcomputer connections the speed is 56K bps or less. If many LAN nodes must communicate with the host, many host ports are required. This not only reduces the number of ports available to the host's terminal users but also is somewhat costly. The cost for host ports can be significant and is burdensome for microcomputers that need only occasional access. Finally, when operating in

Table 16–7 Terminal Emulation Software Capabilities

Scripts	Mouse support	File transfer
Terminals emulated	Network support	E-mail
Phone directory	Text editor	Password entry
Capture of data to a disk		

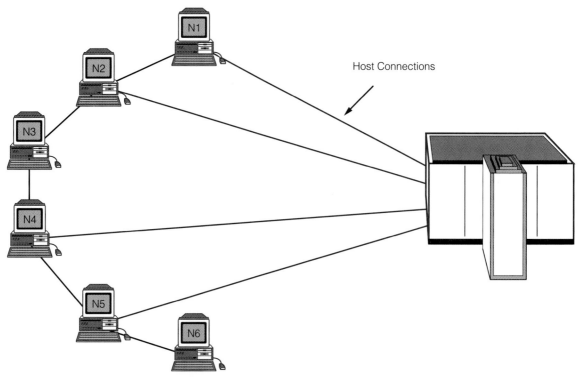

Host Connections

Figure 16–15
Multiple LAN-to-Host Connections

terminal emulation mode, the microcomputer loses some of its processing capabilities. It can essentially do only what a terminal can do. Specifically, the microcomputer can send and receive data but (usually) cannot use this interface to have a local application, such as a database management system, directly access data on the host.

multiplexer A hardware device that allows several devices to share one communication channel.

Multiplexing   A **multiplexer** is a hardware device that allows several devices to share one communication channel. Multiplexing typically is used to consolidate the message traffic between a computer and several remotely located terminals, as illustrated in Figure 16–16. This technique can also be used to allow several microcomputers to share a communication link to a host processor.

communication server A server that monitors connections to the host by determining whether there is a free port to make the connection and granting or denying the request accordingly.

Shared Asynchronous Connections   In some applications, each LAN node needs occasional access to the host but the number of concurrent connections is far fewer than the number of LAN nodes. A dedicated line per node is excessive in such situations. A better solution is to share asynchronous connections. The most common way to share connections is via a **communication server** or front-end processor (FEP), as illustrated in Figure 16–17.

In the figure, the communication server has four connections to the host. A microcomputer needing host services requests a connection through

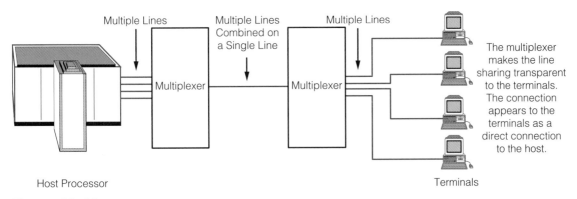

Multiple Lines

Multiple Lines Combined on a Single Line

Multiple Lines

The multiplexer makes the line sharing transparent to the terminals. The connection appears to the terminals as a direct connection to the host.

Multiplexer

Multiplexer

Host Processor

Terminals

Figure 16–16
Multiplexer Connection

the communication server. If all four ports are in use, the request is denied. If a host port is free, the request is honored and the microcomputer is connected to a vacant host port. You might note that the communication server functions much like a telephone switch.

Communication servers also may provide connections for remote hosts. The usual way a connection is made to a remote host is via a modem connection. The line to the remote host may be dedicated or switched. A dedicated line is continuously available; a switched line connection is established on an as-needed basis. The typical example of a switched line is a dial-up telephone line. The link between two devices is made via a telephone call, remains active during the length of the session, and is broken when the session is completed. Rather than providing each LAN node with a dedicated modem, the com-

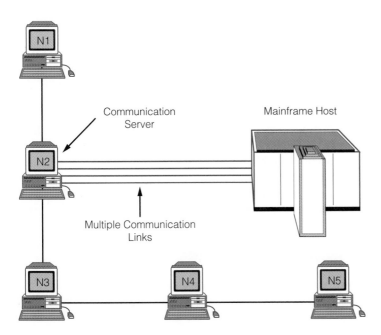

N1

Communication Server

Mainframe Host

N2

Multiple Communication Links

N3

N4

N5

Figure 16–17
LAN-to-Host Connections Using a Communication Server

munication server can provide modem sharing. The technique for doing this is much like the sharing technique described in the previous paragraph.

Other Types of Host Connections

Asynchronous connections are common because they are easily implemented and are supported by most host systems. On the microcomputer side, all that is necessary is a serial port and terminal emulation or file transfer software. The only host-specific characteristic is the type of terminal being emulated or the file transfer software. Other types of vendor-specific connections exist.

IBM System Connections

Because of the dominant role played by IBM systems, many of these connections are based on IBM software and hardware technologies. These connections might also work on non-IBM equipment because many large-computer companies support one or more IBM communication protocols. Two of the most common IBM interfaces are described here.

IBM-3270 Emulation   A mainstay of IBM's communication networks is the family of 3270 terminals. The family consists of a variety of terminals, printers, and cluster controllers. The communication protocol used for 3270 devices is a synchronous protocol, either binary synchronous (BISYNC) or synchronous data link control (SDLC), both of which were discussed in Chapter 11.

IBM-3270 emulation can be effected through a communication server or through individual LAN nodes. When emulation is implemented at individual LAN nodes, a synchronous communication controller must be installed in the microcomputer. The controller provides the necessary line interface. If a communication server is used, the server must have a synchronous communication port. Aside from the protocol interface, the connection works much like the asynchronous connection described earlier.

LU 6.2 Connection   For many years IBM networks have been designed around IBM's Systems Network Architecture (SNA), which is discussed in Chapter 15. In SNA users communicate through sessions and a variety of session types are defined. Logical units (LUs) represent users in establishing, using, and ending a session. One type of session allows programs to communicate with other programs. This type of session is called an LU 6.2 session. Support for LU 6.2 sessions is available for microcomputers and is being increasingly used to establish host connections. The advantage of an LU 6.2 interface is that a microcomputer application can communicate directly with a host application or with an application on another network node (as opposed to the microcomputer simply acting as though it were a terminal).

INTERCONNECTION UTILITIES

Having the ability to establish network connections is one part of communicating among networks. Another part is having utilities that help you use those connections. Many such utilities are available. Some are commercial products and others are available in the public domain for no or little cost. Some utilities you may find useful are briefly described below.

File Transfer Utilities   **File transfer utilities** allow you to move files between network nodes. File transfer capabilities are an intrinsic part of many routers. Part of the TCP/IP protocol suite is a file transfer capability. Kermit is another file transfer utility that runs on a wide variety of computer platforms. It uses asynchronous communication links to transfer ASCII format files. Two common microcomputer file transfer utilities are XMODEM and YMODEM. Kermit, XMODEM, and YMODEM are often included in terminal emulation programs.

file transfer utility An intrinsic part of many routers, this utility allows files to be moved between network nodes.

Remote Logon   **Remote logon facilities** allow users to log onto a remote system. A remote logon essentially establishes a remote user as a local user on the remote node. Once a user has successfully logged onto the remote node, commands issued by that user are processed and acted on by the remote node rather than by the local node. When the user logs off from the remote node, his session is reestablished on the local node.

remote logon facility A network utility that allows users to log onto a remote system by establishing the remote user as a local user on the remote node.

Access Servers   **Access servers** allow remote microcomputers to access LAN resources remotely. Suppose you are working at your home microcomputer and must do some work at your office. Specifically, you may have remembered that you have a report due in the morning. If the software, files, and e-mail essential to creating and distributing the report are available only on the LAN in your office, you have two options: You can drive to the office to complete the work or you can use the facilities of an access server. To access your LAN remotely, you need a serial port and a modem and a modem on the LAN end plus the communication software. This type of connection was described earlier.

access server An interconnection utility that allows remote microcomputers to access LAN resources from remote locations.

Access servers provide more than just modem connections. If you tried to run a LAN application such as word processing remotely, the word processing program would have to be downloaded into your computer. If your line speed is 2400 bps and the size of the application is 360 KB, it will take at least 25 min to download the program (2400 bps is about 240 characters per second). This level of performance is hardly acceptable. An access server is one solution to this problem. The access server runs applications at the LAN end of the connection and passes only the monitor display and keyboard data over the communication link. The remote processing can be accomplished by connections to remote access CPU boards (the user essentially has a dedicated remote CPU at the LAN) or by multiprocessing on a high-capacity microcomputer. The two approaches to access server technology are illustrated in Figure 16–18.

SUMMARY

Networks are not necessarily isolated islands of computing. Often there is a need to connect several LAN segments, connect homogeneous but separate LANs, connect heterogeneous LANs, connect LANs to WANs, connect one

LAN Medium   LAN Medium

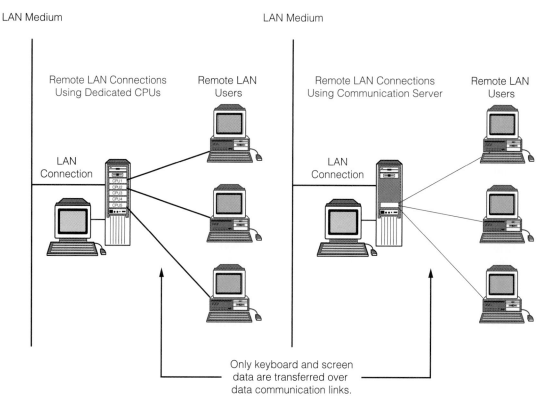

Remote LAN Connections   Remote LAN   Remote LAN Connections   Remote LAN
Using Dedicated CPUs   Users   Using Communication Server   Users

LAN   LAN
Connection   Connection

Only keyboard and screen
data are transferred over
data communication links.

Figure 16–18

Two Remote Access Server Technologies

WAN to another WAN, or connect LANs to a single host. These connections can be made in many ways.

Repeaters are used to connect segments of a homogeneous LAN and thereby extend the length of the LAN medium. Repeaters operate at the physical level. They simply accept a signal from one segment, amplify or regenerate the signal, and forward the signal the next segment.

Bridges connect homogeneous but distinct LANs. A bridge operates at the data link (MAC) level. A bridge receives a packet, looks at its destination address, and, if the address is a node on a LAN other than the one on which the packet was received, the bridge transmits the packet onto another LAN. Most of today's bridges are learning bridges. Learning bridges use spanning tree or source routing algorithms to learn the location of network nodes. Learning bridges can adapt to changes in network paths.

Routers operate at the network layer and can connect homogeneous or heterogeneous networks. A router receives a message, determines the address of the destination, and chooses a route for the message to take. The message may travel through several intermediate networks to reach the destination. Different data link protocols may be used in moving the message from the source to its recipient. Because they operate at the network layer, routers are independent of data link protocols.

A gateway is a name applied to network connections between heterogeneous networks. A gateway must perform translation functions such as packet formatting, speed conversion, and error checking.

Sometimes LAN nodes must be connected to a host machine. A variety of connection types exist. Some hosts can connect directly to the LAN and operate as a LAN node. Asynchronous connections are common and easy to implement but are quite slow. Synchronous connections offer greater speed but usually require additional microcomputer hardware. Because of the wide variety of connection services available, you should be able to find ready-made solutions to most of your LAN connection needs.

KEY TERMS

access server	learning bridge (transparent bridge)
active port	multiplexer
bridge	remote logon facility
brouter	repeater
communication server	root bridge
Connectionless Network Protocol	router
(CLNP)	routing table
dedicated connection	source routing
discovery packet	spanning tree algorithm
file transfer utility	Transmission Control Protocol/
flooding	Internet Protocol (TCP/IP)
gateway	Xpress Transfer Protocol (XTP)
inactive port	

REVIEW QUESTIONS

1. Give two reasons that a company might have two LANs in the same general location.

2. Identify the OSI level at which each of the following operates.
   a. bridge
   b. repeater
   c. router

3. Under what conditions can a repeater be used? What does a repeater do?

4. What does a bridge do? Under what conditions can a bridge be used?

5. What does a router do? Under what conditions can a router be used?

6. Compare the capabilities of repeaters, bridges, and routers.

7. Describe how TCP/IP sends a message from a node on one network to a node on another network.

8. Besides providing network interconnections, list three other functions you might find in TCP/IP.

9. What is a gateway?

10. Describe three distinct LAN-to-host interfaces.

11. What are the advantages and disadvantages of asynchronous LAN-to-host interfaces?

12. Describe two common types of microcomputer interfaces to IBM systems.

PROBLEMS AND EXERCISES

1. Evaluate the following LAN situations. State whether the LANs can be consolidated with a repeater, bridge, or router. Give all possible types of connection. State which connection alternative you would choose and state why you chose it.
   a. A token ring and a token bus.
   b. Two IEEE 802.3 LANs. One LAN has a total cable span of 1000 m and the other has a total cable span of 2500 m.
   c. Two IEEE 802.3 LANs. Each has a total cable span of 1000 m. Assume that the cable being used meets the IEEE 802.3 standard for maximum segment lengths of 500 m and a maximum distance of 2500 m per LAN.
   d. Three Novell LANs. One LAN is ARCnet, one is a token ring, and one is a CSMA/CD bus.

2. Your company has two IEEE 802.3 LANs, one in your eastern office and one in your western office (the distance between them is several hundred miles). The company wants to connect these LANs so users can more easily exchange data. The data being exchanged is primarily small messages, such as e-mail messages and small data files. Occasionally a file several megabytes in size must be exchanged but in these situations, the exchange is not time critical (for example, it could occur overnight). Devise a way to connect these LANs. Describe the type and speed of communication channel you would use to make the connection. Explain your decision.

3. Suppose the two LANs described in Problem 2 were different, such as a token ring and a CSMA/CD bus. Would your decision be different? Explain any differences and the reason for your decision.

4. Suppose the situation in Problem 2 were different in that the large files (2 MB or less) had to be exchanged within 2 min or less. Would your solution be different? Explain any differences and the reason for your decision.

5. A company has two large computers connected by a synchronous communication line having a speed of 56 Kbps. These computers are geographically separated, one in the eastern office and one in the western office. Each location also has a LAN. The company wants to allow all computer users, those connected to the LANs as well as those connected to the large computers, to be able to communicate. Can the connection be made using the existing communication link? Explain your answer.

6. Assuming that the existing communication link described in Problem 5 is used for the long-distance connection, answer each of the following:
   a. How can the LANs be connected to the large systems?
   b. Describe the changes a LAN packet will undergo as it moves from a LAN, to a large system, to the other large system, and then to the other LAN. Assume the LANs are homogeneous.

CHAPTER 17

Network Management Objectives

CHAPTER OBJECTIVES

After studying this chapter you should be able to

- Present a brief history of network management
- List the objectives of network management
- Describe ways of meeting network management objectives
- Explain what ergonomics means and the importance of ergonomically designed terminals
- Describe the network management organization
- Distinguish between managing a WAN and managing a LAN

Once a network is installed and operational, it must be managed. Proper management keeps the network components functioning in an optimal way. In this chapter we look at some techniques and tools for network management. This chapter begins with a discussion of the objectives and functions of network management, and how those objectives can be met. You then learn about generic and specific network management systems and some of the issues surrounding WAN and LAN management.

HISTORY OF NETWORK MANAGEMENT

The network management team has historically been responsible for the selection, implementation, testing, expansion, operation, and maintenance of the data communication portion of the data processing environment because early networks were concerned with the transmission of character-oriented data. Currently, data being transmitted by high-speed networks also includes graphics, voice clips, and video. Some companies are also combining telephone services with computer data on the same medium. With the integration of voice, data, and video transmissions on a common medium, the role of network management is expanding to include management of the entire telecommunication needs of an organization. In the past, voice, video, and data communication were usually separate and were managed by different groups. In today's communication environment, integrating and sharing media and hardware components can produce significant savings for a company. Despite these changes, covering all facets of telecommunication management is beyond the scope of this text. In this chapter we confine the discussion to management of a data communication network.

The role of network manager, like that of database administrator, is a new position within the data processing industry. Both positions were created by the technological expansion of the 1970s and the recognition of the increasing importance of these technologies to the storage, retrieval, and maintenance of business data. These positions are similar in several respects. Both have high visibility among system users. The database administrator is called when required data is unavailable. If terminals do not work or response time is unsatisfactory, the network manager is notified. Both roles are responsible for configurations, planning, tuning, and establishing standards and procedures in their respective areas. Both positions require personnel with a strong technical background, good leadership qualities, and an ability to work well with people who have wide ranges of technical expertise. These positions and the importance of an organization's processing and communication resources have been validated by the new executive position appearing in many companies, the chief information officer (CIO).

In the remainder of this chapter, the terms ***network manager,*** *network administrator,* and *LAN administrator* refer to the function of network management, and therefore to a team of people rather than to a single person.

network manager An individual or management team responsible for configuring, planning, tuning, and establishing standards and procedures for a network. Also known as a network administrator or LAN administrator.

NETWORK MANAGEMENT OBJECTIVES

The three primary objectives of network management are to

- support system users
- keep the network operating efficiently
- provide cost-effective solutions to an organization's telecommunication requirements

If these three objectives are met, the network management team will be successful.

Supporting System Users

Supporting system users means empowering them with the hardware and software tools to do their jobs effectively. Essentially it means keeping the network users satisfied. User satisfaction can also be enhanced by

repair person to travel to the site and run various diagnostic routines and testing procedures. Availability can be defined by the probability function[1]

$$A(t) = \frac{a}{a + b} + \frac{b}{a + b} \times e^{-(a+b)t}$$

where $a = 1/\text{MTTR}$, $b = 1/\text{MTBF}$, e is the natural logarithm, and t is a time interval. The equation gives the probability that a component will be available when required by a user. For a terminal with an MTBF of 2000 hours and an MTTR of 0.5 hours (typical of replacement with an on-site spare),

$$a = 1/0.5 = 2 \quad \text{and} \quad b = 1/2000 = 0.0005$$

Availability for an 8-hour period, then, is

$$A(8) = \frac{2}{2 + 0.0005} + \frac{0.0005e^{-(2+0.0005)8}}{2 + 0.0005}$$

$$= \frac{2}{2.0005} + \frac{(0.0005)(0.0000001121)}{2.0005}$$

$$= 0.99975 + 2.8 \times 10^{-11} = 0.9997$$

On average, an operator can expect the terminal to be unavailable three times in every 10,000 tries. Because the exponential term approaches zero and becomes insignificant as the time interval increases, availability in such cases becomes

$$A = \frac{\text{MTBF}}{\text{MTBF} + \text{MTTR}}$$

Table 17–1 shows availability given different values for MTBF and MTTR.

Availability with Multiple Components If several components—such as terminal, modem, medium, and CPU—must be linked together to make

---

[1] Nickel, Wallace E. "Determining Network Effectiveness." *Mini-Micro Systems,* November 1978.

Table 17–1 Availability for Several MTBF and MTTR Values

	MTBF				
	10	100	1000	10,000	100,000
MTTR					
1	0.90909091	0.99009901	0.99900100	0.99990001	0.99999000
2	0.83333333	0.98039216	0.99800399	0.99980004	0.99998000
5	0.66666667	0.95238095	0.99502488	0.99950025	0.99995000
10	0.50000000	0.90909091	0.99009901	0.99900100	0.99990001
20	0.33333333	0.83333333	0.98039216	0.99800399	0.99980004

the system available to the user, then system availability is given by the product of the availabilities of the component parts (Nickel, 1978):

$$A_s = A_t \times A_m \times A_l \times A_m \times A_c$$

where A represents availability and the subscripts s, t, m, l, m, and c represent the system, terminal, modem, link, modem, and CPU, respectively. If each component has an availability of 0.999, the user will see a system availability of

$$A_s = 0.999^5 = 0.995$$

In this situation, statistically the user would find the system unavailable 5 times every 1000 attempts, or once every 200 attempts. The availability factor is important in determining how many spare components to stock and how much productive time might be lost when the system is unavailable. Figure 17–1 illustrates system availability as a function of MTBF and MTTR.

reliability The probability that the system will continue to function over a given time period.

Reliability **Reliability** is the probability that the system will continue to function over a given operating period. If a transaction requires 3 s for a response to be received, then the reliability of the system is the probability that the system will not fail during that 3 s. Reliability of the network includes error characteristics of the medium and stability of the hardware and software components. More specifically, network reliability is a function of the MTBF. In some cases the user will see circuit errors in the form of slow response times. Data received in error will cause retransmissions, slower response times, and congestion of the medium. If the errors are persistent, the retry threshold for the link might be exceeded and the link consequently removed from service. For some modems, a large number of

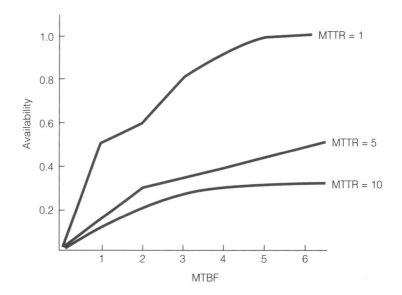

Figure 17–1
Availability, MTBF, and MTTR

errors will cause the modem to change to a lower speed to minimize the impact of the errors. Failure of hardware and software components is usually seen by the user as downtime on the system. With fault-tolerant systems the effect is either negligible or somewhat slower response times, depending on the system load. Even though the processor and all components of the system except one are functioning properly, the user, who is unable to continue working because of that one failed component, views the system as being down.

The reliability function, which is the probability that the system will not fail during a given period, is given by

$$R(t) = e^{-bt}$$

where b is the inverse of the MTBF, as described earlier. The time units used for MTBF and t must be the same. If the MTBF for a terminal is 2000 hours, and a transaction requires 1 min to complete, then the reliability is

$$R(1/60) = e^{-(1/2000)(1/60)} = e^{-(1/120,000)} = 0.999992$$

All times are expressed in hours. This equation shows that if the terminal is available at the beginning of the transaction, the probability is high that it will remain available throughout a 1-min transaction.

Reliability with Multiple Components   Like availability, system reliability is the product of the reliability of its components. If a system consists of a terminal, a medium, two modems, and a CPU, the reliability of the system from the user's perspective is

$$R_s = R_t \times R_m \times R_l \times R_m \times R_c$$

where $s, t, m, l, m,$ and c represent the reliability of the system, terminal, modem, medium link, modem, and CPU, respectively. Figure 17–2 shows reliability as a function of the MTBF.

Overall Effectiveness   The overall **effectiveness** of a system is a measure of how well it serves users' needs. Mathematically, effectiveness is given by the following formula:

> **effectiveness** A measure of how well a system serves users' needs.

$$E = A \times R$$

where E is the effectiveness, A is the availability, and R is the reliability of the system. The formula shows that, for a given system effectiveness, when R is greater than A the amount of time available for repairing a fault increases, whereas if A is greater than R the repair time is reduced (Nickel, 1978). Because R is entirely a function of the MTBF, an increase in R means that more time can be devoted to repairing the system to attain the same overall effectiveness. This is illustrated in Figure 17–3.

Reliability of Backup Components   In many networks, alternative components are available should one component fail. Communication paths

Figure 17–2
Reliability and MTBF

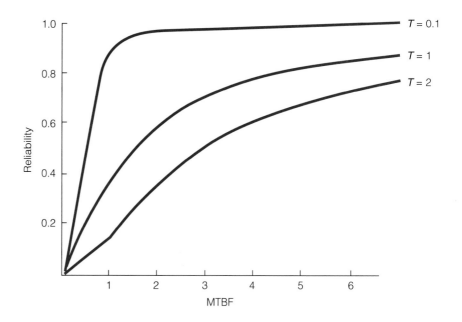

often have alternative links available, and fault-tolerant systems have available a backup CPU, disk drive, or other components. These backup components increase the MTBF of the system, which increases reliability, availability, and effectiveness. With backup components available, the reliability of the components operating in parallel is given by (Nickel, 1978):

$$R_p = 1 - (1 - R_s)^2$$

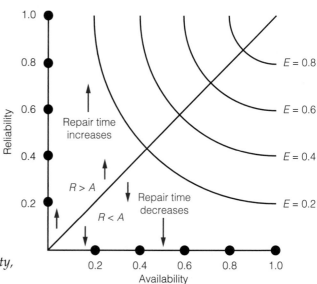

Figure 17–3
Reliability, Availability, and Effectiveness

where R represents reliability, p represents the components operating in parallel, and s represents a single component. If the reliability of a communication link is 0.995, the reliability of the link with a backup is

$$R = 1 - (1 - 0.995)^2 = 0.999975$$

Cost-Effectiveness

The third objective of network management is to provide cost-effective solutions to the data communication needs of an organization. As shown in previous chapters, there are many solutions to communication problems. Network management is responsible for selecting solutions that are feasible and cost-effective. If the network cannot contribute to the financial position of a company, it probably should not be implemented.

Planning   Planning is one way to save money. In configuring a network two basic alternatives exist: installing equipment to meet immediate needs and paying the price of upgrading when the time comes (which sometimes leads to lower immediate costs but a higher cost of expansion) or immediately buying equipment in anticipation of future needs (which creates higher immediate costs, with low-cost, easy expansion). Buying immediately for future needs is sometimes risky because technology changes so quickly. Usually the best alternative is to purchase modular equipment, which can be upgraded in small increments so overpurchasing is seldom necessary and expansion is easy. A variation of this approach is the planned movement of equipment, whereby lower-capacity equipment is gradually pushed outward and absorbed elsewhere in the network as newer, higher-capacity equipment is acquired.

Modular Expansion   Modular growth is available for several network components, the most fundamental being the computer itself. Many computer vendors offer a broad line of systems that allow growth within the product line. Most vendors have several different models spanning the distance between small systems and very large systems, and within each model there is also a certain amount of growth potential. The transition from one model to another is not always easy, often requiring a recompilation of programs and often causing significant rewrites. When an organization has finally reached the top of one model line and is ready to upgrade to the next model, the processors, operating systems, and network software often are not the same as those in current use, even if they are produced by the same vendor.

This approach can be contrasted with systems that allow **modular expansion** from a small system to an extremely powerful one by adding more of the same type of processor. There is no need to remove, sell, or return the existing equipment; it is simply augmented to provide the additional processing power. Computer vendors that offer this capability, such as Compaq Computers and Stratus Computers, often have systems designed for the transaction processing market, where expansion is very common.

modular expansion A single-vendor system that allows the user to upgrade from a small system to a more powerful system by adding more of the same type of processor to the existing system.

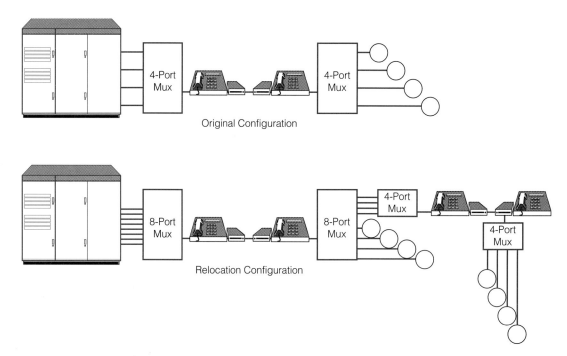

Figure 17–4
Relocation of Components

Modular expansion is also possible with front-end processors (FEPs) and multiplexers. Some vendors offer multiplexers that can be expanded from 4 to 32 or more lines, in increments of 4, 8, or 16 lines, so the user company pays for the cost of expansion only when necessary.

Planned Equipment Moves Planned equipment moves are an alternative when modular expansion is not possible. For example, the central site could begin with a four-port multiplexer, with remote sites also having four-port multiplexers. As the number of applications in a remote site grows, the central-site four-port mux could be moved there, a new eight-port mux added to the central site, and the old four-port mux used in a new location or cascaded off the eight-port mux. This is illustrated in Figure 17–4. Similarly, low-speed modems can be moved to low-traffic locations as they are replaced by high-speed modems. If the older equipment is not needed, it can be kept in inventory to be used as replacements for failed equipment. This type of activity requires longer-range planning than the other options; however, the financial rewards may make it preferable to the disposal of old equipment, possibly at a significant loss, every time a new piece is acquired.

MEETING THE OBJECTIVES

The objectives of network management are met by a combination of competent staff, hard work, careful planning, good documentation, implementing standards and procedures, communicating with users, and being able to work with other people to resolve problems. Although some of these elements may be absent in a successful network, the probability of success is directly proportional to how well these elements are realized.

Competent Staff

The most important element is creating a competent staff that can overcome deficiencies even in other areas. Specific staff qualifications depend on the hardware and software used, but some generalizations can be made. The functions of network management can be grouped into the areas of design and configuration, testing, diagnosis, documentation, repair, and, on rare occasions, coding. The team must have detailed knowledge of both hardware and software; ideally, every member of the team would know both areas, but often one person is an expert on hardware, whereas another's specialty is software. The staff should be versatile and creative in resolving problems because many solutions are ad hoc, temporary ones that require ingenuity. Finally, and perhaps most important, staff should be able to work well with both technical and nontechnical personnel. Being able to describe the technology to those not "in the know" and to elicit the necessary technical information from nontechnical users is critical to the team's success.

Design and Configuration

The staff should be skilled in use of the diagnostic and planning tools described later in this chapter. In design and configuration, they should understand configuration alternatives and their strengths and weaknesses. They must be willing and able to keep up with changes in hardware and software of the existing system as well as capabilities offered by other vendors, including a multitude of different tariff structures from a growing number of common carriers. Furthermore, when configuring clients, the staff should choose equipment with good ergonomic design.

Ergonomics

Ergonomics, also called human engineering, is the science of designing equipment to maximize worker productivity by reducing operator fatigue and discomfort while improving safety. Currently, a very important consideration in terminal and microcomputer design and selection is the unit's human engineering. Several physical problems have been attributed to poor terminal design, including radiation side effects, headaches, eye strain, muscle and tendon problems, and arthritic conditions. Perhaps the major side effect of VDU terminals is their emission of radiation. Terminal and microcomputer monitors emit low-level radiation, and users working near the monitors are exposed to those emissions. Some companies have noted a higher incidence of birth defects among women working at VDUs, and several lawsuits have been filed in this regard. According to U.S. law, radiation emitted from a terminal must be less than 0.0005 rems per hour at a distance of 2 in. from the screen. Radiation reduction is usually achieved by filtering the radiation with a glass screen. Radiation emission is one factor to consider when selecting a monitor.

ergonomics The science of designing equipment to maximize worker productivity by reducing operator fatigue and discomfort while improving safety.

Three other ergonomic factors to consider include monitor position, monitor display, and keyboard position. Among the most common user complaints are head, neck, and eye strain. Head and neck strain can be caused by the user having to adjust to the fixed position of a monitor. An ergonomically designed monitor can be tilted and swiveled to a position that is comfortable for the user. Finger, hand, and wrist strains result from improper positioning of the keyboard. The keyboard should be detached from the monitor so it can be moved to a position comfortable for the user. Computer furniture is also an ergonomic factor to consider. With a chair that can be raised and lowered and a movable keyboard platform, the computer system can be adjusted comfortably to the user. Again, the key is to have a unit capable of adjusting to a user rather than requiring a user to adjust to the equipment.

Eye strain can be caused by poorly formed characters, flickering screens, and poor foreground/background colors. A good monitor has crisp, well-formed characters and images, and the contrast between foreground and background colors should be visually pleasing. Ergonomic studies show that green or amber foreground characters on a black background is easier on the eyes than other combinations, such as white letters on a black background. Another factor affecting eye strain is screen flickering. CRT screen images are constantly refreshed by "repainting" the screen image. Low refresh rates cause screen images to fade before being refreshed, creating a flickering effect that can cause headaches and eye strain.

Ideal Terminal Characteristics   The ideal display should be easy on the eyes, with a nonglare surface. Green phosphor or amber characters on a black background are preferred to white characters on a black background. The display should tilt and swivel for ease of reading. The screen image should be refreshed at a sufficient rate to avoid flicker, and contrast should be adjustable to ease eye strain. Display characters should be well formed and easy to read. The keyboard should be detachable and at a convenient height. Keys should be sculpted and arranged for easy access. The keyboard should emit a click to reinforce each keystroke, and the loudness of the click should be controllable, from inaudible to somewhat loud.

Diagnosis

Skill in diagnosing the cause of problems, often under considerable pressure, is essential. Whenever a problem in a production system is encountered that disables all or a portion of an online application, immediate resolution is needed. A failed system prevents employees from fully performing their job functions and decreases productivity. In some situations, direct revenue is also lost, as in an airline reservation system.

Planning

Planning is another key to success. Because of the dynamic nature of networks, constant planning and replanning are necessary to ensure that objectives are met. Too often, network managers are so caught up in day-to-day activities that they ignore long-range planning. This behavior is both common and self-perpetuating. Without good planning, problems occur more often and require a greater amount of time to be solved. There is often truth to the adage, "If you fail to plan, you plan to fail." Corporate goals are set by upper-level management. Planning that defines the actions essential to accomplishing these goals should include short-term and long-term objectives. Short-term planning includes scheduling of personnel, hiring, training, budgeting, and network maintenance and enhancement activities. Long-term planning involves predicting and resolving expansion issues, integrating new technologies, and budgeting.

Documentation, Standards, and Procedures

Documentation, standards, and procedures are an outgrowth of good planning. Good documentation includes source code listings of the software, logic diagrams, internal and external specifications for the system, wiring and connection diagrams, hardware specifications, and users' manuals. Documentation is used in all phases of network management. Standards and procedures together provide consistency in system management. Standards set minimal acceptable levels of performance and implementation. Procedural guidelines aid in operating and maintaining the system and are especially necessary in resolving problem situations.

In summary, meeting network management objectives requires a group of talented people who

- have the right tools in place
- have a well-defined but flexible direction for the short term and the long term
- are willing to work unusual hours in sometimes difficult or stressful environments
- can work effectively with people at all levels of capability

The growth in network management has placed large demands on the supply of qualified people. As a result, network management personnel are currently among the most difficult to find and highest paid in the computer industry.

NETWORK MANAGEMENT ORGANIZATION

Once a system has been successfully installed, tested, and made operational, the day-to-day management of the network begins. Operations tasks include monitoring, control, diagnostics, and repair. Just as application developers design a system to solve business problems, network managers should design a system—part manual, part automated—that solves the problems of operations. The manual portion of the system is necessary for restoring a down system, a task that cannot be accomplished with software when the hardware is not running.

Control

Control functions to be performed include putting failed lines or terminals back in operation, adding new lines or terminals, and taking failed components out of the system. Control of a geographically separated, multiple-computer network is somewhat more difficult because parts of the control function must also be distributed. The distributed case is discussed here because a subset of it applies to single-node or collocated-node networks.

control center A network component responsible for monitoring the network and taking corrective action when necessary.

Control Center   The **control center** is responsible for monitoring the network and taking corrective action where necessary. In a distributed network, it is not uncommon to have more than one control center. In a network of cooperating, independent users, such as a network of universities, each node can participate in the management and control functions, with each installation being responsible for control of its part of the network. However, the central control site is usually able to resolve any problem.

A processor may be dedicated to the control function in very large networks. Several companies provide computers and software designed specifically for network control. A network control system typically consists of special microprocessor-based modems that collect **network statistics** that are periodically transmitted to the network monitor node for storage and analysis. The monitoring systems gather information such as error rates, data rates, and the number of retransmission attempts resulting from errors. Trend analysis of this data can help determine gradual degradation so faults are immediately reported and corrective measures taken.

network statistics Information, such as error rates, data rates, and the number of retransmission attempts resulting from errors, that is collected to analyze network performance trends.

Network Monitors   The control facility must have at least one hardware/software monitor so the management team can probe every node for problems and gather network parameters and statistics. The monitors also enable managers to make any necessary changes to the system. These include

- bringing lines and terminals into and out of service
- bringing network applications to an orderly halt and start network applications
- altering network parameters, such as the process controlling a terminal
- checking for line errors and implementing corrections
- initiating and evaluating line traces
- running diagnostic routines
- adding and deleting users from the system
- controlling passwords for local and remote nodes
- maintaining the control center database

A network database contains data about the network configuration, the release level of all software and hardware components, the names of contact individuals at remote sites, histories of problems and solutions, outside contact points for vendors, and documentation.

Problem-Reporting System   Ideally an online **problem-reporting system** should also be available for retrieving trouble reports via keywords. This capability is especially helpful in managing a distributed network in which problems can be encountered and resolved in multiple locations simultaneously. An online problem-reporting system can help managers avoid having to repeatedly solve the same problem.

problem-reporting system A system for recording and managing error reports.

Problem-Reporting Procedure

Another important function of a control center is the acceptance and resolution of problems. Some solutions may lie outside the control center itself; however, the center should remain active as an intermediary in resolving the problem. This section describes a prototype control center's operation with respect to problem reporting and resolution. Although a computerized problem-reporting system is assumed, a manual system with the same functionality could exist.

Network managers should publish a problem-reporting procedure that describes the information users must gather to report a problem, and to whom the report should be made. It is assumed that users have been directed to contact their control center about network problems by telephone rather than by any automated problem-reporting system. An end user, such as a terminal operator, ordinarily should not be expected to interface with an automated problem-reporting system. When the problem report call is received, the network manager obtains all relevant information, including

- date and time of the call
- date and time the problem was first observed
- name of the caller and how the caller might be reached
- names and contact information for any other personnel involved in the problem
- a brief but detailed description of the problem
- whether the problem is reproducible or intermittent
- possible contributing external influences such as installation of a new software release, reconfiguration, power glitches, or the equipment being used

A problem report containing the relevant information is generated and a copy returned to the reporting person. As soon as the problem is resolved, the solution is noted in the trouble report, a final copy is sent to the reporting installation, and the trouble report is marked closed. If the solution is not immediately known, the control center begins its evaluation, first searching the problem database to determine whether such a problem was resolved before. If not, problem investigation begins. The first objective of such an investigation is to isolate the problem and pinpoint the source of the difficulty, which can involve looking at statistics and system console or log messages, initiating line traces, using line monitors, taking program dumps or traces, debugging, or running hardware diagnostics. If the problem is isolated to an area of vendor responsibility, such as network control programs, the vendor is contacted and the supporting documentation is passed to the vendor for analysis. The degree of vendor involvement varies among vendors, and even within one vendor company the support level can vary among individual customers, depending on the expertise available. Some users provide a vendor with a complete analysis and suggested solution, whereas others simply report the existence of a problem and leave the diagnostics to the vendor.

Additional Control Center Responsibilities

The additional responsibilities of the control center are creating and maintaining documentation, implementing security, establishing procedures, performing release control, and training personnel. Documentation, which should be kept current, includes operations manuals, procedures for emergency and routine activities, notification lists, contingency plans, inventory, source program listings, and statistics. Security measures include creating and assigning passwords, setting user access levels, monitoring and reacting to unsuccessful logon attempts, ensuring that passwords are changed periodically, and checking physical security where applicable. Procedures should cover normal operating guidelines as well as those for handling abnormal situations such as network failures. Escalation policies that bring problems to the attention of higher management levels if the problem persists and contact names and numbers are also included. **Release control** includes the installation, testing, and implementation of new versions of hardware and software to ensure compatibility of new features with existing software and hardware, and to uncover any new problems, which are often introduced with new releases. Finally, training involves all levels of personnel who use or maintain the network.

release control Procedure including the installation, testing, and implementation of new versions of hardware and software to ensure compatibility of new features with existing software and hardware.

LAN VERSUS WAN MANAGEMENT

In theory, you might expect LAN management to be essentially the same as WAN management. In practice that is not usually the case. WAN management typically involves

- geographically distributed nodes
- some local autonomy in node management and control
- diverse hardware platforms and network protocols
- a variety of media types and speeds
- third-party media vendors

WANs typically grew out of data processing departments and the management concerns are more technically oriented than those for LANs, which grew out of stand-alone microcomputer environments. If a site has interconnected LANs and WANs, responsibility for management of the interconnection interfaces often falls on the WAN management team. This means the WAN management team must be aware of large and small system concepts, whereas the LAN administrator is not usually required to have knowledge of large systems and WANs.

Consider the enterprise network portrayed in Figure 17–5. Each LAN will probably have an administrator who is responsible for keeping the LAN functioning. The WAN managers are responsible for

- keeping all WAN nodes operating properly
- working with common carriers to obtain and maintain links between nodes
- maintaining connections between subnetworks
- coordinating efforts of subnet managers
- managing LANs collocated with the WAN

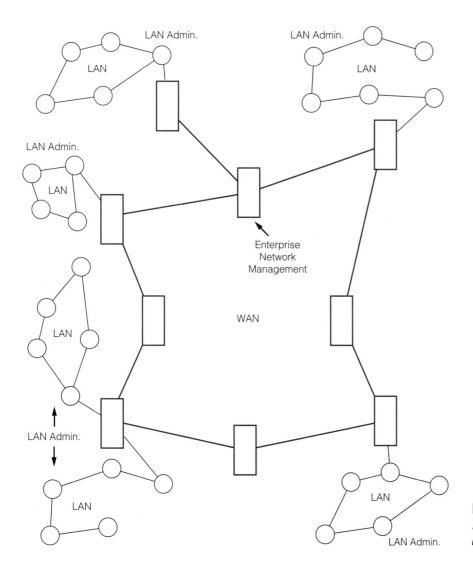

Figure 17–5
Network Management in an Enterprise Network

- establishing standards for workstations
- administering license agreements for all network and workstation software
- maintaining the network notebook
- implementing chargeback policy so that new network products can be funded

Having evolved from mainframe management environments, WAN management personnel are typically highly experienced data processing personnel who know the intricacies of data communication subsystems and large system operating systems. In contrast, a LAN administrator may be chosen from the ranks of skilled microcomputer users. Sometimes personnel chosen for this position have limited technical backgrounds as compared to their counterparts in WAN management. We have already described the profile of a network management team and the skills they need. Let us now look more closely at one of the entry levels of network management: LAN administration.

In a six-person office in which each person has a microcomputer workstation, how do you imagine the management and operations of the workstations are conducted? In most offices

- Each person is responsible for backing up his or her data (if it is done at all).
- Each person is responsible for operating a microcomputer.
- There is no office data processing manager (although there may be a local "expert" on whom others rely for help).
- No provisions are made for security.
- If resource sharing exists, it is done via disk exchange or printer switches.
- If someone makes a mistake or if one system fails, it has little impact on the others.
- A certain amount of software trading occurs because the office does not have one copy for each user.
- Everyone wants the best printer attached to his or her computer.

Now, suppose the office manager informs everyone that a LAN is about to be installed and that, after the dust settles, a more effective computing system will be available. The manager probably is correct with respect to the LAN providing a more effective computing platform. However, let us look at another implication of a LAN: LAN management.

In switching from a stand-alone microcomputer environment to a LAN, it is essential to have two or more people designated as LAN managers. If the LAN is large, several people may be actively involved as LAN managers; if the LAN is small, one person may be the principal manager and the second the alternate. (What constitutes a small, medium, or large LAN is difficult to define. For our purposes, small LANs are those with fewer than 50 workstations and only 1 server; a medium LAN has 50 to 150 nodes and 3 or fewer servers; all other LANs are considered large. Be aware that some small LANs can be as complex to manage as a large one.) The alternate LAN manager assists the primary manager as necessary and fills in when the primary is absent.

During installation, LAN management is a full-time job. After the LAN is in operation, management tasks are less time-consuming. For a small LAN, management tasks may take less than 1 hour a day; for a large LAN, management may be a full-time position and may even require more than one full-time person. It is easy for a business to overlook the costs of LAN management.

LAN Management Tasks

Before the LAN is installed, LAN managers should be hired or existing personnel trained. The amount of training varies according to the complexity of the system. At a minimum, managers should know the fundamentals of data communication and how to

- connect and disconnect workstations
- diagnose and correct medium problems
- add and delete users
- create the users' environments
- implement security
- create, modify, and manage the printing environment
- install and modify applications
- make system backups
- recover from system failures
- monitor and evaluate performance
- add new resources, such as a new server
- maintain LAN documentation and procedures
- assist in setting up LAN interconnections
- detect and remove viruses

Connecting and Disconnecting Workstations A LAN often is not static. New workstations must be added and existing ones moved or removed, particularly during LAN installation and the initial stages of operation. The procedures for installing a new workstation vary from one implementation to another, but usually the following steps are required:

1. Install the LAN adapter in the workstation.
2. Establish a connection on the medium for the new workstation. This may require a new port on a multistation access unit or wiring hub, a new BNC connection on a coaxial cable, or simply a tap into a cable.

3. Connect the workstation to the medium by establishing a connection between the LAN adapter and the medium.
4. Install network software in the workstation.
5. Boot the new workstation and test its ability to communicate over the network.

Once the new workstation is working, the network documentation ought to be updated to reflect the new address and wiring circumstances.

Diagnosing and Correcting Problems   In some LANs, the most common problems are medium faults: wiring breaks, loose connectors, and unterminated cables. Being able to locate and correct these faults is critical to the success of the LAN. A host of other problems can occur as well, including

- improperly installed network software
- improperly installed application software
- user errors
- broken equipment
- improper security settings

Solving these problems requires diagnostic skills and the right set of tools. These tools are discussed in Chapter 18.

Adding and Deleting Users   Each LAN user must identify himself or herself when logging onto the LAN. Each user is authorized to run certain applications and perform a set of actions on selected files. These privileges are described in the following section on security. The network manager must assign user IDs and delete or modify user IDs when a user leaves or changes job functions. Users are usually associated with a group (one for personnel administration, one for payroll administration, and so on). Like users, groups have assigned privileges on the LAN. Again, it is the responsibility of the LAN manager to define the required groups and to assign individuals to one or more groups. Sometimes, the LAN manager will pass user and group administration functions to unit managers.

For each new user, the LAN administrator typically creates or assists in creating the user's environment. Some of the tasks that might be completed are

- creating a home directory for the user
- adding the user to the network mail system
- creating a **user logon script** (a set of actions to be taken when the user logs on, such as setting search paths and initial menus)
- setting default security parameters
- setting limits on resource use, such as the maximum amount of server disk that the user can consume
- setting printer mappings

user logon script A set of actions to be taken when the user logs on, such as setting search paths and initial menus.

Creating User Environments   The LAN administrator must assist in creating the proper environment for each user. This includes providing access to the proper applications, setting up user menus as called for, setting up the proper printing environment, and providing access to the necessary servers. Much of this is accomplished via batch command files and user logon scripts. The key to setting up these environments is to make LAN use transparent, so the user has access to the necessary LAN facilities without being made aware of the details of the LAN itself.

Implementing Security   In making the transition from a stand-alone to a LAN environment, resources that were once private may become shared. A file that resided on a stand-alone system may be placed on a file server, a program that existed on one or two microcomputers may be placed on a file server, or a printer available to only one microcomputer might be attached to a printer server. Being placed in a shared circumstance does not mean, however, that any user should to be able to read or modify the file, run the application, or use the printer. Instead, the LAN manager must create an access profile for each user, group, file, application, and hardware device. Some attributes thus defined are given in Table 17–2.

Table 17–2   Security Attributes

File Capabilities
  Ability to examine a directory listing
  Ability to read or write a file
  Ability to delete, rename, or create a file
  Ability to execute an application
  Ability for several users to simultaneously use a file
  Ability to restrict a file to one user at a time
  Ability to define file ownership
  Ability to pass privileges on to another user

User and Group Capabilities
  Allow file access according to the capabilities just described by user and group
  Require a password
  Require passwords to have a minimum number of characters
  Require passwords to be changed at certain intervals
  Allow logons only during specified times
  Allow a user to logon only from selected workstations
  Include users in a group
  Specify account expiration date
  Restrict amount of disk space used
  Detect multiple logon attempts and deactivate workstation or account

Monitoring Capabilities
  Identify users logged onto system
  View information about users
  View information about jobs
  View a user's activity on servers
  View what is displayed on a workstation
  Take control of a workstation's keyboard

There may be more or fewer capabilities depending on the particular implementation. Additional utilities often can be purchased to enhance the capabilities provided with the LAN software. For example, most LANs do not provide the ability to view what is displayed on a workstation's monitor or to take control of the keyboard, but several utilities exist that can be added to do this.

Creating, Modifying, and Managing the Printing Environment
There can be two types of printers on a LAN: dedicated and shared. **Dedicated printers** are attached to workstations and can be used only by a person at that workstation. **Shared printers** are those controlled by a server and available to designated users. The latter type of printer is discussed in this section.

The general layout for a LAN printing system, a spooler, is presented in Chapter 8. An application might go through the following steps to print a document on a shared printer:

dedicated printer A printer that can be used only by a person at the workstation to which the printer is attached.

shared printer A printer controlled by a server and available to designated users.

1. The application opens a printer port, such as LPT1 in a DOS system, and begins writing to that device.
2. The LAN printer software intercepts the print stream and routes it over the network to the server.
3. The server print collector accepts the print stream and stores it in a file.
4. Steps 2–3 continue until the application closes the connection to the printer port or until a timeout limit of no print output is reached. In either case, the workstation software sends an end-of-job designator to the server.
5. The server closes that print job and schedules the job to be printed.
6. The printer driver looks at the scheduled jobs, selects the one with the highest priority, and prints it on the printer.
7. On completion of printing a job, the printer driver selects the next available job and prints it, and so on.

From each user's perspective, the needed printer is always available and dedicated to that user. It is the **spooler** that provides this virtual printer capability. The spooler can also provide other functions, such as

spooler A software system that collects printer output (typically on disk) and schedules the data for printing. *Spool* is an acronym for *simultaneous peripheral operation online.*

- printing multiple copies
- printing a document on several printers
- holding a document on disk after printing or instead of printing
- printing selected portions of a document
- printing banners before each print job

At the more detailed level, there are many factors to consider and parameters to set when installing and controlling a printing subsystem. The factors are too many to cover in detail here, and the ways in which they are established vary from one LAN to another. In essence, the LAN administrator carries out the following tasks:

- mapping printer ports on workstations to a print queue
- mapping print queues to one or more printers
- associating a printer with one or more print queues
- changing the print queue and printer port configuration
- assigning a printer priority scheme, such as printing small jobs before large jobs
- monitoring the print jobs on disk
- removing print jobs from disk
- starting or stopping print jobs or printers
- adding or deleting printers

Being able to obtain printed output is one of the basic needs of a LAN system. With all the configuration options typically available, the LAN administrator can provide an environment that meets or exceeds the needs of the LAN users; on the other hand, a poorly designed configuration can hinder printing effectiveness.

Installing and Modifying Applications   When installing a new application, the LAN manager must plan how the application will be used, which users will need it, and on which servers the application will reside. Applications not designed for shared use must be installed in a way that prohibits concurrent usage. Applications that can be used concurrently must be installed in a manner that maximizes their capabilities for each user. Most important, the LAN administrator must understand and comply with the application vendor's **software license agreements.** License agreements vary considerably. Some software programs are licensed for only one workstation; some are licensed for a specific number of concurrent users, such as four concurrent users; some are licensed to allow access for all users on a specific server; and some are licensed to allow access for all users on all servers. Obviously, understanding the license agreements is important for application selection and installation.

software license agreement A document provided by the software vendor that specifies the rights and restrictions of using the software.

Each application user ideally is able to match his or her hardware with the application's features. Accordingly, a user with a color monitor ought to be able to tailor the application and have it display that user's preferred foreground and background colors. A user with a monochrome monitor will have a different user profile that runs correctly on his or her workstation. Other features that might be accounted for include the type of graphics adapter, display size, amount of memory available, and so on. Once the application is operational, the LAN administrator is responsible for installing application upgrades. A major application release sometimes provides significant changes in the system operation and the user interface to the system.

The LAN manager must plan for the transition from the old system to the new one. In such cases, it is usually prudent to have both application versions available to make the transition to the new application easier.

Making System Backups   Recall that in the stand-alone microcomputer environment, each user is responsible for backing up his or her data files. On a LAN, this responsibility is assumed by the LAN administrator. The administrator must design a backup policy that allows data files and programs to be recovered. Backup devices and the associated software capabilities were discussed in Chapters 6 and 8.

Recovering from System Failures   The main purpose of making backups is to recover from failures. The LAN administrator must prepare procedures to be implemented if the LAN fails. Because some failures do not affect files, the recovery procedures must encompass more than file recovery. For example, a workstation may fail in the middle of an application. The LAN administrator ought to have a procedure for recovering the application and lost work.

Monitoring and Evaluating Performance   LAN usage is likely to change over time. New users might be added, some workstations deleted, and applications added or deleted. The LAN administrator must monitor the LAN usage and plan necessary changes. If usage increases, a new server may be needed or, if multiple servers exist, the usage may need to be better balanced among them. Things the LAN administrator may monitor include

- printing environment
- disk usage
- number of active users
- application usage
- transmission faults
- server-busy statistics

Based on the performance statistics, the LAN administrator plans corrective action.

Adding Resources   The LAN administrator must plan the acquisition and integration of any new LAN resources into the system. If a file server is added, the LAN administration must decide which files are to be placed on the new server and which users the file server will primarily serve. After integrating the new server, the administrator will monitor the LAN activities to ensure that service is satisfactory and that all components are used effectively.

Maintaining LAN Documentation and Procedures   Much of the success of data processing administration stems from having good, current documentation and procedures. The LAN administrator is responsible for creating and updating this documentation.

Assisting in Setting Up LAN Interconnections   In Chapter 16 you read about the ways in which one network can be connected to another network. The LAN administrator is involved in setting up the proper hardware and software interfaces on the LAN side of the connection. If two LANs are being connected, the administrator may be responsible for all of the interconnection details.

Detecting and Removing Viruses   One concern of network administrators at all levels is the proliferation of computer viruses and similar disruptive programs or code modules. It is estimated that over 100 new viruses are released in general circulation each month; furthermore, recent surveys have estimated that only one-third of the installed virus detection/removal programs are current. Additionally, viruses are taking on new forms. Macro viruses are now imbedded in word processing documents, and new or existing viruses are coded so that their signature can change and thus make them harder to detect. Before macro viruses, a virus was embedded only in executable programs. Because viruses are constantly changing, today's network administrators must have up-to-date virus detection and removal software and procedures as well as employee procedures to prevent the inadvertent introduction of viruses. There are several sources of software for virus detection, and many of them can stay memory resident and provide continuous scanning. All network administrators need to include computer viruses in their planning and procedures.

WAN Management Tasks

The responsibilities of WAN managers differ somewhat from those of a LAN manager. A LAN administrator is an integral part of the network management team; however, in this section the term *WAN management team* refers to the group of network managers whose responsibilities include WAN management. Some LAN management tasks typically not carried out by a WAN manager are

- creating user environments, a task typically carried out by programming personnel
- creating, modifying, and managing the printing environment, a task typically carried out by operations personnel
- installing and modifying applications, a task typically carried out by programming and operations personnel
- making backups, a task typically carried out by operations personnel

A representative list of WAN management tasks is given here:

- connect and disconnect workstations
- diagnose and correct medium problems
- add and delete users
- implement security

- recover from system failures
- monitor and evaluate performance
- add resources, such as a new server
- maintain LAN documentation and procedures
- assist in setting up LAN interconnections
- detect and remove viruses
- interface with a common carrier
- estimate equipment and media costs
- configure network components to meet transmission and cost requirements
- interface with corporate and vendor personnel in devising network solutions
- resolve problems regarding international telecommunication
- develop and maintain network software
- coordinate and consolidate network management

Tasks in this list up to and including detecting and removing viruses are common to LANs and WANs and have been discussed above. Let us look at the management tasks that are unique to WANs.

Interfacing with a Common Carrier   As technology advances, we may see increasing instances of LANs being implemented using a medium provided by a common carrier. Currently, the use of common carrier media in LANs is uncommon, whereas in WANs it is common. In the United States, a company can choose from among several common carriers. Each common carrier has characteristics that set it apart from its competitors. Differences among common carriers may include rates, types of media and services, locations served, and quality of service and support. The WAN management team must be familiar with the advantages and disadvantages of each common carrier and choose the most cost-effective alternatives.

Network problems can be caused by a company's equipment, by a common carrier's equipment, or by the interface between the two. When problems occur that cannot be isolated to the company's equipment, the network management team must work with the common carrier in diagnosing and correcting the problem.

Estimating Equipment and Media Costs   A LAN administrator will also carry out this task; however, the number of options and range of prices are much greater in a WAN. In configuring portions of a WAN, the management team must evaluate several common carriers, perhaps several services per common carrier, and data communication equipment from a variety of vendors. Often the number of possible solutions is large. If a company considers three common carriers, two services per carrier, and five different data communication providers, each of which has three pieces of equipment to consider, the number of combinations of vendors, services, and equipment is 90. Choosing the best one requires considerable analysis and expertise.

Configuring Network Components Like estimating equipment and media costs, configuring network components is a process of evaluating a large number of alternatives. A LAN's standard and topology limit the ways in which network components can be added. In a WAN there are usually fewer restrictions, the configuration task is much more complex, and the cost of solutions is often greater than for LAN configuration solutions. For example, adding a node to a LAN usually means finding the closest wiring hub or cable and attaching the node to it. Adding a node to a WAN often requires obtaining one or more communication lines from a common carrier, deciding which existing nodes the new node is to be linked to, procuring the hardware and software for the new node, preparing the site for installation of the new node, and training personnel to manage the new equipment.

Resolving Problems Regarding International Telecommunication In Chapter 15 you read about international networks. LAN administrators need not be concerned with international issues. Managers of international WANs must address the issues raised in Chapter 15. These issues are

- politics
- regulations
- hardware
- language
- tariffs

The WAN management team must consider these issues in estimating network costs, use, and configuration.

Developing and Maintaining Network Software A LAN administrator is responsible for setting up a user's application environment but seldom gets involved in fixing or writing network software. The WAN management team may need to customize some characteristics of the network or install corrections to faulty network programs. If a company has a unique device that must be attached to the network, the WAN management team may need to write the network interface code or modify an existing interface. When errors are detected in network software, the software vendor may distribute patches to the code. The WAN management team is responsible for inserting the patches and testing the system to ensure that it works properly.

Coordinating and Consolidating Network Management A LAN administrator is usually responsible for one or more LANs in a specific location. The WAN management team is responsible for the coordination and consolidation of all aspects of network management, including the operation and interconnection of subnets. The knowledge and responsibilities of the

WAN management team are far beyond those of the LAN manager. Problems that cannot be solved by local operations or LAN management personnel become the responsibility of the WAN management team. WAN managers must remain aware of problems in all segments of the network to avoid duplicating diagnosis and correction of problems that have already been encountered and resolved.

SUMMARY

As the use of data communication expands, so will the importance of network management. The keys to effective network management are knowledgeable personnel who can work well with a broad spectrum of users, planning, and the effective use of network management tools. Network management is involved in the design, testing, and operation of a system. A certain amount of implementation or development is also required in some installations.

Network management is both a function and an application. The application portion should be designed and implemented like any other business application. The primary functions for computerized implementation are problem-reporting systems, tools, network management software that reacts automatically to problems in the network, and diagnostic systems. With careful management, the network can be a valuable asset to a company; with poor or no management, even the best designed application system can fail. If the network is incorrectly designed, is not modified to meet changing demands, or is often inoperable, and if problems are not readily resolved, users will lose confidence in the system, and the network's effectiveness will be diminished.

KEY TERMS

availability	performance
control center	problem-reporting system
dedicated printer	release control
effectiveness	reliability
ergonomics	shared printer
modular expansion	software license agreement
network manager	spooler
network statistics	user logon script

REVIEW QUESTIONS

1. What are the two main objectives of network management?

2. Why is user satisfaction an important network management objective?

3. Describe the functions performed by the network management team.

4. Why is ergonomic design an important terminal selection criterion?

5. How do problems get reported and resolved? What documents are generated as a result of the problem-reporting system? Who receives copies of these documents?

6. How are statistics used in network management?

7. Describe the documentation created and maintained by the network management team.

8. List ten LAN management tasks.

9. What must a LAN manager do when installing a new workstation?

PROBLEMS AND EXERCISES

1. Identify and describe five subobjectives of network management. Match each subobjective with a main network management objective.

2. Besides the ergonomic requirements of terminals, what other environmental guidelines should be followed with respect to a terminal work environment? What lighting, noise dampening, and furniture should be available to protect the user? How often should breaks be taken?

3. Design a problem-reporting form. What are the essential elements of a problem-reporting form?

4. If you were assigned to recruit a LAN manager, what experience would you require of candidates? What salary can a LAN manager expect?

5. A personnel file contains data regarding an employee's name, address, date of birth, date of hire, performance rating, and salary. You have been assigned to set security for this file for all employees and employees in the personnel and payroll departments. Suppose that you can set security attributes on each data item. What attributes would you assign to
   a. all employees?
   b. employees in the personnel department?
   c. employees in the payroll department?

   Explain your decisions.

6. How are backup files used in recovering from a disk head crash that destroys both the disk and the data stored thereon?

7. A company has decided to install a LAN and has collected data from two vendors regarding their equipment reliability. The figures the company obtained are as follows (in hours):

Device	Vendor A MTBF	Vendor A MTTR	Vendor B MTBF	Vendor B MTTR
Workstation	4000	2.5	3500	1.5
LAN adapter	8000	1.0	8500	1.0
File server	3500	4.5	3500	4.0

Which vendor has the best availability? Which vendor has the best reliability? Which vendor has the best effectiveness?

CHAPTER 18

Network Management Systems

CHAPTER OBJECTIVES

After studying this chapter you should be able to

- Discuss the general workings of a network management system
- Compare the SNMP and CMIP standards
- Explain the capabilities of IBM's Netview network management system
- Explain the capabilities of Novell's Network Management System
- Compare network management tools

This chapter begins with a discussion of a generic network management system (NMS) and NMS protocols, and concludes with a brief look at two NMS implementations: IBM's Netview and Novell's Network Management System. The chapter concludes with an overview of tools used in managing a network.

NETWORK MANAGEMENT SYSTEM SOFTWARE

A network should be under continuous scrutiny to ensure that the objectives of customer satisfaction and cost-effectiveness are met. Too often, network problems surface through user complaints. This is usually not the way a network manager wants to learn about problems. A far better way is to have potential problems detected and reported by a network management system, so problems may be corrected before users become aware of them.

A **network management system (NMS)** is a combination of hardware and software used by network supervisors to monitor and administer the

network management system (NMS) A combination of hardware and software used by network supervisors to monitor and administer a network.

507

network. The NMS must be able to determine the status of network components such as modems, lines, terminals, and multiplexers. If a device's status indicates that malfunctions are occurring, the NMS will either take automatic corrective action or alert a network supervisor of the condition. The network supervisor may then use network control functions of the NMS to take corrective action. An NMS also gathers network statistics, such as line use information, together with capabilities for evaluating those statistics. The information produced assists network supervisors in capacity planning.

In the past, most network software vendors neglected the area of network management. With few exceptions, the network software and hardware were built and installed with little support for managing them. Although management of small networks is not difficult, the composition of networks changed as more businesses made the move to online systems. Two of these changes have had a significant impact on the ability to manage networks. First, the number and complexity of network nodes have increased. Early networks may have consisted of one central processor with communication controllers and terminal devices. The host assumed a supervisory role and provided a centralized point of control and management. Often the communication links were point-to-point leased or switched lines. In contrast, many of today's networks have multiple processing nodes and hundreds or thousands of connected devices. The network may consist of LANs, X.25 networks, leased lines, satellite and microwave links, switched lines, and PBX systems. Numerous interfaces between different types of equipment and networks are common.

Second, many of today's networks are a hybrid of processors, terminals, controllers, modems, and other components from different vendors. Just managing a homogeneous network in which all the components are provided by one vendor is difficult. In the past, effectively managing a large network with components from multiple vendors approached the impossible. Fortunately, this problem is being recognized by network managers and vendors alike, and NMSs are being sold from both network vendors and independent software companies. We first consider the requirements of a generic NMS and then discuss the specific capabilities provided by IBM's Netview, Netview/PC, and Netview/6000. These products were chosen for two reasons: their applicability to a large body of users and their functionality. The reader should be aware that other products exist, some of which provide more comprehensive management features.

A Generic Network Management System

To understand an NMS, consider a hypothetical network of a large, international manufacturing firm. This company has processing nodes in many locations throughout the world. A small portion of this network from one manufacturing location is depicted in Figure 18–1. The backbone network is an SNA network (see Chapter 15), and there are two domains. The major components of the system come from seven different vendors. The host processors in both domains are from Company A. The communication controllers were purchased from Company B, but run IBM NCP (Network

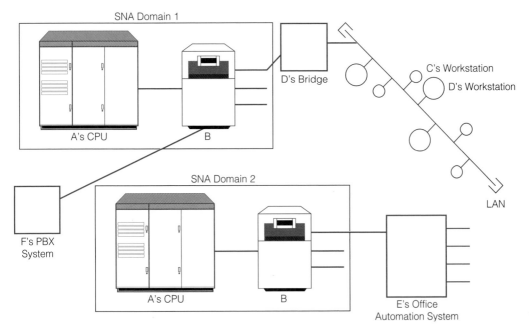

Figure 18–1
Integrated Network

Control Program) software. The engineering and development department has an IEEE 802.3–compatible LAN to support its design efforts. The workstations are special purpose and were provided by two companies, C and D. A bridge to the SNA network is provided using Company D's equipment. The interface to the SNA network is via LU 6.2. The office automation system uses equipment from Vendor E and interfaces to the SNA system in the same way as the engineering bridge. The PBX system obtained from Vendor F is also tied into the network. Modems and multiplexers were all obtained from Vendor G. What will the network management team need to know to keep this network running efficiently? A summary of this information appears in Table 18–1.

In a large network, if all of the data being gathered is sent to the network managers, both the network and the network managers would have a difficult time keeping up with it. Simply receiving the data is not enough; it must be received in a usable format. The NMS is responsible for ensuring that the correct data is received and that it is in a usable format. The network segment illustrated in Figure 18–2 shows a network component, a portion of the NMS, and the connection to the control center. The NMS continually obtains status and operational data from the components it is monitoring. Ordinarily the data is routine, and is either ignored or logged for later evaluation. Specifically, if the component being monitored is a communication line, some of the information the NMS will receive could be the number of errors encountered since the last status report, current status, line quality, number

Table 18–1 Network Management Information

Host Processors	Communication Controllers
Status	Status
CPU busy rates	Processor busy rates
Internal queues, such as on TCP	Buffer use
Transaction turnaround time in the CPU	Queues
Buffer use	Peak activity time
Peak activity times	Performance during peak activity
Performance during peak activity	

Lines	Terminals
Status	Status
Number of failures	Number of failures
Number of retries	Failure types
Aggregate data rate	Number of transactions
Peak activity time	Type of transactions
Performance during peak activity	Transaction response time
Active devices on the line	
Line quality	
Changes in line quality	

Processing Nodes	Modems
Status	Status
Number of transactions	Errors
Response time	
Type of transactions	

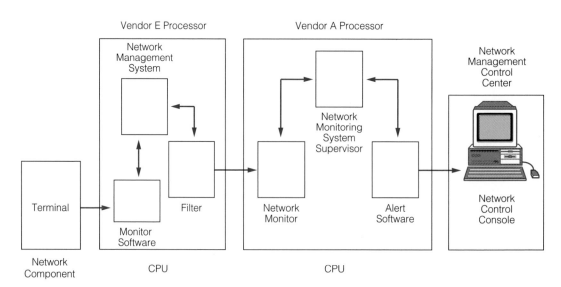

Figure 18–2
Network Management System

of retries on the line, and number of characters transmitted or received. When some statistic changes, it must be brought to the attention of the network managers, which is called an **alert** or **alarm.** If a problem has occurred, the NMS should also assist the managers in solving the problem by indicating the potential causes and perhaps even solutions.

If the values received are within tolerance, and if data collection is enabled, the data is logged. Later it may be evaluated for trend analysis and capacity planning. If the data is not within accepted tolerance levels, this must be brought to the attention of the network managers. An alert is necessary for a data communication line if the line is down, the error rates have exceeded some threshold, the number of retries is excessive, or the line is congested. A change in service level also may be cause for an alert for a component that is being closely monitored. For example, if a line has been operating between 20% and 25% capacity and suddenly experiences 50% load capacity, an alert may signal this change.

When an alert condition has been detected, it must be forwarded to the network management center. Steps that may be taken in this process include

> **alert** A signal given by the network management system that a statistic, such as current line status, line quality, or number of retries on the line, has changed since the last status report. Also known as an alarm.

1. Identification of probable causes of the alert condition.
2. Formatting the message for the NMS presentation services. Component addresses, status, and probable causes must be identified. In Figure 18–2 this function is performed by the software component identified as a **filter,** which is used to screen and format data sent to the management center. A filter can perform many functions, one of which is to control the flow of data to the center. Flow control avoids flooding the control center with repetitious status messages.
3. Transmission of the data to the control center for display.
4. Passing the message through a formatter at the control center, which determines where and how the message is to be displayed. Many NMS presentation services use color monitors to present the data. Warnings may be displayed in yellow, outages in red, and major catastrophes in blinking red with an audio signal. The message is also usually logged to an alert history file.
5. The network management team acting on the alert as necessary and documenting the event and its solution.

> **filter** A software component used to screen and format data sent to the management center.

As mentioned earlier, obtaining the proper information to manage a network is difficult enough in a homogeneous network environment. In a mixed-vendor configuration, additional complexities must be resolved. In Figure 18–2 the network management control center is attached to one of the host processors and uses software provided by that vendor, Vendor A. Vendor A's network management tools are designed to monitor only its own equipment and to present messages in a specific format. In the configuration shown, terminals attached to Vendor E's processors may be involved in a session with a host logical unit. This terminal also may not be supported by the host system.

The problems that must be resolved in this type of environment include obtaining status information from each vendor's equipment, formatting the alerts in a manner consistent with the host's requirements, and routing alerts and their associated data to the host node for display. Once the alert has been raised, the system managers must react to it. For example, if a device is malfunctioning and disrupting the network, the device must be deactivated until the problem is fixed. The NMS provides an interface that allows the network managers to deactivate the device and later bring it back online. If several vendors are represented, each vendor is likely to have different peripheral control utilities and different command languages. In Vendor A's environment the command to bring a failed terminal, such as the terminal known to the system as TERMINAL-X, back online may be RESTORE TERMINAL-X, whereas in Vendor E's system the same command may be DEVICE TERMINAL-X UP. Thus, once the alert has been received, correction in a mixed-vendor network may not be simple. One cannot expect network managers to know the command languages required to remedy faults on several different vendor systems. Even on one system there may be several interfaces for fault correction. One interface may be used for physical devices and another for logical devices and connections. If a terminal has failed and needs to be restored, it may be necessary to activate the terminal on the line via a peripheral utility program and, using a different utility, notify application programs that the terminal is again available.

To reduce the complexities of dealing with multiple-vendor equipment, and sometimes even a variety of interfaces from one vendor, the NMS may provide a command mapping function. This allows the network managers to work with one command language that has a consistent interface. The command mapping function selects the proper interface programs to receive the message and translate the command into a format acceptable to these programs.

NETWORK MANAGEMENT PROTOCOLS

Network interconnection raises an additional network management problem. The problem is how to monitor nodes on one subnetwork from a node on a different subnetwork, such as monitoring a node on a token ring from a network management console attached to an IBM SNA network. To facilitate the exchange of management data among network nodes, a network management standard or protocol is essential. If such standards exist, network designers can build their networks with the ability to exchange management and control data. Two such standards have evolved: the **Simple Network Management Protocol (SNMP)** and the **Common Management Information Protocol (CMIP)**. CMIP is also sometimes called the **Communications Management Information Protocol.**

Simple Network Management Protocol

The SNMP is a part of the TCP/IP suite described in Chapter 16. Originally the protocol was implemented on UNIX systems. Since the first SNMP products appeared in 1988, they have rapidly gained acceptance

---

Simple Network Management Protocol (SNMP) SNMP provides a guideline for creating network management software products. SNMP has four key components: the SNMP protocol, Structure of Management Information (SMI), Management Information Base (MIB), and the Network Management System (NMS).

Common Management Information Protocol (CMIP) ISO guidelines for creating network management products. Also known as the Communications Management Information Protocol.

Structure of Management Information (SMI) A component of the SNMP that details how information is represented in the Management Information Base.

Management Information Base (MIB) A database that defines the hardware and software elements to be monitored in the SNMP protocol.

and popularity. The protocol is endorsed by companies such as IBM, Hewlett-Packard, and Sun Microsystems and is implemented on most microcomputer, minicomputer, and mainframe computers under a variety of operating systems. As the protocol has spread, its capabilities also have been expanded to accommodate new needs. Currently, the SNMP standard is SNMP version 2 (SNMPv2).

SNMP has four key components: the protocol itself, the **Structure of Management Information (SMI),** the **Management Information Base (MIB),** and the **Network Management System (NMS).** The SNMP is an application layer protocol that outlines the formal structure for communication among network devices. The SMI details how every piece of information regarding managed devices is represented in the MIB. The MIB is a database that defines the hardware and software elements to be monitored. SNMPv2 expanded the capabilities of the original MIB and this new version is called MIB II. The NMS is the control console to which network monitoring and management information are reported. The components of the SNMP are shown in Figure 18–3.

Each SNMP device has an **agent** that collects data for that device. The data is stored in the device's MIB. A vendor that creates a device adhering to the SNMP standard will include an agent as one of the device components. Thus, there are agents for routers, servers, workstations, bridges, terminal servers, multiplexers, hubs, repeaters, and concentrators. An SNMP **management component** interfaces with agents to provide network control. The management component uses three basic commands, GET, SET, and TRAPS, to control a device. The **GET** command allows the management component to retrieve data stored in the device's MIB, and the **SET** command allows data fields stored in the device's MIB to be reset. **TRAPS** allows an SNMP device to trap and forward unsolicited data; for example, a trap would be used to notify the management component of an alert condition. One example of a trap is a cold-start trap that notifies the management component when a device has been powered up.

The MIB contains information that the network administrator needs to monitor and control the network. Each device being monitored has its own individual MIB that contains data about only that device. A device MIB has two parts: a proprietary part in which data defined by the device vendor is saved and the part in which data common to all MIBs is stored. The data stored in device MIBs can be collected in a network management MIB that contains data for multiple network components. A new SNMP standard also provides for a **Remote Monitoring MIB (RMON MIB),** which describes nine different device groups. A vendor must choose an appropriate group for a device and is required to support all data objects defined for that group. There is also an ability to support devices that do not directly support SNMP.

SNMP allows network managers to get the status of devices and set or initialize devices. If problems occur, an event mechanism generates a message that is displayed on the network monitoring console. As a simple protocol, SNMP has a few shortcomings. Its command set is limited, there are limited provisions for security, and, because it lacks a strict standard, there is some inconsistency among different vendors' implementations.

Network Management System The control console to which network monitoring and management information are reported in the SNMP protocol.

agent A device component that collects data for the device, which is then stored in the MIB.

management component A component that interfaces with the SNMP agent to provide network control.

GET An SNMP command that allows the management component to retrieve data stored in a device's MIB.

SET An SNMP command that allows data fields stored in a device's MIB to be reset.

TRAPS An SNMP command that allows a device to trap and forward unsolicited data, such as an alert condition.

Remote Monitoring MIB (RMON MIB) An SNMP standard that describes nine different device groups. A vendor must choose an appropriate group for a device adhering to this standard and is required to support all the data objects defined for that group.

Figure 18–3
Details of the SNMP Environment

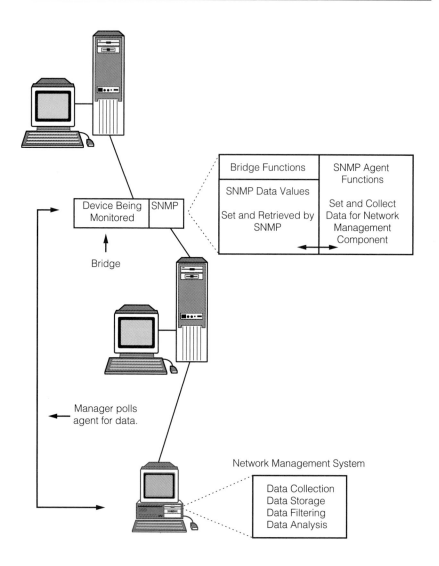

Common Management Information Protocol

In competition with SNMP is the International Standards Organization's (ISO) Common Management Information Protocol (CMIP). CMIP has a more complex protocol for exchanging messages among network components and has the potential for better control and the ability to overcome the limitations of SNMP. Unfortunately, there currently are no provisions for direct interoperability of SNMP and CMIP; however, some NMSs communicate concurrently with SNMP agents as well as CMIP agents. Thus, interoperability may arise through specific NMS implementations. Because CMIP was developed more recently than SNMP, operational systems are just beginning to emerge. It will take some time for CMIP to overcome the market penetration of SNMP. CMIP has been endorsed by AT&T and Digital Equipment Corporation, and its capabilities are being implemented in each vendor's product line.

With this general overview of network management, we now look at a specific implementation of an NMS system, IBM's Netview, Netview/PC, and Netview/6000 products. Netview/6000 supports SNMP and it is realistic to assume that CMIP support will also be implemented.

IBM'S NETWORK MANAGEMENT SYSTEM

Netview and Netview/PC were introduced by IBM in 1986, and another version, Netview/6000, was introduced in 1992. The original Netview consolidated and extended several network management packages that had been used to monitor and control SNA networks. Netview is thus oriented to managing the host SNA environment. Netview/PC contains logic for monitoring IBM's token-ring network, PBX systems, and other vendors' equipment. Netview/6000 runs on IBM's UNIX-based systems and provides support for multivendor networks with no centralized host system.

Netview

Netview runs on an IBM host system and is the NMS for monitoring and controlling an SNA network. The functions it provides include control services and diagnostic control capabilities, such as hardware monitoring, session monitoring, and status monitoring. Hardware monitoring collects status information from physical devices, and session monitoring provides information on SNA sessions. Status monitoring provides display information regarding system components and assists in restarting system elements following a failure. The control function provides the ability to activate and deactivate devices. In addition to the management and control functions, Netview provides two other basic facilities: help and a user interface. The help function provides users with online assistance as well as an operator tutorial. The user interface allows scripts, called Clists, to be prepared by users to monitor devices or to automate startup and shutdown sequences.

Netview/PC

Netview/PC, as the name indicates, runs on a microcomputer. Netview/PC is an important component in IBM's open communication architecture (OCA). IBM recognizes that networks tend to have a mixture of vendor equipment. OCA opens an IBM network from a management perspective by providing other vendors with interface specifications. Through these, other vendors can integrate their equipment more completely into the network. Within Netview/PC this integration is effected through an application program interface (API).

API allows users to write applications that can interface to non-IBM devices. The API applications can be written to have device-specific interfaces as well as a Netview interface; this allows the application to establish the management connection between the device and IBM's network management tools. Within Netview/PC, IBM provides this interface to its token-ring LAN and to computerized PBX systems. Status information collected by the microcomputer running Netview/PC may be stored on the microcomputer's local disk or forwarded to Netview, which runs on the host system. If alerts are received, they either may be handled at the microcomputer or may be forwarded to the host for operator intervention and resolution. The interface between the host and the microcomputer is either via an SNA 3270 terminal or as an LU 6.2 session type.

Netview/6000

Netview/6000 represents IBM's NMS for decentralized networks and networks using the SNMP. Netview/6000 requires fewer system resources than Netview and can run on smaller platforms. Netview/6000 has the ability to monitor up to 30,000 different objects and supports SNA capabilities such as LU 6.2, the virtual terminal access method (VTAM), and advanced peer-to-peer networking (APPN). Netview/6000 also provides support for managing LANs and devices such as bridges, wiring hubs, and routers.

Netview Architecture

The Netview architecture identifies three types of control points: focal points, entry points, and service points. A focal point is a central point for network management and monitoring functions. Focal points provide host-oriented functions including functions related to billing, line optimization, and performance analysis. Entry points relate to IBM or IBM-compatible network elements. Entry point functions include remote management and control modules, which allow the element to be controlled remotely from the control center and to communicate with Netview. Service points are gateways into the Netview system from non-SNA devices. Service points are characterized by Netview/PC and the devices it monitors and controls.

To summarize, through Netview and Netview/PC, IBM has created a system that allows centralized control of a distributed system that consists of IBM, IBM-compatible, and non-IBM equipment. Netview provides the ability to monitor and control the SNA network, and Netview/PC provides the same function for other network components. With Netview/6000, the management and control functions have been extended to include decentralized networks and multivendor networks.

NOVELL'S NETWORK MANAGEMENT SYSTEM

NMS is both a generic term for a network management system and a specific term for Novell Corporation's Network Management System. Novell's NMS contains a collection of tools oriented toward managing LANs using Novell's network operating system. The main functions managed by NMS are network faults, performance, configuration, security, and accounting.

NMS consists of several components, including Network Management Map, Network Services Manager (NSM), and NetWare Management Agents (NMA). The Network Management Map (NMM) is essentially a database that represents all LAN components, such as details about servers, workstations, LAN adapters, wiring hubs, bridges, and routers. The NMM is a resource for other NMS components. In addition to collecting network

Table 18–2   Network Management Systems

Company	Product
Applied Computing Devices	Network Knowledge Systems
AT&T	Accumaster Integrator
Cabletron Systems	Spectrum
Cheyenne Software	Monitrix Network Manager
Digital Equipment Corporation	DECmcc
D&G Infosystems	LANWatchMan
Hewlett-Packard Company	HP Open View Network Node Manager
Hughes LAN Systems	Monet Network Manager
Intel Corporation	LANDesk Manager
MAXM Systems Corporation	MAXM
MCI Corporation	FocusNet
NCR Corporation	NetWare Management Systems
Nynex Allink Company	Allink Operations Coordinator
Objective Systems Integrators	NetExpert Toolkit
SunConnect	SunNet Manager
Systems Center	Net/Master
Unisys Corporation	CNMS
Visisoft	VisiNet Enterprise

configuration data, the NMM can graphically display the complete or partial network configurations.

The NSM and NMA components work together to provide statistics and alerts to the NMS console. The NMS polls NMAs for statistics, similar to the way in which SNMP collects data from device agents. The NSM can organize and report on data collected. A dedicated or nondedicated workstation is used as the LAN administrator's interface to the NMS. Other features found in Novell's NMS include

- application program interfaces to give third-party vendors access to NMS functions
- modules for monitoring packets, protocols, and media
- modules to track wiring hub performance
- automatic server fault detection and alert notification
- an interface to IBM's Netview
- graphical and text reporting
- setting of thresholds for devices

Table 18–2 lists several NMSs and their vendors.

NETWORK MANAGEMENT TOOLS

To carry out its various duties, the network management team often uses a variety of tools. In addition to the tools previously described for managing a LAN, a variety of other tools exist. These can be divided according to their function: diagnostic tools, monitoring tools, and management tools. They differ from the LAN tools discussed in Chapter 17 because they can be used for both LANs and WANs.

Diagnostic Tools

LAN analyzer A diagnostic tool that monitors network traffic, captures and displays data sent over the network, generates network traffic to simulate load or error conditions, tests cables for faults, and provides data helpful for system configuration and management.

LAN Analyzers   **LAN analyzers** are similar to digital line monitors (discussed in Chapter 10). A LAN analyzer monitors network traffic, captures and displays data sent over the network, generates network traffic to simulate load or error conditions, tests cables for faults, and provides data helpful for system configuration and management.

analog line monitor A diagnostic tool that monitors and displays the analog signals on the communication circuit or on the data communication side of the modem, enabling the user to check for noise and proper modulation.

Analog Line Monitors   An **analog line monitor** measures and displays the analog signals on the communication circuit or on the data communication side of the modem, enabling the user to check for noise and proper modulation. Analog line monitors are used primarily by common carriers to evaluate their circuits and are seldom used in a user's environment.

Cable Testers   **Cable testers** are used to detect faults in cables by generating and monitoring a signal along the cable. By monitoring the signal, a cable tester not only can detect faults in the medium itself, or in medium connections, but also can identify the location of the fault.

cable tester A diagnostic tool used to detect faults in cables by generating and monitoring a signal along the cable.

Emulators   An **emulator** is a diagnostic tool that enables the user to check for adherence to a specific protocol. For example, a vendor must have its X.25 software certified by a packet distribution network before being allowed to connect to the system to avoid disrupting other system users; one way the software can be tested is with an emulator. The emulator acts like an X.25 node, generating both correct and incorrect messages to ensure that the system reacts according to the X.25 specifications. Emulators of this type usually allow the user to specify the types of messages to be transmitted. Emulators also can be used during the development process to ensure that the interfaces between software levels are correct.

emulator A diagnostic tool that enables the user to check for adherence to a specific protocol.

remote control software A diagnostic tool that allows a LAN administrator to remotely view a user's monitor and take control of the user's keyboard.

Remote Control Software   **Remote control software** tools allow a LAN administrator to remotely view a user's monitor and take control of the user's keyboard. This capability is helpful during initial diagnostic work because it allows the network administrator to experience the problem firsthand. Sometimes the problem can be resolved remotely, thus providing more immediate correction and a reduction in the diagnostic time required by hands-on diagnostics.

Current Documentation   One of the best diagnostic tools is current documentation, including software lists that reflect the correct release and patch levels, logic diagrams, internal documentation, maintenance manuals, and any other supporting documents. Although documentation may seem obvious as a diagnostic tool, its importance cannot be overstated. Key documents that system implementers need to consult are compatibility lists. Each piece of hardware and software is usually accompanied by a compatibility list. It is important that related products adhere to the same standards because incompatibilities are a major source of system problems.

Diagnostic tools help locate problems in the network, whereas monitoring and management tools are used to avoid problems in the network. Monitoring and management functions include capacity planning, general project management, performance, and configuration. Several of these tools have been developed for microcomputers and are affordable for many users. Capacity planning is an extremely important function of network managers, who must recognize when resources are approaching full capacity and plan for expansion or reconfiguration to avoid saturation and decreased service. Project management tools allow a manager to plan and monitor the progress of projects. System performance and configuration address how well the system is working and the location and types of network components.

Four tools that are very effective in planning for capacity are metering software, performance monitors, simulation models, and workload generators.

Monitoring Tools

Metering Software **Metering software** is used on LANs to enforce adherence to software license agreements. Metering software runs on a LAN server and keeps track of the number of times an application is executed. If an organization has a license to concurrently run 25 copies of a word processing program, the LAN administrator sets the metering count to 25 for that application. Whenever a user starts the application, the counter is incremented by 1, and when a user exits the application, the counter is decremented by 1. If the usage counter is at 25 and a user attempts to start the application, the metering software denies the request.

metering software A monitoring tool used on LANs to enforce adherence to software license agreements by keeping track of the number of times an application is executed.

Performance Monitors **Performance monitors** provide snapshots of how a system is functioning, typically capturing such information as number of transactions, type of transaction, transaction response times, transaction processing times, queue depths, number of characters per request/response, buffer use, number of I/Os, and processing time by process or process subprogram. When collected over time, information of this nature enables the management team to identify trends in the use or misuse of the network, such as whether the number of a specific type of transaction is steadily increasing and whether the capacity for handling that transaction type is being reached, or whether users are playing games during lunch hour when the peak processing load occurs.

performance monitor A monitoring tool that provides snapshots of how a system is actually functioning, which helps the network management team identify trends in the use or misuse of the network.

Simulation Models **Simulation models** allow the user to describe network and system activities and to receive an analysis of how the system can be expected to perform under the described conditions. This service is especially useful during the development stage to predict response times, processor use, and potential bottlenecks. During operations, simulation models help determine what size transaction load is likely to reach or exceed

simulation model A monitoring tool that allows the user to describe network and system activities and to receive an analysis of how the system can be expected to perform under the described conditions.

full capacity as well as the effect of adding transactions, applications, and terminals to the existing system.

A good simulation model in the development stage can avert performance problems during the design stage. Simulation models vary significantly with respect to the amount of information provided and the manner in which the user defines the workload. A simple model for line use and polling overhead might interactively prompt the user for the speed of the line, data link protocol, number of polling characters, modem turnaround time, and number of stations on the line, resulting in a report indicating the processing and line overheads of the polling and the maximum and average wait times a device might expect between polls. A comprehensive model, on the other hand, uses a network configuration file and a transaction file as input. The configuration file will contain the complete hardware configuration, including disk drives, disk drive performance characteristics, line types, data link protocols, terminal types, database files and their locations, and access methods. The transaction file contains a list of transaction types and the activities each transaction type performs, such as number of I/Os to each disk, access method used, number of instructions executed, and number of characters input from and output to a terminal.

In addition to the two user-supplied files, the simulation model is driven by software performance characteristics such as polling overhead, instruction execution times, and disk access times. This type of model outputs information similar to that provided by a performance monitor, including expected response times, line use, processor use, and disk use. The simulation model essentially enables the user to see how an application will run without ever writing it. If the model predicts that a particular communication line will have 300% use and a response time of 10 min, either a faster circuit or more circuits will be needed to support the workload.

The time required to set up a simulation run varies with the amount of detail needed. The comprehensive model just described requires a considerable amount of information regarding the application. Usually it is not necessary to have the correct initial configuration, as the model will indicate areas of over- and underuse. If the processor is 150% busy, either a larger or an additional processor is needed.

Workload Generators   Whereas the simulation model predicts system use, a **workload generator** actually generates the transaction loads and pseudo-application processes for execution on the proposed configuration. If the model and the workload generator were perfect, the results would be identical; in actual practice, however, some variation between the two is likely to occur. A workload generator together with a performance monitor can illustrate how the system will actually function in the proposed configuration. It also can be used for stress testing. As with any model, the above models are only as good as the inputs, the people who use and interpret them, and the closeness of the models to actual use. Their value decreases with the amount of time required to use them and increases with their ability to portray an application accurately. This means they should be used carefully and the results interpreted sensibly.

workload generator A monitoring tool that generates transaction loads and pseudo-application processes for execution on a proposed configuration to illustrate how a system will actually function.

Log Files **Log files** are another tool valuable in monitoring a system. Certain logs, such as a system log or network messages, should be maintained continuously, whereas others can be used only when necessary. A line trace, for example, is a log of the activity on a particular line that is normally used only when a problem has been detected. Some software has been designed to log its activities on demand; the network manager would enable or disable the logging, depending on what information is required. Log files are used for both diagnostic functions and predictive or management functions.

log file A monitoring tool used for both diagnostic functions and predictive or management functions.

Network Configuration Tools **Network configuration tools** are used to plan the optimum network configuration with respect to sources and types of circuits. In the past these have been expensive to purchase or use, and some were limited to one common carrier's facilities or geographical locations. These systems are now available on microcomputers and at more affordable prices.

network configuration tool A monitoring tool used to plan the optimum network configuration with respect to sources and types of circuits.

Management Tools

Menuing and Inventory Software **Menuing software** is used in both LANs and WANs to provide users options via a menu of choices. On LANs, menu software allows a network administrator to quickly implement a set of choices and the actions associated with those choices. **Inventory software** is capable of interrogating many components of a LAN and collecting information on those components. Examples of the data collected include network addresses, CPU types, operating systems, disk use on servers and workstations, and workstation and server memory configurations. Many of the statistics needed by a network administrator in managing and fixing a network are automatically provided and reported by inventory software.

menuing software A management tool used to provide users options via a menu of choices.

inventory software A management tool used to collect LAN component data, such as network addresses and CPU types, that will assist a network administrator in managing and fixing a network.

Project Planning Tools **Project planning tools** are beneficial in the administration of the network, in planning the activities of the team members, in the installation of new equipment and software, and in numerous other management activities. Many of these tools are now available on microcomputers, bringing them to more users at a low cost.

project planning tool A tool used by project managers to define, monitor, and modify project events, resources, and schedules.

Database Management Systems and Report Generators Database management systems and report generators are also useful management tools. The database can be used to store statistical and operational information, which a good query/report writer can select, synthesize, and summarize. These systems can schedule members of the network management team, store and retrieve error and trouble report information, and produce reports on modeling. Database management systems are available on most systems today and can be very useful in storing, modifying, and retrieving data about the network management function. State-of-the-art systems enable users to define a database; enter, modify, and delete information; and generate reports without having to write much code. Many of the microcomputer relational model database systems provide all these features and are oriented toward users with little expertise in programming or systems.

SUMMARY

Managing a network can be a complex task requiring a wide range of information and tools. NMSs and utilities assist the administrator in managing the network and correcting network problems. An NMS collects statistics on network components, provides alerts when proper operation is threatened, and generates standard reports to allow the network manager to monitor performance and take corrective actions before problems develop. Two network management protocols, Simple Network Management Protocol (SNMP) and Common Management Information Protocol (CMIP), have been defined to assist vendors in creating software and hardware that can be monitored. The SNMP is part of the TCP/IP suite and is widely used in a variety of hardware and software platforms. The CMIP is an ISO recommendation for collection and reporting of management information. Although more comprehensive than the SNMP, CMIP is not yet widely implemented.

A number of vendors provide NMSs. IBM's Netview has three variations: Netview, Netview/PC, and Netview/6000. Each is designed to support different network configurations. Netview is designed to support SNA networks, Netview/PC provides interfaces to non-IBM devices in an SNA network, and Netview/6000 is designed for noncentralized networks using a variety of vendor platforms. Novell's NMS is called Network Management System and provides management capabilities for LANs running under Novell's NetWare LAN operating system. NMS services are also provided by a variety of other vendors.

In addition to a comprehensive NMS, a variety of tools and utilities are available to assist network managers in performing their duties.

KEY TERMS

agent
alert (alarm)
analog line monitor
cable tester
Common Management Information
    Protocol (CMIP), or Communications Management Information
    Protocol
emulator
filter
GET
inventory software
LAN analyzer
log file
management component
Management Information Base
    (MIB)
menuing software
metering software

network configuration tool
network management system
    (NMS)
Network Management System
    (NMS)
performance monitor
project planning tool
remote control software
Remote Monitoring MIB
    (RMON MIB)
SET
Simple Network Management Protocol (SNMP)
simulation model
Structure of Management
    Information (SMI)
TRAPS
workload generator

REVIEW QUESTIONS

1. How are statistics used in network management?

2. What functions are performed by network management systems?

3. Describe how IBM's Netview and Netview/PC interact with each other.

4. Compare and contrast Netview and Netview/6000.

5. Describe the capabilities of Novell's Network Management System.

6. Describe the function and use of four LAN management tools.

7. Describe the function and use of
   a. analog line monitor
   b. emulator
   c. simulation model
   d. log files
   e. metering software
   f. menuing software
   g. remote control software

8. How are project management tools used in network management?

9. Compare the Simple Network Management Protocol (SNMP) and the Common Management Information Protocol (CMIP).

10. Why are SNMP and CMIP necessary?

PROBLEMS AND EXERCISES

1. Investigate a network management system other than IBM's Netview. How does it compare to the features provided by Netview?

2. Explain how five of the statistics listed in Table 18–1 might be used in managing the network.

3. Describe two situations in which it would be beneficial to have a LAN utility that allows the network manager to view what is displayed on a workstation's monitor. As a workstation user, would you have any concerns regarding the use of such a tool? If so, what are your concerns?

4. Describe a situation in which it would be beneficial for a network manager to take control of a workstation's keyboard.

5. Find two software applications that perform the functions described in Exercises 3 and 4. What features do these applications provide? What do they cost?

CHAPTER 19

Security, Recovery, and Network Applications

CHAPTER OBJECTIVES

After studying this chapter you should be able to

- Compare the three major classes of security: physical, data access, and encryption
- Describe the functions of the OSI presentation and application layers
- Discuss error detection and recovery capabilities
- Describe data compression techniques and the role of data compression in networks
- Discuss the types and capabilities of groupware

In this chapter we discuss some of the functions found in the OSI reference model's application and presentation layers. Two important functions found at these layers are providing security and recovering from failures. Security helps protect network resources by limiting access by unauthorized users and preventing authorized users from making mistakes and making unauthorized data accesses. Networking, particularly LANs, has given rise to a new class of applications called groupware. In this chapter you will read about several varieties of groupware applications and how they support the interaction of individuals in a workgroup. In providing users access to network applications and utilities, the network administrator must ensure that the software is used in accordance with provisions stipulated by the software vendor. Failure to adhere to these provisions may result in legal action and associated penalties. We begin with a short review of the functions of the application and presentation layers.

525

THE PRESENTATION LAYER

The presentation layer accepts the data from the application layer and provides generalized formatting of the data. Thus, if there are data preparation functions common to a number of applications, rather than being embedded in each application, these functions can be resolved by the presentation services. The types of functions that can be performed at this level are encryption, compression, terminal screen formatting, and conversion from one transmission code to another (e.g., EBCDIC to ASCII).

THE APPLICATION LAYER

The application layer is functionally defined by the user. Application programs sometimes must communicate with each other. The content and format of the data being exchanged are dictated by the needs of the organization. The application determines which data is to be transmitted, the message or record format for the data, and the transaction codes that identify the data to the receiver. An order entry transaction started on a sales node may need to pass product shipping information to a warehouse node. This message contains the ship-to address, part identifiers, quantities to be shipped, and a message code indicating the action to be taken by the receiving application.

SECURITY

Security does not prevent unauthorized access to a system, but only makes such access more difficult. The delay to access the system should be long enough to make unauthorized access cost prohibitive or to give the system manager time to detect and apprehend the perpetrator, or both. In the first case, the rewards of unauthorized access would be less than the cost of breaking into the system. In the second, the attempted penetration would be detected and further attempts blocked. From the system owner's perspective, the cost of security should be no more than the potential loss from unauthorized system access.

Note that levels of security may exist. No security means that any user can access and use anything on the system. On a system with no security, a user could give himself or herself a raise or a good performance rating. On the other hand, total security means no one can access or use anything on the system. Obviously, selecting the proper security level for each user is important. Imposing tighter security makes the system more difficult to use and increases the system overhead. Security should protect data from intentional or accidental loss or disclosure, without adversely affecting employees' ability to perform their jobs.

Security Policy

Security must be planned; therefore, the first and most important element of any security system is the security policy. The security policy is a document that sets forth corporate goals and rules. It indicates how those goals and rules are translated into data access permissions. The content of the policy document varies from company to company because each organization has different security requirements. Some of the topics covered in a security policy are given in Table 19–1.

Vendor-Provided Security

Security needs are as various as the number of users. Each organization has its own security objectives, and it is therefore difficult to provide one security system that meets everyone's needs. Vendors of hardware or system software tend to provide only basic security features. This security is generally found only in vendor-provided user interfaces, such as command interpreters and operator- or programmer-level interfaces. Such facilities are generally limited to user identification and authentication. At the data level, additional protection includes layered security for access to files and operating system safeguards, such as prohibiting one process from interfering with the data of another process and viewing the data of an active or recently terminated process.

   This section addresses security concerns more directly affecting the data communication network, and does not include operating system security.

Physical Security

Physical security means using measures such as door locks, safes, and security guards to deny physical access to areas containing sensitive information. Because physical security is independent of hardware or software, it can be planned long before the installation of a network and hardware. If access is prevented to physical components of the system such as terminals, communication circuits, processors, and modems, the likelihood of unauthorized access is significantly decreased. Physical security will not prevent an authorized user from accidentally or intentionally misusing the system. This is significant because studies have shown that the biggest security risk

physical security Measures such as door locks, safes, and security guards, taken to deny physical access to restricted areas.

Table 19–1   Security Policy Topics

Password administration (see Table 19–2)	Access to outside networks/nodes
Auditing policy	Control on external access (e.g., switched and Internet connections)
Consequences of employees intentionally trying to subvert security	Disaster recovery
Encryption implementation	Designation of personnel for monitoring and implementing security
Virus detection procedures	Managing security threats
Data backup/restore policy	Security training
Introduction of software/data by employees (i.e., using media from outside the organization)	Documentation
	Security review procedures

companies face is the accidental or intentional destruction or misuse of data by employees.

Because of the notoriety given to hackers, for some people security is associated with issues such as user IDs and passwords to protect against unauthorized remote access. However, security was a requirement for some applications before remote access was common and in some current systems that do not provide remote access. Enforcement of security in these systems is easier than it is in most of today's networks. A batch-processing system is an example of a system that might not allow remote access. Consider the security implications of such a system. All the computerized data and devices used to access that data can be contained in a single computer room. Paperwork used to generate batch inputs and printed outputs is the only form of data that needs to leave the computer facility. Security for this system can be satisfied primarily by physical security.

Because gaining access to computerized data in a pure batch facility requires gaining access to the computer room, security locks on computer room doors and proper staff training regarding computer room access provide a security level adequate for many installations. While the computer staff is on duty, they control computer facility access; during off-shift hours, security guards can take over. The hard-copy documents that are removed from the computer room can be controlled through corporate policies for dissemination and protection of paperwork.

A common physical security measure is a surveillance system. Security personnel can use this system to screen entry to the premises. The premises may be the property on which the facility is located, individual buildings, rooms within a building, or combinations of these. Additional security can be provided for sensitive areas with closed-circuit television monitors, motion sensors, alarms, and other such intrusion-detection devices. Many installations can justify features such as closed-circuit television and motion sensors because they provide for equipment protection as well as data protection. Use of these devices may result in reduced insurance rates and partially offset their cost.

Other physical security measures that may be used include the following:

- All equipment should be located in secure areas with controlled personnel access.

- Nonsecure transmission media, such as broadcast radio, should be avoided where possible because they are easier to intercept. Use a conducted medium rather than a radiated one for such transmissions.

- If broadcast radio must be used, all transmitted data should be encrypted (encrypting only sensitive data identifies it as such to a potential penetrator and makes his or her work easier).

- Switched lines should be avoided, if possible. Recall that switched lines are those that can be accessed through the telephone company's switching equipment. If you have a switched line, anyone with a computer and a modem has the ability to access your system. When they are used, switched lines should be physically disconnected during the hours they are not required, thus limiting the potential for unauthorized use.

- Computers used for highly sensitive applications should be disconnected from networks whenever possible, placing an additional barrier to access from other network nodes. For example, some U.S. military computers are connected to a national network, except those that are used for highly classified data.

In most current processing environments, protecting computer rooms from physical access is not sufficient to protect data. Access to data is available via terminals distributed throughout the organization. Many online systems also have the ability to access the system remotely via switched circuits. Because physical security is not enough, other security levels—encryption and access security—must be added.

Encryption

Encryption should be used with all media carrying sensitive data. The encryption algorithm chosen should be capable of deterring unwarranted use by making it too costly or time-consuming to decipher the message.

Data Encryption Standard   One of the most common yet controversial encryption algorithms is the **Data Encryption Standard (DES)** adopted by the National Bureau of Standards. DES is an algorithm that uses an encryption key to transform data, called **plaintext,** into an encoded form called encrypted text or **ciphertext;** likewise, someone who knows the encryption key can retransform the encrypted data to its original plaintext. Making the transformation from encrypted text to plaintext without the encryption key is a laborious and time-consuming process. The controversy surrounds the effectiveness of the standard. In 1976 it was estimated that it would take an average of 91–2000 years to break the DES code. Opponents of the algorithm countered that the code could be broken in 6 min to 12 hours at a cost of $20–$5000. The primary criticism of the DES is that only 56 bits are used for the encryption key. Critics believe that this allows for too few different possible data permutations because systematic attempts to decrypt the message would allow message decryption within a reasonable time. With the increasing speed and lower cost of computer hardware, most critics and proponents agreed that the algorithm had an effective life of approximately 10 years, meaning that it should now be at the end of its effectiveness.

Encryption introduces overhead to a network and can slow communication. This is particularly true if the encryption is done with software. Therefore, most DES algorithms use integrated circuits designed for encrypting and decrypting data. The chips may be integrated onto processor or controller boards or used in stand-alone external boxes. The encryption devices can be placed between individual nodes or at the origin and destination of the message. Figure 19–1 illustrates several configuration options. If the encryption devices are placed at each node, the message must be decrypted at each intermediate node, which increases the likelihood of interception. In end-to-end encryption, only the text body can be encrypted and

encryption A process in which transmitted data is scrambled at the sending location and reconstructed into readable data at the receiving end.

Data Encryption Standard (DES) An algorithm that uses an encryption key to transform data, called plaintext, into an encoded form, called encrypted text or ciphertext.

plaintext The unencrypted or properly decrypted version of a message or data. Plaintext is intelligible. Also known as clear text.

ciphertext The encrypted version of a message or data.

Figure 19–1
Encryption Configurations

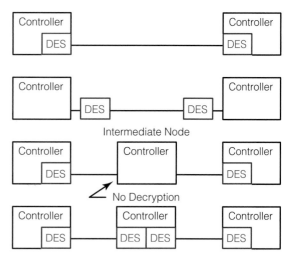

end-to-end addressing must remain clear so intermediate nodes can perform the routing correctly.

Other encryption algorithms have been proposed, although none has gained the acceptance of the DES. One of the more promising, called **trapdoor encryption** or the **public key method,** uses large prime numbers and two keys, one key made public and the other kept secret by the message recipient. The public key encrypts the data; the private key decrypts the ciphertext. A new encryption chip called the Clipper chip is being proposed by the U.S. government for encrypting data on networks and telephone lines. If this chip is installed in telephone and computer equipment, the U.S. government also wants to reserve the right to tap communication lines and decode messages that may pertain to criminal investigations. Most practitioners agree that secure communication is a good idea but have concerns over abuses that might arise if the government has the ability to decrypt all messages.

Key administration is an important function in an effective encryption program. Administration includes

- key creation
- key distribution
- key storage/safeguarding/restoration
- setting standards for frequency key changes

Standards organizations have recognized the critical nature of key management and have adopted several standards to guide key administrators. Among these are ANSI X9.17, which addresses key management for financial institutions, and U.S. Federal Standard 1027, for security requirements for equipment using the DES standard. An organization that is serious about security and encryption should have one or more people designated as security administrators whose function is to implement security and detect

trapdoor encryption
An encryption algorithm that uses large prime numbers and two keys, one key made public and the other kept secret by the message recipient. The public key encrypts the data and the private key decrypts the ciphertext. Also known as the public key method.

attempts to breach security. Security measures that might be implemented are given in Table 19–2.

User Identification and Authentication

Encryption is only one aspect of security. In most systems the first level of security is user **identification** and authentication. User identification runs the gamut from simply providing a user name to biological measures such as retina scans, voice prints, palm prints, or fingerprint identification, which are usually used only in high-security systems such as those of the intelligence and military communities. In business applications, identification is generally supplied by user name or electronic badge. After identification comes **authentication,** which requires the user to provide additional information unique to that particular user, such as a password or a fingerprint.

Passwords   A **password** is the most common form of authentication. It is maintained in a file of information about system users, which typically includes user ID, password, defaulted security attributes for any files created, and possibly an access profile. Because this file contains the information needed to access any portion of the system, it should be carefully secured and encrypted. Passwords should be changed frequently, either centrally by the network administrators or in a decentralized manner by the users. Through central management, passwords are changed regularly and assigned randomly. The major flaw of centralized management is the timing of distribution to users: Dissemination of new passwords must be timely and well coordinated. The logistics in a large, distributed network are considerable. The distribution process also is likely to be the weakest element in the security system: Because passwords are usually distributed in written form via mail or courier, ample opportunity exists for unauthorized users to obtain them. Personal identification numbers (PINs) are passwords associated

identification Information assigned to a specific user of a system for security and control purposes. User identification ranges from simple user names to high-security measures such as voice print and fingerprint identification.

authentication A process in which a system user is required to provide or verify his or her user identification to gain system access.

password A secret expression used by authorized users to prove their right to access a system.

Table 19–2   Sample Security Measures

All users must have a password.	Unsuccessful attempts to log onto the system will be recorded. Data recorded will include the time, terminal from which the attempt is made, and the user ID for which the logon is attempted.
Passwords must be at least six characters long.	
Passwords must be changed at least monthly.	
Passwords will be changed immediately if there is suspicion that a password has been compromised.	Two people will be responsible for encryption key administration.
	No single individual can change the encryption key.
Passwords will not contain user's initials, month abbreviations, or other obvious character strings.	Switched (dial-up) lines will be disconnected when not in use.
Passwords must not be written down.	Manual answer and user verification must be used for all switched connections or call-back units will be used.
Passwords must be created randomly so they do not contain sequence numbers or other instances of succession.	
All unsuccessful logon attempts will be investigated.	Encryption keys will be changed regularly.
All sensitive data will be encrypted.	

with automatic terminal machine (ATM) cards. The card distributor usually mails the card to the user and mails the PIN in a separate envelope. This reduces the risk of an unauthorized person obtaining both the card and the password, but it is not a very secure method. Consequently, some banks now allow users to select their own PINs, which avoids the need to send the password through the mail.

Decentralized password changes rely on users to change their passwords regularly, either by themselves or through their managers. Individual users can change their passwords without leaving any written record of the password, and they can make changes as often as they like. The password file can be centrally examined periodically, and if users have not changed their passwords within a specified time, they can be so notified or their access privileges can be revoked. Some systems contain provisions for password aging. In this case, the security administrator can specify that users must change passwords at least monthly, and users who have not changed their passwords in the allotted time are warned during their logon. The security administrator may allow the user several such "grace" logons. If the user still fails to make a password change under the established rules, his or her account is deactivated. The user then needs to see the security administrator to have the account reactivated. The biggest problem with user-assigned passwords is that they are typically nonrandom because users like to select a password that is easy to remember, such as their initials, birth date, or names of family members. Unfortunately, this type of password is also more easily guessed by a potential intruder. Some dos and don'ts regarding password selection are included in Table 19–2.

Ultrasensitive Applications

Identification and authentication are usually insufficient for sensitive applications because we must also identify what functions a given user may or may not perform. The two most common ways of controlling user access are layers of identification and authentication, or user or application profiles.

Layered IDs   Layers of identification and authentication help to screen access to sensitive transactions. Once users have logged onto the system via the initial identification procedures, they can be asked to provide additional identification and authentication information every time they attempt to access a new application or a sensitive transaction within an application. In a banking application, an operator might be required to provide another password or authorization code to transfer funds from one account to another. The operator uses one user ID and password to gain access to the system. This level of access allows the operator to check account balances and make changes to data other than account balances. If the operator needs to run a transaction that will change an account balance, he or she must first provide another password. If the transaction exceeds a certain limit, an additional password may be required. The advantage of layered IDs is that each application or transaction can have its own level of security, so applications that are not sensitive can be made available to everyone and those that are very sensitive can be protected with one or more levels of security.

The disadvantage of layered IDs is that the user must remember several different authentication codes, thus increasing the probability of the codes being written down and thereby made accessible to others.

User Profiles   A **user profile** contains all the information needed to define the applications and transactions a user is authorized to execute, such as a user in a personnel application who is authorized to add employees, delete employee records, and modify all employee data fields except salary. The profiles maintained in a user file can be very detailed, covering each application or transaction, or fairly simple, including only a brief profile. With a brief profile, a user might be assigned an access level to the system for each of four functions: read, write, execute, and purge. Specifically, suppose a user has been given level 8 read access, level 6 write access, level 8 execute access, and level 2 purge access. Each file or transaction is also given an access profile. A user is granted access to the file or transaction only if his or her access number is equal to or greater than that of the file or transaction. Thus, if the payroll file has access attributes of 8, 8, 10, and 10 for read, write, execute, and purge, respectively, the user just described will be able only to read the information in the file. This is because the user's read access meets or exceeds the file's security profile. A write access of 6 is insufficient to allow the user to write to the file.

The advantage of the brief profile is its simplicity. Its disadvantage is the difficulty in stratifying all users across all applications and files in this manner. Of course, this type of profile could be provided for all files or applications, which then becomes a complex profile that is difficult to maintain and administer. Another effective aspect of user profiles is the restriction of logons to specific days and times. In some systems, the security administrator can define a calendar specifying when a given user is allowed to be logged on. Thus, most workers can be given a profile restricting their access to the system to normal working days and hours. Attempts to log on during times outside this profile will be unsuccessful.

Menu Selection and User Profiles   User profiles can be very effective when used in combination with a menu selection system that displays options on the terminal so the user can select the transactions or applications to perform. If a user profile is available, the menu can be tailored to the individual user, and the only transactions the user will see are those to which he or she has access. In the example above, the user who could only read the payroll file would see only that option displayed on the menu, whereas the payroll manager would probably have all options displayed. The security of the system is enhanced by denying users knowledge of transactions and files that they are not permitted to access.

Time and Location Restrictions   Time and location restrictions play an important part in system security. In a stock trading application, for instance, buying and selling stock on the exchange is limited to a specific period, so any attempt to trade stock outside of that period is rejected. In a personnel application, it would be prudent to restrict transactions that affect employee salary or status to normal working hours. This kind of security can

user profile Information needed to define the applications and transactions a user is authorized to execute.

be further enhanced by making sensitive portions of the application system unavailable during nonworking hours.

Transactions can also be restricted by location. A money transfer transaction would be denied to a bank teller terminal if such transactions had to be initiated by a bank officer. Also, money transfer transactions will always be denied if the terminal is attached to a switched or dial-up communication line. In a manufacturing plant, a shop floor terminal would be unable to start an accounts receivable or payable transaction because those transactions are limited to terminals in the accounting department. This can be implemented either by attaching applications to specific terminals or by terminal identification coupled with its location and a transaction profile. A terminal profile could list the location of the terminal and the transactions valid from that terminal. Time and location restrictions with user controls provide a hierarchy of security precautions.

Switched Ports with Dial-In Access

Perhaps the most vulnerable security point of any system is a switched port that allows dial-in access. The dangers of this should be evident: It enables any person with a telephone and a terminal to access the system. For that reason, extra security precautions should be taken. The switched line should be operational only during the periods when transactions are allowed. In an order entry application, this would probably be between 8:00 A.M. and 8:00 P.M.; in a university environment this might be 24 hours a day. During the period when transactions are disallowed, the line should be disabled. A callback unit, as described in Chapter 10, can be used to ensure that only calls from authorized locations are received.

When switched lines are used, user identification and authentication procedures and restricting transactions are very important to maintain system security. The telephone numbers of the switched lines should be safeguarded as carefully as possible. A manual answer arrangement should be used in high-security installations, thus allowing person-to-person authentication as well as the usual application-based authorization. Another method used to stall unauthorized users of switched lines is to hide the carrier tone until an authentication procedure has been provided, a solution that is most practical when telephones are answered manually. This method is meant to foil hackers who try to gain access to systems by randomly dialing business telephone numbers until a computer installation is reached.

Recognizing Unauthorized Access Attempts

All the security techniques discussed are simply delaying tactics; their implementation alone may not provide adequate security. A tight security system should recognize that an unauthorized access attempt may be occurring and should provide methods to suppress such attempts. In the movie *War Games*, a computer was used to generate passwords until a correct one was found. Even low-security systems would discourage this type of activity. A very simple way to counter such attempts is to retire the affected terminal temporarily, meaning that the system would not accept input from that terminal for a specified period. Such an algorithm might work as follows: After three unsuccessful access attempts, no input from that terminal would be accepted for 5 min. Assuming a 6-character password of only letters and numbers, which gives more than 2 billion possible passwords, if 1 billion of these were tried, with a 5-min delay between each try, more than 9500 years would be needed to gain access. Alternatively, the security system might deactivate the account, disallowing its use to both authorized and unauthorized users. This method is included in a security feature called intruder detection in Novell's NetWare operating systems.

A second algorithm used in some systems simulates a successful logon. After a certain number of unsuccessful logon attempts, the user receives a successful logon message. Rather than actually being granted access to the system, however, the user is provided with a fake session. While this session is being conducted, security personnel can determine the terminal from which access is being made and the types of transactions the user is attempting to run. This type of simulated session can also help keep the penetrator busy while security personnel are dispatched to the location for investigation. Again, switched connections make such an activity more difficult, especially with respect to apprehension.

Automatic Logoff

People are often the weakest link in security. All too often, operators write their passwords on or near the workstation or they leave the area with their workstation still logged on, allowing anyone to perform transactions on their behalf. This not only jeopardizes the security of the system but also can place the employee's job in jeopardy. The system can assist operators by logging off any user who has not entered a transaction within a certain amount of time, such as 2 min. Operators who leave their terminals for more than 2 min must go through the identification and authentication procedures again upon returning. Alternatively, the user can be required to go through an authentication procedure for every transaction. Unfortunately, this adversely affects operator performance. The first alternative is simple to implement on most systems, and in most cases operator efficiency is not impeded.

Transaction Logs

Transaction logs are an important adjunct to security. Every logon attempt should be logged, including date and time, user identification, unsuccessful authentication attempts (with passwords used), terminal identification and location, and all transactions initiated from the terminal by that particular user. If several unsuccessful logon attempts are made, the information could also be written on the console of the operator or security personnel so other actions, such as investigation, can be initiated. Transaction logs are also beneficial to electronic data processing (EDP) auditors and diagnostic personnel.

Computer Viruses, Worms, and Trojan Horses

The need for a new type of security surfaced in the late 1980s with the introduction of computer viruses, worms, and Trojan horses. Most security countermeasures until that time were oriented toward people actively attempting to breach security for personal gain, revenge, or gratification. During this type of security violation, the perpetrator of the breach or the perpetrator's system was actively connected to the network. In contrast, computer viruses, worms, and Trojan horses operate independently of the person who implanted them. A virus infection can be implanted intentionally or accidentally.

A variety of viruses have been discovered and although their implementation differs, there is usually a common objective: to bring down a system or disrupt users. A virus is typically a fragment of code that attaches itself to a legitimate program or file. The virus has the ability to duplicate itself to other programs and files. Once attached, the virus may attack a variety of resources. Some destroy or alter disk files, some simply display annoying messages, and others cause system failures.

Detection and correction of viruses can be time-consuming and expensive. Special antiviral software often is purchased to eliminate and detect viruses. Viruses can be introduced intentionally or accidentally. An unintentional infection can occur when an employee uses an infected disk, unaware that the disk carries a virus. Within a short time the entire network might be infected. Detection may be made more difficult because some viruses remain dormant for a period of time, propagating themselves before becoming active. New virus strains called **stealth viruses** or **polymorphic viruses** also change their appearance by encrypting themselves, which makes them quite difficult to identify.

Antidote programs exist for most known viruses, and using these antiviral programs can help keep a system healthy. Additional measures also should be taken to prevent infections, including procedures to prevent employees from using personal disks in workstations, checking new software on a virus-free system separate from a production system before installing the software for general use, and closely monitoring the source of all new files. Using diskless workstations is another excellent way to limit exposure.

A worm is a self-replicating, self-propagating program. Original worm programs were benign. They were designed to replicate themselves on idle network nodes and carry out useful work. However, the most famous worm program was a rogue known as the Internet worm. The Internet worm surfaced in 1988 on the Internet. It replicated itself primarily on computers using the UNIX operating system. Once established on such a computer, the worm began replicating itself on other network nodes. Eventually, some of the network nodes became saturated with copies of the worm program, reducing the amount of useful work and in some instances causing the computers to fail. Although the worm was not released intentionally, the consequences were far-reaching and the Internet worm illustrated the disruption that can be caused by such programs.

A Trojan horse program contains code intended to disrupt a system. Trojan horse programs are code segments hidden inside a useful program. Trojan horse programs have been created by disgruntled programmers. In one such instance, a programmer inserted code that would periodically activate and erase accounting and personnel records. A Trojan horse program differs

stealth virus A computer virus that has the ability to change its signature of identity, thus making the virus more difficult to detect and eradicate. Also known as a polymorphic virus.

from viruses and worms in that it does not attempt to replicate itself. Although the implementation of viruses, worms, and Trojan horses differs, their consequences are often the same: system disruption. A comprehensive security system must guard against each.

ERROR DETECTION AND RECOVERY

Error detection and recovery, specifically redundancy checks and message sequence numbers at the data link and transport layers, have already been discussed in Chapters 4 and 11. Recall that these checks provide detection of lost or garbled messages, and the recovery technique is usually to retransmit the message or messages that are in error. Another level of recovery in data communication systems is the recovery of the system once a message has arrived and before it is processed. This type of recovery ideally is coordinated with the database recovery system. Although individual implementations differ in their approaches, the basic elements of such a recovery system are outlined in this section.

When a message arrives at a node, a certain amount of processing must be accomplished to satisfy the message requirements. For example, the message is forwarded to the next node and stored. After the message has been stored, it can be delivered to a local application or transmitted to the next node on the path to its destination. During this processing cycle the application(s) processing the message, or the system itself, may fail. This section discusses one option for recovery of a lost message or a failed system.

When a node receives a message and acknowledges receipt to the sender, responsibility for the message is transferred from the sender to the receiver. This means that the receiving node must be able to re-create the message and ensure its correct processing in the event of any possible failure. Designers of simple terminal systems sometimes maintain that it is the responsibility of the terminal operator to resubmit any possibly lost messages in the event of a failure. This approach can be justified only on the grounds that it is easier than implementing more sophisticated software that would resolve most of the problems automatically. Although such recovery systems slow the system and increase processor use, these resources still usually cost less than relying on an operator to recover transactions.

Message Logging

Message logging, also called **safe storing,** means writing the message to a file so it can be reviewed or recovered. To ensure that a message can be re-created, the system should log the message before acknowledging it. The object of the recovery process is to close all windows of vulnerability and create a system in which no messages are lost and all are processed only once. If message receipt is acknowledged and then the message is logged to an audit file, there is a small window of time, perhaps 50 ms, during which a system failure could prevent the message from being re-created. If failure occurs after acknowledgment has been returned but before the write to the log file has been completed, the message is lost. Furthermore, it is not

message logging Also called safe storing, this recovery system writes the message to a file before acknowledgment so the message may be reviewed or recovered later if necessary.

enough to initiate the write to the log file and acknowledge the message before the log write is successfully completed. In this case queues on the log device might delay the write, or a file error could occur that prevents the write from being completed. Thus, the acknowledgment has already been sent and a failure could again cause the message to be lost. Because it is typically the responsibility of the receiver to re-create a message once it has been acknowledged, it is important to design the system so reception acknowledgment is sent only after the message is logged.

Database–System Consistency

In addition to message logging, a transaction must be started for update transactions. A transaction is a logical collection of processing activities that either will be completely accomplished or will leave the database in the same state as it was before the start of the transaction. Although this may sound complicated, it is actually quite simple, as shown by the following example.

Consider a banking application in which a customer wants to transfer money from her checking account to her savings account. We will call the record in the checking account record C and the record in the savings account record S. At the beginning of this transaction, record C has a balance of $1000 and record S has a balance of $3000.

A transaction is started indicating that $500 is to be deducted from the checking account (record C) and deposited into the savings account (record S). After attempting to process the transaction, the database can be in only two possible states: Records C and S contain either $500 and $3500 or $1000 and $3000. The combination of $500 and $3000 and the combination of $1000 and $3500 are inconsistent states. If a failure occurs when record C has attained the value $500 and record S still has the value $3000, recovery must be invoked. The recovery process must either roll the value of record C back to $1000 or roll the value of record S forward to $3500. This transaction is used in the following discussion. Figure 19–2 illustrates the various states of the database for this transaction.

Message Processing

Once the message has been written to the log file, the acknowledgment returned to the sender, the data edited, and a transaction started, the message can be processed. The transaction is forwarded to an application process. The unique transaction ID created when the transaction began is passed along with the message.

Database Update   The application accesses the two records to be updated in the database and issues a database write request for both records. Before the updates are posted to the database, the database management system writes the before- and after-images to an audit file. The **before-images** are balances of $1000 and $3000 for records C and S, respectively. The **after-images** for those records are $500 and $3500. After the audit writes have been completed, the writes to the database can be initiated. Just as it was incorrect to ac-

before-image The status of a record before it has been processed.

after-image The status of a record after it has been processed.

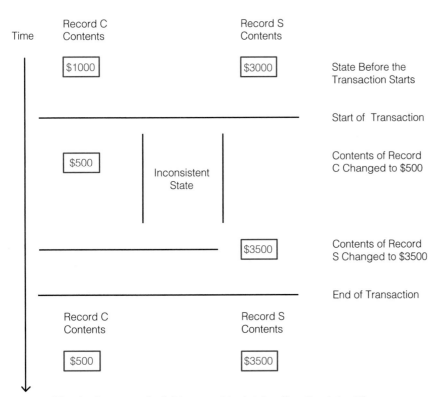

Figure 19–2
Database States During Transaction

*The database must be left in a consistent state, either the state at the beginning of the transaction or the state at the end of the transaction.

knowledge the message before completing the write to the log file, it is incorrect to write to the database before completing the before- and after-image writes; to do so would create a small time window that would make recovery impossible. If a failure occurs before the audit images are captured on disk or tape, the transaction might be unrecoverable. In some systems both the database and the audit writes may be deferred until a later time, with the records held in memory for some time to expedite processing. Deferring the writes does not alter the fact that writes to the audit trail must be completed before the writes to the database.

Response Message   Having completed the database updates, the application prepares a response and returns it to the TCP. The TCP then ends the transaction by writing an end transaction record to the transaction log and ensuring that all audit buffers have been written to the audit file. After both events have occurred, the transaction is completed and the response message can be sent back to the originating terminal.

Recovery After Safe Storing

Recovery following failure is a joint effort between database and data communication systems. At any point after the safe storing of the original message, recovery to a consistent state is possible. Suppose a failure occurs after the application has received the message and modified the first but not the second database record. The database system begins the recovery process first. When the system is restored to operational status, the transaction is labeled incomplete. The database management recovery system uses the before-images it captured to restore the database to its state before the beginning of the transaction. The before-image of the updated record is written back to the database, thus erasing the update. Next, the database recovery process sends a message to the TCP advising that the transaction was unsuccessful and the before-images have been posted. The TCP retrieves the message associated with that transaction, starts a new transaction, and forwards the message to the application.

Retry Limit   It is possible that the same transaction could fail again, which is often a problem if database files are full, access method tables are full, or unusual data conditions exist, such as division by zero. To protect against an infinite recovery loop, the recovery system should have a retry limit that prevents a transaction from being restarted indefinitely. If the retry limit is exceeded, the failed transaction must be handled differently. One outcome is to display an appropriate error message on the computer operator's console and to notify the initiator that the transaction cannot be completed. The computer operator must then follow the necessary procedures to have the problem corrected. When the cause of the failure has been removed, the transaction can be resubmitted from the transaction log or from the user. In some cases it is not appropriate to restart from the transaction log. For example, the transaction may have been to book a traveler on a flight. If the system were unable to process the transaction, the traveler may have booked the flight with another carrier.

Audit Trails   Like security systems, recovery systems are not completely reliable. If system failure includes failure of the device (tape or disk) containing the transaction and database audit logs, automatic recovery becomes impossible. In such instances a database backup version is reloaded and as many after-images as possible are reposted to the database to bring it forward in time. The images on the medium that failed are not available, of course, so some processing is lost. To limit the exposure due to failure of the audit media, many systems allow the user to have multiple copies of the audit trails. Having audit trails on a disk drive is preferable because of the disk's random access capability; a magnetic tape could be used if no disk is accessible. In addition to the recovery methods just described, recovery can be made easier if good transaction design is used.

TRANSACTION DESIGN

transaction A user-specified group of processing activities that either are completed or leave the database and processing system in the same state as before the transaction was initiated.

A **transaction** is a user-specified group of processing activities either that are completed or, if not completed, that leave the database and processing system in the same state as before the transaction started. Thus, a transaction always leaves the database and the system in a consistent state. A transaction is also a unit of recovery, an entity that the recovery system manages. Recovery and contention have a great influence on transaction design. From the perspective of an application, it makes little difference how or when the transaction begins, ends, or is recovered. From a system design and recovery perspective, good transaction design is very important.

Review of Transaction Activities

Before discussing transaction design, it is useful to discuss the activities needed to start, end, and process a transaction. A generic recovery system is assumed; details vary with implementations. Beginning and ending a transaction require a certain amount of work, and additional work is required when processing a transaction. Starting a transaction demands that a unique transaction identifier be generated. A beginning transaction record is then written to the transaction log. Each record updated by the transaction must be locked to prevent concurrent update problems. Some records that are read but not updated also may have to be locked. All updates must be posted to the before- and after-image audit trail before being written to the database. At the end of the transaction all audit buffers must be flushed to disk and end-of-transaction markers written to the audit trail.

A simple transaction that updates one record may therefore result in five writes: the begin-transaction record, the end-transaction record, the before-image, the after-image, and the record itself, as illustrated in Figure 19–3. This may appear to be a rather high overhead, but it is not. The cost of inconsistent data can be much greater, and many systems use techniques to optimize the capturing of audit images. Audit images are like insurance policies: They cost a small amount over time but pay large dividends when needed.

Grouping Activities into a Single Transaction

Transaction design covers two areas: the grouping of activities into one transaction and the implementation of that transaction within the system. The need for a transaction to leave the system in a consistent state often dictates the transaction's composition. In other cases the composition is not quite so obvious. In transferring funds from one bank account to another, for

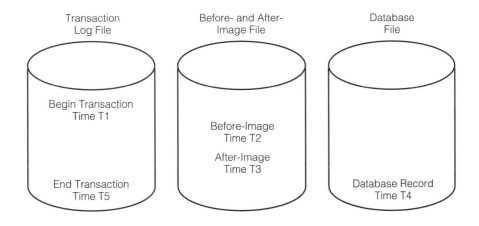

Transaction Log File — Begin Transaction Time T1 — End Transaction Time T5

Before- and After-Image File — Before-Image Time T2 — After-Image Time T3

Database File — Database Record Time T4

Figure 19–3
Records Written for a Simple Transaction

instance, it is clear that the deposit and withdrawal must be placed together in one transaction, for to do otherwise would make the database inconsistent. A trial balance would not balance if funds are taken from one place but not deposited in another.

An example of a transaction with less obvious boundaries is adding an employee to a company database. This statement assumes that the transaction activities required are selection and assignment of an employee number, addition of an employee record, and addition of zero to several associated records (employee history, payroll, dependents, and benefits). The employee number is selected so that employee numbers form an increasing numeric sequence with no gaps. This requires reading a control record that contains the next number in the sequence, incrementing the sequence number on the control record, and rewriting the control record.

Although the employee is not fully entered into the system until all these activities have been completed, it may not be necessary to group all activities in a single transaction. The selection and assignment of an employee number and the creation of an employee record are tightly coupled events. Thus, if an employee number has been removed from the control sequence, there should be an employee record with that number, which should be available for reuse if adding the employee to the file fails. However, adding a dependent record, which requires only that an employee record exist, is not so tightly linked with the process of creating the employee record. Indeed, dependent records are often added long after an employee has been hired. The same can be said for payroll records, benefits, and work history. In this example, there might be one or several transactions.

Advantages and Disadvantages of Single Versus Multiple Transactions

What would be the advantages and disadvantages of making the employee transaction a single or multiple transaction?

Brief Versus Long Transactions   A single transaction requires only one begin-and-end transaction activity. Although not an overriding consideration, there is an overhead to starting and ending a transaction that a careful designer will attempt to minimize. On the other hand, a long transaction has a greater risk, albeit very slight, of a failure that would involve a recovery. Long transactions also require that records be locked for a longer period, which increases both the likelihood of deadlock and the time the records are unavailable. When record locking is used to resolve the multiple update problems of contention (which arise when two or more users attempt to access the same records), deadlock can occur. As discussed in Chapter 8, deadlock results when two different users (in this case, transactions) have control over records and attempt to access records the other user has already locked, as illustrated in Table 19–3.

Multiple Sessions with One Operator   The major consideration in whether to group multiple updates into one transaction is none of the above, however. Because the weakest link in a transaction may be the operator, good transaction design avoids multiple sessions with the terminal

Table 19–3　Deadlock Situation

	Transaction 1	Transaction 2
T	Read and lock record A.	
i		Read and lock record B.
m	Attempt to read record B.	
e		Attempt to read record A.
	Wait	Wait

operator whenever possible. If it is decided when adding a new employee to treat all activities as one transaction, complications could arise, as follows: The terminal operator begins the transaction by entering the employee data, triggering updates to the employee number assignment file, the employee file, and perhaps a number of access method files. All these updates are accomplished by one interaction with the terminal. Having been updated, the employee number assignment record and the new employee record are locked. The operator next enters job history information. If the operator takes a lunch break at this point, putting the transaction on hold with its records locked, then, because the employee number assignment record must be used every time an employee is added, no employees can be added during this interval.

The problem with having a transaction span sessions with one operator is not just the operator's potential absence; it is also the amount of time that a transaction must be held in limbo while the operator enters more information. Compared to the milliseconds required to update databases and process transactions, the minutes required to enter the data are rather long. This situation is further complicated when records are locked across sessions with the operator. Fortunately, techniques exist for avoiding such delays.

How to Avoid Multiple Sessions　　If system design requires all the activities described for adding an employee to be a single transaction, the transaction should be planned to avoid multiple sessions with the operator once the transaction begins. Essentially, the solution is to gather all necessary information before beginning the transaction. One way this could be accomplished is described here. The operator enters the information for the new employee. The data is edited and, if there are no inconsistencies, the record is safe-stored. The operator is then prompted for job history data. Again, edit checks are performed and the record is safe-stored. The same is done for dependent, payroll, and benefits data. If a failure occurs during this process, the data already input is available, so the operator does not need to enter it again. Once all of the data has been entered, the transaction is initiated. The database locks are kept for the minimum required time because no additional sessions with the operator are required. Upon completion, the result is returned to the operator. Should the operator leave the terminal in the middle of the transaction, no records are left locked during the period.

To summarize, transactions should be designed to be as brief as possible and to avoid multiple interactions with an operator. The overriding consideration is to design transactions so the database is always left in a consistent state and so recovery can be ensured. The participation of a terminal operator in the recovery process should be kept to a minimum. Operators should be notified of the last activity completed on their behalf so they can continue from the correct place.

WORKGROUP SOFTWARE

workgroup software
Often called groupware, this software facilitates the activities of a group of two or more workers by reducing the time and effort needed to perform group tasks such as meetings, office correspondence, and group decision making.

Most LAN implementations have the potential for effectively using **workgroup software,** often called **groupware.** In this section, you will learn what a workgroup is and some of the application tools used to increase the group's productivity.

Before you can fully appreciate the functions of workgroup software, you must understand what we mean by a workgroup and the functions needed by the group. First, a group consists of two or more workers. In doing their jobs, these workers must share information, communicate with each other, and coordinate their activities. Specific work tasks that are group activities include meetings, office correspondence, and group decision making. Groupware is designed to make arranging and carrying out these tasks easier and less time-consuming.

The functions performed by groupware are not new. For years they have been done manually or with limited degrees of computer support. Networked systems in general and LANs in particular provide the communication link that was previously missing in computerizing many of these tasks. The groupware applications that have been created thus far fall into the following broad categories:

- e-mail
- conferencing
- work-flow automation
- decision support
- document coauthoring and document management

Mail Administration

Today, many people are aware of e-mail capabilities because they use it at school, work, or on the Internet; therefore, we will not provide a detailed description of those capabilities here. Instead, let us look at e-mail administration. Administering a mail system can be a time-consuming responsibility. User lists and distribution lists must be established and maintained. Periodically, old mail messages may need to be manually removed from the system. There is also the potential for mail to be misused, which may include sending a high volume of broadcast junk mail, hate/love letters, and advertisements for personal gain. One responsibility of mail administration is to set corporate policy for acceptable and unacceptable use of the mail system.

E-mail is becoming a significant communication tool for many companies. It has become the fundamental means of communication for some corporations. In a private mail system where the communication network already exists, an e-mail system can help reduce telephone and postage charges. It allows messages to be quickly composed and delivered. Recipients can review their mail at their own convenience, eliminating some of the interruptions of telephone communication.

Some disadvantages also arise from the use of e-mail. Earlier we discussed the importance of security, and mail system security is one responsibility of mail administration. A secure mail system provides options for controlling mail messages, such as the ability to encrypt messages. Without such safeguards, one employee may be able to access another's mail file and read his or her correspondence. One of the corporate policies should describe penalties for such unauthorized access. On the other hand, in some cases employees have been fired because their mail messages fell into the wrong hands. Like any tool, a mail system can be misused.

E-Mail Interchange Standard X.400

One of the first standards for the application layer of the OSI model pertains to the interface of e-mail systems. The **X.400 standard,** developed by the ITU, provides a platform for the implementation of a worldwide electronic message-handling service. Because a wide variety of e-mail systems are in use today, connecting these systems to provide message exchange between heterogeneous mail systems is the focus of the X.400 standard. X.400 is to mail systems as the OSI reference model is to the interconnection of different networks.

X.400 standard A standard developed by the ITU that provides a platform for the implementation of a worldwide electronic message-handling service.

The implementation of X.400 is based on a hierarchy of entities. The hierarchy is used for implementing worldwide message distribution and for addressing. At the top of the hierarchy is a country, followed by a public administration agency or private regulated operating agency, a company, and a user. Addresses for the senders and recipients of a mail message are generated from this hierarchy. An address consists of a country name, a public utility name, a company name, and a user name.

An X.400 system allows users to exchange electronic messages. The users can be in the same or different companies, can be using the same or different mail systems, and can be in the same or different countries. Mail transfer is accomplished via mail agent processes. Each user has a mail agent called a **user agent (UA).** A user agent allows a user to compose a message, provides recipient addresses, and receives messages. The interface between UAs is accomplished by **message transfer agents (MTAs).** An MTA can serve none, one, or several UAs. The network of MTAs is responsible for taking a message from a sender's UA and delivering it to the recipient's UA. This environment is depicted in Figure 19–4, which shows a U.S. user communicating with an Australian user.

user agent (UA) A mail agent that allows a user to compose a message, provides recipient addresses, and receives messages.

message transfer agent (MTA) An interface between user agents.

The X.400 standard describes two different domains: a private domain, which represents a private e-mail system corresponding to a company in the above hierarchy, and a public domain, which represents a delivery and interconnection network corresponding to the public administration agency in the hierarchy. In some ways the public domain provides a function similar to that provided by an X.25 network: the ability

Figure 19–4
X.400 Connection

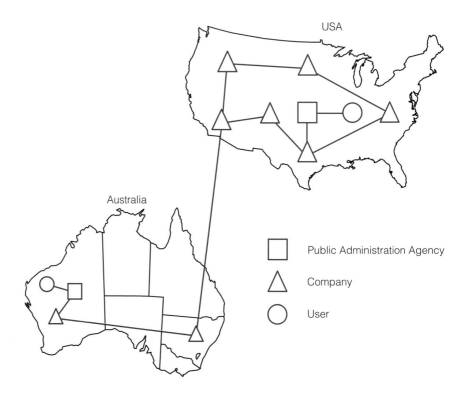

administrative manage-
ment domain (ADMD)
A domain that repre-
sents a delivery and in-
terconnection network
corresponding to a pub-
lic agency in the X.400
standard hierarchy.

private management
domain (PRMD) A do-
main that represents a
private e-mail system
corresponding to a
company in the X.400
standard hierarchy.

X.500 standard A stan-
dard that specifies the
procedure for creating
a directory system to
maintain e-mail user
names and their net-
work addresses, as well
as the names and ad-
dresses of other net-
work resources such as
printers and servers.

to provide connections and message routing among systems. The public
domain is called an **administrative management domain (ADMD)** and
the private domain is called a **private management domain (PRMD).** An
interdomain interface is defined to establish protocols for passing messages among different domains. Protocols are defined for communicating
among ADMDs and between PRMDs and ADMDs, and for the contents
of the message itself. X.400 is significant because it establishes a standard
for user communication. It has been implemented in several systems. If
the standard is universally followed, computer users anywhere can communicate with each other electronically.

The ITU X.500 Standard

Imagine the complexities of managing a worldwide X.400 e-mail system. Currently, there are more than 15 million e-mail users in private
companies who account for 6 billion messages. Keeping track of all these
users and their mail addresses is a complex task that is addressed by the
X.500 standard. The **X.500 standard** specifies how to create a directory
system to maintain e-mail user names and their network addresses. Thus,
a user who needs to send a mail message to another user but does not
know that user's mail address can search the X.500 directory for the necessary information. The directory will contain the addresses of mail users
worldwide.

Electronic Conferencing Applications

Electronic conferencing applications range from simply arranging meetings to conducting the meetings themselves. Arranging a meeting or conference requires that the participants be notified and that a mutually agreeable meeting date and time be set. Conferencing applications provide assistance with one or more of these tasks. If each attendee has an electronic calendar, groupware can book the meeting at the best time. Given an interval during which the meeting must take place, the groupware application consults the calendars of the attendees. It notes the date and time that all attendees are available and schedules the meeting on their electronic calendars. If scheduling conflicts arise, the application can help resolve them. Some schedulers even double-book participants and allow them to choose which appointment to keep. Others report the conflicts and suggest alternative meeting times with no or reduced conflicts, allowing the person calling the meeting to find the best possible time. Once a meeting is scheduled, the electronic calendar software can issue an RSVP notice to the participants. Like personal calendars, groupware calendars can issue reminders of forthcoming events. The reminder might be a mail message or an audio tone. Some groupware allows users to declare meetings to be recurring, such as weekly, monthly, or biweekly. The scheduler automatically books these meetings for the attendees.

If the meeting is held with participants in different locations, teleconferencing groupware can also assist with communication among the attendees. Some teleconferencing applications allow images displayed on one computer monitor to be displayed on remote monitors. Individuals at all locations can modify the screen image and have the changes immediately reflected on the screens of the other participants. Thus, conference attendees can both view and modify computer-generated data and graphs. Viewing and modifying data coupled with audio transmission and freeze-frame or full-motion video allows geographically distributed conferences to be held, saving both travel costs and personnel time. Another conference or meeting communication aid is the creation and distribution of electronic minutes.

Work-Flow Automation

Attendees at a meeting may accept action items they must complete, or a workgroup manager may assign tasks to workgroup members. One responsibility of a workgroup manager is monitoring the progress of such tasks. Progress monitoring is not a new concept. For many years, managers have used **program evaluation and review technique (PERT)** charts or similar methods to track a project's progress and determine its critical path. The **critical path** of a project is the sequence of events that takes the longest to complete. Often, a project can be divided into several tasks. Some tasks can be done in parallel, but other tasks cannot start until one or more tasks have been completed. For example, when you build a house, the roof cannot be put on until the building is framed. Plumbing and electrical wiring can possibly be done concurrently. The project cannot be completed until the path with the longest duration is completed. Thus, project managers pay close

electronic conferencing An application that assists users in arranging and conducting meetings electronically.

program evaluation and review technique (PERT) A technique that tracks a project's progress to determine its critical path and to monitor personnel, schedules, and project resources.

critical path The sequence of events that takes the longest to complete.

attention to the project's critical path to avoid delays. Although some project management work has been computerized for many years, much of the monitoring work was done by people. Groupware has extended the abilities of earlier systems by automating the tracking function.

Figure 19–5 is a PERT chart for selecting a LAN vendor. The critical path for the selection process is indicated by the heavier line. It is the critical path because it has the longest elapsed time between the start and the end points. Groupware helps in monitoring the critical path and keeps the group working together. Through the groupware application, group members can also track the status of other tasks that may affect their work.

With work-flow automation groupware, a manager can assign tasks to individuals or groups (through the group leader). The individual can either accept the task, negotiate a change, or refuse the task. Once a task is accepted, a completion date is set. The worker uses the groupware application to record his or her progress and to signal the completion of the task. The manager can then either agree that the task is complete and close it out or reach the decision that the task has not been satisfactorily completed and refuse to accept the work. In the latter case, the worker is notified and must rework the task until the result is acceptable. The groupware work-flow application tracks all tasks and evaluates progress. The group manager can query the system and obtain reports of each task's status. If several tasks are in progress at once and other tasks are awaiting the outcome of those tasks, the groupware monitors the progress of the critical paths and helps the manager keep the project on schedule.

Other functions that may be simplified with work-flow automation software include

- establishing and monitoring to-do lists
- delegating tasks

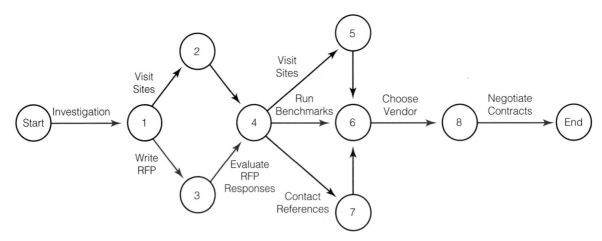

Figure 19–5
PERT Chart for Selecting a LAN Vendor

- holding completed tasks until released by a manager
- deleting tasks
- preventing a worker from modifying an accepted task
- setting or resetting task start and stop times
- adding, deleting, or changing the people responsible for tasks
- providing task and group reports

Document Coauthoring and Document Management

Word processing, text editors, and document exchange software were among the early computer applications. However, most of these systems were designed to allow only one person to manipulate a document at one time. If you have ever worked on a team to write a program, report, or manual, you are probably aware of the limitations inherent in these systems. If you and one of your team members wanted to work on the document at the same time, you found either that it could not be done or that concurrent document updates created contention problems. In a workgroup, it is often desirable and sometimes necessary to have several workers actively working on one document simultaneously. Document coauthoring and management applications provide this capability.

A full-function **document coauthoring system** allows two or more workers to work on one document concurrently. Concurrent processing presents some complex problems regarding posting changes to the same pages. Some coauthoring systems do not provide this ability; however, they do provide the management and control abilities that allow a document to be shared without risk of contention problems. Some document managers help control the flow of documents through the production cycle. Group users are identified as the principal document author, coauthors, or editors. The document manager assists in the production of the document by controlling the flow of the document from one designated user to another.

Document management software can control access to the document by a checkout mechanism. Workers can check out all or portions of the document. Once a portion is checked out, update access to that portion of the document by other users is typically restricted because the worker checking it out may change it. If a worker changes the document, the document management software monitors the changes and records the identity of the person making the change. When the document is ready for review, the application can route the document to the proper reviewers and editors. The reviewers and editors then can make notations and suggestions, with or without changing the document itself, and the application will keep track of the person making those remarks.

Other document management features include document organization, archiving, location, and full file searches. Imagine the number of documents generated per year by a large law office. Some law offices generate more than 50,000 documents per year including wills, contracts, legal briefs, and trial notes. Keeping track of this volume almost necessitates the use of a system

document coauthoring system A system that allows two or more workers to work on one document concurrently.

that allows documents to be stored, archived to backup media, and retrieved when needed. For such large systems, standard directory and file naming conventions are often severely limited. A document management system allows users to store a single document under a variety of different subjects. As in a library card catalog, the document can then be found by attorney, client, subject, date created, last date accessed, project, department, author, and a variety of other descriptive categories. Some systems allow users to specify combinations of these attributes as well. Full file searches systematically search files stored on disk or archival directories looking for user-defined text strings.

Group Decision Support

group decision support software LAN software that facilitates the communication of ideas among members of a group.

Group decision support software on LANs facilitates the communication of ideas among the members of a group. Each participant has a workstation from which to make comments and suggestions, which are exchanged among the users in an anonymous way. This allows the lowest member in the organizational hierarchy to feel free to criticize suggestions made by the highest member. The key to making this work is protecting the source of ideas and comments. Included in the software are tools to gather and manipulate data from a variety of sources, such as a database, a spreadsheet, and graphic images. Companies that use decision support technology find that better decisions are reached in a shorter period of time.

It is important to emphasize that groupware is not intended to replace person-to-person interactions. Our future should not be one in which we get assignments via computers, are computer graded, and are fired or promoted via the computer. Instead, groupware complements person-to-person interactions. Groupware provides a tool for assigning and monitoring the group's tasks with the objective of making the group more productive.

Time-Staged Delivery Systems

time-staged delivery system Software that allows users to identify a transmission package, designate one or more recipients, and specify a delivery priority.

Time-staged delivery systems have some characteristics of a mail system. Time-staged delivery software allows users to identify a transmission package, designate one or more recipients of the package, initiate the delivery of the package, and specify a delivery priority. If we relate time-staged delivery and e-mail to regular mail service, e-mail is like express mail service whereas time-staged delivery is equivalent to parcel post or surface mail. E-mail is usually oriented toward short messages of several pages or less. Time-staged delivery systems may be used for short messages, for transaction routing, or to transmit entire files.

With time-staged delivery, the user specifies a required delivery time. The system then schedules the message transmission to meet the requested goal. Suppose a user needs to send a lengthy report from New York City to each of five manufacturing plants, and that the message must be available at each plant by 9:00 A.M. local time. The report to London must arrive several hours before the one destined for California, so it has a higher priority in transmission than the California-bound package. The delivery system also can use the delivery time to defer transmission until a more convenient time.

Rather than sending data in real time, when the system may be quite busy, it can delay transmission until a less busy time, such as the early morning. In distributed processing environments, the ability to designate transmission packages and delivery times can be an important capability. An example of a time-staged delivery system is IBM's SNA delivery system (SNADS).

SUMMARY

Security is a delaying tactic used to deter unauthorized personnel from gaining access to a system and to provide time to catch those who attempt such access. Security of systems and networks is of growing concern to system managers. Security can be implemented at multiple levels within a system. There is an overhead to implementing security precautions, and the cost of the security system should not exceed the potential loss from unauthorized use of the system.

Reliability and presentation of data are very important to the success of any system. Many software functions in a data communication network handle these requirements. Data is encrypted to prevent unauthorized disclosure, compressed to economize online time and disk storage, edited to eliminate as many errors as possible, and formatted to make it understandable and presentable. Data is formatted for output as well as for exchange between processes and media.

The error detection and recovery discussed in this chapter are different from the error checks made by VRC, LRC, and CRC discussed earlier. This chapter discussed error detection and recovery in connection with system and application recovery. The data communication and database systems should work together to provide a comprehensive recovery that leaves the system in a consistent state, with no transactions lost or processed more than once. The recovery system should also assist with user recovery and establish or help establish users' restart points.

A transaction is defined as a user-specified group of processing activities that are completed or, if not completed, that leave the database and processing system in the same state as before the transaction started. A transaction is also a unit of recovery, an entity that the recovery system manages. Recovery and contention have a great influence on transaction design. Good transaction design is crucial to an effective application system. Related updates should be grouped together in one transaction. To avoid contention issues, long transactions and multiple operator sessions during a transaction should be avoided.

Two network applications that are becoming common in networks are e-mail and time-staged message delivery systems. These provide communication among network users and move data from one node to another in an orderly, timely manner. A variety of applications oriented toward improving group productivity is available on LANs and WANs. Groupware applications include electronic conferencing, work-flow automation, document management, and decision support.

KEY TERMS

administrative management domain (ADMD)
after-image
authentication
before-image
ciphertext
critical path
Data Encryption Standard (DES)
document coauthoring system
electronic conferencing
encryption
group decision support software
identification
message logging (safe storing)
message transfer agent (MTA)
password

physical security
plaintext
private management domain (PRMD)
program evaluation and review technique (PERT)
stealth virus (polymorphic virus)
time-staged delivery system
transaction
trapdoor encryption (public key method)
user agent (UA)
user profile
workgroup software (groupware)
X.400 standard
X.500 standard

REVIEW QUESTIONS

1. What is the greatest security risk a company faces? Why is this so?

2. How has data communication complicated the ability to provide data security?

3. Describe a number of physical security features and how they protect unauthorized access.

4. What is data encryption? What benefits does it provide?

5. What are user identification and authentication? Describe three methods for accomplishing identification and authentication.

6. How can you recognize and overcome unauthorized access attempts?

7. What is a computer virus? How can you protect against computer viruses?

8. Why are error detection and recovery important?

9. Describe the steps a system might take to provide a good recovery environment.

10. What is a workgroup?

11. Describe four classes of groupware.

12. Describe eight features that might be found in an e-mail system.

13. Describe the motivation behind the X.400 and X.500 standards.

14. What is work-flow automation? How does it help promote workgroup productivity?

15. How does a document coauthoring and document management system differ from a word processing application?

16. What are the benefits or uses of a time-staged message delivery system?

17. What are the implications of having transactions involve multiple sessions with a terminal operator? Are there any benefits to having multiple sessions with an operator?

18. What impact do long transactions have on a system?

PROBLEMS AND EXERCISES

1. Investigate the security features of a system to which you have access. Describe the strong and weak points of the security provided.

2. Research the security capabilities of a current version of Novell Corporation's NetWare. Describe how users and groups are managed. What file security attributes are there? What provisions exist for password administration (requiring users to change passwords, time and location restrictions, and so on)?

3. Research the literature and find three incidents of virus infections. What problems were caused and how were the problems corrected? Were the perpetrators apprehended? If so, what happened to them?

4. Computer crime can result from a lack of security. Find three instances of computer crimes (including intentional destruction of data) and describe the nature of each. What security measures could have prevented these crimes?

5. Investigate an e-mail system and determine which features it provides. Does it provide any capabilities not listed in this chapter? If so, what are they?

6. Find a company that uses e-mail (LAN or WAN based). Interview several mail users to determine how often they use the mail, their likes or dislikes of e-mail, and the overall impact of the mail system on how they do business. How would their work be different if e-mail were not available?

7. Some people feel that work-flow management, electronic calendars, and e-mail are intrusive systems because they automatically schedule people for a meeting, monitor their work progress, report back to the originator of a message that the message has been read, and so on. Discuss why people might feel this way. What are your personal viewpoints on these groupware applications?

8. Are there any applications in which long transactions are necessary? If so, give some examples.

CHAPTER 20

Distributed Systems

CHAPTER OBJECTIVES

After studying this chapter you should be able to

- Define the concept of a distributed system
- Trace the evolution of distributed systems
- Describe the functions of a remote file system
- List the advantages and disadvantages of distributed systems
- Discuss the use and problems of database management in distributed systems
- Describe the requirements of distributed systems and distributed databases

Thus far, we have looked at networked systems primarily from the perspective of using them for their communication capabilities. Another application of networking is distributing and sharing resources. One direction of network technology has been creating the ability to effectively distribute processing resources such as hardware, software, and data, as well as the use, management, and control of these resources.

DISTRIBUTED SYSTEM DEFINITIONS

Systems can be distributed in a variety of ways. In Chapters 5 through 15 you read about LANs and WANs, and although it was not explicitly stated, many of those networks' resources were distributed. For example, a LAN's processing load is split among servers and workstations, both acting in concert to help workers attain their objectives. In this use of the system, processing is distributed. Data also can be distributed over two or more nodes, such as on file servers, SQL servers, and workstations. However, although data is distributed, there is not always a distributed data management capability. In these instances, the distributed data is treated as islands of data without the benefit of the comprehensive, coordinated management of a distributed database management system (DBMS). The same may be said for WANs.

The ultimate goal of distributed processing and databases is essentially to make the network the computer. In early computing systems, all data and processing were confined to one computer. In early networks we were able to distribute the computing load among several computers by replicating what was done on individual computers. If a network had three nodes, processing was taking place simultaneously on all three computers, but most of the processing entailed a single program on one system accessing and processing data on the same system. The network was used primarily to transport completed reports, for data input on terminals attached to a re-mote computer, and so on. Ideally, we would like to have the aggregate re-sources of a network applied as appropriate to cooperatively work on problems. In this context, a single transaction might use processing re-sources of several computers, access and update data in a database distrib-uted over multiple disk drives on multiple computer nodes, and perhaps output data in several geographically distributed places. Such distributed collaboration of hardware and software naturally is transparent to users of the system. Before we introduce the technology of distributed processing and distributed databases, we first define more precisely the various aspects of distributed systems.

First, there is a distinction between distributed processing and distrib-uted databases. From the preceding paragraph, you may have an intuitive idea about these distinctions. **Distributed processing** refers to the geo-graphic distribution of hardware, software, processing, data, and control. The data communication system is the glue that holds the distributed sys-tem together and makes it workable. Geographic distribution does not mean great distances. As stated earlier, a LAN is a distributed processing system and, by definition, serves a limited area. A company also can have a dis-tributed system contained in a single computer room. The key factor in hav-ing a distributed processing system is networking two or more independent computing systems in which there is an interdependence among the nodes. The dependence can be for processing power, data, application software, or use of peripherals.

Often, distributed systems also are characterized by distribution of con-trol. If the nodes are placed in different locations, there is local responsibil-ity for each node. A manufacturing organization may have processing nodes in the headquarters offices, regional offices, and warehouses. In each of these locations, there will be an operations staff responsible for running the systems. There may also be a local support and development organization responsible for developing, installing, and maintaining applications and databases.

Data is often one of the objects distributed in a network. People often re-fer to data distribution as a **distributed database.** However, simple data

distributed processing The geographic distrib-ution of hardware, soft-ware, processing, data, and control.

distributed database A database wherein data is located on two or more computing sys-tems connected via a data communication network. The fact that data is distributed should be transparent to database users.

distribution is not sufficient for a distributed database. To have a true distributed database, there must be a comprehensive, coordinated system that manages the data. Later in this chapter, you will learn about the requirements of a distributed DBMS and how it differs from distributed file systems. Because distributed data and databases are an important aspect of distributed systems, a large portion of this chapter addresses the issues surrounding this topic.

One objective of distributed processing is to move data and processing functions closer to the users who need those services and thereby to improve the system's responsiveness and reliability. A second objective is to make remote access transparent to the system user, so the user has little or nothing special to do when accessing the other nodes of the system. How these objectives are met is explained below. First, however, we review how distributed systems evolved.

EVOLUTION OF DISTRIBUTED SYSTEMS

At the dawn of the computer age, computers were big and expensive, and operating systems were either nonexistent or incapable of supporting multiple job streams. As a result, for the organizations that could afford it, computer systems were acquired for every department needing computational power. In a manufacturing organization, one computer would be dedicated to inventory, one to accounting, and one to manufacturing control. These were decentralized processing systems, but they were very different from the current concept of distributed systems in one important respect: the sharing of resources.

Duplicated Databases and Inconsistent Data

Processors in early systems usually were not connected via communication links. As a result, each maintained its own database, often with duplicated data. Both the warehouse database and the accounting department database contained the same customer information, the former for shipping and the latter for invoicing. When a customer moved, the address change was probably not reflected in both databases at once, and in some instances not before a considerable amount of time had elapsed. Such redundant storage of data, with the attendant update problems, created data inconsistencies. Data inconsistencies often are manifested by conflicts in reports. As a consequence, shipments or invoices could be sent to the incorrect address and perhaps be lost. Because each department was essentially the proprietor of its own system, there was little sharing of computer resources. This meant that one system might be inundated with work while another was idle. One possible early decentralized processing system is depicted in Figure 20–1.

Centralization

The early decentralized systems were far from ideal. In addition to data inconsistencies, there were extra costs for hardware, operations, maintenance,

Figure 20–1
*Early Distributed
Processing System*

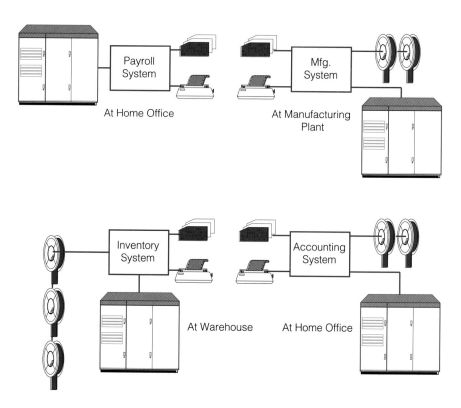

At Home Office   At Manufacturing Plant

At Warehouse   At Home Office

centralized system A
single system capable of
supporting multiple job
functions using shared
resources.

and programming. As systems grew larger and operating systems more comprehensive, there was a movement to large, **centralized systems,** as illustrated in Figure 20–2. Large, centralized systems had the benefits of a single operation center, control, and (according to some) economies of scale, as a single large system was likely to cost less than several smaller decentralized systems. In many organizations with centralized systems, a single programming department was established for all application development and maintenance. To reduce data redundancy and promote data sharing among users, centralized databases also were established.

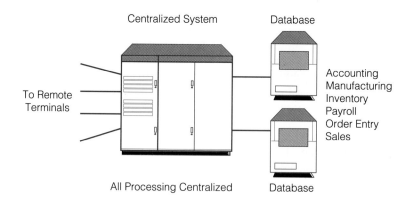

Centralized System   Database

To Remote
Terminals

Accounting
Manufacturing
Inventory
Payroll
Order Entry
Sales

All Processing Centralized   Database

Figure 20–2
Centralized System

Disadvantages of Centralization

It was later found that large centralized systems also have inherent problems. First, if the large central system fails, the entire system fails, and if a component fails, all or part of the application system may be unavailable. In the decentralized approach, failure of one node results in part of the overall system being lost, but many processing functions can be continued. In this respect, decentralized systems are more reliable than a single centralized system.

Many end users—the accounting department, warehouse, and so forth—found that their needs were not met by a centralized system. Because the system was shared, users often found it unresponsive; there was often difficulty running jobs and getting resources for new development. With a departmental system in a distributed or decentralized environment, a user contends only with other users in the department, so it was easy to establish priorities. However, setting interdepartment priorities was not easy sometimes. The same held true for programming. In the centralized environment, a programming team may have been assigned to develop an application or a new report for a department. Because developers were not under the direct control of the department, it was sometimes difficult for the department to change priorities and directions.

Expansion and growth of the large centralized system posed another problem for some companies: that of controlling system growth. Too often growth was not in small, manageable increments but in giant steps, such as conversion to a larger processor with a different operating system. This conversion meant downtime while the new system was being installed. Sometimes programs had to be revised and new program bugs were encountered. The change was usually disruptive to all users. In contrast, when upgrading a distributed system, growth was generally in smaller, more manageable increments. In addition, if a new processor became necessary, only those using that node were affected, not the entire user community.

Networked Systems

Networking provides some of the benefits of both centralized and distributed environments: more localized processing and control with shared data, processing power, and equipment. We again use a LAN as an example; these comments generally apply to WANs as well. In a LAN, end users have a workstation capable of performing a variety of application functions such as word processing and spreadsheets. Each workstation is also able to call on the processing power and database capabilities of a larger system—a server or host processor—to accomplish more complex and time-consuming processing tasks. Some of the data required frequently by a user at a workstation may reside on the workstation's local disk drives. This may include documents in process and budget data for spreadsheets. Data that either is infrequently used or is too big for the workstation's local disks can be maintained at a larger host. Although this data is maintained by another node, the workstation can access that data as though it were stored locally. Workstations are also able to share other network resources such as printers and magnetic tape drives. The key to a distributed system is making resource distribution transparent to the users. When the resources being distributed are data, sophisticated network software is necessary. The software responsible for doing this is called a **distributed file system (DFS).**

DISTRIBUTED FILE SYSTEMS

distributed file system (DFS) Network software responsible for making resources available to multiple users regardless of their location in the network.

In distributed systems, users must have the ability to locate and use remote files as though those files were locally resident. The objectives of a DFS are given in Table 20–1 and are described below. Again, do not confuse a DFS with a distributed DBMS. Although there are similarities between the two, distributed database systems significantly extend the capabilities of a DFS.

transparent access The ability of a user to access distributed files as though they were located on the user's local node.

Transparent Access   **Transparent access** means that a user at one node must be able to access distributed files as though they were located on the user's local node. This means a user should be able to use the file system commands of the local system to access remote files, even if the remote file is located on a node with a different operating and file system.

Operating System Independence   In building a distributed system, a user should be able to configure heterogeneous systems. This may mean that different operating systems and file systems are involved. Not only should designers be able to build a system composed of different hardware and software, but also they must make these differences transparent to users.

File System Independence   With file system independence, different file systems, such as DOS, UNIX, and VMS, may be used in one network. Just as important, the differences among the file systems should be transparent to users. For example, the local file system commands should be functional when a user accesses a file on a remote node with a different file system.

Architecture Independence   The DFS should allow any network configuration (star, bus, ring, interconnected, and so on). Neither the architecture nor the network software should limit the ability to distribute files.

Contention Resolution   The DFS ought to provide a mechanism that prevents data corruption due to contention. Such corruption can result when two or more users try to access and update the same file or record.

Security   A DFS must provide the requisite level of security. Files should be able to be secured for local access only or for remote access. When

Table 20–1   Distributed File System Objectives

Provide transparent access to distributed files	Provide contention resolution
Provide operating system independence	Provide security
Provide file system independence	Provide file directory information
Provide architecture independence	Provide location independence

remote access to a file is allowed, the DFS must be able to grant or deny requests based on the requester's ID. Inherent in this requirement is the ability to provide user identities for users on a node that does not support user IDs (such as a single-user microcomputer) and to reconcile network differences among user IDs.

File Directory Information   The DFS is responsible for transparently satisfying user requests. This means it must maintain a directory of remote files and their locations. When a user requests access to a file, the directory is consulted to find the node that houses the file.

Location Independence   Location independence means that a file can be located at any node in the network. A file also must be able to be moved from one node to another without disrupting applications or user access to that file.

Several DFS implementations exist. The one most often used for networks with equipment from a variety of vendors is the **Network File System (NFS),** developed by Sun Microsystems. It is implemented not only on Sun systems but also on a variety of UNIX-, VMS-, and DOS-based systems. Sun Microsystems has placed the NFS protocol specifications in the public domain to allow other vendors to implement it. The objective of publishing the protocol was to spread its use and establish NFS as a standard.

A UNIX operating system DFS, **Remote File Sharing (RFS),** currently runs only on UNIX-based systems. This protocol is supported by AT&T, the originator of the UNIX operating system. One current limitation of RFS is its restriction to UNIX-based systems. With RFS, files that physically exist on one node can appear as though they reside on other nodes. Thus, a user can access the remote file as though it were a local file.

Network File System (NFS) A distributed file system developed by Sun Microsystems that is also compatible with DOS- and UNIX-based systems.

Remote File Sharing (RFS) A distributed file system that is supported only by UNIX-based systems.

ADVANTAGES AND DISADVANTAGES OF DISTRIBUTED SYSTEMS

Advantages

Each distributed system just described has numerous advantages. For one, storing data close to the location that uses it most in a network situation minimizes the amount of data that must be transmitted between nodes and provides better response times. Because maintenance of the data is a local responsibility, there is more of a vested interest in keeping the data current. Third, nonlocal transactions are still possible, as are transactions that must span several nodes, the only penalty being slower response times due to slow transmission speeds on the communication links. Distributed systems also give local users more control over their data processing system. This provides users with the flexibility to tailor changes to their own needs without disrupting other network nodes. Reliability also is higher than with a centralized system, for the failure of one node does not mean the entire system is down. Each node has most of the data it needs to continue local processing, so applications can continue with only a slight degradation in service.

Disadvantages

There are also disadvantages to the distributed approach.

Multiple-Node Transactions Are Slower   Whenever a transaction must span more than one node, response time is longer than if the transaction ran on one node only. Suppose a salesperson for a computer vendor enters an order for a new system consisting of processors, disks, and terminals. The response time for placing the order will be faster if all the equipment is available in the local warehouse than if each component must come from a different location. In the latter case, a message would have to be sent to the other warehouses in sequence until the order was filled.

Maintaining Transaction Integrity   A transaction is an atomic piece of work—a group of updates that must all be completed for database consistency. In a centralized database, this atomic property is guaranteed by the DBMS's recovery system. However, when a transaction updates files on several nodes, several independent DBMSs are involved. Each may be capable of guaranteeing the integrity of the portion of the transaction processed on its system, but there is no coordination among the various DBMSs. In fact, it may be difficult to establish a consistent, unique transaction identifier for node-spanning transactions.

Contention and Deadlock   Update transactions on multiple nodes increase the risk of contention and deadlock. As discussed in previous chapters, a record being updated is locked until the end of the transaction to avoid the problems of concurrent updates. Because a transaction that spans several nodes is slower than one on a single node (because of data communication transmission time), affected records remain locked longer. Thus, the probability increases that the records will be needed by another transaction, and hence the amount of contention and the potential for deadlock increase.

Potential for Failure   The longer response time for transactions that span multiple nodes also increases the probability of a failure that will produce an unsuccessful transaction.

Determining Participating Nodes

Most DBMSs available today were not designed for distributing data over several nodes. With a transaction that accesses and updates records on multiple nodes, the system must determine which other nodes must be involved. It is unthinkable to require the user to do this because one of the objectives is to make the distributed nature of the system transparent. It is also desirable to reserve the ability to redistribute data and processes without disrupting users.

One approach to identifying the location of resources is to programmatically define the nodes that are to participate by coding the locations into the programs. This requires that the programming staff know the location of data their programs are using. As nodes are added or data is relocated, it is likely that program changes also will be required. This approach is preferable to relying on the user to determine the location of files, but it creates considerable problems with respect to maintaining the system, extending the system, and redistributing system resources.

Network Dictionary of Locations A better way to identify resource locations is to have a network dictionary that describes the locations of all distributed data and processing entities referenced in the system. The application or transaction control process can access the dictionary to learn where the required resources are located. Redistribution of files requires a simple update to the dictionary and programs are not affected by such changes.

Central Versus Distributed Dictionary The dictionary can be either centrally located and maintained or replicated at all nodes. The centralized approach, with several weaknesses, is the less desirable. First, when the central node becomes unavailable, the distributed system is inoperable. Local operations could continue, but finding remote resources would be impossible. The centralized dictionary approach could be augmented by establishing one or more alternative nodes with backup dictionary capability. The backup nodes are used if the primary fails.

A second problem with a centralized dictionary is that additional access time is required to obtain the information, and the possibility exists that the central node will become a performance bottleneck. In a LAN with high-speed links, communication time might not be significant. But accessing data via a slow communication link with several hops through intermediate nodes can significantly slow the application response time, especially if the dictionary must be consulted several times for each transaction.

A distributed dictionary resides on all nodes or strategically located nodes. This provides faster access to the dictionary than in the centralized approach. The disadvantage of distributed dictionaries is the need to keep all dictionaries properly updated, particularly if the contents change often. Despite this shortcoming, a distributed dictionary usually gives better performance than a centralized one.

Routing, Transmission, and Processing

Once the locations of the distributed resources have been determined, a strategy must be developed for accessing and processing the data. Designers of distributed systems have several options in determining how the remote processing and accesses will be handled. In general, the strategy selected depends on the type of transaction.

Remote Access and Local Processing One method for processing with distributed data is remote access and local processing. This type of transaction is used effectively when most of the data being accessed is needed at the local node. Consider a system for a state's highway patrol force. If a state trooper stops a car and inquires regarding the driver's record, the application on a local node issues a read request for the driver's files on a remote node. The set of records for the driver is transmitted to the local node and from there to the display device in the trooper's car. In this case, there was a local request for remote access, and all data satisfying that request was sent to the local node for processing. If the driver is cited for a violation as a consequence of the trooper's work, the driver's record might be modified locally and then a local request for updating the record in the remote file is made. The revised record is transmitted over the network and the database updated as a consequence of the remote update request. The characteristics of the police transaction are that every record accessed was transmitted over the network to the local node, all processing was done locally, and all updates were brought about via local requests. This is similar to the way in which a LAN file server operates.

Partial Remote Processing   A second method for handling distributed processing requires that the remote node perform some amount of application processing. Consider a transaction to list all employees with more than 10 years of service and a salary below $20,000. For a company with 100,000 employees, all 100,000 records must be accessed to satisfy the query. Passing each of the 100,000 records to the requesting node for selection would place a large load on the communication subsystem and take considerable extra time. A much better alternative is to have a server process on each remote node access the records, perform the selection, and then transmit only the results to the requesting node, where the list will be consolidated.

Total Remote Processing   Consider a transaction that updates records at a remote node. When the record is required locally, the remote record is transmitted to the local node, an update is made, and the record is sent back to the remote node for updating in the database. In some instances the entire update can be performed remotely, as in giving an across-the-board pay raise to employees.

Suppose a company decides to distribute the personnel and payroll applications and maintains that data in each of five regional processing centers. A manager in the corporate headquarters may have the responsibility for administering a 6% pay raise for all 100,000 employees. If the first strategy is used, each of the 100,000 records must be read remotely, transmitted over the network, updated, sent back over the network, and updated in the database. For this transaction, however, there is no need to transmit any data to the local node. A better alternative is to send the request to a server process on the remote node and have all the work done there. You should recognize this type of processing as being equivalent to the capabilities of the LAN's SQL server described in Chapter 6.

Many other examples of the division of activity among nodes could be cited. In essence, there are only the three basic methods just discussed: access remote records, pass them to the local node, process the records locally, and then return them to the remote nodes for updating as necessary; send messages to remote application servers that accept and process data and then return only the required information to the requesting nodes; or a combination of the two approaches, which is sometimes the best alternative. The design objective is always to make the transaction as efficient as possible, which means minimizing the transmission of many records between nodes.

DATABASE MANAGEMENT IN DISTRIBUTED SYSTEMS

Having discussed how data can be manipulated with remote file systems, we now look at the more complex problem of distributed databases. Most current DBMSs were designed to operate on only one node. There was no need to keep track of files or databases on another node or to manage transactions that span multiple nodes. In some instances the problem of distributed transactions is compounded by having two different database systems involved. One example is when one node uses one vendor's hardware and software and another node uses a different vendor's hardware and DBMS. In such cases, it is not likely that the DBMSs will cooperate with each other except through user-written programs or routines.

Rules for a Distributed Database

You have already read about the objectives of distributed file systems. A similar set of objectives or rules has been established for distributed databases. These rules, given in Table 20–2, are explained below. Note that in some instances the rules are comparable to those for distributed file systems and that the rules extend the capabilities of remote file systems.

Rule 1   Local autonomy means that users at a given node are responsible for data management and system operation at that node. A local node has a certain amount of independence regarding these local operations. This independence is not unrestrained, however. As with individuals in a free society who have individual independence, the independence extends only where it does not adversely affect another member of the society. Thus, a local node does not typically have the independence to arbitrarily remove its node from the network if that action is detrimental to operation of the distributed system. Another implication of local autonomy is that users at a node accessing only data local to that node should neither experience performance degradations nor need to interact with the system differently as a result of being part of a distributed system.

Rule 2   No reliance on a central site means that all nodes in the distributed system shall be considered as peer nodes, with no node identified as a supervisor. Furthermore, there shall not be one node on which other nodes must rely, such as a single node that contains a centralized data dictionary or directory.

Table 20–2   Date's 12 Rules for Distributed Databases

Local autonomy	Distributed query processing
No reliance on a central site	Distributed transaction management
Continuous operation	Hardware independence
Location independence	Operating system independence
Fragmentation independence	Network independence
Replication independence	DBMS independence

Rule 3 Continuous operation means that adding nodes to the network, removing network nodes, or having one node fail will not affect availability of other nodes. Naturally, a single node failure will probably disrupt access for the users local to that node; however, users at other nodes can continue to use the distributed database, and their disruption is limited to an inability to access data stored only at the failed node.

Rule 4 Location independence means that data can be placed anywhere in the network and that its location is transparent to those needing access to it. Data can be moved from one node to another, and users or programs needing access to that data are not disrupted.

Rule 5 In the personnel and payroll example cited earlier in this chapter, each regional node had personnel and payroll files for the employees in that region. Physically these were separate files, but logically their combination formed the corporate personnel file and payroll file. Fragmentation independence means that data that appears to users as one logical file can be transparently partitioned over multiple nodes. Thus, the personnel file is fragmented over several regional nodes. The corporate personnel director must be able to make inquiries regarding all employees (such as the average salary of all employees) and receive the answer consolidated from all fragments. The manager also must be able to initiate the query in the same way he or she would have if the table had not been fragmented. The distributed DBMS is responsible for making the various fragments appear as a single file.

Rule 6 Storing the same file in multiple locations is called replication. Replication independence means that any file can be replicated on two or more nodes and that such replication is transparent to both users and applications. Replication is desirable for files that must be accessed by several nodes, such as a network directory. Replication can enhance performance and availability. The distributed DBMS is responsible for managing updates to replicated data and keeping the replicated data consistent.

distributed query processing A condition in which a user at one node can start a query involving data on other nodes.

Rule 7 When we discussed access strategies for distributed files, three alternatives were given: remote access and local processing, partial remote processing, and total remote processing. The alternative used depended on the application program's logic. **Distributed query processing** means that a user at one node can start a query involving data on other nodes. Access and processing strategies such as those discussed earlier must be supported. The location of the data must be transparent to the user and the application. The query also must be completed in an optimum way. This might mean that database servers on several nodes cooperatively work on a portion of the query. In this way, the minimum amount of data is transmitted over the network to the requesting node. The DBMS is responsible for determining the access strategy and carrying it out.

distributed transaction management In a distributed database, a transaction may be operated on by several processes in different computer nodes. Transactions of this type must be managed by the distributed database system to ensure database integrity, either by completing the transaction or by reversing any updates done by a transaction that cannot be completed.

Rule 8 **Distributed transaction management** means that node-spanning transactions must be allowed. Moreover, transactions that update data on several nodes must be recoverable. This requires that a transaction started on one node can update records on other nodes and that the DBMSs on those other nodes coordinate their activities regarding locking records and effecting transaction backout and recovery.

Rule 9   Hardware independence means that the distributed network can consist of hardware from a variety of vendors. Nodes in the distributed system can come from a variety of vendors, such as IBM, Hewlett-Packard, or Compaq.

Rule 10   When different hardware vendors supply network nodes, it is likely that different operating systems will be used. This capability is known as operating system independence.

Rule 11   Another consequence of Rule 9, hardware independence, might be that different network architectures, software, and protocols are used. If the vendors design their network systems according to the OSI reference model and related standards, such interconnection is easier. Network independence means that multiple kinds of network software may be used in connecting the nodes together. Some network nodes may be part of an SNA network, others may be members of a DECNET network, and still others may be nodes on an Ethernet LAN. Using disparate network systems must not adversely affect distributed database capabilities.

Rule 12   DBMS independence means that a variety of DBMSs may be used in the distributed database. One node might use an IMS database, another might use DB2, and a third might use Oracle. Each DBMS has a different data access and manipulation language, has different recovery mechanisms, and stores data in different formats. The distributed DBMS must make these differences transparent to both users and applications. A user also should be able to access data managed by such a variety of DBMSs without learning a variety of data access languages. Specifically, the user should be able to access distributed data using the same interface he or she uses to access data stored locally. This rule implies that database recovery systems be coordinated and database language differences accommodated. Implementation of this rule is very complex.

Currently, there is no system that adheres to all of these rules. Creating a distributed environment that encompasses all 12 rules will require a considerable investment. Until then, those who want to implement distributed databases must settle for less than the capabilities implied by these rules. The best way to implement distributed databases today is to use hardware and software from one vendor only and to choose a database system that supports distributed capabilities.

SUMMARY

Distributed systems are becoming viable processing systems. They are currently at the frontier of DBMSs and data communication systems. Many of the problems that impede their widespread use are in the area of database technology rather than data communication. Distributed data and distributed transactions may have a significant impact on the use of network resources. Specifically, data transfers, message transfers, and recovery messages can cause increased media traffic. Development in the problem areas should be spurred by potential advantages of distributing data to where it is most often used, by sharing of processing and data resources, and by providing more control to end users.

KEY TERMS

centralized systems
distributed database
distributed file system (DFS)
distributed processing
distributed query processing

distributed transaction management
Network File System (NFS)
Remote File Sharing (RFS)
transparent access

REVIEW QUESTIONS

1. What are the disadvantages of replicating data on multiple nodes?
2. What types of files are candidates for replication?
3. Describe three methods for keeping replicated files current.
4. What benefits do relational model DBMSs provide in distributed database applications?
5. List four current problems in distributed processing.
6. List four applications that are good candidates for distributed processing.
7. Distinguish between distributed processing and distributed databases.
8. Describe the objectives of a distributed file system.
9. What are the advantages and disadvantages of distributed systems?
10. List and describe the 12 rules for distributed databases.

PROBLEMS AND EXERCISES

1. Research the literature for DBMSs that are or claim to be distributed. Determine how well these systems conform to Date's 12 rules for a distributed database.
2. You have been asked to design the placement of files for a personnel database. Your company has four regions, each of which has a personnel office, and there is a personnel office in a separate world headquarters complex. The files in the system are employee, benefits, job history, payroll, department, skills, insurance, and insurance claims. Devise a plan for placing each of these files, assuming each location has computer facilities. Would you recommend a distributed database solution? If so, would you replicate any files? Would you partition any files? Document your decisions.
3. Research Digital Equipment Corporation's implementation of the remote file system. Describe how files are distributed and how users are able to access them.

Asynchronous Transmission

This appendix supplements the discussion of asynchronous transmission protocols in Chapter 11. You may want to refer to that material before continuing. Asynchronous transmission occurs one character at a time. Sending and receiving stations are not synchronized with each other, which means that a sending station can send a character at any time, with no prescribed interval to the next character. Of course, the receiving station must also be ready to accept a character at any time. In the discussion that follows, an asynchronous point-to-point line with a transmission speed of 1200 bps is assumed (this speed is much slower than current transmission speeds, but makes the calculations easier).

THE UART

At the heart of asynchronous transmission is a processing chip called the Universal Asynchronous Receiver/Transmitter (UART). The UART accepts characters via parallel transmission from the terminal or host and places them on the circuit serially. It also accepts bit serial transmissions from the communication line and passes the characters to the data terminal equipment in bit parallel fashion.

DETECTING INCOMING CHARACTERS

To detect an incoming character, the UART samples the state of the communication circuit at a rate 16 times the expected bit rate. On a 1200-bps line, 1 bit passes every $1/1200 = 0.000833 = 0.833$ ms, so a sampling of the line is taken every 52 microseconds. Figure A–1 illustrates this situation. The line is sampled so often to identify immediately when the state of the line has changed from the mark condition to the space condition. When a line transition is detected, the sampling interval is changed to ensure that the line is always being sampled in the middle of a bit interval. This is far

Figure A–1
Asynchronous Line Sampling

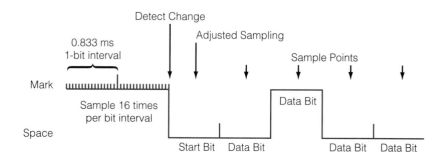

safer than attempting to interrogate the line at the beginning or ending of a bit, when a slight timing error could cause the bit to be missed. Thus, when it appears that a start bit has arrived, there is a delay of 7/16 of a bit interval (0.364 ms in the current example) before the line is sampled again, so that the sample is taken approximately in the middle of the bit interval. If the line is in the space condition, it is assumed that this represents a start bit. Line sampling timing is adjusted to sample the line during every bit interval (every 0.83 ms), and the line is sampled once for each bit and nearly in the center of the bit interval. As discussed in Chapter 11, four items must be agreed on by sender and receiver before asynchronous communications can begin: line speed, number of bits per character, presence of a parity bit, and message termination characters. Line sampling makes use of the agreed-on line speed.

RECEIVING INCOMING CHARACTERS AND PARITY CHECK

Knowledge of the number of bits expected per character is used to receive the bits making up each character. This discussion assumes 7 bits per character plus 1 parity bit. Having detected the start bit, the UART then assembles the next 7 bits that should make up the character. The ninth bit, the parity bit, follows the start bit and the 7 data bits. The parity bit is received and checked against the 7 data bits already received. If parity does not check, then a parity error message is sent to the transmitter so the character can be retransmitted. If parity checks, the next bit is examined to see whether it is a stop bit or a mark condition. If a stop bit or mark condition is not detected, a transmission error is assumed to have occurred. If everything is correct, the UART returns to sampling the line. It is necessary to know how many bits compose a character, as well as whether parity is being transmitted and checked, to know when to expect the stop bit.

MESSAGE TERMINATION

If termination characters have been specified, the communication process driving the line must examine the character to determine whether it matches any of the defined termination characters. If there is no match, the character is placed in memory awaiting the rest of the message. If an interrupt character is detected, appropriate action is taken, depending on the interrupt character.

Suppose two interrupt characters have been designated, a backspace and a carriage return. The backspace is used to cancel a character just received, and a carriage return, to signal the end of the message. If a backspace character is received, it causes the end-of-buffer pointer to be decreased by one, meaning that it essentially erases the previously received character. The next character transmitted (if not another backspace) is placed in the buffer over the previously received character. Because every keystroke in asynchronous transmission is transmitted immediately to the host (with dumb terminals, anyway), hitting an incorrect character followed by backspace transmits two characters to the host: the incorrect character and the backspace character. On the other hand, if the carriage return character is received, the end of the message has been indicated. On receiving this interrupt character, the system makes the data available to the application program.

DATA OVERRUNS

A UART usually has two registers available for receiving data from the line and two for receiving data from the data terminal equipment (DTE). This allows a received character to be checked for parity and placed into memory while another character is being received. Even so, data overruns are still possible, especially when an intelligent or smart terminal is transmitting data from its buffer. At such a time the data may be transmitted at intervals much faster than operator typing speeds. Even when the line speed is not exceeded, the receiving hardware or software may be incapable of receiving a continuous stream of characters at that speed. One solution to this problem is to increase the interval between transmitting characters.

Synchronous Data Link Control

This appendix supplements the discussion of IBM's Synchronous Data Link Control (SDLC) protocol given in Chapter 11. You may want to review that material before continuing. This SDLC discussion focuses on the control field functions and the Ns and Nr message sequencing concept. The control field provides the ability to designate the type of the frame—unnumbered, supervisory, or informational—and to acknowledge receipt of frames.

UNNUMBERED FRAMES

Unnumbered frames are used for control functions such as resetting a station's Ns and Nr counts to zero, causing stations on switched lines to disconnect, rejecting a frame received in error, and transmitting data such as broadcast or status messages that do not need a sequence check. The general format of the unnumbered control field is given in Figure B–1. The first two bits (11) identify the frame as unnumbered. The code bits are used to identify the frame function, initialize station, reject frame, disconnect, and so on. The 5 bits allow for 32 different functions. The existing control functions for unnumbered frames are given in Table B–1.

P/F Bit

The P/F (poll/final) bit, which is common to all control fields, is set when a station is being polled and when the final frame for a message is sent. Just as in BISYNC, messages can be broken into blocks for transmission; all but

| 1 | 1 | Code | P/F | Code |

Figure B–1
*Control Field Format:
Unnumbered Frame*

Table B–1   Unnumbered Control Functions

Code for Unnumbered Control	Function
UI	Identifies an information frame as unnumbered.
SNRM	Sets normal response mode. Resets Ns and Nr count fields.
DISC	Places secondary station in disconnect mode.
RD	Indicates a secondary station request to disconnect.
UA	Signals a positive acknowledgment to an SNRM, DISC, or SIM command.
RIM	Indicates a secondary station request for initialization.
SIM	Primary initializes secondary. Ns and Nr counts are set to 0.
DM	Indicates that a secondary station is in disconnect mode.
FRMR	Signals that an invalid frame has been received.
TEST	Means that a test frame has been sent to a secondary station, which will respond with a test frame.
XID	Requests an ID exchange.

the last such block have the P/F bit set to zero. The P/F bit also is used in loop configurations to specify optional and mandatory responses to polling.

SUPERVISORY FRAMES

The control field format for the supervisory frame is given in Figure B–2. The first two bits (10) designate the frame as supervisory. The P/F bit is as described above. The receive count field (explained below) is used to acknowledge receipt of frames. The code field is 2 bits wide and therefore can represent only four different control functions, three of which have been specified thus far. Two control functions are used to indicate whether the station is ready to receive (RR) or not ready to receive (RNR) data. The third control function (REJ) is used to reject a frame.

INFORMATION FRAMES

The information frame is used primarily to send data; its control field format is given in Figure B–3. Unlike in the other two types of frames, only the first bit (0) is used to designate the frame as informational. The P/F bit is as described above. The send count (Ns) and receive count (Nr) fields are each made up of 3 bits. As discussed in Chapter 11, the Ns field is used by a station to count the number of messages sent to another station. The Nr field is

Figure B–2
Control Field Format:
Supervisory Frame

| 1 | 0 | Code | P/F | Receive Count (Nr) |

Figure B–3
*Control Field Format:
Information Frame*

a count kept by a receiving station of the number of messages received from another station. Each station maintains separate Ns and Nr count fields for each station with which it communicates. When a station is initialized by the supervisor, the Ns and Nr counts are set to zero, so the Nr count becomes the message number the receiving station expects next. The first message sent is message number 0. After either count reaches 7, the next increment rolls the count over to zero, meaning that, at most, seven messages can be sent before an acknowledgment is necessary.

EXAMPLE: HOW NS AND NR COUNTS ARE USED

This example, illustrated in Table B–2, shows the values of the address field, the frame type, the Ns and Nr counts, and the P/F bit, in that order. The supervisor station polls the secondary stations. The supervisor uses a supervisory frame to indicate that it is ready to receive. The P/F bit is set to 1 to indicate that station A is being polled. The Nr count is set to zero, indicating that the next frame expected from station A is frame number 0. Station A has no data to send and thus responds with a supervisory frame, indicating that it is ready to receive and that the next frame expected from the supervisor is frame number 0. The final bit is set to 1 in this instance to indicate that there is no data to send.

Station B is then polled. Station B does have data to transmit and uses the information frame to do so. Four frames are required to transmit the entire message. For the first three frames the P/F bit is set to 0 to indicate that more frames will follow. The last frame in the message has the P/F bit set to

Table B–2   Example of the Use of Ns and Nr Subfields

Supervisor					Secondary Station				
Address	Frame Type	Ns Count	Nr Count	P/F Bit		Address	Frame Type	Ns Count	Nr Count	P/F Bit
A	RR	0	0	1	→					
					←	A	RR	0	0	1
B	RR	0	0	1	→					
					←	B	I	0	0	0 data
		0	1		←	B	I	1	0	0 data
		0	2		←	B	I	2	0	0 data
		0	3		←	B	I	3	0	1 data
B	RR	0	4	0	→					
C	RR	0	0	1	→					

1. The Ns count for station B is incremented with each frame. The Nr count is incremented following the receipt of each frame, although the supervisor sends no acknowledgment in this case until the final frame is received. On receiving the final frame, the supervisor acknowledges receipt of all messages at once with a supervisory frame. The P/F bit is not set on this frame because station B is not being polled. Much of the efficiency of bit-oriented data link protocols stems from their ability to transmit multiple frames without acknowledgment and to transmit in full-duplex mode. This avoids the wait times required by other protocols such as BISYNC, which require that each message be acknowledged before another may be sent.

Acronym Glossary

For a more thorough definition, please refer to the Key Terms Glossary.

ACF Advanced Communications Facility

ACK acknowledgment

ACU auto-call unit

AD administrative domain

ADCCP Advanced Data Communications Control Procedure

ADMD administrative management domain

ADSL asymmetric digital subscriber line

AM amplitude modulation

ANSI American National Standards Institute

API application program interface

APPN advanced peer-to-peer networking

ARP address resolution protocol

ARPA Advanced Research Projects Agency

Arpanet Advanced Research Projects Agency network, original version of the Internet

ASCII American Standard Code for Information Interchange

ATM asynchronous transfer mode

BBS bulletin board system

BCC block check character

BCD Binary Coded Decimal

BDSL Same as VDSL

BISYNC Binary Synchronous Communications (also BSC)

BIU bus interface unit

BPS bits per second

BSC Binary Synchronous Communications (also BISYNC)

CAD computer-aided design

CAI computer-aided instruction

CAM computer-aided manufacturing

CCITT Consultative Committee on International Telegraph and Telephony

CDDI copper distributed data interface

CDPD cellular digital packet data

CICS Customer Information Control System

CIO chief information officer

CIU communication interface unit

CLNP Connectionless Network Protocol

CMIP Common Management Information Protocol

CMIS Common Management Information Service

CPU central processing unit

CRC cyclic redundancy check

CRT cathode ray tube

C/S client/server

CSMA/CA carrier sense with multiple access and collision avoidance

CSMA/CD carrier sense with multiple access and collision detection

CSU channel service unit

DBMS database management system

d-cash digital cash

DCE   data circuit–terminating equipment, data communication equipment, or distributed computing environment

DES   Data Encryption Standard

DFS   distributed file system

DHCP   dynamic host configuration protocol

DNS   domain name system or domain name server

DPSK   differential phase shift keying

DS0   Digital Signal 0, equivalent to voice-grade digital channel of 64 Kbps

DS1   Digital Signal 1, digital line equivalent of T-1 service, 1.544 Mbps

DS2   Digital Signal 2, digital line equivalent to four T-1 lines for data rate of 6.312 Mbps

DSL   digital subscriber line

DSLAM   digital subscriber line access multiplexers

DSU   data service unit

DTE   data terminal equipment

DVD   digital versatile disk

E1   European equivalent to T-1 service, provides 2.048 Mbps data rate

E3   European equivalent to T-3 service, provides 57.344 Mbps data rate

EBCDIC   Extended Binary-Coded Decimal Interchange Code

e-cash   electronic cash

EDI   electronic data interchange

e-mail   electronic mail

FAQ   frequently asked question(s)

FCS   frame check sequence

FDDI   fiber distributed data interface

FDM   frequency division multiplexing

FEP   front-end processor

FM   frequency modulation

FMS   file management system

FQDN   fully qualified domain name

FRAD   frame relay access device

FSK   frequency shift keying

FTP   file transfer protocol

GATT   General Agreement on Trade and Tariffs

GDSS   group decision support system

GUI   graphical user interface

HDLC   high-level data link control

HDSL   high-data-rate digital subscriber line

HTML   hypertext markup language

HTTP   hypertext transfer protocol

Hz   Hertz

IAB   Internet Architecture Board

IEEE   Institute of Electrical and Electronics Engineers

IETF   Internet Engineering Task Force

IITF   Information Infrastructure Task Force

InterNIC   Internet Network Information Center

IP   Internet Protocol

IPC   interprocess communication

IPng, IPv6   Internet Protocol, next generation or version 6

IPX   Internet packet exchange

IRC   Internet relay chat

ISDN   integrated services digital network

ISO   International Standards Organization

ISP   Internet service provider

ITU   International Telecommunications Union

LAN   local area network

LAPB   Link Access Protocol, Balanced

LATA   local access and transport area

LDAP   Lightweight Directory Access Protocol

LLC   logical link control

LRC   longitudinal redundancy check

LU   logical unit

MAC   media access control protocol

MAN   metropolitan area network

MAU   multistation access unit

Mbps   million bits per second

MIB   management information base

Mips   million instructions per second

MNP   microcomputer network protocols

MTA   message transfer agent

MTBF   mean time between failures

MTTR   mean time to repair

mux   multiplexing

NAK   negative acknowledgement

NAP   network access point

NAU   network addressable unit

NC   network computer

NCP   Network Control Program

NDS   Novell Directory Services

NFS   Network File System

NIA   network interface adapter (also NIC)

NIC   network interface card (also NIA) or Network Information Center

NMS   Network Management System

NOS   network operating system

NPA   Network Performance Analyzer

NPDA   Network Problem Determination Aid

NTS   NT Server (Windows)

OLE   object linking and embedding

ORB   Object Request Broker

OS   operating system

OSI   Open Systems Interconnection reference model

PAD   packet assembly/disassembly

PBX   private branch exchange

PC   personal computer

PCI   peripheral component interconnect

PCM   pulse code modulation

PCS   personal communication services

PD   public domain

PDN   packet distribution network or public data network

PDU   protocol data unit

PERT   program evaluation and review technique

PGP   Pretty Good Privacy

PNW   Personal NetWare

POP   point of presence or Post Office Protocol

POTS   plain old telephone service

PPP   point-to-point protocol

PRMD   private management domain

PSE   packet-switching equipment

PSK   phase shift keying

PSN   packet-switching network

PTT   postal telegraph and telephone

PU   physical unit

PUCP   Physical Unit Control Point

PVC   permanent virtual circuit

QAM   quadrature amplitude modulation

RADSL   rate adaptive digital subscriber line

RAID   redundant arrays of independent disks

RBOC   regional Bell operating company

RFI   request for information

RFP   request for proposal

RFQ   request for quotation

RFS   Remote File Sharing

RIP   Routing Information Protocol

RJE   remote job entry

RMON MIB   Remote Monitoring Management Information Base

RPC   remote procedure call

SAA   System Application Architecture

SAP   service access point

SBT   six-bit transcode

SDLC   Synchronous Data Link Control

SDSL   single-line digital subscriber line

SDU   service data unit

SET   secure electronic transaction

S-HTTP   Secure HTTP

SLIP   serial line Internet protocol

SMDS   switched multimegabit data service

SMI   Structure of Management Information

SMP   symmetrical multiprocessing

SMTP   simple mail transfer protocol

SNA   Systems Network Architecture

SNADS   SNA Distribution Services

SNMP   simple network management protocol

SONET   Synchronous Optical Network

SPX/IPX   Sequenced Packet Exchange/Internet Packet Exchange

SQL   Structured Query Language

SSCP   Systems Services Control Point

SSL   secure socket layer protocol

SSR   spread-spectrum radio

STDM   statistical time division multiplexing

STE   signaling terminal equipment

STP   shielded twisted pair

SVC   switched virtual circuit

T-1   transmission facility transmitting data at 1.544 Mbps

T-3   transmission facility transmitting data at 44.746 Mbps

TCP   Transmission Control Protocol or transaction control process

TCP/IP   Transmission Control Protocol/Internet Protocol

TDM   time division multiplexing

TSAP   transport service access point

UA   user agent

UDP   User Datagram Protocol

UPS   uninterruptible power supply

URL   Uniform Resource Locator

UTC   Universal Time Coordinated

UTP   unshielded twisted pair

VADSL   very-high-speed asymmetric digital subscriber line

VAN   value-added network

VDSL   very-high-speed digital subscriber line

VDT   video display terminal

VDU   video display unit

VHF   very-high-frequency radio waves

VPN   virtual private network

VRC   vertical redundancy check

VTAM   Virtual Telecommunications Access Method

W3   World Wide Web

WAIS   wide area information server

WAN   wide area network

WATS   wide area telecommunication or telephone service

WWW   World Wide Web

WYSIWYG   what you see is what you get

xDSL   generic abbreviation for various digital subscriber line configurations, such as ADSL and HDSL

XNS   Xerox Network System

XTP   Xpress Transfer Protocol

Key Terms Glossary

100BaseFX   IEEE specification for fiber optic cable Ethernet LANs with a speed of 100 Mbps.

100BaseT   IEEE specification for twisted-pair wire Ethernet LANs with a speed of 100 Mbps.

100VG-AnyLAN   IEEE specification for twisted-pair wire or fiber optic cable Ethernet LANs with a speed of 100 Mbps.

10Base2   IEEE specification for thinnet coaxial cable Ethernet LANs with a speed of 10 Mbps and segment length of 185 m.

10Base5   IEEE specification for thicknet coaxial cable Ethernet LANs with a speed of 10 Mbps and segment length of 500 m.

10BaseF   IEEE specification for fiber optic cable Ethernet LANs with a speed of 10 Mbps.

10BaseT   IEEE specification for twisted-pair wire Ethernet LANs with a speed of 10 Mbps.

10Broad36   IEEE specification for broadband Ethernet LANs with a speed of 10 Mbps.

802.x   Generic designation for IEEE subcommittees responsible for developing specifications for LANs and MANs.

access method   A software subsystem that provides input and output services as interface between an application and its associated devices. It eliminates device dependencies for an application programmer.

access security   Security that controls a user's access to data. The controls may regulate a user's ability to read and update data, delete files, and run programs.

access server   An interconnection utility that allows microcomputers to access LAN resources from remote locations.

access time   The total time required in accessing a disk, including seek time, latency, and transfer time.

acknowledgment   A message returned to the sender of a block of data indicating that the block has been received error-free.

acoustic coupler   An acoustic coupler converts digital signals to analog and analog to digital. It is used mostly in switched communication and uses the telephone handset to pass data between a terminal or computer and the acoustic coupler.

active hub   A node connection hub used in an ARCnet LAN that provides signal regeneration and allows nodes to be located up to 2000 ft from the hub.

active node   A node capable of sending or receiving network messages.

active port   The status of a bridge port that will accept packets from the LAN end of the port.

adapter   A device that connects one system to another and allows the two systems to interoperate.

adaptive routing   A routing algorithm that evaluates the existing paths and chooses the one that will provide the best path for a message. Routes may change due to congestion and path failures.

address resolution protocol (ARP)   A protocol used to convert an IP address to the hardware address of a node. For example, if a node on an Ethernet network has an IP address, an Internet message will refer to the IP address. The ARP protocol is used to convert the IP address to a hardware address so the message can be delivered over the Ethernet network.

administrative management domain (ADMD)   A domain that represents a private e-mail system corresponding to a public delivery network in the X.400 standard hierarchy.

Advanced Communications Facility (ACF)   Facility that provides interdomain communication, improved error and testing capabilities, and dynamic device configuration.

Advanced Data Communications Control Procedure (ADCCP)   An ANSI standard bit-oriented data link control. Pronounced "add-cap."

advanced peer-to-peer networking (APPN)   An IBM network technology that allows two nodes to communicate directly with one another. Under IBM's Systems Network Architecture, communication between two entities generally requires the involvement of the Systems Services Control Point (SSCP), which runs in an IBM host computer. With APPN, involvement of the SSCP and host node is not required.

advanced program-to-program communication   In IBM's Systems Network Architecture, the ability for two programs to communicate with each other via an LU 6.2 session.

Advanced Research Projects Agency (ARPA)   A U.S. Department of Defense agency responsible for funding research in a variety of areas. ARPA funded the Arpanet, which grew into the Internet.

after-image   The status of a record after it has been processed.

agent   A device component that collects data for the device, which is then stored in the management information base. In client/server computing, an agent performs information preparation and exchange on behalf of a client or server process. In e-mail systems, agents can act on behalf of users to operate on mail. For example, a vacation agent could automatically file mail messages and forward them to another user.

aggregate data rate   The amount of information that can be transmitted per unit of time.

alert   A signal given by the network management system that a statistic, such as current line status, line quality, or number of retries on the line, has changed since the last status report. Also known as an alarm.

American National Standards Institute (ANSI)   A U.S. standard-making agency.

American Standard Code for Information Interchange (ASCII)   A code that uses 7 or 8 bits to represent characters. One of the two common computer codes. See also *EBCDIC*.

amplitude   The height, magnitude, or energy of a waveform.

amplitude modulation (AM)   One method of changing the properties of a wave to represent data.

analog line monitor   A diagnostic tool that monitors and displays the analog signals on the communication circuit or the data communication side of the modem, enabling the user to check for noise and proper modulation.

analog transmission   Refers to measurable physical quantities, which in data communication take the form of voltage and variations in the properties of waves. Data is represented in analog form by varying the amplitude, frequency, or phase of a wave or by changing current on a line.

application layer   One of the layers of the ISO's (OSI) reference model. The functions of this layer are application dependent.

application program interface (API)   In LANs, the interface between application programs and the network software.

application server   A node that provides application-oriented processing on the server side of client/server computing.

application software   Software that solves a business or scientific problem, as opposed to system software, which makes the system easier to use.

Archie   An Internet service that allows a user to search for documents at FTP sites.

ARCnet   LAN implementation based on Datapoint's attached resource computer network.

Arpanet   A packet-switching network implemented by the U.S. Defense Department's Advanced Research Projects Agency. The Arpanet evolved into the Internet.

asymmetric digital subscriber line (ADSL)   A digital switched technology that provides very high data transmission speeds over telephone system wires. The speed of the transmission is asynchronous, meaning that the transmission speeds for uploading and downloading data are different. For example, upstream transmissions may vary from 16 Kbps to 640 Kbps and downstream rates may vary from 1.5 Mbps to 9 Mbps. Within a given implementation the upstream and downstream speeds remain constant.

asynchronous transfer mode (ATM)   A high-speed transmission protocol in which data blocks are broken into small cells that are transmitted individually and possibly via different routes in a manner similar to packet-switching technology.

asynchronous transmission (Async)   The oldest and one of the most common data link protocols. Each character is transmitted individually with its own error detection scheme, usually a parity bit. The sender and receiver are not synchronized with each other. Also known as start–stop protocol.

AT&T divestiture   In 1984, AT&T was broken up into independent RBOCs and a separate AT&T company. The divestiture ended the regulated monopoly of AT&T as well as freeing AT&T and the RBOCs to enter into business areas previously denied to them.

attenuation   A weakening of a signal as a result of distance and characteristics of the medium.

authentication   A process in which a system user is required to provide or verify his or her user identification to gain system access.

authorization   A security procedure that ensures that the entity making a request is allowed to carry out all the activities implied by the request.

auto-call unit (ACU)   A device used to place a telephone call automatically without manual intervention.

availability   All necessary components of a network are operable and accessible when a user requires them.

backbone network   A network used to interconnect other networks or to connect a cluster of network nodes.

backup software   Software that is responsible for reading the files being backed up and writing them to the backup device.

baluns   Adapters that change coaxial cable connectors into twisted-pair wire connectors, allowing transfer from one medium to another or from a connector for one medium to a different medium.

bandwidth   The difference between the minimum and the maximum frequencies allowed. Bandwidth is a measure of the amount of data that can be transmitted per unit of time. The greater the bandwidth, the higher the possible data transmission rate.

Banyan Vines   A leading LAN operating system implementation produced by the Banyan Corporation.

baseband transmission   Sends the data along the channel by means of voltage fluctuations. The entire bandwidth of the cable is used to carry data.

batch applications   A style of computing in which inputs are collected over time and then processed as a group. Processing is carried out without interaction with a user.

Baudot   A code obtained from the telegraph industry that is used in data communication with telegraph lines or equipment originally designed for telegraphy. It is limited in its number of representable characters.

baud rate   A measure of the number of discrete signals that can be observed per unit of time.

before-image   The status of a record before it has been processed.

benchmark   A test in which one or more programs are run on a proposed hardware configuration to verify the ability of the hardware to meet a system's application requirements.

binary-coded decimal (BCD)   A coding scheme for the storage of data in digital computers. The code may either be 4-bit or 6-bit.

Binary Synchronous Communications (BISYNC or BSC) protocol   A transmission protocol introduced by IBM as the data link protocol for remote job entry. It later became a de facto standard for many types of data transmission, particularly between two computers. Data is transmitted a block at a time, and the sender and receiver must be in time with each other. Specific control characters are used to indicate beginning of text, end of text, start of header, and so on.

bit-oriented synchronous data link protocol   A data link protocol in which one or more bits are used to control the communication link. Bit synchronous protocols are commonly used on both LANs and WANs.

bit parallel transmission   The simultaneous transmission of bits over a wire medium.

bit rate   One method of measuring data transmission speed (bits per second).

bits per second (bps)   The number of bits that can be transferred over a medium in 1 second; a measure of data transmission speed.

bit stuffing   The implementation of transparency in SDLC through bit insertion.

block check character (BCC)   In the error detection methods of longitudinal redundancy check or cyclic redundancy check, an error detection character or characters, called the BCC, is appended to a block of transmitted characters, typically at the end of the block.

block mode   A mode in which data is entered and transmitted in one or more sets or blocks.

breakout box   A passive, multipurpose diagnostic device that is patched or temporarily inserted into a circuit at an interface.

bridge   The interface used to connect networks using similar data link protocols.

broadband transmission   A form of data transmission in which data is carried on high-frequency carrier waves; the carrying capacity of the medium is divided into a number of subchannels, such as video, low-speed data, high-speed data, and voice, allowing the medium to satisfy several communication needs.

broadcast message   A message sent to all users on a network.

broadcast radio   Uses AM, FM, and shortwave radio frequencies, with a total frequency range from 500,000 Hz to 108 MHz. Its primary applications include paging terminals, cellular radio telephones, and wireless LANs.

broadcast routing   Routing in which the message is broadcast to all stations. Only the stations to which the message is addressed accept it.

brouter   A term used to describe bridges that are able to connect two LANs using different data link protocols.

browser   A program that allows a user to navigate the Internet using hypertext links. A browser supports one or more Internet protocols, such as HTML.

buffer overflow/overrun   A situation that arises when the buffer is either too small or too full to receive the transmitted data. In either case there is no place to store the arriving characters, and the data is lost.

bulletin board system (BBS)   A hardware/software system that provides dial-in access for services such as file archives, message posting, and business functions. Many BBS functions have migrated to the Internet.

bus   A communication medium for transmitting data or power. A LAN topology.

bus interface unit (BIU)   In a LAN, the BIU provides the physical connection to the computer's I/O bus.

byte count protocol   A type of synchronous protocol that delineates data by including the number of characters being transmitted within the message.

cable modem   A modem that provides an interface between a user's system and a cable TV provider. Cable modems allow users to access resources such as the Internet via a high-speed cable TV connection.

cable tester   A diagnostic tool used to detect faults in cables by generating and monitoring a signal along the cable.

cache memory   High-speed memory that improves a computer's performance.

call-back unit   A security device for switched connections. It operates by receiving a call, verifying the user, severing the call, and calling the user back.

call clearing   The process that dissolves a switched virtual circuit.

carrier sense with multiple access and collision avoidance (CSMA/CA)   A media access control technique that attempts to avoid collisions.

carrier sense with multiple access and collision detection (CSMA/CD)   A media access control technique that attempts to detect collisions and is the most common access strategy for bus architectures.

carrier signal   A wave that continues without change. The carrier signal can be modulated by a modem so a receiver can interpret the information.

Carterphone case   A U.S. lawsuit between Carter Electronics and AT&T. A consequence of the decision was that any company could develop equipment and attach it to a telephone company's network as long as the attached device met FCC approval.

cascading   See *daisy chain*.

cellular digital packet data (CDPD)   A technology that uses idle cellular radio broadcast time to transmit digital data.

centralized system   A single system capable of supporting multiple job functions using shared resources.

Centrex service   A telephone company service that provides PBX capabilities to a company. With the Centrex service, the PBX equipment is located on the telephone company's premises.

character-count termination   A transmission termination technique in which a transmission is complete when a specified number of characters have been received. Allows the computer to save the data in blocks and avoid buffer overflow.

character synchronous protocol   A type of synchronous protocol oriented toward specific data codes and specific characters within those codes.

chat room   A virtual location on the Internet in which users can congregate and converse.

chatting Using the Internet to carry on conversations with other Internet users. The Internet supports chatting protocols and various sites provide chat rooms wherein users can meet and converse.

checksum A technique used to check for errors in data. The sending application generates the checksum from the data being transmitted. The receiving application computes the checksum and compares it to the value computed and sent by the sending station.

chief information officer (CIO) An executive corporate position responsible for communication, data processing, and information management.

ciphertext The encrypted version of a message or data.

circuit Either the medium connecting two communicating devices or a path between a sender and a receiver that may include one or more intermediary nodes. The exact meaning depends on the context.

circuit switched cellular (CSC) radio telephone A common carrier service that provides communication for cellular telephones, pagers, and other mobile devices.

circuit switching A connection in which a dedicated path is allocated for two participants of a session. All packets are forwarded over the established circuit. Contrast with connectionless services such as packet switching.

class A address An Internet address space that allows 127 subnets and 16 million nodes per subnet.

class B address An Internet address space that allows 16,000 subnets and 64,000 nodes per subnet.

class C address An Internet address space that allows 2 million subnets and 256 nodes per subnet.

class D address An Internet address space that is used by nodes willing to accept broadcast messages.

client A software application that requests services from the server in a client/server computing environment. Some systems may call the client a requester.

client/server computing An application framework in which the processing load is divided among several processes called clients and servers. Clients issue requests to servers, which provide specialized services such as database processing and mail distribution. Within this framework, clients are able to concentrate on business logic whereas servers can use specialized hardware and software that allows them to provide their services more efficiently. When clients and servers are located in different computers, application processing is distributed over multiple computers and, in effect, the network becomes the computer.

closed system A proprietary system wherein the interface specifications are not made readily available to other manufacturers. A closed system does not provide support for OSI or ANSI standard protocols and interfaces.

cluster controller A device that manages multiple terminals by buffering data transmitted to and from the terminals and performing error detection and correction.

cluster server A collection of servers in which failover capability is implemented. With failover, if one server in the cluster fails, one or more of the remaining servers will absorb its workload.

coaxial cable A transmission medium consisting of one or two central data transmission wires surrounded by an insulating layer, a shielding layer, and an outer jacket. Coaxial cable has a high data-carrying capacity and low error rates.

code independence The ability to transmit data regardless of the data code, such as ASCII or EBCDIC.

collision In a CSMA/CD media access control protocol, a collision occurs when two stations attempt to send a message at the same time. The messages interfere with each other, so correct communication is not possible.

common carrier A public utility that provides public transmission media, such as the telephone companies and satellite companies.

Common Management Information Protocol (CMIP) Guidelines issued by the ISO for creating network management software products. Also known as the Communications Management Information Protocol.

Common Management Information Service (CMIS) An ISO standard for services to be provided by a network management system. CMIS and the Common Management Information Protocol form the ISO network management protocol.

communication controller A computer that serves as a front-end processor for a host machine. The communication controller provides the data link protocols and controls the physical devices attached to communication lines.

communication interface unit (CIU) In a LAN, the CIU provides the physical connection to the transmission medium.

communication server A server that monitors connections to the host by determining whether there is a free port to make the connection and granting or denying the request accordingly.

computer-aided design (CAD) An application of computers in the design process. One component is computer drafting.

computer-aided instruction (CAI) The use of computers to facilitate education.

computer-aided manufacturing (CAM) The use of computers to solve manufacturing problems. CAM includes robotic control, machine control, and process control components.

concentrator A computer that provides line-sharing capabilities, data editing, polling, error handling, code conversion, compression, and encryption.

conditioning A service provided by telephone companies for leased lines. It reduces the amount of noise on a line, providing lower error rates and increased speed.

conducted media Media that use a conductor such as a wire or fiber optic cable to move a signal from sender to receiver.

congestion control The reduction of transmission delays.

connectionless A session type in which no formal setup is required between session participants. Packets sent between source and destination may take different routes. Contrast with connection or circuit-oriented sessions.

Connectionless Network Protocol (CLNP) The ISO counterpart to the Internet Protocol, this protocol provides message services such as message priorities, route selection parameters, and security parameters.

connector Establishes the physical connection between the computer and the medium.

consistency A consistent system is one that works predictably with respect both to the people who use the system and to response times.

Consultative Committee on International Telegraph and Telephony (CCITT) An international standard organization within the ITU.

contention A convention whereby devices obtain control of a communication link. In contention mode, devices compete for control of the line either by transmitting directly on an idle line or by issuing a request for line control.

contention mode A mode in which the host and the terminal contend for control of the medium by issuing a bid for the channel.

context data A requirement of multithreaded processes that entails unifying the work by keeping track of the completed parts as well as the parts yet to be worked on, and ensuring that an interrupted transaction is restarted at the correct point.

control center A network component responsible for monitoring the network and taking corrective action when necessary.

controller See *disk drive interface.*

conversational mode A mode in which the terminal and the host exchange messages.

cooperative computing A data processing model in which two or more processes collaborate on the processing necessary for a single transaction or application. The cooperating processes may reside in different computers.

copper distributed data interface (CDDI) An ANSI LAN standard for twisted-pair-wire LANs providing speeds of 100 Mbps. An extension of the fiber distributed interface LAN.

corporate license A license that gives a corporation unlimited use of software at all locations.

CPU time The amount of time required for the CPU to execute a transaction's instructions, including those executed by the database management system, operating system, data communication software, and application programs.

critical path The sequence of events in a project that takes the longest to complete.

crosstalk When the signals from one channel distort or interfere with the signals of a different channel.

current loop A transmission technique that uses changes in current flow to represent data. Does not require a modem and operates at speeds up to 19.2 Kbps.

Customer Information Control System (CICS) A TCP provided by IBM. Its primary function is as an interface between terminal users on one side and application programs or the database on the other.

cyclic redundancy check (CRC) An error detection algorithm that uses a polynomial function to generate the block check characters. CRC is a very efficient error detection method.

daisy chain   A connection arrangement in which each device is connected directly to the next device. For example, a daisy chain of devices A, B, C, and D might have A connected to B, B connected to C, and C connected to D. Also known as cascading.

database management system (DBMS)   A system that organizes data into records, organizes records into files, provides access to the data based on one or more access keys, and provides the mechanism for relating one file to another.

database server   A computer that allows microcomputers on a network to request database processing of records, returning a single-figure answer rather than the set of records essential to determining the answer.

data communication   The transmission of data to and from computers and components of computer systems.

data communication equipment (DCE)   One class of equipment in data communication, including modems, media, and media support facilities.

Data Encryption Standard (DES)   An algorithm that uses an encryption key to transform data, called plaintext, into an encoded form, called encrypted text or ciphertext.

data entry application   Applications that consist of lengthy inputs with short responses.

data flow control layer   Layer 5 in IBM's SNA networks. The data flow control layer provides a set of protocols between two users. These protocols provide for the orderly flow of information between the two users.

datagram   One connection option for a PDN. The message fits into the data field on one packet. There is less accountability for packet delivery than in other connection types.

data link control layer   Layer 2 in IBM's SNA networks. The data link control layer is responsible for protocols in node-to-node transfers, such as synchronous and asynchronous transmission. The data link control layer is also responsible for error detection and recovery across a link. Similar in function to the OSI reference model data link layer.

data link layer   One of the layers of the ISO's OSI reference model. The data link layer is responsible for node-to-node message transfers.

data link protocol   Convention that governs the flow of data between a sending and a receiving station.

data set/modem   A device that changes digital signals to analog signals for transmitting data over telephone circuits. Also used for some fiber optic transmission (digital fiber optics do not require a modem) and any transmission mode requiring a change from one form of signal to another.

data switch   A device implemented on sub-LANs to provide connections between microcomputers.

data terminal equipment (DTE)   The second class of equipment in data communication, including terminals, computers, concentrators, and multiplexers.

deadlock   A state in which two or more processes are unable to proceed. It occurs when two or more transactions have locked a resource and request resources that other processes already have locked.

dedicated connection   A connection providing direct access to the host using non-LAN resources for communication between the host and the microcomputer.

dedicated printer   A printer that can be used only by a person at the workstation to which the printer is attached.

dedicated server   One or more computers that operate only as designated file, database, or other types of servers.

dibits   A transmission mode in which each signal conveys 2 bits of data.

differential phase shift keying (DPSK)   A modulation technique that uses phase modulation. DPSK changes phase each time a 1 bit is transmitted and does not change phase for 0 bits.

digital cash   Electronic money. Digital cash may take various forms, including credit/debit card numbers, smartcards, and electronic scrip issued by an electronic cash agent.

digital subscriber line (DSL)   A switched telephone service that provides high data rates, typically over 1 Mbps. See also *asynchronous DSL, rate adaptive DSL, high-data-rate DSL, single-line DSL,* and *very-high-speed DSL.*

digital subscriber line access multiplexer (DSLAM)   A device that splits communication over a DSL into a data switch or voice switch depending on the type of data being transmitted.

digital transmission   A transmission mode in which data is represented by binary digits rather than by an analog signal.

digital versatile disk (DVD)   An optical disk standard that extends the capacity of compact disks to 4.7

GB by increasing recording density, to 8.5 GB by having two recording layers per side, and to 17 GB by using both sides of the disk.

direct sequencing Sends data out over several different frequencies simultaneously to increase the probability of success.

discovery packet A packet sent by the sending station on all available routes to evaluate and determine the best route from the information collected by the packet.

disk caching Similar in function to cache memory except that main memory serves as a high-speed buffer for slower disk drives.

disk drive interface/controller Sets the standards for connecting the disk drive to the microprocessor and the software commands used to access the drive.

diskless workstation A workstation that has no local disk drives, reducing the ways in which a virus can be introduced.

disk seek enhancement An I/O optimization technique that reduces the head movement during seeks and improves performance.

distributed applications Applications in which the data, the processing, or both are distributed among processing units.

Distributed Computing Environment (DCE) A standardization for middleware established by the Open Software Foundation that specifies the use of remote procedure calls, security, name services, and messages for client/server computing.

distributed database A database wherein data is located on two or more computing systems connected via a data communication network. The fact that data is distributed should be transparent to database users.

distributed file system (DFS) Network software responsible for making network resources available to multiple users regardless of their location in the network.

distributed processing The geographic distribution of hardware, software, processing, data, and control.

distributed query processing A condition in which a user at one node can start a query involving data on other nodes.

distributed routing determination A routing algorithm in which each node calculates its own routing table based on status information periodically received from other nodes.

distributed transaction management In a distributed database, a transaction may be operated on by several processes in different computer nodes. Transactions of this type must be managed by the distributed database system to ensure database integrity, either by completing the transaction or by reversing any updates done by a transaction that cannot be completed.

distribution list A predefined list of users, represented by a single e-mail address, that replaces the need to enter each user's address when sending a message to them collectively.

document coauthoring system A system that allows two or more workers to work on one document concurrently.

document management system A system that helps an organization manage and control its documents.

domain In IBM's SNA, the network components managed by a Systems Services Control Point. In the Internet, domains refer to the hierarchy of organization. Top-level domains include *gov*, *mil*, *org*, *com*, *net*, and *edu*. In Windows NT a domain is a collection of resources that are grouped together for ease of access and administration.

domain name server A server that resolves domain names to network addresses.

Domain Name Service (DNS) A distributed database and query system that allows a user to reconcile an address name to an Internet address.

dotted quad The four-octet address representation on the Internet.

double buffering Used when buffer overflow/overrun occurs to avoid losing characters.

downloaded The process of transferring data or an application from the server to the workstation.

DS-1/T-1 through DS-4/T-4 High-speed data transmission circuits from a common carrier.

dumb terminal A terminal that passively serves for input or output but performs no local processing.

duplexed servers The fault tolerance technique in which one server can fail and another is available to continue working.

dynamic addressing The assignment of an Internet address to a node that does not have a static address.

dynamic host configuration protocol (DHCP) The most common mechanism for dynamically assigning Internet addresses.

E-1 European equivalent to T-1 service. E-1 provides a 2.048-Mbps data rate.

E-3 European equivalent to T-3 service. E-3 provides a 57.344-Mbps data rate.

echo The reflection or reversal of the signal being transmitted. Also, a transmission convention in which the receiver of data sends the data back to the sender to assist in error detection.

echo suppressor A device that allows a transmitted signal to pass in one direction only, thus minimizing the echo effect.

effectiveness A measure of how well a system serves users' needs.

electronic appointment calendar A workgroup productivity tool that is stored on the network, so that users can consult each other's appointment calendars.

electronic cash (e-cash) See *digital cash*.

electronic conferencing An application that assists users in arranging and conducting meetings electronically.

electronic data interchange (EDI) The standardized exchange of business data.

electronic mail (e-mail) An online service that allows users to exchange messages with other users electronically.

electronic meeting system Network software that allows participants to exchange machine-readable information in the form of graphics, text, audio, and full-motion video.

emulator A diagnostic tool that enables the user to check for adherence to a specific protocol.

encryption A process in which transmitted data is scrambled at the sending location and reconstructed into readable data at the receiving end.

end office A telephone company office to which a subscriber is connected. Also called a class 5 office.

end-to-end reliability Message error checking performed by the source and destination nodes of the message. Contrasted with node-to-node reliability. End-to-end reliability is a function of the OSI transport layer.

end-to-end routing In SNA, routing for which at least one of the nodes is a type 5 physical unit or terminal and the path is determined and maintained through the entire session.

enterprise network A network of two or more LANs connected to each other, or one or more LANs connected to a WAN.

ergonomics The science of designing equipment to maximize worker productivity by reducing operator fatigue and discomfort while improving safety.

Ethernet A LAN implementation using the CSMA/CD protocol on a bus. The IEEE 802.3 standard is based on Ethernet. A popular LAN implementation.

exclusive open mode A file open mode in which an open request is granted only if no other user has the file opened already.

extended addressing In SNA a 23-bit address space, as opposed to a 16-bit address.

Extended Binary-Coded Decimal Interchange Code (EBCDIC) A code that uses 8 bits to represent a character of information. One of the most common computer codes. See also *ASCII*.

external specification Specifications detailing end-user interfaces to a system and information available to the user.

failover A fault tolerance capability used in clustered servers. With failover, if one server in the cluster fails, one or more remaining servers in the cluster will absorb the work of the failed server.

fair protocol A protocol in which each node has equal access to the medium.

fast Ethernet See *100BaseFX, 100BaseT, 100VG-Any-LAN*, and *gigabit Ethernet*.

fault tolerance A combination of hardware and software techniques that improve the reliability of a system.

fiber distributed data interface (FDDI) An ANSI LAN standard for fiber optic LANs spanning a distance of approximately 200 km and providing speeds of 100 Mbps.

fiber optic cable A transmission medium that provides high data rates and low errors. Glass or plastic fibers are woven together to form the core of the cable. This core is surrounded by a glass or plastic layer called the cladding. The cladding is covered with plastic or other material for protection. The cable requires a light source, most commonly laser or light-emitting diodes.

file exchange utilities A workgroup productivity tool that allows files to be copied easily from one network node to another.

file management system (FMS) A system that provides a subset of a database management system's capabilities. An FMS provides functions such as storage allocation and file access methods for a single file.

file server A computer that allows microcomputers on a network to share resources such as data, programs, and printers. The file server's software controls access to shared files, as opposed to the operating system of the microcomputer.

file transfer protocol (FTP) A capability of the TCP/IP protocol suite that allows files to be transferred from one node to another over the network.

file transfer utility An intrinsic part of many networks, this utility allows files to be moved between network nodes.

filter A software component used to screen and format data sent to the management center.

finger A utility that provides retrieval of user information.

flaming Severe criticism or condemnation of a user via e-mail.

flexibility The ability to have both growth and change with minimal impact on existing applications and users.

flooding A technique used by a bridge to locate a destination address not present in the bridge's routing table by sending a packet out on all possible paths. An acknowledgment from the receiving station contains the destination address of the packet, which can then be added to the bridge's routing table.

flow control A mechanism used by network protocols to provide message pacing so the sender does not send data faster than the receiver is able to accept it.

fractional T-1 A T-1 service that fills the void of high-speed transmission options between 64 Kbps and 1.5 Mbps by providing a portion of T-1 line to customers.

frame A term used to describe a transmission packet in bit-oriented protocols.

frame relay A fast packet-switching protocol that is similar to X.25 packet switching. Frame relay does not perform as exhaustive error checking as X.25 and is thus able to switch packets at a higher rate than X.25.

frame relay access device (FRAD) A device that provides the interface between a customer's communication equipment and a frame relay network.

framing protocol A synchronous protocol that uses reserved characters or bit patterns to delineate data and control fields within the message.

freenet A community-based organization that provides free access to the Internet or to a bulletin board system.

frequency division multiplexing (FDM) A technique that divides the available bandwidth of the circuit into subchannels of different frequency ranges, each of which is assigned to one device.

frequency hopping Data is transmitted at one frequency, the frequency changes, and the data is transmitted at the new frequency. Each piece of data is transmitted over several frequencies to increase the probability that the data will be successfully received.

frequency modulation (FM)/frequency shift keying (FSK) One method of changing the characteristics of a signal to represent data. The frequency of the carrier signal is changed. Often used by lower-speed modems.

front-end processor (FEP) A communication component placed at the host end of a circuit to take over a portion of the line management work from the host. Also called a communication controller or message switch.

full duplex A data transmission mode in which data is transmitted over a link in both directions simultaneously.

Fully Qualified Domain Name (FQDN) The computer.domain notation used to specify addresses in the Internet.

functional specification An agreement between management and designers outlining design objectives, such as the product to be produced, and design constraints, such as time and cost.

functional testing Testing individual modules to ensure that they produce the desired results.

gateway The interface used to connect two dissimilar networks or systems by providing conversion from one network to another.

Gaussian noise See *white noise.*

General Agreement on Trade and Tariffs (GATT) An organization of 97 nations that has proposed an international treaty that includes stipulations regarding the use and cost of private lines.

geosynchronous orbit A satellite orbit in which the satellite is stationary with respect to the earth. The satellite is always positioned over the same location.

GET An SNMP command that allows the management component to retrieve data stored in a device's MIB.

gigabit Ethernet   A standard for 1-Gbps Ethernet LANs using twisted-pair wires or fiber optic cable.

Gopher   An early Internet service that provides an easy way to browse the net.

group decision support system (GDSS)   System that assists individuals and groups in the decision-making process and helps them set objectives.

groupware   Workgroup productivity tools that allow a group of users to communicate and to coordinate activities.

guardbands   Subchannel separators that are implemented in frequency division multiplexing to avoid crosstalk.

half duplex   A data transmission mode in which data can travel in both directions over a link but in only one direction at a time.

half-session layer   Represents a single layer (transmission control, flow control, and presentation service) in the four-layer definition of SNA functional layers.

Hertz (Hz)   The term used to denote frequency; 1 hertz is 1 cycle per second.

heterogeneous   In networks, a network made up of a variety of equipment, particularly equipment and software from a variety of vendors.

hierarchical topology   A network topology in which the nodes are arranged hierarchically. Also known as a tree structure.

high-data-rate digital subscriber line (HDSL)   A digital switched technology that provides very high data transmission speeds over telephone system wires. The transmission speeds are equivalent to T-1 speeds (1.544 Mbps) or, in Europe, to E-1 speeds (2 Mbps). In contrast with ADSL, the transmission speed is synchronous, meaning that the speed is the same in both directions. See also *digital subscriber line, asynchronous DSL, rate adaptive DSL, single-line DSL, very-high-speed DSL,* and *very-high-speed ADSL.*

High-Level Data Link Control (HDLC)   A positional synchronous protocol that operates in full-duplex mode in both point-to-point and multipoint configurations. Data is transmitted in fixed-format frames consisting of start flag, address, control, information, block check character, an end-of-frame flag. HDLC is an ISO standard similar to IBM's SDLC.

hop   In network routing, hops are a measure of the distance from source to destination. In some contexts, the number of hops is the number of routers through which a packet must travel to reach its destination.

hub   A wiring concentrator for connecting workstations on a token-ring or 10BaseT LAN.

Hush-a-Phone Case   A U.S. case that set a precedent regarding attaching equipment to telephone networks.

hypertext   A document that contains links to other documents or parts of a document.

hypertext markup language (HTML)   A language used to create and format hypertext documents.

hypertext transfer protocol (HTTP)   A protocol used on the World Wide Web to transfer HTML documents.

identification   Information assigned to a specific user of a system for security and control purposes. User identification ranges from simple user names to high-security measures such as voice print and fingerprint identification.

IEEE 802.1 High-Level Interface Subcommittee   Addresses matters relating to network architecture, management, and interconnections.

IEEE 802.2 Logical Link Control Subcommittee   Defines the functions of the logical link control sublayer of the OSI reference model data link layer. The objective of the LLC is to provide a consistent, transparent interface to the media access control (MAC) layer, so the network layers above the data link layer are able to function correctly regardless of the MAC protocol.

IEEE 802.3 standard   A standard that covers a variety of CSMA/CD architectures that are generally based on the Ethernet.

IEEE 802.4 standard   A subcommittee that sets standards for token bus networks.

IEEE 802.5 standard   A subcommittee that sets standards for token-ring networks.

IEEE 802.6 standard   A MAN standard similar to the FDDI family of technologies. The IEEE 802.6 standard has also been adopted by ANSI. The standard is also called the distributed queue dual bus (DQDB) standard. As the name *DQDB* indicates, the architecture uses two buses. Each bus is unidirectional, meaning that data is transmitted in one direction on one bus and in the other direction on the second bus.

IEEE 802.7 Broadband Technical Advisory Group   Provides guidance and technical expertise to other groups that are establishing broadband LAN standards, such as the 802.3 subcommittee for 10Broad36.

IEEE 802.8 Fiber Optic Technical Advisory Group Provides guidance and technical expertise to other groups that are establishing standards for LANs using fiber optic cable.

IEEE 802.9 Integrated Data and Voice Networks Subcommittee Sets standards for networks that carry both voice and data. Specifically, it is setting standards for interfaces to integrated services digital networks.

IEEE 802.10 LAN Security Subcommittee Addresses the implementation of security capabilities such as encryption, network management, and the transfer of data.

IEEE 802.11 Wireless LAN Subcommittee Sets standards for multiple wireless transmission methods for LANs.

IEEE 802.12 Demand Priority Access Method Subcommittee Developed the specifications for the 100VG-AnyLAN protocol. The protocol specifies 100-Mbps speeds over twisted-pair wires.

impulse noise A noise characterized by signal spikes. In telephone circuits it can be caused by switching equipment or by lightning strikes and in other situations by transient electrical impulses such as those occurring on a shop floor. A common cause of transmission errors.

inactive node A node that may be powered down and is incapable of sending or receiving messages.

inactive port The status of a bridge port that will not accept packets from the LAN end of the port.

Information Infrastructure Task Force (IITF) A U.S. government task force charged with guiding the formation of the information superhighway.

information superhighway A national information system geared toward moving the raw materials (data) and finished goods (information and ideas) of information to their needed locations.

infrared transmission Uses electromagnetic radiation of wavelengths between visible light and radio waves. It is a line-of-sight technology used to provide local area connections between buildings and is also the medium used in some wireless LANs.

inquiry/response applications Applications in which inputs generally have only a few characters and output responses have many.

Institute of Electrical and Electronic Engineers (IEEE) A professional society that establishes and publishes documents and standards for data communication.

IEEE has established several standards for LANs, including IEEE 802.3 and IEEE 802.5.

integrated services digital network (ISDN) The integration of voice and data transmission (and other formats such as video and graphic images) over a digital transmission network. This network configuration is offered by numerous common carriers.

integrated testing A procedure that ensures that all parts of a system are functionally compatible.

intelligent terminal A terminal that has both memory and data processing capabilities.

interactive application A computing paradigm in which users interact with the programs.

interconnected (plex or mesh) network A network topology in which any node can be directly connected to any other node.

intermodulation noise A special form of crosstalk, which is the result of two or more signals combining to produce a distorted signal.

internal specification Specifications for developing a software system.

International Standards Organization (ISO) An organization that is active in setting communication standards.

International Telecommunications Union (ITU) An international standard organization. See also *CCITT*.

Internet A specific collection of interconnected networks spanning most countries of the world. When used with a small letter *i*, an internet is any interconnection of two or more computer networks.

Internet Architecture Board (IAB) A group responsible for the architecture of the Internet.

Internet Engineering Task Force (IETF) An open committee that proposes Internet protocol standards.

Internet Packet Exchange (IPX) The network layer protocol used by Novell NetWare LANs.

Internet Protocol (IP) The network layer protocol used on the Internet and many private networks. Different versions of IP include IPv4, IPv6, and IPng. Ipv4 was the version of the protocol in use in 1997. IPv6 and IPng (*next generation*) refer to the same version of IP and are the replacement for IPv4.

Internet relay chat (IRC) A UNIX utility that allows one or more users to communicate interactively. IRC is used on the Internet for chatting.

Internet service provider (ISP) A company that provides Internet connections and services.

InterNIC An Internet organization that provides Internet services such as name and address allocation and database services.

interoperability The ability of all network components to connect to the network and communicate with shared network resources.

interrupt A signal issued by hardware or an application requesting a service from the operating system.

interrupt characters A set of characters that terminate a message or cause an interruption in transmission to perform a special action, such as a backspace.

intranet A private network that uses Internet technology such as hypertext documents and Internet protocols to store and retrieve data.

IntraNetWare The current flagship of the Novell NOS line.

inventory software A management tool used to collect LAN component data, such as network addresses and CPU types, that will help a network administrator manage and fix a network.

inverse multiplexer A mux that provides a high-speed data path between two devices by separating data onto multiple lower-speed communication circuits.

I/O driver The part of the operating system that manages the input/output subsystem by providing low-level access to devices.

I/O optimization A variety of ways to optimize the task of file access, which increases the performance of the server.

IPng See *IPv6*.

IPv6 Version 6 of the Internet Protocol. IPv6 supersedes and provides significant improvements to IPv4. One major improvement is the expansion of the Internet address space from 32 bits to 128 bits.

ISO 2110 A functional interface standard similar to the functional portion of RS-232-C. It describes which signals will be carried on specific pins.

ITU V.10 and V.11 Electrical interfaces for data transmission.

ITU V.24 A functional interface similar to RS-232-C.

ITU V.25 A specification for establishing and terminating sessions with an auto-call unit.

ITU V.28 A specification for electrical interfaces similar to that of RS-232-C.

ITU V.32 A modem standard specifying trellis encoding techniques to represent signals.

ITU V.34 A modem standard for speeds up to 28.8 Kbps using trellis encoding.

ITU V.35 A standard for data transmission at speeds up to 48 Kbps using a 34-pin connection.

ITU V.42 A modem standard that defines error checking capabilities using cyclic redundancy checking.

ITU X.20 and X.21 Standards that cover the interface between DCE and DTE for packet distribution networks.

ITU X.24 A functional interface for packet distribution networks.

Java A platform-independent programming language used extensively to create World Wide Web applications (sometimes called applets).

Jughead A Gopher add-on utility that allows a user to search Gopher servers for menu items containing specific words in their titles.

key disk A security system in which a specific floppy disk must be in the disk drive when the application is run.

LAN analyzer A diagnostic tool that monitors network traffic, captures and displays data sent over the network, generates network traffic to simulate load or error conditions, tests cables for faults, and provides data helpful for system configuration and management.

LAN Server (IBM) An example of LAN software that runs under OS/2.

latency The average time required for the requested data to revolve under the read/write heads.

learning bridge Bridge that builds its own routing table from the messages it receives, rather than having a predefined routing table. Also known as a transparent bridge.

leased lines Lines leased from common carriers. Lines are leased when the connection time between locations is long enough to cover the cost of leasing or if speeds higher than those available with switched lines must be attained.

license agreement An agreement that covers the rules under which you are allowed to use a product.

Lightweight Directory Access Protocol (LDAP) A protocol used to define access to directory services based on the X.500 directory.

line driver   See *repeater.*

line monitor   A device used to diagnose problems on a communication link. Also known as a protocol analyzer.

link   The circuit established between two adjacent nodes, with no intervening nodes.

Link Access Procedure, Balanced (LAPB)   A bit synchronous protocol similar to high-level data link control. LAPB is the protocol specified for X.25 networks.

local access and transport area (LATA)   The region served by a regional Bell operating company (RBOC). Following the divestiture of AT&T the U.S. was divided into local access and transport areas. LATAs are not rigidly defined, but calls within a LATA are handled exclusively by the RBOC (the call is not handled by a long-distance carrier but still may be a toll call).

local area network (LAN)   A communication network in which all of the components are located within several kilometers of each other and that uses high transmission speeds, generally 1 Mbps or higher.

local procedure calls   In programming, one procedure in a program can call another procedure in the same program. The called procedure carries out a processing task for the calling procedure. Generally, the two procedures exchange information through a list of parameters that are passed between the calling and the called procedure.

locks   Record or file-level control that overcomes the problem with file open contention.

log file   A monitoring tool used for both diagnostic functions and predictive or management functions.

logical link control (LLC)   A sublayer of the OSI reference model data link layer. The logical link control forms the interface between the network layer and the media access control protocols.

logical unit (LU)   In IBM's SNA, a unit that represents a system user. Sessions exist between LUs or between an LU and the SSCP. Several types of LUs have been defined.

longitudinal redundancy check (LRC)   An error-checking technique in which a block check character is appended to a block of transmitted characters, typically at the end of the block. The block check character checks parity on a row of bits.

LU 6.2   An SNA logical unit type representing a program-to-program session.

mail agent   A software module that can automatically act on behalf of a user to forward mail or alert other users that the recipient is unavailable.

Management Information Base (MIB)   A database that defines the hardware and software elements to be monitored in the SNMP.

matrix switch   A device that allows terminal connections to be switched among the available processors.

mean time between failures (MTBF)   A measure of the average amount of time a given component can be expected to operate before failing.

mean time to repair (MTTR)   The average amount of time required to repair a broken piece of equipment and restore it to service.

media access control (MAC) protocol   A sublayer of the OSI reference model's data link layer. The MAC protocol defines how a station gains access to the media for data transmission. Common MAC protocols are carrier sense with multiple access and collision detection and token passing.

medium   In data communication, the carrier of data signals. Twisted-pair wires, coaxial cables, and fiber optic cables are the most common LAN media.

memory management   Functions provided by an operating system or program, such as a TCP, that manage the system or program's memory area.

menuing software   A management tool used to provide users options via a menu of choices.

message logging   Also called safe storing, this recovery system writes the message to a file before acknowledgment so the message may be reviewed or recovered later if necessary.

message sequence numbers   A system in which each transmitted message is given a sequential number, allowing multiple messages to be transmitted without acknowledgment.

message transfer agent (MTA)   An interface between e-mail user agents.

metering software   A monitoring tool used on LANs to enforce adherence to software license agreements by keeping track of the number of times an application is executed.

metropolitan area network (MAN)   A high-speed network that services an area larger than a LAN but smaller than a WAN. The area served is on the order of 100 mi of cabling, and can thus serve the major portion of many cities.

microcomputer network protocols (MNP)   A set of modem protocols providing for data compression and error checking, such as MNP level 4 and MNP level 5.

microwave radio A method of transmitting data using high-frequency radio waves. It requires a line of sight between sending and receiving stations. Capable of high data rates, microwave is used for WANs and wireless LANs.

middleware A software interface that functions as an intermediary between clients and servers.

MILNET Military network. A U.S. Defense Department network that was once a key subnet on the Internet. MILNET is no longer an Internet subnet.

mirrored disks A fault tolerance technique in which two disks containing the same data are provided so that if one fails, the other is available, allowing processing to continue.

mobile computing Has expanded the role of broadcast radio in data communication. It requires a wireless medium such as cellular radio, radio nets, and low-orbit satellites.

modem Short for *modulator–demodulator*. A device that changes digital signals to analog signals for transmitting data over telephone circuits. Also used for some fiber optic transmission and any transmission mode requiring a change from one form of signal to another.

modem eliminator A device that allows data transmission over short distances without a modem. Provides for signal timing as well as data transmission.

modem turnaround time The time required for a modem to make the transition from sender to receiver on half-duplex links. It includes the time for the old sender to drop the carrier signal, for the new sender to recognize that the carrier signal has been dropped, and for the new sender to raise the carrier signal that must be detected by the new receiver.

modular expansion A system that allows the user to upgrade from a small system to a more powerful system by adding more of the same type of processor to the existing system.

multidrop See *multipoint connection*.

multimedia technology Technology that extends a computer's capabilities by adding audio and video to data.

multimode graded-index fiber Refracts the light toward the center of the fiber by variations in the density of the core.

multimode step-index fiber The oldest fiber optic technology, in which the reflective walls of the fiber move the light pulses to the receiver.

multiple access The ability of nodes to access a medium that is not carrying a message.

multiplexer A hardware device that allows several devices to share one communication channel.

multiplexing A line-sharing technology that allows multiple signals to be transmitted over a single link.

multipoint connection A connection in which several terminals share one communication link.

multistation access unit (MAU) In an IBM token-ring LAN, a MAU is used to interconnect workstations.

multithreading The capacity of a process to work on multiple requests at once.

negative acknowledgement (NAK) Notification of the sender of a block of data that the data has been received in error. The block is typically retransmitted.

Netview IBM's network management system. Netview has three major subsystems: Netview, Netview/PC, and Netview/6000.

NetWare A leading example of the integrated LAN operating system software approach by Novell.

network Two or more computers connected by a communication medium, together with all communication, hardware, and software components. Alternatively, a host processor together with its attached terminal, workstations, and communication equipment, such as transmission media and modems.

network access point (NAP) A NAP is an Internet connection and exchange point. It provides high-speed connection to major ISPs and to other NAPs.

Network Addressable Unit (NAU) In IBM's SNA, any device that has a network address, such as logical units and physical units.

network architecture The way in which media, hardware, and software are integrated to form a network.

network computer (NC) A low-cost computer designed to provide efficient access to the Internet and support Internet protocols and software. Some NCs use televisions as the monitor to further reduce the cost of the system.

network configuration tool A monitoring tool used to plan the optimum network configuration with respect to sources and types of circuits.

network control Involves the sending and receiving of node status information to other nodes to determine the best routing for messages.

Network Control Program (NCP) A data communication program that helps manage a communication network. Specifically, a program that runs in IBM's 37xx line of communication controllers.

network directory services A database that contains the names, types, and network addresses of network resources such as users, printers, and servers. The directory database may be replicated on several network nodes, thus allowing users and processes to locate resources they need to complete their work.

Network File System (NFS) A distributed file system developed by Sun Microsystems that is also compatible with DOS- and UNIX-based systems.

network layer One of the layers of the ISO's OSI reference model. The network layer is responsible for end-to-end message routing.

Network Management System (NMS) A combination of hardware and software used by network supervisors to monitor and administer a network.

network manager A person or management team responsible for configuring, planning, tuning, and establishing standards and procedures for a network.

Network Performance Analyzer (NPA) The NPA provides performance information for the system, including information on lines, buffers, errors, queue lengths, and data transmission rates.

Network Problem Determination Aid (NPDA) The NPDA collects, maintains, and reports information on error conditions within the network. It also allows testing of the system, concurrent with production operations.

network routing manager A designated node that has an overview of network functioning, location of any bottlenecks, and location of used facilities.

network routing table In the process of message transmission, a table in which the network layer looks up the destination address to find the next address along the path.

network statistics Information, such as error rates, data rates, and the number of retransmission attempts resulting from errors, that is collected to analyze network performance trends.

network topology A model for the way in which network nodes are connected. Network topologies include bus, ring, and star.

neutral working A method of transmitting data in a current loop, where current represents a 1 bit and the absence of current indicates a 0 bit.

newsgroups, Internet See *Usenet*.

next received See *number received*.

next sent See *number sent*.

node A processor in a LAN, MAN, or WAN.

nondedicated server A computer that can operate as both a server and a workstation.

null modem A cable in which the transmit and receive leads are crossed. A null modem allows two devices to communicate over short distances (typically 50 ft or less) without using a modem.

number received (Nr) subfield In bit synchronous transmission such as HDLC, a field on the transmission frame used to represent the frame sequence number the receiving station expects to receive next.

number sent (Ns) subfield In bit synchronous transmission such as HDLC, a field on the transmission frame used to represent the frame sequence number being transmitted.

Object Request Broker (ORB) A standardization for middleware established by the Object Management Group that ensures hardware and software independence by locating a server that is capable of satisfying a client's request.

octet A group of 8 bits used in bit synchronous protocols. Data, regardless of its code, is treated as octets.

office automation systems A special case of a distributed system, with both data and processing distributed among several different components.

open architecture Architecture whose network specifications are available to any company. This allows a variety of companies to design hardware and software components that can be easily integrated into new and existing networks.

open system See *open architecture*.

Open Systems Interconnection (OSI) management framework The part of the OSI reference model that provides the model for network management standards.

Open Systems Interconnection (OSI) reference model A seven-layered set of functions for transmitting data from one user to another. Specified by the ISO.

operating system (OS) The overall manager of the computing system that performs all of its functions, transparent to the application program and the programmer.

operation interface An interface that enables a user to use, monitor, and control a system.

overlay module A memory management technique wherein the program is divided into two distinct segment types: the resident or main segment and the overlay segments. Overlay segments share the same memory area. Typically, only one of the overlays is in memory at any given time. When a different overlay segment is required, it replaces the memory resident overlay segment.

pacing See *flow control*.

packet A unit of data transmission. The packet consists of the data to be transmitted together with the headers and trailers affixed by the various layers in the OSI reference model.

packet assembly/disassembly (PAD) A function in a packet-switching network that breaks messages into packets for transmission and reassembles packets into messages at the message's destination.

packet distribution network (PDN) See *X.25 network*.

packet switching The transmission of a message by dividing the message into fixed length packets and then routing the packets to the recipient. Packets may be sent over different paths and arrive out of order. At the receiving end, the packets are reordered. Routing is determined during transmission of the packet. Also known as packet distribution network, public data network, X.25 network, or value-added network.

packet-switching equipment (PSE) Equipment that accepts and forwards messages in a packet distribution network.

packet-switching network (PSN) See *X.25 network*.

parity check/vertical redundancy check (VRC) The same as parity error checking. For each character transmitted, an additional bit, the parity bit, is attached to help detect errors. The bit is chosen so that the number of 1 bits is even (even parity) or odd (odd parity).

parity data In RAID technology, additional data that provides the ability to reconstruct data that has been corrupted.

passive hub A node connection hub used in an ARCnet LAN that does not provide signal regeneration, so nodes can be located no farther than 100 ft from the hub.

password A secret character string used by authorized people to prove their right to access a system.

path A group of links that allows a message to move from its point of origin to its destination.

path control layer The third layer in IBM's SNA. Path control provides end-to-end routing.

peer layers Corresponding layers in the OSI reference model. For example, the network layers in two nodes are peer layers.

peer-to-peer A type of communication in which any two devices can communicate on an equivalent basis. A peer-to-peer architecture is a LAN option that allows nodes to communicate on an equal basis and share resources (as opposed to a server-based LAN).

performance The predictability of transaction response time.

performance monitor A monitoring tool that provides snapshots of how a system is functioning, which helps network managers identify trends in the use or misuse of the network.

permanent virtual circuit (PVC) One of three types of connection for a packet distribution network. A PVC provides a permanent link (like a leased line) between two nodes. It is usually selected when two nodes require continuous transmission.

personal communication services A mobile communication service providing cellular radio, paging, and other mobile communication services.

Personal NetWare (PNW) An NOS for small workgroups who simply want to share applications and printers.

phase jitter A variation in the phase of a continued signal from cycle to cycle.

phase modulation A change in the phase of a carrier signal. Commonly used alone or in conjunction with amplitude modulation to provide high-speed transmission (4800 bps and higher).

phase shift keying (PSK) A form of phase modulation.

physical control layer Layer 1 in IBM's SNA networks. The physical control layer covers physical interfaces, similar to the physical layer of the OSI reference model.

physical layer   One of the layers of the ISO's OSI reference model. The physical layer specifies the electrical connections between the transmission medium and the computing system.

physical security   Measures, such as door locks, safes, and security guards, taken to control access to restricted areas.

physical unit (PU)   In SNA, a hardware unit. Four physical units have been defined: type 5, host processor; type 4, communication controller; type 2, cluster or programmable controller; and type 1, a terminal or controller that is not programmable.

Physical Unit Control Point (PUCP)   In IBM's Systems Network Architecture, a PUCP resides in nodes that do not contain a Systems Services Control Point. The PUCP is responsible for connecting the node to and disconnecting the node from the network.

ping   A utility that allows a user to determine whether a given system is active on the network.

plaintext   The unencrypted or properly decrypted version of a message or data. Plaintext is intelligible. Also known as cleartext.

point of presence (POP)   In the U.S. public telephone network, a point at which a transfer is made from a local telephone company to the long-distance carrier.

point-to-point connection   A connection using a communication line to connect one terminal or computer to a host computer.

point-to-point protocol (PPP)   A protocol used to provide serial transmission to the Internet over serial point-to-point links such as switched telephone connections. Also, a protocol that allows routers to establish data link connections and to exchange configuration information.

polar working   One method used to implement current loop transmission.

polling   The process of asking terminals whether they have data to transmit.

polymorphic virus   See stealth virus.

port concentrator   A device that allows multiple input streams to be passed to the host through a single communication port.

port selector   A device that helps determine which users are granted access to applications when the number of potential terminal users far exceeds the number of available lines. Also known as a data switch.

positional protocol   A type of synchronous protocol that delineates fields by the use of fixed-length fields on the message, by indicating the size of the message with a character count embedded in the message, or both.

presentation layer   One of the layers of the ISO's OSI reference model. The presentation layer addresses message formats.

presentation services layer   Layer 6 in IBM's SNA networks. The presentation services layer is involved in formatting data received from and sent to a user.

Pretty Good Privacy (PGP)   A popular encryption algorithm for protecting files and e-mail.

primary center   A telephone company class 3 station. A primary center is one station higher than a toll center.

printer driver   A software module that determines how to format data for proper printing on a specific type of printer.

print server   A computer that allows several users to direct their printed output to the same printer.

private branch exchange (PBX)   Telephone switching equipment located on corporate premises and owned by the corporation. A PBX allows telephone calls within an office to be connected locally without using the telephone company's end office or transmission circuits.

private lines   Communication lines owned by a user, or communication lines leased from a common carrier.

private management domain (PRMD)   A domain that represents a delivery and interconnection network corresponding to a company in the X.400 standard hierarchy.

problem-reporting system   A system administration feature that records, assigns, and tracks problems.

program evaluation and review technique (PERT)   A technique that tracks a project's progress to determine its critical path and to monitor personnel, schedules, and project resources.

project management system   A management tool that assists in planning projects and allocating resources.

project planning tool   A tool used by project managers to define, monitor, and modify project events, resources, and schedules.

propagation delay   The amount of time it takes for a signal to travel from its source to its destination.

protected open mode   A file open mode that is granted only if no other user has already been granted exclusive or protected mode.

protocol Convention used for establishing transmission rules. Protocols are used to establish rules for delineation of data, error detection, control sequences, message lengths, media access, and so on.

protocol control information (PCI) A header attached to a service data unit. The PCI and the service data unit form a protocol data unit.

protocol converter A special-purpose device that allows a terminal to look like a different type of terminal in order to facilitate interconnection between different computer systems.

protocol data unit (PDU) A unit of information exchanged between peer protocols in the OSI reference model.

protocol stacks A protocol stack allows a collection of protocols to interoperate. The stack defines the order of operation of the protocols. The top of the stack is oriented toward the application layer and the protocols at the bottom of the stack deal with communication protocols, such as those at the data link and network layers.

proxy agent Software that provides an interface between different network management protocols.

public data network (PDN) See *X.25 network.*

public key encryption An encryption algorithm. Two keys are created, the public and private keys. Encryption is accomplished with the public key and decryption is done with the private key, or vice versa.

pulse code modulation (PCM) A method for transmitting data in digital format.

punchdown block A connector used as a terminal point for multiple-wire cables.

quadbits A technique in which each signal carries 4 bits of data. Requires 16 different signals.

quadrature amplitude modulation (QAM) A modulation technique using both phase and amplitude modulation.

quality of service A capability that distinguishes between classes of messages and gives priority to message forwarding. For example, real-time video and audio messages should have low transmission delay and would therefore be given priority over file transfer messages.

queuing time The amount of time a transaction must wait in queues for service.

radiated media Media that use radio waves of different frequencies or infrared light to broadcast through air or space and accordingly do not need a wire or cable conductor.

rate adaptive digital subscriber line (RADSL) A DSL service that adapts the speed of transmission to the quality of lines being used and the distance from the subscriber to the telephone end office.

read-after-write A fault tolerance capability wherein data is read from disk immediately after being written. This allows immediate detection and correction of write errors due to system problems or bad disk sectors.

recovery The act of restoring a system to operational status following a failure.

redirector A software module that intercepts and reroutes network application I/O requests before they get to the workstation's OS.

redundant arrays of independent disks (RAID) A fault tolerance disk storage technique that spreads one file plus the file's checksum information over several disk drives. If any single disk drive fails, the data stored thereon can be reconstructed from data stored on the remaining drives.

regional Bell operating company (RBOC) The AT&T divestiture resulted in the formation of RBOCs and a separate AT&T company. An RBOC is responsible for local telephone services within a region of the United States.

regional center A class 1 telephone station.

release control Procedure including the installation, testing, and implementation of new versions of hardware and software to ensure compatibility of new features with existing software and hardware.

reliability The probability that the system will continue to function over a given time period.

remote control software A diagnostic tool that allows a LAN administrator to remotely view a user's monitor and take control of the user's keyboard.

remote data access (RDA) An OSI standard that defines a service that allows application programs to access data located on another node. RDA is intended to allow such access independent of the database management systems or operating systems being used.

Remote File Sharing (RFS) A distributed file system that is supported only by UNIX-based systems.

remote job entry (RJE) An application of data communication. Batches of data are collected at a remote site and transmitted to a host for processing. In early implementations the input was card format and the output was printer format (between the remote terminals and the host processor).

remote logon facility   A network utility that allows users to log onto a remote system, thereby establishing the user as a local user on the remote node.

Remote Monitoring MIB (RMON MIB)   An SNMP standard that describes nine different device groups. A vendor must choose an appropriate group for a device adhering to this standard and is required to support all the data objects defined for that group.

remote procedure call (RPC)   A remote procedure call is similar to a local procedure call except that the calling and called procedures are not a part of the same program. The called and calling procedures may be located in the same computer or in different networked computers.

repeater   A device used to amplify signals on a network. Repeaters allow the medium distance to be extended.

request for information (RFI)   An informal method of investigating hardware and software solutions by presenting a brief statement of a problem to be solved and a list of questions soliciting solutions to the problem.

request for proposal (RFP)   Sometimes called a request for quotation, a formal document describing the problem to be solved and asking qualified vendors to submit plans and costs for solving the problem.

response time   The amount of time required for a user to receive a reply to a request. Usually the time elapsed between the user pressing a key to send the request and the return of the first character of the response.

reverse channel   Allows transmission in both directions on a line that is essentially half duplex. The reverse channel generally has a lower transmission rate than the forward channel and is used to acknowledge receipt of data. Reverse channels help reduce the need for modem turnaround.

ring topology   A network configuration commonly used to implement LANs. The medium forms a loop to which workstations are attached. Data is transmitted from one station to the next around the ring. Generally the access protocol is token passing.

root bridge   The bridge assigned the highest priority.

router   A network interconnection device and associated software that links two networks. The networks being linked can be different, but they must use a common routing protocol.

routing   An algorithm used to determine how to move a message from its source to its destination. Several algorithms are used.

routing information protocol (RIP)   One of the protocols used by routers to exchange routing information and thus update their network routing tables.

routing table   An information source containing node or network addresses and the identification of the path to be used in transmitting data to those nodes or networks.

RS-232-C standard   An Electronic Industries Association standard for asynchronous transmission.

RS-366 standard   An Electronic Industries Association standard for automatic-call unit interface.

RS-449 standard   An Electronic Industries Association standard that improves on the capabilities of RS-232-C.

RSA encryption   A public key encryption algorithm named for its developers, Ron Rivest, Adi Shamir, and Leonard Adleman.

satellite radio transmission   Transmits data via VHF radio waves and requires line-of-sight transmission between stations.

search engine   A software system that allows users to search for files or keywords. Two popular Internet search engines are Yahoo! and Lycos.

sectional center   In the telephone network, a class 2 station.

secure electronic transaction (SET)   A standard developed by credit card companies. SET uses encryption to provide secure credit card transactions over networks, specifically for the Internet.

Secure HTTP (S-HTTP)   One of the most commonly used protocols for securing electronic transactions. S-HTTP was developed by Enterprise Integration Technologies and is used by Spyglass, Open Market, and several other software companies.

secure socket layer (SSL) protocol   A protocol used to provide secure network transactions, particularly on the Internet.

security   Controls and procedures implemented to delay unauthorized access to a system and thus to protect data.

seek time   In disk accessing, the time it takes to move the read/write heads to the proper cylinder.

sensor-based application   An application in which the processor receives data from sensors and, if necessary, acts on that data.

serial binary transmission   The successive transmission of bits over a medium.

serial line internet protocol (SLIP)   A protocol used for Internet access over serial lines, such as dial-up telephone access. SLIP has been generally replaced by the newer point-to-point protocol.

server   In client/server computing, the software application that provides clients with the services they request. A computer that provides LAN services.

server license   A license that allows an application to be installed on one server.

service bureau   A data processing organization that provides computing resources for other companies.

service data unit (SDU)   The basic data unit consisting of data assembled at the application layer. Protocol control information is attached to the SDU, forming a protocol data unit.

session   The dialogue between two system users.

session layer   One of the layers of the ISO's OSI reference model. The session layer is responsible for establishing a dialogue between applications.

SET   An SNMP command that allows data fields stored in a device's MIB to be reset.

shared open mode   A file open mode that allows several users to have a file open concurrently.

shared printer   A printer controlled by a server and available to designated users.

shielded twisted-pair (STP) wires   Twisted-pair wires that have a metallic or foil outer covering to reduce the probability of noise affecting the signal transmitted over the wires.

signaling terminal equipment (STE)   Node used to provide an interface between two different packet-switching networks.

simple mail transfer protocol (SMTP)   A protocol within the TCP/IP protocol suite. SMTP is an application layer protocol used to implement mail services and message transfer.

Simple Network Management Protocol (SNMP)   SNMP provides a guideline for creating network management software products. SNMP has four key components: the SNMP protocol, Structure of Management Information, Management Information Base, and Network Management System.

simplex transmission   A mode of data transmission in which data may flow in only one direction. One station is always a sender and another is always a receiver over a simplex link.

simulation model   A monitoring tool that allows the user to describe network and system activities and to receive an analysis of how the system can be expected to perform under the described conditions.

single-line data digital subscriber line (SDSL)   A digital switched technology that provides very high data transmission speeds over a single telephone line. The transmission speeds are equivalent to T-1 speeds (1.544 Mbps) or, in Europe, to E-1 speeds (2 Mbps). In contrast with ADSL, the transmission speed is synchronous, meaning the speed is the same in both directions. See also *digital subscriber line, asynchronous DSL, rate adaptive DSL, high-data-rate DSL, very-high-speed DSL,* and *very-high-speed ADSL.*

single-mode transmission   The fastest fiber optic technique, in which the light is guided down the center of an extremely narrow core.

single threading   A technique in which only one operation is processed at a time.

site license   A license that gives the user unlimited rights to use the software at a given site.

Six-Bit Transcode (SBT)   A 6-bit computer code developed by IBM primarily for RJE.

sizing   The analysis conducted to determine the amount of hardware required to support a system. Sizing must consider the system throughput and the required transaction response times during peak processing periods.

smartcard   A wallet-size card with updatable memory and often with an embedded microprocessor. A smartcard may be used in a variety of ways. One use is to initialize the card with a certain amount of money. The card can then be used for financial transactions, such as paying for telephone calls. One use of monetary smartcards is for Internet transactions.

smart terminal   A terminal that can save data entered by the operator into memory.

SNA Distribution Services (SNADS)   An SNA facility that provides asynchronous distribution of documents throughout a network.

socket A combination of a transmission control protocol port number and an Internet address. Sockets are used in TCP/IP and other systems to provide connections between two entities.

software license agreement A document provided by the software vendor that specifies the rights and restrictions of software users.

source routing A learning bridge algorithm in which the sending node is responsible for determining the route to the destination node. The routing information is appended to the message and the bridges along the route use the routing information to move the message from the source to destination.

spamming The practice of inserting extraneous words into World Wide Web documents or the sending of hundreds or thousands of e-mail messages to a user. In the latter case, the people responsible for spamming typically take retribution for some perceived wrong by overwhelming the user's mailbox and disrupting their use of the Internet.

spanning tree A method by which learning bridges build their own routing table.

spanning tree algorithm A learning bridge algorithm in which bridges exchange routing information. Based on the routing information thus received, each bridge maintains a routing table that shows how to route messages to other LANs.

spooler A software system that collects printer output (typically on disk) and schedules the data for printing. *SPOOL* is an acronym for *simultaneous peripheral operation online*.

spread-spectrum radio (SSR) The primary application for data communication is for use with wireless LANs. It has a characteristic reliability in environments where signal interference is likely.

StarLAN A configuration similar to the basic star topology in that each workstation is connected to a wiring hub. The primary medium used for implementations is twisted-pair wires.

star network A network topology using a central system to which all other nodes are connected. All data is transmitted to or through the central system.

star topology A network topology using a central system to which all other nodes are connected. All data is transmitted to or through the central system. Also known as star network.

star-wired LAN A variation of star topology in which a wiring hub is used to form the connection between network nodes.

static routing A form of routing in which one particular path between two nodes is always used.

statistical time division multiplexing (STDM) A technique that provides improved time-sharing efficiency by transmitting data only for lines with data to send, rather than allowing idle lines to occupy carrying capacity of the communication circuit. Also known as a stat mux.

stealth virus A computer virus that has the ability to change its signature or identity, thus making the virus more difficult to detect and eradicate. Also known as a polymorphic virus.

store-and-forward system When transmitting data between two nodes, the messages are logged at intermediate nodes, which then forward them to the next node.

StreetTalk (Banyan) A database that provides network directory services.

stress testing A procedure that ensures that the system can sustain the designated workload.

Structure of Management Information (SMI) A component of the SNMP that details how information is represented in the Management Information Base.

Structured Query Language (SQL) A relational database language developed by IBM and later standardized by the American National Standards Institute.

subarea A portion of an SNA network consisting of a subarea node (a host node or communication controller—PU types 5 and 4, respectively) together with all network resources supported by the subarea node.

sub-LAN A network that provides a subset of LAN capabilities, primarily peripheral sharing and file transfer, but has lower data transfer rates and transparency than a LAN.

subnet A portion of a network.

subnet address The first set of numbers in an Internet address, representing the identification of a node's network.

subnet address mask The ability to apply a bit mask to an Internet node address space and thereby decompose the node address space into local subnets.

switch A device that links devices such as computers, terminals, and printers, and provides a mechanism to connect one device to another and allow the two to communicate directly.

switched connection A communication link established when one station dials a telephone number to connect to another station. A switched connection uses voice circuits. The circuit exists for the duration of the session.

switched multimegabit data service (SMDS) A high-speed connectionless digital transmission service.

switched virtual circuit (SVC) One of three types of circuits in a packet distribution network. When a session is required between two users, an end-to-end circuit is determined and allocated for the duration of the session. Similar to a switched connection.

symmetrical multiprocessing An SMP system has CPUs that are alike and that share memory, processing responsibility, and I/O paths.

synchronous A transmission protocol in which the sender and receiver are synchronized. Data is generally transmitted in blocks, rather than a character at a time, as in asynchronous transmission.

Synchronous Data Link Control (SDLC) An IBM positional synchronous protocol that operates in full-duplex or half-duplex mode in point-to-point and multipoint configurations. Data is transmitted in fixed-format frames consisting of start flag, address, control, information, block check character, and end-of-frame flag.

synchronous protocol See *synchronous*.

Systems Network Architecture (SNA) IBM's architecture for building a computer network. Encompasses hardware and software components, establishment of sessions between users, and capabilities such as office and message/file distribution services.

Systems Services Control Point (SSCP) In IBM's SNA, the process that controls a domain. It is responsible for initiating network components, establishing sessions, and maintaining unit status.

T-1 service A high-speed common carrier service that provides 1.54 Mbps. T-1 service is also known as DS-1 signaling.

T-2 service A high-speed common carrier service that provides 6.3 Mbps. T-2 service is also known as DS-2 signaling.

T-3 service A high-speed common carrier service that provides 45 Mbps. T-3 service is also known as DS-3 signaling.

T-4 service A high-speed common carrier service that provides 274 Mbps. T-4 service is also known as DS-4 signaling.

talk A UNIX utility that allows one user to communicate instantaneously with another user.

Telecommunications Act of 1996 U.S. legislation that increased competition among intrastate and interstate communication companies and deregulated the cable television industry.

Telnet A TCP/IP protocol that allows entry from a keyboard to be passed from a local system to a remote system. Through this protocol, an application on the remote node believes it is communicating with a locally attached device.

terminal An input/output device that can be connected to a local or remote computer, called a host computer.

terminal emulation A software program and a hardware interface that allow one microcomputer to function as a variety of terminals in support of changing requirements.

terminator A resistor at a cable end that absorbs the signal and prevents echo or other signal noise.

thermal noise See *white noise*.

think/wait time The amount of time an operator will wait or think while entering data for each transaction.

throughput The amount of work performed by a system per unit of time.

time division multiplexing (TDM) A technique that divides transmission time by allotting to each device a time slot during which it can send or receive data.

timeout interval A period of time allowed for an event to occur. If the event does not happen, the timeout expires and the process initiating the event is notified.

time-staged delivery system Software that allows users to identify a transmission package, designate one or more recipients of the package, and specify a delivery priority.

token A special frame that is passed between nodes on a LAN. The node that receives the token has the right to transmit data. In some LANs, only one token is allowed to circulate. In MANs such as FDDI, several tokens may circulate at one time.

token passing A media access control protocol in which a string of bits called the token is distributed among the network nodes. A computer that receives the token is allowed to transmit data onto the network. Only the stations receiving a token can transmit. Token passing is implemented on ring and bus LANs.

token-passing bus A LAN architecture using a bus topology and token-passing media access control protocol.

token-passing ring A LAN architecture using a ring topology and token-passing media access control protocol.

toll center In the telephone network, a toll center is a class 4 switching office. Also called a class 4 station.

topology The physical layout of a network. Common LAN topologies are bus, ring, and star. Common WAN topologies include star, hierarchical, and plex or interconnected.

Tracert A tool that allows a user to trace the round trip between the user's node and another node on the network.

transaction A user-specified group of processing activities that either are entirely completed or leave the database and processing system in the same state as before the transaction was initiated.

transaction control process (TCP) A process that receives inputs from terminals and routes them to the proper application processes. TCPs also may edit input data, format data to and from a terminal, log messages, and provide terminal job sequencing. Examples include IBM's CICS and Tandem's Pathway. Also called a teleprocessing monitor or message control system.

transaction log Records all of the data received and is used in recovering from failures and in system auditing.

transaction routing The routing of a transaction received from a terminal to one or more application programs.

transaction services layer Layer 7 of IBM's SNA networks. Transaction services addresses application level processing.

transceiver A device that receives and sends signals. A transceiver helps form the interface between a network node and the medium.

transfer time The amount of time required for the data to be sent over the channel to the CPU's memory.

transistor A solid-state device used to control the flow of electricity in electronic equipment.

transmission control layer Layer 4 of IBM's SNA networks. Transmission control addresses initiating and terminating sessions, flow control, and message sequencing for end-to-end reliability. Transmission control contains functions found in both the session and transport layers of the OSI reference model.

Transmission Control Protocol/Internet Protocol (TCP/IP) A suite of protocols developed by the U.S. Department of Defense for internetwork file transfers, e-mail transfer, remote logons, and terminal services.

transparency The ability to send any bit string as data in a message. The data bits are not interpreted as control characters.

transparent access The ability of a user to access distributed files as though they were located on the user's local node.

transparent bridge A learning bridge. Transparent bridges are able to use information contained in the data link packets to determine the path along which to send packets.

transponder In satellite communication, a transponder receives the transmission from the earth (uplink), amplifies the signal, changes frequency, and retransmits the data to a receiving earth station (downlink).

transport layer One layer of the ISO's OSI reference model. The transport layer is responsible for the integrity of end-to-end transmissions.

transport service access point (TSAP) An address used by the transport layer to uniquely identify session entities.

trapdoor encryption An encryption algorithm that uses large prime numbers and two keys, one made public and the other kept secret by the message recipient. The public key encrypts the data, and the private key decrypts the ciphertext, or vice versa. Also known as the public key method.

TRAPS An SNMP command that allows a device to trap and forward unsolicited data, such as an alert condition.

tribits A method of modulation that allows 3 bits to be represented by each signal.

twisted-pair wires A type of wire that consists of pairs of wires (typically two or four pairs) in a LAN. Each pair of wires is intertwined to reduce noise from adjacent pairs and to enhance their ability to transmit data. Twisted-pair wires can be shielded or unshielded.

Uniform Resource Locator (URL) A string representation of an Internet address. A URL is the address used to access pages on the World Wide Web.

uninterruptible power supply (UPS) A backup power unit that continues to provide power to a computer system during the failure of the normal power supply. A UPS is often used to protect LAN servers from power failures.

unipolar signaling A digital transmission signaling technique that uses a single voltage to represent a 1 bit and zero voltage to represent a 0 bit.

UNIX A popular multiuser operating system. UNIX is available on a wide variety of hardware platforms and has numerous capabilities that make it effective as a network operating system.

unshielded twisted-pair (UTP) wires A type of twisted-pair wire that has no metal covering to shield the wires from external interference.

uploading The transfer of files or programs from the terminal to the host.

Usenet or newsgroups A worldwide bulletin board. Usenet is organized into hundreds of interest groups in a variety of categories such as computers, social issues, business, and recreation.

user agent (UA) A mail agent that allows a user to compose a message, provides recipient addresses, and receives messages.

User Datagram Protocol (UDP) An Internet standard connectionless transport layer protocol.

user logon script A set of actions to be taken when the user logs on, such as setting search paths and initial menus.

user profile Information needed to define the applications and transactions a user is authorized to execute.

user-to-modem ratio For an ISP, the number of users compared to the number of available modems. If the user-to-modem ratio is large, such as 50-to-1, it means that for every 50 users only one modem is allocated, so users often may be unable to obtain an Internet connection.

value-added network (VAN) See *X.25 network.*

Veronica An Internet search capability similar to Jughead.

vertical redundancy check (VRC) See *parity check.*

very-high-speed digital subscriber line (VDSL) A digital switched technology that provides data transmission speeds between 12.9 and 52.8 Mbps. See also *digital subscriber line, asynchronous DSL,* and *rate adaptive DSL.*

video display unit (VDU) A terminal that uses a technique such as a cathode ray tube or liquid crystal display to represent data. Also called a video display terminal or cathode ray tube.

Vines (Banyan) An example of LAN software that runs under an existing OS, UNIX.

virtual circuit A connection, established in setting up a communication session, between a sender and a receiver in which all messages are sent over the same path.

virtual memory management A memory management technique that uses disk as an extension of memory, thereby allowing virtually unlimited memory capacity for applications and data. With virtual memory one can run programs that do not reside entirely in memory.

virtual private network (VPN) Using shared communication systems such as the Internet to establish links for a corporate network. VPN software typically uses strong encryption and authentication algorithms to ensure the privacy of the company's data.

virtual routing No permanently established path exists; instead each node consults its routing table to determine which node should next receive the message.

Virtual Telecommunications Access Method (VTAM) One of IBM's telecommunication access methods.

virus A program or program segment that reproduces itself on computer systems by incorporating itself into legitimate programs or system data areas. A virus typically is designed to disrupt or disable normal computer operations.

virus detection software Software that analyzes a system and attempts to discover and remove any viruses that have infected it.

Web page A World Wide Web accessible document. A Web page may contain text only or may also contain links, images, or other information.

weighted routing When multiple paths exist, each is given a weight according to perceived use. A random number is generated to determine which of the available paths to use, based on their weights.

white noise One source of data communication errors. It results from the normal movements of electrons and is present in all transmission media at temperatures above absolute zero. Also known as thermal noise or Gaussian noise.

WHOIS database A repository of data about domains and users.

wide area information server (WAIS) An Internet document search system allowing searches based on keywords.

wide area network (WAN) A network that typically covers a wide geographical area and operates at speeds lower than LAN speeds.

wide area telecommunication or telephone service (WATS) An inbound or outbound telephone service that allows long-distance telephone service. In the United States the inbound service is associated with toll-free (800, 888, and 877 area code) numbers.

Windows NT A leading example of the integrated LAN operating software approach by Microsoft.

wireless LAN A LAN implemented without using conducted media. A wireless LAN may use spread-spectrum radio, broadcast radio, microwave radio, or infrared light transmission to connect the workstations together. Some LANs may use both conducted and wireless media.

wiring hub Used by some LAN implementations to provide node-to-node connection.

workgroup software Often called groupware, this software facilitates the activities of a group of two or more workers by reducing the time and effort needed to perform group tasks such as meetings, office correspondence, and group decision making.

workload generator A monitoring tool that generates transaction loads and pseudo–application processes for execution on a proposed configuration to illustrate how a system will actually function.

World Wide Web (WWW or W3) A hypertext-based distributed information system used on the Internet.

worm A computer program that replicates itself, typically on multiple nodes in a network. Originally worm programs were designed to find and legitimately use underused systems. More recently, worms have gained a reputation similar to that of viruses.

X.25 network A network defined by CCITT X.25 standard. An X.25 network uses packet switching, and is also known as a packet-switching network or value-added network. See *packet-switching network*.

X.400 standard A standard developed by the ITU that provides a platform for the implementation of a worldwide electronic message-handling service.

X.500 standard Specifies the procedure for creating a directory system to maintain e-mail user names and their network addresses as well as the names and addresses of other network resources such as printers and servers.

Xpress Transfer Protocol (XTP) An extension of TCP/IP that enhances performance by reducing the amount of processing and allowing some functions to be worked on simultaneously.

zero-slot LAN A low-speed LAN using standard microcomputer components that do not require an additional slot on the motherboard for a LAN adapter.

Index

Note: italicized *f*'s and *t*'s following page numbers refer to figures and tables, respectively.